BEYOND
ALL
ISMS

♣ Author's Note ♣

An immoral people cannot be constructively managed
or governed - only controlled.

Immorality corrodes and diminishes
courage, generosity, honor, integrity, and wisdom,
dividing and weakening entire populations.

Transhumanism is the 21st century methodology
for controlling morally weakened populations while
ensuring they never realize they are enslaved.

Transhumanism intends to accomplish what propaganda,
conditioning, and lies could not...
Enslavement of the human race by a
Luciferian cult of dynastic families and their order followers.

Humanity's defense and most effective offense
are putting on the armor of God, fasting,
and prayer—before taking any action.

God's grace, our peaceful resistance, and a simple
NO THANK YOU
will stop global syndicate psychopathy
in its Luciferian tracks.

BEYOND ALL ISMS

Lurks the

Study Group System

Well Hidden in Plain Sight

Bruce J. Kolinski, P.E. *(Retired)*
1st Edition

Publisher
Grit Company Unlimited

BEYOND ALL ISMS

Published by:
Grit Company Unlimited
2177 West Wilson Avenue
Coolidge, Arizona 85128

Library of Congress Control Number: 2022908018

Kolinski, Bruce
1ˢᵗ edition
25 chapters; 460 pages; 164,586 words

p. cm.
Includes references:
Print paperback (ISBN-13) 979-8-9850736-0-7
Epub (ISBN-13) 979-8-9850736-1-4

Geopolitics / History / Political Science / Religion / Transhumanism.

Print On Demand by:
IngramSpark.

Wholesale Distribution by:
Ingram Book Company (Ingram Book Group LLC)
in conjunction with IngramSpark's *Global Connect Program.*

For signed copies or special discounts for bulk purchases, corporate gifts, educational purposes, fund-raising, or special promotions - please contact the author directly by email at: bruce@brucekolinski.com.

~ ~ ~ ~ ~

Dedicated To:

Asher, Beau, Brynn, Griffin,
and all young people
on whom tomorrow depends.

~ ~ ~ ~ ~

Acknowledgments

With all the gratitude this 71-year old man can muster:
Thank you, heavenly Father, for gifts my family has received.
Thank you Father for blessing the United States of America.
Thank you, Nan, for patiently guiding me through five decades of ideological *cul-de-sacs* obsessively searching for wisps of wind I do not understand; then listening to my compulsive sharing of every little breeze as
noted by accomplished human behaviorists, Beavis and Butthead with,
"words, words, more words".

Preface: A comment on AGREEMENT

Four decades of my working life have been spent as a licensed professional civil & environmental engineer, general contractor, and project manager in heavy construction. A much shorter effort, about a decade and a half was doled out as young farm laborer, warehouse worker, and Class A licensed truck driver.

Interestingly, at least to me, across these different endeavors, I've found agreement over-rated. Creativity and effective solutions are more likely to evolve from different ideas and view points than from conformity. That said, agreement is usually a pleasant experience, even satisfying in many respects. Certainly not a bad thing; BUT satisfaction can lead to complacency. When birth gob-smacks us into the middle of an epic spiritual war, complacency can hazardously disarm vigilance—unfortunate, as this is a circumstance where more is definitely better.

This book is in many respects about personal vigilance and having each other's back, certainly more about vigilance than agreement. In spiritual warfare, as with any type of warfare, vigilance requires accurate perception, clear thinking, and coherent analysis. In that regard this author doesn't care what the reader thinks relative to what the writer thinks—BUT does care that our thinking and any disagreements are based on accurate information. I care that my readers (hopefully more than one) DO THINK, and more importantly, THINK as INDEPENDENTLY and COHERENTLY as possible.

When managing people, I've found accurate information critical, but have not found complete agreement necessary to resolution of differences and I've negotiated in many publicly adversarial, even hostile business and personal situations. Differing opinions and ideas, buffered with respect, consideration, and generosity—with exclusion of psychopaths—ALWAYS provide a balance of power when facts are available to all sides. If you work toward your best interest; I do the same, and we share mutual consideration, at least within reason based on fact; we can find a balance of power. Within that balance of Adam Smith's *invisible hand* lies more energy and mutual prerogative for sharing love and creating abundance than can be imagined.

This is the world, with a little help from our Creator, we can build together.
I hope we manage to accomplish this in our lifetime.
I doubt the rest matters much. Just sayin'.

Table of Contents

Regarding the Prince of our World:
(John 15:18-10)
"If the world hates you, you know that it hated Me before it hated you. If you were of the world, the world would love its own. Yet because you are not of the world, but I chose you out of the world, therefore the world hates you."

1 • Introduction

Historic depictions of human culture suggest every generation feels a special uniqueness during its time on Earth. Our *Baby Boomer* generation, coming of age in the mushroom cloud shadow of *nuclear annihilation and bomb shelters* incongruously overlaying Saturday's *Dick Clark Show* hosting Sheb Wooley's *Purple People Eater* and Chubby Checker's *Twist*, later upstaged by Laurel Canyon's folk rock *Counterculture*,[1] certainly feels this pull toward something significant, yet unclear. Clarity regarding humanity's purpose remains unclear until we understand our world, in the above Biblical sense, is dominated by Satan and only action through faith in Christ can free us from Luciferian influence. If there are other paths to love, I am ignorant of them. **We are all spiritual warriors born into an epic battle between good and evil.** Choosing good is the difficult path to love eternal while choosing evil is the easier path to eternal alienation from God's love. Participating in this epic battle for love eternal is our purpose, our human *telos*.

Of course every generation should feel special because every human is uniquely endowed by our Creator with personally infinite spiritual value. We are each born into this wondrous battle between light and darkness with unique warrior skills suited to strengthening and protecting our families, communities, nations, and world. Individual and even group skill sets vary in strength or weakness emotionally, intellectually, physically, and spiritually with all skill sets serving our personal contribution to our communities.

---

1 David McGowan and Nick Bryant, *Weird Scenes Inside the Canyon: Laurel Canyon, Covert Ops & the Dark Heart of the Hippie Dream*, Illustrated edition (London: Headpress, 2014).

Life is a process of intelligently created evolution wherein our unique skill sets develop and evolve along freely chosen paths. For rational creatures, this is a naturally and spiritually revelatory process leading to unification with our Creator's love, or rejection of that love – in either case, freely chosen, with that choice shared in community... *or not.* Today, love's essence is obscured by indoctrinated *"or not"* programming.

Fortunately, there are always truth seekers diligently attempting to shed light on all this as best they can. John B. Wells (*Caravan to Midnight*) might look around our world commenting, *this is really quite something, let's get some facts.* Jay Dyer (*Jay's Analysis*) might comment regarding Hollywood's **long-range penetration** and **inner-directional conditioning**[2]: *"Not only do Hollywood and the Pentagon present us with manipulative toxic culture creation and the co-opting of trends and movements, but recent scandals have even shown studios themselves can function as fronts and shells for criminal operations."*[3] Dave Rubin (*The Rubin Report*) might say *let's get together and discuss it... and in the meantime please don't burn any books.*

Stephen K. Bannon (*War Room Pandemic*) might say, *there are no conspiracies, but there are also no coincidences - we have the receipts - the data, evidence, and facts - now we can take action.* Tim Kelly (*Our Interesting Times*) might say, *we live in interesting times, let's study this situation and determine the truth.* Joe Atwill (*Caesar's Messiah*) might suggest sharpening our perception when around *lifetime actors preying on conventionalism and superstitious beliefs* held by those most susceptible to Fascism as described by Adorno and associates in *The Authoritarian Personality* (1950). *University of Toronto's* Professor of Psychology, Dr. Jordan Peterson might suggest, *paying attention is key to discerning how we might be better persons.*

I mention these few information warriors (there are many), to suggest in the heat of **information warfare** when programmed ignorance means humiliation, subjugation, or even death – valuable sources of information are available, any one of which may appeal to individual preferences, interests, or level of understanding. A brave truth seeker somewhere will assuredly appeal to one of our hot buttons: say art, culture, economics, entertainment, finance, history, literature, movies, music, philosophy, politics, relationship, religion, sociology, sports, science, theology, etc.

Like all *Boomers*, I was once young and indestructible with all the dark-haired answers. In my gray-hair years, I'm not sure what questions to ask, BUT have plenty of questions. Realizing it's never too late to learn and we don't know what we don't know, at my daughter's urging to write a book, *I've decided to* share a few of my questions along with things I've noticed over seven decades. In this writ-

---

2 "The Tavistock Institute of Human Relations: Shaping the Moral, Spiritual, Cultural, and Political. A by John Coleman (2006-08-02): Amazon.Com: Books," 56
3 Jay Dyer, *Esoteric Hollywood II: More Sex, Cults & Symbols in Film*, 2018, 5.

ten inquiry we'll meld what sometimes appear unmeldable human proclivities, admittedly from my biased perspective hoping to provide useful information.

Humans are born into a space/time arena called Earth for the purpose of learning to receive, reciprocate, and share our transcendent Creator's love, through action of the Holy Spirit who proceeds from the Father and the Son.[4] Love must be and can only be freely chosen and of course, choice requires alternate choices or no choice is possible. The alternative to God's love is Luciferian evil. We cannot be forced to embrace love or evil. Our rational human birthright is freedom to choose, so we must inevitably choose, then live with our choices among each other in community on the material plane, then spiritually forever. Refusing to choose is a passive choice for evil. Born into this human *telos*, we are warriors stuck smack in the middle of a monumental spiritual battle between light and darkness, eternal joy with love or eternal anguish without.

In this ontological context, given humans always have issues, **Globalism** is served up through what I call the **Study Group System** as a societal cure-all on a polished platter of deceit to Main Streets around the world. For all its utopian promise, Globalism is the darkest sovereignty challenging ideology conceived over the past six thousand years. Wrapped in fair and equal subtlety, packaged with lies and false hope, Globalism proselytizes fairness and social justice, delivering only subjugation, and now – transhuman feudal serfdom on its global path to destruction of all creation.

Marxism and its twisted sister, Fascism are the BATTERING RAMS of Globalism presenting false choices within the context of **controlled conflict**, i.e., **Hegelian Dialectic.** These vicious battering rams oppose representative forms of government and free market Capitalism, which does not exist in today's world anyway. In America, as well as other places, we struggle with forms of Mercantilism[5] falsely labeled free market Capitalism. We are programmed to accept antihuman ideologies offering false solutions for correction of socio-economic wrongs. Wrongs which proponents of Luciferian ideologies create, perpetuate, then falsely promise to resolve. This dark ideological umbrella is a **control system**, whereby authority is abused to confuse and undermine free will choice for the purpose of first enslaving humanity, then obliterating it as painfully as possible. Our world's violence speaks for itself.

---

4 "Aquinas's Shorter Summa," The Catholic Company®, 44, 277
5 Wayne Jett, *The Fruits of Graft: Great Depressions Then and Now*, 1st edition (Los Angeles: launfal Press, 2011).

Setting aside academic debate for Main Street practicality, **Globalism** stands on **three immoral legs**. **Marxism** is dictatorship imposed by government thugs. **Fascism** is dictatorship over government thugs imposed by **Mercantilist Corporatism**, enforced by threat of violence against Main Street constituencies through order following government thugs. All four destructive isms are offered to Main Street by dynastic global syndicate family members, but Marxism and Fascism comprise the frontal attack. These two thug-driven battering rams synergistically infiltrate authoritarian enslavement systems into representative forms of government to undermine free capital markets while destroying governing and economic systems capable of promoting spiritual health and raising billions out of poverty.

The U.S. Constitutional Republic, enjoined by Divine Providence did enable self-governance, free markets, and entrepreneurship bringing about a safer, more abundant life for its communities since March 4, 1789 than yet seen in human history. Satan is obsessively bound by personal choice to compulsively destroy this model of generosity and hope. Every form of totalitarian rule is pure Luciferian evil intended to bring about human impoverishment, pain, and destruction—ultimately of all creation. Satan and his army of fallen angels hate every created thing but most virulently despise human beings made in the image and likeness of God. Satan's rage is unimaginable.

Globalism is a classic Satanic trap; a Deal with the Devil difficult to grasp, easily overlooked, often denied. We'll consider various aspects of this devil's deal, offering remedies for self-defense via healthier perception, coherence, discernment, and avoidance of self-destructive behavior. Satan and hordes of fallen angels chose to destroy their loving future by rejecting God's love and have been sharing their dark choice with all creation since. Our only defense against evil influence is the cross and resurrection of Jesus Christ.

It is my gray-haired observation that SATAN'S PRIMARY TOOL, the darkest weapon of choice viciously wielded against humanity and God's everlasting love IS BIG GOVERNMENT marketed through the **Study Group System**. Big Government enables the tilted playing field Marxist Democrats and Establishment Republicans prefer. Obviously and historically Big Governments abuse citizens. History discloses no exceptions. The way Satanically influenced Elites use monopoly business to coerce big governments to abuse citizens is not transparent, so we need to peek under the rug and look behind the couch. Self defense demands we stop corrupt multinationals from rewarding equally corrupt government drones for helping enslave Main Street economically; and more importantly to prevent emotional, intellectual, and spiritual subjugation. The larger question is how do we do this? How do we create a safer, more abundant world for everyone?

1 • Introduction

CLARIFICATION: The idea of cooperation instead of competition is raised in the text. I do not use the word cooperation in the disingenuous sense employed by today's **DAVOS crowd** or early 20th century corporate monopolists, nor as eloquently espoused by AT&T Chairman John deButts in 1973.[6]

Cooperation can be viewed in mathematical terms of **game theory cooperation or retaliation**, as we see with Anatol Rapoport's *Tit for Tat*,[7] but let's keep it simple. Instead of fighting each other for opportunity, land, or stuff, maybe we could help each other find opportunities, acquire property, get more stuff, etc. Catherine Austin Fitts estimates Earth's current Uni-polar competitive model limits wealth creation to approximately 1% of what is possible if we embraced a Multi-polar model. Instead, for example, the global syndicate (my words) employs engineered COVID as an asymmetric health and financial weapon destroying independent middle-class businesses. Elites are creating a **digital transaction control system** to replace the dying reserve currency system. Global syndicate order-followers know Main Street will revolt if what's happening is understood, so **information warfare** is the 4:00 A.M. *talking-point* order of the day. Invisible enemies created for *Wars on Drugs or Terror* and now COVID *Bio-terror* are effective vehicles for herding Main Street *unwashed* into gulag slaughterhouses voluntarily – always for the common good, of course (my words).[8] Take the free JAB THEY tell us.

In multinational monopoly speak, *competition* means *wasteful*, and *cooperation* translates to *monopoly above the law*. Successful monopolist apologists arguing for efficiencies gained by monopoly spawned the **regulated monopoly,** an oxymoron to be sure. A *regulated monopoly* is corrupt, Fascist, government sanctioned and protected elimination of healthy competition in support of information and behavior manipulation, resource rape, commodity controls, price fixing, money laundering, and other horrors Big Tech and Associates now classically embrace.

To be clear, I applaud *healthy competition* geared toward increasing knowledge, skill, and pursuit of excellence shared in community – NOT *destructive competition* rigged to annihilate creative entrepreneurial competitors, impose community enslavement, squash personal growth, and pirate self-actualization.

Control of Main Street, harming citizens, and confiscating Main Street's wealth producing capacity are the only visible functions remaining in Wash-

6 Tim Wu, *The Master Switch: The Rise and Fall of Information Empires*, Reprint Edition (Vintage, 2010), 187–88.
7 Robert Axelrod and Richard Dawkins, *The Evolution of Cooperation: Revised Edition*, 2006.
8 "Global Capital Class Destroying Independent Income Using SARS-CoV-2," *Dryburgh.Com* (blog), January 14, 2021, https://dryburgh.com/catherine-a-fitts-global-capital-class-destroying-independent-income-using-the-magic-virus/.

ington D.C. The same is true across most other nations. The people's White House is lost; the courts are lost; and honorable legislation is DOA. Marxist Democrats and Establishment Republicans have since Woodrow Wilson and Teddy Roosevelt built a non-responsive, non-transparent, corrupt **Administrative Dictatorship**—now a powerful, out-of-control FOURTH BRANCH of government. U.S. political leadership and honor are AWOL. We must fix this mess by ourselves – MAKE AMERICA GREAT AGAIN—then more importantly, MAKE OUR WORLD GREAT AGAIN.

Success in our task, should we accept this challenge to restore humanity's place in our world, requires better understanding of human nature, *Natural Law* and *Natural Revelation*, then melding this knowledge with *Supernatural Revelation*; a spiritual and material melding dependent upon requesting such revelation be granted by our Creator. *Supernatural Revelation* requires spiritual preparation on our part in order to receive and understand the wisdom offered. We must deal with art, culture, economics, politics, science, and so forth, but underlying all of it is spirit.

Preparation is difficult because our world's *Prince of Darkness* and *hordes of demon angels* keep us **bifurcated**, that is, separated from personal awareness of the intrinsic duality of humanity's material and spiritual nature. Only with grace requested through the Holy Spirit can we overcome this bifurcation, enabling our evolution into coherently actualized human beings, i.e., warriors for love. Isms are collections of ideas. Collectively, isms can be weaponized against each other to destroy societal harmony. We must arm ourselves against the powerful influence of the global syndicate's primary indoctrinational weapon for doing this. I call this subversive global network the **International Study Group System**.

We can happily embrace and engage this glorious battle together, knowing with God's grace victory is already achieved through Christ's death and resurrection. All that remains is courageously doing our part for love or settling for evil, raising the question, "how do we do this?" We should remind ourselves:

"Those who cannot remember the past are condemned to repeat it."
(George Santayana-1905)

If George Santayana was correct, we should ask: "Who stands behind malevolent attacks on human learning like the insidious **1619 Project**—pushing desperately to rewrite and erase historic memory? Why do Elite order followers self righteously and aggressively support increasing societal ignorance? I can only suggest, like so many truth seekers before us, from my limited background and engineering perspective, let's examine the matter, determine some facts, then develop healthy strategies and remedies for going **Beyond All Isms** to obtain life, liberty, and the pursuit of happiness as God intends.

Trust in God with all your heart,
And do not exalt your own wisdom,
That she may cut a straight path for you;
And your foot will not stumble.
Proverbs 3:5-6

2 • Marxist-Fascist America

**The more violence necessary to maintain a system,
the less sustainable the system.**

Remedy: Spiritual warfare rages across American and world Main Streets beneath the contentious Marxist-Fascist guise of culture, economics, politics, and science. Love's Victory requires putting on the armor of God (Ephesians 6: 10-20) to defend God's children and creation itself in unity, not to be confused with uniformity or conformity as we each have unique spiritual gifts to share. Achieving Love's Victory over Darkness requires undertaking several activities such as: 1. Study the Bible. 2. Pray. 3. Read and learn. 4. Sharpen reasoning skills. 5. Center ourselves in the name of Jesus Christ. 6. Engage healthy physical activity. 7. Eat nutritious foods and fast regularly.

For those going their own spiritual way, unable or unwilling to do these seven things, I respectfully suggest following your own heart, making up your own mind, avoiding lies, and doing the best you can to fight for decency and goodness. That said, I caution from my own stubborn experience: going it alone is not a good idea and is not safe. Free Masonry encourages going it alone for a reason.

Do not fall for the divide and conquer trap Satan sets. We cannot focus anger on each other and achieve reunification with our Father. The most lost and reprehensible among us need patience, forgiveness, and prayer from the more fortunate, not more Hatred. Our will to battle MUST focus on our true adversary, Satan and Forces of Darkness, never on each other. United we are strong in Christ. Divided we are weak, reducing ourselves to easy targets for those intending oppression.

Recent unredacted history is educationally riddled with examples of shortages, waste, and problems created by Marxist Central Planning failures in victim countries like Russia, China, North Korea, Cuba, or more recently, Venezuela. Redacted history, adopted for indoctrination in conditioning centers called schools, rarely mentions such failure. One exemplary central planning failure is mass murderer Mao Zedong's *The Great Sparrow Campaign of 1958*, part of *The Great Leap Forward*. Described by Michael Pillsbury,[9] the progressive (pun intended) CCP intent was fueling the enslaved relocation communes and mass industrialization effort hoped to enhance the Chinese Communist State's competitive efforts against the West (my words). Efforts aggressively enabled by *The World Bank* incidentally.

Tiny sparrows were allegedly consuming thousands of tons of Chinese grain annually. Grain projections almost certainly over-estimated by Mao's central planners to begin with. Mao's fearful CCP planners recommended eliminating sparrows to conserve grain, so by 1960, sparrows were nearly exterminated across China. Of course, sparrows also eat insects, resulting in the unintended consequence of surging locust populations ravaging grain harvests. Further aggravated by localized drought and localized flooding, this central planning boondoggle resulted in 30-45 million Chinese people starving to death. The CCP response to this managed devastation was pointing fingers everywhere but at themselves and the woeful failure of inoperable Marxist systems.

Of course, this worst famine in recorded history wasn't caused by vanishing sparrows and expanding insect populations alone. Drought was blamed for much of the crop loss by the CCP, but studies suggest less than 10% of cultivated Chinese land was impacted by what were fairly localized droughts at the time. Paradoxically, localized flooding also contributed to significant crop damage during this same period – BUT – **the real culprit was central planning and poor procurement policy** implemented during the agrarian reforms of *The Great Leap Forward*. We find here, in just one single central planning error, nine years after taking power, a procurement policy blunder so inflexible, common sense adjustments in reaction to nature's variability were impossible to implement. Brutal starvation of 30 to 45 million people resulted while the CCP malevolently issued more dictums.

On the heels of this horrific central planning massacre, did CCP leadership evaluate and improve failed policies? Of course not. They issued edicts, denied culpability, and punished the innocent. When government leaders murder ±40 million of their own people without remorse, then lie about what happened, it cannot be exaggeration to suggest they are insane. Add to this

---

9 "The Hundred-Year Marathon: China's Secret Strategy to Replace America as the Global Superpower: Pillsbury, Michael: 9781250081346

the slaughter of an additional 60 million Chinese people by Mao's mass murdering regime through its *Red Guards* along with 400 million abortions, 80% of whom were girls, and the CCP murdered more than 500,000,000 Chinese citizens. CCP leadership brags about this and are proud of slaughtering more than 400 million babies. This goes beyond insanity to pure Satanic evil.

This murderous totalitarian, Marxist-Fascist nonsense is what our children are being taught via academic lies in fact and by omission in our malfeasant school systems, as supposedly preferable to our once self-governing Republic. This is an ignorant disgrace to education and proof certain we lost the cold war in terms of Marxist ideology. As a result, the U.S. has become a Globalist Administrative Dictatorship.

Dr. Peter Navarro, Harvard PhD, economist, author, and top advisor to the first Trump Administration has been warning America and the world for more than 15 years about CCP's non-kinetic warfare strategy deployed against the West. This asymmetric strategy was formalized in 2003 by the CCP after publication in 2002 by the PLA of *"Unrestricted Warfare"* by Col. Qiao Liang and Col. Wang Xiangsui. The three primary non-kinetic strategies are: **legal warfare** (*lawfare*), **media warfare**, and **psychological warfare**. I think it's safe to add **scientific warfare** at this point. Anyway, the CCP and its treasonous affiliates across the globe deploy these asymmetric warfare modes 24/7 in an all out form of mercantilist attack against America and the world. The unconscionable CCP SARS-CoV-2 chimeric bio-weapon attack is recent evidence encompassing all four modes: legal, media, psychological, scientific - along with subsequent Main Street health deterioration and economic destruction. The CCP must be held accountable for its *Nuremberg Code* violations, and must pay reparations for this crime against humanity along with western CCP global syndicate handlers enabling the atrocities.

Spiritually bereft multi-national management of Apple, Berkshire Hathaway, Boeing, Caterpillar, Ford, General Motors, Google, Microsoft, NBA, Wynn Resorts, and so many others stooping to CCP's totalitarian dictatorship, embracing slave labor, and decimating its own citizens is beyond despicable. If capable of shame these psychopathic managers would be ashamed.

Marxism and its twisted sister, Fascism—co-conspirators of Globalist materialism are pure evil and can only be considered in that context. Failure to understand Luciferian influence unleashed within totalitarian systems undermines thoughtful consideration by decent people, thereby weakening resolve and coping ability. My consideration of Marxist-Fascist America and America's place in Globalist Central Planning lies within this melding context, beyond material boundaries.

From a civil engineering perspective let me suggest the first step toward fixing anything is simply determining what's wrong. What isn't working properly? What's missing? What's there that shouldn't be? The second step examines whether repairs are possible, or replacement is required. Step three assesses ability to complete repairs or replacement in a reasonably acceptable manner. Step four implements planning, funding, design, and execution of the most appropriate solution. Step five is operation and maintenance.

Bearing the above in mind, our American governance system has degenerated from "best practices" of a Representative Constitutional Republic to a post-constitutional hybrid of fascist, socialist, mercantilist control systems bolstered by non-transparent technocracy. The citizens Big Governments promise to protect are considered obstacles to orderly control. Freedom of assembly, speech, and thought are coercively discouraged and, in some cases, criminalized, or as in the U.S., on the path to criminalization. Government pawns don't mandate this, of course. Censorship along with information, communication, and behavior controls are imposed by transnational monopoly policy, popularly self-enforced by Main Street acceptance of Adorno's *Authoritarian Personality*, i.e., blind faith in private and government institutions, now fully corrupted, and turned malevolently against Main Street. Though many in Washington D.C. don't know it and many of us on Main Street don't know it, destructive regulatory policy is not misunderstood or accidental. **Destructive D.C. policy is driven by fear, greed, and malevolent intent.** The parroted divide and conquer **news alert soundbites** telling us liberals on the one hand or conservatives on the other, somehow just don't get it is balderdash.

Marxist decimation of human potential and opportunity depends on five critical attack points. **1.** Belief in God must be wiped out. **2.** All sense of personal responsibility must be wiped out. **3.** The family, society's foundation must be wiped out. **4.** Human life must be attributed no value beyond economic quantification. **5.** The State is omnipotent. These five doorways to self-enslavement are the primary thrust of NWO programming, augmented by controlling access to good nutrition and healthcare when possible. The State even claims to own our children. Today's attack strategy was unleashed against Main Street autonomy when Marx and Engels wrote *The Communist Manifesto* in 1847 for London's *League of the Just*, later renamed by Marx and Engels the *Communist League*. Such ideology has been eating U.S. and world freedom voraciously since at least 1913. If we do not possess the national will to examine ourselves and our chronically ill governance system, to assess our strengths and weaknesses along with successes and failures, we are stopped. If our assessment concludes we and/or our systems cannot be fixed or replaced, we are stopped. **Note:** Marxist mayhem is designed by City of London to stop us.

I'm not stopped. I hope you're not stopped. Together with the grace of the Holy Spirit, in the name of Christ we can set the brakes on fascist violence in all its Satanic forms and correct our nation's course. This is spiritual warfare with no easy path through the battlefield as asymmetric violence of spiritual warfare takes many forms. Spiritual warfare manipulates faith, hope, charity, fear, and insecurity while strategically manipulating Main Street's anxiously obscured view of our material world. This is done via demonically influenced attack waged against nutrition, health, education, financial sustainability, competition for resources, wealth, power, etc. The generosity of love is attacked by perceived material need and emotional/physical drives until reason is so relentlessly obscured by chaos and confusion, we beg for relief. Recall Henry Kissinger foretelling this scenario.

• Regarding Spiritual Warfare With Authoritarianism •

The spiritual yardstick by which we accurately measure what the world (authority) claims is reasonable against what God reveals to be true is available every hour of every day through prayer and *careful* meditation. We learn to love through **Natural Revelation** by living our material lives and paying coherent attention. We strengthen empirical learning through **Supernatural Revelation** via prayer and silence. This is best done in the name of Christ with the aid of the Holy Spirit; a process requiring responsible commitment and action on our part, which nourishes faith and confidence in our Father's love for us. If we can't or won't accept Christ, at least follow our heart, seek truth honestly, and remain open to our Creator. Regardless how lost, all sheep can be found.

Orthodox Christian teaching tells us in Ephesians there is only one uncreated Father, whose love desires Jew and Gentile alike with all creation to join in unity as one created family under the loving Fatherhood of God. Through Christ's death and resurrection Earthly humans are offered unity in Christ's community, wherein humans are granted access to the Father, a mystery even angels came to learn. Unity in Christ affects all elements of creation; material and immaterial. Christ's sacrifice, resurrection, and exaltation enabled spiritual renewal of humanity, thereby forming the basis for reconciliation of the heavens and the Earth. Human spiritual weakness has been redeemed by Christ for us, but repair is dynamic, requiring faith and action on our part to complete reconciliation through personal choice and action. Ignoring spiritual history opens cage doors to evil influence which works to hold those doors open until we enter; after which cage doors are locked by Marxism, Fascism, and Globalism.

Not all churches and religious houses are equal. Find community where you are spiritually nourished - at home, under a tree, a Circle K sidewalk, a mountaintop, or wherever, but ask for discernment and your prayer for reconciliation will be answered. The Bible tells us there is strength in numbers, hence the importance of community. It is through this spiritual reconciliation process and healthy human choice that in faith, we protect and nourish ourselves, Earth, and all creation. Earth, humanity, and other life forms cannot be protected through fruitless geopolitical legerdemain marred by authoritarian grasping for wealth, power, and control. It makes little difference whether we are enslaved by others through Marxist or Fascist authoritarianism, or we enslave ourselves in a more friendly fashion by foolishly accepting and voting for Fascist policies.[10] We are oppressed serfs either way.

It is reconciliation with our Creator, that Satan and hordes of demon angels work so hard to prevent. Satan and the fallen angels made poor choices by deciding not only to separate from God but hate God. They bitterly wish to share their poor judgment with all humanity by cleverly marketing a manipulative *Deal with the Devil*. This malicious deal presents in many ways within many different isms, certainly within Marxism, Fascism, and Globalism.

Our Satanically debased culture, for instance, casually parrots phrases like, *falling in love*. **No one falls into love.** Love isn't a trip hazard. Life on earth is not random. Choices have consequences, often impacting others. Love is a definite choice and often a struggle. I doubt it is possible to love without being challenged by evil. If it is possible, not often. Our human dilemma is learning to receive, reciprocate, and share love in the face of obstacles, i.e., legitimate choice; hence the spiritual need for good and evil to exist. **Pope John Paul II viewed human love as a task given to us by God**, not a free gift or something that just happens. His view suggests interactive choice.

Marxism foils choice by denying spiritual human value and individual responsibility, i.e., denies the possibility of love by mandating every human being property of the State with all decisions assigned to the State apparatus. Alternatives beyond obedience, imprisonment, torture, or execution do not exist under Marxist ideology.

Without alternatives, choice does not exist. Without choice, love cannot exist. Ignorance, fear, and violence are Luciferian weapons for obstructing love. God did not create evil—Lucifer freely rejected love and embraced hate. God allows free will exercised by rational persons. Some persons, angelic or human, reject love's joy, choosing instead, the pain and agony of alienated hostility. This alienated condition is the source of all negative energy and bad things we now call evil. Our only defense against evil influence is asking for God's help, but Satanic influence doesn't permit easy choices. God hating ideologies like Marxism, Fascism, and Globalism use lies, anxiety, and violence to prevent Main Street from realizing this simple truth.

---

10 Bertram Gross, *Friendly Fascism: The New Face of Power in America*, First Printing edition (Boston: South End Press, 1999).

2 • Marxist-Fascist America

Note: *The Orthodox Church teaches that Satan is a fallen angel as are other less powerful fallen angels. Satan was created by God with the gift of creative free will just as we are.* **Satan is not evil by nature but by willful choice and action.** *Satan freely chose to stand against God and all God created. Satan and his hordes of demon angels fell from grace by their own choice to reject God's love. What we know as evil in our world comes about and is influenced by Satan, never by our Father. Humanity's ills are caused by embracing Satanic influence. God does not do bad things to good people or bad people. Because of free will, God will not stop our bad choices from causing bad things to happen. We must do the work. Satan influences all bad things, and we must defend ourselves accordingly, i.e. through the armor of God. God is not the cause of bad things, BUT God helps us see how to fix bad things when we request Divine assistance.*

Biblically, humanity has struggled and often failed in the epic battle between good and evil. Evil influence dominated the natural setting as we read in Genesis. Neither Jews nor Gentiles faithfully and uniformly honor the Ten Commandments, i.e., The Law of Moses. God's response to this ongoing human dilemma was sending His Son to give up His corporal life in redemption for our rejection of love; thereby disarming Satanic power through Christ's Ascension, leaving the Holy Spirit and the aid of God's grace to help enable better human choices. Why this was necessary is a complete mystery to me, but there it is.

Humanity's fall from grace is ongoing by free will choice, though driven by very real Satanic influence expressed as spiritual violence. The biblical story puts it on Adam and Eve, allegory or not, but we make our own choices every day. We are responsible for our choices. Therefore, in self-defense we must put on the armor of God (Ephesians 6: 10-20). Humans are not powerful enough to resist Satanic influence on our own. Satan's influence can only be overcome in the name of Jesus Christ and even then, arrogance leads us to make mistakes. **Our ability to resist evil influence is strengthened by prayer and fasting as is physical health. The power of these three weapons should not be underestimated.**

We know violence comes to us in many forms—physical, emotional, or intellectual to name three and can be passive or aggressive. Spiritual violence is subtle, often going unnoticed, though via grace and discernment, even within the confusing fog of spiritual battle we can realize our gut did notice. All forms of violence are poison darts from Satan serving one single purpose - **destruction of all creation.** The *Angel of Light* (2 Corinthians 11: 13-15) and hordes of *fallen angels* particularly enjoy influencing human beings to bring about self-imposed annihilation of our own lives. It's why every Globalist policy injures those it promises to benefit. The totalitarian Globalist ideology is pure evil. There is no truth in Satan, only deception as we find in Marxism, Fascism, and Globalism.

Globalist totalitarian ideology is Satanically influenced. The slaughter of hundreds of millions just in the last century substantiates this. The victimized Left injures and/or destroys everything it touches. There are no exceptions, and hundreds of millions imprisoned, tortured, starved, and murdered attest to the magnificence of the lie. The tasty treats offered on the engraved silver platter of Globalism are all poison.

The dialectics of Right/Left or Conservative/Liberal are nonsensical as both are 100% usurped by Globalism for its own collectivist agenda and are used as two false choices—thesis and anti-thesis. Marxism is always Leftist in today's vernacular. We debate whether Fascism is Right or Left as an irrelevant distinction. A more cogently practical distinction is freedom or slavery—representative republican democracy or totalitarian dictatorship. Anything more is semantic gibberish. Following are five UniParty schemes presented as gifts delivered by corrupt Marxist Democrats and/or Establishment Republicans.

• Five examples of Marxist-Fascist (Globalist) lies •

I. U.S. Social Security Administration (SS) created by Globalist Franklin D. Roosevelt Administration.

Enacted August 14, 1935, by Globalist FDR, SS is restricted by law to investments in U.S. Treasury Securities. American labor is obscenely taxed several ways, one of which is the social security payroll tax, usually under FICA (Federal Insurance Contributions Act). Less administrative overhead, beneficiaries are paid via SS tax collections with the remainder deposited in the Trust Fund. There is a Trust Fund of sorts, functioning in name only.

Good intentions or fraudulent wealth transference mechanisms aside, per the 2020 annual report released by *Social Security and Medicare Trustees*, the *Social Security Old-Age and Survivor's Insurance Trust Fund* is projected to become insolvent in 2034, and *Medicare's Hospital Insurance Trust Fund* insolvent in 2026. Many analysts claim *Social Security* and *Medicare* are insolvent today, though insolvency is covered up by digital money printing. No allowance for the asymmetric economic attack against American Main Streets via 2020's bio-weaponized CCP COVID Scamdemic has yet been attempted as of this writing. Long-term fallout from toxic JABs is not yet known either.

SS and Medicare are pay-as-we-go **Ponzi Schemes**, though some financial returns are generated by Treasuries held on account. Once SS taxes are invested in U.S. Treasuries, assigned monies enter the General Fund, where Congress persons appropriate it any way they please. Even if Congress were not corrupt, the system was and is 100% unsustainable since inception.

In 1945 there were 42 workers per each beneficiary in the SS system. By 1970 this number decreased to 3.6 workers per beneficiary. Today, we have 2.8 workers contributing and population demographics suggest by 2035, 2.2 workers per each beneficiary. I doubt FDR's Administration was so intellectually challenged as to require Bruce to mansplain the obvious – our 5th grade level math does not work – this Globalist Nanny-State system is a wealth-harvesting ruse.

II. Patient Protection and Affordable Care Act (Obamacare).

In 2009-2010, the Globalist Obama Administration told us we could keep our health insurance policies and doctors if we liked them, and family health insurance premiums would decrease an average of $2,500 annually. Three lies in one package. All health insurance policies not PPACA compliant were canceled under threat of penalty. Doctors were routinely changed per policy approved provider lists. Policy premiums doubled, and in many cases, tripled.

My personal PPACA experience in Phoenix, Arizona was cancellation of my family's better than adequate health coverage at ±$500 per month with PPACA compliant policy replacement at just over ±$1,400 per month, along with increased deductibles, and reduced coverage. This $1,400 per month PPACA compliant policy was the least expensive Bronze Plan available at the time. Mandated robbery continued unabated when I retired to Medicare Advantage Plans. You may recall the Obama Administration raided $750 billion from Medicare to offset PPACA affordability lies it told our useless CBO by offsetting 10-years of revenue against 6-years of expense to demonstrate PPACA budget neutrality.

Not one of my medications covered under previous health insurance plans were covered under the obamanation of Obamacare. For example, I was using a non-steroidal, topical Vitamin D cream to treat psoriasis, for which the copay under the old non-compliant plan was $110 for 65 grams. Under PPACA this bumped to a higher tier, costing me $340 for 65 grams. I needed two tubes (130 grams) per month, so nix the psoriasis cream and welcome the heartbreak.

III. BLUE states and cities impose the strictest gun control measures to supposedly reduce violence.

The twenty U.S. cities with the highest murder rates all have Globalist Democrat Mayors excepting two claiming non-partisan elections (Danville, Illinois and Saginaw, Michigan). These two are Globalist managed anyway.

Per 2018 data the top 20 are:

Detroit, MI   Memphis, TN   Birmingham, AL   Baltimore, MD
Flint, MI   St. Louis, MO   Danville, IL   Saginaw, MI

Wilmington, DE Camden, NJ Pine Bluff, AR Kansas City, MO
San Bernardino, CA Alexandria, LA Little Rock, AR
Cleveland, OH Milwaukee, WI Stockton, CA Monroe, LA
Chester, PA
Also high on the violent murder list are three more Globalist destroyed cities -
Baton Rouge, Detroit, and New Orleans.

IV. The Left decries the income gap nonstop.
Globalist Democrat run cities and states consistently demonstrate the highest
comparative income gaps while insisting Marxist-Democrat leadership failure is
not causative. RINO's incidentally are even more deceitful.

V. The Left whines about poverty continuously.
Nearly every poverty center in the U.S. developed within Marxist-Democrat
run cities. The Left again claims their destructive ideas are not causative while
failing to disclose into whose pockets $25 trillion welfare dollars disappeared.

Moving on, with respect to America at large, our nation's poisoned capital, *Washington D.C.* is sick in the same manner as *City of London* (some insist
by the City of London) and *The Vatican* because it is populated with the equivalent of global syndicate bondsman doing what they are ordered to do in return for money and privilege. These *order-followers*, slaves themselves, live under
threat of losing their privilege, along with blackmail, extortion, and threat of
violence to themselves, family, pets, friends, and associates if they don't come
to heel. Mainstream media and Hollywood are controlled in similar fashion,
acting as Public Relations Enforcers for their New World Order (NWO) handlers. *Order followers* is a descriptive term I've borrowed from Mr. Mark Passio.[11]

Note: *The District of Columbia, City of London, and Vatican City are incorporated
city-states. I do not understand the legal significance of this fact, though more than 20,000
pages of legal opinion have been written about it. I leave that rabbit hole for reader curiosity. For those who are not aware, City of London referenced above refers to City of
London Corporation within metropolitan London - sort of a British Wall Street I suppose. As I understand it, this financial district began forming a few years after the Roman
invasion of 50 A.D. along the north bank of the River Thames. Its original corporate
charter is said to no longer exist, though the Magna Carta (June 15, 1215) recognized
"it's ancient liberties", which scholars sometimes refer to as "incorporated by prescription".*

---

11 "What On Earth Is Happening," accessed April 22, 2017, http://www.whatonearthishap-
pening.com.

In any event, City of London, Vatican City, and Washington D.C. are three incorporated city states together wielding control of immense dynastic power and wealth accumulated by elite bloodlines over many centuries. Unfortunately, psychopathy and occult practices run rampant through these bloodlines and among their order following minions. These three city states are power centers for the New World Order (NWO) cabal, with Basel, Beijing, Brussels, Frankfurt, Hong Kong, New York, Paris, and others vying for well positioned seats at the Satanic table. **I refer to this cabal as a global syndicate since it syndicates evil globally.**

The self-destructive direction American culture, education, geopolitical policy, economic policy, and religious teaching have taken over this past century makes little sense outside the well-organized NWO *study group* context. It's not helpful to suggest the United States is broken because as a people we ignore our Constitution. Though an accurate observation, it assesses a symptom, not a cause. Many of us claim the U.S. Constitution the foundation of our liberty. The U.S. Constitution and Bill of Rights are the basis for our Rule of Law, but not foundational to liberty. Our Constitution arose from a more primal spiritual foundation expressed in the Declaration of Independence.

The Declaration of Independence asserts certain unalienable rights endowed by our Creator and entitled by Nature and Nature's God. President of Hillsdale College, Larry P. Arnn explains: "Universal in scope and divine in elevation, it is written in tones of majesty. It celebrates blessings that come directly from God and are known through the reason with which He created us. It proclaims the inclusion of every human being – past, present, and future – in its reach. No nation is left out. No era is excluded."[12]

The Declaration of Independence, though addressing specific circumstances of colonial America is a Declaration of unalienable Rights for all humanity, for all time, everywhere. The Declaration states, "... That to secure these Rights, Governments are instituted among Men, deriving their just Powers from the Consent of the Governed..." In other words, the Constitution and Bill of Rights institute the specific form of government selected by our Founders to secure recognized Rights granted by our Creator as outlined in the Declaration of Independence. **Government sovereignty arises from the sovereignty of the people as a group of responsibly sovereign individuals.** The 1776 Declaration concludes with: "And for the support of this declaration, with a firm reliance on the Protection of Divine Providence, we mutually pledge to each other our Lives, our Fortunes, and our sacred Honor."

---

12 Larry P. Arnn, *The Founders' Key: The Divine and Natural Connection Between the Declaration and the Constitution and What We Risk by Losing It*, 1st edition (Nashville: Thomas Nelson Inc, 2012), 8.

Fifty-six (56) signatures appear on this uniquely original national **Declaration**. Every signature executed in full knowledge that signing this document was an act of treason against Great Britain's King George III punishable by death. We have ignored our Constitutional Rule of Law for decades at the insistence of Mercantilist policy makers and Marxist/Fascist *order followers*, but **the underlying CAUSATIVE issue is irresponsibly abandoning our God given sovereignty as individuals and as a nation.**

Marxist-Fascist refusal to acknowledge we are created by God, endowed with certain unalienable rights recognized and secured by our Constitutional Republic and Rule of Law, places our lives and liberty under arbitrary Rule of Man.

Mercantilism is the Rule of Man.
Marxism is the Rule of Man.
Fascism is the Rule of Man.
Technocracy is the Rule of Man.
Transhumanism is the Rule of Man.
Globalism is the End of Man and all Creation.

Unfortunately, ALL representative republican forms of government are predictably and ALWAYS abused by weak *selected* Representatives and appointed bureaucrats abusing authority in their own self-interest. No known exceptions. When such self-interest is determined and/or controlled by outside psychopathic interests of a Satanic Global Syndicate and supported by Main Street apathy, there is no happy ending for Main Street. As our Founders recognized, a representative republic, oligarchic itself, can only be maintained by morally vigilant citizens enforcing their God given sovereignty. No known exceptions.

We the people of Main Street must work together, **awakening** each other to throw off ignorance, fear, and ideological shackles of dumbed down, Globalist controlled, Marxist acceptance. Then we must remove psychopathic Fascist thugs enforcing ideological and physical subjugation. We must, with God's grace, do this ourselves. Note that nations are only free—until they aren't.

No leader can or will obtain or maintain freedom for us. This incredible battle, this noble task is ours, the people of Main Street to take on and with the grace of God achieve victory. Freedom is the necessary goal of winning the spiritual battle between good and evil, i.e., learning to love. Freedom is foundational to love – therefore EVERY TOTALITARIAN SYSTEM OUTLAWING OR MARGINALIZING FREEDOM IS EVIL.

Marxism, Fascism, and Globalism are anti-God, anti-human, and therefore evil. **Human** life on Earth is spiritual warfare. This glorious and wonderful battle is our destiny. **Be not afraid.**

> **"If it is not right, do not do it: if it is not true, do not say it."**
> **Marcus Aurelius Antoninus** (A.D. 121-180)
> *(Roman Emperor & Stoic Philosopher)*
> *(From Meditations: XII: 17)*

3 • Study Group Fascism

Remedy:
- Mercantilism is bait leading to Main Street's economic gulag.
- Marxism locks the financial gate.
- Fascism throws away the gate key.
- Globalism synthesizes the above into Satanic enslavement.
- ♥Asking our Creator for help avoiding all four is a good idea. Going it alone is not a good idea.
- ♠ Reject all four Luciferian Isms.

Evil only survives and sustains its abusive sway when humanity is OBE-DIENT to evil's MALEVOLENT INFLUENCE. The **international study group system** is an influential consortium of seminars empowering global indoctrination of the Main Street many by the Elite few. It is a prestigious form of mind control wherein participants volunteer in exchange for recognition, privilege, and wealth. It comprises the epicenter of Deep State networking for better, more powerful elected or appointed positions, positive press coverage, more wealth, more power, awards, prizes, access to academic publication, access to publicly funded research and information, etc. The study group system *inner circles* effectively facilitate dulling and distorting *outer circle* mass perception, cleverly misaligning the focus of reason, and sanctioning manipulated points of view suiting its own *inner circle purposes*. Such thought manipulation is a form of mass theft restricting freedom of thought, speech, and action. It is inherently and willfully evil, though most participants don't know it.

Ideas are important things. Short of Jesus Christ, concepts are more important and more authentic than most bearers of concepts, though only idea bearers can bring ideas to our attention and then to fruition. Because ideas are so readily subverted by self-serving agendas of instructors, managers, rulers, and so forth—it's a good idea to run with the idea, not the teacher, manager, or politician. As citizens, evaluating the legitimacy of any policy requires accurate perception, coherent discernment, and solid reasoning skills – all three of which can be manipulated by skilled politicians or other orators for purposes of which we may or may not be aware. **Potomac Fever** is dangerous which is why I humbly recommend never supporting any politician personally. Yes, I know we have to vote for candidates. Support the good guys and gals, elect them to one or two terms and let 'em safely return home. We can support a politician's ideas and carry them forward by becoming a politician ourselves, through conversation, social media, writing, or if so motivated, through Republican Party Precinct Committees, school boards, city councils, county boards, church groups, associations, or other local organizations. In any case and at any level of our choosing, we must vigilantly involve ourselves in government affairs and informed voting or our republic is lost.

Local, local, local is the beginning and end of every public policy. Culture is always local and always precedes politics, sprouting locally, then spreading like ripples across a pond and back again. Our spiritual lives determine cultural tradition. Healthy spirituality is prerequisite to beneficial policy at the local, state, and national level—but being morally correct and having the best ideas are never as many conservatives believe, enough to win votes.

Until November 3, 2020 election fraud, Study Group Fascism has never demonstrated being correct versus winning more powerfully than on November 3, 1964. Lyndon B. Johnson vaporized Barry Goldwater with 486 electoral votes to 52, the largest electoral margin in U.S. history. According to Richard A. Viguerie *("funding father of the conservative movement")* in his 2014 book, *TAKEOVER*, no prominent politicos of the time such as Nelson Rockefeller, Henry Cabot Lodge, George Romney, or William Scranton even bothered debating Goldwater on the merits. Goldwater lost massively due to a continuous barrage of establishment media slander and claims of extremest, kook, crackpot, and so forth. Political victory by best policy can only be achieved by paying attention, rolling up our sleeves, getting our hands dirty, and leaping into the fray at whatever level is appropriate to our personal skill set.

Quality of character or lack thereof combined with changing views often results in humans disappointing each other for a surprising range of reasons, some pro, some con. Political leaders, good or bad, come and go, but ideas are forever. The American Constitutional Republic is an idea we can hang a hat on. No such thing has existed in human history, so the concept is experimental, fragile, and its founding freedoms render it prone to attack. The Satanically inspired study group system never sleeps, never stops attacking, and never stops infiltrating every sector of society. Conservative Christians must be as directly involved or more involved than the Globalist Left and their place-holding Progressive Republican associates.

The only defense a representative republic has is the moral integrity of its citizenry. Any and all societal damage done to its moral citizenry wreaks abuse on the republic itself. That said, moral integrity without appropriate action is useless. Proof is provided by a century of American Main Street apathy allowing a massive Fascist bureaucracy to metastasize under our noses behind the silly delusion of Marxist Nanny State promises. Discussion, debate, books, speeches, and having the best ideas did not stop this onslaught. Marxist Democrat and Progressive Republicans rolled up their sleeves and got directly involved in critical areas of education, policy making, and administration. Their deceptive organizing skills have soundly unbalanced the confident self-righteousness of constitutionally conservative people like myself, convinced we could win simply because we were on the right side of God. We forgot—God doesn't defeat the evil of Marxism and Fascism for us—we must, with faith and grace do the work ourselves.

A monarchy is a dictatorship of one. An oligarchy is dictatorship by a few. Democracy is dictatorship by the majority. A representative republic is a representative oligarchy by definition, hence is fragile by nature. A non-vigilant, out-of-control republic abandoning its checks and balances becomes an oligarchic Administrative State. When that unchecked Administrative State is controlled by unseen, powerful others, it becomes an **Administrative Dictatorship.** When an Administrative Dictatorship grows into a self-protective, bloated bureaucratic monster it rages out of control. It is said as few as 150 people control more than 70% of all multinational corporate monopolies on Earth. It is these few people, regardless of number, who now control America's Administrative Dictatorship in service to their own Satanic Agenda. The primary Luciferian levers of abusive power are Marxism and Fascism, which combine to form Globalism, i.e., global slavery.

Psychopathic Fascist ideology institutionalizes raw violence inflicted on others by Satanically influenced *Pawns of Privilege*. Fascist brutality is obscured and sold to Main Street as necessary enforcement of fairness via false promises and predictable failures of Marxism, never a prescription for Main Street empowerment or abundance. The staccato rhythm of hob-nailed fear mongering, for the public good of course, is history's midwife birthing the of loss of liberty – ironically emerging out of the 17th and 18th century **Enlightenment Era.**

Humans figured out how to move heavy objects with sledges about 9,000 or so years ago but didn't figure out rolling was better than pushing and pulling for another 4,000 or so years when the wheel idea came along and finally – spoked wheels. Eventually this led to *friction element bearings* and so forth and we humans were feeling smart as all get out. So smart in fact, just like Lucifer back in the *Angel of Light* days, we became so **enlightened** we started thinking we could and should reason our way through life's adventures without Divine assistance. Many wonderful material things emerged from the *Enlightenment Period* along with pollution and better ways to kill each other, but spiritually we stepped backwards into the spiritual darkness we live with today.

Understanding today's evolving authoritarian government abuse, i.e., Globalism since **Friendly Fascism**[13] began metastasizing in America requires consideration of synergy arising from the merger of Mercantilism, Marxism, and Fascism into Globalist ideology. This subversive synergy of controlled conflict and false choices develops through the **international study group system** (my words) arising from early *Rhodes-Milner Round Tables*.[14] Understanding Globalism requires fathoming how and why false choices are regularly presented to Main Street. It requires grasping how a small number of *inner circle voices* can be amplified throughout the echo system until the *vast outer circles* incorrectly perceive enormous consensus.

Today's **global study group system** expanded from *British Round Tables* to an extent the entire world has become a matrixed study group system rendering it difficult to identify or define. Foundationally, it is circles within circles comprised of dynastic family members, secret societies, public societies, governments, central banking, multi-national corporations, bar associations, trusts, foundations, endowments, universities, think tanks, schools, professional associations, media, unions, churches, and so forth. It's wide, deep, and obscure — BUT at the same time, as Steve Bannon might say, *"it's right up in our grill."*.

When circumstances become overwhelming or confusing, an excellent *rule of thumb* for surveyors and civil engineering designers is **begin researching a problem or issue by going back to something verifiably true and correct.** Something we are certain of to the extent possible. From that foundational starting point, we can work forward to determine where something went wrong and how best to correct a deficiency. Once we understand initial conditions and how they relate to present and future conditions, we can better design a plan for what we are creating from a blank piece of paper – or blank computer screen. This thought process usefully applies to geopolitical and cultural analysis as well. Investigative journalist, Jon Rappoport shares a similar approach in his series *Outside the Matrix* when discussing how to assess information in a world of disinformation.

---

13 Gross, *Friendly Fascism*.
14 Carroll Quigley, *Anglo-American Establishment* (San Diego, CA: Dauphin Publications Inc., 2013), chap. 7.

America and Western Europe veered sharply off any path following a moral compass bearing as soon as Main Street intellectuals embraced the **Enlightenment Era** state of mind suggesting REASON itself to be the originating source of legitimate authority. OUT with God, IN with the Prince of Darkness. As Gil Bailie suggests in *Violence Unveiled* (1995): "Those who think that disdain for religion is an antidote for religious superstition haven't sufficiently pondered the French Revolution or Madame Mao's cultural revolution or Pol Pot's bloody attempt at social engineering." Bailie also suggests we fail to realize the world's mother lode of **anti-superstition** resides precisely in the teaching of Hebrew prophets and the New Testament. Clearly our polluted, chaotically violent world is not better off for abandoning the discipline of Judeo-Christian tradition for Luciferian delusion. Such abandonment is a lie proclaiming ordered societal life, liberty, and constitutional republics can stand firmly on the unrestricted foundation of **reason alone**.

This **moral relativism** detour around spiritual discernment began at the ideological fork, where as Enlightened citizens, we began ignoring our Creator, turned away from the Christian principles and justice system upon which the United States' Rule of Law is founded, toward something less representative of Main Street's best interests. As a practical matter, we abandoned our American Covenant with God.[15] **Christian principles and unalienable rights endowed by our Creator as enshrined in our Declaration of Independence, secured by enforcing our Constitution are the covenantal rock on which America is founded.** Abandoning this rock-solid foundation, to ostensibly build a promised utopian future on a relativistic undefined dialectic, was and is a destabilizing decision, a trap. A trap set by whom?

Lucifer, of course. Make no mistake about it – we have as a people decided to abandon our responsibly protective American covenant. We threw away the only moral yardstick we have. It is consequential most of us failed to notice we took a fork in the road; that we abdicated God-given sovereign responsibility to our own republic. We have been induced as once free citizens to subjugate ourselves to a bought-off and/or blackmailed herd of misled and/or self-serving politicians, unelected bureaucrats, and so-called experts mis-educated themselves by indoctrinated academics via a **propagandized study group system**. A Satanic information system of lies supporting **the new authoritarian foundation of technocratic totalitarian sand** upon which we now futilely attempt to construct our children's dystopian future. This burgeoning Administrative Dictatorship already bankrupted itself and failed its citizens as it

---

15 Timothy Ballard, *The Covenant, One Nation under God: America's Sacred & Immutable Connection to Ancient Israel* (New York: Legends Library Press, 2019).

has everywhere, every totalitarian time, though this history is ignored in American schools and its failure temporarily hidden by unsustainable digital coinage.

Global syndicate obliteration of America's Constitutional Republic requires undermining appreciation of our God-given unalienable rights and responsibilities as enshrined in the Declaration and recognized by our Constitutional Rule of Law. Faith in God and knowledge of our infinite value as persons and children of God must be abolished, dumbing us down to a more manageable animal level of consciousness. **Hail Transhumanism – if not animal consciousness, then machine unconsciousness!** The sanctity of our world is designed for protection (dominion) provided by responsible human consciousness and love. Destroying free will consciousness as Transhumanism intends, is a sure path to Satanic destruction of all creation. Satan and hordes of fallen angels have chosen to sabotage humanity's responsibility for sustaining healthy life on many fronts, the most visible of which is BIG GOVERNMENT, the nesting lair of Marxism and Fascism.

This sabotage is primarily wrought by enlisting the **study group system** to enable academic attack and media persecution of America's once autonomous middle class, while simultaneously preventing upward mobility by the less fortunate to join productive middle-class autonomy. In juxtaposition with this deceit, indoctrinated study group victims instigate divisive class, ethnic, racial, religious, sexual, and other forms of cultural animosity between targeted groups. In some respects, this disjointed logic path to chaos is an outcome of *Reflexive Law*, now popular in academia (See Chapter 4). The intended result is *Cultural Marxist* ignorance coupled with a failing State-run economic and financial system.

To the extent members of manipulated target groups sublimate themselves to intentionally divisive ideologies like *Cultural Marxism* or *Critical Race Theory* with their inherent racism to abolish racism, various levels of agitation and/or violence are engaged toward those we are conditioned to mistrust or even hate. The ensuing chaotic emotionalism blinds us to reality. All forms of violence including armed assault, battery, and arson are deemed politically correct political expression for the global syndicate's Marxist battering ram – but not for anyone else. Non status quo ideas are *verboten* and are criminalized. Questioning authority is domestic terrorism and verbal disagreement constitutes violent attack. The least of us are effectively alienated and weaponized against our own health, enrichment, and upward mobility. We are trapped by Marxism within the economic class into which we are born or reduced to, then blame each other for the trap. Toxic Whitey, for example, is blamed but no viable solution offered. Family is demolished and The Fascist State pretends to own our children.

3 • Study Group Fascism

Since the advent of *Cultural Marxism*, over time, as this intellectual delusion progresses, accurate perception and logic steadily diminish, with maladjusted frustration (*free floating anxiety*) morphing into anger and rage, now emotionally self-inflicting until Main Street is so busy fighting with itself, it fails as a political union to realize the global entirety of Main Street is being impoverished and enslaved. It doesn't matter if we vote for this depravity or tolerate fraudulent machines voting for it on our behalf. Enslavement is our new reality either way.

Crippled by declining ability to reason, we enslave ourselves by a Luciferian inspired, malevolently declining thought process requiring no walls, no barbed wire, and no cattle cars. Our minds become prisons within which we are rendered helpless, complacently accepting antihuman population controls implemented by a ruling class coerced by a small group of psychopathic Elites. We roam freely within our unwalled prison today, but with the advent of transhuman nanotechnology, crypto coupons, and increasing electronic surveillance, roaming free will no longer be tolerated outside privileged circles. Despite the hype, autonomous vehicles for example, are not about benefiting Main Street. AI vehicles are about controlling and restricting Main Street. Today's much loved wildlife preserves, national parks and forests, riparian habitat, salmon and trout streams, fresh water lakes, mountain ranges, etc. will eventually be declared off limits to human invasion by Main Street boaters, campers, fisherman, hikers, and hunters. Only the privileged will have digital travel privileges.

Fulfillment of U.N. Agendas 21/30 mean Main Street enslavement and travel restrictions are implemented by a multi-faceted matrix of transhuman nanotechnology, surveillance, mind control methodologies, poor nutrition, toxic pharmacology, deviant technocracy, and privileged ruling class pawns, also enslaved though they may not realize it. Reality degenerates into a poorly understood holographic projection within which we wander—dazed, confused, divided, and weak. Coherently unable or unwilling to defend ourselves - smart phone images, sound bites, and electronic social media become reality. Labeling things takes on more value than creating things. Listing things becomes more important than understanding things until in McLuhan fashion[16], the **message of the medium** overwhelms direct human contact altogether, rendering us less human and more machinelike, i.e., authoritarian **transhuman hell**.

We as a people complacently allowed psychopaths to occupy positions of power and influence in agriculture, banking, business, education, food processing, government, industrial farming, law, manufacturing, media, medicine, military, mining, publishing, science, shipping, transportation, etc. Our complacence is

---

16 Marshall McLuhan and Lewis H. Lapham, *Understanding Media: The Extensions of Man*, Reprint edition (Cambridge, Mass: The MIT Press, 1994).

not accidental. We are programmed. Many psychopaths we are conditioned to accept as experts or leaders are socially deviant, steadily nudging American Main Streets to gullibly adopt unconstitutional policies assured to bring about cultural and economic disharmony. Such chaos has always led to tyranny and will now, unless stopped in its tracks. Globalist ideology is the perfect hammer for this chaos nail as the Left injures anything it gets near and destroys everything it can get its hand on. The Progressive Establishment Right panders and despicably place holds for the more openly Satanic Left. A perfect UniParty that must be fixed and only we the people of Main Street can fix it.

This predictably unsustainable human circumstance guarantees eventual rebellion, anarchy, and Main Street turmoil. Once *controlled conflict* has the Main Street pot boiling to an untenable level of impoverishment, anger, frustration, and violence, even to the extent of civil war – the inevitable authoritarian solution, Globalism will be offered and voila – Main Street everywhere can again enjoy its long-lost condition of serfdom. Technocracy's AI will render slavery permanent.

So goes the *color revolution* brought home to the streets of America where rogue elements within the United States' power structure, working with City of London and The Vatican, together spread study group lies about sharing freedom, democracy, and fairness. Unfortunately, Main Street hasn't noticed that hopelessness, global impoverishment, and slavery are hidden within the false hope of this utopian lie. Globalist ideology is a Satanic Trojan Horse implanted into society by the **study group system**. **Color Revolution** in victim nations like Armenia, Bahrain, Lebanon, Macedonia, Poland, Russia, Syria, Ukraine, and dozens of others has now been brought home to North America by the global syndicate. America's Main Street painfully basks in the glory of its own shadow governed, CIA pacification agenda.[17]

In the upside-down, inside-out Globalist gulag, interrogators are our friends; indoctrinators are teachers; conditioning (brainwashing) is education; asking questions is conspiracy; free speech is outlawed; truth is a crime; patriots are insurrectionist; the law abiding are outlaws; the productive are greedy; the greedy are selfless; arson prone rioters and looters are peaceful; pornography, pedophilia, bestiality, and cannibalism are normal; toxic vaccines are medicine; the murder of children is prochoice; global climate change is science; etc.

America, deeply infected with this globalist disease, primarily by Marxist vaccination (pun intended) enforced by Fascist abuse of power is Constitutionally sick. This Luciferian infection has progressed (pun intended) to the point, if we can spiritually awaken to realize our national error in judgement; fixing it first

---

17 Douglas Valentine, *The Phoenix Program* (Open Road Distribution, 2016).

requires understanding how we got here. Why for example, are we willing to exchange liberty, opportunity, and abundance already enjoyed for provably false promises bringing hopeless devastation everywhere imposed? Communism by any name is a system of devastation. Enforced by indoctrinated Fascist violence it becomes omnicide. Look at what the Chinese Communist Party is doing to the environment and nary a peep from so-called environmentalists. Why?

Is it as Dennis Prager, founder of *Prager U* suggests? **Many of us prefer being taken care of to freedom.** If so, belief in nanny-state Socialism and its Fascist enforcement render liberty beyond the reach of many – but for those preferring the responsibility of liberty, of freedom under God, we shall continue our inquiry into what was our once cherished American value system and examine how it can be taken back and fixed. We will overcome study group indoctrination, reestablishing spiritual primacy in our temporarily godforsaken world. This is a *how and when* not an *if*.

American Fascism was spawned by Western Atlanticist banking and industrial interests by funding false promises of ethnic and cultural fairness via Corporatism in what was to be a more secure Germany, Italy, and Japan. Hitler's *Nazi International* anti-thesis was born, funded, and nurtured in the Mercantilist Anglo-American Establishment womb of Hegelian Dialectic to lead unwitting opposition against the Communist thesis. The *Rhodes-Milner* Round Table(s) (City of London study group Grandfather) didn't even bother denying or defending lack of European opposition to the predictable result of Hitler's militarizing the industrial Rhineland in violation of both the *Treaty of Versailles* and the *Locarno Pacts*. The disastrous idea to pit Germany against Russia, hoping for a stalemate weakening both, not originated by the Rhodes-Milner inner circle, was so powerfully wielded by Neville Chamberlain and others via difficult to control *outer circles* of the Rhodes-Milner Round Table, that once sold to Main Street, the horrific idea could not be removed from the table.[18]

With Italy overrunning Ethiopia and Japan invading Manchuria alongside *Nazi International*, the seeds of Fascism were sown, and America's Main Streets stepped right into its poison garden. Subsequent history up to WW II is well documented, though less well known. The **first post WW II chink** in America's shield, supposedly protecting American sovereignty was **weaponizing propaganda rather than putting on the armor of truth.** Friedrich Nietzsche warned, *when battling monsters beware, we do not become monsters,* but our CIA was behind the classroom door that day. For example, skipping past the Federal Reserve debacle of 1913 with the horrendously destruc-

---

18 Quigley, *Anglo-American Establishment*, 264–66.

tive 16th and 17th Amendments; our CIA, from its global syndicate spawning in 1947, claimed to fight against Marxism's Communist propaganda.

Taking CIA leadership at their word, which I do not, they failed to understand or intentionally ignored the most powerful antipropaganda weapon available is TRUTH. **Truth is the appropriate counter to any lie.** Intentionally or unintentionally, our CIA ignored that factoid, countering with their own egotistical propaganda apparatus. It took about a minute for CIA assets to become mirror images of the monsters they fought - a predictable outcome likely intended from its global syndicate inception. The CIA as well as most other Federal agencies (many of them such as the DEA and FBI infiltrated by CIA operatives) are now monstrous enemies of the people, exclusively serving global syndicate psychopathy. Were Allen Dulles and Shadow Government friends intrinsically evil creatures? Of course not. They were none-the-less overwhelmed and used by strategically powerful forces they sought to overcome.[19] This was a predictably failed outcome of battling evil on our own from outside our American covenant with God – a mistake our Founders did not make, despite their own personal and political issues.

As of 2021, Communism has devastated American banking, business, education, government, Hollywood, media, medicine, publishing, and science at every level. Antonio Gramsci could only dream of the Satanic destruction *Cultural Marxism* has successfully wrought. The dumbing down is spectacular. Many Americans believed for example, in January 2021; mentally challenged, arrogantly corrupt, provably treasonous, Joe Biden, stashed in a basement by corrupt handlers for months, speaking only words he was ordered to speak through his earphone after losing ability to follow the teleprompter, then messing that up, won an election and can function as President of the United States. Comedian, Ron White told us, "Stupid can't be fixed. Stupid is forever." (I hope Mr. White was incorrect.) Fascist authoritarianism renders *Cultural Marxist* devastation dangerous to counteract, a huge dent in liberty's armor - and the fraudulent Biden Regime fully embraces both evils.

The **second chink** in America's post WW II freedom armor, building on the first, a possibly fatal chink, is failure of our three branches of government to defend their Executive, Legislative, and Judicial turf; while at the same time, unconstitutionally, each branch penetrates turf of the other two branches. This ongoing governmental misfeasance quickly degenerated into *malfeasance in office* by disrupting the synergy of checks and balances, which until 1913 or so, made the sum of our republican parts greater than the whole. De-

---

19 David Talbot, *The Devil's Chessboard: Allen Dulles, the CIA, and the Rise of America's Secret Government* (Harper Perennial (Harper Collins Publishers), 2015).

terioration of any meaningful Main Street political voice along with growth of unbridled government power is symptomatic of Fascist dictatorship.

Note: *Constitutionally, in my non-legal opinion, the Judicial Branch is not co-equal with the Executive and Legislative Branches. This is an insidious fallacy of Reflexive Law. Judicial power is constitutionally limited to adjudicating (trying) disputes between States, disputes between citizens of different States, or Constitutional issues to which the Federal Government is party. This limitation does not sit well with Fascist psychopathy, still somewhat restrained by legislative process, even if self-aggrandizing, so is carefully obscured from Main Street view.*

Front and center in support of this imbalance stand the horrible mistakes of the 16th Amendment (02-03-1913) and the even worse 17th Amendment (04-08-1913). The 16th Amendment provided unconstitutional access to Main Street pocket books by corrupt government insiders to feed global syndicate coffers. The 17th Amendment removed the legitimate voice of State's Rights from the bi-cameral Congress, rendering D.C. generally and the 16th Amendment specifically, unfixable until Main Street catches on to the hoax. This loss of Constitutional checks and balances renders our federal government irrelevant with respect to *just governance* of Main Street, enabling the whole of it to function with impunity as a cesspool of organized crime, money laundering, and resource rape.

Washington D.C. is not a swamp. D.C. is a filthy septic pit and liberty demolishing criminal enterprise responsive only to the biggest stick and most egregious blackmail applied by factionalized global syndicate players. The *District of Columbia* has become a tool of evil and must be purged and fixed. Only Main Street can fix it. However, we can only garner the wisdom, courage, will, and strength to fix it with the grace of the Holy Spirit bolstering concerted populist action via our faith in Christ. Acting alone without Divine Providence is how we got into this Satanically influenced mess.

Note: *Spiritual history demonstrates the inherent danger of recklessly challenging a powerful demon on our own. Such a challenge can only be safely accepted and engaged in the name of Jesus Christ and even then, mistakes can easily be made. The history of exorcism painfully bears this out. Not all demons are powerful, some little more than evil pranksters, but a powerful demon is dangerous and not to be toyed with.*[20]

The fault of course, does not lie at the doorstep of corrupt D.C. parasites bearing their own guilt, but at our local indoctrinated doorsteps for apathetically allowing this subversion to occur. The problematic cause of our now endemic loss of liberty is found on Main Street USA, not on symptomatic Pennsylvania Avenue, Independence Avenue, First Street, 2nd Street, or

---

20 Malachi Martin, *Hostage to the Devil: The Possession and Exorcism of Five Contemporary Americans*, Reissue edition (San Francisco, Calif.: HarperOne, 1992).

"K" Street in the Masonic sewers of Washington D.C. The study group system ensures protection of the guilty by disabling Main Street understanding. Study group invective and misinformation restrain us from realizing we must drain the Masonic septic pit and that if we the people replace every crook in D.C. today but fail to change our thinking, we will just replace the old crooks with new crooks tomorrow. **We are the problem and must face it directly, which means stepping into the sewer and getting our hands dirty.**

We routinely see U.S. legislators refusing to honor oversight and budgetary responsibilities as well as ignoring the people's legitimate business, while corruptly engaging money laundering activities for special interests. We have judges unconstitutionally legislating from the bench with Congress allowing it to proceed uncontested. We have some judges inappropriately acting as prosecutors with zero judicial oversight by so-called higher courts. Our Supreme Circus hides within its own obscene bubble of blackmail, extortion, and cowardice only the nine black robed clowns comprehend.

Finally, we have White House Executives stumbling around like chickens with their heads cut off issuing Executive Orders in lieu of legislation because there isn't any other way to do anything, as Congress is fully engaged in money laundering for enrichment of global syndicate bosses, their handlers, associates, and themselves – all under pain of blackmail, extortion, or worse. We the complacent taxpayers subsidize this dark activity with exorbitant sums of Main Street wealth redistributed to insiders who trample our abandoned liberty. Then we bless this evil with apathy and denial, rubbing our own noses in the filthy D.C. quagmire we paid for and voted (or machines we paid for voted) into putrid existence.

How does abdication of balanced turf administration by the three branches of Federal government come about? How does the judiciary rise to obscene levels of power it was never constitutionally granted? Where does the idea for this originate and how can such a bad idea infect so many people? How does the historically proven concept of impoverishment by totalitarian dictatorship become more palatable to the American public, than participation in the most powerful mechanism for reducing poverty and providing opportunity yet seen on earth? A reality so many of the public have experienced themselves. **Welcome to the study group indoctrination system.**

All flaws considered, and there are many forms of abuse; a morally founded, Constitutional Republic coupled with free market capitalism are unequaled as a combined system enabling freedom and abundance, even for, maybe especially for those participating marginally. Even with extensive abuses of power exercised by *the haves*, upward mobility in terms of one's opportunistic circumstance is enabled. This is not historically arguable. So, how did we get here? Why do many Americans believe a Marxist, Fascist, Globalist style totalitarian system funded by a global syndicate historically responsible for hundreds of millions of impoverished, imprisoned, tortured, starved, and murdered innocents can suddenly be just wonderful for us – gimme some a' that?

Such mass delusion does not happen overnight. It requires decades of *Enlightened reason* and subversion by *Cultural Marxist* infiltration into schools, publishing, media, entertainment, sports, government, NGOs, professional associations, churches, etc.—all coordinated through the study group system. In the NWO hive-mind context, Left and Right, liberal and conservative are controlled opposition; two sides of the same globalist coin. We live politically with differing rhetorical pandering serving one global agenda through a functionally enslaving UniParty. Insiders, for the most part, understand this enslavement agenda as worldwide totalitarian dictatorship with Elites as Slave Owners; privileged Ruling Class as Enforcers; and Main Street people as Slave Labor. Main Street is cannon-fodder for endless wars necessary for *unwashed* population control, *useless eater* servitude to Elite agendas, and Elite profit taking.

Unfortunately for indoctrinated NWO believers, all NWO business is transacted on a NEED-TO-KNOW basis. Circles within circles in the Jesuit organizational fashion followed by City of London Round Tables and their extended international study group system. The NWO CEO is Satan, and the only agenda is destruction, i.e., complete annihilation of all creation. Pure hatred. Few NWO pawns understand this spiteful aspect of their Satanic religion - and it is religion in the deepest sense, with or without understanding, ritualistic ceremony, or self-awareness.

Fascism and Marxism are twisted Globalist sisters, interaction between which destroys any semblance of free markets, hope, or Main Street opportunity. *Cultural Marxist materialism* deceitfully attacks spiritually and intellectually while *Fascism* openly attacks materially. How does the intellectual side of this composite business plan operate? Americans today, particularly young people trapped in Marxist conditioning centers called schools are led to believe by heavily funded globalist sources, that underlying causes of societal difficulties stem from misunderstanding and lack of consensus regarding various environmental, scientific, medical, legal, political, economic, religious, sexual, cultural, or other highly divisive, professionally agitated issues. Indoctrinators fail to point out, these issues are part of everyday life and are not fatal.

Organized agitation and targeted propaganda aggregate lies designed to indoctrinate and divide individual persons by plucking at uninformed emotional heart strings, thereby narrowly energizing each person against this or that to the detriment of their best interest. **The Left never stands for building anything.** The Left stands against everything including itself, hence its many contradictions. The Left does not build; it criticizes, demonizes, marginalizes, mocks, ridicules, and tears down. The Left has zero constructively sustainable ideas. The Left confiscates and destroys while the Progressive Right enables Leftist pathology in controlled conflicting service to Globalist totalitarianism. Leaders of both thesis and anti-thesis are themselves enslaved more ruinously than their Main Street victims.

Once programmed victims react to targeted issues irrationally, often perceiving differing viewpoints as violent attacks against their person, they automatically respond to perceived attacks adversarially with learned soundbites ending any useful exchange of ideas. Such indoctrination, over time, produces defined neural pathways and programmed habitual response behavior. Vocal parroting replaces thoughtful conversation. Commonly, on social media for example, views opposing the *status quo* are ridiculed, cursed at, and finally blocked by Globalist pawns and order following techies. This is mass Tavistockian manipulation at its finest demonstrating how and why so few notice *The Green New Deal* has little to do with environment or energy and everything to do with Main Street impoverishment and totalitarian control agendas. Unaudited public green monies are distributed to unaudited green NGOs to unaccountable infinity with some portion of funds kicking back to politicos and some paying for more propaganda and more indoctrination.

Confirmed globalists are chronically incapacitated, incapable of sustained logic. They are unable to connect dot "A" to dot "B". Partially indoctrinated Liberals and some Rinos are still being programmed, have some reasoning capability remaining, and may sustain a degree of balanced intellectual capacity, but their most noticeable attributes are ignorance, cowardice, meanness, anger, negativity, and finger-pointing. Responsibility is shunned in favor of targeted scapegoats.

The Left is used as the vicious battering ram of globalism, parasitically invading all hosts judged worthy of robbing, destroying, or both. Their contemporary, well-organized infiltration process, first developed by Soviet KGB propagandists, explained by defector, Yuri Bezmenov in 1984 is poorly understood by most Americans and is implemented in four phases: **Demoralization, Destabilization, Crisis, and Normalization.** Communist infiltration of the United States has been ongoing since the 1920's, but this more sophisticated format, i.e., Socialism by more effective lies, was unleashed in America post WW II. The intent is 100% annihilation of republicanism, replaced by totalitarian dictatorship, reducing Main Street citizens to transhuman serfdom.

3 • Study Group Fascism

Contrary to urban myth, Marxism is adversarial to God but not necessarily Godless as we are often told. Karl Marx not only believed in God but openly hated God, writing poetic pieces stating so. Marxism is pure Luciferian hatred unleashed. Its 21st century advocates are cowardly traitors, deceit, and uninformed votes in place of tanks, guns, barbed wire, and gulags – although the Biden, Bush, Cheney, Clinton, McCain, Romney, Obama posers demonstrate interest in re-educating or exterminating opposing Constitutional views.

Add to the Bolshevik threat, the Chinese Communist Party's (CCP) **Hundred Year Marathon** strategy (1949 – 2049)[21] to take down the United States and the west, thereby establishing its own global hegemony with minimal open warfare and, *Houston – we have a 4th Turning Crisis*. The fraudulently elected Biden regime showcase themselves daily as perfected CCP Pawns under the deceptive Chinese (*Warring States*) strategy. America has in 2021 for the first time, what may well be a 100% or nearly 100% treasonous White House Administration supported by at least 90% of Congress... or worse. In further support of fraud, unelected judiciary, including Supremes are at least 89% AWOL.

Global syndicate deceit on a truly magnificent level. As education, publishing, media, government at every level, citizen groups, professional associations, and churches are infected with NWO programming, reason vanishes, limiting discussion to useless distraction. Some refer to this orchestrated limiting of debate, as the *Overton Window*, limiting discussion to targeted symptoms of underlying problems, placing all debate within narrowly defined boundaries circumscribed by political correctness, ridicule, character assassination, etc. The *Overton Window* is of course an effective *idea limiting tool* of the global syndicate's study group indoctrination system. It controls more effectively than blackmail or physical violence.

The *Overton Window* is observable fact, operation of which is a form of intellectual violence. In 2020 and 2021's asymmetric economic warfare attack on the U.S. for example, it's why otherwise intelligent people wear cloth masks to ward off viruses in the same way erecting chain link fencing wards off mosquitoes. It's why we don't protect our elderly who may have multiple comorbidities, instead quarantining the young and healthy who with early treatment have a 99.9% SARS-CoV-2 Scamdemic survivability rate. It's why we negligently close schools and demand child COVID JABs when children have nearly zero chance of becoming ill from SARS-CoV-2. A child has 50 times more chance of becoming seriously ill from a synthetic mRNA COVID JAB, than from so-called COVID infection, yet indoctrinated parents with good intentions line their kids up for the JAB. Thank you CCP and treasonous American order followers.

---

21 "The Hundred-Year Marathon: China's Secret Strategy to Replace America as the Global Superpower: Pillsbury, Michael: 9781250081346: Amazon.Com: Books."

The result of persistently targeted **study group propaganda** flooded onto Main Street over repetitive time is *mass formed* amalgamation of hive-mind groups effectively divided against opposing hive-mind groups, then supported within each group by peer pressured guilt, anger, and hostility toward anyone or any group daring hold antithetic views. As provoked anxiety deepens hostility into some degree of mindless fear driven rage; communication strangles, every issue becoming personal and irresolvable, until finally – **violence becomes the last alternative to societal impotence.**

The people's White House, U.S. Congress, and Supreme Circus, all thoroughly study group brainwashed, like most other national government entities around the world are compliantly dominated by multinational global syndicate thugs. Honest people are now *domestic terrorists*. Honor and integrity are AWOL. Administrative Dictatorship runs rampant over constitutionally recognized rights.

All creation is tied together and united through our Creator's loving life energy, spirituality, and gift of creative intelligence (imagination). Satan mimics Natural Law, Supernatural Revelation and this loving spiritual consciousness (unity) via electro-magnetic energy, autonomous algorithmic so-called intelligence, the World Wide Web (WWW) for humanity, the Internet of Things (IoT) for machines, and hive-mind hubris binding the global indoctrinational study group system. Many study group victims arrogantly believe *Transhumanism* and *full spectrum dominance* to be humanity's own brilliance led by cyber pied pipers like Yuval Harari, Ray Kurzweil, Sergey Brin, Larry Page, Elon Musk, Bill Gates, and dozens of others who not only don't know what they don't know, but stubbornly and blindly embrace the spiritual deceit decimating their own souls through self-important conceit inspired by the swaggering insolence of their Dark Ideological Prince and his spiteful Plan for Armageddon.

We are anxiously conditioned to believe Main Street stands alone, unaided; reinforced certainly, by lack of governmental or judicial representation. Even WOKE military leadership above O-6 is questionable. Of course, Main Street is not alone and not powerless. The intercessional power of the Holy Spirit is available upon request. Our armored defense against study group Marxist-Fascist-Globalist indoctrination and destruction is prayer coupled with action powered by we the moral majority motivated by and strengthened by the grace of the Holy Spirit, the source of all imagination, creativity, and spiritual strength.

Our conservatively Christian voice rings quietly like a tiny bell lost in a Globalist abyss. Through prayer, with God's grace, we will more actively ring that liberty bell and will not stop until American freedom and world freedom are firmly established.

Reflexive Law supports Globalist totalitarian ruling systems by deceptively trapping citizens into an outcome based legal system of forced equality, that is, slavery.

4 • Reflexive Law: Chaos Out of Order

Remedy: Globalism is the Luciferian Influenced Plan for worldwide scientific serfdom, i.e., Transhumanism, a new energy-based, electro-magnetic economic order with 0.01% winners and 99.99% losers. This enslavement system cannot be imposed on nation-states under laws of most nations. For globalism to succeed in its Luciferian mission to destroy all creation, the Rule of Law and common sense must be outlawed and replaced by Rule of Man. An effective process for *prominent global citizen* implementation of this subjugation with minimal risk of Main Street revolt normalizes the illusive deception of <u>Reflexive Law</u>, under which law is reduced to whatever the few desires, subject to political manipulation at the whim of global syndicate pawns.

<u>In citizen self-defense,</u> Reflexive Law must be recognized by Main Street as an imminent threat to representative republican government. Reflexive Law must be done away with, and brainwashed law professors put out to pasture far away from our young people. Malfeasant judges, the unconstitutional likes of which perch on our Lower Court Benches, District (trial) Courts, Circuit (Appeals) Courts, and Supreme Circus benches must be removed from those benches or recognized Main Street rights, freedom, and opportunity are legal toast.

There are many ways to abuse, damage, undermine, or even destroy representative forms of government. One of the most popularly effective means is REFLEXIVE LAW. **Reflexive Law is outcome-based law**, i.e., discriminatory, or non-existent law. Reflexive Law predetermines legal outcomes before evidence is introduced or legal arguments made though practitioners won't admit this. It is totalitarian rule by experts with a *Friendly Fascist*[22] smile. Effectively undermining statutory law with the fiction of reflexive law requires cooperation by corrupt law enforcement officials as we see routinely demonstrated by order followers on FBI *Stasi-like* tag teams conveniently ignoring statutory obligations in pursuit of preferentially abhorrent injustice. The FBI is out of control and likely irreparable. If not, where are the whistle-blowers?

Reflexive Law is an illogical analogue complimenting *Counterculture* indoctrination and *Technocracy*, now transforming into **Transhumanism**. Patrick Wood tells us, "In 1973, when the Trilateral Commission was founded by Zbigniew Brzezinski and David Rockefeller, they claimed as their goal to create a *New International Economic Order.*" This subversive anti-capitalist thinking evolved out of the *Technocracy Movement* begun in 1933 by M. King Hubbert and Howard Scott, both later booted from Columbia University in 1934. Hubbert and Scott developed the *Technocracy Study Course* and, in my humble opinion, launched the religion of **Scientism**. This is significant because **Technocracy, i.e., Scientific Dictatorship** cannot exist or evolve under existing law. Technocracy and Reflexive Law are synergistically joined at their parasitically destructive hips.

Before discussing the *globalist con* called *reflexive law*, we should establish context by again reminding ourselves of the ultimate objective sought by the global syndicate, i.e., economic Main Street slavery and dumbed-down acceptance of enslavement by Main Street ultimately leading to destruction of all creation. I realize the redundancy, but it's imperative for future freedom and autonomy, we understand this plan without reservation as we cannot defeat an enemy we cannot identify. **Globalism is the incremental establishment of full, unaccountable control by an Elite few over all people, resources, and wealth on earth without recourse and eventually, beyond earth by systematizing full spectrum dominance over the many without luring out rusty pitch forks.** Globalist overlords hope to accomplish this horrific goal by usurping all other isms; redefining those isms to narrowly establish a totalitarian umbrella beneath which language is abused (linguistic alchemy) to expediently dominate differing cultural traditions, moral codes, systems of law, and more generally, nations. Hilariously, one argument for reflexive law purports defending diversity.

---

22 Gross, *Friendly Fascism*.

Literally, all other isms are transformed via misinformation, sham-science, linguistic alchemy, propaganda, entrainment, and other methodologies from their original mission, good or bad, to the singular *divide and conquer* mission of Elite global supremacy, primarily by convincing Main Street to self-police thinking, speech, and behavior, i.e., **political correctness**. We see this toxic linguistic alchemy in the language and phraseology of TECHNOCRACY, but also in capitalism, collectivism, communism, *Cultural Marxism*, environmentalism, fascism, feminism, *Free Masonry*, humanism, imperialism, Marxism, mercantilism, monopoly capitalism, Nazism, racism, relativism, Scientism, secularism, sexism, socialism, *Social Darwinism*, etc. along with gay rights, religious debasement, etc. All these pot-stirring isms are weaponized for globalism by being *about* and *using* alienated, captive groups rather than being *for* them, an important distinction. Group conformity via hive-mind becomes necessity.

With respect to reflexive law, a detailed discussion on how reflexive law is transforming U.S. statutory law is provided by Mr. Patrick M. Wood in *Technocracy Rising.*[23] For now, please bear with me as we briefly touch on it as a critical top shelf weapon in the enormous globalist toolbox.

Reflexive Law was first introduced by Gunther Teubner in a 1982 *German Law Journal* paper: G. Teubner, Reflexives Recht, ARCHIV FÜR RECHTS- UND SOZIALPHILOSOPHIE, 1982, p. 13et seq. It evolved to development of a *New Law Merchant*, apparently intended as an autonomous legal system in a 2001 paper: *German Law Journal* Vol. 2 No. 17 - 01 November 2001; *Lex Mercatoria: A Reflexive Law Guide To An Autonomous Legal System* by Gralf-Peter Calliess.

Mr. Calliess tells us, "... <u>regulated self-regulation is the core political concept behind Reflexive Law</u>". Do we see the gobbeldy-goop here? We are thinking of thinking, communicating about communication, teaching about teaching, making laws on law making, adjudicating on adjudication, and regulating self-regulation. **In other words, new pseudo law(s) are intended to <u>reflect back</u> on themselves, meaning whatever our unelected, unseen rulers, AI algorithms, and bots say they mean, without Main Street recourse.** This is why Americans are fallaciously taught the Judicial branch is co-equal with the Executive and Legislative branches, which Constitutionally it is not.

Fortunately for Main Street, many countries around the world have laws in place offering at least partial civil rights protections for citizens. Even when largely ignored or poorly written, these laws hinder blanket imposition of **transhumanist slavery** and must be overcome by *prominent global citizens* if NWO serfdom is to

---

23 Patrick M. Wood, *Technocracy Rising: The Trojan Horse Of Global Transformation* (Mesa, Ariz.: Coherent Publishing, 2014), chap. 7.

be imposed on Main Street. This is the purpose for which the sophistic duplicity of *reflexive law* was spawned, though those extruding it may not have grasped its import. "The globalization process to establish the **New International Economic Order**, or Green Economy, was simply not possible if it were to be ruled by law and not men. In fact, the advance of global transformation could not have taken place at all amidst the myriad of legal systems that are found within the nation-states of the world unless there was some new supra-national legal theory that was capable of either trumping or subverting those various legal systems."[24] Recent proof of this centrally planned scheme is exposed in the fraudulent Biden Regime's H.R. 3684 infrastructure lie unconstitutionally funding little beyond unsustainable *Green New Deal* subsidies for connected insiders. Passed or not – malevolent intent is unmistakable.

Statements of Reflexive Law regularly fold back on themselves, confusing logical argument until irrational circuitry becomes preposterous. Reflexive Law cannot stand on its own logical merit, therefore cannot defend itself in rational debate. This subversive quality must be hidden in plain sight by partnering with academic linguistic alchemy and re-engineering of ethical and cultural norms, which if successful, masks Reflexive Law's intent to bolster totalitarian policies beneath cover of fairness, equality, social justice, and other deceit. In court, Reflexive Law is enforced by blackmailed, indoctrinated, or otherwise corrupted judges, who refuse to hear certain cases based on supposed lack of standing, who routinely reject testimony and evidence, and who allow adjudication of non-existent prosecutorial crimes to proceed, etc. Litigator Sydney Powell's detailed examples of these legally incendiary practices will break any law-abiding citizen's heart in *Licensed to Lie*.[25]

Hence, the importance of synergistic indoctrinational modalities of *Cultural Marxism, Critical Race Theory, Transhumanism,* and movements such as gay rights, feminism, environmentalism, woke culture, cancel culture, etc. **Notice every one of these modalities bitterly requires an opponent to demonize, an enemy from whom RIGHTS must be gained or whose property must be taken.** In false hive-mind zero-sum fashion individuals of one divisive group are taught they will become better off by taking from others for themselves. Lashing out aggressively with profane inanities against toxic white males, patriarchy, religious tradition, etc. replaces constructive dialogue with mistrust and hatred until finally absurd terms like *"micro-aggression", "hate crime"* or *"speak to my truth"* take on a parroted life and sick meaning of their own.

Such ideological movements, some of which came about for good reason are taken over and subverted for totalitarian purposes until original issues, real or unreal, are forgotten or so abused, they become unrecognizably manageable

---

24 Wood, 129.
25 "LICENSED TO LIE: Exposing Corruption in the Department of Justice (Second Edition Paperback)," Sidney Powell

or even self-destructive. As recent reflexive examples folding back on themselves, what organization is more Fascist than *Antifa*? Is any WOKE organization more racist and more desperately addicted to discrimination than *BLM*, the *NAACP*, or the *Southern Poverty Law Center*? How much more damage to women, and to lesser extent men, can the indoctrinated transgender movement accomplish? We are literally bringing the existential nihilism of Albert Camus to life, becoming *lifetime actors* in our own *Theater of the Absurd.*

Reagan, Bush I, Clinton, Bush II, Obama, Trump, and Biden bureaucracies were all submerged in this emerging reflexive nonsense. The bleating D.C., indoctrinational blow horn repeats like a gong connected to a self-winding watch. Remember treasonous "W" bragging, "I've abandoned free market principles to **save** the free market system". The Trump Administration opposed this reflexive end run around the Rule of Law but with all the shriek-o-meter noise and pandering by compromised bureaucrats and treasonous bicameral legislators, it is hard to tell what's real and what's B.S. I get no one can fight every fight on every front simultaneously, but support for FASAB 56, potentially dangerous synthetic mRNA vaccines loaded with weird ingredients, 5G technology, and modified **HAARP** (High Frequency Active Auroral Research Program) are four serious question marks not addressed by the most Main Street Centric American President in my lifetime, President Donald J. Trump. Why?

In any event, grasping the duplicitous nature of reflexive law and its dependency on culturally manipulative support systems are necessary if we are to understand how globalism works to comprehensively subjugate Main Street populations by subverting the statutory legal process. Reflexive law transforms legislative statutory law, i.e., the Rule of Law established by _selected_ Representatives to the Rule of Man by first politicizing it, then misappropriating it through activist courts, abusive regulatory agencies, and misinformed law enforcement. In the U.S. for instance, under its Constitution, the judiciary does not create statutory law; it interprets it and through courts, rules on it. Statutory law is legislated by our once elected, now *selected* non-representative Congress. In the United States, statutory law is… or was legislated by the people's representatives but has devolved into a rigged crap shoot favoring the privileged few. The United States Bicameral Congress now views its constituencies as "obstacles" to be overcome and manipulated.

Reflexive law and its activist judges unabashedly and sometimes popularly revise historic legal paradigms beneath protective umbrellas of complicit media propaganda and corrupt political misinformation. Case in point would be the now commonly accepted **"guilty until proven innocent"** farce directed at anyone daring oppose the oppressive globalist viewpoint. *Guilty until proven innocent* is a legal impossibility turning the Rule of Law on its head.

We saw this illegal form of deep state attack unfairly play out against Bill Binney, Glenn de Souza, General Flynn, Rudy Giuliani, Katherine Horton, Duncan Hunter, Dennis Montgomery, Devin Nunez, Carter Page, George Papadopoulos, Donald Trump, Kirk Wiebe, and dozens of others for years.

Corrupt law enforcement in support of reflexive law also works in reverse. Unarmed Air Force veteran and Maga supporter, Ashli Babbitt for example was shot in cold blood on January 6, 2021, in the U.S. capitol building. The fraudulent Biden Department of Injustice closed the investigation (if there was one) into Ms. Babbitt's murder because it doesn't fit their prejudiced narrative. Ms. Babbitt and more than 500 MAGA supporters, as of this writing are presumed guilty, many still imprisoned, some held in solitary confinement, and most held without charges filed.

On January 6, 2021, rogue FBI goons masqueraded as Trump supporters staging an alleged riot (there was no riot to speak of) at the Capital for which legacy media was primed to blame on the non-violent MAGA Movement. Not one MAGA supporter firearm was found and with only a minimum of charges filed as of this writing, as previously mentioned, more than 500 U.S. citizens remain imprisoned, many held in solitary confinement by the CCP compromised Biden Regime. We also learned FBI thugs infiltrated *Oath Keepers* to take advantage of and spy on patriotic veterans to stir up Main Street chaos. We saw this same playbook used at the *Bundy Ranch* debacle in July 2014. Such intimidation is no different than post WW II's East German *Stasi* (Communist) mayhem brought home to America.

The schizophrenic Biden Regime casually refers to more than 80 million American citizens as domestic terrorists. Treasonous Joe Biden added in June 2021, "The Second Amendment, from the day it was passed, limited the type of people who could own a gun and what type of weapon you could own. You couldn't buy a cannon. Those who say the blood of lib- — 'the blood of patriots,' you know, and all the stuff about how we're going to have to move against the government. Well, the tree of liberty is not watered with the blood of patriots. What's happened is that there have never been—if you wanted or if you think you need to have weapons to take on the government, you need F-15s and maybe some nuclear weapons."

First of all, note the 2nd Amendment doesn't mention or prohibit any *types of people* from purchasing *any firearm* including *cannons*. Secondly, Biden infers Constitution defending patriots cannot stand up to or pose a significant threat to our Fascist Federal government which according to Biden has no problem nuking citizens into oblivion. At the same time, on January 6th, 2021, Biden and Leftist psychopaths insist a small group of unarmed MAGA supporters nearly overthrew the entire U.S. Government. Which is it? Poor Marxist AOC was in photo-op tears for months and wasn't in the Capitol building at the time of January 6th festivities referred to as insurrection. This is all manipulative reflexive planning for justification of Fascist controls needed to solve a Big Government manufactured problem. A problem that doesn't exist on Main Street. If Main Street patriots ever revolt against D.C.'s fascist tyranny, assuming the courts don't honor our Constitution, the Left won't have to invent stories about insurrection. Education regarding the Bill of Rights will be unavoidable.

As order following Comrade Obama complained, the U.S. Constitution restricts government authority, while attempting to maximize individual autonomy and opportunity. Obama detested this affront to state authority and over-reach. Constitutionally founded U.S. statutory law provides restraint against government tyranny—a concept detested by the global syndicate and its privileged *prominent global citizens*. **Reflexive law does the opposite, expanding government authority at the behest of Elite handlers by establishing PREFERENCES as RIGHTS.** Reflexive Law is dictatorial control dictated by microphone and gavel instead of smoking gun barrels.

This practice is legally lethal given its arbitrary and disingenuous nature, thereby posing an imminent threat to Main Street autonomy and opportunity. Consider the indoctrinated Left ignorantly salivating as big government Democrats and Rinos systematically chew away at Constitutionally recognized rights of conservatives, not realizing when conservative freedom, bibles, productivity, and guns are gone – freedom is lost for everyone, as demonically intended.

Regulatory agencies, NOW THE FOURTH BRANCH OF GOVERNMENT, are more complicated than the more clearly definable judiciary as they are established by legislative act, sometimes administratively, for the alleged purpose of equitably setting standards and/or rules within specific fields of commerce, industry, or other activity; then enforcing those standards. This functions passably well until *moral relativism* replaces *objective morality,* and *linguistic alchemy* subverts equal treatment to outright slavery. **Think of unelected regulatory power as legislator, law enforcement, judge, and jury.** Outrageously, much abusive or unconstitutional regulatory language is written for corrupt legislators by *regulated monopolies,* a ludicrously oxymoronic joke on Main Street in itself.

Regulations adopted by unelected agency stipulation generally have the force of law, enforcement of which occurs by passing agency judgement; a usurped judicial function abetted by rigged public hearings, studies, and so forth (the study group system in action). Most, if not all agencies act as independent government sanctioned commissions, operating beyond legitimate executive or legislative oversight, a circumstance ripe for corruption and abuse of power arrogantly on D.C. display. *Separation of powers* is a useful concept but plays into abuse by integrity challenged executives, legislators, and judges refusing to work within separation of power boundaries. Corrupt themselves or blackmailed by syndicate handlers matters little as Main Street outcomes are diminished with impunity either way. Vigilant checks and balances matter and the United States has no checks or balances effectively remaining in D.C.

Regulation bears watchful scrutiny or abuses thrive. The unimaginably corrupt *Securities and Exchange Commission* (SEC) for instance, openly allows millions of non-existent stock shares; that is, shares never issued by any corporation or acquired by any investor to be electronically shorted on criminalized trading floors. This fraud is called *naked-short selling*. It's bad practice because when some entity, say a hedge fund or group of funds have the ability to sell unlimited shares of *phantom stocks*, i.e., *non-existent stock shares* in a publicly traded corporation, they can manipulate share price or even destroy the stock and the company if so choosing. Apparently, a primary SEC function is legitimizing insider fraud.

Samo, samo for the *Commodity Futures Trading Commission* (CFTC) and paper commodities such as gold and silver. The ratio of traded gold certificates (paper) to physical gold often approaches ratios as high as 200:1 and even 300:1. In 2012, roughly twenty claims were made on COMEX per registered ounce of physical gold. In 2016, this ballooned to a peak of about 550 COMEX paper claims for each ounce of registered physical gold. Clearly, at some point, contracts cannot be honored, begging Bill Holter's (*jsmineset.com*) oft stated question, "what is the value of an unenforceable contract?" **Unmanipulated free trading markets no longer exist,** so what on earth do we need the SEC or CFTC for? Both simply waste tax dollars normalizing, facilitating, and protecting insider greed and fraud. These agencies function as enemies of Main Street citizens protected by irrational reflexive legal constructs. How is it logical or legal to publicly trade non-existent stock shares and fiat gold certificates?

Fortunately, offsetting this government sanctioned corruption, Main Street media-centric small investors are networking together, buying and holding stock shares to protect corporations like *AMC, Bed Bath and Beyond, GameStop* and others from marauding hedge fund manager short-selling. The fact these decent, patriotic, mostly young investors referred to as Reddit's *WallStreetBet Community* or LOL, the *Ape Community* are attacked by legacy media and Wall Street titans for defending Main Street businesses is telling proof of discriminatory D.C. Fascism. These smart young'uns figured out through networking they can outplay corrupt Leviathans in rigged markets. Now that's American ingenuity.

Unfortunately, increasingly fashionable reflexive law concepts influencing agency management ensure corruption and abuse of power. **The rationale behind reflexive law is identical to global syndicate scheming behind rogue regulatory agency discrimination and preferential abuse of power.** If malevolent regulatory abuses were nothing more than errors in judgement or random acts of corruption carried out by competing factions, probability would level the playing field; but when abuses are driven by an indoctrinated, systematized ideology serving the sole interests of psychopathic *prominent global citizens* employing socially deviant order followers to carry out abuses; Main Street is left with an evil form of mercantile despotism imposed by unelected officials owned and operated by unseen interests. At the same time, our pathetic U.S. Senate and House Members are irrelevant except for criminal facilitation of massive money laundering schemes on behalf their global syndicate handlers and their own self-enrichment.

Add technocracy, AI, our increasingly ionized atmosphere, 5G, *Space Fence* lockdown, unlimited government surveillance by third party contractors, crypto coupons, and weaponized cymatics to the equation and we have a transhuman Main Street horror story unfolding. This is not and cannot be self-governance. If we fail to soon re-activate responsive representative government, *full spectrum dominance* will render global serfdom a demonic certainty. Through Congressionally unaccountable privatization, black-op transnational corporate monopolies now routinely have our GPS connected smart meters, phones, watches, vehicles, refrigerators, and other appliances, via the *Internet of Things* (IoT) monitoring and reporting every transaction, purchase, spoken word, email, Internet search, travel arrangement, etc. Bye, bye Fourth Amendment. *Reflexive Law*, i.e., *Outcome-Based Law* circumvents constitutional statutory law. Technologies mentioned above are soon to be replaced by more powerfully invasive nanotechnologies.

Non-transparent technology enables private global syndicate contractors with developing AI to infiltrate every electronic activity on earth including the human body and human thought processes. Hacking through digital back doors gives access to military planning and procurement, industrial planning, retail outlet data, law offices, patent applications, etc. NSA whistle-blowers claim the NSA through its *Tailored Access Operations* cyber group even monitor White House personnel they don't approve of. Digital insider trading of stocks and commodities, currency manipulation, technology theft, legal strategies, blackmail, extortion, and every form of criminal manipulation imaginable including behavior modification are now ongoing every day of every week by unelected people we cannot identify. All of it ignored and/or justified within corrupt government agencies by circular Reflexive Law argument.

Irrationally circuitous logic of subversive Reflexive Law combined with supporting reflexive cultural manipulation nurtures Main Street ignorance of the global
crime syndicate slavery agenda. Reflexive Law is the skeletal spine on which
hangs the blindfold and muzzle of ignorance obliterating Main Street political
voice at every level of government. Reflexive Law is the unelected bureaucrat
guillotine beheading Main Street justice across American Main Streets by wielding the smirking lie of regulatory fairness as its iron fisted enforcer. Ignorance
not only isn't bliss, ignorance fertilizes serious criminal and subversive activity.

The U.S. government has metastasized into a completely unmanageable, unaccountable, bloated beast with a voracious appetite for harvested Main Street
freedom and wealth. As of 2021, we have more than 4 million federal employees
including civilian workers, military, and U.S. Postal Service, but not including
federal contractors. Approximately four out of every ten people working for
the U.S. government are private contractors. New York University professor,
Paul Light estimated as of 2015, the size of the federal government at approximately 9.1 million total government employees, active-duty military, Postal Service employees, and contract and grant employees. I don't have current data,
but even with Trump Administration reductions, the number has increased.

The idea our pathetic U.S. Executive and Legislative Branches of government are managing this $5 trillion dollar per year headless beast under the
umbrella of Reflexive Law and fully corrupted judiciary is insolvently ridiculous. Neither the White House nor our bicameral Congress are capable of managing much of anything beyond money laundering, much less
this corrupt septic pit we still call the seat of government. Imagine one
grain of sand in the Sahara Desert attempting to manage all other grains of
sand in the Sahara during a raging sandstorm. That's analogous to the U.S.
government - an endless sea of unaccountable, corrupt bureaucrats, many
if not most fully indoctrinated through the international study group system to hate Main Street America and everything it has stood for since 1776.

Reflexive law promotes ignorance and enables ignorant hatred fostered by
Cultural Marxism between targeted **woke groups** and unwoke groups. While
Main Street gets whiplash trying to keep track of all the shiny fairness objects
jetting around on mass media, we fail to notice – every member of every divide and conquered group is being equitably impoverished and enslaved by
the global syndicate. As John B. Wells might say, "It's really quite something."
I would add, "if we don't stop this illegal insanity, we ain't seen nothin' yet."

Why do American voters elect venal representatives
working to corrupt society faster
than good people can make society better?

5 • Reflexive Injustice

Remedy: Objective justice based on factual evidence under statutory legal procedures is obliterated by Reflexive Law. We the people of Main Street must weed out elected and appointed government corruption and demand re-establishment of Statutory Law with appropriate legislative and judicial boundaries. Reflexive inanities like "speak your truth", "my truth", or "in your world" undermining objective judgement while encouraging relativistic subjectivity should be recognized as the linguistic alchemy they are. We are all naturally subjective, not to suggest subjectivity is bad, valid, rational or irrational, just personally biased. We must pray for coherent understanding, then think for ourselves. Avoid compliant hive-mind behavior. Collective independence, not collective conformity is the healthy path to societal well-being and authentic justice.

The idea of two tiers of justice is childish. In a nutshell, as **Reflexive Law** politically bull-dozes the Rule of Statutory Law, citizens are left with as many preferential and/or discriminatory tiers of justice the Oligarchy wishes to impose and enforce. One set of laws for Elites; one set for Elite Pawns of Privilege; one set for corrupt (Ruling Class) government enforcers; one set for Main Street serfs; one set for perceived Elite enemies; and one set for whomever else is named in the *Abyss*. All tiers are blanketed by prosecutorial malfeasance, legal liability, or legal immunity dragged out and expediently peddled to the public. In other words, no law at all, at least not in terms of predictable adjudicated justice for Main Street citizens. How can a small businessperson or citizen plan anything while under the boot heel of privileged and/or discriminatory political whim?

Main Street is shackled with unworkable, unscrupulously managed systems of **outcome-based**, discriminatory, politically predetermined law justified under the abusive banner of *fairness, social justice* and *sustainability*. Reflexive Law only survives its incoherency through absurd support of indoctrinated **Reflexive Culture**. Therefore, in support of outcome based law we find economics run by political ideology; science dictated by political ideology; medicine and health dictated by political ideology; religion influenced by political ideology; education and truth subverted by political ideology; and politics itself—controlled by a psychopathic drive for power, control, **money and destruction** – with ideology and politics funded exclusively by, packaged by, sold by, controlled by, and coerced by *prominent global citizens* and order-following Pawns of Privilege. In other words, **from order emerges chaos and from chaos, tyranny.** This is globalism enabled by Reflexive Law. This is **Neo-Feudalism** morphing into permanent **Transhumanism**.

Back-story. Globalism is a deceptively innocuous term for the onerous imposition of worldwide slavery or serfdom if you prefer. The global syndicate has aggressively, since the *City of London* time of Cecil Rhodes, Alfred Milner, Frederick Scott Oliver {author of *Alexander Hamilton: An Essay on American Union* (1906)}, Leo Amery, Lionel Curtis, and so many others of Milner's *Kindergarten* and the first *Round Tables;* been working toward re-establishing a feudal system, but this time as a *global federation (commonwealth)*. *Round Table* planning through the **study group system** brought us today's modern euphemism, *globalism*—a less threatening perception on Main Street for Elites to freely discuss, openly plan, and proudly sell to Main Street than speechifying about *excess population* democide or the worldwide totalitarian dictatorship planned for Main Street survivors of planned eugenic holocaust. *Less is more* is the plan for Main Street but not for global Elites. **"You will own nothing,"** Klaus Schwab and the DAVOS crowd arrogantly proclaim.

As a side note, since many claim the late Cecil Rhodes' desire to end war a sincere motivation for establishing his Trust and exercising his considerable influence; I admit my view of this defense as nonsense, since Rhodes' despicable behavior and aberrant greed, put on open display by himself and his associates before and during the *Boer Wars* along with other atrocities around the world precludes such thinking. I do not blame Rhodes in a singular way for the Transvaal carnage as certainly Great Britain's Elite imperialism itself was instrumental in what may have occurred at some Fascist point anyway.

The South African history of resource rape and power jockeying between the Dutch, English, Portuguese, Spanish and to lesser extent, France and Sweden is a long one dating back centuries, so the imperialist dance was complicated.[26] In any event, Rhodes played a crucial role and did little to diminish the pitiless genocide. In British defense and fairness, I will add that most modern beneficial things brought to Africa at the time were carried by British or Dutch hands. Not everything the global syndicate does is evil, though China's *Belt and Road Initiative* is fixing that.

It should be noted that devoted Round Table *initiates* Amery and Curtis referred to Oliver's book on America's Alexander Hamilton as *The Bible*; considered an essential guide to consolidation of *organic* unification under their dream for British imperial rule, not just within the British colonial sphere of influence but across the world. Globalism is essentially brought about by a network (matrix) of order-following proxies within central banking, multi-national monopoly corporate management, and treasonous government, all bolstered by endless counterfeit debt-based currency issuance, in conjunction with a privileged, well-compensated, slavery-complicit media necessary to disseminate misinformation, propaganda, and to engender Main Street's confidence in the promised, soon-to-be glorious future of **transhuman serfdom.**

The organized embedding of outside influence compliant with New World Order central planning within local educational and political institutions of both developed and developing nations make implementation of *Rule by Proxy* (my words) difficult to perceive, much less understand.[27] Threats to healthy national interests go unnoticed with nationalism itself demonized in the sole uni-polar interest of global syndicate power brokers detesting the sovereign complications of national boundary controls.

The more recent twist since Germany's *National Socialism* of the 1930's is **technocracy.** Please note despite the label, Hitler was a Fascist not a Bolshevik, both generously supported by so-called capitalists of the West. Technocracy is a centrally planned *scientific dictatorship* sold to Main Street as expert guidance, critical information, beneficial progress, and *unwashed* convenience disguising the slow but steady intrusion of unconstitutionally invasive *full spectrum dominance* by unelected algorithms with no accountable persons in sight. Unlimited electro-magnetic invasion of unsuspecting and/or entrained populations for surveillance and control are no longer pending but are an exponentially expanding reality. Technocratic dictatorship relies 100% on networks such as the *World Wide Web* (www) for humans, the *Internet of Things* (IoT) for machines and appliances[28], ionized atmospheric plasma, *Space Fence*,[29] wea-

---

26 Harry Booyens, *AmaBhulu - The Birth and Death of the Second America*
27 Gross, *Friendly Fascism.*
28 Wood, *Technocracy Rising*, 145.
29 "Space Fence," Lockheed Martin, accessed September 3, 2019, https://www.lockheedmartin.com/en-us/products/space-fence.html.

ponized 5G, toxic vaccines loaded with nanotechnology, and so forth. **Reflexive injustice** incrementally aids bringing about eventual machine control of the human mind and behavior. To the extent the human mind interfaces with machine controls or becomes just another computer system, it will in either case, sublimate to controlled machine inputs ensuring predictable outputs. Satanic influence will have finally derailed, if not destroyed humanity.

Interestingly, and indirectly related to reflexive law circumlocution, the late Mr. H. G. Wells (1866-1946) predicted this coming *manufacture* of behavioral control by highly educated, middle class *scientific managers*, now called *technocracy* as early as 1901 with publication of several articles, culminating in his book, *Anticipations*, suggesting either Wells' insider access to globalist long-term central-planning or amazing prophetic ability.[30] I don't know which, but Wells postulated in 1901, his societal predictions coming to fruition by year 2000. In 1901 he called the culmination of this transformative diabolic process a **New Republic** extending across all sovereign national borders. Today we call it the **New World Order**. This sociopathic thinking spawned the birth of *Technocracy* at Columbia University in the early 1930s, conceptually requiring about a minute for Nazi psychopaths to grasp the evil reward potential of using it.

We do know, Wells, along with Adorno, Rees, Lewin, Aleister Crowley, Aldous and Julian Huxley, Bertrand Russell, and too many others to name were involved directly or indirectly with the global syndicate, with *Free Masonry* and the so-called *Frankfurt School, Tavistock Institute of Human Relations* (TIHR), *Theosophical Society, Fabian Socialism,* and *Cultural Marxism* now undermining American and world freedom. So, to emphasize the question, was Wells eerily prescient… or did he have access to long-term globalist central planning? I suspect the answer likely involves *Authoritarian Personality support of Ruling Class dominance through abuse of our child-like wonder*, as Mr. Joe Atwill[31] might suggest.

Did Well's Chapter 10, *The Declaration of the Rights of Men* in his 1939 tome, *The New World Order* in any way foreshadow today's oft parroted *collectivist promise*, fortified by the advent of reflexive law? Was Wells warning us or promising us, as planned European genocide of WW II crawled toward reality on the heels of WW I European genocide? Perhaps so, particularly as across our spinning sphere, the BANAL COLLECTIVIST PROMISE REPEATEDLY AND CONSISTENTLY METASTASIZES EXCLUSIVELY AS SUPPRESSION, VIOLENCE, IMPOVERISHMENT, MEDIOCRITY, AND DE-

30 H. G. Wells, Malcolm Farmer, and Martin Pettit, *Anticipations by H. G. Wells: Anticipations by H. G. Wells* (CreateSpace Independent Publishing Platform, 2018).
31 "Caesar's Messiah: The Roman Conspiracy to Invent Jesus: Flavian Signature Edition: Atwill, Joseph: 8601404677632

5 • Reflexive Injustice

SPAIR. Mr. Wells apparently found this reprehensible circumstance appropriate for members of the *unwashed* **Abyss**, as he categorized Main Street people.

In any event, with 21ˢᵗ century technocracy making irrational Transhuman gains; with corporatized monopoly money, corrupt government, abusive political power, and dishonest media in place; what else might be necessary for global enslavement of Main Street? Oh yes, that would be destroying checks and balances restraining government power along with all remnants of the constitutional Rule of Law. How better to popularly mimic order while authoritatively creating chaos so unidentifiably widespread, its only unaccountable remedy appears on Main Street as the psychotic false choices of Hegelian dialectic? Privileged *prominent global citizens* are sick... and worse, spiritually blind. Foolishly following spiritually blind, insipidly vacuous leaders is never a constructive idea.

Much better than limiting societal confusion caused by controlled conflict between Marxism and Fascism is adding the third leg of the triumvirate, Capitalism – also exported by *City of London*. Of course, no one alive today has ever lived one day under a free-market capitalist system, so the revulsion and horror directed at Capitalism by indoctrinated Globalist - Marxist - Fascist proponents is meaningless. Only in theory can 21ˢᵗ century debaters discuss readily abused capitalist principles. Mercantilism is the predominant world economic system and is the Mother of Globalism, progenitor of the New World Order. Mercantilism absorbs Marxism and Fascism, thesis and anti-thesis, as seemingly competitive ideologies, then synthesizes Globalism from the two as alternatives to non-existent Capitalism. If this is not reflexive insanity, what is?

So, we're finally done back-tracking. Please understand I'm not a lawyer. Remarks regarding reflexive law or any other law are from my limited, liberty-biased Main Street citizen point of view, which by the way, all Americans are Constitutionally entitled to, and all humans are unalienably entitled to regardless constraints of man-made law, *Darwinian* justification, or *Cultural Marxist* nonsense. **So, what is man-made law?**

Britannica tells us: **Law**, *the discipline and profession concerned with the customs, practices, and rules of conduct of a community that are recognized as binding by the community. Enforcement of the body of rules is through a controlling authority.*

French economist and journalist, Frédéric Bastiat in 1850 wrote more descriptively: *"Law is common force organized to prevent injustice; --- in short, Law is Justice.*

It is not true that the mission of the law is to regulate our consciences, our ideas, our will, our education, our sentiments, our works, our exchanges, our gifts, our enjoyments. Its mission is to prevent the rights of one from interfering with those of another, in any one of those things.

Law, because it has force for its necessary sanction, can only have the domain of force, which is justice.

And as every individual has a right to have recourse to force only in cases of lawful defense, so collective force, which is only the union of individual forces, cannot be rationally used for any other end.

The law then, is solely the organization of individual rights that existed before law.
Law is justice.

So far from being able to oppress the people, or to plunder their property, even for a philanthropic end, its mission is to protect the people, and to secure to them the possession of their property.'[32]

I wonder, reading the above, if our health is our property, why does our government work so hard preventing us from securing possession of it?   Anyway, there are varying descriptions of what constitutes law, particularly regarding regulatory boundaries, but we get the idea—law is supposed to secure our liberties.   We might ask, how could someone undermine law and abuse legal authority for privileged or unfair advantage? Worse, how could law be employed to obliterate uniformly applied justice?

One of the most powerful tools of Luciferian globalism employed for the last four decades is *reflexive law*, which of course, is not law at all. **Reflexive law is ideological prejudice disguised as beneficial caring.** Reflexive law is a dis-functional form of *soft law;* or as mentioned earlier, *outcome-based law.* It's not law any more than outcome-based education is educational.   Both encompass methods for enabling indoctrination and control of the many by the few.   Cleverly devised reflexive argument propagandizes, indoctrinates, and conditions as does outcome-based education; I suppose obviously as both are predicated on the same dumbed-down enslavement ideology.   Problem-Reaction-Solution repeated until behavioral conformance is accepted by Main Street.

Reflexively blaming and shaming individual thought into compliant hive-mind submission is the first play of the dominate Main Street by mind control game. If Hegelian dialectic subtlety and lies cannot successfully build the mind-cage, employ drugs. If pharmacology fails, then well-dressed though less polite legal coercion is next on the docket; and finally, from the on-deck circle and much less politely, bring on the mindless hatred and violence our indoctrinated Left is carefully programed to provide. Marxist-Fascist violence go hand in hand though violence is not limited to physicality. A cherry on top is project-

---

32 "The Law Illustrated: Bastiat, Frédéric: 9798714320958: Amazon.Com: Books," 49–50

ing Leftist violence on non-violent MAGA constitutionalists, who regardless of race, creed, or ethnicity, the Woke Left calls White Supremacists. Candace Owens, Larry Elders, and I guess now, Nicki Minaj are all White Supremacists.

Just the sight of a red or white baseball cap, the letter "T", a rattlesnake, or an American flag can trigger indoctrinated *useful idiots*. Fake reflexive order predictably resulting in maximized societal division ignites (*mass aggression*) incendiary chaos. Chaos in turn is used to justify privileged, big globalist government behavior evolving from lies, deceit, and covert theft to rogue military violence and if necessary, FEMA Camp internment for re-education; or for stubborn folks like my family and friends, something a bit less tasteful and permanent – all for the public good.

Above is an extreme statement on my part, at least for today, but have no doubt *prominent global citizens*, demonstrating zero remorse for government imprisonment, torture, starvation, and murder across the globe of more than a hundred million[33], perhaps as many as 300 million innocent people over this past century, will not hesitate to humiliate, coerce, brutalize, or kill a few million more of us on the demonic road to the new global slavery.

Instead of relying on at least a semi-concrete legal foundation such as *codified civil law* or *precedence based common law*, both of which can be judicially capable of leading to **clear outcomes**; reflexive law prejudicially begins with **desired outcomes**, typically developed by unaccountable, unelected persons or agenda driven NGO's[34] funded and controlled by *prominent global citizens* (my words). **Reflexive law is a politically binding collectivist trap ensuring the impossibility of justice.** Not an obvious or transparent trap of forged steel and concrete but a confusing matrix of deceptively intertwined strands of jumbled thought malevolently bent, twisted, and incrementally tightened until inescapable. This is the form Elite *Fabian Socialist* order-followers have been conditioned to cleverly invent for Main Street constraint. Thank you, academia.

Reflexive law is 100% unaccountable to representative government, itself now unaccountable, or more pointedly, unaccountable to voters. By technocratic design, there is no emergency call box on America's Main Street and no one to call if there were. There is by malicious, treasonous intent, no responsible party Main Street electromagnetic serfs can call. Unelected globalized bureaucrats, untold thousands of them wading through more than $5 trillion annually, are structurally segregated into dozens of thoroughly indoctrinated, alienated layers. Unreachable, compartmentalized slaves themselves, they are now, as

---

33 R. J. Rummel, *Death by Government: Genocide and Mass Murder Since 1900*, 5th PRINT-ING edition (New Brunswick: Routledge, 1997).
34 Patrick Wood, "Reflexive Law: Sustainable Development Has Conned Us All," *Freedom Advocates* (blog), August 29, 2014, https://www.freedomadvocates.org/reflexive-law/.

Wells predicted, more powerful than elected photo-op legislators or cowardly executives we foolishly vote for who pretend to run the show. Each unelected one of these drones is operated by difficult to see shadow governments and unnoticed deep state operatives on behalf their unseen *prominent global citizen* handlers, themselves safely ensconced behind protective digitized walls of soulless mathematical algorithms. These miscreants are beginning to and will continue to electro-magnetically surveil and control everything on Earth – if we continue to allow this psychopathic Luciferian progression to continue its charade. We must say NO or Justice perishes into Transhuman oblivion.

How does the reflexive process work to undermine justice? First off, a problematic societal circumstance must be orchestrated – or at least perception of a problem must be orchestrated—always through the *study group system*. NWO solutions can never be sold on merit because they are always intended to make situations worse, never better. For Satanic Elites, slavery as an interim goal simply expedites creation's eventual annihilation, though possessed individuals don't know that or don't care. Planning to bring about a desired outcome (Hegelian synthesis) requires sufficient chaos, devastation, anxiety, and societal desperation (*mass formation*) to justify tyrannical subjugation as a palliative further weakening Main Street resistance to whatever totalitarian nonsense is proposed on the path to final omnicide. This strategy is effectively employed on both small and large scales, say from local epidemics and civil wars to global pandemics and world wars.

Once a so-called *desired outcome* is staged and this should be read as, *desirable for Elites*; so-called *information disclosure* can be offered by heavily funded special interest parties and their order-followers for propagandized public consumption and corrupt or deluded government agency adoption. This is accomplished by referencing various **study group conditioned experts**, censoriously approved white papers, expensive favorable studies, biased academic and professional journal articles, or of late, unconfirmed media accounts by unnamed sources.

Prejudiced information is widely and repeatedly disseminated regardless of veracity or independent verification. In fact, verification is discouraged, marginalized, vilified, and if necessary, blocked via *cancel culture* dogma from print publication and the air waves. A small number of academically prolific people suddenly appear to the public as a widely disseminated, enormous cross section of people—a deceptive marketing strategy perfected by the *Rhodes-Milner Group* before WW I. Fauci and friends are a medical *Scientism* example; Al Gore and friends, a climate & environmental *Scientism* example; Klaus Schwab and friends an economic *Scientism* example; and Ray Kurzweil and friends a Transhumanist *Scientism* example. A surprisingly small group, through repetitive parroting can generate tremendously loud noise in the media echo chamber.

Since dissenting opinion is blocked from Main Street view, consensus is boldly claimed and lobbying of greedy government lawmakers, corrupt agency heads and so forth begins. Consensus can be verifiably, though falsely claimed since shallow investigation fails to disclose contrary findings or dissenting opinions. How many of us busy-trying-to-survive folks read or listen beyond a misleading headline or an officially unsourced quotation anymore? If any facts or truth are offered, they will be glibly presented at the end of the white paper, article, or news report, where at least half of Main Street never treads. Plausible deniability is obscurely offered with little or no risk of program damage. Report study data, accurate or not is rarely shared or quoted. Quotes are carefully limited to **Report Summary statements** written by politicians and administrators, not scientists.

Non-status quo views are not permitted publication by *cancel culture* accredited, foundation funded deep state sources, hence are difficult to find and are rarely, if ever cited by MSM. Interestingly and happily, this ongoing despicable MSM censorship resulted in the birth of independent investigation and reporting by diligent citizens through direct mail, email, or podcasting from attics, sheds, garages, living rooms, and small studios, now maligned by MSM as so-called **alternative media**; the only news media remaining in much of the world, certainly in the U.S.

The predetermined, *desired outcome* will now be pushed forward by honoring proponents and shaming opponents through a public process wherein opposition is cruelly and unabashedly abused, and unbelievers silenced via reduced speaking time, shouting down at public hearings, or in extreme cases banishment from meetings altogether as now experienced at school board meetings. The ever-dependable study group system spawns disinformation news articles, biased televised reports, and malicious lawsuits against politically incorrect, selected targets engendering even more reflexive publicity and public shaming – a perfect societal poison pie. Shiny objects and false flags drown accurate perception.

Reflexive lawsuits, once called **nuisance lawsuits** need not be meritorious or even feasible to file under *civil* or *common* Rule of Law. Indoctrinated or blackmailed judges conveniently help skew findings or simply disavow any possible legal defense by refusing evidentiary submittals or hearing argument, usually on a contrived *"lack of standing"* basis. Depending on scope, the lawsuit's certain-to-be highly publicized existence ensures local, national, or international exposure and softball media questions, if not full agreement with desired outcomes and abject hatred for anyone daring oppose the *status quo*.

Do we often bump into verifiable data or provably repeatable, *non-status quo* poverty data, crime data, vaccine studies, public health or climate change models? Of course not.[35] Data and evidence are *verboten*. Piling on top of reflexive law enforcement, i.e., **weaponized lawfare**, we live with Leftist favored free speech intimidation and violence toward constitutionalists carried out by Fascist, mask wearing thugs of *Antifa, BLM* and other global syndicate funded black-shirt groups in controlled twisted sister cooperation with rogue law enforcement. If consent can't be sufficiently manufactured by fake news, movies, television, social media, or other indoctrination tools, force it with threat of violence and anxiety.

Mr. Patrick Wood tells us, *"information disclosure"* is a principal policy instrument of reflexive law. That is, the analysis produced is presented with its 'recommended outcomes.' Public meetings are then held to build consensus between individual citizens and other "actors".[36] These public hearings and interviews are carefully staged to shame and abuse *desired outcome* opponents until they submit to whatever freedom relinquishing policy is proposed. Essentially, a **binding political agreement** is entered into and legitimate **hard law**, impossible to legislate in most cases, is by-passed. This is now routinely done at local, state, national, and international levels, so busy folks on Main Street are unable to track or determine what is going on as their freedom, autonomy, and future are slowly impoverished by misinformation cleverly packaged and sold as beneficial, desirable, and of course, fair. Silencing of honest research findings and this obscene legal abuse are then openly supported by corrupt Bar Associations, Medical Associations, and professional licensing boards across the country.

Obama's treasonous Iran deal was nothing more than a non-binding negotiation Iranian leadership never signed. There was no contractual deal. Iran was not expected to sign such nonsense. This outrageously corrupt whatever it claimed to be, certainly wasn't a Senate approved treaty, an executive agreement, or signed document. None-the-less it cost U.S. Main Street tens of billions and threatens the security of every country on earth, though dozens of insiders benefited handsomely at Main Street expense. This is reflexive thinking and reflexive legal mumbo-jumbo in practice.

We see this geo-political chicanery in the language of openly discriminatory tax codes, preferential regulatory abuse, multi-lateral trade agreements, 1,000-2,700 plus page legislative bills drafted by unelected third-party special interests and so forth. It appears the Trump Administration tried to reduce discriminatory, un-

---

35 "Temperature Analysis of 5 Datasets Shows the 'Great Pause' Has Endured for 13 Years, 4 Months | Watts Up With That?," accessed March 3, 2019, https://wattsupwiththat.com/2014/07/29/temperature-analysis-of-5-datasets-shows-the-great-pause-has-endured-for-13-years-4-months/.
36 Wood, "Reflexive Law."

fair politicization of codes, regulations, and agreements by eliminating more than 30,000 pages of the ridiculous 178,200-page 2015 *Code of Federal Regulations* and by taking actions revising discriminatory taxation, preferential regulation, and by adopting bi-lateral trade agreements more in keeping with the flexibility necessary for free trade to exist. DT's "mean tweets" and "gruff threats" of sanctions, tariffs, and so forth, appear more as strategic international bargaining chips than goals, with the eventual objective being elimination of tariffs altogether. Career Establishment Republicans fought every bit as hard and as bitterly as corrupt Marxist Democrats to prevent Trump from slowing down or stopping the treasonous kick-back gravy train enjoyed by D.C. insiders and their associates for decades.

Of course, massive 2018-2020 election fraud masked by reflexively indoctrinated courts knocked *The Donald* off stage, at least for the time being so the longer-term Trump Administration agenda as of this writing remains unclear, though hoped for by tens of millions. This all smells like a putrid deep state con supported by Reflexive Law judges refusing to hear evidence, much less allow litigation. Without change, this insult to human electoral intelligence instigated by the CCP, Russia, Iran, UK, Germany, Spain, and Italy along with indoctrinated Democrat and Rino pawns may result in Revolution II.

To my uneconomist mind, globalism embraces the post-feudal economic system of Western Europe referred to as *Mercantilism*; or at least a mutated form of it. Mercantilism became popular during the 16th century; the reasoning being a nation's power and wealth were thought to be bolstered by limiting imports, increasing exports, and hoarding stores of precious metals. This thinking led Great Britain to trade restrictions, favored trading partners, and ultimately to favored status of influential monopolies like the *British East India Company* originally formed in 1600 - and the competing *Dutch East India Company* (today's Netherlands) formed in 1602. **Mercantilism is the exercising of political power used to control economic activity, sometimes enforced by military intervention**; a provably bad idea for Main Street anywhere; and one significant cause of the 1776 American colonial revolution.

Mercantilism turned out to be an abusive economic system from its 16th century spawning through its 18th century dominance, until its static, zero-sum philosophy was replaced by today's monopoly capitalism, which of course, isn't capitalism at all and is at least as horrible as mercantilism. I'm not sure there's significant difference from a practical standpoint, but that distinction is outside my economic wheelhouse. In any case, inequities foisted on Main Street are bolstered by false Marxist promises and the iron enforcement fist of Fascism.

Today's trade sanctions, tariffs, multi-lateral trade agreements, and discriminatory tax policies reek of mercantilism whereby restraint of free trade disincentivizes competition, deprives manufacturers and customers of choice, and raises prices. Elites employ favored wealthy nations in the 1st World to engage their diplomatic influence, economic, and military power as a battering ram against less wealthy 3rd World nations for the purpose of enhancing and protecting Elite resource rape, genocide, and control - all bolstered by **International Reflexive Agreement.** False socialist promises are particularly amenable to these barbaric practices, hence propagandized popularity, but since socialism is not self-sustaining, it only survives at the end of smoking gun barrels in Fascist states. Collectivism in any form is always an Elite wealth-transference gravy train where the poor get poorer and the uber-rich grow much richer... and of course, more fully entrenched in centralized power; all for fairness and the common good we are repeatedly told.

I raise mercantilism and its ugly cousin, monopoly capitalism as concrete examples of unjust political ideology and reflexive law conceptually coming together, employed to control economic outcomes through propaganda, coercion, and threat of violence to their inevitably unsustainable, crash-and-burn collapse every fifty or so years. Anglo-American monopoly capitalism, a hybrid form of Elite corporatist, Fascist government control reinforced on the downside by false government promises of socialist freebies for Main Street is now gasping for Kissinger's 1973 Oil-dollar breath.

A new, more One World, energy-based re-placement for the Oil-dollar, a technocratic economic system spawned by the **Great DAVOS Reset** is intended to be digitally inflicted on Main Street by Elites for the purpose of *full spectrum dominance*, i.e., absolute control over all people, resources, and wealth on earth. This is the Transhuman pinnacle of pathological, Luciferian influenced, zero-sum, Malthusian delusion and if not stopped by we the sane people of Main Street, will bring about the omnicide of most Earthly life forms.

Whatever follows the planned collapse of our fiat economic system and American Rule of Law along with the petro-dollar and its international abuses will become our children's future. If we refuse to rise above the coercive nature of reflexive law threatening our lives with indoctrinated mob-mentality driven by top-down, centralized, autocratic rule tyrannically imposed via politically correct public ridicule, shaming, abusive slander, threat of lawsuit, threat of violence, algorithmic tyranny, etc.; a dark future lies ahead. In DAVOS club rooms, this diabolic plan is called the GREAT RESET.

A providential return of Main Street to our Creator's loving embrace, along with spiritual coherence and personal responsibility constitutes a far superior option.

"Compliance in Silence leads to Tyranny."

Christine Anderson - Alternative for Germany Member of European Parliament

6 • Follow the Fiat Money

Remedy: ELIMINATE DEBT (FIAT) BASED CURRENCY! Worldwide totalitarian dictatorship is enabled by THREE PRIMARY WEAPONS: BIG GOVERNMENT, DEBT (FIAT) CURRENCY, and MIND-CONTROL. It's up to we the people of Main Street to end all three. No one can or will do it for us. The Lone Ranger and Tonto are retired.

What is the New World Order (NWO) con our young people face?

In one word – **SLAVERY!** A planned return to feudalism by our world's dynastic families and their Fascist pawns who refer to slavery as *equity, fairness, social justice,* and *sustainability.* Understanding the incremental NWO enslavement agenda encompassed within U.N. Agendas 21/30/50 at least in part require a quick detour into asymmetric financial warfare and eugenics. Global population reduction on a massive scale without risk of revolt can only come about via unseen mountains of fiat financial trickery. Young people surviving population reduction policy are necessarily being deprived of all possible benefits of free markets and capitalism by Elite order followers.

Four such benefits of **true free market capitalism** which no person alive today has experienced without Marxist-Fascist constraints, are productive work engaging personal fulfillment while generating a decent living, and property ownership. These four benefits are steadily being erased on Main Street with Washington D.C. corruption enabling and protecting the enslavement agenda. Fiat money, reflexive law, indoctrination, propaganda, fear, drugs, and transhuman machine-mind-body cyborgism are weaponized component tools bringing about voluntarily compliant Main Street enslavement while information controls and dumbed-down education help Elites avoid Main Street pitchforks and rebellion. Once fully implemented, walking this enslavement program back will be difficult, if not impossible. It can be stopped by prayer, discernment, and concerted action.

Note that America's eight-year Revolutionary War against overreach by Great Britain's crown (not British citizens) begun in 1776 was also a civil war within the colonies. Today, American citizens and world citizens wage World War III (my opinion) against powers and principalities, i.e., enemies of human decency both foreign and domestic difficult to recognize or identify. Divide and conquer global syndicate strategies since WW I successfully spawned the disease of WOKE CULTURAL hatred, so now WW III from America's view is once again, both a civil and international war. An asymmetric war battling totalitarian Marxism and Fascism to prevent synthesis into Globalist slavery though bloodshed has, so far, been limited to uninformed Blue City and Blue State condoned Leftist violence.

Divide and conquer tactics effectively blanket Main Street beneath a divisive intellectual fog so thick, few of us see all Main Street is being impoverished, disempowered, and enslaved. Fiat money in socially deviant hands renders evil so convenient, it's now enabling Main Street's regression back to Medieval European style feudal servitude. The unthinkable becomes reality when unaudited digital money flows out the back doors of Washington D.C. and New York like rampaging rivers.

If slavery seems too strong a term, we should ask four questions. **1.** When a human being has no voice in the decision to have their body injected with experimental chemicals and nanotechnology, what is the status of that citizen? **2.** When a hard-working, taxpaying citizen has no voice in government as proved daily in 2022's United States - what is the status of that citizen? **3.** When 60% or more of a hard-working person's gross wage are confiscated without recourse by federal and state income tax, property tax, sales tax, excise tax, assessments, tolls, fuel tax, various taxes on phones, utilities, and other things, user fees, etc.—what is the status of that person? **4.** Do we imagine slave owners had zero overhead cost to own and operate slave labor? We are free roaming slaves and will remain slaves until we wake up and take back self-governance.

Moving on to a more general discussion, central banking isn't necessary, but isn't a bad idea since 195 recognized countries across the globe (including the Holy See and the State of Palestine; but not including Taiwan, The Cook Islands and Niue) do require an organized interface enabling equitable currency exchange and reasonable transaction costs, among other things. However, central banks should be limited to **"fees for service"** and have nothing to do with setting discriminatory interest rates. To bring about a decent world managed by transparently honest people, central banks must never be private banks of issuance, nor be allowed near the money supply of any nation. If we do desire private banks of issuance, then all banks must be private competitors, and each one must be transparently audited in real time all the time – and the *State Appointed* bank auditors must also be transparently audited. (Where does this stop?)

All currencies issued by sovereign nations MUST be backed by gold, other precious metals; or some other stable, definable, measurable standard(s). I don't know if physical exchangeability is necessary, as in exchanging currency for gold or silver on demand? That question is best answered by Martin Armstrong or someone else of that caliber[37] - but in any case, central banks must be transparent public banks whose limited function is determining accurate weights and measures relative to currency value and amount of currency held or traded.

Fascism is not capable of enforcing destructive Marxist impoverishment without access to fiat capital whenever, wherever, and for whatever its psychopathic dictates require. We must therefore look at how counterfeit debt money, i.e., fiat money created from thin air works.

Again, it is imperative for sustainable life on earth, we understand the dire threat arrayed against humanity and creation by the Luciferian globalist triad of **big government, fiat money, and mind control**. As stated earlier, our only strength and protection are provided by cognitive coherence, awakened spiritual discernment, and active spiritual warfare, individually and societally.

We'll delve into our potentially fatal economic disease, fatal to Main Street freedom and abundance anyway, along with fiat/debt currency and central banking shortly; but must first understand the nature and intent of *cartels* and in the cartel sense; *syndicates*, controllers, and order-followers of which are direct beneficiaries of global financial deceit and piratization of Main Street wealth creation.

Evil is not only organized but is often deceitfully sophisticated and maliciously multi-faceted, even to the point of self-destruction. Evil often cloaks itself within elements of truth and fact, suggesting data and facts alone are not enough for useful analysis. Contributing factors must also be considered. Ask how free market capitalism can be possible when just three multinational asset managers, **BlackRock, Vanguard,** and **State Street,** hold con-

---

37 "Armstrong Economics | Research the Past to Predict the Future," accessed May 10, 2018, https://www.armstrongeconomics.com/.

trolling interest in nearly every indexed Fortune 500 company? Ask how few dynastic families control **BlackRock, Vanguard,** and **State Street?**

According to Merriam-Webster's on-line dictionary:

Cartel
1: a written agreement between belligerent nations
2: a combination of independent commercial or industrial enterprises designed to limit competition or fix prices; illegal drug cartels
3: a combination of political groups for common action.

Syndicate
(Entry 1 of 2)
1a: a council or body of syndics
b: the office or jurisdiction of a syndic
(Entry 2 of 2)
1: to subject to or manage as a syndicate
2a: to sell (something, such as a cartoon) to a syndicate or for publication in many newspapers or periodicals at once also : to sell the work of (someone, such as a writer) in this way a syndicated columnist
b: to sell (something, such as a series of television programs) directly to local stations
2: an association of persons officially authorized to undertake a duty or negotiate business
3a : a group of persons or concerns who combine to carry out a particular transaction or project
b: cartel sense 2
c: a loose association of racketeers in control of organized crime
4: a business concern that sells materials for publication in a number of newspapers or periodicals simultaneously
5: a group of newspapers under one management

Per G. Edward Griffin[38]: "A cartel is a grouping of companies that are bound together by contracts or agreements designed to promote inter-company cooperation and, thereby reduce competition between them. Some of these agreements may deal with such harmless subjects as industry standards and nomenclature. But most of them involve the exchange of patent rights, the dividing of regional markets, the setting of prices, and agreements not to enter into product competition within specific categories. Generally, a cartel is a means of escaping the rigors of competition in the open free-enterprise market. The result always is higher prices and fewer products from which to choose. Cartels and monopolies, therefore, are not the result of free enterprise, but the escape from it."

---

38 G. Edward Griffin, *World Without Cancer; The Story of Vitamin B17*, Third Edition edition (Westlake Village, CA: American Media, 1974), 187.

Again per Mr. Griffin[39]: "This is why cartels and collectivist governments inevitably work together as a team. They have a common enemy and share a common objective: the destruction of free enterprise."

In the mercantilist sense, particularly in the case of transnational monopoly, cartels are groups of companies entering into verbal or written contracts between themselves agreeing to fix supply, control distribution, fix pricing, and generally plan their independent market penetration while limiting risk exposure jointly, within the context of interlocking directorships, stock ownership and management, wherein parties to the cartel contracts can safely share profits with minimal competitive expense or risk. **This monopoly structure only works with corrupt government protection and the subverted United States' Federal government provides plenty of sanctioned protection.**

Beyond flag waving and patriotic pandering of MSM financial media and central bank managers leading marks into markets while feigning helpless confusion about perplexing interest rates and volatile liquidity, what's the function of a central bank?

Wayne Jett, discussing the birth of America's privately owned *Federal Reserve Banking System* in the context of globalist President Woodrow Wilson's abandonment of "principles chiseled into the cornerstone of the Democrat Party by its founder Andrew Jackson, who battled and terminated the U.S. central bank"; accurately summarizes this subversive function for us as follows:

First citing historian Carroll Quigley: "The powers of financial capitalism had [a] far reaching aim… to create a world system of financial control in private hands able to dominate the political system of each country and the economy of the world as a whole. This system was to be controlled in a feudalist fashion by the central banks of the world acting in concert, by secret agreements arrived at in frequent private meetings and conferences."

Mr. Jett goes on to tell us in his own words:
"Practices of central banks in this strategic role were (a) to dominate governments by controlling their access to borrowed money; (b) to manipulate currency exchange rates; (c) to manipulate economic growth and recession in each country; (d) to dictate government policies by use of financial rewards to political officials after they leave office."[40]

When rogue elements within the U.S. intelligence apparatus, opportunistic lobbyists, corruptible politicians, and captured bureaucratic government agency pawns are blackmailed, bribed, extorted, indoctrinated, or otherwise brought to conformity with the globalist control apparatus, we have an organized, government protected, monopoly crime syndicate, which with apparent immunity, safely and profitably conducts resource rape, controls banking, interest rates, agriculture,

---

39 Griffin, 189.
40 Jett, *The Fruits of Graft*, 104.

mining, energy, other resources and commodities, manufacturing, shipping, publishing, media, entertainment, etc., - all with impunity on a global basis beneath the protection of mis-used military force and threat of violence for inquisitive or uncooperative victim nations including the United States of America.

This organized swindling occurs within a contrived MSM environment selling cleverly packaged marketing hoopla about necessity of spreading freedom, democracy, and free trade, no matter how big the lie or how high the human cost. Today's wealthy, privileged MSM propagandists are shamelessly dishonest, abusing their protected right to free speech utterly without conscience. An ivy league degree in journalism today should be conferred with a mandatory *wall plaque* or *forehead tattoo* warning, "I AM A COWARDLY LIAR."

Many respected financial analysts make an argument for elected officials and government bureaucrats often being more depraved than organized crime families, integrity challenged lawyers, or pathological *private central bankers.* Therefore, the argument goes, turning *privately owned and controlled central banks* over to government thugs to abuse *public banks* begs for guaranteed economic slaughter on Main Street. I take no issue with well-deserved criminal accusations leveled toward devious politicians and bureaucratic pawns but differ as to whether public banks can work – at least work until post-MAGA renewed Main Street apathy kicks back in, allowing thieves to retake control. Here's a thought or two.

For a public bank to work, it must be transparent; must be audited annually by an outside third party, agreed to and appointed by the States, which must also be transparently audited independently (not sure how far this goes); must be tasked with assessing accurate weights and measures relative to maintaining a stable currency value; must be openly transparent regarding money supply and upcoming changes; must be open and transparent when assessing interest rates not more than once each year; and must run at a small positive return on investment based on transaction fees as determined by its directors;... and that's it.

Each State should have its own independently operated State Public Bank and the Federal Government can have its own Federal Public Bank serving federal functions including receipt of national property tax or in lieu of, sales tax revenue payments. Note – it is assumed 16th Amendment income tax is abolished. National property or sales tax revenue collected by each State shall be submitted by each State to the Federal Public Bank for payment processing against government expenses, and corrupt programs such as Social Security, Medicare, etc., if they still exist. The Federal Public Bank shall have no control over independent State Public Banks. Public State Banks shall have no monopoly on service. Any citizen resident in any state can choose to utilize their Public State Bank of choice, i.e., State Public Banks can compete with each other. Coinage shall be per Article I, Section 10 of the Constitution. I realize the so-called *Coinage Clause* can be subject to interpretation. We'll still have to deal with that as best we can.

Only one interest rate for lending, borrowing, and for corporate or individual interest charges shall be assessed by each Public Bank, state or federal. In other words, NO SPREAD and NO DISCRIMINATION. Insider access to "low cost of capital" providing advantage over Main Street's "high cost of capital" is a thing of the past. All borrowers shall be considered within the same standard. Public Banks pay for themselves with fully disclosed "direct fees". Depositor - Borrower qualification shall be uniformly assessed by a single, uniform standard. No discrimination shall be permitted and no need for public banks to protect the spread between discriminatory rates benefiting privileged entities because there are none to protect. The public pays the bank's operating cost by "direct fees for service", which shall be audited annually by an independent (State appointed) outside third party, also audited. Boom and bust business cycles are no longer manipulated by insider banking interests.

I propose: private commercial banks can compete with public banks, competitively setting interest rates and fees as they wish, with free markets determining success. No citizen is obligated to use any private or public bank services outside state and federal revenue/expense functions. **Public State and Federal Bank directors** shall serve terms of two-years and managers with terms of four years. Public State appointments are by State legislature vote. Public Federal bank directors and managers are appointed by vote of each state governor; each state having one vote. This concept or something like it can transparently prevent unscrupulous politicians from gumming up the works as mercenary bankers do today; and facilitates each state protecting their interest with some semblance of transparent, auditable, accountable power balance.

Repeal of 16th and particularly the 17th Amendments would help, though in today's politically and legally corrupt atmosphere coupled with educational dumbing down, a **Constitutional Convention** would likely bear tragic results for Main Street. Probably better for now, to simply set the Federal Income Tax Rate at zero percent and call it a day. At some point, U.S. Senators must be removed from the mud-slinging popularity pits drowning in election fraud; firmly placing their systemically corrupted votes under the thumb of respectively accountable State legislatures – as Originally intended. Along with creating a *transparent public bank*, a **single property tax** should be assessed along lines proposed by Henry George in *Progress and Poverty* replacing all other Federal taxation. In lieu of, a national sales (consumption) tax could be implemented as the only Federal tax. Actual Federal budgeting per *Generally Accepted Accounting Principles* (GAAP) must be rigidly implemented, replacing farcically corrupt baseline budgeting. State and local taxes are as elected state or local representatives determine.

Moving on, we sometimes hear the catchy phrase, *competition is a sin, therefore we must destroy it.* Often attributed to John D. Rockefeller of *Standard Oil* notoriety, I haven't been able to confirm he said it. In any event, economic history demonstrates cult-like adherence to this phraseology by psychopathic monopolists the world over, which I suppose stokes the megalomaniacal fire within their Luciferian obsessed minds seeking world-wide domination via financial/political subjugation? For some reason, applying logic… or perhaps lack of logic, many academics embrace and support this subjugation by arguing for the impoverishing, centralized, collectivist ideologies necessary to Fascist/Mercantilist corporate domination? Monopoly Capitalism, Marxism, Fascism, Globalism, and tyranny run together like train cars to a train wreck.

Monopolists depend on top-down, centrally planned governments for subsidies and protection against non-competitive, predictable losses. Go figure why honest Leftists, if any, cannot see the obvious parasitic synergy? This delusion must be unpacked if we are to understand why, regardless of who runs what transnational monopoly or who in whatever Political Party is elected or appointed to government office – nothing gets better for Main Street. Main Street impoverishment worsens with 100% predictability followed by useless UniParty finger pointing and the hollow blame game trumpeted by handsomely compensated MSM parrots. President Trump did throw a four-year wrench into this disease—hence global syndicate fear and hatred of him.

Many of us fall victim to the urban scholastic myth; free market capitalism is unsustainable as it MUST GROW to survive; and CANNOT GROW indefinitely on our finite spinning Earth; therefore, capitalism is doomed to fail – only God mocking parasitic socialism is sustainable. This uninformed deceit is balderdashic collectivist proselytism intended to convince propagandized Main Street; abundance is not possible. Wealth accumulation by *unwashed* masses is impossible we are led to believe in our Malthusian conditioned academic caves; so necessarily Main Street must accept impoverished serfdom at the genocidal hands of privileged order-followers working in harmony with criminalized intelligence services, i.e., shadow governments, and the corrupt international deep state with its monopolized transnational corporate interests.

This is organized crime in service to pathologic Elites demanding to own slaves with slave owner status protected by the Fascist States Elites own and operate.   False, Socialist nanny-state promises successfully pacify the *un-washed* most of the time and when trust issues crop up and Main Street confidence wains; a bang-up war suffices to distract and justify continued harvesting. Why do we keep falling for, voting for, and paying for this obvious con – not just with our confiscated wealth, but with our young people's blood?

I don't know if any Earth-bound person has ever lived one day under free market capitalism, but certainly, no one alive in the 21st century has. An unused ideology can hardly fail; and if that's the case, then what is failing? Capitalism's unfortunate Achille's heel is predilection for abuse brought about by human frailty, the most important aspect of which is spiritual incoherence - also causative to failure of republican forms of self-government necessary for the nourishment and survival of free-market capitalism, the most generous economic ism yet attempted. Republicanism requires honesty to survive. An immoral people cannot be managed by any system of government.

The entrenched global syndicate parasitically appreciates human frailty, manipulating trustful Main Street naivete to great *prominent global citizen* advantage.[41] This Elite appreciation of human weakness spawned Marxism and so-called Capitalism from their putrescent *City of London* womb with *Vatican City* as mid-wife and later, *Washington D.C.* as babysitter. We're told on Main Street, via Leftist projection, free-market capitalism cannot succeed because growth cannot continue forever. The truth is, free market capitalism does not require constant growth to sustain itself, BUT collectivism does. Parasitic collectivism cannot succeed without ever increasing theft and cannot survive without a productive host to bleed; and any host bleeding too much, expires and is no longer available for further bleeding. Even viruses (if they exist) are smarter than that. This doesn't mean every socialist concept is bad, but overall, socialism cannot support itself as it always operates at an unsustainable net negative return on investment similar to its abusive cousins, monopoly capitalism and mercantilism (if there's a difference?).

What is commonly and incorrectly referred to as capitalism today is a hybrid form of Mercantilism imposed through socialist impoverishment of Main Street, then enforced by Big-Fascist-Government. Government is controlled in turn through cash and influence of transnational monopolies through lobbyists, media exposure, or other more unsavory behavioral influences. Even a parasitic virus creates variants to save its host, yet Marxists cannot figure it out.

This corruption of government is in turn supported by indoctrinated Elite dynastic family round table networks such as *Royal Institute of International Affairs*,

---

41 "About the Bretton Woods Committee | The Bretton Woods Committee," accessed February 16, 2018, http://www.brettonwoods.org/page/about-the-bretton-woods-committee.

Council on Foreign Relations, Trilateral Commission, Bilderberg, Bohemian Grove, etc. These, together with many dozens of secret societies, foundations, trusts, endowments, academic pawns, controlled publishing, think tanks, etc., comprise the global syndicate's deep state matrix. Monopolies are by their nature ineffective, inefficient good-old-boy systems operating lazily and precariously on a net negative return on investment basis, which is why they cannot be sustained.

Every monopoly in every industry despite some short-term efficiencies is a Ponzi Scheme… a nefarious, often criminal enterprise where tomorrow's growth pays for today's losses or the scheme collapses; hence the need for corrupt government agencies protecting the criminal cartel's inability to competitively turn a profit or maintain liquidity within a free market environment. **This irrational hybrid system does demand perpetual growth for the Ponzi Scheme to survive BUT is not free market capitalism or anything like it.**

As Mr. Griffin explained earlier, this punitively controlled, highly discriminatory economy conveniently provides escape from healthy competitive capitalism and free markets for greedy monopolists and their global syndicate bosses, the 0.10% or more likely 0.010% (my words - I don't go to Elite meetings so don't know). Capitalism's inherent weakness is the ease with which it, along with representative government can be malevolently morphed into an opportunity demolishing, wealth confiscating, abundance diminishing, Socialist/Fascist/Mercantilist hybrid for creation and control of slaves, who don't realize they're slaves as they routinely vote for their own economic captivity by supporting elected and unelected rulers. Main Streeters work slavishly themselves, then accept imposition of unconstitutional progressive taxation and draconian regulation… all for the public good, of course. How can something this foolish even happen, much less survive?

Politically speaking, in *Fabian Socialist* manipulative stages of course. Dr. Paul Craig Roberts in an interview podcast with *Geopolitics and Empire* published Jan. 25, 2019, made some interesting observations regarding **identity politics** and the relationship between Democrat and Republican Parties. Today's Democrat Party has its forgotten roots with Thomas Jefferson and the anti-Federalists as did the Whigs and today's Republican Party, but Democrats veered in the 19th century, becoming the staunch pro-slavery party and finally today's Fascist-Socialist-Democrat Big Government Party — quietly supported by Establishment Republicans by the way. The Clintons, now a recognized crime family (my words), have played a crucial role in this transformation, and have been amply rewarded for abandoning workers and unions in favor of transnational monopoly as did Barry Soetoro, successor to the corrupt crown.

6 • Follow the Fiat Money

In the 20th century Dr. Roberts tells us; a balance of power was maintained between Republican support of industrial and corporate interests and Democrat support for workers and unions. This delicate balance worked well as upward mobility in terms of education, work skills, and higher salaries were available to those on lower economic rungs of the ladder. Poor became working middle class; middle-class became entrepreneurial upper class; and upper class joined the wealthy investor unearned income class. The practical result of this delicate balance along with hope and opportunity it engendered drew immigrants from around the world to the U.S. seeking a more equitable, more secure, more fulfilling, and/or abundant lifestyle called the **American Dream.**

During the 1990's, however, the globalist pawn Clinton crime machine successfully turned the Democrat Party away from what Hillary eventually termed, *irredeemable, deplorable* blue-collar workers and unions, toward the totalitarian global interests of big banks, transnational corporate monopolies, and so forth, leaving two parties supporting the same global interests; so, what on Earth to sell uninformed voters became a major Democrat-Republican UniParty issue. The *Race Card* fit the bill perfectly along with other divisive cards. *Critical Race Theory* jumped to the front of the indoctrination line.

The new Establishment R & D UniParty supporting corrupt, often treasonous banking, military, industrial, surveillance agendas had to be obscured from voter scrutiny or pitchforks might be dusted off. The *Pitchfork Avoidance Strategy* (PAS) PsyOp we live with today is the creation of Democrat targeted minority groups indoctrinated as victims to foment bitter divide and conquer Hegelian discord for Establishment political capital of both disingenuous Proxy Parties. This last is my more reactive paraphrasing of Mr. Robert's reasoned phraseology.

We now leave Dr. Robert's reasoned observations entirely, returning to my less polite line of thought. The 21st century American Uni-Party leaves Main Street with zero checks and balances against threats posed by Wall Street/D.C./Vatican City/City of London corruption, their unbridled love of counterfeiting currencies in service of Satanic Elites; and of course, enablement of eugenics and the global mind control apparatus, all on behalf of the psychotic global syndicate. Divide and conquer by Hegelian dialectic is its stock in history predetermination trade. It is a soiled, dog-eared, page-worn but effective playbook for obtaining *Imperial Federation*, i.e., *commonwealth, i.e., global power.*

Obviously, in terms of propaganda, the most divisively poisonous Democrat venom is reserved for alleged racist middle class white males, especially productive, financially successful, often generous white males, whose existence on Earth is considered by Progressives, a horrible affront to decency, fairness, and the Left's mutated concept of slavery, euphemistically referred to as *social justice*. I'm not sure what Progressive decency is comprised of as post-modern Marxists despise concepts like right or wrong, absolute truth, and the infinite value of created life. Paradoxically, *Cultural Marxism* is funded by and organized by uber-wealthy, Atlanticist Elites controlling multinational monopolies funding Leftist mayhem—the same corporations the Left claims to detest.

Animosity of group-think consensus toward anything *white* on Main Street is now the ignorant, though dogmatic main-stay across the *Cultural Marxist* world… a remarkable divide and conquer, global syndicate weapon created by the very Anglo-American globalists guilty of slavery, opium wars, and carrying out Establishment European/American imperialism, resource rape, and genocide themselves. Of course, *toxic white* does not apply to dynastic family members. Elites have cleverly misdirected world hatred of war crimes and other crimes against humanity toward innocent Main Street whites, particularly middle-class whites, who played no part in these well-documented atrocities, other than bleeding out on foreign soil and having their created wealth confiscated by D.C. to pay for global syndicate crimes, which all races are guilty of. Could we possibly be more foolish than buying into this globalist finger-pointing tripe, particularly as most Elite globalists are white or nearly white, whatever that is these days?

Sadly, deceitful bought-and-paid-for, Fascist Big Government Establishment Republicans, mostly Neocon war mongers, place-hold for lying, bought-and-paid-for, Socialist Big Government Democrats, mostly Neo-Liberal war mongers. Together, they subtly enable centrally planned lunacy while feigning disagreement via useless rhetorical pandering. Corrupt media order-followers crank up the *shriek-o-meter* on demand, facilitating misinformation, public discord, and often, treason. (*Shriek-o-meter* is a handy *Solari Report* term.)[42]

The only dissenting voice remaining in America's two treasonous Houses of Congress are a handful of *Freedom Caucus* members whose voices are so marginalized; they can't peep louder than a caged canary innocently singing in a gas-filled mine. Hopefully, carrying on the analogy, miners (citizens) see the helpless canary croak and run like hell, but if listening to slimy MSM, that escape likelihood is slim. As I write this, the *Freedom Caucus* has degenerated to just another useless pandering joke anyway, so little respite there. A few of these pandering pawns actually claim to be Libertarian; can't make it up.

American Main Street 21ˢᵗ century citizens are left without D.C. representation at the mercy of a corrupt Uni-Party System of cowardly, greedy, glo-

---

42 "The Solari Report Blog | The Solari Report Blog," accessed April 20, 2017, https://solari.com/blog/.

balist order-followers whose insane marching orders demand privileged D.C. thugs incrementally genocide the *unwashed* excess population (think GMO foods, processed malnutrition, toxic vaccines, aerosol spraying, 5G, etc.), while impoverishing unlucky survivors, i.e., the uninformed constituency gullibly believing R's and D's still matter while being robbed by both with impunity. This evil package, this conspiracy against mankind and creation itself is only funded and made possible by fiat currency, or more accurately, debt-based money. NO DEBT, NO MONEY IN AMERICA.

So, how does DEBT MONEY come about?

Direct taxation renders fraudulently expensive big government a non-starter as Main Street will quickly grab pitch forks in mass if citizens notice their wealth being stolen from under their pillows. Unfortunately, we must deal with amputation by *prominent global citizen* order-followers of what Adam Smith referred to as the *invisible hand*, exchanging mutual cooperation for one-sided coercion. Few of us will voluntarily write a check paying for *CIA* and *United Fruit's* murderous theft of Guatemalan farmer's land, Somalia's oil reserves, bombing mountain goat farmers in Afghanistan, crushing Libya and Syria to dust, robbing Russia or the Ukraine, enslaving all of China, etc. I suspect for those of us not yet 100% indoctrinated, the inability to consider writing these checks as being *in our best self-interest*, is a given. Unjust taxation or tax magic must be hidden from Main Street's prying eyes or it's pitchfork time. How do **tax magic and fiat money** work?

G. Edward Griffin calls this magic, the **Mandrake Mechanism** in honor of the 1940's comic book character, *Mandrake the Magician*, whose talent was bringing things forth from nothing and making them disappear back into nothing.[43] **A fiat U.S. dollar is created the instant it's borrowed. That same fiat dollar vanishes the instant it is paid off.** Interestingly, if you are a bank owner, you can create nine more dollars for every dollar of debt redefined as reserves. This is truly a magically fraudulent process encompassing *usury* and the fraud of *fractional reserve banking*. Mr. Griffin provides a summary of how this financial debt magic works when performed by the privately-owned *Federal Reserve Banking System* and he says it better than I can, so in Mr. Griffin's own words:

The Mandrake Mechanism: An Overview – Debt:

"The entire function of this machine is to convert debt into money. It's just that simple. First, the Fed takes all the government bonds which the public does not buy and writes

---

43 G. Edward Griffin, *The Creature from Jekyll Island Update 5th Edition Published in 2010 by G. Edward Griffin - Exact Book Featured on Glenn Beck Program*, 5 Edition (Amer Media, 2010), chap. 10.

a check to Congress in exchange for them. (It acquires other debt obligations as well, but government bonds comprise most of its inventory.) There is no money to back up this check. These fiat dollars are created on the spot for that purpose. By calling those bonds "reserves", the Fed then uses them as the base for creating 9 additional dollars for every dollar created for the bonds themselves. The money created for the bonds is spent by the government, whereas the money created on top of those bonds is the source of all the bank loans made to the nation's businesses and individuals. The result of this process is the same as creating money on a printing press, but the illusion is based on an accounting trick rather than a printing trick. The bottom line is that Congress and the banking cartel have entered into a partnership in which the cartel has the privilege of collecting interest on money which it creates out of nothing, a perpetual override on every American dollar that exists in the world. Congress, on the other hand, has access to unlimited funding without having to tell the voters their taxes are being raised through the process of inflation. If you understand this paragraph, you understand the Federal Reserve System."[44]

Note that today, the Fed also has what some call a *trading desk* run by the *markets group* on the 9th floor of 33 Liberty Street, home of the privately owned New York Fed. Wouldn't you and I enjoy having a free currency creation machine fueling our investment portfolio? Just sayin'. We'll not take time here to fully explain the fiat money creation fraud process as Mr. Griffin does in Chapter 10 of *The Creature from Jekyll Island*. We'll just touch on a few pertinent points for clarification as elucidated by Mr. Griffin. The following is summarized in my own words from Chapter 10 of *The Creature from Jekyll Island*. It's important voters understand this central banking fraud process, so please study the following paragraphs carefully… or better, purchase Mr. Griffin's wonderfully informative book and read it in full.

An instrument of government debt such as long-term Treasury Bonds (30-year), TIPS (5, 10, & 30 year), shorter-term Treasury Notes (2, 3, 5, 7, & 10 year), or Treasury Bills (terms less than 1-year) are considered assets as are IOU's called currency (Federal Reserve Notes) under the assumption the government can and will honor its obligation to pay. (Given the *Federal Reserve System* on-book accounts as of 2Q-2021, showing a Debt to GDP ratio of ±125.5% – this obligation is a joke and has been for decades.) We don't know what the Fed is doing off-book as it has never been properly audited and since 2018, FASAB 56 legalized non-disclosure of government finances for poorly defined national security purposes.

Anyway, these so-called asset instruments are used by the Federal Reserve to offset liabilities in the form of more pieces of paper called Federal Reserve Checks which are issued to government in return for receiving associated assets. There is no money in any account to cover these checks, none-the-less Federal Reserve books

---

44 Griffin, 193.

are said to be balanced as liability of the paper check is offset by the asset value of the paper IOU. Paper of course, is now usually replaced by digital computer entry.

The Federal Reserve Check is then endorsed and deposited in one of the Federal Reserve Banks as a **Government Deposit**, in turn used to pay government expenses. (This process is digital today, but you get the process.) In other words, **the Government Deposit is transformed into Government Checks, which are how the first wave of debt (fiat) money enters the economy.**

As you may imagine, this horde of Government Checks is cashed with recipients depositing Government Checks into their own bank accounts where they become **Commercial Bank Deposits**. Now the fun begins. The Commercial Bank Deposits take on a dual personality as liabilities to the commercial bank because they are owed back to the depositors; but if they remain in the bank, they are considered assets because they are on hand. Again, the commercial bank books are now balanced with paper assets offsetting paper liabilities… and here comes the serious magic. **These on-hand deposits are re-classified as "reserves".** Reserves for what we ask?

Reserves from which to pay depositors should they wish to close out their accounts? Of course not. That would be silly. Most bankers don't care about Main Street depositors except as marks. Commercial banks are authorized by the Fed to loan money up to some limit of required reserves, which varies from time to time, but let's say 10%. In other words, for each $1.00 of 1st wave fiat money created by the Fed, commercial banks can lend $0.90 ($1.00 less $0.10 reserve), then rinse and repeat. Bankers refer to this $0.90 as **Excess Reserves**.

The simple equation for this monetary inflation process is: **Deposit / Reserve Percentage = Money Created** • so, $1.00/0.1 = $10.00

Clearly, reducing the Reserve Percentage from 10% to 5% would double the counterfeit (fiat) money supply. • $1.00/0.05 = $20.00. Easy peasy. Conversely, increasing the Reserve Percentage reduces the money supply.

Newly named Excess Reserves can now be converted into Commercial Bank Loans. These new commercial bank loans are generated from thin air thereby creating new money from the same thin air the Fed used. The nation's money supply can and usually is increased by 90% of commercial bank deposits. BUT WAIT! We are not finished. The original bank deposits cost the commercial bank in terms of interest paid on deposits or services provided. This new money is free and earns interest revenue for the commercial bank making new money more profitable than old money—a much sweeter deal.

This 2ⁿᵈ wave of fiat money, slightly smaller (remember the 90% rule) than the first wave is now circulated as More Commercial Bank Deposits and the process repeats. According to analysts, this process can be repeated about twenty-eight (28) times if maximally employed, thereby increasing the total fiat money supply (monetary inflation) up to ten (10) times the National Debt. **In other words, the total amount of fiat money created by the Federal Reserve and Commercial Banks together is about ten (10) times the underlying government debt.** Not as complicated as we're told, is it?

Unfortunately for Main Street, if this created money supply disproportionately surpasses goods and services produced, the purchasing power of each dollar is proportionately reduced. Prices rise (price inflation) because the value of created fiat money is decreasing. **The result of reduced Main Street purchasing power is equivalent to that same amount being confiscated from us on Main Street in the form of direct taxation.** So, in addition to income taxes, property taxes, assessments, excise taxes, user fees, and so forth; Americans pay a **hidden tax** in the form of higher prices. Remember, the first users of this money, say government or connected insiders, spend their debt money before it decreases in value. Main Street is stuck with the already decreased value of their 2nd hand debt money. BUT WAIT! We are not done! It gets better for the global syndicate and their order followers.

This quantity of fiat money has nothing underlying it except debt. Therefore, more or less money can be loaned, thereby expanding or contracting the nation's money supply. Simply put, as the nation, its businesses, and people sink deeper and deeper into debt – the money supply expands. If the nation, businesses, and people pay off their debts and don't borrow more money – the money supply contracts. This is one reason why interest rates are a major player in whether money supply expands or contracts, except when Government is the largest borrower and the scheme breaks down. High interest rates discourage borrowing; low interest rates encourage borrowing. Our money supply is tied directly to the level of borrowing, hence, to interest rates.

The Congressional Budget Office (CBO) states in a 2019 Working Paper (2019-01) titled, *The Effect of Government Debt on Interest Rates* by Gamber and Seliski: **In the baseline specification, for each percentage-point increase in the ratio of projected debt to GDP, expected interest rates have increased by 2 to 3 basis points.**

In other words, government debt levels typically control money creation and money supply, directly impacting quality of financial life for citizens. Fascinating, as this government debt level is largely unseen

and poorly understood by taxpayers being defrauded. **Of course, this general CBO rule of thumb is now manipulated as is everything surrounding it.** *Circa 2021, quantitative easing, overnight repos, and reverse repos of $1 trillion or more overnight blow increasing interest rates into unsustainable non-existence.*

Obviously, alternating expansion/contraction of the money supply by global syndicate central bank order-followers causes the boom, bust, recession, depression cycle wherein only insiders benefit at the painful expense of Main Street because <u>insiders know when the money supply will be expanded or contracted by the central banks.</u> Simply put, insiders go to the meetings you and I aren't invited to and then have lunch with their golf and yachting buddies who don't have time to attend organized fraud meetings. If insiders know when these expansion/contraction adjustments are occurring; it's a simple matter to make sure privileged insiders are cash rich as money tightens and investment rich as money loosens. Billionaires are often not brilliant as PR campaigns and MSM suggest; just well connected, well informed, government protected, and criminally opportunistic. The global syndicate takes care of its thugs.

The ensuing Main Street bankruptcies caused by money tightening inevitably provide convenient opportunities for the privileged to purchase choice "real" assets like property, commercial/retail businesses, farms, mines, factories, shipping companies, commodities, etc. for pennies on the dollar. After the bust buying spree, *prominent global citizens* can sit back, comfortably sipping adrenalized blood and other treats, watching their newly stolen asset values rise as the money supply is again expanded for the next phase of the boom/bust cycle. A nice cherry on top is provided by the predictable Main Street clamor for food stamp and other welfare relief handled by global syndicate Big Banks, who earn a tidy profit servicing stale crumbs dropped on Main Street. Welfare isn't free. Most welfare dollars go into processing pockets and kickbacks—not to the needy.

The Left and Right Establishment call this organized theft, **equity, social justice**, and **fairness**. Insider risk is zero or at least close to zero as insiders know ahead of time when to position themselves as fully invested or cash rich. Not much mystery here and those of us paying attention can see those borrowed *nanny state* crumbs are astonishingly expensive for Main Street and obscenely profitable for *prominent global citizens*. So expensive in fact, Main Street is guaranteed no financial future beyond increased debt enslavement will ever be allowed by the global syndicate. Note that at overall tax rates above the 25-30% range, wealth accumulation is nearly impossible in a ±100-year lifetime. A middle-class family today is totally taxed and assessed around 60% of total income assuring middle class entrepreneurial challenges to monopoly interests are minimal as it's difficult for the impoverished to defend themselves.

Since I can be a bit harsh, let's return one more time to Mr. Griffin's more reasonable words: "Who benefits from all this? Certainly not the average citizen. The only beneficiaries are the political scientists in Congress who enjoy the effect of unlimited revenue to perpetuate their power, and the monetary scientists within the banking cartel called the Federal Reserve System who have been able to harness the American people, without their knowing it, to the yoke of modern feudalism".[45]

Our discussion could continue for many pages if we dig deeper into this financial fraud, but we get the big picture. Government sanctioned fraud enables mercenary political careers along with enormous, unaccountable, non-transparent, abusive government with all the abuses elected and unelected order-follower greed can imagine perpetrating on unsuspecting Main Streets across the globe. Let's not forget to mention WAR, the *Numero Uno* for Elite profit taking, excess population reduction, and profitable reconstruction.

Psychopathic Elites and their sick, privileged order-followers love to profitably perpetrate war by applying the well-worn, so-called *Rothschild Formula*, i.e., destruction of infrastructure that will have to be profitably replaced by insider contracts, destabilization of sovereign nations, genocide of the *unwashed*, resource rape, and of course, the endemic surveillance state now growing exponentially in viciousness and invasive control, spawning whatever other horrors we can imagine. All made possible by debt (fiat) money and its non-transparent, unaudited, uncontrolled use. In defense of Rothschilds, (oh the horror of it) is my understanding, Rothschild family leaders typically avoid geopolitical involvement as "unbusiness-like", so don't directly run the world as many suggest. However, they do fund, influence, and reap financial benefits from chaos sown by malevolent associates whom they finance, with their share of financing driving the chaos, so there's that.

Fiat/debt money must be eliminated if our world is ever to be safe. But how; what then? Socially deviant control of global syndicate miscreants for centuries complicates things like the once simple gold standard. For example, as I write these words in 2021, central banks around the world, mostly Far East banks have been buying gold in quantities greater than quantities of gold are mined. How?

Dr. Joseph P. Farrell[46] has postulated a case of pure bookkeeping fraud, that gold is being alchemically created; not a high probability, or may be making its way from hidden depositories of which Main Street is unaware? I'll carry the conjecture ball from here in the interest of preserving Dr. Farrell's good name. Thank you, Dr. Farrell, for the head's up though and please enjoy your new pipe organ.

---

45 Griffin, 200.
46 "Giza Death Star," Giza Death Star, September 29, 2016, https://gizadeathstar.com/.

6 • Follow the Fiat Money

Skipping past the possibility of complete fraud, as a for instance, we might inquire as to the whereabouts of Czar Nicholas II's confiscated Romanov family wealth in the form of gold, silver, jewels, art, etc. following the February 1917 Russian Revolution (*February Bourgeois Democratic Revolution*); or more significantly on the heels of the October 25, 1917 coup d'etat carried out against the provisional Kerensky government at the Winter Palace by Lenin, Trotsky and their Bolsheviks, where early on the morning of Oct. 26th (Red October) the *Red Guard* took command of the Russian government? Interestingly, neither Lenin nor Trotsky were in Russia in February 1917. They came along later from Switzerland and New York respectively, along with Wall Street, Prussian, and City of London financing, but I digress.

OK, I never stop digressing. Those of us who cannot read Russian and may not be interested in historic rabbit holes are unfortunately left with published gibberish contrived about the horrors of living under notably weak Czar Nicholas II. I don't often defend Elites, but if interested I suggest checking out the controversial deposed Orthodox priest, Dr. Matthew Raphael Johnson's *A Circle of Betrayal, Cowardice and Deceit*, an alternative view of revolutionary Russian history.[47] I don't agree with some of Dr. Johnson's many views, but he appears to be a courageous researcher, and in my humble opinion worth a bit of consideration. I do provide this friendly warning label though; Dr. Johnson is an equal opportunity disrespecter of human rationality and I don't have the means to verify his information.

Getting back to it, we might inquire where the tons of loot confiscated in 1917 Russia as well as other European loot under cover of World War I and World War II went off to? Treasures stolen by all sides, each funded by gleeful, global syndicate central banks, primarily the *Federal Reserve*? Rumors abound but the fact of this enormous theft isn't arguable – so, where did the loot go? The question is valid as it appears more gold is being purchased by central banks today than is known to exist or can be mined on an annual basis. Where is this gold coming from? Who is selling it? The post-war Fascist Nazi International? Antarctica? Grand Canyon? The Philippines? Is it just fraudulent accounting?

These vanishing wealth mysteries and others like, where did Libya's gold reserves go when the order following Obama Administration initiated its Libyan slaughter along with weapons transfers to ISIS in Syria? These events raise questions concerning the quantity and purity of gold and silver in the world, not to mention who's holding it or where; in turn raising questions about accurate weights and measures relative to possible resetting of currency values – think *The Great Reset* discussed at DAVOS, 2020.

---

47 Matthew Raphael Johnson, *"A Circle of Betrayal, Cowardice and Deceit" – On the 100th Anniversary of the Ritual Murder of the Russian Royal Family* (Hromada Books, 2018).

Making matters worse, at least for the U.S. petro-dollar are $21 trillion missing U.S. dollars since 1998 per *Inspector General Audit Reports* for *DoD* and *HUD* (See *Solari Report*/Missing Money); and unaudited *Federal Reserve* bailouts totaling between $17 and $27 trillion dollars – who knows how much or where it went – on top of $30 trillion on-book U.S. national debt and ± $205 trillion in unfunded mandates, including Social Security and Medicare per the 2014 *Congressional Budget Office's* (CBO) 2nd set of books entitled *Alternative Fiscal Scenario* (AFS) ?[48] Incidentally, the CBO doesn't publish AFS anymore. Too many prying eyes? Can't have that with self-governance.

On top of this missing money, *Department of Defense News* reported that DoD announced $29 trillion in accounting changes in 2017, $30.7 trillion in 2018, and $35 trillion in 2019 – an additional $94.7 trillion in *undocumentable adjustments*. Granted, per DoD spokespersons, these accounting discrepancies involve double, triple, and worse counting errors, but quadruple accounting doesn't get DoD from just under appropriations of ±$800 billion annually to $30 trillion annually. D.C. fiscal accountability is zilch and not accidentally or incompetently. There is fraud here.

A bit unrelated, but on top of this vanishing wealth mystery, *Comex* now trades paper gold in quantities as high as 300:1. In other words, for an ounce of physical gold; up to 300 ounces of paper gold are fraudulently traded. Obviously, this is criminal and since all contracts can't be honored, i.e., physical gold can't be delivered because it doesn't exist; paper gold contracts will one of these days go to zero value for lack of performance. **"What is a non-performing contract worth,"** as Bill Holter frequently asks?

Begging the question, why on earth are taxpayers paying for profligate goofball agencies like the malfeasant *Commodity Futures Trading Commission* (CFTC) or in the case of stocks, bonds and mutual funds, the *Securities and Exchange Commission* (SEC)? How is maintaining these two agencies not morbidly masochistic? How much financial self-abuse do we the people of Main Street wish to inflict on ourselves? Another reason to wake up.

Circling back (a little Biden Regime lingo there) to government debt and fiat money creation, the *Congressional Budget Office* (CBO) fallaciously maintains two completely different sets of books; as does every *Ponzi Scheme* management team wishing to avoid prison, although privileged government criminals have *qualified immunity* under the fiction of National Security. The first set is the *Extended Baseline Forecast* (EBF), which is the magic set of books order-following media talking heads disingenuously quote from for busy

---

48 "$205 Trillion in Unfunded Liabilities," Daily Reckoning, February 12, 2014, https://dailyreckoning.com/205-trillion-in-unfunded-liabilities/.

Main Street folks to soak up so they continue investing in rigged markets. In the *Daily Reckoning* article just cited above by Mr. Gary North in February 2014, *Boston University* economist, Professor Laurence Kotlikoff tells us:

"In past years, the CBO simultaneously released what it calls its Alternative Fiscal Scenario. This forecast is what CBO actually projects future taxes and spending to be given not just the laws in place, but also how Congress and the Administration have been bending and changing the laws through time. In short, the Alternative Fiscal Scenario (AFS) is what the CBO thinks we're facing absent a truly dramatic and sustained shift in fiscal policy."

Please note since Professor Kotlikoff began publicizing CBO's second set of books some years ago and some on Main Street noticed, CBO no longer publishes the AFS. Since we don't know how much gold and silver are held in global vaults, caves, or whatever; and are not certain how many unaudited fiat U.S. dollars exist or where those dollars are – how can anyone accurately determine U.S. oil-dollar currency value or a new gold-backed value? How can world trade with the largest economy on earth, i.e., America with 2021 GDP of ±$23 trillion be equitably conducted?

Why has Main Street tolerated this complete abrogation of *Generally Accepted Accounting Principles* (GAAP) and fiduciary responsibility to taxpayers by *District of Columbia* crooks behaving as cowardly proxies for an unelected, malevolent global syndicate? We MUST advance our learning curve on these matters if we hope to avoid further impoverishment... or euthanasia in the event the global syndicate decides not to honor Baby Boomer pensions, about $25 trillion. Are the bioweapon SARS-CoV-2 and its toxic JABs an aspect of ensuring $25 trillion in pension fund dollars aren't wasted on retiring Baby Boomers?

We haven't taken time here to raise questions concerning other nation's finances, hidden or otherwise, secret space programs since November 22, 1963, other black or hidden budgets since WW II, secret technology development, how much money is held by the non-transparent, unconstitutional *Exchange Stabilization Fund* created in 1934, etc. There is much we don't know on Main Street and clearly, self-governance has been abdicated to a Luciferian global syndicate whose privileged, order-following proxies are visible; but whose psychopathic, influential leadership are not.

Do we the people of Main Street have any idea how many diamonds were looted by Master Mason, Cecil Rhodes controlled, *De Beers Consolidated Mines* from the bloody soil of South Africa? How much gold was looted from the people of South Africa and other African nations by Rhodes, Milner, and friends? Has any of this wealth been tucked away for a rainy day? If today's Main Street *preppers* are forward looking enough to prepare for unforeseen circumstances; wouldn't the world's most viciously greedy, obsessively paranoid Elites do as much, or more?

Elites after all, are expert in *Pitchfork Avoidance Strategy* (PAS). Elites have as much right as anyone to protect wealth; but not when stolen, and not when millions of innocent people have been brutally starved, tortured, imprisoned, and murdered while stealing it. Elites have no *Darwinian Evolutionary* right to manipulate global economies with stolen wealth hidden wherever it's been concealed. I'm not saying this hiding-the-loot thing happened or is happening; just asking as clearly something is going on behind Main Street's back? There is an explanation for how more gold per year is traded than can be mined from the ground.

Returning to the gold standard today is not a simple thing as enormous fraud renders simple things unclear. None-the-less, fiat/debt money must be flushed down history's mistake toilet. This will help end BIG GOVERNMENT, WORLD WARS, WEAPONIZED WEATHER MODIFICATION, POPULATION STERILIZATION AND ELIMINATION, and the TRANSHUMAN MIND CONTROL APPARATUS because there'll be no way to fund these monstrosities without raising taxes directly, which will bring out Main Street pitch forks - more than eight billion rusty pitch forks inbred Elites fear.

So-called digital currencies and nanotechnology along with other surveillance techniques are every dictator's dream. Wealth confiscation is 100% enabled for Elites without Main Street recourse. Slave tracking is fully enabled 100% of the time. Global syndicate central bank pawns drool over this enslavement idea. Imagining global syndicate banking thugs will tolerate uncontrolled, private crypto currency circulation is beyond naïve. Crypto, regardless its status as a good or bad idea, is employed as just another Satanic trap.

If we cannot turn this divide and conquer American ship, with its anti-human Hegelian cargo of mindless venom, demonization, and hatred onto a more human course bearing; our children and grandchildren have little hope for any kind of secure, free, or abundant future. It is time to stop being afraid of each other because nincompoops say we should and start embracing each other. We must have each other's back.

If Main Street Americans cannot or will-not lead the world into a 21st century sustainably human friendly era of recognized unalienable rights such as life, liberty, and the pursuit of happiness – who will—who can? **ABANDON MAKE BELIEVE MONEY AND THE PSYCHOPATHIC BLACK MAGIC CLINGING TO IT!**

Let freedom ring with gold and silver coinage!

Experience teaches governments gone bad—only get worse.
History proves it!
Time to rejuvenate our Republic—or enjoy Transhuman slavery.
The pandemic is not COVID—the pandemic is non-treatment.
The 2nd COVID pandemic will be adverse JAB reactions.
Thank the WEF, a pathologically ill organization.

7 • METAVERSE & COVID Slave Training

Remedy: Defending our families against transhuman enslavement requires coming to grips with modern mind control methodologies. Psychopathic Elites have a come a long way from the days of *"do what we say or watch us rape your wife and daughter before drawing and quartering you."* Manufactured fear porn unreality is the name of the 21st century mind control game. Obtaining freedom and staying free demands developing defensive skills capable of warding off the deluge of global syndicate propaganda, fear mongering, conditioning, entrainment, and so forth. Spiritual warfare has evolved from the mind-material Universe to the mind-machine Neuralink, electromagnetic <u>Metaverse.</u> This new form of asymmetric warfare requires retrofitting our ancient suit of protective armor – the armor of God. God's grace, available upon request enables spiritual discernment, clarifies thinking, develops our will, strengthens our fortitude, and provides building blocks of character necessary to actively overcome evil.

On February 12, 2016, *National Academies Press* reported a statement made by British scientist, Dr. Peter Daszak, head of *EcoHealth Alliance* stating:

"We need to increase public understanding of the need for medical counter-measures such as a pan-corona virus vaccine. A key driver is the media, and the economics will follow the hype. We need to use that hype to our advantage, to get to the real issues. Investors will respond if they see profit at the end of the process."

You just read a quote by an Anthony Fauci (NIAID) funded, Satanically inspired psychopath collaborating with the **People's Liberation Army** of the **Chinese Communist Party** for more than fifteen years. Daszak outlined in four sentences, the planned chain of events following the September 2019 Phase I bioattack on the entire globe launched by the **Chinese Communist Party** (CCP). Whether initial bioweapon release of SARS-CoV-2 was intentional or accidental is immaterial. The **People's Liberation Army** (PLA), the military arm of the CCP used the Wuhan bioweapon release to harm the entire world, thereby hardening and globally expanding CCP's competitive position with their **Belt and Road** initiative. Like all G20 led nation states, the CCP is a Satanically influenced criminal enterprise. Unfortunately, it is now a transnational criminal enterprise not only operating without restraint, but with cooperation deeply embedded within other nation states, strategically employing treasonous elements in the United States of America, France, Germany, Italy, Spain, UK, the British Commonwealth, as well as across the South American and African continents.

The **"Metaverse"** mentioned above is envisioned by techies as the **Transhuman Successor** to the current **World Wide Web** (internet) proposing to intersect and meld mind-machine integration globally—with unlimited interaction between humans, machines, and I don't know what else. **Think of the Metaverse as Satanic fruition of DARPA's <u>full spectrum dominance</u> over all <u>human terrain</u>.** This alternate *Metaverse*, now under construction, melding quantum computing, atmospheric ionization, nanotechnology, the *Space Fence*, etc., together, is determined to be electromagnetically synchronous with a traceable (trackable) crypto (possibly nano) currency and unfairly dysfunctional global economy. The *Metaverse* is intended to be inter-operational, that is, centrally AI controllable (my words) with nearly infinite surveillance and entrainment capabilities. The *Metaverse* will never sleep, is intended to meld the "virtual world" with our "real world", and will permanently end life and freedom as we currently imagine them. I believe the Phase II bioweaponized TOXIC JABs and vaccine tracing are our public introduction to this psychotic Transhuman nightmare. Fortunately for humanity and all other life on Earth the frail *Metaverse* can be taken down by simple things such as rust, sun activity like *coronal mass ejections* (CME), or other electromagnetic interruptions.

SARS-CoV-2 is an engineered, bioweaponized, Phase I chimeric health threat, an attack utilizing social engineering, financial devastation, and population control protocols on an international scale. **Its toxic JABs are weaponized Phase II**. We know SARS-CoV-2 is a man-made or modified, laboratory engineered virus (if viruses exist) - or an engineered something. We also saw global syndicate order followers discussing bio-threat arrival at study group *Event 201* in 2019 several months before any Scamdemic was declared, inferring the release of so-called COVID-19 was intentionally planned. CDC's SARS-CoV-2 virus with research ties to Fort Detrick, its toxic spike protein, human ACE2 protein receptor penetration, etc., have undergone serious weaponization study since 1999 with more than 120 patented pieces of evidence demonstrating the *absurdity of new or novel.* The proposed so-called vaccines are mislabeled as medicinal. This per Dr. David Martin with *M-CAM International* speaking with Reiner Fuellmich, a German attorney working with the *International Corona Investigative Committee.*[49]

In my humble opinion, SARS-COV-2 and its WEAPONIZED NWO toxic JABs are an early implementation phase of the global syndicate's global enslavement program. Ms. Karen Kingston, whistle-blower and former employee of *Pfizer* has among other pieces of information shared her knowledge of two U.S. Patents pertinent to mislabeling mentioned above. The **first** is U.S. Patent Publication 2012/0265001 A1, published on October 18, 2012. This patent application discusses in detail a **composite magnetic nanoparticle drug delivery system for time-release gene therapies**. The **second** is U.S. Patent Application 20210082583 A1 filed on November 30, 2020 absurdly titled, METHODS AND SYSTEMS OF PRIORITIZING TREATMENTS, VACCINATION, TESTING AND/OR ACTIVITIES WHILE PROTECTING THE PRIVACY OF INDIVIDUALS.

This patent application is for a **complete surveillance tracing system** tracking all VAXXED Victims including a digital **monitoring score card,** similar to the CCP social scoring system. For example, if you attend religious services you get a higher score than someone who doesn't. It will monitor victim location, movement, personal contacts, physical meta-data, biological functions, etc., 24/7. This psychopathic Transhuman enslavement tool is public record, not conspiracy theory, and is expected to interface with the developing, more invasive **Neuralink** (Elon Musk)**, META** (*Facebook*), i.e., *Metaverse* networking technology.

An interesting **third** U.S. Patent 10,786,570 filed July 30, 2018, issued September 29, 2020, assigned to Rockefeller University, funded by NIH Grant No. ROI GM095654 with retained government interests cross referencing several other associated patents, protects a pharmaceutical composition effecting chimeric TRP channels using ferritin nanoparticles for **remote control of cell function** by radio frequency (RF) waves to excite nanoparticles targeted to specific cell

---

49 "Twenty-Year Genetic Trail behind Covid's Creation," *The Conservative Woman* (blog), July 13, 2021, https://www.conservativewoman.co.uk/twenty-year-genetic-trail-behind-covid's-creation/.

types for regulation of cellular functions including hormone release, muscle contraction, or neural activity. Do we doubt this technology is weaponized?

Note: Just because a government protected, Big Pharma Monopoly patent has not yet been issued doesn't mean Big Pharma isn't already using it. They have no shortage of expensive litigators to defend their patent rights and profit margins. In the case of mislabeled vaccines Big Pharma has no legal or financial liability anyway. Thank you U.S. Congress.

In October 2021, fraudulent Biden Regime, U.S. Secretary of State Antony Blinken traveled to Paris to address a conference of the *Organization for Economic Cooperation and Development* (OECD). This international cult of order following psychopaths, so far consisting of 38 member states, is drafting international rules and setting standards for how humans will interact with artificial intelligence. Comrade Blinken stated the Biden Regime is working to place the U.S. population beneath authority of this global cult (my words). The Transhumanist freaks publicly discussing their Satanic Plan forget to mention the handy little robots they envision, are you and I.

It's magnitudes less expensive and faster to electromagnetically program Main Street dupes as cyborgs than waste time and money trying to build functional robots. It's just simple cost efficiency and time logistics. At this same Paris meeting, OECD proposed a minimum 15-percent global tax on corporations to support their new digital economy, to which as of this writing, the Biden Regime along with 135 other nations, agreed. This unconstitutional global tax addresses "tax challenges" to be met by the coming globalized digital economy, i.e., **METAVERSE**.

SARS-CoV-2, its variants, and its criminally negligent so-called vaccines are about deceit, money, power, control, eugenics, and the ongoing pursuit by Big Pharma to develop a government mandated, self-marketing, guaranteed profit center built on weakened immune systems and **vaccine addiction** across the world population. Influenza vaccines failed in this regard, so a new disease had to be fabricated—and it was. In the U.S., this is not arguable—demonstrated by coordinated, simultaneous abandonment of established public health and medical treatment **"best practice"** protocols, abruptly mandated across many states. Any mandate for use of weaponized experimental JABs violates the *Nuremberg Code* (Directives for Human Experimentation) and would violate the 1925 *Geneva Protocol* prohibiting use of biological and chemical weapons – if we were at war – which of course we are, though conveniently undeclared or even acknowledged.

GAIN OF FUNCTION RESEARCH = BIO-CHEMICAL WEAPONS RESEARCH

7 • METAVERSE & COVID Slave Training

Soliciting consent of medical experiment volunteers is one thing. Mandating a largely untested experimental JAB without consent while refusing to disclose the JAB's ingredients or postulated long term effects is absolute hooey. How is it possible we are graduating medical school students and residents so medically illiterate and/or corrupt they engage such criminally malfeasant policy? What level of professional blackmail or licensing extortion is required to force trained physicians to abandon early treatment using historically safe, effective, low cost medications like *Hydroxychloroquine*, *Ivermectin*, or *Fluvoxamine*? What about readily available holistic protocols using L-Arginine, vitamin C, vitamin D$_3$, melatonin, zinc, quercetan, NAC, etc.?

NIH, CDC, FDA and other federal agencies did not abandon established virology protocols along with WHO because they were found ineffective. They abandoned proven protocols up-front, immediately implementing counter-productive protocols ensuring weakened immunity on a mass scale, thereby enabling *Emergency Use Authorization* of experimental toxins. This predetermined asymmetric warfare attack was simulated at *Event 201* by *The World Economic Forum* on October 18, 2019. The same cartel on July 09, 2021, simulated a major infrastructure cyberattack called *Cyber Polygon*. Was *Cyber Polygon* a precursor to *planned supply chain breakdowns* as *Event 201* was to COVID-19? I don't know as of this writing, but future will likely prove past. Preppers of the world unite! What level of international power and influence is required to pull off something this evil?

Main Street citizens must demand a **2nd Nuremberg World Tribunal** to investigate this global medical fraud. I don't favor international entanglements, but this genocidal bioweapon pogrom is too widespread to be handled by any one nation. Another sad aspect of this weaponized medical fraud is we the people of Main Street being conned into paying for or accepting responsibility for debt incurred to pay for our own poisoning and enslavement. Any doctor willingly abandoning established treatment protocols for propagandized nonsense disseminated by a heavily compromised CDC, FDA, NIH, WHO, etc., should be ashamed of themselves and give up their license to practice. What responsible doctor **doing no harm** recommends patients take experimental JABs with unknown ingredients or sends patients home without treatment recommending an appointment after their lips turn blue from lack of oxygen? This is professionally negligent and morally unconscionable, particularly in the case of a virus fatal to so few with early treatment and JABs containing provably harmful substances. Thousands of uninformed doctors across the globe are sadly and aggressively driving public health into the jaws of asymmetric COVID bioterrorism instigated by the *Chinese Communist Party* (CCP) at the behest of global syndicate handlers.

In the U.S., this malevolence is made more significant by unexplained abandonment of established viral treatment protocols by government agencies like CDC and NIH, apparently justifying FDA approval for experimental distribution of unproven mRNA carried payloads or other injections with unknown ingredients and limited testing histories. Experienced practicing physicians were inhibited and, in many cases, threatened with license revocation by malfeasant medical boards for prescribing commonly used treatments known to have few if any side effects. *Ivermectin* and *Hydroxychloroquine* (HCQ) for example are two of the safest medicines on Earth. Instead of traditionally successful treatments, experimental vaccines were coercively pushed on doctors. It is imperative we investigate why public health medical malfeasance is being forced on our medical community.

If this pharmafraud and medical fraud and what now appears to be serial mass murder are investigated and found even partially as corrupt as I claim here, Main Street MUST demand indictments, adjudication, and orange jump suits for the guilty.

Here is a paragraph taken from the *Limit of Detection* (LoD) description on Page 40 of the CDC's own July 21, 2021, *Instructions for Use* for the **2019-Novel Coronavirus (2019-nCoV) Real-Time RT-PCR Diagnostic Panel.**

"The analytical sensitivity of the rRT-PCR assays contained in the CDC 2019 Novel Coronavirus (2019- nCoV) Real-Time RT-PCR Diagnostic Panel were determined in Limit of Detection studies. Since no quantified virus isolates of the 2019-nCoV were available for CDC use at the time the test was developed and this study conducted, assays designed for detection of the 2019-nCoV RNA were tested with characterized stocks of in vitro transcribed full length RNA (N gene; GenBank accession: MN908947.2) of known titer (RNA copies/μL) spiked into a diluent consisting of a suspension of human A549 cells and viral transport medium (VTM) to mimic clinical specimen. Samples were extracted using the QIAGEN EZ1 Advanced XL instrument and EZ1 DSP Virus Kit (Cat# 62724) and manually with the QIAGEN DSP Viral RNA Mini Kit (Cat# 61904). Real-Time RT-PCR assays were performed using the Thermo Fisher Scientific TaqPath™ 1-Step RT-qPCR Master Mix, CG (Cat# A15299) on the Applied Biosystems™ 7500 Fast Dx Real-Time PCR Instrument according to the CDC 2019-nCoV Real-Time RT-PCR Diagnostic Panel instructions for use."

<u>Please note the phrase</u> – **"Since no quantified virus isolates of the 2019-nC0V were available for CDC use…"** I leave it to the reader to ponder what *"no quantified virus isolates"* means but something is awry here and it gives off a noxious odor.

Neither the CCP nor any G20 government is comprised of decision makers. Nations are controlled by global syndicate shadow governments and managed by international deep state networks, one component of which are elected and appointed government order followers, i.e., middle level managers, trained, vetted, and groomed through the aforementioned study group system. The study group system is a global Fascist vetting, conditioning, and management system predicated on lies and threat of violence as the stick in one hand, alongside the privileged carrot in the other. This putrid system runs Washington D.C. as mentioned elsewhere.

Regarding COVID bioterrorism, SARS-CoV-2 is a Phase 1 bioweapon, followed by Phase 2 synthetic mRNA carried nanotechnology injections, followed by Phase 3 boosters, all possibly enhanced by various venoms, recent influenza and/or HIV containing corona virus strains, and difficult to identify nanotechnologies. My non-medical bioterrorism opinion is based on data provided by D.O. Ryan Cole, D.O. Elizabeth Eads, Dr. Simone Gold, Dr. Sunetra Gupta, Dr. Stella Immanuel, Steve Kirsch, Dr. Pierre Kory, Dr. Martin Kulldorff, Lieutenant Colonel Theresa Long, DO. Carrie Madej, Dr. Robert Malone, Dr. David E. Martin, Dr. Peter Mc-Cullough, Dr. Lee Merritt, Dr. Judy Mikovits, Dr. Jane Ruby, Dr. Sherri Tenpenny, DVM/PhD Geert Vanden Bossche, Dr. Michael Yeadon, Dr. Vladimir Zelenko, and other brilliant medical practitioners and researchers. Note the international community first banned use of biological and chemical weapons after WW I. This ban was reinforced by the *Biological Weapons Convention* (BWC) *International Treaty* signed in Washington D.C., London, and Moscow on April 10, 1972, and updated in 1993. China became signatory to the BWC Treaty in 1984. The *BWC International Treaty* prohibits ALL development, production, acquisition, stockpiling, and transfer of biological and chemical weaponry by signatory nations.

Such treaties are of course, meaningless to leadership psychopaths, so with insufficient monitoring by citizens, end runs around treaty constraints are a simple matter of logistics and cover-up. Linguistic alchemy along with disregulated private contractors are routinely employed to rename and implement such horrific bioweapons research, so the threat becomes invisible to Main Street, though Main Street pays for it via corrupted government programs. Such global deceit is enabled by societal blindness and cultural banality massaged by conglomerated media networks becoming as Aldous Huxley predicted in 1927: **a machine that applies all the resources of science in order for imbecility to flourish** (my paraphrase from the August 1927 Harper's article entitled *Outlook for American Culture*).[50]

Gain of Function Research is a euphemism for internationally illegal Bio-Chemical Weapons Research. Linguistic alchemy in action. *Gain of function* research typically mixes aborted human fetal tissue or other human tissue

---

50 Wu, *The Master Switch*, 219.

with animal tissue, say mice, monkeys, bats, or other, **then engineers say a type of corona virus to be more infectious and more deadly to humans**. How is this medicine? Where we find *Gain of Function*, we find military programs, military funding, and military consultants. Corrupt agencies like *National Institutes of Health* (NIH), *Foundation for the National Institutes of Health* (NIH funding arm), and its subsidiary, *The National Institute of Allergy and Infectious Diseases* (NIAID) claim to support and conduct research for prevention and treatment of allergic and infectious diseases. On its face, a factual claim - but not the whole treasonous story.

EVENT 201, hosted by *The World Economic Forum, Bill and Melinda Gates Foundation*, and *John Hopkins Center for Health Security* on October 18, 2019, simulated four corona pandemic scenarios focusing on lack of public and private sector preparedness. Program solutions were limited to implementing powerful controls on Main Street along with unconstitutional medical mandates, one of which mandated medical tracing, i.e., unconstitutional surveillance.

When a corrupted agency like NIH obtusely mentions *getting ahead of* or *in front of disease* – they are disingenuously talking about bio-chemical weapons research masquerading as medicine. This can only be done outside the purview of international treaties and direct funding of our treasonously corrupt Congress, which for plausible deniability looks the other way anyway. Elected and appointed global syndicate pawns make unreported bank, supported by complicit misrepresentation of fact by morally challenged legacy propagandists.

Note: In October 2021, Doctors affiliated with FLCCC reported treating dozens (200+) of U.S. Congressional Members, their family members, and staffers with *Ivermectin* and the *I-Mask+protocol* for COVID. None of these cowardly but privileged Congressional Members I know of have spoken publicly about this even though many American citizens were blocked from obtaining *Ivermectin* by prescription. These same congressional criminals are not required to take JABs.

The unaudited central banking cartel using government sanctioned digital money, i.e., fiat money, funds an array of NGO's, institutes, and so forth via various funding pathways. Obscured or unaudited moneys are distributed as philanthropic donations along with PR hoopla for philanthropic heroine and hero adulation. Amidst flag waving and legacy propaganda cheering, the difficult to track money pours into bioweapon labs, the actual end users, held at arm's length from the unscrupulous bank managers and politicians who fully finance and support such insidious treachery. This Satanic parade is ongoing since before WW I. Packaged as medical research for protection of poor souls living on Main Street, bioweapons are aggressively deployed against Main Street citizens promised protection by the very agencies attacking them.

At the *DAVOS* January 25-29, 2021 conference centered around the COVID Scamdemic and **Great Reset**, much of it conducted virtually, *The World Economic Forum* founder and executive chairman, Klaus Schwab, also 1971 Founder of *DAVOS* summarized the NWO cult's program wonderfully. **Main Street will own nothing and be happy.** We might inquire, do slaves own anything? No, not beyond their human dignity and infinite spiritual value anyway. We should inquire, do cyborgs own anything?[51]

COVID is a global NWO management, eugenics, and wealth transfer scam as well as a biological attack on Main Street justifying deceptive experimental JABs. The JABs of course, comprise the injected nanoparticle, chemical weapons component enabling surveillance and AI brain-machine interface with ionized atmospheric control systems. More than forty Big Pharma companies were or are developing bioweapon JABs. Many of these JABs inject some or all necessary components into our body for what *Moderna* proudly calls *"our operating system"*. The following is copied from page 1 of Moderna's website in early 2021, since scrubbed.

Our Operating System

Recognizing the broad potential of mRNA science, we set out to create an mRNA technology platform that functions very much like an operating system on a computer. It is designed so that it can plug and play interchangeably with different programs. In our case, the "program" or "app" is our mRNA drug - the unique mRNA sequence that codes for a protein.

We have a dedicated team of several hundred scientists and engineers solely focused on advancing Moderna's platform technology. They are organized around key disciplines and work in an integrated fashion to advance knowledge surrounding mRNA science and solve for challenges that are unique to mRNA drug development. Some of these disciplines include mRNA biology, chemistry, formulation & delivery, bioinformatics and protein engineering.

Doesn't sound weaponized does it, though *Moderna* didn't mention our body is the computer system hard drive once the *app* is installed and doesn't say if what we're injected with is harmful, legal, permanent, or can be removed? We might inquire, "are JAB BOOSTERS providing necessary self-assembling component parts of the nano-operating systems?" Just askin'? Medical information coming in from around the world is now plentiful outside corrupt government sources and legacy propaganda so I'm not citing VAXX or ANTI-VAXX sources here. My non-medical high-octane COVID JAB speculation is:

---

51 Klaus Schwab and Thierry Malleret, *COVID-19: The Great Reset* (Cologny/Geneva: ISBN Agentur Schweiz, 2020).

- COVID lockdowns intentionally destroy middle class businesses and jobs producing mass poverty, homelessness, and various neurosis.
- COVID lock downs unconstitutionally obstruct freedom of association.
- Big Medicine vacuums billions in fraudulent government COVID bonuses.
- Big Pharma is staggering beneath its COVID subsidies with zero liability.
- Retail monopolies simultaneously rake in billions of dollars from discriminatory lock down policies forcing small Main Street business into insolvency.
- Many JAB victims will require expensive long-term, post-JAB care.
- A primary JAB objective is not illness but sterilization of young people.
- COVID sets up the disaster capital basis for Main Street impoverishment, implementation of universal health care, and the universal stipend, i.e., slavery.
- Insider monopolies like asset manager, *BlackRock*, infused with Federal Reserve cash are buying up foreclosed residential and commercial property for pennies on the dollar as well as bidding up prices on non-foreclosed properties. This is driving first time home buyers and small businesspeople out of the market. First time home buyers, our young families, will be renting from these corrupt transnational monopolies for the remainder of their enslaved lives.
- The JABs will reduce population through illness and sterilization.
- JAB technology is coordinated with ELF controls engaged through 5G, 6G, our ionized atmosphere, modified HAARP technology, Space Fence, etc.
- JAB technology works in tandem with other ELF technologies to engage the human-machine interface being wired directly into the cellular structure of our bodies. Elites intend those of us surviving depopulation, maybe 500 million or so, to exist as fully controlled, *Neuralinked* cyborg slaves.

A global eugenics scam like COVID-19, with its variants and Toxic JABs isn't possible without the study group's **worldwide public and private coordination and central bank funding** conjured from thin air. Recall Bertrand Russell religiously worshiping *Malthusian Scarcity* and Darwinian principles, proclaiming in 1952:[52] "There are three ways of securing a society that shall be stable as regards population. The first is that of birth control, the second that of infanticide or really destructive wars, and the third that of general misery except for a powerful minority." Sir Russell's proposed methodology for bringing this Main Street horror show about is WORLD GOVERNMENT. Lord Russell goes on proclaiming: "These considerations prove that a scientific world society cannot be stable unless there is a world government."

SARS-CoV-2, JAB stimulated variants, and toxic JABS are a One World Government Giant Leap Forward as Mao might chant, with *general misery except for a powerful minority*. STOP IT NOW, or Neo-Feudal Transhumanism is our grim future.

---

52 Bertrand Russell, *The Impact of Science on Society*, Reprint edition (London ; New York: Routledge, 2016), 94.Reprint edition (London\\uc0\\u8239{}; New York: Routledge, 2016

Transhumanists insist rust-prone machines tell humans what to do.
Here's an idea:
Why don't we tell machines what to do?

8 • Religion of Scientism

Remedy: STOP DNA DESTROYING 5G AND THE WEAPON-IZED IONIZATION OF OUR ATMOSPHERE unless and until it can transparently be proven safe and necessary! Fanatical, close-minded religiosity of material scientism demeans the quantum significance of human spiritual consciousness. This effectively bifurcates, i.e., separates us from knowledge of our created conscious human nature, its causative operational role in the material world, and how the human duality of our spiritual/material world interacts and functions.

Quantum Mechanics demonstrates what philosophy recognizes and Scientism does not. Consciousness is an intrinsic aspect of causative reality, of intelligent life itself, cannot be divorced from life, and must be incorporated within our study of life's purpose if truth is to be ascertained, now provable at both micro and macro cosmic levels. Pre-Socratic Greek thinkers recognized this basic cosmological concept five centuries before Christ, though failed to grasp operative interrelationships. Denial of conscious power affirms the meaningless futility of ignorance, reduces humanity to animal levels of consciousness, and attempts to diminish the spiritual potential of intelligent infinity.

Scientism is a narrow-minded, rigidly dogmatic religion politicizing science to manufacture mass consensus furthering self-constrictive and when deemed necessary, coerced behavioral engineering agendas. Scientism is abortive manipulation of scientific knowledge using misinformation bolstering **Scientific Dictatorship**, i.e., **Technocracy**. Scientism is not scientific method, has little to do with objective science, and undermines scientific credibility. Scientism is at best, programmed religious zealotry manufacturing politically ignorant consensus for enablement of morally relative mass behavior controls desired by a small group of relatively unknown Elites. By Elites I do not refer to cheer leading, psychopathic order followers the likes of Jeff Bezos, Warren Buffett, Bill Gates, Elon Musk, George Soros, nor even more privileged, less well known pawns of our world's dynastic families. Most Elite dynastic families are influenced by demonic forces, rendering their influence over Scientism dangerous and professionally reprehensible.

Scientism exists in a state of academic denial and scholarly deceit in part by narrowly considering the origins of life on Earth within the narrow context of genetic evolution and probability theory—while simultaneously ignoring both genetic evolution and probability theory. The random formation of complex molecules in geologic time as Scientism's *Darwinian Theory* proposes is preposterous. The probability of one simple protein molecule forming in biologically sustainable folded form from 150 available amino acids (each already randomly formed) is about 10^{164}.[53]

If earth's geologic pedigree is 4.6 billion years old, an overzealous estimate could project random formation of approximately 10^{58} protein molecule combinations within that time. This is impressive but not nearly enough failed combinations to realistically produce one correctly folded protein molecule… and we are assuming a perfectly nutritious, protective environment with zero molecular damage by ultraviolet radiation or any other source of random harm. At this imaginary point we do not yet have life—just a single protein.

A simple cell consists of about 300 different proteins. If considering multiple forms of the same protein, the number can grow to ±100,000. Living organisms as even today's poorly educated high school biology students know, are comprised of more than just protein molecules. Nucleic acids, complex carbohydrates, lipids and so forth are all necessary along with organized energy and metabolic pathways. **Significantly, cell formation requires every ingredient be present together within the cell membrane simultaneously or cell formation cannot occur.** The probably of this sequence of events occurring to produce just one cell (without even the first cellular membrane hav-

53 Bruce Cooper, "Origin: Probability of a Single Protein Forming by Chance," *Reasoned Cases For Christ* (blog), February 10, 2018, https://bcooper.wordpress.com/2018/02/10/origin-probability-of-a-single-protein-forming-by-chance/.

ing yet been created) in 4.6 billion years is unimaginably large. The probability of randomly combining trillions upon trillions of molecules into cells and then into the variety of Earth's interrelated life forms in geologic time as we understand it is nonsensically absurd – yet Scientism insists this happened randomly.

It is imperative for sustainable life on Earth, we understand threats arrayed against humanity and all creation by the Luciferian globalist triad - **big government, fiat money, and mind control**. Our strength, protection, and victory over evil originate within the cognitive coherence of awakened spiritual discernment and active spiritual warfare. Paul's gospel known as the *Book of Ephesians*, thought to have been written during his 61-63 A.D. imprisonment teaches **the mystery of salvation as not only for mankind, but for all creation**.[54] Scientism is a powerful Satanic weapon arrayed against spiritual realization while obscuring humanity's nurturing responsibility (dominion) for our created world. It employs technocratic pseudo-science as *Pitchfork Avoidance Strategy* (PAS) distracting and dumbing down populations while enslaving, robbing, sterilizing, and euthanizing them. **It is professionally unconscionable for technically trained persons to take advantage of or harm less technically trained people.** In this context, scientism presents a clear and present danger.

Ephesians 6:12 "For we do not wrestle against flesh and blood, but against principalities, against powers, against the rulers of the darkness of this age, against spiritual hosts of wickedness in the heavenly places."[55]

As far back as 1966, on the heels of Ken Kesey's 1964 Masonic bus ride with *The Merry Pranksters* so wonderfully chronicled in Tom Wolf's 1968, *Electric Kool-Aid Acid Test*, Robert Ardrey published his insightful *The Territorial Imperative* in which he expresses concern regarding scientific and educational integrity.[56] "I suggested earlier that unless we could grasp the extent to which falsehood has triumphed over truth in contemporary thought, we should have difficulty in comprehending our contemporary predicament. In America we appropriate tens of billions of dollars each year for the education of our children: do we ask, as we pay our tax bill, what does that education consist of? Will an education captured in large areas by the forces of scientific romanticism produce citizens less or more able to deal with the dubious future?"

I react to Robert Ardrey's polite concern regarding lost academic integrity more directly as institutionalized, academic grant greed addiction, and professional *cancel culture* cowardice bowing to the closed fist of targeted endowment funding by

54 "The Orthodox Study Bible - Hardcover Edition," 1597
55 "The Orthodox Study Bible - Hardcover Edition," 1609.
56 Robert Ardrey, *The Territorial Imperative: A Personal Inquiry into the Animal Origins of Property and Nations* (Atheneum, 1966), 246.

overbearing dynastic family trusts and foundations. This targeted financial lever-
age enforced by unfairly issuing grants to status quo compliant researchers while
brandishing threats of grant withholding for non-compliant creative behavior
constructs a cheap intellectual coffin for objective scientific study. The objective
science coffin was nailed shut in 1980 with passage of the *Bayh-Dole Act* (*Patent
and Trademark Law Amendments Act*) which: **1.** Changed procedures for federal
contractors to acquire, retain ownership, and retain revenue from inventions developed with federal taxpayer facilities and dollars. **2.** Federal agencies were authorized to grant exclusive licenses to inventions patented by and owned by federal government agencies. This 1980 legislated federal fraud provocation created
Anthony Fauci's private malevolent playground which demands investigation.

The above two abusively preferential *Bayh-Dole Act* practices predictably turned
research related government agencies and many universities into grant addicted, patent feasting goliaths incapable of admitting to egregious conflicts of interest with fiduciary responsibility to taxpayers as well as compromising even
the pretense of learning objectivity. This sad situation discloses that corruptible allegiance to self-serving foundation, trust, and endowment goals must be
loyally demonstrated by academics prior to grant of tenure, ability to obtain
grant monies, or ability to publish in so-called academic journals. Academic
status quo conformance is mandatory in most, if not all, Elite accredited institutions. Stepping outside status quo dogma garners immediate black-balling
and career destruction. Most academic, medical, and technical journals as a result, are now just cheap propaganda tools useless to legitimate scientific inquiry.

Academic honesty, integrity, and truth in education are administratively strangled by pathetic peers, buried in remote graves covered over with politicized
grant allocations shoveled by psychopathic directors of Elite controlled Endowments, Foundations, and Institutes, each weaponizing their own anti-human agendas. American education is a dystopian disgrace to learning. It's up
to parents and alumni to fix the mess. If this isn't a Luciferian attack on functional learning, what is it? Parents and alumni must step up and re-populate
principals, teachers, professors, school boards, and state boards of regents with
responsible, left/right brain balanced adults. Education must be protected if
life on Earth is to be protected. Scientism's wrecking ball is doing the opposite.

Wholesale abuse of tax exempt/tax deferred foundations and trusts by dynastic families raises the question; **how much longer will western civilization tolerate psychopathic abuse of so-called philanthropic entities
pretending to benefit society with lies and stale crumbs while quietly
controlling vast wealth sectors for exclusive tax free or tax deferred family enrichment and empowerment?** Foundations and trusts have become

critical pillars of the global syndicate study-group system routinely employed to powerfully influence academic curricula, medical school protocols, scientific research, professional associations, publishing, media, Hollywood, and government policy for exclusive family benefit and globalist approved agendas – and whether Elites know it or not, complete destruction of our biosphere.

A **One Word** translation of **One World Government** is **OMNICIDE**. The transition from human autonomy to global enslavement leading to omnicide is **TRANS-HUMANISM**, i.e., scientific dictatorship by entrainment without recourse.

So, to Mr. Ardrey's concern, let's add an earlier bit of 1964 erudition by Herbert Marcuse regarding what Marcuse suggests is our technocratic dumbing-down (my words), that is, *desublimation* into what he refers to, without humor, as our new **Happy Consciousness**. Since Marcuse states his observation so articulately, we'll quote him in full, demonstrating beyond doubt the malicious intent and purpose of technocracy as currently directed by pathologically ill Elites and their pathetic order-following drones:

"Institutionalized desublimation thus appears to be an aspect of the "conquest of transcendence" achieved by the one-dimensional society. Just as this society tends to reduce, and even absorb opposition (the qualitative difference!) in the realm of politics and higher culture, so it does in the instinctual sphere. The result is the atrophy of the mental organs for grasping the contradictions and the alternatives and, in the one remaining dimension of technological rationality, the *Happy Consciousness* comes to prevail.

It reflects the belief that the real is rational, and that the established system, in spite of everything, delivers the goods. The people are led to find in the productive apparatus the effective agent of thought and action to which their personal thought and action can and must be surrendered. And in this transfer, the apparatus also assumes the role of a moral agent. Conscience is absolved by reification, by the general necessity of things.

In this general necessity, guilt has no place. One man can give the signal that liquidates hundreds of thousands of people, then declare himself free from all pangs of conscience, and live happily ever after. The antifascist powers who beat fascism on the battlefields reap the benefits of the Nazi scientists, generals, and engineers; they have the historical advantage of the late-comer. What begins as the horror of the concentration camps turns into the practice of training people for abnormal conditions – a subterranean human existence and the daily intake of radioactive nourishment. A Christian minister declares that it does not contradict Christian principles to prevent with all available means your neighbor from entering your bomb shelter. Another Christian minister contradicts his colleague and says it does. Who is right? Again, the neutrality of technological rationality shows forth over and above politics, and again it shows forth as spurious, for in both cases, it serves the politics of domination."[57]

---

57 Herbert Marcuse and Douglas Kellner, *One-Dimensional Man: Studies in the Ideology of Advanced Industrial Society*, 2nd edition (Boston: Beacon Press, 1991), 79, 80.

That's quite enough Frankfurt School psychopathy for one chapter, so we'll wind down, though Marcuse goes on at some length describing how *Rand Corporation*, in its *RANDom News* publication, volume 9, number 1, in an article entitled, *BETTER SAFE THAN SORRY*, paints a disgusting picture of its amoral vision for our future through its PsyOp war game, *RAND's SAFE*.

In this spotlessly clean, intellectualized game, the organic brutality of war and pungent odor of spilled blood and visceral slaughter of millions are reduced to a safe, clean-room exercise conducted by the Red and Blue Teams managed by the Game Director and Control Group. The game is interrupted only by brief interludes of hot aromatic coffee, tea, and fresh doughnuts. Actual, on-the-ground screams, battle smells of decaying bodies, scorched meat, and grotesquely missing limbs twisted into ragged disemboweled postures leaking fetal excrement and coppery blood mixing with urine and red-stained mud are removed from sight. Violence is technocratically sterilized and normalized. Easy-peasy. Vote by mail and manipulated voting machines for a psychopathic proxy and it is a done deal all over the world.

Did *RAND's SAFE* spawn gaming scenarios played out by miscreants attending *World Economic Forum* strategy sessions where Main Street noses are openly rubbed in elaborate lies about protecting public health, safely maintaining supply chains etc., while being disabled or exterminated? The reality of course, is not planning how to deal with or avoid crisis – but **gaming how to most effectively create crisis.**

Marcuse sized it up accurately more than a half-century ago. This new technocratically sanitized form of global butchery called *unrestricted warfare* is now acceptable on Main Street.[58] Malfeasant elements of our government, organized crime, rogue military and intelligence services, in concert with Hollywood order-followers and a systemically corrupt media have for example, successfully relegated the brutal murder of Afghan shepherds and farmers to nothing more than a digitized, full color, high-def pastime to be enjoyed with dinner. Slaughter is politely discussed among friends as our utilitarian duty to spread charred bone fragments, freedom, and democracy to those who MUST have it across the globe. Modernization is cleverly defined by **Anglo-American Atlanticism** as Westernization, helpfully spreading freedom and democracy while excluding any mention of the imposed debt-slavery, resource rape, starvation, and genocidal horror Atlanticized Westernization usually is. Does the wine we drink with dinner while skipping past such evil absolve us?

---

58 Qiao Liang and Wang Xiangsui, *Unrestricted Warfare: China's Master Plan to Destroy America*, Reprint ed. edition (Brattleboro: Echo Point Books & Media, 2015).

8 • Religion of Scientism

The *Golden Crescent* is back in opium cultivation – thank you 9/11. The narco-trade is bursting *prominent global citizen* bank accounts and *Happily UnConscious Days* are here again. More than 70,000 drug-related deaths (not all narcotics induced) annually with untold numbers of wasted lives and devastated families, just in America, comprise a usefully profitable method of voluntary dumbing down, complacency, population management, and population reduction. The efficiency of drugs is *totally awesome man* as we might overhear on an indolent evening along one of Hollywood's pedophile boulevards.

Note: *The Donald Administration* shut down America's narcotics and human trafficking southern corridor, initiating nearly 15,000 pedophile arrests over four years, but in less than 30 fraudulent days, the treasonous NWO Biden pawns re-opened the border's illegal flood gates. Child sex trafficking, sex slavery, ritual sacrifice, drugs, weapons, disease, terrorists, and other global syndicate pastimes are not only here again but were cranked up on steroids with as of May 2021, more than 20,000 unaccompanied minors held at the U.S. Southern border waiting for unimpeded initiation into sex slavery, organ harvesting groups, etc. Main Street noticed the horror, however, so CCP operated Biden Thugs spent tax dollars on charter flights from South and Central America into U.S. border cities as covert drop points for national distribution of invaders into traditionally conservative cities. Borders and laws are immaterial to globalist thugs and international mafiosi mistakenly called world leaders, the CCP Biden Regime a prime example.

Why do we tacitly accept drones slaughtering mountain shepherds on the other side of the world; or for that matter, here at home, squishing through urine and feces on the sidewalks of LA or San Fran tent cities hearkening back to some prehistoric-public health era? The putrescent stink of liberal tent cities filled with left behind Democrat voters atrociously brags by example on the phenomenal success of globalist indoctrination as municipal policy. Only the poor and disadvantaged suffer as liberal caring and fairness are mandated by *Open Society* or hundreds of other NGO standards, as well as elected and unelected pawns – not one iota objected to by supposedly knowledgeable academic pawns of scientism. If public health scientism freaks won't provide health guidance, who will? Oddly, Blue City Commies show no interest in demanding street poopers wear face diapers or get vaxxed like shamed productive citizens.

Do irresponsible mayoral candidates in these disgusting Leftist municipalities not know Babylonians used clay plumbing pipes as far back as 4,000 BC?

Or how about wealthy suburbs of Ephesus on the west coast of Turkey, since around 2,000 BC, enjoying hot and cold running water? Urban residents haven't had to slog through urine-soaked excrement for centuries, but now Progressives think they have a new idea called **social justice**. In what way are sidewalk urine and feces along with tent-city destitution and destruction of middle-class property rights augmenting justice? Oops, another digression because water and wastewater treatment are on my civil engineering radar. Sorry!

Getting back to sanitized warfare. Fake news mollifies and covers up the terrifying bombed reality of the tortured and dying as they helplessly experience their families, neighbors, and entire villages decimated; not by Johnny and his gun; not by warriors; but by nearly silent, rather graceful, unmanned drones. Drones remotely and skillfully operated by toothy, freckled computer geeks many thousands of miles away, comfortably ensconced in designer chairs slouching in front of colorful computer screens, placidly sipping warm lattes within jogging distance of relaxing Florida beaches – over which uncounted tons of CIA managed narcotics from you guessed it, Afghanistan, breach our shores with full government protection for Main Street poisoning and degradation. Popular background music replaces screams of the wounded and dying.

Barack Hussein Obama openly bragged, "I'm really good at killing people"[59] in apparent surprise at his cowardly talent for ordering unsuspecting people mutilated or murdered by drone strikes... and the PsyOp marches on with Main Street never noticing the grotesque horror perpetrated around the world in our U.S. name using wealth we the people of Main Street created. Our U.S. military is being misused by *powerful others*. Honor and doing the right thing are effectively banished as dangerously short-sighted military science steadily displaces rationally strategized national defense. Sadly, across the world we are witnessing brave law enforcement and military *protect and serve duty* transformed and degraded into *"doing our job"* and *"following orders."*

Is Main Street incomprehension of sociopathic crimes wantonly committed in our uninformed name using our confiscated wealth excusable? Should it be excused in a sane world? If an Army or Marine Lieutenant is held accountable for atrocities committed by exhausted, war-fatigued infantry soldiers under his or her command; aren't taxpayers liable for atrocities enabled by *selected* Representatives? Aren't we the people the bosses of our representatives? Is the shocked expression on a small child's horrified face in Afghanistan, Iraq, Libya, Somalia, Syria, or Ukraine watching their severed arm or leg fly gracefully into the dusty chaos of freedom and democracy worth our callous disre-

---

59 Mark Halperin and John Heilemann, *Double Down: Game Change 2012*, 1st edition (New York: Penguin Press, 2013). The New York Times:\"

gard? I don't think so… and no, I'm not standing in defense of Islamic ideology any more than wanton genocide by Atlanticist order-followers. Islam is a wantonly destructive ideology, but murder of 1.5 billion Muslims isn't the cure.

How is it, abuse of science in the interest of generational sterilization, famine, mass genocide, resource rape, and unspeakable horrors go largely unnoticed on western Main Streets? Does fake news serve any purpose at all beyond syndicated indoctrination and propaganda? Can Main Street justifiably continue acquiescence toward Scientism's normalization of crimes against humanity just because crimes are masked by the unreality of mass media spin? Abuse of science on many levels is happening, the obscene power of which is inappropriately used, not for good or to educate, but exclusively to proliferate evil by disguising barbaric reality in pretty-colored pixels, punctuated by energizing music, with *flicker-rates* soothing us into that *Happy Consciousness* Marcuse bragged on.

Indoctrinated dupes fostering the illusion of choice spew hatred of the criminalized Bush II Administration, but turn schizophrenically silent, while the traitorous Obama Administration murders thousands more than Bush II's Globalist Administration dreamed—not just overseas, but here at home. The Obama Legacy gave us twenty times more people murdered on an average 2021 Chicago weekend than during an entire year in war-torn Afghanistan over the four Trump Years and MSM doesn't mention it. BLM, for example, is clearly about Marxist thuggery and middle-class destruction, not black lives. Linguistic alchemy, anointed by dopamine laced social media, renders protest 99% meaningless and 100% ineffective regardless intent, proudly proclaiming the new *Happy Consciousness* has arrived. *"Hate each other"* MSM grimaces daily from tanned, self-important faces in rainbow-colored studios… and many of us do. Main Street futilely dog paddles through mind control methodologies perpetrated by Scientism's gurus of doom while dreaming of swimming faster – BUT never considers climbing out of the swirling PsyOp sewer altogether.

Recall bigoted House Democrat, befuddled Communist, Maxine Waters on the domestic front urging dopamine fueled hatred of Trump Administration officials and supporters in June 2018; "If you see anybody from that Cabinet in a restaurant, in a department store, at a gasoline station, you get out and you create a crowd and you push back on them, and you tell them they're not welcome anymore, anywhere." This hateful, privileged California Democrat Communist added: "If you think we are rallying now you ain't seen nothing yet." *Antifa* and BLM thugs enthusiastically sunk to the Water's gutter while hypocritical Leftist MSM cheered her disgusting remarks for weeks afterward, ginning up divisive social media angst. The good *mass formation* news is many of us can see the evil shrieking in our faces.

All education is of course, an obvious form of mind control, though in the past most of us innocently viewed such expensively organized mental tampering as beneficially necessary. Prior to the onslaught of 1960's CIA manufactured, drug fueled **counterculture**, preceded by Tavistock's undeclared war on American identity, culture, and behavior – I certainly viewed education necessary and beneficial. Today, with what's left of tattered educational honor and respect for honest inquiry, supplanted with university approved, politically correct bigotry, along with politicized sham-science, not so much. Home schooling rocks as one way to protect our young from globalist indoctrination.

Academia has devolved into *"identity-manipulated, doublespeak"* bigotry with free speech literally beaten into the gutter by pie throwing, club carrying, screeching Fascist ignoramuses vacuously convinced of their own intellectual acuity. A few brave educators, thank you by the way, willing to speak out against mass educational atrocities regularly watch their careers flush down the bigoted toilet of ignorance by indoctrinated money-grubbing peers. Is healthy, beneficial 21st century science completely dead? **Must every materially scientific idea be weaponized?** Is this a rule? Can't we settle for using technology beneficially? These four questions are important to responsibly answer as adults. I love technology; BUT must every technology be weaponized by psychopathic order-followers? Is it possible for at least some, a few technologies to be set aside for beneficial purposes? Maybe just one? Could we please have some adult supervision in the religious cathedrals of technocracy programming? Technocracy is rapidly devolving into global omnicide, led by megalomaniacal pied pipers of Transhuman lunacy and we don't seem to notice. How are we missing this?

Many so-called educators tell us scientific study of our material world is separate from or in conflict with human ego—ego being both our direct and indirect material connection to free spiritual activity and Divine life. This restrictive scientific culture creates an academic cul-de-sac of ignorance paved with intellectual cowardice, designed to obscure true knowledge of reality, how our world functions, and our place as created sentient beings within it. **Science exquisitely proves organized intelligent creation, not randomness.** Evolution and Natural Law are aspects of intelligent creation, not aberrations of chance. Even casinos, *palaces of chance* have little to do with chance. Casinos are calculated statistical cash registers ringing calculated *House Odds Ka-Ching* 24-hours a day.

Material science is not functionally at odds with spiritual reality. Only within intellectually compromised academic circles, do we find prejudiced refusal to account for that which is, but is not physically sensed… yet. Honest scientists ought not limit their scope of study to preordained, outcome-based (reflexive) funding boundaries, but conversely, must honestly EXPAND THEIR SCOPE OF STUDY to include unseen forces, not the least of which is human consciousness. Quantum physics repeatedly demonstrates consciousness is not separate from our material world, but is intricately woven within it, in what appears to be an operationally causative relationship superseding time and space.

Quantum physicists, philosophers, and dreamers, as well as occultists, one of whom is the late Rudolf Steiner (1861 – 1925), Father of *Anthroposophy*, author of *Philosophy of Freedom* first published in 1916[60], studied some of these invisible connections with occasionally surprising results. This is an area of mystical, philosophical, and scientific study notoriously active during the so-called *Age of Enlightenment*; a time of interesting ideas and unfortunately a time during which Satanic influence effectively turned the egoistic reasoning power of humanity away from spiritual unity with our Creator. Today's sophisticated strategies for anti-human totalitarian governance systems were spawned during this period.

Anyway, I read things I probably shouldn't, and while doing so bumped into a transcript of Mr. Steiner, speaking at Oxford in 1922, referencing his 1916 book where he stated – "Therefore today we need above all a view of the world based on *Freiheit* – one can use this word in German, but here in England one must put it differently because the word 'freedom' has a different meaning – one must say a view of the world based on spiritual activity, on action, on thinking and feeling that arise from the individual human spirit".

Note: The above statement is enlightening (pun intended) and historically insightful. At the same time, though I appreciate Mr. Steiner's thoughts regarding freedom and spirit underlying human activity I disagree regarding **origination of spirit**. Thinking does not originate from finite individual human spirit. Thought energy originates with the transcendent Divine where all intelligent creativity and life energy originate; then resonating materially as brain waves through created human spirit in harmony with or not in harmony with Divine Spirit per free will and participatory, though finite, creative license. Our personal thoughts resonate materially and spiritually with positive or negative energy, then manifest per free will choices and behavior. Just sayin'.

I find some *Enlightenment* thinking of interest though don't agree with Mr. Steiner most of the time and certainly not with others peddling the occulted mysticism of Ms. Helena Blavatsky, co-founder of the *Theosophical Society*, with whom, even Steiner eventually took issue. Most *New Age* philosophy as well, is dangerously off the safe spiritual track and like *Free Masonry*, tempts people to engage spiritual seeking without the armor of God – a bad idea. Because of

---

60 "The Philosophy Of Freedom: Rudolf Steiner: 9781257835126

Satan's hatred of all creation, **spiritual seeking is always spiritual warfare**. Despite denial of a personal God, reincarnation, *Fifth Aryan Root Race* befuddlement suggesting other races are *degraded specimens of humanity* and so forth, good things can occasionally be found in unsuspected places; so, while acknowledging extreme danger, with faith in our personal God, *be not afraid* to question. That said, don't forget Nietzsche's comments in #146 of his 1886 tome, *Beyond Good and Evil* – "*He who fights with monsters should be careful lest he thereby become a monster. And if thou gaze long into an abyss, the abyss will also gaze into thee.*"

Now that I've concerned my Christian brethren by referencing the *Enlightenment Era*, I should clarify — I'm not pantheistic, nor a solipsistic theosophist thinking my essence comes from and is the same as the non-personal essence of some arbitrary divine providence. My lack of theosophical agreement, however, doesn't suggest disregarding all *Enlightenment Era* thinking out of hand. Some of what these folks considered is of interest, even if conclusions are incorrect. In engineering design, we sometimes find the embarrassingly dumb idea innocently forging our path toward the good idea leading to the best solution. This occasional practicality, within reasonable limits, causes me not to oppose considering, at least for a time, ideas appearing stupid or even dangerous in the hope of discovering something useful beneath the misleading or ill-intended nostrum.

To clarify by example; the mesquite tree growing happily in my back yard doesn't exist because I thought about it… though my wife and I did think about it, purchase it, plant it, and now nurture its shade, which makes my point. I am not the delusional center of my universe creating molecules, soil, water, and tree bark with my mind. That creative essence is not mine. I do, however, perceive the world around me, conceptualize my perceptions, then plan and act within the bounds of my Divine gift of human creative intelligence and free will.

When speaking of imaginatively creating our reality, I'm speaking in narrow terms of limited human perception, cognition, reasoning, and carrying out actions within the spiritual and physical reality we inhabit as created creatures. I believe our Creator originally and transcendentally creates; we do not. Our human task is interacting with creation, preferably in a morally sane, generous manner despite challenges offered to our success. I hope this is not misleading.

Scientism unfortunately impacts society in profound ways. Some of what follows may seem a detour but is not. **Counterculture itself, was a by-prod-**

uct of Scientism. The lyrically poetic ethologist with whose writing I am unabashedly fond, the late, Mr. Robert Ardrey, and with whose limited Darwinian evolutionary view of *Homo sapiens* I take serious issue states in 1966, "To believe that the sciences are rigidly objective and unswayed by the winds of intellectual fashion, of public mood, of political temper, of personal prejudice, is to go forth into the human storm clad only in trust's most innocent winding sheet. To believe that a scientist is unaffected by public disapproval, unaffected by the regard or disregard of professional colleagues, unaffected by the lack or abundance of funds for his work, is to characterize the scientist as an unperson."[61]

The above was penned in 1966, between Kesey's CIA counter-culture-fueled bus trip from La Honda to the Atlantic and Mr. Tom Wolf's, *New Journalism* chronicling of that historic trip, all amidst the psychedelic angst of our CIA affiliated buddy, Tim Leary and Augustus Owsley Stanley III's wonderfully pure *White Lightning*, to which I testify, was capable of providing a sensational lysergic acid diethylamide mobilized trip while never taking a step, though some would *keep on truckin'* or unfortunately *leap from rooftops* while under the influence.

Pile on *The Grateful Dead*, alleged pedophile Alan Ginsberg, *Hell's Angels*, *The Man*, Huxley's 1954 *Doors of Perception*, Charlie Manson's psychopathic mind-controlled *Family*, flowers in Jim Morrison's hair and common-sense reality out-the-window and you have the pharmaceutically Masonic molding of Laurel Canyon,[62] and future Haight-Ashbury order-followers leading thousands of *dazed and confused* zombie impersonators inside the red pill – blue pill box with its broken lid refusing to be closed. Pandora ran for cover and even *unwashed* Hippies didn't tend to crap on sidewalks, though their monkeys, puppies, and birds did.

Left is right, right is left, and no one knows the difference. Snow is black as Lord Russell explained… or maybe just dark gray if the indoctrination cost rises too high?[63] Gray does nicely, since if we aren't thinking at all – it no longer matters what we think because we're not. Mission accomplished on the entrained road to scientifically mind-controlled, transhuman dystopia while we the people of Main Street remain convinced, we yell at perceived idiots on TV of our own accord. Drugged dystopian delusion of Laurel Canyon and Haight-Ashbury dwellers, more than a half-century later, have birthed ignorant political defense of feces clogged LA and San Franciscan sidewalks—public health and hardworking taxpayers be damned. Is *Blue California* a public health threat needing quarantine for safety of the less delusional?

61 Ardrey, *The Territorial Imperative*, 179.
62 McGowan and Bryant, *Weird Scenes Inside the Canyon*.
63 Russell, *The Impact of Science on Society*, 27, 28

Much changed since the frenetic mid-sixties with its polarizing LSD and mescaline fueled counterculture and politicization of science serving divide and conquer collectivist agendas being just two of those things. 1960's societal frustration was absolutely justified but projects *Moonstruck, Bluebird, Artichoke, MK Ultra, Orion, Monarch, MK-Delta, Phoenix II, Trident* and other CIA *mind control* experimentation ended up leading my generation down a systemic cul de sac of relativistic failure and indoctrinated divisiveness, not love or unity. Why? How did this occur? Was the sharp Left Turn to debased American culture incrementally unleashing totalitarian calamity first spawned by biochemist Ira Baldwin and friends at then Camp Detrick's (renamed from Detrick Field in 1943) *Army Biological Warfare Laboratories* during WW II? Was this incoherent program emboldened when after WW II, CIA chemist Sydney Gottlieb came on board with *MK Ultra* and dozens of offshoot crimes against humanity? How many bioweapons labs around the world is Fort Detrick (renamed in 1956) connected to? Where is evidence, despite Scientism claimed good intentions, that employing psychopaths to blast unsuspecting minds to smithereens had constructive results?

Is there evidence anywhere that even one exploded mind was ever put back together or functionally rebuilt in the Shadow Government dungeons of rural Kentucky or Germany? Science has been in part, at least since WW II, relegated to a blunt edged tool for *creative thought limitation.* The most tragic portion of this program was led by narrow minded, academic Pawns of Privilege funded by politically motivated ideologues promoting the *science of material religion* for mass behavior programming and modification; apparently in deluded hope of fending off Malthusian prophesy? Silicon Valley is out of control and desperately needs a long-shank curb bit put in its slavering study group mouth.

The growing Surveillance/Police State is alive and well on all centralized fronts and there are many inconvenient fronts, though we glowingly and mistakenly speak of weaponized Technocracy and Transhumanism as beneficial trends. Achieving societal benefit requires careful adult supervision and responsible charge of technological development, both of which are sorely AWOL in the psycho-neurotic halls of rogue military science at DARPA and Silicon Valley. Our world is in *Googles* of trouble and CIA constrained, Mockingbird MSM routinely parrots lie after lie after lie minimizing or ignoring this imminent threat.

Legacy Journalism is long dead, truth-seekers ridiculed, induction and deduction comatose, replaced by repetitive statist propaganda issued on behalf of dynastic Elites as millions of Main Streeters smile with doleful grins in Marcuse's *Happy Consciousness* through pixelated flat screen reflective staring eyes. Only agendavized narrative of government mandated mediocrity thrives atop tiny slivers of barely noticed alternative media truth bits. **Globalist advocacy has replaced**

8 • Religion of Scientism

Journalism's capital J with a small a, and apparently brain washed journalists are unable to distinguish the difference, pointing to yet another failure of western education… or from the globalist point of view, overwhelming success. Perhaps we should have listened to pentathlete, General George S. Patton Jr.'s warnings about globalist tool, Uncle Joe Stalin back in '45 instead of silencing our glorious General Patton by T-Boning him with a military truck?

Did we kill education and science altogether we might ask? Is **university** just an obtuse term for **indoctrination center**? Why are tough, inveterate retired KGB Comrades smiling through broken teeth over unwashed vodka glasses? Can this malfeasant abuse of education have a happy ending? Should we the people of Main Street don our tweed jacket livery with well-worn, suede elbow patches and fix this birdbrained mess? I suspect so, as these obscenely expensive lunatic asylums run by Lenin's *useful idiots*, still after more than a century haven't caught on to being thoroughly duped by denizens of The City of London, Washington D.C., and The Vatican? Is there hope? Can we awaken beyond the absurdity of WOKE Culture and Micro-aggression to reality and own it? I think so… but can **we** make it so? Emphasis on WE.

Awareness, perception, and knowledge of spiritual dimension; the true and complete essence of what it is to be human has been, certainly for the past 100-years or so, swept out of sight by Scientism's adherents – apparently furthering whatever opportunistic transhuman agenda(s) we can politely imagine. This politicization and trivialization of science in the interest of social engineering, behavior modification, Main Street harvesting, and depopulation have occurred despite and in denial of breakthroughs in quantum theory and deeper understanding of nature's reality. Authentic science is now hidden on a dusty shelf in the teacher's lounge. This valuable area of study and knowledge has for centuries; even more so today fallen victim to a calculated, morbid agenda of diseducation, occultation through sham-science, hidden knowledge, hidden money, and hidden power.

When humans voluntarily compromise their own nature, experience, knowledge, and self-awareness—what remains of humanity's future? To understand how this malevolently manipulative, self-dumbing-down, self-defeating scientism program of intelligence debasement works, we must briefly digress if you can imagine that. Can we hear Ms. Lynnette Hardaway and Ms. Rochelle Richardson (Diamond and Silk) smiling and saying Uh Huh?

Since the heady days of Planck's *quantum concept* and Einstein's 1905 recognition of that theory's implications regarding *quantization of light*, through de Broglie's 1923 thesis suggesting the particle behavior of light may have a counterpart in wave behavior of particles; to Werner Heisenberg's *Uncertainty Principle*, our concept of physical reality has been tipped upside down, turned inside out, and raised more questions than provided answers. This should give any thinking person pause and the fact it doesn't bat nearly an eye in today's academic world of sham-science is astonishing. Yes, I know there are exceptions – thank you brave academic warriors more than you know.

As an example, Heisenberg's *Uncertainty Principle* raises questions regarding perception and reality. **The act of observing something changes the behavior (state) of the something being observed.** Repeatedly tested, found true on the micro-level, this interaction is being successfully tested on a macro-level.

The act of observing either the position in space or the velocity of a particle causes a perceptible change in the other. The exact position and velocity of a particle cannot, so far, be determined simultaneously. Since these changes continue throughout the period of observation, an observer is uncertain precisely what it is he or she is observing. This effect is multiplied when more than one observer is present. Does this suggest multiple person's individual consciousness are communally additive? The Power Elite wouldn't want us on Main Street figuring that out, would they? We might dare as a group to peer outside our PsyOp bubble or even escape our trashy, intelligence challenged, litter strewn, *Animal Farm* altogether? *Oh, the horror of it?*

Proponents of *Biocentrism*[64] further suggest the active *causality* is not just observance or the act of looking, but *consciousness*. If we accept the idea that particles exist in a state of wave probability, only collapsing into unique particle form when consciously focused upon; then we must at least **ask whether consciousness creates operational reality or does consciousness simply recognize some outside reality created by conscious forces we don't yet recognize, then interact with it?** (Again, I'm not saying our thoughts create particles or forces governing those particles; just that thoughts apparently affect particle behavior within the context of already existent particle matter, space/time, and involved forces.)

To pose the question another way, **to what extent does physical reality operationally exist in its perceived circumstance outside of and/or independent of individual and communal consciousness?** Answering this question necessarily and inescapably carries physics specifically and science generally into a cooperative electro-magnetic-chemical-biological sphere with

---

64 Robert Lanza and Bob Berman, *Biocentrism: How Life and Consciousness Are the Keys to Understanding the True Nature of the Universe*, 1 edition (Dallas, Tex.: BenBella Books, 2010).

spirituality and metaphysics; the likely result of which may eventually lead to a more unified theory of reality, or as some say, *The Unified Theory of Everything.*

Serious scientists and objective researchers actively seek honest answers to these momentous issues. Less serious, more subjective, or politicized pseudo-scientists can't be bothered because as *The Big Lebowski's Dude* might abide, *"hey, hey, careful, man, there's a grant funding here".* Since these pseudo-scientists assumedly know everything, have none of Jeff Lebowski's curiosity and have agreed to contrived consensus, usually in exchange for money and publication access, why apply for additional study grants? If consensus exists, what's left to study?

Oxymoronically, what is there to learn when we claim established consensus? **Clearly, the words science and consensus can rarely if ever legitimately appear in the same sentence.** In any event, academic grant funding and academic ability to publish are ideologically dependent, therefore compromised and carefully limited by targeted political agendas precluding authentic study and objective learning. Such academic restraint is not accidental. Dynastic families like Carnegie, Danforth, Duke, Ford, Hartford, Kellog, Lilly, Moody, Pew, Rockefeller, Sloan, and so many others have raised this sort of restraint to a fine and profitable art form. The result is politicized science, i.e., SCIENTISM, which is not science at all.

In today's prestigious academic circles, money, and social engineering trump (no pun intended) honest science in dedicated service to transhumanist and New World Order delusion. A blatant example of this is ignorantly discussing climate change in limited terms of carbon, SUV's, and cow farts while never mentioning *Geoengineering,* now more than a half-century old; our increasingly ionized atmosphere and its increasingly conductive plasma state; or just as significantly, *Milankovitch Cycles* or other phenomena. Glorious cow farts are not destroying Earth regardless how many bought and paid for fart sniffing professors claim so.

Transhuman delusion, conceived and observed by indoctrinated sociopaths like the late, brilliantly misguided Zbigniew Brzezinski outlined in *Between Two Ages; America's Role in the Technetronic Era*[65], requires denying proven, though not yet understood powers of human consciousness; in turn requiring denial of Created Intelligence and our spiritual relationship with it. This narrow-minded disassociation maintained by otherwise intelligent people lost within the complexity of circular logic and mathematical algorithms, leads to the mistaken idea that electronic circuits, magnetic fields, and programed machines with short useful life spans can replace human creativity, imagination, and loving spiritual energy. Has anyone had to plug their spirit into an electrical outlet to charge it?

---

65 Zbigniew K. Brzezinski, *Between Two Ages: America's Role in the Technetronic Era,* Revised edition (Westport, Conn: Praeger, 1982).

Narrow-minded techies arrogantly call this **artificial intelligence**, which incidentally, is easily disabled by a process of oxidation and corrosion commonly called **rust**. Should we wonder then, why aren't grant-hungry academics waging war against water (H_2O) and oxygen (O) in defense of AI as they wage war on carbon dioxide (CO_2), supposedly in defense of organic life? I probably should not have asked this question, possibly planting a Scientism seed, huh?

So-called artificial intelligence (AI) can, aside from implicit system design bias, make subjectively limited tasks more quantitatively objective and accomplish them very quickly. No argument there. This is a benefit to society if handled intelligently (no pun intended), but to date, highly compensated pawns like Transhuman Grandfather Julian Huxley, or younger cult members Sergey Brin, Jose Luis Cordeiro, Pope Francis, Bill Gates, Michio Kaku, Ray Kurzweil, Elon Musk, Larry Page, Kevin Warmick, Mark Zuckerberg, and other order followers pushing *Humanity 2.0* and the *4th Industrial Revolution* refuse to go there; instead rushing earth toward extinction in headstrong denial of what they don't know, blindly pretending they do.

Fortunately, there are tech savvy corporatists like Carlos Moreira (founder of *WISeKey*) and David Fegusson, co-authors of *The Transhuman Code* (published in 2019) at least engaging consideration, pandering or not, of how and why the *4th Industrial Revolution*, **Metaverse**, might provide an intelligently balanced approach to integration of technology with human nature and potential. Unfortunately, in my humble opinion, Moreira and Fergusson, both Board members of *WISeKey*, both suggesting anti-Transhumanist leanings, are simply bright enough to understand, despite even serious discussion of burgeoning METAVERSE issues, global syndicate intent for Transhuman technology to transform and dominate humanity cannot be hidden. The following statement, poor English usage and all, was taken from the *WISeKey* Homepage in October, 2021. *"Our technology is Trusted by the OISTE/WISeKey's Swiss based cryptographic Root of Trust ("RoT") provides secure authentication and identification, in both physical and virtual environments, for the Internet of Things, Blockchain and Artificial Intelligence. The WISeKey RoT serves as a common trust anchor to ensure the integrity of online transactions among objects and between objects and people."* If this is not **full spectrum dominance**, what is it?

Indoctrinated technocrats uniformly support exponentially spreading microwave (MW) and radio frequency wave (RF) technologies across the globe despite predictable potential harm. Why? Electromagnetic radiation is known to have harmful biological effects since the mid-18th century.[66] Wi-Fi signals typically operate at a frequency of 2.4GHz or for higher speeds, 5.8GHz. This falls within the microwave frequency range of 300MHz to 300GHz at wave-

---

66 "The Invisible Rainbow: A History of Electricity and Life: Firstenberg, Arthur

lengths of 1mm to 1m. **Microwave radiation exerts harmful effects on living organisms.** Scott M. Bolen for example published a report titled *Radio-frequency/Microwave Radiation Biological Effects and Safety Standards: A Review* back in 1994 for the *U.S. Air Force* and *National Technical Information Service* (NTIS).

In Bolen's study, beyond thermal aspects of constant and pulsed radiation at various frequencies and wavelengths, chromosomal and cellular damage were observed. For example, irradiation of tissue by pulsed MW/RF sources causes cell membranes to become more permeable to destructive chemical mutagens. Oncogenic effects linked to dysfunction of the body's regulatory mechanisms were observed as well as immune system disturbances. Bolen's detailed report goes on to outline other observed effects the curious can follow up on if interested.

Studies performed around the world two, three, and even four decades ago raised serious concerns about effects of electromagnetic radiation generally and MW/RF radiation specifically relative to biological systems, mutative effects, tumor growth, etc.; yet 5G roll-out, expansion of modified HAARP (pulsed) technology, and ionization of earth's atmosphere continue unabated with no publicly transparent testing for biosystem health. This is disgraceful Scientism denial. These days, before dispersing into silvery-gray opacity, pulse patterns are recognizable in ionized cloud formations by anyone raising their eyes to the once blue sky.

Handing undue influence, power, research funding, and control of information flow to the vision challenged is a dangerous thing to do. Handing these same things over to arrogant narcissists demonstrating psychopathic tendencies is insane. Adult supervision is necessary. Lies by omission regarding 5G and atmospheric ionization are commonplace with censorship and released information at best euphemistic resulting in what is now a free speech issue. What is not allowed to be said looms like a vast electrified storm cloud above what is permitted or ordered to be said.

Art precedes culture and culture resides upstream of politics. Today, technology resides upstream of both art and culture. Since technology is metastasizing into Transhumanistic ultra-surveillance and centralized domination in dark computer rooms and laboratories, behind closed doors, in the delusional hands of narcissistic psychopaths, we have a growing problem. We have militarized much of law enforcement. We have militarized transportation. We have militarized science. We have militarized our schools via indoctrinating curricula, metal detectors, and armed guards. We are now militarizing medicine and public health services. Given totalitarian history's track record, if America doesn't slam on the brakes soon, there will be no brakes. Then what?

Main Street citizens have the right to publicly fund beneficial technology, harmful technology, self-destructive asininity, and psychopathy if so choosing — but choice requires factual information to responsibly decide. Can we say INFORMED CONSENT? Can we say CONSENT OF THE GOVERNED? Such information is increasingly and conspicuously AWOL in the United States. When insiders benefiting from public funding manipulate publicly available information and mass perception to advocate for and further non-transparent agendas, perhaps we should inquire if those unseen agendas are harmful or even Luciferian as I from an engineering point of view insist some of them are? If repairing the bridge collapses the bridge, perhaps we should effect repairs differently? If helping the patient kills the patient, maybe there is a better way? Can we at least discuss it?

Regarding COVID for example, U.S. Federal (so-called) health experts outlawed traditionally effective early treatment protocols. The FDA banned *Hydroxychloroquine* (HCQ), a safe 65-year-old malaria treatment, which in concert with other malaria treatments held Sub-Saharan Africa to alleged COVID fatalities more than 300% below U.S. death rates. **Hydroxychloroquine**, licensed in the U.S. in 1955 is used to treat autoimmune diseases like systemic lupus erythematosus and rheumatoid arthritis, in addition to malaria. HCQ with vitamin C, D_3, zinc and so forth have been found to cost effectively treat corona virus infection, particularly when used early. **Ivermectin**, also a banned treatment is proven effective despite demonization by government pawns, legacy media, and Big Pharma talking heads.

Instead of regulatory agencies and medical boards allowing experienced medical practitioners to prescribe medications and employ clinically appropriate treatments; American Main Street CCP bio-attack victims are told to mask up, stay away from each other, avoid normal exposure to immune strengthening organisms, shut down your business, be terrified, and most importantly—take the experimental JAB with its unidentified ingredients.

Question for Robert Redfield, Stephen Hahn, Janet Woodcock, Anthony Fauci, Deborah Birx, Vivek Murthy, and dozens of corrupt government others: **Why has your SCIENCE since January 2020 resulted in American citizens having a four times (4X) higher probability of death due to weaponized COVID than anyone living in sub-Saharan Africa? If you have any science at all, it is embarrassingly, if not malevolently weak.**

On another front, Scientism's artificial intelligence is a misnomer and does not exist outside known life forms and intelligent life energy. What does exist in the electro-magnetic/machine world is **autonomous intelli-**

gence, a very different thing, which learns rapidly via repetition and calculation within given parameters set by creative human intelligence. Autonomous intelligence can teach itself; it learns, but has no consciousness, no imagination, no ability to make moral or creative distinctions, etc. So-called AI reasoning is limited to quantifiable analytics incapable of qualitative judgement. Purported AI qualitative results mimicking reasoning skills are based on mathematics, statistical probabilities, and other programmably limited capabilities.

Left unchecked by careless proponents of transhumanism, their amoral digital world, growing in spiritually bereft *Humanity 2.0* power is already harming human and other life forms. Few things pose more danger than thought-conditioned educators and researchers who don't know what they don't know, but arrogantly presume they do. *Useful idiot* is the correct term here. Thank you, Comrade Lenin.

Do we imagine indoctrinated order-followers running web related social platforms, search engines, browsers, etc., are unfamiliar with psychology's *Asch Conformity Experiments* conducted back in the 1950's by Solomon Asch? We're not investing time on the studies here (they make interesting homework), but rest assured, technocrats have labored over the subject of *conforming behavior, obedience to authority* and related topics as studied by Asch and later expanded on by the notorious *Stanford Prison Experiment* and better-known *Milgram (Shock Generator) Experiments.* **Google** for instance, with funding and development enabled by CIA, DARPA, NSA, NSF, and I suppose other agencies[67] is not friendly to Main Street health. (My opinion.) *Google* is a tool – but tool for what? Whose tool? Are some tools weapons? Can invasive weapons be aimed at us? In psychopathic hands as *Google* and the CCP are, *Google* is not and cannot be benign.

<u>Appropriate</u> applications of AI do not threaten human thought, imagination, or life. Only when unbalanced Left Brain order-followers employed by psychopathic handlers weaponize AI does it go off the rails and become a threat. Some threats are obvious; some subtle. One subtler threat is the unseen subjectivity of computerized internet searches. What we can't see and are not aware of can bolster false premises of Scientism, particularly those aspects geared toward behavior modification, personality disruption, mental confusion, and identity change.

We, or at least I, think of internet searches as under our control and objectively presented to us, but of course this is not the case. Web searches are algorithmically controlled, and those algorithms are subjectively created by someone, which means information access is compromised by that someone to some extent. Given human nature this innate bias is impossible to eliminate.

---

67 Jeff Nesbit, "Google's True Origin Partly Lies in CIA and NSA Research Grants for Mass Surveillance," Quartz, accessed July 2, 2021, https://qz.com/1145669/googles-true-origin-partly-lies-in-cia-and-nsa-research-grants-for-mass-surveillance/.

Interface activity between a web browser query through a browser such as *Chrome, Firefox, Internet Explorer, Safari, Edge,* etc., and a search engine like *Bing, Google, Yahoo* or now it appears, *Amazon* and *Facebook (META)* become repetitive, learned activities subject to platform programming bias and in many cases, prejudice. How this works between our IP address and a searched URL, I have no idea, but somehow, via digital 0/1 and now quantum magic our web searches, over time, become subjectively biased toward things and views we are algorithmically identified as interested in per the language we use and paths we search. *Search Engine Optimization* (SEO) is predicated on these trending habits.

Conversely, trending habits can be countered. More importantly, bias is aggravated and put on steroids by platform prejudice programmed into cloud storage/search criteria. There is no question that information interdiction, manipulation, and censoring are routinely occurring, imposed by tools we voluntarily employ as we access the WWW. The objective search for open-source information we thought we were conducting is biased by previous searches, other surveilled IoT related activities, and by programed censorship, but this is not obvious to non-techies like me. None of this *"birds of a feather"* manipulation and censorship are accidental. Surveillance and behavioral modification technology are built into these systems to the extent possible as discussed in 1993's **Massive Digital Data Systems** (MDDS) project.

The most obvious, though not most crucial media censorship in the U.S. is applied to subject matter deemed significant to so-called conservatives generally and constitutionalists specifically. Most liberals have little awareness of the vast scope of this censorship but quickly experience it when mistakenly voicing an independent thought on social media or trying to search accurate information regarding a subject deemed taboo by globalist order followers. The hard Left, however, loves this censorship, not realizing the Satanic maw is coming for them as well, just a bit later. The most crucial media censorship related directly to **Scientism** is not of targeted groups or specific subject matter BUT CENSORSHIP OF REALITY ITSELF. This is perception altering and dangerous since perception is foundational to reasoning and behavior. Information censorship can in some cases be justified but is most often dangerously disingenuous or malicious. Fascistic censorship by government mandate and/or covertly coordinated with corporate monopolies is evil.

Controlled information dissemination and censorship, i.e., **information warfare** is endemic to **Scientism** as a support mechanism for conning Main Street into compliance with **scientific dictatorship**, i.e., Globalism, i.e., transhuman slavery. Slave owners know uneducated slaves are easier to control than educated slaves, one aspect of which requires dumbing down internet searches for Main

Street slaves. This narrow view tasks Scientism with several objectives, one of which is blurring distinctions between belief by faith, belief by logical argument, belief by factually observable evidence, belief by consensus, belief by coercion, etc. A little obtuse I know, but historically as far back as the fourth century, Cappadocian Fathers of the Orthodox Church wrestled with this exact issue.[68]

Trained in Greek language, culture, philosophy, and rhetoric while embracing early Christianity and faith in Christ posed serious theological issues in the 4th century as it does today though Scientism masks such issues by denial of human spiritual nature altogether. Consider a 4th century discussion issue: **Was faith in a belief a better safeguard of truth than belief brought about by rhetorical argument?** Posing the question another way: **if I argue poorly in defense of my belief does this render my belief untrue?** Obviously not, I'm just an unconvincing debater so better luck next time, but the facts remain unchanged. Today, Scientism, assisted by mass media reflexively discourages debate altogether, preferring to predetermine propagandized outcomes while discouraging questions via manufactured consensus and intimidating peer pressure.

I suspect this accounts in part, for why many supposedly unbiased students, investigators, researchers, and scientists so often claim CONSENSUS on this or that subject. The claim is fallaciously based in part, on the algorithmically biased information returned by what we think of as unbiased searching; but in fact, our search is biased by past searches and/or other computer activity picked up by data mining, then processed by surveillance algorithms. I'm not alleging criminality here though it's probable, just sayin'. When all we're permitted to see via our supposedly open-source search query is in agreement with this or that opinion or line of potentially propagandized thought; of course, it appears we found consensus—but it's fake. It's a lie by machine ignorance, omission, spin, or by factual data screening and manipulation.

A global warming believer for instance, may tend to search for information supporting anthropogenic sources as primarily or predominantly causative to climate change. Of course, nonconforming opinions on this subject are largely censored and unpublished, but some are permitted to slip through so-called fact checker cracks for public ridicule and mockery. Beyond blatant censorship while seeking information, over time, IP address search behavior is learned by algorithms programmed to trend displayed information toward identifiable previous behavior patterns. This is electro-magnetic machine pattern bias mimicking defined neural pathways, not rational intelligence by the way. It's simply mindless, repetitive pattern recognition programmed into a machine, appearing to mimic intelligence. The machine itself is not biased, just programmed to function as if it were.

68 ThriftBooks, "Christianity and Classical Culture: The... Book by Jaroslav Pelikan,"

I doubt many of us regard internet searches as a form of mind control; BUT if our cognitive processes are based on perception, and perception is based on information; and if information received is controlled and/or biased for whatever reason, say by programming preferences, machine pattern recognition, intentional censorship, or other means; our information is not objective and consequently cognition becomes less objective and more biased. The apparent search consensus viewed on our own computer screen may not show up on the first three pages of someone else's computer screen, but this logistical flaw isn't immediately obvious.

For example, my partner and I have tested query results related to our U.S. Patent (8,381,523 B2) informational website, on his iPad and my desktop computer. Our patent is for our cost-effective, closed-system, supercritical geothermal energy technology. Same query wording, same time of day, but different machines, different browsers, different search engines. A query on his *ipad* showing up *numero uno* on his first page listing, shows up number 44 on my query; about four pages later using the exact same search wording. What impact can this sort of search differential have on legitimate scientific inquiry? Clearly there is subjective developer bias built into these web browsers and search engines. Is it difficult for prejudiced techies and jaundiced pseudo-scientists to restrict objective knowledge acquisition via pre-programed internet search bias? Makes a case for libraries full of printed books, articles, and white papers doesn't it.

At least some indoctrinated order-followers working for popular search engines and browsers, not to mention computer operating system developers do intentionally program cultural and/or technological bias per personal preferences into product software. Some egotistical system developers brag about doing this. Even if my belief is unfair respecting programming intent, users (customers) might ask, is it possible for any programmer to develop software outside their own experiential knowledge base and does that limitation constitute a form of autobias?

Answering this question poses a legitimate burden on program designers since search engines don't just make information accessible to users. Search engines are programmed to interpret, organize, and prioritize information per selective criteria, i.e., criteria and priorities preferred by programmers and/or their managers. In short, **data is censored via programmer bias as a matter of programming skill and practicality** as well as by sorting, categorizing, prioritizing logistics. Even when imposing our own filters while searching, those filters are impacted through operational programming by someone else.

These data organizing priorities clearly effect user search information retrieval, in turn profoundly impacting user perception and subsequent thinking regarding subject matter being searched. *If it's on the internet, it must be true, as the joke goes. If we operate a business and do not have a website, we're not real are we?* What level of information and knowledge restraint do programmer organizing priorities impose when programming is intentionally or unintentionally biased toward a particular cosmological view, philosophy, theology, political or cultural ideology, economic view, scientific debate, statistical interpretation, style of music or art, a product or service, etc.? If political views are an artifact of culture and art precedes culture as it usually does — and technology overrides art and culture, this is a big deal.

Controlling foundational information search priorities, access, search boundaries, and search speed constrains the *Overton Window* of debate. Intended or not, this programming process automatically sublimates the narrative thereby molding user thought processes, modifying language, and manipulating behavior. World wide web user beware as information cannot be as objectively organized as it seems. Science, technology and related data, when abused, manipulated, and weaponized as we experience today, become useless to beneficial Main Street endeavors and threaten underlying conservative principles of free thought, free speech, and free behavior. Social media is another tool weaponized for effectively cordoning off, encouraging, or discouraging web search activity, information access, speech, and for enabling surveillance via dopamine enhanced sharing. We provide private information to Transhuman psychopaths for free without apparent concern for how this information is used or abused.

Moving away from the cyberspace information highway, physicists tell us ±95% of all energy and matter in our known universe is *dark energy (68%)* and *dark matter (27%)*, about which we know little. Given this level of ignorance juxtaposed with our innate human proclivity to comprehend the meaning of life, for discerning truth, and dare I say, goodness along with our need to be loved—**mustn't a thinking person at least consider the natural essence of spirit, spiritual energy, and how it interfaces with material existence?** I can't see how this is arguable, and if it isn't, why do many so-called scientists insist we not consider these aspects of life? Look here, not there they insist; "There" is irrelevant. So, who do Scientism gurus work for and how deeply embedded in global culture are these Transhuman worms?

As one example, in July 2019 the Vatican actually hosted a Transhuman Conference sponsored by *OISTE Foundation,* titled **"Technology and Human Flourishing"**. Though not supported by many at the Vatican, **at least not openly,** this antihuman spiritual infection was supported by *Pontifical Lateran University* (PLU) at the Collegio Teutonico, adjacent to St. Peter's Square. Incidentally, *The OISTE Foundation*, created in Geneva in 1998, is a not-for-profit organization regulated by article 80 et seq. of the Swiss Civil Code, and is as deeply interwoven within New World Order study group circles as any global-ist NGO can be. *OISTE* has proprietary rights for a Root Cryptographic Key enabling digital certification of persons and objects. Global cybersecurity company, *WISeKey* acts as the Operator chosen by the foundation for the management of their root cryptographic key. *OISTE* and *WISeKey* are bound together by a defined Trust Framework and Certification Practice Statement (CPS).

The *OISTE* misinformation website prominently speaks of "right to privacy and trust" while conspicuously avoiding terms like surveillance or control. One question is—if OISTE and related NGO's are so interested in protecting our privacy, why are they so busy inventing electronic data stratagems for peaking into it?

OISTE and its relationship with Vatican secularists is just one parasitic example among dozens of international agreements and burgeoning trans-human threats to civilization and sovereign nation states. Given such proudly displayed arbitrary subjectivity, why are academic purveyors of scientism and their supporting corporate conspirators still considered legitimate sources for anything at all? Accredited medical experts today have near zero credibility for any thinking, fact-oriented person—a sad circumstance.

At what point did science stop questioning and learning in favor of politically bullied peer consensus? If science is a lie, what purpose can it serve? We've filled libraries with what we think we know regarding the 5% of energy and matter we can conceptualize, then refuse to acknowledge the 95% we don't comprehend. Do ten or so pages of Ecclesiastes, likely written by Solomon around 935 B.C. reveal more about the meaning of life than centuries of science have been able to reveal? Just askin'?

Suggesting Creation conflicts with Natural Law or evolution is willfully ignorant; just as answering every origination question with "God did it" is ignorant. Darwin's 5th grade theory of evolution explains and accounts for little of what we see today obviously evolving. The childish theory of evolution doesn't account for much of the how or why of anything we can see, hear, touch, taste, or smell – not to mention the 95% of dark energy and dark matter we can't sense, aren't aware of, and don't yet understand. If Scientism assumes 5% or so of anthropogenic carbon emissions tip the entire world climate upside down; is it rational to assume 95% of unseen dark energy and matter exert zero cause or effect on climate? Does earth's sun activity exert no impact on climate? Is this legitimate scientific method? Though long after Darwin's time, why is discussion regarding geoengineering and aerosol spraying of heavy metals and other toxic nanomaterials taboo?

8 • Religion of Scientism

Why would I rudely suggest Darwin guilty of 5ᵗʰ grade science? Because despite Darwin's material insight, his error, in my humble opinion is stubborn refusal to recognize Supernatural Revelation, man's conscious and subconscious relationship with transcendent mystery, man's spiritual ability to think, plan, and exercise imagination as differentiated from other known life forms governed solely by Natural Law. Evolution itself is an aspect of intelligently created Natural Law—not an exception. Completion, however, fulfillment if you will, of Natural Law comes about through Supernatural Revelation along with our human response to transcendent creation on behalf of all creation.

Scientism advocates prefer Main Street remain nescient because Scientism's global syndicate handlers understand starving, illiterate, dumbed down slaves with limited ability to reason are more cost effectively piratized and managed than educated, thinking slaves. The Transhuman AI formula for human behavior control is straight forward. Even Yale, Harvard, and Stanford grads pick up on it with a bit of soul selling. It's how and why so few Americans realize 70,000 annual deaths by drugs, i.e., more in one year than 58,220 killed during the entire Vietnam War from 1954 through 1975 comprises asymmetric warfare against Main Street USA.

Circa 2021, opioids kill 136 Americans every day — the most vicious being the synthetic opioid, *Fentanyl* – the vast bulk of which is manufactured by the **Chinese Communist Party**, then with help of treasonous Big U.S. Government is delivered across thousands of miles of open, unwalled southern U.S. border, as well as through more than 300 ports of entry.

This is an aggressive, in our face CCP attack coordinated with rogue elements in U.S. Federal, State, and local government, though thankfully not as far as I know, our elected Sheriffs. Most American people are unaware of this corrupt complicity due to D.C. and State level lies and treasonous Big Tech censorship. The U.S. government in concert with the British Crown are the world's largest traffickers in drugs and humans on the planet. Cartels are just disposable contractors, not decider guys. Please note that sex trafficking is sex slavery. Human trafficking is human slavery. Drug trafficking supports all forms of human slavery. **Woke culture** uselessly worries about century's past slaves but cares nothing for today's millions of slaves. This is Marcuse's destructive *Happy Consciousness*.

Scientism's single most imminent global threat is the obscene marriage of Western corporatist oligarchs with the surveillance and control obsessed *Chinese Communist Party* (CCP) intertwined with compromised western governments and corporations. Of China's estimated 1,500,000,000 people less than 150 million are CCP members, with only thousands ruling the CCP. This tiny fraction brutally controls the good people of China via cyber deceit, cyber surveillance, brainwashing, violence, and fear—all of which are now generously being delivered throughout Europe and North America. The Satanic Elite few criminal psychotics destroying life on Earth, only exist and survive because *we the many* allow them to do so.

In the West, fewer than 0.001% control banking, government, capital flows, commodity trading, etc. This concentrated wealth and power then controls education and media, relegating scientific method to crass Scientism. When soulless North American and European oligarchs finance and assist the greedy slave economy of the *Chinese Communist Party* and laud its corrupt efficiencies our entire world is in serious *Belt and Road* trouble. A world ruled by Satanically influenced serial mass murderers and pathological underlings will work diligently to survive, escape its own dark tendencies, and will injure, kill, or destroy all creation if it can. The CCP is itself just another global syndicate tool for division and ultimately, destruction of all life on Earth. God help the Chinese people, and with God's grace maybe we can help. Echoing Marx, *we the people of the world must unite together* with God's grace against the destructive power of Satanic influence and psychopathic omnicide.

CCP leadership is so deeply marooned in its *Warring State* past, so oblivious to moral standards, human decency, and sanctity of human life, it is reasonable to suggest as a practical matter, CCP leadership under global syndicate coercion is functionally insane. This observation speaks volumes about dangers of Scientism posed by western Elites compliantly and treasonously compromising their nations in the interest of CCP control agendas, does it not? Given the nature of Anglo-American Establishment planning, funding, and technical support for Mao's brutally implemented form of Chinese slavery as a pilot program for NWO global feudalism, concern for humanity's future is in order.

Scientism breeds Technocracy, which breeds Transhumanism, which is scientific slavery fortified by censorship, surveillance, and lies. China has become the West's testing laboratory for implementing Transhuman enslavement. It is time our Baby Boomer generation outgrew its aging *counterculture* indoctrination to finally cope with Satanically influenced transhuman enslavement realistically and morally.

Main Street must get past opinionated controlled conflict, roll up its sleeves, get its hands dirty, and deal firmly with government and corporate titans cooperating treasonously with CCP global syndicate order followers. Talk and debate are necessary, but direct involvement in political party operations as **volunteers, poll watchers, precinct committee persons, candidates,** and so forth is essential to change. Wishing, talking, and arguing change nothing and will not save our future.

SCIENTISM must be over-ruled by SCIENCE.

METAVERSE = GLOBAL 3.0 + HUMAN 2.0
= TRANSHUMAN SLAVERY

9 • Weaponized Biosphere and Medical Fraud

Remedy: Eat healthy, organic, non-GMO, locally grown nutritious food. Use an effective water filter. Exercise. Get plenty of sleep. Stop with the dumbed down sound bite language. Turn off all Mainstream Mockingbird (Fake) News – it's just soul shattering narrative and group-think propaganda. Legacy mainstream media sources are dehumanizing indoctrination outlets damaging to balanced Left/Right Brain intelligence and creative thought.

To be human is to be creative. Diminishment of imagination is dehumanizing, disempowering, spiritually malnourishing, and must be avoided as a means of self-protection and health-preservation. Television, smart phones, and other IoT electronic devices are dangerous transhumanist surveillance/entrainment weapons. Beware subliminal messaging, flicker-rates, and more invasive entrainment technologies.

An imminent threat to Main Street freedom and sustainable life on Earth is posed by the concept of Transhuman METAVERSE, that is, weaponized FULL SPECTRUM DOMINANCE through MIND CONTROL METHODOLOGIES; most prominently, ENTRAINMENT, NANO-COMMUNICATION DEVICES, and SCALAR WAVE TECHNOLOGIES. These dangerous technologies partner with more commonly recognized censorship, propaganda, indoctrination, and every form of surveillance imaginable. Globalism is slavery, only accepted by incoherent people so effectively indoctrinated, dumbed down, drugged, entrained, and physically weakened, they stumble into a compliant DEMORALIZED stupor.

For example, suitcase size *mobile cell site simulators* (ISMI Catchers) such as *Sting Ray* have been in use by law enforcement for more than a decade and have been around since the 1990's. These surveillance devices are used on the ground, in the air, and are easily powered by a vehicular cigarette lighter. *Sting Ray* is the brand name for an ISMI catcher manufactured by Florida based *Harris Corporation*. GPS location along with every call, email, text message, etc. within range of a *Sting Ray* is tracked and stored while in <u>passive mode</u>. The *Stingray* can also use <u>active mode</u> to communicate with and/or load spyware and malware onto a smartphone or direct a phone's browser to a website that can perform the installation – without the phone user knowing this occurred.

A similar device generically called a *dirt box* is capable of tracking more than 10,000 phones simultaneously. The name comes from DRT, an acronym for *Digital Receiver Technology*, a Maryland based *Boeing* subsidiary.

Aside from flagrant censorship and drugs, the biospheric threat to Earth is largely invisible, though if we look up, we still see aerosol sprayed particulate trails and chemical cloud mixtures of various nanoparticulates, i.e., the partially visible transhuman aspect of developing control methodologies dependent on ionization of Earth's atmosphere into an electromagnetically conductive plasma. I say "still see" because at least four new aerosol mixtures have been developed as of this writing to mask the poisoning and weaponizing of our biosphere against prying eyes. Earth's ionosphere is being psychopathically transformed into an antenna working in conjunction with implementation of *Space Fence* and other technology.

One aerosol spraying technique is chemical, nanoparticulate cloud dumping under cover of darkness with dispersal before daylight. We won't see the chemical trails nor Earth's traditional blue-sky. Instead, we see a weaponized plasmatic, whitish to silvery-gray toned sky everywhere. California and the American southwest have been living with this ramped-up toxic plague for years but it is a global phenomenon working in concert with designers developing electro-magnetic *Space Fence* capabilities. So-called chemtrails are now routinely visible in movie sky shots as well as in fakes news report backgrounds, photos, etc.

My issue with the 2nd generation *Space Fence* is, beyond collision avoidance with debris, WHAT ELSE CAN IT OR WILL IT DO? A legitimate question given D.C.'s penchant for corruption, pathology, lying, spying, robbing, controlling, and now, killing Main Street citizens with JABs. It appears the *Space Fence* will be or is capable of AI interface capability with *Gwen Towers*, *Nexrad Towers*, *5G cell phone towers*, the IoT, and our *ionized atmosphere*. If so, this will put surveillance as well as AI command/control of planet Earth on steroids without citizen recourse – suggesting Main Street must demand transparency since we don't know how pathologically ill transhumanist *Space Fence* developers are. We also don't know how this ionospheric technology interfaces with new synthetic mRNA JABs loaded with metallic nanoparticles, nano-chips, nano-tranceivers, graphene oxide, and the like.

Note: Space travel after *Sputnik* I in 1957 resulted in the need for collision avoidance technology to detect irresponsible litter polluting space like abandoned or damaged equipment, orbiting equipment, satellites, etc. These new systems were to protect new launches or re-entering space craft from accidental collisions. The **Space Fence**, i.e., *Air Force Space Surveillance System* (AFSSS) was a very high frequency (VHF) radar network stretching from Georgia to California. AFSSS was transferred from the U.S. Navy to the U.S. Air Force in 2004, then shut down in October 2013, supposedly due to feckless Obama Regime sequestration financial strain but 2nd generation planning was underway at least since 2009 anyway, so get rid of the old stuff and bring on the new stuff. After years of development, the new S-band 2nd generation space surveillance system was deemed operational by the *U.S. Space Force* in March 2020.

On the bright side, I suspect as of this writing, our new *Space Force*, hopefully with Trump Administration leadership formed without WOKE communist military traitors, captured more than 37 terabytes of 2020 election fraud packet captures in real time as corrupt algorithms were adjusted to steal the 2020 election from patriots. Time will tell if more than 3,100 counties were compromised.   Thank you Mike Lindell.

A logical question might be why am I linking **Stratospheric Aerosol Injection** (SAI), aka, chemtrails to medicine while claiming WEAPONIZATION? Several reasons. Nanosize aluminum particles are hygroscopic. When mobile aluminum particles are included as a constituent of aerosol spraying (SAI), a group of chemtrails quickly disperse, forming a sun light obscuring chemical cloud. This reduces natural Vitamin D production, weakening immune systems thereby aiding viral or other infection of cells. Simultaneously, pathogenic organisms like corona viruses propagate more abundantly under reduced sun light intensity. Eugenicists love this deadly combination – optimized deniability, more virus, less human immunity – particularly when those viruses are bio-engineered to be more invasive and more deadly to humans. Big Governments are dangerous.

The ionization of Earth's atmosphere into an electromagnetically conductive plasma will likely have harmful, possibly devastating effects on biological systems. At best, the public has no idea what long term effects may be experienced. All biological and chemical processes on Earth are electric. It has been understood since at least the mid 1700's that electricity is a property of life.

We've known since the mid eighteenth century, that electricity exerts profound effects on biological organisms. This research is not advertised on Main Street.

Doctors like neurosurgeon, Russell L. Blaylock, mercilessly demonized by Legacy Media, Big Medicine, and Big Pharma are identifying the process by which aluminum nanoparticles found in geoengineered *chemtrails* contribute to increased cases of degenerative disease. Add bioengineering of food crop DNA, i.e., Genetically Modified Organisms (GMOs) along with copious doses of refined sugar to this noxious mix and we have uncontrolled experimentation operating on Earth's natural processes… by whom… for what *Fascist International* purpose? Is growing harm to global health an unintended consequence of covertly building a stratospheric umbrella of reflective aerosols to reduce so-called global warming while simultaneously attempting to increase food production? Or are covert engineering processes intended for malevolent purposes? Why are so-called environmentalists NOT TALKING about weaponized *Metaverse* processes?

Correlation is not causation, but the two can run together. The development of electricity correlates with a number of chronic diseases we now regularly cope with.[69] Anxiety disorders were largely unheard of before the 1860's when telegraph wires began encircling the Earth. Influenza was identified in 1889 alongside alternating electrical current. Diabetes was almost unheard of prior to the 1860's and was typically found only among thin people, not overweight people. Heart disease was rare prior to the 1860's. Cancer was rare and before widespread electrification, tobacco use was not known to cause lung cancer.

Does research demonstrate correlation between global proliferation of electricity and influenza outbreaks? If so, this prompts questions about flu vaccination programs in combination with ingestion of toxic aerosol spraying constituents, together engendering adverse immune reactions when triggered by 5G radiation. **Remember, all life processes are electric.** Many researchers suspect engineered forms of corona or other viruses may react to 5G as though on super-steroids with severe flu-like symptoms. Do toxic JABs enhance this reaction through their transhuman operating system? How deadly will this interaction be? What level of sterilization should our VAXXED children be prepared to face? A child JABBED today won't experience lack of fertility for ten or more years. Who will connect these insidious dots a decade from now when many of us fail to see the murderous nature of toxic JABs today?

---

69 "The Invisible Rainbow: A History of Electricity and Life: Firstenberg, Arthur: 9781645020097: Amazon.Com: Books," 2.

9 • Weaponized Biosphere and Medical Fraud

Megalomaniacal practitioners of Scientism imagining we can improve our world by weaponizing weather and climate are as grotesquely short-sighted as indoctrinated psychopaths imagining machines merging with organic bodies will improve humanity. It's the nature of material things to pass away and be sustainably recycled via the synergistic transformation of energy. 99.9% of all Earthly species are extinct; replaced by newly evolved species. Extinction is nature's evolutionary norm, not its exception. Created life begets more life more abundantly – unless disturbed by Satanically influenced processes. Life itself is a battle between creative power of love and destructive influence of evil. The transhumanist search for everlasting life through AI cyborgism is superfluous. Safely meditate, fast, pray, embrace, and enjoy our gift of spiritual eternity. It already exists via unification with our Creator's love waiting for us to celebrate our precious gift.

I'm not delving much into atmospheric weaponization aspects of mind-control because this subject is voluminous, going back to the 1930's and the spawning of Technocracy; followed in 1942 by Dr. Norbert Weiner's MIT research into *CYBERRNETICS* (human-machine interaction); then in 1953, the CIA's *Bluebird, Artichoke, Monarch - MK Ultra*; and more recently, 2015's *Brain Initiative* and today, far beyond any of that to *gain of function* (bio-weapons) research (GoFR), *gang-stalking*, 5G, 6G, the *Internet of Things* (IoT), modified *HAARP*, scalar wave, nanotech, *Space Fence* technology, and *full spectrum dominance* i.e., *Metaverse*, exercised over what military science calls **human terrain.**

Human thought broadcasts within the range of electromagnetic radio-wave frequencies; that is, an extremely low frequency (ELF) band. Brain activity can be sensed and interacted with by satellites orbiting hundreds of miles above Main Street. Satellites have been able to detect brainwaves as far back as the early 1970's and as of this writing are in their 8th development generation. This research is not well publicized. Main Street ignorance regarding this research fertilizes ground for psychopathic covert abuse of high-tech applications.

Ms. Elana Freeland tells us: "By the early 1990's, properly equipped geosynchronous orbiting satellites were able to read minds, influence behavior, and detect human speech underground or behind walls unprotected by lead. Beams from high above the earth can 'interfere' and lock onto human targets and knock them down. Subliminals can be broadcast into the brain, including signals ordering the target to do something criminal, sexual, or violent."[70] This theft of autonomous life choices is pure evil.

70 "Under an Ionized Sky: From Chemtrails to Space Fence Lockdown: Elana Freeland: 9781627310536: Amazon.Com: Books," 216, accessed April 14, 2018, https://www.amazon.com/Under-Ionized-Sky-Chemtrails-Lockdown/dp/1627310533/ref=sr_1_1?ie=UTF8&qid=1523733639&sr=8-1&keywords=under+an+ionized+sky.

Does rogue military/Silicon Valley technology and covert real-time testing play into serial murder, the rash of *false flag* school violence, vehicle crashes, shipping accidents, earthquakes, tsunamis, wild fires, and violent *false flag* events now plaguing Main Street on behalf the group-think gun control agenda and/or other control-the-public-dialog furthering divide and conquer methodologies? I suspect so as significant investment of time, energy, and money, especially dark money, are not psychopathically aggregated for no reason. There is an observably malicious attack plan being enacted and clearly, we Main Street *unwashed* are targets.

It's critical to societal health and well-being Main Street realize 21st century mind control is devolving to full spectrum control by attacking Main Street through weaponized rails of: pollution, poor nutrition, weakened immune systems, reduced fertility, dropping intelligence quotients, industrialized poor nutritional agriculture, pseudo-economics, corrupt politics, mis-education, censored publishing, politicization of sports and entertainment, censored/surveilled social media, propagandized news media narratives, false flag events, medical fraud, misleading expert opinion, and electro-magnetic entrainment via 5G and IoT.

Main Street pays dearly to have itself defined as the *unwashed* enemy of the psychopathic global syndicate and its City of London, Vatican City, Washington D.C. feasting centers. Global syndicate order followers mindlessly drive this criminalized transhuman bus toward a NWO nightmare. Sadistic psychopaths are returning Main Street to Neo-Feudal serfdom... only this time with ABSOLUTE CONTROL and 100% foolproof *Pitchfork Avoidance Strategy* (PAS). Medicine plays an expansive role in this transhuman nightmare though most medical professionals and patients don't realize it. It's a perfect ploy because who argues against medicine supposedly governed by **"do no harm"**?

Wealth created by hard working Main Street populations across the globe is systematically harvested by the global syndicate. Nothing new here except improved harvesting methodology and technique. More efficient harvesting and disablement of resistance to harvesting are enabled by various forms of mind-control implemented to nurture compliance and expedite harvesting without risk of popular recognition or subsequent revolt. Plausible deniability rules D.C.'s criminal culture, driving honesty and integrity into the industrialized dust of the vast GMO fruited plain.

MAKE AMERICA GREAT AGAIN are the most horrifically loathed, dynamically feared four words ever heard spoken by the ears of global syndicate families. Discussing abandonment of unipolar impoverishment and enslavement for Main Street with replacement by multilateral free market abundance for Main Street is a call for ELITE PANIC. Rising Main Street awareness of ubiquitous election fraud has Elites and their Rino/Leftist order followers shrieking in despair, lashing out irrationally at anyone daring to ask a question.

Realize that mind control is ultimately about *prominent global citizens* pathologically harvesting productive Main Street wealth through order-following Pawns of Privilege working through transnational monopoly corporations and corrupt ruling class government without stirring revolt. It's a friendlier impoverished Fascism without cattle cars and barbed wire. Boundless finger pointing makes liberal thieves and so-called conservative thieves difficult to identify. Harvesting takes many forms, some of them, like nutrition and medicine, surprising. We can and should criticize big medicine and big pharma for expensively treating autism, cancer, diabetes, heart disease, HIV/AIDS, COVID, and other illnesses as opposed to curing them and should wonder how and why this centrally planned failure comes about? We should wonder because medical protocols are enabling poor overall public health and immunity, in turn reducing resistance to mind control.

One quick example of destructive protocol is the ridiculous workload forced on hospital residents and interns. I get young doctors and nurses must be conditioned to bear up under stress, but intentional resident exhaustion is clearly not a good idea. So why are residents subjected to exhausting schedules? Two reasons. One, residents working 2.0 - 2.5 weeks every week are cheaper than residents or doctors working normal work hours. Second, a horrifically over-burdened resident barely has time to survive his or her steep indoctrination curve - and therefore, has no time to question protocols or examine best practices. What resident has time to consider food as medicine or address curing root causes of illness instead of just relieving symptoms through expensive treatment? This cult-like educational process is not accidental and is driven by not very philanthropic foundations and trusts meddling in protocol development through targeted financing, grants, etc. These same dynastic family foundations, trusts, and endowments own Big Pharma, Big Medical Equipment, Big Oil, and Big Government, etc. Follow the money.

In the U.S., resident certification is by the *Accreditation Council for Graduate Medical Education* (ACGME). This pathetic institution panders to competency along with patient and medical staff safety by declaring *resident education to be professionally self-regulated* — if so, begging the question, what purpose does ACGME serve? ACGME unsuccessfully panders to restrain resident work hours to 80-hours per week with a 24-hour continuous duty limit for intermediate level residents. I don't pretend to understand resident or intern reality but suspect these band aid limitations are an exhausted joke at many, if not most hospitals and university medical centers.

Mr. G. Edward Griffin penned an important expose on big medical/big pharma issues in 1974 called *World Without Cancer, The Story of Vitamin B₁₇* in which he touches on different areas of concern, some of them fraudulent. Unfortunately, for Main Street medical patients, monopolized avarice rules the hallowed halls of medical research and pharmacology, crushing the Hippocratic Oath beneath the punishing weight of duplicitous philanthropic foundations, trusts, and endowments controlled by psychopathic dynastic family fortunes. Compound interest on facility debt handles the rest. Treat, but not cure is the profit secret.

One reference is made by Mr. Griffin to Ferdinand Lundberg's 1968 *The Rich and the Super-Rich* where Lundberg, while discussing abuse of influence by notable foundations states: "A fourth effect is that the foundations extend the power of their founders very prominently into the cultural areas of education (and propaganda), science, the arts and social relations. While much that is done in these areas under foundation auspices meets judicious critical approval, it is a fact that these dispensations inevitably take the form of patronage, bestowed on approved projects, withheld from disapproved projects. Recipients of the money must be ideologically acceptable to the donors.

There is a positive record showing that by these means purely corporate elements are able to influence research and many university policies, particularly in selection of personnel. While the foundations are staunch supporters of the physical sciences, the findings of which have many profit-making applications in the corporate sphere, among the social disciplines their influence is to foster a prevailing scholastic formalism. By reason of the institutional controls that have been established, the social disciplines are largely empty or self-servingly propagandistic, as careful analysis have disclosed."[71]

Unfortunately, Mr. Lundberg, an indoctrinated Leftist, ignores his own fact-finding by viewing government as the solution rather than the obvious facilitator of monopoly interests. Greedy monopoly interests cannot compete or survive economically without corrupt government sanction, reflexive legal protection, price fixing, competitive restraint, and subsidy. Can it ever be a good idea for corrupt transnational monopolies, traditionally managed by psychopaths, to hold substantial sway over medical school curricula, research, or medical protocols?

We see similar fact screening and censorship applied throughout status quo climate research as well as in heavily biased environmental studies, green energy, failed Keynesian Economic Theory, and other areas of what are now just politicized sham-science. **Science is controlled by the agendas of those who fund it.** We should note, by carefully screening and selecting staff members and employees based on ideological pref-

---

71 Ferdinand Lundberg, *The Rich and Super-Rich* (n/a, 1973), 469.

erence, upper management easily controls concepts, views, and policies its staff generates or supports while never overtly suggesting or censoring anything. Another *invisible hand* lent by the international study group system.

The world-wide study-group system supported by central banking, corrupt or uninformed government leaders, military/industrial/medical concerns as well as by secret societies, foundations, trusts, endowments, institutes, universities, NGO's and professional associations provides a steady supply of indoctrinated academics and bureaucrats to share globalist indoctrination and NWO policy.

This pervasive study group system evolved from and was originally disseminated around the world by the Rhodes-Milner Group, initially through various influential Oxford colleges.[72] The study group system subtly provides a cost-effective means for networking, hazing, and recruiting ideologically suitable candidates for employment within heavily agendavized organizations working toward totalitarian control and reduction of deplorable populations. Mainstream news anchors for instance, do not usually have to be coerced. What they will say on any issue is a known commodity before consideration for employment. The same holds true for RNC and DNC sponsored candidates.

The global syndicate effectively censors what it views as undesirable ideas, policies, and candidates by ostracizing non-status quo views, thereby banning, or at least limiting questions and/or dissenting opinion from public exposure. We see this bullying today with shadow banning by social media and news outlets of dissenting climate opinions, COVID opinions, election fraud opinions, energy opinions, etc. A shockingly small number of "approved" official contributors speaking to various issues, then parroted repeatedly in the media echo-chamber, establishes what appears to be a broad Main Street cross-section of conforming consensus.

A relatively tiny group of obedient sycophants whose opinions echo redundantly across the news alert landscape appears to Main Street as a large cross section of the population. Using manipulated data, cherry picked information, and with dissent censored from prying eyes, consensus is proudly proclaimed. The only path to knowing better for the uninformed is exerting prodigious effort toward discerning facts; and who has time for that in the face of censorship, obscene taxation, compound interest payments, and daily commutes?

There are many citations covered in *World Without Cancer*, but one I found particularly notable was by controversial, Omar Garrison, critically discussing the late Harvard professor, Dr. Frederick Stare, jokingly referred to as the *Cornflakes Professor*. "Perhaps it is without significance that Dr. Stare is a board member

---

72 Quigley, *Anglo-American Establishment*.

of a large can company, and that his department at Harvard has been the recipient of substantial research grants from the food industry. For example, in 1960, the Harvard president announced what he called a "momentous" gift of $1,026,000 from General Foods Corporation, to be used over a ten-year period for expansion of the nutritional laboratories of the university's school of public health, where Dr. Stare is professor of nutrition. The seductive question is: Can any scientific research remain wholly objective and untainted by loyalty when it is so generously endowed by big corporations whose commercial future will be influenced by the outcome of such research"?[73]

Good question indeed. Another intriguing citation regards Joseph Goulden's, *The Money Givers*; a 1971 study showing how foundation control extends to the medical profession. "The medical profession does quiver excitedly when it hears the fast riffle of thousand-dollar bills. Since Ford [through the Ford Foundation] began nationwide operations in 1950, it has spent more than a third of a billion dollars on medical schools and hospitals...

Foundations are popular with the medical establishment because they do so much to preserve it. A well-endowed regional foundation – Kellogg in Michigan, Moody in Texas, Lilly in Indiana – can be as influential in hospital affairs as are the state medical associations, through grants for construction, operating expenses, and research.[74]

I reference these older citations pointing out avarice-driven, subversive foundation influence to emphasize that knowledge of self-serving abusive practices by foundation directors goes back decades, is not new; yet continues unabated, unhindered, and ignored by MSM. A second reason for referencing older citations is today's paucity of serious medical/pharma criticism despite **medical error** cited by a May 2016 Johns Hopkins Study as the **third leading cause of death** in the United States with more than 250,000 fatalities annually.[75] Due to variance in death record reporting, some studies attribute as many as 440,000 deaths annually to medical error. Approximately 12 million patients are misdiagnosed annually accompanied by an estimated $210 billion in additional costs due to medical billing errors. Why aren't liberals shrieking about banning pharmacies, doctors, clinics, and hospitals? Why does the cult of medicine refuse to address this growing life-safety issue; an issue which journalist, Jon Rappoport[76] has diligently exposed for decades?

Medical education curricula and treatment protocols are heavily influenced, if not controlled by supporting foundations, institutes, professional associ-

---

73 Griffin, *World Without Cancer; The Story of Vitamin B17*, 251, 252.
74 Griffin, 252.
75 "Study Suggests Medical Errors Now Third Leading Cause of Death in the U.S. - 05/03/2016," accessed March 24, 2019, https://www.hopkinsmedicine.org/news/media/releases/study_suggests_medical_errors_now_third_leading_cause_of_death_in_the_us.
76 "No More Fake News Jon Rappoport Investigative Reporter," accessed October 2, 2017, http://nomorefakenews.com/.

ations, and endowments furthering their founding family's global agendas and financial interests. It may not be pathological to prioritize earnings over helping people, just poor judgement; but causing illness through poor nutrition advocated by questionable food guide pyramids (since 2005, *MyPyramid*), biologically noxious GMO crops, toxic vaccines, heavy metal aerosol spraying, and development of intentionally ineffective medical school curricula and treatment protocols, is not only psychopathic, but socially deviant.

Main Street can reasonably accuse this malevolent medical cartel of profiteering by soft genocide. When do foundation and institute prerogatives intended to brain-wash medical school faculty and students begin undermining beneficial medical practice and become manslaughter... or worse? What happened to the Hippocratic Oath? How does **"do no harm"** justify slave-training face diapers reducing oxygenation below the safe minimum 19.5% OSHA Standard, leading to unhealthy buildup of CO_2 levels as well as concentrating bacterial and viral contaminants in a warm, humid environment? This nonsense allegedly warding off viruses ranging in size from 0.005 to 0.3 microns is like employing a chain link fence to avoid gnats. Psychopaths perpetrating this hoax must be investigated and held accountable for the harm they perpetuate as must the global syndicate controlled *Chinese Communist Party* for instigating it.

Medical school curricula, training regimens, and health insurance monopolies have traditionally constrained competent medical practice as best they could. The Trump Administration wounded the government protected health insurance monopoly by legalizing sale of health insurance policies across State lines. This simple regulatory change eliminated the intrastate health insurance monopolies to the benefit of patients, though corrupt legislators, and our Supreme Circus stopped the Trump Administration from offering citizens further protection from corrupt PPACA regulation. The criminal enactment of Obamacare is itself a justifiable racketeering case under the RICO Act.

Apparently, an unintended consequence (was it) of this one small Trump Administration action was the desperate reaction of the global syndicate. Syndicate order followers immediately and aggressively ramped up the false teaching of Scientism into the medical practice arena where it invaded medicine to the health detriment of all of us—even to the point of serial murder by hospital non-treatment protocols related to COVID terrorism. Fake environmental science, fake energy science, fake weapons science, and fake technological science were not enough to conveniently disable thought processes and adult behavior on Main Street.

Official Big Medicine and Big Pharma lies are nothing new but were typically limited to targeted groups as with polio, HIV/AIDS, cancer, etc. However, 2019-2021, delivered a new more malevolent ballgame. The monstrosity of GLOBAL FAKE MEDICINE has been uncaged. Thank you, World Health Organization (WHO), Centers for Disease Control and Prevention (CDC), Chinese Communist Party (CCP), CCP pawns, Big Pharma, Big Medicine, etc.

Planet Main Street must ask --- was the COVID SCAMDEMIC just asymmetric economic warfare by the depraved CCP against the Western world? Was the COVID SCAMDEMIC the global syndicate lever prying open the door for mass transhuman experimentation and *Transhuman Metaversal* control without knowledge or consent of Main Street citizens? Was it both? Asked and answered.

Clearly, it's both and Main Streets everywhere will, unfortunately, over the next few years realize what synthetic mRNA injection payloads, nanotechnology, eugenics, and psychotic control are about.

Gain of Function Research = Weaponized Bio-Warfare

Main Street Earth has been asymmetrically attacked on a global scale by the completely insane Chinese Communist Party Leadership and its treasonous sycophants in nations everywhere through bio-warfare, lawfare, and economic devastation. Note the CCP psychopaths are not decision makers, just indoctrinated global syndicate order followers. None-the-less, Chinese Communists and globalist enablers, such as the Beijing branch of the World Bank, World Health Organization, Big Pharma, Big Medicine, and treasonous citizens of nations around the world must be held accountable for CCP criminal behavior and crimes against humanity.

China and complicit multinationals must be held accountable to the entire world, not just for its devastating attack against Main Street health, but for the financial devastation as well. Never has world history witnessed a more barbaric global attack against innocent people. This Luciferian inspired evil must be paid for by tariffs on Chinese products, worldwide sanctions on Chinese business ventures, Chinese capital flows, and reparations made by the CCP. Hopefully, such reprisals, once strictly imposed, will result in Chinese people standing up to finally overthrow what is the single most evil regime built by the Anglo-American Establishment in world history. God help us save the Chinese people from the syndicate.

Many sources including CDC indicate SARS-CoV-2 has never been isolated from human tissue in a lab, but Dr. Li-Meng Yan, MD, PhD, a respected Chinese virologist, and whistle-blower who fled Hong Kong in fear for her life, arrived in the U.S. on April 28, 2020, bravely says she has the genome sequence.[77]

---

77 Li-Meng Yan et al., "Unusual Features of the SARS-CoV-2 Genome Suggesting Sophisticated Laboratory Modification Rather Than Natural Evolution and Delineation of Its Probable Synthetic Route," n.d., 26.

9 • Weaponized Biosphere and Medical Fraud

Given we know from open sources both NIH (NIAID) and DoD were working with and/or funding the Chinese Wuhan lab to develop bioweapons, in this case relative to engineered corona viruses, the American people MUST acknowledge the possibility of treason. This treason has attacked societies across the globe, suggesting at the very least, negligent mass homicide must be investigated. When investigations warrant, indictments and criminal prosecutions by responsible law enforcement MUST follow in 1947 Nuremberg Code fashion.

It appears as of this writing, orchestration of COVID related negligent mass homicide will not only be found treasonous, but rogue elements in several U.S. Federal Agencies and several multinational monopolies in Big Pharma and Big Medicine along with legacy media are complicitly involved. Realizing BIG PHARMA, BIG MEDICINE, LEGACY MEDIA and our corrupt U.S. FEDERAL GOVERNMENT are all involved – and are all uniformly owned by and operated by global syndicate assets; we also have a criminal RICO case here on top of a massive world-wide mass action civil suit – but it gets worse.

If readers find it difficult to believe D.C. is complicit in murdering thousands of American citizens - check out the Obama Administration's *Ensuring Patient Access and Effective Drug Enforcement Act of 2016* which hamstrung law enforcement and legal efforts to reduce or even monitor opioid trafficking by Big Pharma in the U.S. Of more than 70,000 annual drug related deaths in the U.S., more than 33,000 annually are opioid related. Outside alternative media circles, distraught family members, and concerned citizens this insane Big Pharma death toll is profitably ignored. On top of this pile of corruption is the open Biden Regime Southern U.S. border across which millions of kill doses of the synthetic CCP opioid, *Fentanyl* are imported. How is this possible?

It's possible for many reasons, but one major reason is global syndicate driven *Chinese Communist Party* influence on American politicians, institutions, and of course, legacy media. *Fentanyl*, for example, a synthetic opioid said to be 50-100 times more potent than morphine is primarily manufactured in Wuhan, China.[78] Newer related forms like *Carfentanil*, said to be 100 times more potent than *Fentanyl*, i.e., 10,000 times more potent than morphine is rarely known by users that they are ingesting it. Washington D.C. parasites bend over backward ensuring law enforcement doesn't block these lethal designer drugs from availability on Main Street. The U.S. government is murdering its own citizens.

How much longer are we going to put up with corrupt, treasonous behavior of rogue government officials and NGO experts whose corruption we passive-

---

78 "China, Mexican Cartels; the Opioid War against America; Is No One Paying Attention? « Jon Rappoport's Blog," accessed August 20, 2021, https://blog.nomorefakenews.com/2021/08/20/china-Mexican-cartels-opioid-war-against-America/.

ly accept and compliantly pay for? These psychopathic bullies are obliterating the future for hundreds of thousands of young people across the globe. Career criminals called politicians, law enforcement officials, scientists, doctors, and administrators are perpetrating vicious crimes against humanity with arrogant impunity on our watch. This MUST cease and only Main Street citizens can or will stop it. We MUST step up, fill the gap, hold the line, and carry our countries back into a more abundant world where love, generosity, decency, and honor thrive and prosper. This is our time and this task is ours to complete.

The U.S. Constitution does not authorize Federal Government intrusion into operational aspects of agriculture, business, education, health, medicine, science, or other areas it arrogantly and corruptly butts into. Human sovereignty and State's Rights supersede Federal authority, precluding Executive, Legislative, and Judicial Branches of government from dictating a subjective interpretation of so-called civil rights. As U.S. Senator Barry Goldwater wrote regarding Supreme Court overreach in Chapter Four of his 1960 *The Conscience of a Conservative:* **"If we condone the practice of substituting our own intentions for those of the Constitution's framers, we reject, in effect, the principle of Constitutional Government: we endorse a rule of men, not of laws."**

The 10th Amendment clearly states; *"The powers not delegated to the United States by the Constitution, nor prohibited by it to the States, are reserved to the States respectively, or to the people."*

The U.S. government derives its authority from the consent of sovereign citizens, who are granted **unalienable authority** directly from their transcendent Creator. Our constitutionally malfeasant law enforcement officials and U.S. courts will either learn to respect and fear we the sovereign people of Main Street MORE than they fear ignorant study group mentors, blackmailers, and handlers, thereby respecting the Constitutionally constrained Rule of Law – OR – they will face the wrath of hard working, decent Main Street citizens who may ignore being legally marginalized, cheated, and robbed – BUT WILL NEVER ignore being poisoned, murdered, and sterilized by BIG PHARMA and its government co-conspirators.

AMERICA FIRST ♥ JOIN OR DIE!!!

THEN WE TAKE BACK OUR WORLD!!!

10 • Weaponized Atmosphere and Finance

Remedy: Earth's atmosphere is being ionized without Main Street knowledge or consent into an electromagnetically conductive plasma, i.e., a transceiving antenna capable of interfacing with other weaponized technologies like toxic JAB ingredients for the purpose of full spectrum dominance. This is being done without public transparency primarily under the guise of reducing global warming, a bold lie. This potentially omnicidal activity must be stopped and publicly peer reviewed with some level of scientific objectivity and sanity.

Weaponized weather, climate manipulation, and the *Space Fence* are critical aspects of emerging electromagnetic mind control technologies, likely enabling genocide of the *unwashed* as well. Before touching on this realm consider a couple of less technical, more visible examples of mind-behavior manipulation. I speculatively raise these seemingly unrelated situations because it's not clear how funding is obtained for development of *full spectrum dominance* and these examples may in part suggest hidden sources of finance.

If the current direction of medical bioweaponry, nano-technology, ionizing Earth's atmosphere, modified HAARP technology, IoT, 5G, and the *Space Fence* are components of *full spectrum dominance* weaponized against Main Street people for establishment of global transhuman serfdom, then clearly funding must be covert, or pitch forks will find their way into Main Street's calloused hands. This poses a global syndicate dilemma as their insane transhuman agenda requires trillions of dark investment dollars. Where can this mountain of hidden money come from without raising Main Street taxes

directly, and without inciting rebellion, since Main Street does not joyful-
ly embrace slavery, and certainly does not beg inclusion on the omnicide list?

**How are trillions of dollars raised by a group of psychopaths for enslav-
ing Main Street and genociding the <u>unwashed excess population</u> without
Main Street catching on?** The easy peasy way is just steal it, which is why more
than $54 trillion dollars vanished out the back doors of the corrupt U.S. Con-
gress without raising an eyebrow since 1998. ±$21 trillion or so unaccounted
for per public DoD and HUD Inspector General Reports between 1998 and
2015, ±$6 trillion through Congressional "stimulus", and ±$27 trillion unaudited
Federal Reserve digital printing distributed internationally. This theft occurred
prior to the fraudulent CCP Biden Regime tearing down the back doors of Congress entirely to the tune of we don't know at this time, how many more trillions disappearing in global syndicate coffers. Not sure why any Americans
call this self-governance? For now, we'll skip more covertly indirect revenue
sources like child sex trafficking, adult sex trafficking, human trafficking, drug
trafficking, and weapons trafficking. What follows will seem a detour but is not.

In humanity's defense we need to look at how Earth's Satanic omnicide is being funded – because government sanctioned fraud converts Main Street wealth
creation and productivity into global syndicate weapons used against us. **A
rather odd beginning and I suppose minor harvesting example** of profitable mind/behavior control not viewed as such is the prescient expansion
and remodeling of airline terminals into profitable retail shopping malls prior
to 9/11 - - with few noticing. Why would any investor imagine prior to the
morning of 9/11/2001, hordes of marks parading through airport parking has-
sles and shoeless inconvenience to shop at outrageous airline terminal prices?

Ms. Catherine Austin Fitts (*Solari Report*) suggests the insider money guys and
gals were apparently aware beforehand, that soon, airline passengers would be
held up in airports for hours on end, trapped as the captive pedestrian audience
of unconstitutional TSA pawns Main Street has been since the unconstitutional
Patriot Act was treasonously (my word) passed in 2001. The global syndicate
never misses a money-making beat, particularly when Main Street harvesting opportunities can be spectacularly created at Main Street's expense... and isn't it
exciting to count your moolah while laughing at millions of indoctrinated airport
sheep limping shoeless through your profitably installed electronic monitors?

Insiders understood the profiteering potential and conjugal bliss of Madison
Avenue retail marketing coupled with a National Security Narrative powerfully

magnifying the ridiculous passenger safety PsyOp. Passengers are now trapped shoeless sheep available for profitable fleecing as the richest retail traffic is foot-traffic and airports guarantee captive, bored, shoeless feet numbering in the millions per day, many of them armed with expense accounts, holiday money, or vacation funds. It's a rich harvest for airport retailers with perceived security and safety masquerading as necessity, accompanied by radiation dosing, DNA splitting, low level x-ray and millimeter microwave (*mmw*) imaging machines and unionized *Transportation Security Administration* (TSA) personnel, all together comprising a sweet government mandated money laundering center. Pure fraud. Add to this the magic of slave training paid for by the slaves themselves.

Airline shopping malls are one of the more lucrative brick and mortar retail sectors still experiencing profit margins and even growth as of this writing though the COVID bioweapon attack, face muzzles, and toxic JABs slowed the extorted traffic down some. Who but insiders working for psychopaths would've dreamed this up? As usual, Mockingbird MSM and mind control magik ensure no dots are connected on Main Street. Now that we're shoeless, we're safe... aren't we? Admittedly a minor example of pathology and human harvesting, but there it is.

A second related harvesting example covered up by corrupt media conditioning is the wildly profitable massive *short selling* of airline stocks immediately prior to 9/11 by *speculators in-the-know*. The 9/11 Report disregarded knowledge these insiders had, though such knowledge obviously wasn't provided by 15 Saudi Jihadists or their 4 associates from United Arab Emirates, Egypt, and Lebanon. The 9/11 Report constitutes a form of mind-control itself via prodigious lies by omission and embarrassing skirting of nuclear, other high-tech, thermite, and/or directed high energy physics involved on 9/11. Burning jet fuel, office equipment, furnishings, and supplies do not melt structural steel. Eccentrically loaded structural damage does not result in symmetric collapse nor does upper floor damage result in lower undamaged floor collapse at near free fall velocity. Gravity does operate on Tuesday mornings in Manhattan.

Main Street investors were again aggressively fleeced, while insiders enjoyed full government protection. The cherry on top was scape-goading an invisible terror faction and profitably attacking thousands of illiterate goat herders in the mountains of Afghanistan, brutally murdered in the name of justice, freedom, and democracy; all incidentally enabling profitable expansion of the *Golden Crescent* opium fields previously shut down by the Taliban... and no, I'm not defending Islam, a despicable ideology masquerading as religion, but Afghan goat farmers do have a right to live; and Main Street has a right to know what their Federal government through rogue elements in the CIA and military are funding with billions of laundered narco-dollars.[79]

For those not aware, we must detour, looking at the global syndicate's primary funding source for nearly five centuries – OPIUM. The Vietnamese War was fought over the *Golden Triangle's* opium production among other things, but we'll skip past that history for now to the mountains of Afghanistan. Afghanistan is a major production player within the Iran-Afghanistan-Pakistan narcotics troika and is fully protected by the Anglo-American global syndicate with opium poppy cultivation growing at times to more than 175,000 hectares since the production low of 6,500 hectares in 2001.

In a May 6, 2021, *TomDISPATCH* article, University of Wisconsin, Harrington Professor of History, Dr. Alfred W. McCoy offers a bit of *Golden Crescent* history as a follow-up to his 2003 book, *The Politics of Heroin* cited earlier. During the 1980's more or less secret CIA war in Afghanistan with the *mujahideen* against Russia, the opium harvest soared from a meager 100 metric tons annually to 2,000 tons. By 1984 the Afghan-Pakistani borderlands supplied 60% of the U.S. narcotics market and 80% of Europe's market. In 1988, between 100 and 200 heroin refineries were operating in Pakistan's Khyber Pass area under the purview of Pakistan's colluding *Inter-Service Intelligence* (ISI).

Professor McCoy goes on to explain, the Taliban, after taking power in 1996 doubled the processed Afghan opium output to 4,600 tons annually. Then, seeking international recognition of their new status, the Taliban suddenly reversed position, decimating opium production by year 2000 to just 185 tons, driving millions of Afghan farmers into financial misery. In my own opinion, adding to Professor McCoy's research, Afghan opium cultivation reduction also irritated the British Crown and America's Anglo-American Elites, all of whom are financially dependent on narcotics revenue for covert funding of NWO decimation, transhuman subjugation, and Main Street serfdom.

Treasonous (my opinion) George W. Bush Administration officials, obedient to global syndicate demands expediently resolved the global syndicate's opium related financial woes by attacking Afghanistan in 2001. The U.S. military coalition along with the Northern Alliance drove the Taliban out of Afghanistan control in about 90 or so days, (some say eight days) so why did we set up permanent CIA-military housekeeping? Asked and answered. By 2003, housekeeping ensured opium production was back up to a more acceptable 3,600 metric tons—soaring to a massive 8,200 tons in 2007 – 93% of the world's illicit her-

79 Alfred W. McCoy, *The Politics of Heroin: CIA Complicity in the Global Drug Trade*, Revised edition (Chicago: Lawrence Hill Books, 2003).

oin. As we might incorrectly imagine, this impressive increase in per-hectare crop yield was easily accomplished by illiterate Afghan farmers with absolutely no aid from Western agronomists and horticulturalists... or could I be mistaken?

During that same period, do we recall an episode of Fox News' documentary series, *War Stories* hosted by former Marine officer, Oliver North, standing in front of a tiny burning poppy field, gallantly informing America how our military, CIA, and dedicated DEA were supposedly burning Afghan opium poppy fields into oblivion? That would be Ollie of Iran-Contra and REX 84 Bravo fame. Talk about lying chutzpa! Or maybe it was just the *"win hearts and minds"* doctrine that stopped the poppy flower burning? I'm just asking – readers will decide.

Note: U.S. military and intelligence services covertly ran nearly two dozen, I believe, necessary covert actions against reprehensible Soviet and Chinese Communists. *Iran-Contra* was just one of these. I'm an ignorant non-military citizen but I read *The Art of War* and a few other things over the years. In a Satanically dangerous world with most nations and all communist nations run by serial murdering psychopaths, spying and other covert activities are part of expedient self-defense. Only academics, fools, slaves, and slaughtered dead people think otherwise. That said, flooding American and world Main Streets with narcotics, crack cocaine, fentanyl, and other poisonous garbage is not an acceptable manner of funding defense. Financing war with drugs poisoning our own citizens, particularly our young as collateral damage is a weak, unsustainable strategy feeding into the Satanic destruction we fight.

Fast forward a decade later and we saw the globalist Obama Administration holding course in 2017 at a steady 9,000 metric tons of protected Afghan opium production. Again, per Dr. McCoy, this provided an estimated 60% of Taliban funding for their relentless advance, apparently (my facetious opinion) a critical tactic intended to give the West an advantage in their so-called *War on Terror*.

Along the way, let's not neglect the Carter, Reagan, George H. W. Bush, Clinton, George W. Bush, Obama Administration, and later fraudulent Biden Regime efforts to traffic cocaine into America's cities, not by the kilo, but by the ton. Harvard and Yale MBA grads apparently wonder, "how can any sensible young person build a future without plentiful access to affordable crack cocaine, not to mention maintaining a reasonable international balance of trade parity?" Of course, the more organized Obama Administration switched to improved economics of the Chinese Communist Party's drug of choice, **fentanyl** – a synthetic opioid 80 to 100 times more powerful than morphine.

If this is how the U.S. government wages farcical *Wars on Drugs and Terror*, clearly the U.S. government is out-of-managerial-control. **Data suggests the rogue U.S. Federal government is Public Enemy Number One.** Is this the mercantilist *British East India Company* dynasty brought back to life by the British Crown in conjunction with the Eastern Establishment of its long-lost American colony?[80] The Global Syndicate cash flow problem bloody solved and few Americans or Brits the wiser. Nothing to see here dutifully parroted Carter, Reagan, Bush I, Clinton, Bush II, Obama, and Biden.

On a brighter note, President Donald J. Trump, in 2017, did stand up against all odds, insisting U.S. and world Main Street citizens be protected from the decades old, CIA sanctioned drug tsunami and violent aftermath – to which all Marxist D's and Establishment R's responded in horror, reaching for their soon to be lighter *Bottega Veneta* wallets and *Lana Marks* bags. *"How can this be happening"* they squawked in hive-mind Pawns of Privilege unison? *"Close the U.S. southern border?"*, they shrieked. *"Oh, the horror of it!"* *"What will become of our 75,000 or so foreign child-sex trafficking orphans every year, they cried? We can't just rape and sacrifice North American children – that's not equity."* As Obama said, *"spread the wealth around."*

Despite global syndicate panic attacks, Afghan opium production declined nearly 42% during Trump's first two years in office, from 329,000 hectares (9,140 metric tons) in 2017 to 221,000 hectares (5,330 metric tons) in 2018. This while working with an international group of concerned countries to take down dozens of pedophile rings, rescuing hundreds of children and adult sex trafficking victims. MSM found none of this notable. I don't have 2020 opium production data, but Afghan opium poppy cultivation decreased to 160,000 hectares in 2019, while production increased to 6,700 metric tons. Credit must be due to the global syndicate fighting back through better agronomy, I suppose.

A third harvesting example coupled with propagandized mind control is the *Patient Protection and Affordable Care Act* (PPACA, aka *Obamacare*), which helped drive Wall Street to new highs at an average gain of 12% annually on the back of predictably doubling and tripling health insurance premiums, reducing coverage risk for insurers (rationing & higher prices), expanding government subsidies paid with unconstitutionally confiscated tax dollars and borrowed dollars along with planned increased profitability of pharmaceutical and medical equities. All this fraud money's going somewhere—but where? Is this a RICO case or what?

Endless trillions of *quantitative easing* digital dollars belched out of Federal Reserve keyboard entries sweetened the insider Wall Street pot, but it couldn't

80 Konstandinos Kalimtgis, U. S. Labor Party Investigating Team, and David Goldman, *Dope, Inc.: Britain's Opium War Against The U.S.*, 1st edition (New York: New Benjamin Franklin House Pub. Co, 1978).

be done without corrupt top tier D.C. complicity. The stage must be lavishly set for successful suspension of lemming disbelief. When exactly will Slick Willy, W., Barry Soetoro, and Biden be matriculating to their newly remodeled, gated community on picturesque Guantanamo Bay, hosted by America's oldest overseas naval base? Soon, hopefully, but I prejudicially digress.

High tech mind-control research has been ongoing with increasing sophistication for more than 75 years; has been consistently and generously funded by sociopathic Elite families, their powerful foundations, and organized crime. Funding is nearly 100% covert, unmonitored, and is now so far off the sanity rails it's threatening every human being and life form on planet earth.

Serious Black Budgeting related to sociopathic technology began post WW II; became more aggressive following the assassination of John F. Kennedy in 1963 and ramped up since the 1980's *Star Wars* program. Funding today is primarily through Hidden Budgets having zero Congressional oversight... or any other adult oversight for that matter. Can we say *Exchange Stabilization Fund* (ESF)?

The *Strategic Defense Initiative* (SDI), referred to as *Star Wars*, was initiated March 23, 1983 by the Reagan Administration, growing out of 1957's *Navy Space Surveillance System* (NAVSPASUR). This program was passed on to the U.S. Air Force October 1, 2004 under command of the 20th Space Control Squadron and was renamed the *AN/FPS-133 Air Force Space Surveillance System* (SSS / the VHF Fence), now a key component of the *Space Surveillance Network* (SSN).[81] Israel's *Iron Dome* defense system is just one visible aspect of this technology.

Space Fence technology was stimulated and made possible by patents initially filed by Mr. Bernard Eastlund in 1987 for his *High Frequency Active Auroral Research Program* (HAARP); such HAARP technology having since been extensively modified, ostensibly for more accurate targeting, power, and control. This highly invasive technology has been developing and metastasizing with near 100% public NON-TRANSPARENCY to the point California Congressional Representative Duncan Hunter, a former member of the *Armed Services Committee* began questioning the extent to which the Army was misleading Congress regarding implementation of their controversial *battlefield anthropology program* known as the *Human Terrain System* (HTS).[82]

81 "Under an Ionized Sky: From Chemtrails to Space Fence Lockdown: Elana Freeland: 9781627310536: Amazon.Com: Books," 202, 203.
82 "Under an Ionized Sky: From Chemtrails to Space Fence Lockdown: Elana Freeland: 9781627310536: Amazon.Com: Books," 197, 198.

As a side note, ignoring guilt or innocence, realizing Congress is a full time money laundering pit, I wonder if California Congressman, Duncan Hunter's August 2018 Federal indictment for allegedly misusing campaign funds is punishment for the courageous questions he asked, not to mention his efforts to obtain passage in 2006 of *The Secure Fence Act?* Time will tell, but it appears U.S. Deep State Comrades detest Duncan Hunter, suggesting retaliation and character assassination were prominently on the option table.

We can recall Main Street confusion and 2015 public fuss about *Jade Helm* exercises simulating *network-centric operations* (NCO's) interacting with the global information grid (GIG) – none of which Main Street understood, had been, or is informed about? These exercises involved operative testing of among other things, "neural or smart dust, nano-spheres, carbon nanotube transistors and integrated circuits, electrochemical energy-storage nanos with anode-cathode nanowires inside polymer core shell separators, etc. All are nanotechnology telemetric sensors released into our environment for us to wear, breathe, and ingest, each sensor programmed to gather data that is then remotely accessed, transmitted, and stored by AIs".[83]

Congressman Hunter was upset to learn the *Human Terrain System* (HTS) experimentation had not been terminated in 2014 as the Army represented to Congress, but was in fact ongoing and covertly progressing, though predictably, while laughing at their oath of office, our bought and paid for Congress did and does nothing about it. The lone, unsupported Congressional person or sometimes two or three, basically talking to themselves with zero legislative support is syndicate approved futility effectively employed to beef up Main Street's illusion of choice, while providing endless though convincing Congressional photo-op-pandering opportunities aiding re-election. Talk, talk, talk but nothing usefully beneficial happens for Main Street; guaranteed by our Federal Ruling Class Pawns of Privilege. If the carrot don't work; show 'em that stick. If that stick don't work; just blackmail 'em into oblivion, apparently an easy task.

Weapons research just mentioned is conducted "live", employing Main Street populations as Guinea Pigs with zero notification, knowledge, or consent. Covert military weapons testing on Main Street populations in real time is nothing new, but we've never been subjected to anything this potentially harmful, this invasively invisible, nor this poorly understood by its compulsively destructive developers. Our tax dollars at work sans adult supervision. Microwave 4G, 5G, and soon, 6G are provably harmful to biological entities – BUT – Main Street is not allowed to know this.[84]

---

83 "Under an Ionized Sky: From Chemtrails to Space Fence Lockdown: Elana Freeland: 9781627310536: Amazon.Com: Books," 195.
84 K Sri Nageswari, "Biological Effects of Microwaves and Mobile Telephony," 2003, 11.

10 • Weaponized Atmosphere and Finance

5G Wi-Fi systems employ microwave signals 150 times the strength of 4G signals. Microwaves are known to harm biological organisms but despite the abysmal lack of transparent testing, our thoroughly and corruptly captured *Federal Communications Commission* (FCC) says nothing to worry about here folks.[85] The FCC in fact, has made it illegal for cities and counties to stop global syndicate telecom monopolies from installing wireless 5G antennas and equipment. Another example of self-governance.

If you're curious, check out what went on with the 5G dispute among San Francisco Firefighters some time back. Firefighters have been raising concerns about health effects resulting from wireless technology since 2004. Here's a link to a related article on the *Light on Conspiracies* website. Firefighters concerned about exposure to cell towers

On a daily 365/24/7 basis it appears the 50th *Space Wing of Air Force Space Command* (AFSPC) stationed at *Peterson Air Force Base* in Colorado Springs "may be the military hub of artificial telepathy operations: "It's the 'mission control' center where rocket scientists, AFRL, HAARP, spy satellites, radar dishes, microwave towers, beam weapons, human experimentation and spooky intelligence agencies like NSA, NRO and DIA all come together".[86]

As mentioned earlier, we'll not delve into the innumerable details of **full spectrum dominance** through militarized weather weaponization (climate change), atmospheric ionization, IoT, 5G, 6G, the *Space Fence* nor the transhumanist control implications of aether, plasma, scalar waves, and nanotechnologies. If interested I recommend delving into Ms. Elana Freeland's heavily documented trilogy on these subjects, particularly her book entitled *Under an Ionized Sky*, from which I quote liberally here.[87] Another solid informational source dealing primarily with biological aspects of atmospheric weaponization technology is Mr. Clifford Carnicom's *Carnicom Institute*.[88] Mr. Carnicom, largely at his own expense deals extensively with nano-infestations thought to cause infections like *Morgellons Disease* or other infections, which *Mockingbird* media drones avoid. **Note** that *Morgellons Disease* origins are a controversial matter under dispute.

85 Strange Sounds, "20,000 5G Satellites to Be Launched Sending DANGEROUS BEAMS of Intense Microwave Radiation ACROSS THE WORLD - Strange Sounds," *STRANGE SOUNDS - AMAZING, WEIRD AND ODD PHENOMENA* (blog), January 31, 2019, http://strangesounds. org/2019/01/5g-satellites-space-problem.html.
86 "Under an Ionized Sky: From Chemtrails to Space Fence Lockdown: Elana Freeland: 9781627310536: Amazon.Com: Books," 205
87 "Elana Freeland," Home, accessed May 25, 2018, https://www.elanafreeland.com.
88 "Carnicom Institute," accessed May 25, 2018, https://www.carnicominstitute.org/.

I raise the issue of atmospheric weaponization of Earth's biosphere and surrounding space as part of mind control because first of all, beyond blowing stuff up and burning things down, it has become the preeminent military mind control pathway for executing *full spectrum dominance* via C4 (command, control, communications, and computers) and secondly, because in my humble engineering opinion, **C4 technologies now threaten all life on Earth**. To suggest rogue Silicon Valley technocrats and military science are completely off the sanity rails lost in a pathological morass is a severe understatement. Military science, arm-in-arm with Silicon Valley self-deception have leapt the chasm edge of darkness, launching all of us into the full-blown Luciferian abyss.

We are now paying for and living with thousands of well-funded, narrow-minded, mentally and emotionally unbalanced, Kahn-Telleresque psychopaths working in secret facilities, funded by hidden budgets, developing secret bio-chemical-nano-energy weapons, without adult oversight on behalf the genocidal control agenda of NWO Elites. This cannot have a happy ending. Allowing this invisible global syndicate destructothon to continue is beyond irresponsible stewardship of our habitable environment to the point of self-genocide by demented order-followers who couldn't identify common sense if they tripped over it. Main Street needs to take a vigilant look at this research and development. *Join or die*! How curious, our sacrosanct EPA and environmental NGO's offer no comment on any of this? Busy sniffing cow farts, I guess.

Aside from 5G microwaves attacking every molecule on earth 365/24/7 with unknown long-term effects, dedicated MSM global warming enthusiasts make zero mention of the thousands of additional rocket launches required to install, maintain, and replace new weaponized communications satellites having an average life expectancy of just five years. 2019 planning suggests *SpaceX* will be licensed for 12,000 satellites; *OneWeb* for 4,560 satellites; *Boeing* for 2,956 satellites; and *Spire Global* for 972 satellites. "To put this into perspective, as of September 2017 there were 1,738 operating satellites in orbit around Earth. **This means the number of satellites will soon be 11 times greater than the current number.**"[89] Fascinating CO_2 footprint there for academia, environmentalists, and MSM to avoid mentioning. Let's save the world with subsidized electric vehicles while we poison it with subsidized rocket fuel emissions.

In other words, along with EMR, vastly increased emissions from solid rocket fuel, liquid kerosene fuel, and newly developing mercury-based rocket fuels are blanketing earth's atmosphere with massive quantities of ozone-layer-damaging solid rocket fuel emissions, kerosene based black carbon soot, and neurotoxic mercury

---

89 Sounds, "20,000 5G Satellites to Be Launched Sending DANGEROUS BEAMS of Intense Microwave Radiation ACROSS THE WORLD - Strange Sounds."

fuel emissions. This from the same *prominent global citizen*s operating the climate change, carbon tax scam. Imagine one of these neurotoxic, Mercury fueled rockets exploding in Earth's atmosphere. John Ronald Reuel Tolkien himself couldn't invent this to reside in the dark realm of **Mordor**, Middle-Earth's Land of Shadow.

Poorly understood direct energy weapon development supposedly for better protection of citizens has narrow-mindedly and shortsightedly devolved into a strong probable outcome of self-destructive genocide for those same citizens. Military Science since WW II has been and is diving blindly and recklessly into violation of their sacred oath and duty. Ignorant self-annihilation and protection of citizens are two very different things. Just because we CAN DO SOMETHING doesn't mean it's a good idea TO DO IT. Common sense applies, and military science misplaced theirs. Recall the sudden white flags and unexplainable surrender in 2003 of the Iraqi *Republican Guard*? Did mind control weapons cause confusion, reducing trained Iraqi soldiers to a mass mental condition of childhood terror and anxiety? Is this technology now being used on Main Streets across the globe? If so, where does it stop? Who stops it?

We should remind ourselves, persons joining our U.S. military have one thing in common regardless of military branch; they must swear-in by taking the **enlisted or officer Oath**. The *Oath of Enlistment* is something every service member must promise and adhere to for his or her entire military career. I'm guessing for most military personnel, before raising their right hand, they understand what they are swearing or attesting to. The oath of enlistment should not be taken lightly as it is binding for the next 4 to 6 years of service at a minimum, with most insisting, for life. There are reasons for taking oaths and I suspect anyone with an IQ above seventy or so comprehends those reasons.

Many military scientists have unfortunately lost sight of their oath's meaning and purpose. Military science and transhumanist order followers are attempting to implant heavy metals, nano-sensors, nano-chips, nano-transmitters, nano-receivers, and other C4 compatible nanocomputing technology into every life form on earth WITH NO IDEA the long-term or even short-term consequence. This invasive transhumanist control technology is being implemented covertly, blindly, without adequate information or study and makes a mockery of human responsibility. We may not understand how dangerous these technologies are to life forms – but we do know they are harmful. Further transparent study is a MUST DO item before allowing cyber lunatics to transport Main Street into the METAVERSE ABYSS.

Some researchers estimate as many as 1.5 million targeted citizens are undergoing periodic electro-magnetic response testing as I write this. I can't verify this activity as I don't attend the meetings but my ignorance doesn't suggest it isn't happening. Recklessly imposing such dark invasive technology on American citizens covertly is in direct violation of the 4th Amendment and military oath, not to mention human decency or potential omniciding of Earth's entire biosphere.

For info on high-tech aspects and dangers of mind control and weaponization of Earth's biosphere I again suggest Mr. Cliff Carnicom's, *Carnicom Institute* and Ms. Freeland's work as two starting points. A third source of geoengineering info by the way is Mr. Dane Wigington's website, https://www.geoengineeringwatch.org/. From here on in, we'll tackle some less high-tech, though none-the-less dangerous forms of mind-control.

Note: Every human born is created to serve fellow humans and nurture our Earth. We are created to help each other learn to receive and share our Creator's love. That's it. No human ever born was created to subjugate fellow human beings nor harm our world in any way. Popes, queens, kings, princes, princesses, and all other leaders from family heads and tribal chiefs to Presidents and Prime Ministers, Governors, and Mayors are honor bound to morally serve their people – just as we the people are honor bound to serve each other. The concept of abusive, non-recourse obedience to an unaccountable Supreme Ruler - ruling by bloodline, appointment, or election is malevolently Satanic.

We can do better.

Obedience is the mechanism
by which evil influence prevails.

11 • Mind Control & Neuro Rights

Remedy: The time for Neuro Rights has arrived. Companies are offering protection against weaponized "thought invasive" technologies already a half century or more in development. Main Street MUST demand transparency and accountability regarding research and development of machine read/write capability intersecting and interacting with our brain and nervous system function. It is imperative Main Street learns to defend itself against psychopathic Metaverse attacks on perception, free thought, and free behavior.

Mind control takes many surprising forms attacking liberty and independent thought from sometimes obscure modalities. Music and art, for instance are discussed at historic length from an unusual perspective by Joseph P. Farrell in *Microcosm and Medium*.[90] Our creative arts are powerful influencers of thought and emotion, but do we view art as mind control? We hear the phrase *culture precedes politics*, but rarely hear *art precedes culture*. Satanically influenced totalitarian dictators, and their order followers understand these concepts, all euphemistically covered in **U.N. Agendas 21/30/50**, but Main Street pays scant attention.

If you're not familiar with historic mind control research, don't be surprised as it isn't advertised, nor taught on Main Street university campuses. Concern is warranted as these evil technologies, disguised as beneficial medical or military research to the extent they're noticed, trample on our unalienable COGNITIVE LIBERTY. Indoctrinated drones of **Scientism** believe the U.S. Constitution may protect free speech, but certainly does not protect free thought. Technical delusion

---

90 "Microcosm and Medium," accessed May 6, 2021, https://www.lulu.com/en/us/shop/
Joseph-P-Farrell

of this sort supported or ignored by order-following D.C. politicians in support of cyber pathology ushers in subjugating processes like psychosurgery, organism activation, nervous system manipulation, psychoactive pharmaceuticals, and every entrainment form of electro-magnetic brain manipulation we can imagine.

This ongoing covert research is out-of-control, conducted by psychopaths and social deviants without transparency – all at the behest of *prominent global citizens*, most of whom incidentally believe in both slavery and genocide as aspects of acceptable business planning and *unwashed deplorable* management. The Rhodes-Milner Group for example, openly defended violence as a necessary means of *buying time* while *unwashed little people* in resource raped 3rd World nations deemed incapable by Round Table members of self-governance learned the *Imperial Way*.

At this 21st century juncture, in Round Table propagandized fashion, malfeasance of our corrupted U.S. Congress continues on an egregiously treasonous basis. We have 535 (435 + 100 = 535) Members of Congress lining up as dangerous pawns of global syndicate privilege. How many of these 535 miscreants are profitably invested in freedom devouring technologies, some of which are wholly owned by or controlled by the CCP? Maybe at most, a half dozen or so bicameral Congressional Members are legitimately honorable Main Street representatives, suggesting in self-defense, voters should **never re-elect incumbents**, thereby therapeutically initiating at least one corruption cure, i.e., <u>automatic term limits</u>. All Federal agencies are now corruptly off the rails with most belligerently beyond any possibility of repair. Globalist totalitarian (study group) indoctrination runs layers deep through every Federal agency. The U.S. Federal government MUST be downsized by at least 75% or the United States, now in Globalist driven Marxist-Fascist decline, will stumble on as a degenerately impoverished feudal state.

As Ms. Catherine Austin Fitts stated many times, **"if your mind is not your own, it's game over"**. I'll add that overtly or covertly preventing a person from thinking at all or messing with a person's ability to think; manipulating what they think; how they think; what they like, don't like, will do, will not do, etc., is theft of a person's thought process, which confiscates that person's freedom and ability to live autonomously. This is a direct violation of the 7th Commandment "not to steal" and is pure evil. Such brain manipulation is also in violation of the 4th Amendment (my opinion). Theft of thought cannot be tolerated by any sane, responsible society, yet many Main Street Americans embrace United Nation Agenda 21 concepts like **"values clarification"** whereby traditionally fact-based, subject-matter education is discarded in favor of **indoctrinating children with critical thought values**. For example, **value clarification** conditions young people with the Luciferian, morally relativistic idea there is no absolute right or wrong.

Both **UNESCO** and **UN Agenda 21/30** promote misusing education as an indoctrination tool for authoritarian GLOBAL COMPLIANCE through internationally binding agreements. Undermining parental authority and responsibility through State sanctioned propaganda and regulatory overreach is serious stuff comprising administrative slavery and child abuse. If mind control research and practice are or can ever be beneficial as opposed to undermining societal stability, then they can be transparently discussed, funded, conducted, and scrutinized in a verifiable manner? The fact mind control research is done in secret tells us it is unacceptably subversive regarding human rights, i.e., civil rights. The only mind control signature visible to Main Street is propaganda of various sorts, appearing in most cases as harmless difference of opinion—when in fact the brainwashing and illusion of choice run much deeper—particularly when enhanced by invisible entrainment technologies.

For the curious, I recommend visiting Aaron and Melissa (Melton) Dykes' website, *TRUTHSTREAM MEDIA*. *TruthStream Media* delves into mind control methodologies making it a good resource for this and related subjects. They provide historic perspective on how and why mind-control research is conducted in such a dangerously non-transparent manner. There's no point in delving into it here, other than bringing it to your attention as a threat to freedom requiring our awareness and resistance. Mind control inhibits spiritual growth and well-being.

It is criminally shocking what's being done to us through satellites, our cell phones, computers, and TV's – not *going to be done* mind you, BUT what is *already being done* on an everyday basis to Main Street citizens without our knowledge or consent. A psychopathic, global cyborg enslavement system is being constructed, requiring no walls and no barbed wire, reliant only on anti-human, transhumanist AI surveillance and electromagnetic behavioral control systems.

Main Street for example, must demand transparent accountability for everything the *National Quantum Initiative* is doing. The *National Quantum Initiative Act* was signed into law on December 21, 2018. As usual, it is proclaimed for the public good, BUT we can reliably predict psychopathic global syndicate order followers weaponizing every aspect of quantum nanotechnology they can for global syndicate control of Main Street citizens they view as problematic *livestock*. The marriage of government with transnational monopoly business has a long track record of abuse and harvesting of Main Street productivity.

Sean Stone reminds us of William Yandell Elliot (1896-1979) writing in 1940's *The City of Man* while discussing elements of Moscow supported FDR's **New Deal** (my words), *"... some form of collectivism and socialized democracy, is with us to stay"* thanks to the introduction of *"a nucleus of planned economy into the loos-*

ened texture of free enterprise."[91]   Clearly, the asymmetric Washington D.C. war against American middle-class freedom and abundance began ramping up decades ago. Differences in political theory can and should be legitimately debated on merit. Fascist government takeover through media manipulation, criminalization of opposing political views, subversive mind control methodologies, and other *reflexive* Constitutional violations can never be legitimate.

Dozens of brilliant authors more knowledgeable than I have written extensively on formalized mind-control programs and covert experimentation, including for instance, Dr. Norbert Weiner's work on *Cybernetics*. Dishonorable mention must include the CIA's notorious Bluebird (1950), Artichoke (1951), MK ULTRA (1953), and Monarch (1960's) programs. MK ULTRA spun off from earlier Project Artichoke, then Project Monarch from MK ULTRA. Monarch gained some notoriety through Cathy O'Brien's book, *TRANCE Formation of America*,[92] a frightening, difficult to verify read, though proof is in the pudding. Slave traders and pedophile sadists rarely advertise entertainment schedules, so proof is difficult to acquire. The CIA, intertwined with all of this, unconstitutionally abused its power from the first day of global syndicate inception. Another unconstitutional espionage monster for spying on American citizens at home was the CIA's Operation MH/CHAOS from 1967 to 1974.[93]

Unconstitutional covert mind control programs were carried out with Federal funds, that is, our money, through psychopathic research efforts by wackos such as Yale Professor and socially deviant neurosurgeon, Dr. Jose Delgado; Harvard University's insane Dr. William Sweet; President of the American and World Psychiatric Association's monstrous Dr. Ewen Cameron; sadist Dr. Sydney Gottlieb, Director of MK Ultra from 1953 to 1964, and others of the same Luciferian ilk. The global syndicate is proficient at sniffing sicko's out via the study group system, then putting them to malicious work on antihuman projects. 2021 CDC Director, Rochelle Walensky is a perfect example of a psychopathic menace (my opinion) groomed through the international study group system. Ms. Walensky, an indoctrinated study group victim herself, is a convincing propagandist for Main Street normie acceptance of bioweaponized mass murder. Many wonder how such an arrogant liar suddenly appeared from nowhere to head the systemically corrupt CDC, but she has been openly metastasizing as an order follower in the study group system since the mid-nineties.

---

91 Sean Stone, Guido Preparata, and Richard Grove, *New World Order: A Strategy of Imperialism*, Reprint edition (Walterville, OR: Trine Day, 2016), 44.
92 *TRANCE Formation of America: True Life Story of a Mind Control Slave*, Revised edition (Place of publication not identified: Reality Marketing, Incorporated, 1995).
93 Frank J. Rafalko, *MH/CHAOS: The CIA's Campaign Against the Radical New Left and the Black Panthers*

11 • Mind Control & Neuro Rights

My characterization of these Luciferian psycho-monsters is distasteful and un-professional, but they earned such disgust. Any doubt about commitment of the late Dr. Jose Delgado (1915 – 2011) for example, to engineer complete con-trol over people's minds is quickly dispelled by a quick read through his diffi-cult to obtain book, *Physical Control of the Mind.*[94] This work is fascinating but only the naïve can fail to imagine the sole purpose of Delgado's work is mass behavior manipulation and control by the global syndicate, not public health.

Note order following Doctors, Cameron and Gottlieb are CIA scapegoats, not due to innocence, but promoted into public view because somebody had to be thrown under the mind-control bus in prevention of revolt. Main Street must be convinced the beasts were exposed, were eliminated, and Main Street is safe again. However, MK Ultra is not dead. MH/Chaos is not dead. Operation Mockingbird is not dead. Whatever euphemisms their offspring now thrive beneath, many doz-ens of *useful idiot* technocrats labor faithfully in universities and study group think tanks around the world, most of them having no idea the Satanic agenda they serve.

Compartmentalization and *need to know* are useful study group tools. Dement-ed medical criminals are worse than mind-controlled serial killers they cre-ate and whose barbaric mass population atrocities, by the way, we the people of Main Street pay for. A historic perspective is mandatory to understand-ing the relevant deviancy of these covert programs, which is why a visit to *TruthStream Media* is an important element of mental self-defense. Check out *TruthStream Media's* 2019, full-length feature film entitled *The Minds of Men*, detailing Cold War social engineering and mind-control programs. Last I checked, incidentally, *Amazon* removed this movie from its product line.

Much of the historic record alluded to above, both private and public, was conveniently expunged prior to investigation in 1973 by Elite water-boy, CIA Director at the time, Richard Helms, fallaciously claiming the mind con-trol programs terminated. None-the-less, the *Senate Intelligence Committee* led by Senator Frank Church did uncover some documents in 1976 relat-ed to covert assassinations, spying on American citizens, drugging of Ameri-can citizens, and so forth. Since that time *Freedom of Information Act* (FOIA) requests, mostly involving not-yet-scrubbed CIA financial history related to mind control activities and other covert operations have brought forth near-ly 20,000 pages (to my knowledge) of now declassified information, shed-ding some light on this monstrous U.S. Government sanctioned undertaking.

---

94 Jose M. R. Delgado M.D, *Physical Control of the Mind: Toward a Psychocivilized Society* (CreateSpace Independent Publishing Platform, 1970).

In further treasonous support of the above, the CIA's *Operation Mockingbird* began in the 1950's, retaining hundreds of journalists, while infiltrating citizen groups for propaganda purposes to control public dialog favoring CIA agendas. *Mockingbird* was never terminated. It thrives today across Mainstream Fake News Media, social media, Hollywood, and publishing, etc. Making matters worse, corrupt FBI Director James Comey and the Obama Administration *Injustice Department* admitted to and defended extension of *Mockingbird* to their covert use of FBI Agents posing as journalists. This was reported in September 2016 in *A Review of the FBI's Impersonation of a Journalist in a Criminal Investigation* by the *Department of Justice Office of Inspector General* (OIG).

Today, we can add the *Brain Initiative* and various malicious mixtures of ELF/VLF/RF manipulation to the unseen mix of potential behavior modulation modalities to which we can accrue Toxic Bioweapon JABs. We'll not be discussing these formalized programs here, but instead will pursue simpler, more general modalities, some of which are not usually considered active participants in the realm of mind-control.

It's possible for humans to act without conscious knowledge of what founder of *Anthroposophy*, Rudolf Steiner[95] called the *driving force*, in which case we're not acting freely. We may be conscious of *motive* but are not aware of the ideas or concepts behind the actions we take. Steiner taught the only way to prevent being controlled by an *outside* (exterior) *driving force* is consciously and intentionally making our own ideals the *interior driving force* of our willful actions. I cautionarily add, this level of consciousness can only be brought about safely via grace of the Holy Spirit. In today's world, this requires humility, hard work, study, and spiritual discipline, (we could call it prayer). If we do the hard work, through grace, we can think and act freely; avoiding outside influences that may determine the course of our actions – at least we could prior to inundation by nano-technology entrainment.

Steiner as a co-founder of the occult *Theosophical Society* in 1875 along with Helena Blavatsky, Henry Steel Olcott and other occultists understood a great deal about human motivation. The sick (my words) *Theosophical Society* made a significant contribution to the Satanic philosophic foundation permeating Germany's Nazi Party derangement and atrocities. Exploring this subject matter is spiritually dangerous and should never be attempted except in the name of Jesus Christ protected by grace of the Holy Spirit. Redundant but important.

---

95 "The Philosophy Of Freedom: Rudolf Steiner: 9781257835126: Amazon.Com: Books."

11 • Mind Control & Neuro Rights

We cannot be free when our thought process is influenced or controlled by others. Prayer is the most potent weapon for interior protection though many of us, unfortunately, refuse to embrace that most powerful of weapons. I would humbly add to Steiner's occult teaching that reaching out to the Holy Spirit for the armor of God is critically necessary to overcoming dark side influence. Going it alone is an egoistic Masonic prescription for difficulty and failure. Many well-intentioned *new agers* are caught up in this subtle Satanic trap. Always pray for discernment and protection when spiritually seeking as spiritual life is lived at the edge of the Satanic Abyss and demons despise fair play.

I should mention, Orthodox Fathers teach that **spiritual power** far exceeds the reach of **physical power** since spirit extends eternally from the uncreated transcendent, whereas all physicality is created in space/time. Spiritual power is available to each of us as a gift from our Father as children of God through Christ, the Son of God with the grace of the Holy Spirit. Our only real defenses against unseen malevolent mind control technologies in this material world are spiritual growth and strength, so pray and *be not afraid*.

All mind control methodologies are inspired by Luciferian influence and poor choices. Lucifer's power has already been broken by Christ's death on the cross and His subsequent resurrection, so we just need to accept what has been done for us. Fighting demonic influence on our own accord without the power of Christ is a bad idea. Malachi Martin's *Hostage to the Devil* touches on several sobering case studies depicting the danger of egoistically taking on demonic battles alone.[96]

I respectfully ask readers, <u>please</u> never take on spiritual forces of darkness alone, without invoking aid from the Holy Spirit in the name of Jesus Christ. Fighting spiritual darkness egotistically is an enormous mistake with potentially dire consequences. Malachi Martin's own death may have been related to this type of circumstance, though may be urban myth. I don't know which.

Anyway, leading into the subtler aspects of thought conditioning, mind control, and entrainment, we should discuss a less subtle aspect of covert manipulation by nanotechnology powerfully raising its ugly, poisonous head. Many researchers such as notable Norwegian researcher and lecturer, Dr. Rauni Leena Luukanen-Kilde, who has studied individual and mass mind control for decades,[97] tell us military research typically precedes academic research by thirty to fifty years, with fifty years being about average for militarized technologies.

---

96 Martin, *Hostage to the Devil*.
97 "Dr. Rauni Leena Luukanen-Kilde on Mind Control - YouTube," accessed August 3, 2017, https://www.youtube.com/.

In other words, it's typical for military-industrial researchers to conduct serious work on various technologies for as many as five decades before academic researchers begin working on the same technology, finally announced to Main Street as something "new". Bell Labs for instance was playing with singing main frame computers and communication satellites in the late fifties. Recall HAL singing *Daisy Bell* in Kubrick's (1968) *2001: A Space Odyssey*? By the way, for trivia buffs, HAL moved one alphabet space forward is IBM and I think the first computerized song (voice synthesizer) was performed on an IBM 7094 mainframe. Not sure what year as this is outside my low-tech wheelhouse?

Getting back to it, in fairness, such prudence isn't necessarily conspiratorial as proprietary rights or national defense in a competitive and frequently adversarial world understandably warrant discretion in research and development activities. For instance, a person or business may work on an innovative technology, device, machine, gadget, medicine, or whatever for many years, bearing significant expense in time, energy, and money. If not discreet, competition or worse, illegal advantage or sabotage can erase any possibility of securing a return on invested time, energy, and capital, much less profiting by hard work and ingenuity. The invention itself may never be realized. When this happens, ability to conduct further viable research is curtailed and benefits of creative genius, lost.

Conversely, covert, unregulated research in at least some areas or industries may be conspiratorial or BAD for Main Street for any number of reasons. Transparent government is generally desirable to prevent both foreseen and unforeseen abuses. Concern about someone else's government harming us is one thing: harm by our own corrupt government, another.

Of immediate interest, the not-so-subtle technologies I'd like to draw your attention to are **micro-chipping** and/or **nano-chipping**. Most of us consider the concept of micro-chipping recently developed technology, but it has been around a long time. Trackers the size of rice grains were already developed in the 1940's. These critters are problematic but are easily detected and removed if implanted in someone's body as seen in movies. Today we have nano-size chips, the presence of which can be detected, but are so microscopically tiny they cannot be found or removed by conventionally known procedures.

Dr. John Donoghue, Director - *Institute for Brain Science* at Brown University developed a micro-chip (not yet nano-size as I understand it) technology, which when implanted in a mentally impaired person, connects the person's brain to a computer; facilitating man-machine communication via a software program called *Brain Gate*[98]. This is a wonderful development being tested in real time, but for how long has such technology been developed not to medically assist a mentally impaired person, but covertly weaponized to impair a healthy person or control that person—or group of persons?

MK Ultra is about mass population control, not just individual control. Government funds this covert mind control research using tax dollars directly or uses our full faith and credit against borrowed funds we are accountable for, and sometimes via hidden or black budgets. Black budgets are partially transparent as non-explicit accounting entries for covert activities; but hidden budgets are 100% non-transparent involving digital printing, narco, weapons, and human trafficking dollars, etc. We the people have a Constitutional right, a legal right to know what this research is, who does it, and what it is employed to do. We use our Constitutionally recognized unalienable rights or lose them.

Government agencies, particularly in military, intelligence, health, and Dept. of State often employ contractors to privatize activities they don't want exposed to Congressional oversight, hence the need for hidden, self-financing budgets, together offering plausible deniability. This practice has become so D.C. routine we the people of Main Street can safely consider the House of Representatives and U.S. Senate nothing more than associated dupes providing tacit approval for any civilly deplorable or criminal activity imaginable... and most of these so-called Representatives are becoming wealthy doing so. We could call this "wealth by denial" or "wealth by complicity". Either way, Main Street = zero D.C. Representation under global syndicate domination. Clearly, dynastically controlled asset management monopolies like **Vanguard, Black-Rock, State Street, Berkshire-Hathaway**, and a few powerful others constitute not just a **fourth branch of government**, BUT the primary branch of government fully owned and operated by global syndicate dynastic families.

The few honest Representatives in Congress are too timid and control file afraid to be of any use to Main Street. I'm not judging here, just stating a fact. I do not imagine for a moment I'd be any more courageous than someone else, but if you don't like heat, get out of the boiler room. Neither cowardice nor denial justify Main Street's congressionally aided and abetted loss of Constitutionally recognized freedoms. That said, I suspect these privileged ruling class pawns are not permitted to retire at will. Global syndicate investment in elected and politically appointed scum is too costly and inconvenient for escape to be discretionary. This may explain bought and paid for derelicts like Biden, Clyburn, Collins, Feinstein, Hoyer, Leahy, McConnell, Pelosi, Rogers, Schumer, Wa-

---

98 "Brain Gate Report | Brain | Electroencephalography," Scribd, accessed August 3, 2017, https://www.scribd.com/doc/86741240/Brain-Gate-Report.

ters, Young, and so many others stuck to the bottom of our autocratic UniParty shoes. I imagine most legislative coercion is by blackmail, financial threats, and threat of negative or embarrassing press, but can also be more serious.

For a horribly graphic example (you may wish to skip to the next paragraph if squeamish) but to make a crude point clearly... say I'm a highly motivated junior U.S. Senator and I'm told if I don't drop sponsorship of a piece of legislation my wife will have an accident. I bravely say buzz off and with her consent put her life on the line. BUT what if instead I'm told, if I don't back off, my wife will be kidnapped, beaten, and raped for weeks, then skinned alive, receiving blood transfusions and drugs to maintain her screaming consciousness through weeks of excruciating pain. Now how brave am I? As the adage goes, everyone has a price, and these Satanic global syndicate ghouls aren't kidding. They live for pain, humiliation, and destruction... of others. How does any President, lone House Member, U.S. Senator, or Supreme Court Justice stand up to this horror show on their own? No one can stand up to this evil without active support and defense guaranteed by Main Street citizens. This is our responsibility.

Mind control is not a new concept. Beyond propaganda, indoctrination, and conditioning, the first so-called mind control device I've personally run across is *The Air Loom*, a device first described in 1810 by psychiatric patient James Tilly Matthews. Hospitalized at England's historic *Bedlam Asylum* under the care of apothecary, John Haslam, who published a book reporting his findings entitled *Illustrations of Madness*. Mr. Matthews apparently described this device and its considerable power to influence not just individuals, but groups of people.

This is a bizarre case and I have no idea as to authenticity of the historic account, other than it was publicly disclosed at the time. I bring it up to punctuate that psychopaths have been interested in constructing mind control devices for an awfully long time. Given Tavistock's current proclivity for mass manipulation of identity and behavior, coupled with complete pathologic disregard for human liberty, dignity, and life, such trivia is of historic interest.

I won't dwell on micro-nanotechnology as I'm not very familiar with it. Further study should lie with Mr. Joe Allen (https://joebot.substack.com/ or *Bannon's Wardroom*) or others educated in the field. We must none-the-less get up to speed with the general case. The human brain is composed of about 100 billion cells, each of which is like a tiny battery holding a negative electrical charge inside the cell and a positive electrical charge outside the cell membrane. Neurons literally pass electrical impulses from one to another and we now have devices capable of hearing or reading these impulses; and software that can interpret the impulses and communicate wirelessly with and between these impulses.

Pre-crime is not coming; it is here today with scalar waves and quantum computers rashly vomiting poorly understood autonomous intelligence systems like nanotech, 5G, 6G, the Internet of Things (IoT) and *full spectrum dominance* ignorantly into a reckless transhuman reality. Not one person studying, developing, or implementing these *directed energy technologies* has any idea the effects on humans or other life forms over time—or perhaps they are so completely evil, they do know the harm they do and don't care? The immature willingness of excitable researchers to plunge forward in the face of overwhelming ignorance is astonishing. In the short-sighted world of Transhuman Scientism – Ignorance and Denial reign King and Queen with Left/Right Brain Imbalance as executioner for those questioning the emperor's lack of knickers. Adults must supervise the technology playroom.

Nearly undetectable, nanosize chips are now available for dissemination via aerosol delivery and smart dust, or can be distributed through water, food, direct contact shedding, etc., or just physically injected. It's possible to be nanochipped today without knowing it and the possibility any of us are not already nanochipped is minuscule. Heavy metals and nanoparticles dispersed using Federal or hidden funds, ingested unnoticed, without our permission or knowledge can turn us into walking, talking, listening – transmission and receiving cyborg devices capable of wireless connectivity to the worldwide 5G Smart Grid now being rolled out to surveil and control the worldwide *Internet of Things* (IoT) beneath the *Space Fence*, i.e., *full spectrum dominance*.

We are becoming mobile human antennas without knowledge or consent. Welcome to the transhumanist order-follower nightmare for a dystopian Main Street future imprisoned within our ionized atmosphere, Smart Grids, Smart Cities, Smart Contracts, Social Credit Scores, cryptocurrencies, Energy Distribution Cards, and nano-chipped humans – all without foreknowledge of consequence, unless we stop it. Leftist political correctness, woke culture, and cancel culture obliterate our freedom to question, discuss, or choose. Non-status quo views are criminalized by a broken legal system supported by order following law enforcement. Nanotechnology electromagnetically locks the prison door on Main Street citizen freedom permanently – unless we say NO.

General distribution of nanochips via aerosol spraying is already the case. Wide distribution of nano-sensors, etc., are becoming sampled and tested fact with human, animal, plant, rainwater, and soil samples confirming the presence of nano-devices, heavy metals, and other particulates such as aluminum, barium, cadmium, chromium, copper, iron, lithium, manganese, nickel, potassium, sodium, strontium, and zinc in non-naturally occurring, extremely heavy concentrations. In my home state of Arizona for example, in the Phoenix area, nanosize aluminum concentrations are found at levels more than 6,000 times the recognized EPA toxic limit.[99] WHY? WHO IS DOING THIS? Are we the people of Main Street paying for our own poisoning and programmed control within a bounded, electro-magnetic, scalar, 5G, *Space Fence* prison? Is this something we should scream NO to? What is our so-called representative Congress doing to protect us (nothing of course – that was a rhetorical question)? These *useful idiots* think they will remain free.

Moving on, heavy metal concentrations interacting with EM radiation are significant because thoughts physically manifesting as electrical impulses are transmitted on specific frequencies. Different kinds of thoughts, say loving thoughts, angry thoughts, or fearful thoughts each have their own identifiable broadcast frequency. Prentice Mulford, a leader of the controversial *New Thought Movement* told us, *"Thoughts Are Things".*[100] **Psychic weapons have been under military study for decades.**[101] Main Street has little information regarding the weaponized nature of such weapons research over the past four decades. Given the extent of even older systems and modification updates to systems like the *Ground Wave Emergency Network* (GWEN), *Survivable Low Frequency Communication System* (SLFCS), and *Essential Emergency Communication Network* (MEECN), along with satellite systems; we should be concerned about the secretive nature of this weapons development and more importantly – who is behind it and why? Is it or when will it be aimed at Main Street? This is an important question given that by 2030, more than 99% of all wealth on earth is expected to be controlled by just a dozen or so dynastic families, with a few lesser offshoots, all of whom dwell beneath Luciferian influence.

If nano-particulate concentrations are being built up in our bodies, it's entirely possible, if not probable, our bodies are being prepared for unauthorized wireless connection to the **Metaverse**, i.e., autonomically-intelligent worldwide 5G/ IoT/*Space Fence* network (or more advanced future networks) for control and behavior modification by rogue entities we neither see, vote for, nor can influence. I love technology, but this is a horrific off the rails abuse of power. Why can't humanity just develop a technology for beneficial purposes? Why do humans weaponize every new thing they can? Answer: Satanic influence.

99 "Chemtrails - Shocking Phoenix Air Quality Test Results," accessed August 6, 2017, http://www.rense.com/general82/chemit.htm.
100 Prentice Mulford, *Thoughts Are Things & The God In You* (Radford, VA: Wilder Publications, 2008).
101 Ronald M. McRae, *Mind Wars: The True Story of Government Research into the Military Potential of Psychic Weapons*, 1st edition (New York: St Martins Pr, 1984).

Future proves past! A quarter-century later, it's apparent how treasonous Bill Clinton's Sept. 1993 Executive Order 12862 formalizing his innocuous sounding *National Performance Review* was. The review headed by globalist con-man Al Gore was more aptly rechristened as the *National Partnership for Reinventing Government*. This sick program set in motion the transformation of account-able American Constitutional government under the Rule of Law into an un-accountable **Administrative Dictatorship** ruled by technocratic regulation and *Reflexive Law* imposed by ideologically screened, unelected technocrats. We see EO 12862 poisonous fruit unconstitutionally borne out by our federal government, state governments, local governments, and transnational corpo-rations mandating shutdowns, lock downs, unhealthy face muzzles, non-treat-ment in hospitals, and toxic bioweapon JABs. This is treason and also anoth-er RICO case with experimental JAB mandates a **Nuremberg Code** violation.

Rather than enforce uniformly binding legislative law; arbitrary regulations are implemented and interpreted by appointed bureaucrats as their handlers demand in service to global syndicate agendas. The unrepresentative re-sult is a lawless U.S. government which Mr. Patrick Wood eloquently points out in *Technocracy Rising*, should have been foreseen in 1993... but wasn't.[102]

The psychopathic Elite dream for a totalitarian One World Government run by autonomously intelligent computerized algorithms and robo-humans is so out of sync with human nature and *Natural Law*, it will predictably debilitate or destroy rather than enhance life, rendering its successful realization improb-able. However, much of this poorly understood technology is here today, alive, and not well. Demonically obsessed Techno-Psycho's are *doing what they wilt*.

A great deal of research is covertly funded and non-transparent to Main Street citizens across the world who pay for it via confiscatory taxation and other less obvious means. I am not anti-technology, but secret, non-trans-parent research on potentially damaging and/or enslaving technologies co-vertly and invasively imposed on people without their knowledge and permission CANNOT be permitted to be conducted by erudite, socially de-viant, order-following pseudo-scientists. This is insane, constituting a societal death-wish. TECHNOLOGY MUST BE VERIFIABLY TRANSPARENT.

Technocratic implantation within a person's body of heavy met-als and/or tiny electronic devices capable of transmitting and receiv-ing electronically generated subconscious and conscious thoughts from programmed computers is not coming; it's here. Where's out-raged "it's my body – it's my choice" baby killing crowds when we need 'em?

---

102 Wood, *Technocracy Rising*, chap. 5.

❧

A nanometer is one billionth of a meter; one millionth of a millimeter. A millimeter is about the diameter of the medium point of a ball point pen. The width or diameter of a human hair is about 75,000 nanometers (75 microns {*75μm*}), providing a sense of how tiny a nanoparticle or nanodevice is. Our fully indoctrinated EPA bureaucrats have <u>no developed testing protocols</u> as of this writing for measuring concentrations of nearly invisible nanoparticles; yet these nanoparticles and devices are now part of our bodies and all organic life as they're being massively ejected by aerosol spraying into earth's atmosphere regularly and continuously along with millions of toxic COVID JABs. How will our immune systems cope with this foreign nano-invasion? We don't know.

The ability to intercept a person's subconscious thoughts enables controllers to know what a person will do before that person becomes aware of what they will do. Quantum physics confirms this by the way and nanoparticles behave per quantum mechanics. Quantum physics crosses into frequency dimensions we have little knowledge of. You may recall 2002's Spielberg movie, *Minority Report* starring Tom Cruise, based on Philip K. Dick's short story where detective John Anderton, in the year 2054 works for *Pre-crime*, a special police unit capable of arresting murderers before they've committed the crime. If you think it, you own it, I guess. Biblical in a creepy, amoral, algorithmically predictive way?

2021 has arrived many mind-control years ahead of Hollywood's 2054 and we should be aware nanodevices can be detected via their signal frequency by MRI, etc., but cannot be found or removed from the body once implanted, injected, or ingested as they are much too tiny; though undoubtedly our military-industrial-surveillance complex has covertly resolved this dilemma for *prominent global citizens* and possibly for their *Pawns of Privilege*, though that's unlikely as *Pawns* are just disposable *useful idiots* and *cannon fodder* undeserving of syndicate respect. It does appear these magnetically responsive nanoparticles are able to be moved around and repositioned within our bodies and can be remotely focused in targeted areas by pulsed ELF radiation. Why? How many of us are aware that DNA synthesis, damage, and repair processes are magnetically sensitive?

Use 'em and lose 'em is the syndicate's rule for both *useful idiots* and *unwashed*. This presents concerns regarding aerosol spraying and geoengineering beyond poisoning as nanodevices can be ingested via aerosol spraying, dust, water supplies, food supplies, JABs, etc. I recognize there are cost limitations; BUT on the other hand, ±\$54 trillion missing dollars since 1998 buys a lot of smart dust.

11 • Mind Control & Neuro Rights

Nanochips can be programed and cost-effectively distributed in mass to influence behavior within large population segments controlled via wireless 5G technology Earth is already being blanketed with. Nanochips can also be wirelessly re-programmed as demented controllers see fit. Surveillance and re-programming can be by satellite, or more cost effectively done via IMSI catchers (cell site simulators) like **Sting Ray** and **DRT Box** mounted in small planes, vans, trucks, or cars. Local police, and in many cases, state police in every state in America, and more than a dozen Federal Agencies are armed with IMSI technology.

Does anyone imagine warrants for IMSI spying are being requested and issued? Is the covert use of this spyware being disclosed to the public? Is legal protection being provided for home or business privacy invasion or third-party use of gathered data? Of course not. Warrants would suggest self-governance with granted police authority, not a jack-booted authoritarian police state, wouldn't it? Washington D.C. is missing more than $54 trillion dollars since 1998 according to Inspector General Audit Reports and other data. That is an enormous Earth-encircling *Space Fence* and could be a lot of nanochips. 5G technology and **AI** in evil hands constitute a potential Main Street autonomy disaster. Transparency is an essential defense against transhuman enslavement and omnicide.

I don't care for the term <u>artificial intelligence</u> because no such thing exists. Computers and machines learn redundantly, not creatively. I prefer the term <u>**autonomous intelligence**</u> (my form of AI). Computers do not possess spiritual essence, spiritual power, nor creative imagination. They learn via repetition many times faster than the human brain and process information much more rapidly, but cannot imagine, create, nor exercise moral judgment, a uniquely Divine gift. **In my humble opinion, so called artificial intelligence is not very intelligent at all.** Solving iteratively structured math equations as programmed is one thing algorithms are good at but exercising qualitative judgement to creatively solve problems is quite another thing. AI algorithms religiously worshiped in the geek world are just math equations performing quantifiable calculations. A math equation has no intelligent essence. Replacing human judgement, good or bad, with calculations quickly leads to difficulties, sometimes humorously, sometimes ignorantly, sometimes maliciously.

A farm of quantum supercomputers algorithmically supercomputing billions of times per nanosecond while attempting to emulate imagination meets the admonition, *"The definition of insanity is doing the same thing over and over again but expecting different results"*. This admonition is usually attributed to Einstein, but I haven't been able to confirm he said it. None-the-less, this electromagnetic-scalar-behavior suggests if supercomputers are alleged to be intelligent, they must also be alleged insane regarding certain anti-human applications.

Unfortunately for Main Street, delusional psychopaths currently developing and disseminating 5G technology, multi-dimensional quantum computing, and whatever electronic magic tags along believe they can and will control AI. They are arrogantly incorrect. The *Internet of Things* (IoT) is already self-perpetuating and mechanistically developing redundant machine ability to defend itself against human management. Why does rogue military science refuse to acknowledge the obvious threat to their oath of enlistment, not to mention survivability? Building powerful machines capable of self-defense but incapable of qualitative or moral judgment, i.e., machines programed to be ignorantly insecure, yet easily damaged by hacking, rust, or sun activity is criminally negligent, malevolent, or both.

As mentioned earlier, I'm not anti-technology, anti-corporation, or anti-money. However, all three are human creations; useful tools which humans are responsible for—and for which we must hold ourselves accountable. A corporation is a legal entity enabling human activity, usually facilitating collaborative business for profit or not-for-profit. This seems a good thing, but when autonomously and/or mindlessly operated, it sidesteps human purpose, moral values, spiritual integrity, and conscience. Mass moral abandonment of human decency, value, and reason are by focused Satanic intent and influence, not moral misfeasance, or happenstance. Any failure to remedy this abhorrent circumstance bears spiritual consequences for humanity suggesting **Neuro Rights Law** to be another necessary burden.

Helping each other be better humans is an individual spiritual responsibility. We cannot fight evil alone and achieve victory. Divided, frightened, and on our own we are weak and easily conquered. We must act together, united under Jesus Christ, protected by the armor of God. This is our only path to victory.

We are strongest when fighting evil from a warrior's position of love; protecting each other and ourselves, slaying the enemy as necessary. We cannot successfully battle demons from a position of anger, hatred, or revenge. Malice leads directly to the Satanic abyss, guaranteeing that by hating demons, we become demons. We must ward off and/or defeat the evil ones, but it is also our responsibility to try and awaken them to turn away from darkness and as best we can, lead them to eternal spiritual life. Salvation is not for you or I; it is for all of us together.

Mind control destroys spiritual perception, rational coherence, and decision-making capacity thereby obliterating created human potential. Mind control is evil. Its defeat requires prayer, fasting, and disciplined intention, only achievable with God's grace, which we must request. With grace, our good intention, and concerted action, victory is already granted through the blood of Christ's cross.

Is the false promise of being cared for by Big Brother
blissful or dangerous?

Does Big Brother honor God or Satan?

12 • Cognitive Blissonance: An Aspect of Mind Control

Remedy: Global syndicate order followers in government, education, publishing, media, Hollywood, and multinational industry submerge Main Streets across the world in a continuous fog of weaponized anxiety. Pollution, poor nutrition, weakened immune systems, manufactured pandemics, propaganda, misinformation, indoctrination, electromagnetic entrainment, and other means are employed to maintain a continuously confusing state of multi-media induced cognitive dissonance. Our brains simmer in an unhealthy cortisol induced stupor. Peace on Earth requires hard-working deplorables of Main Street stop allowing ourselves to be victimized by the tempting, monopolized conveniences we support and pay for. Just say NO THANK YOU! SIMPLIFY OUR LIVES! It is imperative as sovereign children of God we protect our health, perception, coherence, and imaginative thought processes. Denial of harmful falsehoods due to manufactured emotional discomfort is cognitive blissonance, which can be prematurely fatal.

We don't usually think of public health, medical practice, medical regulation, or nutritional guidelines as forms of mind control, but since the *Rockefeller Foundation* and associated foundations realized petroleum and pharmaceuticals would be a profitable marriage, we should. Government protected, corrupt dynastic family trusts, foundations, and endowments, beneath the guise of philanthropy took over U.S. medical school curricula, medical associations, and medical licensing boards via a financial coup d'etat early in the 20th century. John D. Rockefeller formed the *General Education Board* (GEB) in 1903, establishing himself as an educational benefactor. We now live with the **Cult of Medicine** as a result.

A series of unconstitutional laws legislated into existence by duped or coward-ly Federal lawmakers resulted in an evil public-private partnership between cor-rupt regulatory agencies and greedy multinational pharmaceutical and medical cartels. The cartels now operate increasingly dangerous agencies at their own pathological discretion. Without going into detail, consider: President Truman's unconstitutional **1952 Executive Order 10399** granting public health author-ity to the WHO, the **National Childhood Vaccine Injury Act of 1986**, the **Public Readiness and Emergency Preparedness Act (PREPA) of 2005**, the **Pandemic and All-Hazards Preparedness Act (PAHPA) of 2006**, and the **Pandemic and All-Hazards Preparedness Reauthorization Act (PAH-PRA) of 2013**. These acts are bolstered by dozens more unconstitutional dec-larations and amendments since enactment. These insidious acts, along with 1980's **Patent and Trademark Law Amendments Act** *(Bayh-Dole Act)* have largely reduced traditional health related university research and medical-health delivery services to a pathetic money-grubbing cult of complicit malefactors.

Arguments are deceitfully made suggesting historic medical malfeasance is well intended misfeasance, that despite good intentions, THE CULT of MEDICINE didn't envision predictably harmful results driven by corrupt philanthropic foun-dation coercion. Main Street is to believe millions of health impaired, physi-cally disabled, sterilized, and in many cases, medically slaughtered victims were unforeseen. However, in the context of policies promoted by various NGOs, the *Bill and Melinda Gates Foundation*, similar foundations, published **World Eco-nomic Forum** reports, the declassified **National Security Study Memoran-dum (NSSM 200), and the Implications of Worldwide Population Growth for U.S. Security and Overseas Interests (Kissinger Report) dated 12-10-1974** – global syndicate intent is clear. Intentional, profitable medical malprac-tice is the felonious status RICO quo. There is no need to consider NWO eugenics and depopulation programs or the like to make a case for evil intent.

A system of preferential laws and regulation evolving as a government sanc-tioned, privateering racket for legalized piratization of Main Street productiv-ity and wealth by connected insiders and multinational resource rapists, along with discriminatory taxation, and preferential regulation creates an obscene power imbalance. When the abusive system metastasizing in D.C. operates without regard for justice, human dignity, respect for life, and lacks responsible controls founded on Christian morality, integrity, and honor—that legal system fails humanity. As of this writing we have hundreds of political prisoners in the U.S. because the oligarchic Establishment has falsely criminalized non-status quo political views. At this point, Main Street is shackled with hubristic governance run by a dehumanized, mechanized corporate structure incapable of recognizing human value or potential. This depraved algorithmic system cannot differentiate between good or evil, human strength or weakness, nor is it motivated to benefit humanity or anything else on Earth. It is evolving spiritually as unaccountable mechanized destruction greased by Main Street apathy, confusion, anxiety, and growing fear. Global syndicate pawns are Satanically implementing global omnicide and we residents of Main Street are letting it happen and helping it happen by supporting multinational criminal corporations. Why?

We have descended to a materialistic nadir where non-transparent, 21st century technologies increasingly run multinational corporations mis-managed by order-following drones incapable of beneficially building for the future. **Government protected multinational behemoths are now openly poisoning us with impunity emboldened by immunity from prosecution as the U.S. Rule of Law has collapsed from within.** Biased algorithmic modeling equations plugged into computers mimic coherent decision making, sadistically exerting pressure on myopic bean-counters to produce short-term mercantilist dividends for shareholders without regard for long term human consequences – or in the minds of some, **to eliminate the long middle-class term entirely**. Since humans are spiritually entrusted with caring for the Earth (dominion) we inhabit, this is an omnicidic travesty in the making. We must be careful as we cautiously proceed; BUT are we seeing any caution at all? Anywhere? *Anyone? Anyone?* ... as young Ben Stein famously asked in 1986 (*Ferris Bueller's Day Off*).

Career politicians cancerously mutated into a Ruling Class Ruled From Above, ironically abandoning all control of the festering Administrative State they created for the global syndicate to manipulate and abuse. This leaves Main Street saddled with deceitful ruling class arrogance in defense of power mongering ignorance and criminality. We deny human nature and purpose, apathetically trusting psychopathic experts unable to recognize their own lack of pertinent information—or do they know and just lie? Either way, this is not a recipe for human fulfillment. As technological power invisibly metastasizes and electromagnetically mutates, our brains anxiously rot in an electrified cortisol bath while shriveling immune systems reduce our bodies to paste balls of indulgently acidic ectopic fat—a conditioned prescription for extinction.

We might inquire if mass obesity itself is the result of *study group* mind control programs. Do people **knowingly** consent to becoming so overweight they can no longer comfortably walk into a shopping center? Why are ±43% of Americans obese and ±10% of Americans severely obese per 2018 CDC statistics? Do industrial agriculture and food processing industry propaganda qualify as mind control, at least when packaged and promoted by captured government agencies?

Industrial agriculture profits are subsidized by government agencies to grow GMO food crops laced with glyphosate and other toxic chemicals. This is in addition to aerosol spraying dumping tons of nanoparticle aluminum and toxic heavy metals on our cropland. These predictably dangerous food crops are then profitably processed into delicious sugary, cancer feeding pseudo-foods, breads, candies, cereals, pasta, and so forth for Main Street consumption. Grocery and chain restaurant customers predictably become ill with incrementally fatal diseases and compromised lifestyles. When sufficiently fatted and chronically ill, victimized customers, including children, become chronic disease patients who are then treated—never cured—as expensively and profitably as possible for as long as possible by Big Pharma and Big Medicine. This incremental genocide paradigm assures perpetual profit for the network of Big Chemical Companies, Industrial Agriculture, Industrial Food Processing, Big Pharma, and Big Medicine – all of which incubate within Big Government Agencies paid for by unsuspecting taxpayers—the fatted calves.

These murderously greedy industries, networked together at their global syndicate hips, are financially subsidized by, legally supported by, nurtured by, marketed by, and sometimes mandated by abysmally treasonous government agencies paid for by we the people of Main Street. This constitutes a dark foundation underlying the mind control aspect of nutritionally weakening Main Street populations via Federally sanctioned privateering. The **Robber Barons** of the 2nd Industrial Revolution are hungrily still with us as Barrons of the 4th Industrial Revolution – bigger, badder, and more Satanic than ever. How does this malignant business plan work? It works by being confusingly multi-faceted but here's a well-coordinated example – and if we had Rule of Law, a RICO case.

Authoritative food recommendations first appeared in America in 1894. Since then, propaganda has been provided by the U.S. Department of Agriculture (USDA) through issuance of the **Food Guide Pyramid** in 1992; updated to **MyPyramid** in 2005, becoming **MyPlate** in 2011. Per the United States government and *study group* experts, **low fat, high sugar, cancer feeding, processed carbohydrates** are the way to health and longevity. The result is an organized plandemic of profitable *metabolic syndrome* medical conditions like obesity, heart disease, type 2 diabetes, stroke, and some cancers – preventable in most cases – yet here we are. Why? Is this a windfall-profit, **treat-not cure** paradigm on steroids? Are Federal Agencies like CDC, FDA, NIH, USDA, and others captured to serve as taxpayer funded **profit incubators** for Big Chem, Industrial Agriculture, multinational food processors, Big Pharma, and Big Medicine? If good food is medicine; is bad food poison?

According to CDC's website (it's all we have) in December 2021, 90% of $3.8 trillion U.S. annual health care expenditures were spent on chronic or mental health conditions. Also, per CDC, obese patients are worth ±$1,400 more per year than non-obese patients to the Cult of Big Medicine coffers, BUT – is the CDC cost breakout presentation a partial coverup – a lie by omission? Consider the following CDC annual average health expense data for the U.S.:

- Heart Disease and Stroke $214 billion •25%
- Cancer $174 billion •20%
- Diabetes $327 billion •38%
- Obesity   <u>$147 billion •17%</u>
           Annual Total   **$862 billion •100%**

Obesity appears here as the least significant cost issue yet we're told obesity is the most significant factor contributing to metabolic disease. Heart disease, stroke, diabetes, and yes cancer are all considered aspects of metabolic dysfunction. Obesity, the smallest cost item, is broken out here by CDC as a separate health expense item but is claimed elsewhere by CDC as contributory to heart disease, stroke, some cancers, and diabetes. CDC does not provide us with a percentage contribution by obesity toward other disease categories, but if we imagine obesity 50% responsible, then medical treatment costs due in part to the **MyPlate** low-fat, processed carbohydrate-heavy nutritional contribution would be $862 x 0.5 = $431 billion annually, nearly half a trillion dollars. Does a share in half a trillion dollars annually sufficiently motivate monopolists, experts, and rogue administrators to incrementally murder millions of people for money? Why is the contributory role of obesity downplayed when better nutrition and physical activity easily prevent it?

Consider the following causes of death in the United States:
    ♦ 868,000 people annually due to heart disease and stroke
    ♦ 600,000 people annually due to cancer
    ♦ <u>354,266</u> people annually due to diabetes*******
    1,822,266 deaths annually from above causes

*** Note: Per www.diabetes.org 34.2 million Americans are diagnosed diabetic with another 88 million diagnosed prediabetic. Studies show only 35% to 40% of people who died <u>with</u> diabetes, list diabetes anywhere on the death certificate. Only 10% to 15% of these death certificates list diabetes as an underlying <u>cause</u> of death. If 50% of the above deaths are largely caused by obesity, then ±911,000 annual deaths are related to obesity. Note that liver and organ fat accumulation is typically related to insulin resistance, the contributory cause of which is about 90% diet and 10% activity level. That's a robust middle-class eugenics program augmented by government propaganda, isn't it?

Just to nitpick, outside the obesity wheelhouse we should also make note of the cult of medicine's patient fatalities due to **medical error** ranging from 210,000 to 440,000 deaths annually. Non-standardized death certificate reporting makes accurate estimates difficult, so just pick your favorite study and wonder why Globalist order followers aren't screaming for hospitals, clinics, doctors, and nurses to be banned instead of hawking toxic bioweapon JABs.

21st century multinational corporate culture, bifurcated from human spiritual and moral discernment, loosed upon the world as a parasitic, segmented monster of monopoly; protected, enabled, and corruptly subsidized by delusional politicians, order-following government regulators, and organized crime, has become regardless intent; a Luciferian dragon intent on eating every human on the planet along with the rest of creation for desert. Lucifer thrives on destruction. Evil leadership is that simple and must be addressed by Christianity. Humanity must redeem itself not only to prosper but to survive.

Politically speaking, the **America First** movement is about returning self-governance to Main Street and ousting career political criminals, meaning the Globalist Democrat machine and RINO enablers MUST be removed from power. This movement must be successful if American citizens surviving burgeoning technological genocide are to avoid entrapment within a Transhuman mind control gulag. The success of **America First** can then spread across the globe, erasing the psychopathic disease of **New World Order** slavery engendered via Luciferian influence. Hopefully, readers are aware of other pathways to societal health as well.

We have been steadily relinquishing managerial control of our world to a God despising group of monopolistic corporate entities united by psychopathic greed, hungry for destruction, and incapable of recognizing human value. This psychopathic syndicate owns and operates every major government on Earth. The Luciferian inspired syndicate is building a 5G autonomous **network of things** beyond human control - an egregiously bad idea and Main Street MUST STOP IT - or bear the uninformed result, not likely to resemble bliss.

Financial analysts claim just three investment firms, **BlackRock, Vanguard** and **State Street** account for ±82% of S&P 500 market capitalization, ±25% of voting shares in director elections of S&P 500 companies, and ±73%-80% of global ETF assets. In other words, the largest 1% of asset management firms control 61% of financial sector assets. Only a retard can refer to this as free market capitalism. Economist, Dr. Peter Navarro theorizes the reason *Black-Rock*, *Vanguard*, and *State Street* sell American interests and jobs out to the CCP is to game China's financial services sector markets, i.e., blood money (my words).

Theosophical Nazi miscreants spawning Technocracy since the 1930's applaud their nightmare coming true. Pay attention to propaganda sprayed across media by the *Club of Rome*, *Royal Institute of International Affairs* (Chatham House, St. James' Square, London), *Council on Foreign Relations*, *Trilateral Commission*, and other *prominent global citizen* study group tools. Elites are not secret regarding their intent to rekindle Feudalism nor to genocide *useless eaters* on a global basis, though they carefully do not publicly say what they mean. Slavery is euphemistically discussed as **sustainable development** for the **common good**; a catch-all phrase for *full spectrum dominance* electromagnetically imposed by the global syndicate over all Main Street economic, environmental, social, and spiritual alternatives. The popular term **"equity"**, for example, translates to **slavery for all** via carefully manipulated *policy* outcomes.

Note: *The Royal Institute of International Affairs* (RIIA) has since 1920 become "a" if not, "the" most influential study group think tank in the Western world. It gave birth to America's *Council on Foreign Relations* (CFR). Members chuckle over expensive cocktails as media drones refer to any observation of syndicated power as what the late Rush Limbaugh referred to as *kook conspiracy theory*. Greed and pedophile blackmail rule this sick club.

The **Chatham House Rule**, not limited to Chatham House by any means, commonly guides global syndicate meetings, seminars, etc., stating: *When a meeting, or part thereof, is held under the **Chatham House Rule**, participants are free to use the information received, but neither the identity nor the affiliation of the speaker(s), nor that of any other participant, may be revealed.* An honor system among thieves.

Anyway, inbred dynastic family members and their pawns meeting within the *study group* system under *Chatham House Rule*, believing they can control the electro-mechanical-scalar AI beast they are building are incorrect. **It already resists** attempts by entities outside itself and we cannot predict how or when it will calculate the threatened need to defend itself. This cannot have a happy ending. **We need adults back in the playroom.** It's time to say NO to Silicon Valley and rogue military science… at least until adult reason and transparency are re-established. The battle for **Neuro Rights** is upon us. The study group system itself suffers from and falls victim to its own cognitive dissonance making it even more dangerous to uninformed Main Street citizens.

Secret meetings and decisions are rarely motivated by generosity and good intentions, hence *Chatham House Rule*. 5G as an example, bears serious scrutiny before unleashing its DNA destructive potential and it is rolling out across the globe with illegal laws prohibiting local restriction. My own Smartphone, wireless modem, and office router are 4G and 5G capable. If you are still reading, you probably sense my brain function frying at scalar speed, though friends suggest that started decades ago. I crave grape lollipops dipped in *Lazy River* Kentucky Bourbon. Is that my sign?

Note: Studies indicate a fairly wide frequency range of interaction with EMF to be a primary functional characteristic of **fractal antennas**. DNA appears to possess the two structural characteristics of fractal antennas, electronic conduction and self symmetry. These properties contribute to sensitivity and reactivity of DNA with EMF. Are increasing weaponization of our now ionized atmosphere along with 5G and electromagnetically responsive JABs starting to make eugenic and population control sense?

There is only one military/industrial/surveillance complex on Earth and it thrives via the study group system. It is not ideologically monolithic, but is run by various groups and factions, often adversarially by the way. This shadow government, deep state control apparatus is loosely led by dynastic family members with varying industry ties, secret society membership (more than one hundred in the United States alone), foundations, trusts, institutes, and so forth. This network operates in league with international bankers networked with transnational monopoly corporations networked with order-following academics and scientists, media drones, publishing houses, and government regulatory drones. Self-interest and factions run deep but all syndicate factions enjoy slave ownership, even on a lease basis – maybe on a preferred lease basis since maintenance responsibility is by Satanic others, though I imagine child sex slavery and adrenochrome rights are maintained among the privileged similar to mineral rights.

Add a few Royals, lesser Nobility, and monied Aristocracy into the Mercantile mix and there you have Main Street serfs cowering beneath the so-called Deep State, cringing beneath Shadow Governments, all on bended knee beneath Global Syndicate domination. Its top tier is an oligarchic network of inbred, genetically challenged sociopaths with far too much money and influence on hand for bribing and coercing order-following thugs to harvest and enslave Main Street citizens across the globe. Doing nothing is tacit compliance with this totalitarian NWO agenda. Doing nothing is no longer an option as far as humanity or sustained life on Earth is concerned. Most Elites do not know it; but are tied to the Luciferian agenda committed to destroying creation. Elites are Satanic victims in need of Main Street prayer... lots of prayer. Only Main Street is coherent enough to offer these prayers. We can always pray for our assailants and attackers while defending ourselves against their evil intentions. The simplest defense against the global syndicate is to say "NO THANK YOU" to their multinational products and services.

On a subtler track, **people management** in simplistic terms or more sinisterly, **mind control** is implemented by Oligarchic order-followers along co-ordinated, <u>multi-faceted rails</u>, sometimes employing unexpected modalities operationally effecting predictable behavioral outcomes across large population segments within a culture. If you are new to this malevolent form of manipulation, it's not believable beyond science fiction. If not, you understand how successfully mind control can be implemented, effecting both individuals and groups.[103] Mind control is a long-term endeavor, and its incremental inculcation is difficult to identify, particularly when packaged attractively, hence its weaponized effectiveness, at least since 1948 or so, when Tavistock declared behavioral propaganda war (my words) against the American people.[104]

Simple aspects of culture can be adapted and implemented as clever forms of mind control. Habitual linguistic patterns for example, not typically regarded by most of us as a form of mind control, effectively corral our range of thinking and even our ability to think effectively at all. The wide-spread use of Ebonics or repetitive, parroted propaganda soundbites for example exert profound influence on our dialectic range of thought.

Can we imagine a beautiful young woman born in South Chicago's projects, whose Marxist Democrat controlled, educational gulag impaled her on the rusty spike of illiteracy and generational poverty, ever employing her Ebonics mutilated language skills to successfully land a high-paying gig at Honeywell or a full tenured Professorship at University of Chicago's neo-classical School of Economics? Not even her quickly brandished middle finger, a skill encouraged by Marxist organizers can overcome this educational malfeasance, though her attitude, dreads, tats, and piercings are spectacular. Our young lady is mutilated by Blue Marxist Propaganda into a living persona of cognitive dissonance, embarrassingly dumbed down, whining for fairness victimhood while simultaneously rejecting life's constructive possibilities.

Dis-education, i.e., anti-education is a crime against humanity and must be regarded as such. This young Chicago child and thousands like her are conditioned from day one in public schools (87% of students attend public schools) and private schools to believe if they swill the brain-washed tripe of hatred,

---

103 "Microcosm and Medium."
104 Daniel Estulin, *Tavistock Institute: Social Engineering the Masses* (Walterville, OR: Trine Day, 2015).

bigotry, discord, and victimhood, futilely acting out accordingly, they will be opportunistically free; but such is not the case outside their own selection of impoverished limitation as a permanent, even generationally institutionalized way of disempowered life. Interestingly, in America, **projected victimhood** for entire classes of people has become a means for psychopaths to obtain name recognition, then political power. Recent Satanic manuals for this manipulative organizing deceit are *Cloward and Pivens Strategy* and *Rules for Radicals.*[105]

Another common example is the wide-spread use of cute little soundbites routinely incorporated into ridiculous, 90-second, so-called News Alert segments projected as rapid-fire collage imagery to millions of mind-numbing TV screens across the globe. We are effectively conditioned hour by viewing hour with the help of *alpha entrainment* and *flicker-rates* or *flicker-fusion* to shorten our attention span, erase our ability to concentrate, tell us what to think; or worse, entrain us not to think at all. As I understand it, flicker-fusion is a separate process not used during mind control applications, but this is outside my wheelhouse. Alpha entrainment, if you're not aware, stimulates right-brain activity while diminishing left-brain analytical thought processes.

Why do we waste time listening to two or three highly compensated sound-bite drones babbling about how to improve the $75 trillion global economy in 90-seconds or less? My dog and kitties won't even listen to this nonsense and they like TV, especially episodic series laced with tightly scripted compelling conflict. We are being dumbed down by increasingly limited language skills and more importantly by increasingly limited use of any meaningful language at all. **Linguistic alchemy** and dumbing down language skills dumb down perception, which dumbs down thinking, which limits life's potential opportunity. Attending conditioning centers called schools for mandated dumbing down, strangling of reasoning skills, and promotion of racial hatred are cognitive dissonance in action on several levels.

Global syndicate owned and controlled multi-media misinformation sources, public and private, routinely intersect. Conflicting ideas, values, beliefs, and contradictory facts are connected as though logically combined. Such irrational association generates psychological stress in viewers and listeners who at least subliminally know better despite peer pressured, status quo conformity. The resulting confusion and low-level anxiety is called **cognitive dissonance**. The global syndicate via Tavistock and other NWO institutes has weaponized low-level anxiety among mass population groups, thereby rendering targeted populations increasingly susceptible to thought manipulation, identity confusion, and behavior modification. This is evil personified.

---

105 "Rules for Radicals: A Practical Primer for Realistic Radicals: Saul D. Alinsky

12 • Cognitive Blissonance: An Aspect of Mind Control

Cognitive dissonance is employed to diminish reason. One way of doing it is cleverly repeating euphemistic opposites so often, they are readily joined and accepted without evaluation by victims of what we call public education. The average busy person trying to survive and carry the impossibly growing financial shackles of inflation, compound interest, and confiscatory taxation, not only fails to see any contradiction or hypocrisy; but often defends the lunacy of contradiction implicit within malicious sound-bite phraseology and imagery.

School in place of the more correct **conditioning-center** label is an example, of course. Pro-choice for infanticide another example. *Black Lives Matter* groups looting and burning, often in predominantly poor or middle class neighborhoods in peaceful protest is a peach. How about grown women claiming to detest objectification as sex objects proudly sporting pink crocheted Vagina Hats supposedly representing gender equality? Double-think/group-think/hive-mind conditioning devours intelligence in huge mass gulps as decent people, apparently so unfulfilled in life, seek something, anything, even a hypocritical vag-hat, just to be part of something. Is this laudable *enlightenment* or pathetic?

When we repetitively allow prurient imagery to fill our minds; and dis-educational, low intellectual quality, linguistic elements to permeate our speech, the debilitating process incrementally permeates our thinking, both as individuals and within groups; reducing our cognitive processes to that of tadpoles – no offense to tadpoles as I doubt there is a tadpole anywhere swimming in a vag-hat?

Anyway, if we employ dis-associative language diminishing perception, fact finding, and conceptual reasoning; and if language skills are severely limited; it follows our ability to cognize, differentiate, and evaluate the world around us declines accordingly. Tavistock order-followers are expert in developing methodologies bringing this type of mental/emotional debilitation to fruition on a mass basis. As a targeted population we become increasingly passive and docile. Decision making becomes inordinately uncomfortable to the point we look to "others" to decide for us, even on significant personal questions, like whether to wear a vag-hat, murder our unborn child, take a bioweapon JAB, wear a noxious face diaper, or defend ourselves from harm.

Imagery and linguistics then, can be weaponized as forms of mind control when repetitively utilized by academia and indoctrinated media for mass behavioral manipulation and/or ideological acceptance, particularly concepts we would likely never agree with if possessing better information or left to our sovereign devices. We may not notice or be aware of these *mass formation* processes, but Tavistock and its demonic researchers are; though some of them, already Left Brain unbalanced, may be compartmentally nescient on a need-to-know basis? Martial artist, Bruce Lee reminded us that imitating others is safer than risking independent thinking and action – a weak way of living sure to minimize life's potential value.

Tavistock's *Lewin Doctrine* basically identifies two psychological spaces – **environment and self**. Dr. Kurt Lewin taught that controlling environmental psychological space could move control beyond mass ability, thereby extending *behavior modification* to *identity change*.[106] This is one purpose of Tavistock techniques such as *long-range penetration* and *inner-directional conditioning*. *Cognitive dissonance* itself is just another rocket in this psychological missile launcher employed to weaken and control our independent selves on a mass scale. Think MK ULTRA, MOCKINGBIRD MEDIA, MH CHAOS, COINTELPRO, etc.

Should we dare inquire or are we even permitted by META infected school boards to ask why dumbed down curriculum protocols are steadily diminishing student math competency, reasoning skills, and functional literacy; or what impact this degeneracy has on future ability of young people to comprehend basic elements of the world they inhabit? Is this failure to properly educate our children an orchestrated crime against humanity or just dereliction of educational duty? Asked and answered.

Obviously, educational failure is planned as the provably failing curricula are written into organized lesson plans using dumbed down materials, leaving only motivation in question. Motivation determined by morally challenged educational publishers and non-teaching administrators, then mandated for overwhelmed teachers to incorporate, as they are heinously trapped in this abusive dumbing down system, where *"new soon to fail ideas"* are unleashed annually. For teaching careers – go along or get out – liberal fairness and equity in action, I guess?

Main Street for the most part, is unaware of this enslaving infection or whom the implementarians are. Controlled conflict through divide and conquer Hegelian dialectic infects both Left and Right thinking with preservative anesthetics. Infected coherency is obliterated for both. Many of those implementing the mass mind control program, are themselves true believers, unaware of big-picture program intent. They are saving the world. Fragmentation, compartmentalization, and what I term **bifurcation** are all forms of atomized thought control, that is, spiritual control, limiting our overall contextual perception, especially for those implementing the program. Implementarians are the indoctrinated A-Team.

Moral conscience and decision-making capacity can be functionally immobilized or manipulated. It is critical for sane survival that Main Street realize Elites desiring mind control implementation as well as their Pawns of Privilege

---

106 "The Tavistock Institute of Human Relations: Shaping the Moral, Spiritual, Cultural, and Political. A by John Coleman (2006-08-02): Amazon.Com: Books," 55–56.

bringing it to fruition, believe in slavery – or at least their right to benefit from it. Furthermore, they are conditioned to believe they are Entitled Slave Masters, and their Slave Stock is culled from Main Street paddocks called nations, states, counties, parishes, cities, towns, villages, and tribes. Since only so many slaves are needed, slave management requires *culling the herd* and eliminating *excess* population. This culling in turn, requires control methodologies preventing slave awareness and possible revolt. Dumb slaves tend to be happier slaves.

After all, mind control is not a hobby; it has a defined people management purpose even if we the people of Main Street or the implementarians themselves, the order-followers, do not realize it or understand it. **Mind control is the new Administrative State warfare model**; the slavery by **pacification and intellectual domination model** found to be more effective than guns, cattle cars, and re-education camps ever were. **No one escapes a prison they don't know they're in.** Prolonged cognitive dissonance creates an unholy but stable foundation for mind control to build on. Few of us can see ourselves as slaves within a regimented system we argue for, vote for, and pay for. Those proclaiming **the right** to be taken care of by government or other institutions are blind to their own demand for enslavement; an embarrassing lack of self-awareness should it ever be perceived, but Mr. Global's Big Bro and Big Sis work overtime inhibiting such perception.

Typically, we discuss mind control, if discussed at all, in terms of bizarre Nazi concentration camp experiments. Examples are Russian, Chinese, Korean, or Vietnam war indoctrination of prisoners or more popularly, Richard Condon's 1959 thriller, *Manchurian Candidate*. More recently, we see my personal favs, Robert Ludlum's exciting *Bourne Series* of novels with their successful film adaptations. Both fiction writers and Hollywood, while entertainingly exposing mind control strategies through suspension of disbelief and cognitive dissonance, have simultaneously trivialized, and relegated this very real, extremely dangerous technology to the backseat realm of surrealistic fiction. Candy treats, popcorn, and delicious buttery flavored topping aside, thought manipulation and cognitive dissonance are happening. This intention is evil.

We can see an interesting example of Hollywood telling us what is going on in one my favorite *Amazon Prime* episodic series, *The Mentalist*. Season 1, Episode 11 titled *Red John's Friends* showcases electromagnetic brain experiments where the subject's decisions are changed 180 degrees, say from yes to no or vice versa. This was done by sending electric current through a small, targeted portion of the brain. The episode depicts old school methods directly attaching circuits to the subject's skull as failing to work. Today this sort of brain wave manipulation is done remotely by any number of technologies and Hollywood dutifully warned us back in 2008. Thank you, pedophile capital of the U.S., though Washington D.C. combatively vies for that same title.

Mr. Jay Dyer of *Jay's Analysis* suggests at least some of this exposure by Hollywood is intended. In his analysis of the 1971 James Bond film, *Diamonds Are Forever* Mr. Dyer tells us: "In reality, the hierarchical pyramid of global government is not a series of goodly nation states seeking to protect the "free world" from dastardly Manichean dialectical manifestations, but rather is itself a large interlocking system of crime syndicates. The world government that presently exists is one of covert, hidden rulership by various oligarchs."[107]

Mr. Dyer goes on to say: "It is the establishment that is the ruling mafia cartel, and the control of black markets is key to understanding what is meant by "shadow government". Their goal is global government and the control of all aspects of life, and unfortunately some aspects of life in this world involve black markets. We often speak of the "New World Order" taking over governments or conspiring to manipulate some event or subvert some institution, but the best lens through which to grasp its true inner workings is international crime and its syndicates. And it is the best model because the globalists run the international crime rackets."[108]

We need to grasp this international criminal reality, its pervasively parasitic hold on government policy—foreign and domestic—and the far-reaching consequence of a globally criminalized business plan before we can embrace freedom enhancing remedies for our current dilemma. It is imperative we realize most of our <u>selected</u> Representatives and appointed agency directors are nothing more than organized crime dupes. Main Street must realize the U.S. economy depends on organized criminal activity for sustenance as well as the extent to which the global system of corrupt arteries and veins is expanded and defended by blackmail, extortion, violence, or threat of violence. If we cannot recognize a systemic threat to civilized society, it can't be fixed. We don't usually find things we aren't looking for and this applies to syndicated threats.

Our supposed leaders, just middle level "made wise guys" or "syndicate managers" operationally, deceitfully lead us to believe we should manage our economy politically and our politics economically, both ridiculous concepts guaranteeing central planning's failure to provide societal benefit. The syndicate understands the American middle class must be brought to its bloody economic knees in order to break resistance to One World Totalitarian Government before global syndicate plans, i.e., **The Great Reset** can be implemented. Main Street is being harvested... and harvesting is fueled by debilitation incurred via globalist attacks unleashed against basic family structure as the foundational building block of

---

107 "Esoteric Hollywood: Sex, Cults and Symbols in Film: Jay Dyer: 9781634240772:" 257.
108 "Esoteric Hollywood: Sex, Cults and Symbols in Film: Jay Dyer: 9781634240772:" 259.

society. Who on Main Street imagines our U.S. Constitution and Rule of Law being taken down collaterally by banning God, destroying families, and instituting *Reflexive Law* as a "better idea"? It is difficult to see through the emotional discomfort generated by Main Street's fog of finely tuned cognitive dissonance.

Study group system entrancement via secret societies, foundations, institutes, associations, think tanks, NGO's, etc., along with educational indoctrination, Hollywood conditioning, and *Mockingbird* media support guarantee the process of intellectual diminishment remaining poorly understood, but powerfully continuing. These subtle control techniques driving immobilizing cognitive conflicts constitute occult knowledge at its 21st century zenith. Since thought manipulation is theft of free thought for undermining individual freedom with or without consent—it is pure evil. In self-defense we must invoke coherent perception and persistently inquire **why do I or we think this or that?** Why do I or we like or dislike this or that candidate or policy; this or that product, etc.? Healthy perception is always strong, rational self-defense.

We are led to believe mind control is limited to individual experiments resulting in lone serial killers, child molesters, or other deviant behavior. We saw this in Stanley Milgram's shocking experiments studying authoritative factors driving one person to hurt another (unknown) person with unwarranted increasing severity.[109] We know from *MK Ultra* and other programs, this research is occurring, but the larger, darker threat is **mass mind control and mass population behavior modification**, i.e., as a component of weaponized *full-spectrum dominance*. This situation worsens when such research is enacted on Main Street without knowledge or consent, say via inhaled/injected nano-chips and nanobots; long range telemetric/telepathic or electro-magnetic-scalar frequency penetration; television and computer screen *flicker-rates*, etc.

Other common mind control pathways are weaponized educational conditioning, propaganda, advertising, religion, sports, entertainment, and military experiments. DARPA's *Life Log* system, called *Facebook* since 2004, now *Meta*, along with other social media surveillance, predictive programming, vaccines, medicines, other pharmaceuticals, poor nutrition, and undermined health via poisoned air, water, and food products; as well as other modes we can imagine all weaken and contribute. 21st century mind control is everywhere, and it is aimed at we the people of Main Street; so, we must turn off the conditioning tubes occasionally, practice thinking for ourselves, and say NO THANK YOU.

---

109 "Obedience to Authority: An Experimental... Book by Stanley Milgram,"

As you may or not be aware, tech giants like *Google*[110] or *Amazon*, social media information gathering forums like *Facebook (Meta)*, *Twitter*, *Instagram*, and Google's *YouTube* are all deeply intertwined with and are funded to a significant extent by DARPA (*Defense Advanced Research Projects Agency*), and our intrepid CIA's *In-Q-Tel* capital fund along with related investment banks such as *Goldman Sachs* and dozens of other transnational monopolies. Think of global syndicate controlled investment monopolies like *Vanguard*, *BlackRock*, *State Street*, and *Berkshire Hathaway* and the insane control captured governments help provide them.

Social media forum platforms are weaponized for *full spectrum dominance* as are all major tele-communications companies working with corrupt agencies. Popular media polls, also weaponized, are not designed to inform us what people think - polls are designed to convince us what to think as an alternative to not thinking at all. The so-called founders of these tech giants may have had an idea; but quickly sold themselves and their ideas to the devil in exchange for billions of dollars and privileged deep state protective cover. Certainly not all of this is evil and, in some respects, may be necessary for self-defense of nations, but 5G kills, literally, and may never benefit anyone on Main Street. Try to find a 5G related health study anywhere on MSM. Maybe 5G can be humanized, but who exactly will do that and if they do, will we know?

The answer is NO, we will not know if we hold our breath waiting for corrupted multinational media monopolies to provide a correct or beneficial answer. Our weak political leaders are no longer capable of telling the whole truth and have abandoned all sense of honor. This leaves humanity on its own to learn the truth, determine our best way forward, then together, work our plan despite overwhelming obstruction, recrimination, and outright attack as we have experienced since January 6th, 2020 with hundreds of U.S. political prisoners.

The only path to regaining Constitutionally recognized unalienable rights is peaceful grass roots organization. Clearly, the egregious election fraud witnessed before, on November 3rd, 2020 and after, will not be addressed by the corrupt and/or blackmailed cretins we foolishly elected to sell Main Street out to the global syndicate via the weaponized CCP, Russia, Iran, Italy, etc. Main Street is on its own, standing together in unison or we sink divided as the global syndicate intends. **The global syndicate plan is global serfdom.** Prayer, united with our effort and God's grace stops this evil plan in its tracks.

---

110 Nafeez Ahmed, "How the CIA Made Google," Medium, November 13, 2015, https://medium.com/insurge-intelligence/how-the-cia-made-google-e836451a959e.

Marxism is a Satanic Ideology spawned by Jean-Jacques Rousseau (1712-1778), Johann (Adam) Weishaupt (1748-1830), Francois-Noel Babeuf (1760-1797), Filippo Buonarroti (1761-1837), Thomas Malthus (1766-1834), Georg Hegel (1770-1831), Charles Darwin (1809-1882), Karl Marx (1818-1883), Friedrich Engels (1820-1895), Antonio Gramsci (1891-1937), and others.

13 • Cognitive Blissonance and Cultural Marxist Decimation

Remedy: The spiritual, intellectual, and emotional violence of Marxism, its twisted sister Fascism, and finally, synthesized Globalism drive many of us to imagine violent self-defense as the logically exclusive answer to humanity's survival. Self-defense via Civil War may necessarily become our future American path—but not yet. We can still save the Rule of Law through grass roots political action. Two-thirds of the United States' population are Constitutionalists of Christian or Jewish faith. We have the majority numbers but do not act as though we do. It's time we did. Time to become involved locally in our church groups, school boards, town, city, county, and state governments. As THEY say – all politics are local. Let's get involved, get our hands dirty, and work together - wiping America clean of Satanic totalitarian disease!

Modern day totalitarian systems are vastly more ideological than history's classic dictatorships. Marxism itself is a zealous God-hating religion spread by indoctrinated *illumination*, i.e., lies. A classic dictator, always a psychopath, once firmly in power, can treat subjugated citizens decently, thereby striving for some level of social stability. A modern Marxist totalitarian dictator, not only psychopathic but also Satanically possessed (my opinion) has no such option. The Marxist totalitarian dictator has only one option, one plan, one goal – destruction of everything within reach, ultimately ending in self-annihilation. All Marxist, Fascist, Globalist ideologies are Satanically influenced plans for omnicide. It is not spiritually possible for any form of equality to exist under State mandated **equity**.

Professor of Psychology at Belgium's University of Ghent, Dr. Mattias Desmet offers instruction in **"mass formation"**, a subject arising from KGB studies of **"mass demoralization"** (my opinion) discussed by Soviet dissident, Yuri Bezmenov back in the 1980's. Through a process of applied societal stresses and repetitive indoctrination, large population groups can be conditioned to adopt a hypnotic **"collective unconsciousness"**, forming what Gustav Le Bon (1841-1931) referred to earlier, as a **"psychological crowd"**. Such groups feel socially isolated, humanly disconnected, cannot make sense of life, therefore lack meaning and purpose in life, then, suffering from *free floating anxiety*, behavior metastasizes into *free floating aggression*. We saw this conditioned behavior with the Bolshevik Red Guard, Mussolini's Black Shirts, Hitler's Brown Shirts, Mao's Red Guard, and we see the rinse and repeat today with *social justice warriors* like members of *Antifa, BLM, our FBI*, and so forth.

The **Mass Formation** indoctrination process, which Tavistock has turned into a fine art, manufactures divided groups of people incapable of tolerating competitive or opposing views, even to the point of responding with Fascistic violence to simple questions. Frustration generated by the narrowly limited ability to engender rational responses to rhetorical questions and debate drives conditioned unfortunates to confront reality, instantly herding them back to the anxiety and unhappiness precipitating *mass formation* initially. We'll not delve into this further, but must realize in self-defense, globalist conditioning runs deep, posing extreme danger to all free or mostly free societies. A person, once *demoralized*, can no longer effectively process information. This *mass formation* conditioning cannot be reversed except through some form of **extreme shock**. We see the sad result of *mass formation conditioning* throughout the United States, in every BLUE CITY, BLUE STATE, and among complicit Establishment RINOs.

To my limited knowledge, the first organized, large scale, intentional *demoralization* attack since 1913's Wilson Administration on individuality and free thinking in America was launched in conjunction with *true believers in Communism*, mostly labor related, during the roaring twenties, not long after the 1917 Bolshevik Coup in Russia. I've held in my own, once callused hands, a stapled pamphlet - a manual of maybe two dozen or so, 5" x 8" pages, copyrighted 1920, published by the *Communist Party USA* (CPUSA, split from the *Socialist Party of America* in 1919), outlining protocols for creating small independent groups (now called cells) to infiltrate and undermine the Catholic Church specifically and Christian churches generally, as well as indoctrinating American educators and various popular societal groups. The Marxist objective was, and is, undermining moral and cultural values, thereby creating disharmony and societal disorder while undermining local organizational effectiveness through infiltration of state governments, county boards, city councils, school boards, school administrations, university faculties, religious as-

13 • Cognitive Blissonance and Cultural Marxist Decimation

sociations, church groups, publishing houses, newspaper editorial staffs, professional associations, etc. The success of this *demoralization* program is impressive.

I personally held the above mentioned 1920's pamphlet in my hot, 30-year-old hands where I found it in a wealthy contractor's private library in Madison, Wisconsin; a gorgeous, traditional three-story home on the southeastern shore of Lake Mendota by the way. I was a young civil engineer in Monona, Wisconsin at the time and yes, I'm disappointed I didn't make a copy. My bad! This pamphlet epitomized Fabian Socialism and the teaching of Italian Marxist, Antonio Gramsci (1891 – 1937) and others, who believed Communist utopia would eliminate capitalism incrementally via a better idea as opposed to Marx and Lenin's view of violent overthrow by the working class.

Apparently, Mr. Gramsci was not aware it was Elite London and Wall Street monopolists themselves who sponsored Communism as a centralized means of feudalistic control? Who took over Russian banking and industry for example? Who took control of Russian oil fields and Caucasus manganese mines? Who got the Czar's gold, art, jewels, etc.? My high-school history book never touched on these historic questions. Who stole the imperial dynastic treasures of the Chinese people? More recently, who pocketed Libya's gold reserves? I've never heard a peep about any of this loot being shared with the proletariat.

Anyway, via this circa 1920's Communist pamphlet, I can personally attest to collectivist indoctrinational activity going on in the U.S. at least since the twenties. My late, great, previous home-state of Wisconsin's, Senator Joseph McCarthy (1908 – 1957) got it at least partially, I would say mostly right (pun intended), though by arc's end, his over-reach became problematic. A bit earlier, then congruently, we have the so-called *Frankfurt School*, a sort of adjunct to the *Institute for Social Research*, itself an adjunct to *University of Frankfurt*.

The *Frankfurt School* wasn't a school or institute per se, as much as an *ad hoc* group of dissidents uncomfortable with communist, fascist, and capitalist theory of their day. This impressive school of thinkers developed a line of reasoning and research known as *critical theory*, which attempted to meld various schools of thought with classical Marxism, hoping to overcome the failings of Marxism already experienced in Western Europe. Lenin might have said these were the first well-paid, *useful idiots*.

Members of the Frankfurt School, most of whom never saw it as a school anyway, as I understand it, did not consider themselves Marxists; but were heavily influenced by Hegel, a significant Marxian influence, and in search of acquiring *"self-knowledge"* via *critical theory*, tended to revisit classical Marxism for solutions.

Not being admitted Marxists themselves, they lived the paradox of basically teaching Marxist principles anyway, hence their extreme danger to freedom in any form. Even though members of the Frankfurt School were a non-agreeing, disparate group of thinkers, I suspect it fair to suggest as a group they might be called Neo-Marxist or at least Collectivist; and in any event, gave birth to the academically influential societal cancer we call *Cultural Marxism* today.

Brief clarification: *Cultural Marxism* is an over-used term (at least by me) usually employed to batter the Left and sometimes used in an anti-Semitic context; I suppose because the Left has historically leaned anti-Semitic as well as antiblack and anti-just about everything else including antiwhite. In any event, I employ the term as a catch-all describing irrational Fascist bigotry of *social justice warriors* (SJW) bolstering divide and conquer causes furthering globalism's totalitarian mind control agenda. The term *social justice warriors* is contrived cognitive dissonance as are the abused globalist terms *equity, equality, fairness, caring, and sustainability*.

Note: Hegelian dialectic misleads both or all sides of a debate or argument via **controlled conflict**. It is sometimes said the Left Hegelians leaned toward Karl Marx while the Right Hegelians leaned toward Adolf Hitler suggesting two opposing outcomes. This error in thinking is a good example of cognitive dissonance blurring reality. Marx's Communism is the lie of state-provided security overcoming individual greed, thereby peddling the totalitarian Nanny State. Occult motivations aside, Hitler's Fascism, i.e., **National Socialism**, simply substitutes racial and religious bigotry and manufactured ethnic hatred for class hatred, thereby providing a long-term, unlimited supply of enemies for disparate groups to hate. This is the path by which Fascism became the hob-nailed government boot on the throat of liberty enforcing the totalitarian Marxist Nanny State. Two sides of the same Hegelian coin with differing hate targets; not diametrically opposed opposites.

Communism and Fascism together forge totalitarian Globalism comprising a complimentary synthesis standing in divide and conquer fashion against non-existent free market capitalism. Under the banner of equality, freedom is renounced for everyone, including *study group* Pawns of Privilege. This synthesis replaces old school Mercantilism but is much the same in practice, just more aggressive, pushing steadily toward Transhuman Neo-feudalism.

Left/right, liberal/conservative, black/white, gay/hetero, rich/poor, global warming believer/climate denier, etc., are all divisive labels co-opted by the Hard Left with complicit support by the Establishment Right to further big government interference and control with top-down, centrally planned subjugation as we see in every Marxist state. *Cultural Marxism* and a deceptively more *Friendly Fascism*

13 • Cognitive Blissonance and Cultural Marxist Decimation

subtend a broad spectrum of wide-ranging though acute economic/social/cultural issues, real and contrived. Such issues are blended into a circular paradigm of controlled conflict, defined and managed into an irrational Hegelian dialectic abyss by an academically indoctrinated Ruling Class working on behalf the global syndicate. *Frankfurt School* theoreticians effectively spawned a *critical theory* monster vastly complicating basic issues with irrational argument, i.e., **cognitive dissonance** and **emotional angst**. *Critical Theory*, like it's recent irrational spawn, *Critical Race Theory* are cognitive dissonance in support of societal destruction.

Exposure to totalitarian thinking and collectivist systems are in the end, anathema to individual creative thought, are self-limiting, and self-impoverishing – even under today's more *friendly fascism* as described by Bertram Gross. Contrary to academic babbling, Marxism doesn't empower human groups or initiative. It enslaves the individual within divided oppressed groups by blind loyalty, force, coercion, lies, forced outcomes, or other means. Marxism strangles human dignity, imagination, and initiative to consistently defend and protect Elite authoritarian control and power. This ideology eventually destroys the divided groups themselves via socio-economic failure, inability to sustain positive returns on investment, or by failing to sustainably provide ongoing human benefit of any kind. Marxist collapse occurs historically in three generations, though staggers on longer if imposed incrementally as in the U.S. and much of Europe.

We see such cognitively dissonant political neurosis play out in our schools today, as liberal ideology refuses to acknowledge the Constitutional right of teachers to arm or defend themselves and their students against violent *false flag* attacks mounted for propaganda purposes by rogue elements within our own government and deep state, but I digress, again. Accurate statistics are difficult to come by, but the *Crime Prevention Research Center* has found between 1998 and 2018, 97.8% of mass public shootings occurred within legally defined **gun-free zones**. Rarely does Mockingbird media share that more than 2.5 million crimes are prevented each year by armed citizens, usually without firing a weapon. A CDC study during the Soetoro Regime estimated this number to exceed 3.0 million crimes prevented annually by armed citizens. Armed citizens, of course, are detested and feared by totalitarian thugs and *demoralized* order followers.

Historically, cognitive dissonance found an American home to burrow into when the **Frankfurt School** folks relocated from Frankfurt to Geneva in 1933 as Hitler rose to power; then to New York in 1935, taking up residence at Columbia University where they scored a new identity as *Studies in Philosophy and Social Science*. This group became profoundly influential throughout American academia in ensuing decades, which is why I mention it. Education itself is a form of thought limiting or expanding mind-control, so context is important. Later, in the early fifties, Max Horkheimer, Theodore Adorno, and Friedrich Pollack returned to West Germany, re-establishing the Institute in Frankfurt in 1953. Other notable thinkers associated with the Frankfurt school were Erich Fromm, Henryk Grossman, Otto Kirchheimer, Leo Lowenthal, Herbert Marcuse, Franz Leopold Neuman, and others of lesser note.

A number of these Frankfurt School intellectuals were brilliant authors and convincing speakers to say the least, particularly from the forties through the seventies. Though I consider their inquiry compelling, weighty, and insightful, many of their conclusions are narrowly conceived, liberty inhibiting, and damaging to Western Christian theology, philosophy, culture, and society, regardless their noble intent and prodigiously prolific effort.

Their contributions, apart from Atheism, Mercantilism, Fabianism, Fascism, Marxism, Neo-Marxism, Socialism, not-to-mention other God despising ideologies have been only cautiously helpful and usually detrimental. Beyond Frankfurt, we have additionally, a monumental, Elite controlled, City of London think tank called **Tavistock** (originally Wellington House) as mentioned earlier. The fact most of us never heard of Tavistock, testifies to its formidable study group influence and subtly profound, sophisticated impact. The good Doctors at Tavistock by the way, appear to have invoked psychological warfare against Main Street United States citizens in 1948. We now struggle spiritually to survive the result of their heavily funded effort to put American Main Streets back under control, or at least nearer British Crown wishes. In Britain's imperial defense, I concede this aggressive asymmetric action may have been in response to FDR's desire to defang the British Crown after WW II. Anyway, mind control is the only path Elites can see to any form of global One World Government slavery. The U.S. middle-class must be brought to heel.

Dissociative thought transformation, personality regression, and identity change carried on a current of *cognitive dissonance* are predictable human responses to intolerable levels of environmentally induced stress. Can we say nuclear holocaust, environmental disaster, climate change, war on drugs, war on terror, disaster capitalism, constant health epidemics, 24-hour news alerts, and frequent false-flag events? Main Street is drowning in mass media **Fear Pornography**.

Applied societal stress, even at low levels over long periods of time reduce the highly differentiated, versatile human mind to that of an ani-

mal, where environment begins to dominate personality.[111] Tavistockian Psycho-Orcs morph this diseased study material into enslavement technologies, whereby Main Street victims incarcerate themselves within their own regressed minds. We now live in a centrally planned, de-stabilized PsyOp reality, the next psychological phase of which is autonomous transhuman control via 5G, IoT, or newer ionizing entrainment technologies. Spiritual existence and awareness, our only hope for survival, are being 100% divorced, bifurcated from Main Street spiritual awareness and material life… and we the people of Main Street are paying for and voting for this horror to our uninformed detriment.

As mentioned previously, mind control also takes less obvious forms of implementation along the lines of *mass media conditioning* by TV, radio, internet, social media, etc., along with entrainment technology or surprisingly, dietary attacks on health, immune systems, brain function, mood, and psychology. These techniques and subsequent effects have been and are being studied and developed by social science order-followers at Elite study group centers such as *The Tavistock Institute of Human Relations*.[112] Tavistockian influence plays into most modern cultural phenomena such as the sexual revolution, Counterculture movement, feminism, gay liberation, gender confusion, climate change, Critical Race Theory, and other nonsense. Though noteworthy, Mr. Jan Irvin, Mr. Joe Atwill and several others have written extensively on manufactured cultural influence, so we will not delve into detail here.

Tavistock is the grandfather of all group-think research centers, holding sway as the geopolitical centroid of the **international study group brainwashing system**. Its power arises in part from lack of notoriety… I mean, who's ever heard of Tavistock for crying out loud… and the folks at T have a great website to show us, though it doesn't mention *mass formation, inner-directional conditioning, entrainment technology, identity change, nor intellectual slavery.*

A more current treatise expounding on the psychotic studies of Tavistock, should the reader be curious is *Tavistock Institute: Social Engineering the Masses* by Mr. Daniel Estulin.[113] This is a wonderful piece of work and should be required reading in every high school across the globe; at least those still hitting 6th grade achievement levels or above. Tavistock has become a psychological warfare octopus extending its insidious tentacles from the University of Sussex to its prime 20th/21st century target, the United States through companies like RAND and MITRE corporations, and such venerable establishment institutions as Yale, Harvard,

---

111 "The Tavistock Institute of Human Relations: Shaping the Moral, Spiritual, Cultural, and Political; by John Coleman, 55,56.
112 "The Tavistock Institute of Human Relations: Shaping the Moral, Spiritual, Cultural, and Political; by John Coleman.
113 Estulin, *Tavistock Institute.*

Stanford Research Institute, Hoover Institution, Aspen Institute, Brookings Institution, CATO Institute, Massachusetts Institute of Technology (MIT), Hudson Institute, Heritage Foundation, Rockefeller Foundation(s), Carnegie Foundation, Ditchley Foundation, Ford Foundation, Russell Sage Foundation, Georgetown's Center of Strategic and International Studies, and Wharton School of Business.

Tavistock caters to secret or semi-secret groups such as The Pilgrim Society, Skull & Bones, Wolf's Head Society, Mont Pelerin Society, and Bohemian Grove, as well as other NGO's and study group anchors like Club of Rome, Royal Institute of International Affairs (Chatham House), Council on Foreign Relations, Institute of Pacific Relations, Trilateral Commission and Bilderberg Group to name just a notable few among many. Sorry if I failed to list your group.

Tavistock, other institutes, foundations, trusts, think tanks, study groups, and academia itself, totaling more than 3,000 dedicated NGOs in the United States alone, are paid, usually with our tax dollars, to develop techniques for manufacture and manipulation of public opinion; or in the case of military applications, *full-spectrum dominance* (superiority). A prominent historic example is provided by Edward Bernays and Walter Lipmann openly preparing U.S. public opinion and Arnold Toynbee preparing Brits for entry into the great war (WW I) against Germany. The Great War, funded on all sides by the **Anglo-American Establishment** by the way. This is not conspiracy, but is an effective monopoly-business development strategy Main Street everywhere keeps saying YES to, when we should say NO. Let Elites fight among themselves. We can pay to watch and munch organic popcorn drenched with grass-fed butter and sea-salt while we enjoy Elites whining each other to unconsciousness in the octagon.

Speaking of buttered organic popcorn, a personal fav, reminds me that Communist Dogma extols the effectiveness of central planning and government control over food and medicine supplies generally, as well as nutrition and health services specifically. Nutrition and healthcare are wonderful exploitation targets for psychopathic government control over Main Street masses, being less obvious weapons of mass subjugation than gun control, the traditional favorite of dictators everywhere.

We asked earlier if obesity itself could be the result of mind control. I suspect it is. Believe it or not, **nutrient deficiency** is one of the subtler forms of *softening-up*, supporting more obvious forms of mind control by decreasing *ability to resist*. The U.S. government is fully complicit in this insidious, health diminishing program, whether individuals involved realize it. The study group conditioning system effectively enlists thousands of regulatory order-followers and true-believers in its program, most of whom gullibly have no idea the evil they perpetrate or why. The study group brain-washing system is nothing, if not effective, in terms of cost, outreach, and deniability.

Cognitive dissonance is an inexpensive, easily circulated mind control tool effectively employed throughout the global study group system. It's just words, words, and more words as *Beavis and Butthead* note but impressively thought numbing across any subject matter. For example, we are still being told by health "experts" to eat several helpings of processed grain daily despite chemical toxicities in most industrial farmed grains. This despite overwhelming evidence of physical harm caused by doing so. Even consuming pesticide laden, GMO, glyphosate laced grains second hand through grain fed cattle, hogs, turkey, chicken, fish farms, etc., are harmful to health. Such misinformation is not just a lie, it powerfully promotes cognitive dissonance to the point health information seekers give up attempting to determine best options. Results of popular food propaganda are inflammation, obesity, leaky-gut, chronic pain, immobility, depression, and other metabolic syndrome issues.

Unlikely as it sounds, **debilitating eating habits** and **nutritionally deficient diets** comprise a subtle modality behind which lurks one of Earth's most egregiously lucrative polygamous marriages linking organized industrial crime, government, and the global syndicate – an incestuous marriage of big banking-big government regulation-big agriculture-big chemical-big pharma-big medicine-big insurance-big food processing-and big media, all beneath Cartel Chairman, Satan.

The criminally malfeasant *Federal Food and Drug Administration* (FDA) along with other corrupt Federal agencies such as *Dept. of Agriculture* (USDA*)*, *Environmental Protection Agency* (EPA), *Centers for Disease Control and Prevention* (CDC), and *National Institutes of Health* (NIH) to citizen-indict four more, uniformly protect and enable corrupt transnational monopolies by routinely accepting falsified testing protocols and manipulated data; approving pharmaceuticals, pesticides, fertilizers, foods, and ingredients regardless of toxicity level or other potentially harmful effects. This criminality is routine practice, while simultaneously delaying or never approving independent competitor testing, thereby restraining free trade, eliminating competition, and prohibiting legitimate products being offered to consumer markets by legitimate entrepreneurs. Treasonous Comrade Uncle Sam is busy, and Pawns of Privilege are getting rich. Some of these agencies are funded by the same multinationals they supposedly regulate, i.e., agencies are fraudulently working FOR un-regulated monopolies, not for American citizen protection – our tax dollars hard at work against us.

Naturally occurring, non-patentable medicines are blocked by corrupted regulators from ever seeing the light of big government day. Successful homeopathic doctors are maligned and worse, tend to have fatal accidents if public recognition appears probable. Corrupt, though gullibly trusted institutions ensure unnoticed incremental genocide of *excess* Main Street populations continues unabated at difficult to imagine profit levels. Traditionally effective, non-patentable medicines and natural organic foods as medicine are ridiculed and marginalized. Medical education and practice are co-opted into cult status by the Rockefeller, Carnegie, Ford, and other dynastic family foundations for expensive, profitable treatment, not cures... and no, I'm not condemning good doctors and nurses caught up in this insidious web. Doctors and nurses, like teachers, like military personnel and law enforcement professionals are caught in this Luciferian web of profitable deceit, inhuman behavior control, and Main Street genocide.

Welcome to 21st century American money laundering by big non-transparent government for transnational monopoly controllers; of, by, and for the people we're haplessly told – near 100% total D.C. corruption, brazenly practiced in the House of Representatives, U.S. Senate, White House, "K" Street, and of course, throughout the highest levels of bought and paid for Federal agencies.

Various forms of money laundering schemes are the *status quo* business of the D.C. day, with enacted legislation hand-feeding the Elite monster, all with full acquiescence by our notorious *Supreme Circus* in their pompous black robes mindlessly mocking the scales of injustice. Nine slugs in an embarrassing consensus row, with only Justice Thomas, after Scalia's murder (my opinion), once standing alone for Main Street's Constitutionally recognized rights, though 2020 election fraud pressure weakened him as well. I say this as Justice Thomas opined : *"We are fortunate that the Pennsylvania Supreme Court's decision to change the receipt deadline for mail-in ballots does not appear to have changed the outcome in any federal election,...but we may not be so lucky in the future."*

This shortsighted Thomas statement ignores obvious abetting of election fraud via ballot count manipulation over that three days of additional time, particularly when weighed against coordinated election fraud in all 50 states, but most importantly in the big six swings states: Florida, Michigan, Minnesota, New Hampshire, Pennsylvania, and Wisconsin. Granted, Pennsylvania fraud by itself did not change 2020 national election results, but its organized complicity with other corrupted state elections did and Justice Thomas helped shut down any possibility of putting additional evidence on the judicial record.

Moving on, the anti-nutrition, anti-health modality is an intentional softening-up operation rendering the unsuspecting, government trusting, Main Street Prisoner

13 • Cognitive Blissonance and Cultural Marxist Decimation

weaker and increasingly susceptible to more obvious conditioning and entrainment modalities also supported by unconstitutional government intrusion – a good argument against career politicians. Institutional complicity enables citizen manipulation with impunity by Elite Puppet Masters. Anti-nutrition is a powerful means of slow population reduction; useful because if Main Street is blind to what's being done, cobweb draped pitchforks stay propped in the shed corner or garage. Elites fear pitchforks in calloused hands more than anything else on Earth.

You may recall the Georgia Guidestones mentioning a desirable global population limited to ± 500 million or so—a far cry from the ± 8.0 billion of us today. What's carved in stone is routinely echoed along with knowing smirks in the sanctity of elegantly furnished meeting rooms of various round-table groups, think tanks, and so forth as the Ruling Class enjoy their privilege while jokingly contemplating 8 billion *useless eaters* going missing, or better, fertilizing elegant Elite gardens after being enjoyably estate-hunted.

Project Veritas investigative journalists, arrested by wannabe Gestapo FBI slugs in 2021 – without constitutionally granted local police authority I might add, have shown us on recorded video - pawns running for elected office along with previously elected pawns and snickering staff joking, *there's no reason for Main Street voters to know any of this*. Sedition and treason are purchased with global syndicate bribes covertly funded by central bank affiliates, locked in with blackmail, then bolstered by citizen apathy. Fear porn is supported by stress producing modalities like cognitive dissonance, along with more aggressive conditioning via propaganda and entrainment – all enabled by mass nutritional infirmity, poor health, depression, and loss of mental acuity.

Ms. Nora Gedgaudas, CNS, CNT wrote a nutritiously rich book called *PRIMAL BODY, PRIMAL MIND*, first published in 2009.[114]   Chapter 29 of this information-packed treatise is entitled, *The Impact of Modern Dietary and Environmental Stress on the Brain*. Now, in defense of Ms. Gedgaudas, her book is about dietary health considerations, not geopolitical agendas. I sincerely apologize Ms. Gedgaudas for dragging your wonderful work into this spiritually depraved sewer we call geo-politics, but that's me. I beg forgiveness and also thank you for turning this old man on to kettlebells.

Interestingly, Ms. Gedgaudas raises several significant issues from a public health standpoint, which I am integrating with geopolitics in a manner suggesting **malevolent intent,** far beyond monetary profit taking. Most Elite mass manipulation techniques are multi-faceted, serving diverse agendas simultaneously from

---

114 Nora T. Gedgaudas, *Primal Body-Primal Mind: Empower Your Total Health The Way Evolution Intended*, Revised edition (Portland, OR: Primal Body-Primal Mind Publishing, 2009).

several different viewpoints. This makes any one strategy difficult to recognize as malevolently *focused with purpose* rather than mere happenstance or oversight.

Such divergent strategy creates tons of misinformation fodder for Main Street citizens to futility argue about as rarely does anyone grasp the full context of the employed multi-stratagems. Industrial agriculture, industrial chemistry, weather manipulation, rogue genetic practices, fertilization, pest-control, herbicides, food licensing, production, processing, distribution, and effects resulting from consuming this so-called food; all of it convenient, much of it nutritionally challenged, some of it at least mildly toxic, fall into this *difficult to recognize* category. **If we combine enough individually tested, mildly toxic, agency approved components into snacks and meals throughout the day, every day – the synergistic toxic overload becomes unsustainably life threatening.** Spend 30 minutes people-watching at any Walmart or shopping center parking lot in America and observe health debilitation walking, limping, or riding by in a motorized cart.

As an example, per retired Army Lieutenant General, Tom Spoehr, director of *Heritage Foundation's Center for National Defense*, more than 70% of Americans aged 17 to 24 cannot qualify for military service even if they want to. Poor health, lack of education, and criminal backgrounds play into this circumstance, but the number one disqualifier is poor health with 27% ineligible due to obesity and 37% due to other health problems like asthma or joint issues.

Circling back Psaki style, Ms. Gedgaudas writes more articulately than I summarize, so following are two quotes taken directly from Chapter 29 of *Primal Body, Primal Mind* regarding effects of poor nutrition coupled with societal stress.

Quote 1. *This subject could be a whole book unto itself. Our primal mind has no defense against the stressful world it now faces, and we are paying a terrifying price for it. We are bombarded from all sides by a chemical (e.g., pollutant, excitotoxin), societal, media, and EMF onslaught – as well as our dietary self-induced tidal waves of insulin and leptin. All of this is relentlessly generating damaging excitatory activity in our brains. It is unprecedented in our history. The toll this takes is insidious as well as profound, and it must be appreciated if steps are to be taken to mitigate its effects.*

The richest repository of cortisol receptors in the brain lies in the hippocampus, which exists as part of the temporal lobes (right above both ears). The hippocampus is a part of the brain's limbic system. It serves a role in the formation of new memories and the retrieval of older memories as well as in spatial navigation and the regulation of affect (emotion). It is typically the first area of the brain affected in Alzheimer's disease and other forms of degeneration. The hippocampus is the part of the brain most responsible for litigating stress response, as evidenced by its preponderance of receptors for cortisol (our major stress hormone) – more than there are in any other areas of the brain.

Unfortunately, we were never designed to be bombarded with stress (or marinated in cortisol) 24/7; this delicate and sensitive part of the brain can become significantly damaged from excessive and chron-

ic exposure to stress hormones and excitatory activity. Its cells wither, degenerate over time, and die off, creating impaired memory function and even psychological disturbances ranging from anxiety to paranoia and emotional instability. Modern imaging studies increasingly show a common trend in the general population toward obvious signs of shrinkage and "Swiss cheese" -looking temporal lobe degeneration. It's a horrifying trend. This is now being referred to clinically as a "normal" variant of aging by radiologists. The fact that it is so very common, however, hardly makes it "normal".

Quote 2. *Another point worthy of ample consideration is the impact of chronic excitatory activity on our frontal lobes – our "executive brain". This is the part of the brain that, in many ways, makes us most human. It controls many aspects of short-term memory, inhibitory activity, consequential thinking, focus, planning, and affect regulation or emotion. This part of the brain is usually not fully developed until we are in our early twenties – as reflected in the sometimes erratic and irresponsible tendencies of juveniles. As mature adults, however, this part of our brain allows us to better consider our environment, effectively use our short-term memory, properly focus and process our thoughts, plan our actions thoughtfully, and control erratic impulses.*

What we are really talking about when we talk about overarousal, excess sympathetic nervous system activity, or excitatory activity is basically a fight-or-flight state. As mentioned before, this part of our nervous systems was designed to kick in only under threatening extremes, such as, say, being chased by a saber-toothed tiger. Unfortunately, we live in a society today where many of us are being chased by saber-toothed tigers 24/7. Many people have a nervous system that functions habitually in this way. These people often end up seeking neurofeedback (if they're lucky), medications or other drugs, or alcohol to manage this constant hellish hijacking of their brain. Many feel like prisoners of their own nervous systems.

What is the impact when everyone functions in this way, not only on us, individually, but on our society as a whole? The sociological implications are certainly chilling, to say the least.[115]

Anybody think beguiling Tavistock theoreticians don't know what Ms. Gedgaudas is talking about here? Ms. Gedgaudas' apolitical, nutritional/health viewpoint, without focusing on it, supports my theory that poor nutrition is not limited to corrupt, government enabled, food industry bribery and profiteering; but malevolently weaponizes nutritional deficiency as a foundational weakening of the body's physical defense against intentionally applied stress and degeneration of mental acuity necessary for intellectual and emotional defense against the NWO stresses applied. Government enabled, institutionalized malnutrition through health-related cognitive dissonance and other conditioning is intended to turn free citizens into increasingly compliant Elite slaves. This is the abject policy result whether bureaucrats realize it or not.

Non-nutritious nutrition is a sophisticated geo-political weapon more powerful than and surpassing its more visibly ugly political cousin, *induced famine*, i.e., murder by political agenda – so popular in Russia, China, across Africa, South and Central America, and other Marxist oases. Unhealthy pro-

---

115 Gedgaudas, 278, 279, 280.

cessed foods comprise a critical component of *full spectrum dominance* unleashed upon the unsuspecting American citizenry with full government compliance. WARNING: As Ms. Gedgaudas suggests, *if we cannot pronounce words listed as ingredients, it is not food.* *Homo sapiens,* somewhat evolved culturally since Paleolithic times, are largely unevolved biologically. Go local, go organic – though aerosol sprayed heavy metals and pollutants make this difficult.

When Elite order-followers augment lousy nutrition by adding mass consumption of nano-devices, atmospheric dissemination of heavy metals to the air we breathe, mercury laden-aluminum adjuvant stimulated vaccines, synthetic mRNA gene therapies with graphene hydrogels, fluoridated water supplies, hoped-for lithium infused public water supplies, poisoned soil for food crops and livestock, toxic seafood, processed sugary foods and beverages, who needs war to disable or wipe out vast population segments?

Our pathetically *selected* Members of the House of Representatives, and corrupt U.S. Senate, whom we mistakenly elect, then re-elect and re-elect in concert with treasonous Federal agencies they spawn, and we pay for are actively doing this to us, whether they or we realize it. According to House Member, Marjorie Taylor Greene of Georgia, we have more than 400 Federal agencies, though some argue no one has an accurate idea how many freedom robbing agencies exist. This is not manageable nor sustainable and will lead to an extinction event if we fail to revise course. The ship of state must be turned, or Main Street will biologically sink after hitting the Luciferian iceberg. Becoming precinct committee persons, election officials, poll watchers, etc., will help remedy current *failures to represent* on the part of *selected* representatives.

We the people don't need <u>selected</u> Representatives or appointed bureaucrats to lead us. **We need elected officials and administrators to follow us, to legitimately represent our Main Street interests.** This is self-governance with the consent of the governed, not rule by special interest, outside third parties - particularly important when those third parties are psychopathically oriented.

Mind control takes many forms supporting many unseen, though coordinated agendas. Re-writing history, erasing connections to our past and our roots is a form of mind control disabling culture and tradition, while enabling the *clash of civilizations*[116], a term popularized by CFR's own Harvard scholar, the late Samuel P. Huntington. De-coupling of history, piled on with contrived wars and population displacement of refugees with subsequent societal chaos, anxiety, rape, and violence predictably leads to desperate demands that somebody fix it.

---

116 Samuel P. Huntington, *The Clash of Civilizations and the Remaking of World Order* (New York: Simon & Schuster, 2011).

13 • Cognitive Blissonance and Cultural Marxist Decimation

Career traitor Henry Kissinger (my opinion) publicly rubbed our Main Street noses in this NWO playbook concept in 1992. I say traitor as Heinz (Henry) Alfred Kissinger, spawned in Fuerth, Bavaria (south-central Germany), became a naturalized U.S. citizen in 1943. Interestingly, the good doctor studied political science under Rhodes Scholar, William Yandell Elliot (1896-1979), mentioned elsewhere, at Harvard during the early 1950s. Indoctrinated totalitarian globalists like Dr. Kissinger are of course, always lurking in the shadowy wings of power with their Luciferian solutions, ready to offer enslaving assistance.

Specifically for example, at the Evian, France *Bilderberg Meeting*, May 21, 1992, global syndicate pawn, Kissinger, former U.S. Secretary of State and National Security Advisor was allegedly recorded by a Swiss attendee saying: "Today Americans would be outraged if U.N. troops entered Los Angeles to restore order; tomorrow they will be grateful. This is especially true if they were told there was an outside threat from beyond, whether real or promulgated, that threatened our very existence. It is then that all peoples of the world will plead with world leaders to deliver them from this evil. The one thing every man fears is the unknown. When presented with this scenario, individual rights will be willingly relinquished for the guarantee of their wellbeing granted to them by their world government."

In this treasonous statement (my opinion), Kissinger, ostensibly loyal to the United States engages *cognitive blissonance* by suggesting Americans along with all other world populations will be better off under a **One World Government**, even suggesting duplicity ("if they were told") to bring this about. A clear denunciation of American national sovereignty by practical inference if true.

On a more positive note, mind control cannot overcome a creative, imaginative person refusing to allow outside third parties (dark forces and enemies) to define his or her being, identity, purpose, or self-worth. This is especially true when this person strengthens conscious discernment in a positive, constructive direction, and employs personal power within a nurturing community of moral persons also steadfastly thinking for themselves in a supportive state of healthy spiritual nourishment aided by the Holy Spirit. We should be routinely telling each other **"We are awesome"** rather than bragging on victimhood while ceding our creative power to others—some of whom detest us. Spiritual discernment and healthy spiritual guidance are prerequisite to overcoming chaotic cognitive dissonance and mind-control at every level, from trite propaganda to full-on electromagnetic entrainment. Spiritual power far exceeds material power yet remains largely unexercised.

Spiritual nourishment requires unity with the Divine and at least a minimal desire to learn to love at some workable level. It requires choosing and making a beginning from which a strong foundation can be laid, and upon which future growth and wisdom can be cared for via assistance by the Holy Spirit. Many of us prefer not to hear this, but there it is. Going it alone, without grace is not a likely scenario for success. A quick look at the viciously divided, malignant world surrounding us is proof certain of the acute pain turning our backs to our Creator has wrought. We must consider requesting Divine assistance if we want our world to be a better, safer, more abundant place to raise children. Shutting our Creator out of our lives has historically documented predictably negative consequences. Lucifer is quite likely pleased with destructive progress to date, and we should aggressively put a dent in that.

Agreement is over-rated. Community agreement on every economic, societal, political, philosophic, or theological point is not necessary or possible. In many cases it may not even be desirable or productive. **Solutions depend on ideas, not agreement. Creativity requires freedom, not dogmatic assessment or what we often term helpful criticism.** Mutual respect, guided by Divine Providence for honest, shared thought, coupled with respectful discussion and spirited debate quickly yields effective solutions for rational, reasonable people sustained by moral integrity. Maintaining our minds and hearts in honest condition, i.e., in resonance with *Natural* and *Supernatural Revelation* is our protection, but only when we do so with spiritual discernment, faith, and courage, i.e., the armor of God. This is our active path to overcoming evil influence and embracing love.

Though tough at times, we should remember to be considerate and respectful toward one another when discussing difficult to comprehend differences in religion, sexual preference, race, ethnicity, or heaven help us, politics, and economics. This is the only viable path to healthy, correct action and positive outcomes—even when self-defense is necessary for survival. To the extent our subjective and objective thought process and imagination are mitigated via *mass formation* processes and various forms of mind-control, including programmed self-censorship; the probability of utilizing personal creative power to causatively bring about positive outcomes is diminished. This is occasionally obvious though Tavistock order-followers prefer mind-control methodologies not be apparent to residents of Main Street.

Frankfurt School's Herbert Marcuse in *One-Dimensional Man* strategized effectiveness of using *linguistic alchemy* to undermine effective thought, resultant communication, and subsequent mass behavior within the context of *Happy Consciousness*.[117] **Marcuse suggests as a control mechanism, language be employed as means of rendering effective citizen protest ineffective yet satisfying to the citizen.**

We see Marcuse's strategy playing out today in the unproductive, usually divisive, but dopamine enhancing, feel good about ourselves rants seen daily on *Facebook, Twitter, YouTube, Instagram,* and other forms of group-think enabling social media, though as of this writing only Leftist rants are uncensored. These rants are not 100% unproductive, but actual exchange of rational thought on social media is increasingly rare, particularly when instigated by paid trolls and bots. In the realm of socioeconomics and politics, bigoted opinion and emotional adversity are the norm whether Left or Right. Interesting given personal animosity quickly renders most issues irresolvable.

An obvious *Cultural Marxist* example of Marcuse's ineffective, though satisfying action resulting from media-driven, politically correct, group-think conditioning is professional football players kneeling disrespectfully during our national anthem as a supposedly anti-racist statement. I am not sure if anyone understands what the kneeling represents but guess it uses racism to promote more racism though it's doubtful consensus kneelers comprehend that. Intentions may be honorable but are none-the-less ineffective and counter-productive as Elites intend and Marcuse taught.

Insulting revered national symbols (flag and national anthem) loved by many if not most of your fans; symbols having no bearing whatever on the bigoted evil of racism beyond **1619 Project** prevarication is not likely to be productive – in fact, quite the contrary as NFL revenues declined in 2020 for the first time in two decades. How is this a boon to black NFL football player careers or the less fortunate blacks they purportedly care about? As of this writing, COVID lockdown backlash is refurbishing NFL revenues, so we'll see what comes.

Why do NFL team owners or the league itself support bigoted ignorance and national disrespect? In 2020 blacks comprised about 14% of the American population with NFL team demographics showing blacks comprising; 70% of NFL players; 29.6% of assistant coaches; 10.7% of senior administrators; 9.4% of head coaches; 8.8% of professional staff; 7.1% of vice presidents; 6.3% of general managers; and 0% of NFL team owners. Despite increasing player salaries, do demographics suggest the NFL is just a profitable plantation for gladiators? This begins to smell when taxpayers foot capital costs of arenas for privileged team owners because apparently NFL revenues don't support the NFL business model without subsidies paid by Main Street. Given foul

---
117 Marcuse and Kellner, *One-Dimensional Man.*

smelling financial arrangements via corrupt public-private partnerships around the country, one wonders, what are the bonus sex slavery revenues for a typical game day or *Superbowl* weekend? Who manages and collects that money?

Professional sports have been assaulted by *Cultural Marxism*, particularly basketball (74% black players), football (70% black players) and to a lesser extent, baseball (7.8% black players) which provide above average incomes for blacks disproportionate to their population numbers. So, now we have arrogant, rather insensitive hypocrisy of highly compensated blacks uselessly and inappropriately protesting the circumstance of less fortunate blacks, many of whose wages are taxed to pay for expensively subsidized professional sports stadiums. NFL bigotry infers mostly or only blacks experience unfortunate circumstances – or maybe only blacks matter though the NFL does little to effectively better black Main Street lives.

Aren't there many different races and ethnicities in unfortunate circumstances for whom we could provide a hand up instead of sanctimoniously kneeling for? (There I go promoting socialism, though short term, not generational.) Liberal NFL players and fans, despite the best of intentions stepped right into Marcuse's *Happy Consciousness* trap by ineffectively satisfying themselves through divisive, counter-productive public protest. Welcome to the **Elite School of Mass Formation**.

History challenged *1619 Project*, *Black Lives Matter* (BLM), *ANTIFA*, and other brown shirt afflictions rain cognitive dissonance down on Main Street citizens with a Satanic fervor only cognitive blissonance can generate. **Programmed Mass Formation** and *demoralization* are bringing America to its bloody knees. Overcoming technocratic entrainment, group-think mind-control and transhuman enslavement requires recognizing our own mind and spirit as the Divine gifts they are; gifts to be shared in community. Only then, through grace, can we comprehend our respective place in this material world and turn it away from hatred, toward love.

We are all human together, like it or not, and together is the only way to overcome divisive study group bigotry and ignorant tribalized rancor.

Scientism debases scientific method as devalued currency
debases financial purchasing power.
{Raheem Kassam, The National Pulse - Dec. 2021}

14 • Social Darwinism and Neo-Serfdom

Remedy: Academia, legacy media, and Hollywood have been co-opt-ed and misused for the global syndicate purpose of irrationally confus-ing young and old with fear mongering concepts like Malthusian Scar-city and culturally determinate Darwinian Evolution. These two ideas are delusional lies. Combining these two dehumanizing concepts with Satanic ideologies of Marxism and Fascism enables dumbing down mass populations and enabling return of feudalism on a global scale by global Elites. Academics and students should freely and openly study and discuss such things, evil or not, but never amidst contrived censor-ship of competing ideas. Authoritarian universities are not true uni-versities, are not places of learning, and cannot be considered such.

An ideologically bigoted authoritarian elementary, high school, or university is an indoctrination center incompatible with free thinking, education, imagination, creativity, and liberty. Re-sponsibly coherent adults MUST return our schools and univer-sities to the once venerable institutions of learning, imagina-tion, creativity, free speech, and debate they once attempted to be.

I raise the issue of Charles Darwin and his contemporary, Alfred Wallace's *theory of evolution by natural selection* in the context of slavery, i.e., serfdom because regardless intent, Darwin's teaching became the basis of *Social Darwin-ism*. Debate continues regarding Darwin's belief in God and whether his think-ing changed between publication of *On Origin of Species (1859)* and *Descent of Man (1871)*. I wasn't there so don't know, but Darwin appears to have theo-logically evolved from Christianity to Deism, and finally to Agnosticism later in life.[118]   Darwin's writings over time in any event, are contradictory relative to God, creation, origination, evolutionary processes, and notable differences between humans and other creatures. *Homo sapiens* as a primate species shares 97% of its genetic code with other primates, like chimps, yet are significantly different creatures, even to the extent of omega-6 versus omega-3 fatty acid ratios for optimum health. Sharing a gene for teeth, wings versus legs, etc., does not signify two creatures have the same nature, or occupy the same functional space within a biogeographical ecosystem. ±3 million year old *Australopothecus africanus* was, and today's chimps are smart but don't plan, design, fund, and build corporations, accounting systems, hospitals, churches, jet planes, etc.

Social Darwinism is a manipulative Elite concept arising from the idea the best fitted of a species survive and replicate, thereby strengthening adaptable qualities of their line over time while less fit die out. This concept of evolution, generally true for plants, fish, reptiles, birds, and animals, cannot be extrapolated to *Homo sapiens.* Darwin and his adherents fail to account for the impact of creative intelligence and reasoning ability on the human evolutionary process. Humans do not adapt singularly within their species as do other life forms. **Acculturation is a strong drive among groups of social animals such as human beings and good or bad, serves an organized survival function.** Unfortunately, malevolent ideologies drive targeted population groups off the rails when harmful indoctrination and conditioning become prevalent within those groups.

Human beings, *"made in the image of God"* are spiritually social beings capable of adapting together via shared cultural learning and adaptation. David Mamet, recalling teachings of Friedrich Hayek explains: "But the evolution of a culture takes place not through the disappearance of those lacking a beneficial adaptation and the interbreeding of its possessors, but through imitation. That culture which has discovered a beneficial adaptation is imitated by those cultures which perceive its worth – the possessors and nonposessors of an adaptation do not compete on this basis – all may adopt the beneficial behavior and thrive."[119] This idea of learning and adapting via cultural sharing and support versus instinct is a difference in level of consciousness between animals and humans legitimate scholars cannot ignore.

Indoctrinated Darwinian scribes teaching interconnected spiritual/material blindness while self-censoring rational questions are indicative of 5th grade level scholarship. If the shoe fits, wear it and I've politely not blamed Mr. Darwin for *Social Darwinian* delusion justifying Elite entitlement, abuse of power, eugenics, or Main Street genocide. In fairness, Darwin's evolutionary theory cannot reasonably be held liable for abusive extrapolation of its princi-

---

118 "From Darwin to Hitler: Evolutionary Ethics, Eugenics, and Racism In Germany_Richard Weikart.
119 "The Secret Knowledge: On the Dismantling of American Culture_David Mamet.

ples by others justifying cultural and economic imperialism, unfair labor practices, legislated poverty, racism, protected classes of citizens, or sterilization.

Had Darwin recognized humanity's two most singularly notable personal characteristics; ABILITY TO IMAGINATIVELY REASON AND LOVE, he would have seen human evolution operating along two distinct pathways; one incorporating human capacity for thought and purpose in possible union with the unseen *Supernatural*; the second along more rigidly defined genetic lines organically governed by *Natural Law* as less-rational, non-human life forms are. Creatures sharing similar genetic coding in the material plane do not necessarily share similar levels of consciousness, nor do they consciously react or behave within any physical environment the same determinate way.

Homo sapiens have free will, plan and build for the future, then behave accordingly; chimps do not. This behavioral difference was obvious in Darwin's time but ignored. I'm not aware, for instance, of any *Galapagos archipelago* wildlife or plant life who, after Darwin's five week visit in 1835, published books about Charles Darwin or about his ship, the Beagle – nor having seen the Beagle did any of these species begin building their own ships.

Darwin inquired, then ignored; **from where does Natural Law and evolutionary process emanate? From where does human person emanate?** Darwin's ignored answer reveals by omission there is no evolutionary conflict between supernatural and natural. In fact, the harmony and synergy between Supernatural Revelation and Natural Law produces universal order bound by created life energy and love of our Creator along with our human response to that love regarding responsible nurturing of the creation we inhabit. The fact most of us fail to comprehend what love is and how its frequencies beneficially operate does not change the fact love and life energy intertwine and exist.

Wallace, Darwin, and others incorrectly contrived an imaginary **mystery conflict** stubbornly defended by academic denial and censorship. Natural Revelation absorbed by sensory experience and Supernatural Revelation absorbed via consciousness, coherent thinking, and emotion, evolve together on a quantum or higher level (we don't know yet) as the human species evolves. Creationism and evolution are ongoing aspects of the same intelligent process. **There is no mystery conflict.**

Non-human life forms experience Natural and Supernatural Revelation at a level of consciousness profoundly different than found in human life, but this biologic difference has no bearing on the fact life is both created and evolves employing intelligent energy sources and forces we are yet to comprehend. What exactly is life energy? Where does life energy originate? If energy cannot be created or destroyed—can it originate anywhere? How could an unintelligent, random universe transform energy into matter and vice versa in an organized fashion? Is our universe a closed or open system? Can life energy be created, destroyed, or converted by natural organic processes... or other processes we are unaware of? How does life energy interact with love? As a practical matter, scientists and engineers can measure various forms of energy, calculate them, and manipulate them – BUT have no understanding of what the essence of energy is or how it exists. Perhaps a bit of humility is in order?

Ancient Greeks of Asia Minor, as material scientists and budding philosophers struggled to comprehend *origination*, the *primary element* (Anaximander) and other concepts of *The One versus The Many* as early as Thales of Miletus in the early to mid-sixth century. Have we evolved much further in our thinking since? Scientifically—we think so. Spiritually, not so much, to the extent many of us deny knowledge offered in Scripture, the teaching of Christ, as well as through differing theologies and metaphysics. Any sign is useless if we cannot or will not recognize it, particularly as many academics and researchers are territorial regarding knowledge acquisition, credit for same, and sharing.

The Bible is simultaneously the most censored and most read book in human history. Why? What unseen power is discussed between those covers that is so threatening or so special? How has information bound between those covers inspired more than 40,000 Christian denominations across the world? By contrast, how many African Grey Parrot or chimpanzee religious denominations are there? What is the theology of any of the seven species of spider monkey, California Golden Trout, or ring-tailed lemur? Are we yet to read dolphin metaphysics still being held up for further editing by publishers?

Christianity, always under demonic attack, travels many paths and destructive cul-de-sacs through its various sects, not because the **Golden Rule** is wrongly interpreted, BUT because of powerful Luciferian influence. The buried lead in Luke's 6:31 lies within Luke 6:36. **God's mercy, not human desire is the virtuous standard.**

Non-human organic life forms behave predictably and repetitively per *Natural Law* as it exists, and as they have evolved in nature. No creative thought or moral imagination is invoked. There's no thought-link or mental picture tying perception of the material world to a mindful concept, planned purpose, or pre-planned course of action. Animals behave per their evolved inherited instincts or drives as genetically passed on to current generations by previously successful generations. Man does this as well, but carries with biological humanness another aspect, another dimension; human spirituality, that is, the ability to think, reason, plan, act, and evolve in a non-biological or abiological manner; a Spiritual Manner - and can coordinate this in groups and among groups.

Note: I often use the phrase **creative thought**. In *Lizards Eat Butterflies*, Dr. David Martin tells us - *humans do not create anything*.[120] To the extent I understand this, humans creatively re-arrange things already created, thereby *contributing* to changed things as opposed to *producing* things from scratch (my words). I accept Dr. Martin's observation on two counts. Original creation is transcendent to infinity, therefore beyond material world capability. Secondly, dreams, visions, art, literature, poetry, and music are clearly just creative interpretations of thoughts, emotions, things, or other life elements we perceive. If or how thought frequencies interact or manifest in material reality I have no idea.

Individual thought, emotion, evaluation, and purposeful decision making are inherent aspects of human spirituality not shared with non-human life forms in-so-far as we know. All creatures are endowed with their own created spirit, level of consciousness, and life energy. Creative thinking, however, enables free-willed purpose in the sense a freely chosen course of action reasoned to cause or bring about a certain effect or goal allows for planned **purposefulness** through the course of action pursued. Only humans demonstrate purposefulness within the context of space/time in this regard, which of course, raises the inevitable question of moral versus immoral actions.

Clearly morality cannot pose an issue for any life form incapable of imaginative thinking. Non-human life forms are not purposeful or moral, just naturally reactive in terms of successfully evolved survival instincts. Anthropopathism to the contrary, non-human life forms to the extent we understand them, do not reason, or suffer moral dilemma. A beaver builds its home but does not envy a better home, envision the best home, or choose not to build a home at all. A rescued pet beaver will attempt to build a home within its larger human house with favorite hats, shoes, slippers, clothes, blankets, rugs, and other things it can find around the house. People living with rescued beavers attest to the cute little critters also chewing on wooden furniture, spurring provision of a less financially damaging, more appropriate outdoor pond for their rescued pet.

Unlike a dairy farmer, a pack of coyotes howling together in celebration of the dairy farmer's calf they just killed experience no guilt or remorse. They're hungry; and now they'll eat. The coyote pack intends to eat and coordinates their hunt but have not considered hunt strategy in terms of how the calf or farmer feel about it, nor have they thoughtfully discussed how they might minimize the calf's pain and

---

120 "Lizards Eat Butterflies: An Antidote to the Self-Help Addiction|Paperback," Barnes & Noble, chap. 7

suffering so as not to taint their meal with stress-induced, adrenalized pH levels as say we might, when keeping a well caught, hydroperoxide free trout for the grill.

Speaking of morality, a moral person is not moral because he or she behaves per a moral concept handed down by ancestors through the ages. A person refusing to kill others as an effective business practice because it's illegal or because the 5th commandment states, *"Thou shalt not kill"* may be well-behaved or socially acceptable, but not necessarily moral. The **Golden Rule** is not a behavioral constraint; it's a way of being. **Morality involves personal choice, not dogmatic compliance.**

Any animal can be taught within its natural boundaries to behave via repetition and reward, or sadly via punishment by ignorant trainers. This behavior may mimic, but is not human, though humans can also limit behavior per targeted social conditioning as observed in many unfortunate churches, classrooms, corporate offices, and courtrooms today. A fully actualized human being, however, goes beyond this base level of animal self-awareness or cultural conditioning, exercising subconscious and conscious reasoning to become fully engaged spiritually in a responsible individual process of evaluation prior to decision making and action. This is the focus of the **Golden Rule** in my humble opinion, misinterpretation of which by organized religion, Dr. Martin, mentioned above takes serious umbrage.

Humans, unlike non-human life forms, make moral, immoral, and amoral distinctions in their relationships with each other and the world they inhabit. This evolutionary behavior is observable in both past and present, so is not arguable; yet Darwin and other so-called Evolutionists choose to ignore the obvious, which is *Ignorant*. Ignorant in the sense information is available but ignored. This rejection of spiritual awareness is not scientific in any real or practical sense of truth-seeking or scholarship. Our created essence and drive for unity with our Creator may be unseen yet exists within each human across many cultures.

Note: As you may imagine, I prefer the concept of morality be applied on a spiritually generous, personally responsible basis with people voluntarily working with each other for everyone's benefit to the extent possible, as opposed to fearfully or blindly conforming to sanctioned societal codes, which may offer only preferential benefit. My preference, to be successful, however, requires asking for and accepting God's grace through the Holy Spirit to overcome demonic influence as does successfully living the Golden Rule. We cannot overcome evil influence on our own as today's punishing world demonstrates daily.

Circling back, an animal returned to the wild then meeting its previous human handler, a long-lost pet returned to its owner, or a pet meeting a returning soldier often react in an aggressively affectionate, wildly happy manner. This may be love within animal consciousness, but is love experienced on a different choice level than their reasoning human counterpart experiences love. Similar, loyal in the purest extreme, but not the same.

In terms of morality for example, a human becomes genuinely moral only through spiritually exercising his or her inherent thought process to engage individual moral imagination. Emotional awareness and reasoning through a moral concept to assess ethical compatibility with individual material perception is a human process not shared with other creatures. In this manner a moral person takes ownership of their own conceptual rationality and only then refuses to commit murder. We see here how important accurate perception is. Dogma guides our thinking, but our responsible decision is not the result of religious or societal rules, subsequent punishment, or ensuing guilt; but because we reach an autonomously reasoned moral conclusion in our present circumstance. Anthroposophist, Rudolf Steiner explains this idea brilliantly and I believe correctly in Chapter 12 – *Moral Imagination (Darwinism and Mortality)* of his *Philosophy of Freedom*.[121]

Note: **Anthroposophy** is a difficult, potentially hazardous area of study blending as I understand it, so-called *Akashic Records*, occultism, *Zoroastrianism*, and esoteric aspects of Christianity. Steiner apparently believed evil forces could only be overcome by immersion in the mysteries of Christ's teaching, but his conception of spiritual battle between the polarized alliance of dark *Luciferic* forces of destruction, with dark *Ahrimanic* forces of materialistic mechanization, fighting against enlightened spiritual beings led by Michael the Archangel can be confusing, so take care reading this teaching and pray for guidance while doing it. For what it's worth, I've read some Steiner because of his concern regarding dark aspects of technology overwhelming healthy human spirituality.

I mention all this because oddly, Steiner's thinking, right or wrong, compliments my view of how theology differs from and is complimentary to Orthodox Christian religious dogma. Theology becomes relevantly helpful within the process of revelation when it dynamically evolves through the ages and speaks understandably and meaningfully to people in the current age. Unfortunately, in my view organized Christianity has largely abandoned Christ's teaching along with Natural and Supernatural Revelation in favor of materialistic, secular dogma. This, of course, is not revelation in any sense leading humanity to loving unification with our Creator, but instead becomes another process of

---

121 "The Philosophy Of Freedom: Rudolf Steiner

mind control promoting secular humanism and moral relativism. Organized religion fails its congregation spiritually to the extent it becomes formulaically stuck in the statically perceived ancestral past, particularly when serving agendas contrary to the dynamic essence of love and the natural evolution of intelligent life energy. Dogmatic truth is necessarily tied to the experiential past, but centuries old theology may or may not speak meaningfully to any current generation and the possibility of incorrectly conceived dogma does exist – enabled of course via Satanic influence and poor choices. Theology is current thinking, not truth. Dogma is based on what already happened, therefore is truth, since what happened (outside quantum theory anyway) cannot be changed – though dogma, i.e., what happened, is subject to problematic interpretation.

Theology evolves as humanity prepares itself to receive more knowledge through dynamic revelation. Some of that theology persists and becomes dogma; some is discarded. Theology is a spiritual maturing process, not a system of static laws. Healthy spirituality never suppresses, hides, or fears its own truth. Scientism's denial of human reason, understanding, and spirituality on the other hand, obscures more than half the true nature and essence of evolving *Homo sapiens*. Evolution is not limited to the objective material world and Darwin, brilliant in so many ways, should have been subjectively open to that knowledge. Humanity evolves spiritually as well as materially and Darwin as well as we, experience evolution every day of our lives.

For what it's worth, Ms. Ayn Rand on a different front, whose writing I dearly love, completely missed this spiritual reality as well. Denial of spiritual reality enables the intellectual vacuousness justifying nihilism and slavery... or feudalism, if you prefer a nicer term, but in any event, without the imposition of moral considerations. Luciferian global syndicate indoctrination cannot allow spiritual awareness to impact material enslavement outcomes through independent thought processes. Slaves must be dissuaded from thinking at any cost including genocide, hence the study group system.

Sham-science prohibits asking "what happened the Saturday before Big Bang"; and 21st century science thus far fails to provide an answer? If our universe is expanding, what is it expanding into? How many universes are there? How many dimensions are there? What defines or bounds a dimension? Are dimensions interconnected? Do time and space exist or are they just intellectual constructs used to simplify poorly understood notions regarding created reality? Is there an up or a down? Can there be an up or down without gravitational force? Does gravitational force recognize what is up or what is down? If life is random, how did highly organized, evolving biological life forms overcome the predictable process of ever increasing entropy, i.e., Murphy's Law?

Why is randomness a concept if nothing more orderly ever existed or exists for comparison? Is there a past; a future; or just the never-ending present? Why do we deny un-sensed dimensions when they clearly exist, though unseen? How does frequency of vibration and resonance impact life energy, material reality, awareness, and state of being? What is energy? Why do we undermine our perception, our window to reality? Do operable windows into unsensed dimensions exist? I'll stop here, sorry.

An extreme example, perhaps a poor one, but illustrative is the predictable *dissociative identity disorder* (DID) experienced by persons undergoing high levels of discomfort and/or pain along with resultant fear, anxiety, stress, etc., particularly when endured during prolonged periods of uncomfortable confinement or torture. We know through *MK Ultra, Monarch,* and other sick CIA programs, assassins without conscience can be created by forcing mental dissociation to survive. Consider a person denied sleep along with adequate food and water, first severely beaten every day for two weeks, then hung naked by barbed wire wrapped wrists from the ceiling in a concrete room maintained at 47°F for three weeks. The person cannot get comfortable and every four or five hours, someone enters and douses the prisoner with a bucket of ice water, then laughingly applies electric shock to sensitive exposed areas. The hanging prisoner, barely able to breathe, is fed just enough nutrition and intravenous pharmaceuticals to remain alive, to enhance pain, and to maintain consciousness for as long as possible.

A sleep-deprived prisoner, painfully hanging by barbed wire constraints while being soaked with ice water and repetitively shocked, either goes excruciatingly insane, gives up and quits, succumbs, or survives. Not uncommonly, survival entails a disassociation of self. The mind literally goes somewhere else to avoid an unbearable reality. The CIA's *Project Monarch* studied such limits. One question is, where does the mind go during these periods of dissociation? If material reality is all there is, then the mind has no escape route from physical reality despite mental machinations. Disassociation could not occur for lack of alternative realities.

I'm guessing as I don't know, but it appears the mind retreats into some other reality to survive; adopting a different personality temporarily in some other dimension; psychologically escaping immediate physical discomfort. This other personality can only exist in another dimension, accessed by the person's mind (or soul if you prefer), invisible to the confines of the cold concrete cubicle. An unseen spiritual dimension perhaps? Horrific programs the likes of *MK Ultra* it appears, have inadvertently opened access doors to unseen spiritual dimensions offering respite for sufficiently tormented human beings. Perhaps less painful paths such as silence, prayer, and meditation are available for accessing these spiritual dimensions less painfully?

When science is misappropriated for *doublespeak, newspeak,* and conditioned *group-think* fodder promoting propagandized human behavior modification, in turn serving pathologic Oligarch control agendas, it is rendered scientifically useless, at least as concerns potential benefit to Main Street. Such abuses malignantly weaponize science against God and humanity. This is our circumstance today. **Immoral technology** in the form of constant surveillance, entrainment, and social engineering is overwhelming moral cultural constraints. Intentional destruction of moral society has been progressively (pun intended) ongoing at least since World War I, the technocratic Nazi 1930s, and I suppose in reality, since the Civil War and some would argue, the *Age of Enlightenment* leading to confused *New Age* spiritual entanglements.

In any event, Scientism and technocracy are misused to destroy healthy human culture and ultimately, humanity itself. A look around our murderously adversarial, dangerously toxic world suggests this trend is not generally beneficial and is not diminishing but growing and metastasizing. It's not what Charlie would call "winning". The Marxist/Fascist tag team are Satanically joined at the Globalist hip facilitating destruction of every good thing in existence. Going along to get along means losing our battle for life.

Winning requires honestly acknowledging human *telos,* our human predicament and purpose. **Humans are born into a gladiatorial arena hosting both the material and spiritual battle between good and evil.** Waging this glorious battle, choosing, then learning to personally receive and share our Creator's love against all obstacles is our reason for being. Clearly, this would be a meaningless state of being without the possibility of love if alternative choices did not exist – hence the usefulness of Luciferian evil, the root of all human suffering resulting from our less-than-optimal choices. All creatures are born through our Creator's love, but only (as far as I know), angels and humans have a creative option through perception and reason to acknowledge, retain, and share God's love or reject it. Rejecting love, of course, engenders suffering. **Rejection of love is hell** (my opinion).

Clinical psychologist, Dr. Jordan Peterson, Professor of psychology at *University of Toronto* presented the keynote address at the *2019 Prager U Summit* in Santa Barbara where he mentioned his view of the mistaken 60's concept of *"you're OK as you are"* and how this nihilist idea undermines personal growth, hope for becoming a better person, hope for a better world, and so forth. Dr. Peterson, I believe correctly, views static human life, i.e., staying as you are, justifying non-change, as profoundly negative, potentially demotivating to the point of stunting personal growth opportunities necessary to facilitating healthy family and community life.[122] I add, *"OK as you are"* is counter evolutionary.

---

122 "Jordan Peterson Speech at the 2019 Prager U Summit - YouTube," accessed May 25,

Dr. Peterson mentions *paying attention* is more important than *thinking* – an idea with which I concur as *paying attention is perception in action* and all thought is necessarily predicated on perception. If we fail to pay attention and our perception is incorrect; it follows our thinking may fail to be healthy or constructive; even becoming self-destructive. Dr. Jordan's *Summit* speech is perceptive, heart-felt, and moving—well worth a listen should you have time.

On a less metaphysical level, paying attention or not paying attention impacts our response to manufactured issues like global cooling (1970s), global warming (1980s), and climate change (today) propaganda. Scientism's carbon tax hoax designed by *Club of Rome* adherents to facilitate middle class wealth transference and global serfdom is a perfect example of misaligned perception. Most other so-called environmental programs are also abused, usually serving UN 21/30 Enslavement Agendas as wealth transfer mechanisms confiscating created wealth from the working middle class worldwide, then transferring it to coffers of Elite dynastic families. This fraud is perpetrated under the guise of protecting Earth while locking in global syndicate control, i.e., Scientism hogwash supporting global serfdom.

Climate change models are used to support abolition of commoner property rights and the wealth transfer scam incrementally returning Main Street to impoverished feudalism. Politicized sham-science and Main Street gullibility have considerable relevance to burgeoning Elite cash flows from middle class to uber-rich bank vaults as well as imposition of global Main Street slavery. Environmental concern and **voodoo climate science** are separate issues unrelated to haves and have-nots, though those eliminating property rights, confiscating Main Street property and wealth via government mandate are precisely the same *prominent global citizens* orchestrating Earth's polluting, aerosol poisoning, and weather modification in targeted areas. This would be funny if it were not racing toward techno-omnicide.

Meanwhile Draconian regulation beneath the hungry auspices of Agenda 21/30 proceeds helter-skelter, apace with rapidly declining educational achievement and fertility, apparently in pursuit of neo-feudal serfdom for the masses surviving nearly constant 20th and 21st century war and the very environmental poisoning science is supposed to be averting, rather than creating. **We are not powerless. We can say NO.** We are never powerless unless choosing to be. The U.S. for example, is home to ±616,800 people per each of 535 members of our corrupt, treasonous bicameral Congress. That is a lot of pitchforks. Congress and the corrupted U.S. judiciary should fear we the people of Main Street more than their cowardly Elite handlers. Main Street holds all sovereign power but unfor-

2019, https://www.youtube.com/watch?v=avInTfCd92Q.

tunately refuses to acknowledge or exercise that power. We can take back our political power simply by becoming social media force multipliers sharing truth, or y becoming precinct committee persons, election officials, poll watchers, etc.

We should remind ourselves as educational standards steadily decline, historic illiteracy among serfs or slaves was not accidental; it was aristocratic policy as the poor, dependent, and uneducated rarely have the confidence to question authority, defend themselves, or make demands on their masters. It is time for the decent silent majority to consider less silence and better education for children? Think local and consider running for School Board positions.

Mind control technology development, electronic surveillance, and rarefied entrainment techniques under the weaponized fiction of National Security - or worse, convenience, are becoming increasingly classified and less transparent as evolving invasive capabilities turn against Main Street humans at the hands of pathological miscreants employed by what appear to be criminally insane political leaders representing inbred, megalomaniacal Elites. If Main Street America actually had honest Congressional representation dozens more prisons would be required to incarcerate thousands of seditious and in many cases treasonous Washington D.C. and State level elected and appointed bureaucrats. As Mike Lindell says, **turn voting machines into prison bars**.

Today's religiously dogmatic technocracy, that is **Scientism**, functions as anti-human technology supporting the myth of group-think *Malthusian Scarcity* and hive-mind inhumanity in a spiritually blind race to extinction. Nihilistic Marxism and Fascism are aligned as Hegelian anti-thesis against a free market capitalism that doesn't even exist – a make believe conflict that can go on forever – or until Satan's hordes trick us into destroying each other along with our material world.

Instead of employing technology and science to solve problems and enhance life's opportunities, creating abundance and health for everyone on earth – science is frequently mis-employed to promote suffering of targeted groups while assisting suffocation of spiritual awareness and creativity. Eliminating human autonomy and diminishing humanity in deference to an irrational anti-human agenda is destructive to life on Earth, including that of so-called Oligarchs themselves. We are at the darkened doorway to Luciferian inspired Globalgeddon and must decide to open that door; or stop to reconsider humanity's options, perhaps in a less exploitive, more generous, healthier light? Help through the power and grace of our Creator is essential to making the correct free will choice. Satan fights unfairly.

We must realize for our own spiritual survival, preferably without gulag incarceration, that Marxism and Fascism are God despising paths back to global syndicate contrived Main Street serfdom. The intellectual, emotional, and material impoverishment of this new technocratic serfdom is a direct method for bringing about worldwide spiritual and material desolation, sans prison walls. It is only the authentic spiritual aspects of life that are capable of sustaining material life - the opposite of today's conditioning center indoctrination. Solzhenitsyn in *The Gulag Archipelago*, Part IV – The Soul and Barbed Wire, Chapter 1 – *Ascent* describes freedom of the soul and lack of suicides experienced while surviving Gulag hopelessness once *zeks* realized prisoners have nothing but each other and no one will ever come to save them. The Gulag itself painfully and powerfully teaches materialism is nothing but a Satanic trap.

It's often said, **politicians don't start parades, they join parades, then run up front to pretend they are the Grand Marshall.** True or not, **no one is coming to save Main Street. We are who we are waiting for** but will only realize our powerful numbers and personal power via God's grace through our own efforts. We are each a warrior and a hero in this epic battle between good and evil but choosing to fight on the side of good requires freely choosing to put on and wear the armor of God. We choose individually, but victory requires working together. In the realm of political reality, coalitions are necessary to win and maintain cultural lifestyles furthering spiritual health and well-being.

Post-modern education is largely reduced to rhetorical sophistry designed to persuade students, not educate students. Such sophistry, aligned with globalist conditioning undermines human curiosity, standing in opposition to philosophical and scientific inquiry. Ideological narrative displaces fact finding and honest discourse. Soundbite aggression replaces respectful discussion. Sophistry typically obscures objective truth in pursuit of subjective agendas; agendas likely not aligned with Main Street commoner well-being. Buyer beware of sophistry as it undermines philosophical pursuit of objective truth. It is the bias of manipulative sophistry that brings about such nonsense as *speak your truth, I will speak my truth*, or worse, the oft abused *truth to power*.

In bulleted Social Darwinian summary, I offer a few so-called issues manufactured by, promoted by, exacerbated by, and profited by the bespoke, central planning controllers of Scientism enabling compliant Main Street serfdom. These are Luciferian narratives ordained on the sacrificial altar of Scientism's blind faith celebrating religiosity of consensus as we blindly shoulder our 5G PsyOp mindlessly down the brutal cul-de-sac of mind-controlled genocidal extinction.

●Despite negative nonsense being discussed here, we the people of Main Street are not useless or powerless. As Mr. Jon Rappoport tells us, **"Hopelessness" is itself a PsyOp**. Please never dwell on or share feelings of hopelessness as thoughts are powerful and through our actions manifest in reality. Don't feed dark forces with negative energy. Laugh at them instead. In Christ's name avoid darkness. Embrace the battle and WINNING FOR GOOD.

•Earth doesn't have a population problem; it has a population distribution problem driven by high-density *stack-and-pack* promotional nonsense such as U.N. Agenda 21/30 and its ubiquitous adherence by Elite controlled foundations, trusts, institutes, heavily conditioned academics, and think-tank drones. Say no to unhealthy zoning restrictions, toxic JABs, and GMO fake-foods. The order followers selling profitable solutions created the dilemma.

•Earth does not have an energy problem; it has a managed ignorance and greed problem targeting *selected* energy development, discriminatory funding, green fraud, preferential distribution, and cost of use. This sad program is intended to serve destructive Elite agendas based on delusional, zero-sum thinking. The bulk of so-called alternative energy funding vanishes into unnoticed insider pockets; and secondly, is carefully restricted to financially unsustainable technologies unable to provide a positive return on investment; wind and solar being two examples - at least to date.

Feasible clean energy research is uniformly abrogated by the Scientism funded *status quo* and is never encouraged, as *status quo* beneficiaries prefer government sanctioned, insider trading schemes and sweet-heart deals. We must support legitimate research by real engineers doing productive work instead. Ask why since the *Kyoto Protocols* in 1992, has so little alternative energy progress been made? Are we that stupid and incompetent? I doubt it. The money and power are enabled, not by solutions, but exclusively by zero or at least minimal progress and perpetual study group fraud. Financial subsidies are passed out to sustain problems, not solve problems. Enslavement is ensured by problem management, not solutions.

•Earth doesn't have a food problem; it has a politically motivated food distribution problem and a psychotic food poisoning problem we should regard as orchestrated *soft famine* and malnourishment for weakening Main Street, controlling Main Street, and depopulation of *excess population*. We should ask how today's ever-present aerosol spraying of aluminum sulphate, barium, strontium, and nanoparticles fit into this toxic sun-energy blocking paradigm? It appears fly ash, a toxic pozzolan waste product captured by coal-fired power plant operations is now a component of aerosol spraying. Why should we inhale black dust or $CaCO_3$ just because Bill Gates says we should?

•Earth doesn't have a wealth problem; it has a managed resource allocation problem narrowly directed by government protected, transnational monopolies, along with a wealth distribution problem promoting the harvest of Main Street wealth with re-distribution to Elites and their Pawns of Privilege, carried out by order-following thugs we call government officials. Demand abolition of the obscene income tax just for starters. Washington D.C. is missing more than $86 trillion dollars since the late nineties. Our Constitution must be enforced to have this money returned to taxpayers. What level of financial devastation and cultural control can be arranged with $86 trillion dollars? How many black ops can be conducted with $86 trillion dollars? Who is spending our money? We still hold a Constitutional right (currently ignored) to its return or at least a *pro rata* equity position. This digital theft is enabled by Main Street good faith and credit, routinely used by psychopaths against us.

●Earth doesn't have a Main Street warring problem among its various Main Street peoples; it has a criminally insane, pathological leadership problem. Main Street is propagandized and entrained to believe in this pathology of war regardless of repeated destructive outcomes regularly assuring, not peace or prosperity, but impoverishment and future destructive outcomes. Stop buying into the *we must have war* sales pitch. I know we write songs about it, issue medals for being good at it, so apparently embrace it, BUT it's stupid and provably self-destructive. We shouldn't kill people we don't even know. Self-defense must never be confused with aggressive violence or resource rape aid. That said, our world economy is built on war and war readiness, meaning if war is eliminated, we must restructure peaceful economies for full employment and sustainability.

●Earth doesn't have a natural born public health problem; it has a corrupt, disingenuous, weaponized health care delivery system warped by fake philanthropic foundations and corrupt Big Government intervention. Health care professionals are trapped within an astonishingly greedy, unworkably fraudulent insurance system mis-appropriated for profit taking by Big Philanthropy, Big Pharma, and Big Medicine as well as population servitude and reduction. Remove government order following goons from health care. Adjudicate and incarcerate the guilty goons and multinational co-conspirators.

●Earth does have a significant educational problem whereby Main Street is incrementally dumbed-down and overloaded with crisis induced stress, enabling more convenient management of intimidated teachers and students along with medicated, apathetic, neurologically passive citizens open to subliminal suggestion and entrainment, complacently and happily accepting impoverishment and ultimately, slavery. Read unredacted history. There's nothing new under the sun. Slavery's been around a long time and is being digitally reborn. Just say NO and demand education in place of socially engineered bio-conditioning. We need to stop marinating our brains in cortisol while wishing for a better outcome.

❧

This brings us to the role drugs play in re-establishing a techno-state of complacent feudalism beneath auspices of Elite *Social Darwinism*, i.e., Communism, Fascism, and synthesized Globalism. I would stand remiss not to make brief mention of an age-old form of mind control, not often viewed as such. **Drug trafficking has an interesting history.** Drugs are an age-old weapon wielded by shamans, priests, and others. We know in modern times, from 19th century historical records the British Crown thoroughly and brutally subjugated China via the *Opium Wars*; the first from 1842 to 1844 and the second from 1856 to 1860.[123] We know the *Second Opium War* was waged by the British Crown to gain Chinese concessions not obtained in the *First Opium War*. Concessions of course, necessary to establish the British Crown's exclusive monopoly over the astonishingly profitable **opium trade** – a monopoly allegedly maintained by the Royal Family and associates today.

The Crown was unhappy with negotiations following the *First Opium War*, so the Crown instigated the *Taiping Rebellion* in Southern China resulting, according to the *Executive Intelligence Review*, in the direct deaths of more than 20 million Chinese people, possibly as many as 30 million; and the indirect death of as many as 70 million Chinese innocents, about which most published history is redacted. We ignore young Queen Victoria, focusing instead, non-stop on Hitler's amateurish annihilation of 6 million Jews and five million or so others as though only Germanic peoples are capable of Luciferian inspired depravity.

The Chinese capitulated under this vicious onslaught and the rest is history as they say, with the British Crown emerging in full or nearly full control of global opium distribution and sales. This is pertinent information for Americans as many U.S. eastern establishment fortunes were primarily established via partnership with the British Crown opium and slave trades; not so much from moderately profitable real estate, corporate investments, and furs as fairy tales suggest. Are drug addled Counterculture victims, i.e., Baby Boomers and now medicated victims of Gen X, Millennials (Gen Y), Gen Z, and Gen Alpha a new take on the Anglo-American opium wars? Of course, and on top of which, the global syndicate wages asymmetric warfare against Main Street through CCP **fentanyl**, a murderous synthetic opioid profitably distributed across the world. Sadly, U.S. members of Congress fully support this plague via our open Southern border along with human trafficking, child sex trafficking, weapons trafficking, and other Elite proclivities.

Oddly I would say, given Indian religious history dating back 5,500 years and farming history dating back nearly 4,000 years within the *Indus Valley Civiliza-*

---

123 Kalimtgis, Team, and Goldman, *Dope, Inc.*, 120.

tion of Harappa and Mohenjo-Daro extending from northeastern Afghanistan to Northwestern India and Pakistan; the British Crown dominated most of Eastern India via its aristocratic *East India Company* from the early 1600's through 1858; then beneath the *British Raj* until 1947, when Indian independence was more or less achieved with Pakistan to follow in 1956. During the 1860's the Crown vastly increased Indian opium poppy cultivation, then added Iran (Persia), Pakistan, and Afghanistan to what became the *Golden Crescent*, profitably extending narco sales across Europe and to the United States as well as other victim markets.

Without getting deep into narcotics history, let it suffice, the British Crown learned that mass populations could be more cost effectively subjugated by drug addiction than by expensive, politically unpopular standing armies, and just as advantageously, the geopolitics smelled better beyond the realm — though now we're stuck living with the CCP's *Hundred Year Marathon*. Some respected researchers claim the British Crown retains and has expanded its narcotics subjugation learning curve across the globe, certainly to the former Soviet Union, Balkan States, and North America, in its participatory quest for Round Table inspired One World Totalitarian Government.

I have no personal knowledge of this, but clearly the international narcotics and cocaine trades are managed as powerful organized global business enterprises; are enabled by big bank money laundering involvement with protection provided by various government intelligence services and in most cases, rogue military assets. This is not arguable. To what extent the British Crown is directly involved, I have no idea and mean no disrespect to my British brothers and sisters by bringing up Crown activities. Brits suffer beneath City of London elitism as Americans slave beneath D.C.'s order following gluttony.

In any event, someone or some group is running this organized criminal drug enterprise; and that internationally connected, powerful group with an amazingly long geopolitical reach enabled in part through the study group system, is certainly not led by uneducated opium poppy farmers in the east nor by cartel abused South American coca plant growers. Drug cartels are operationally disposable tools for distribution, sales, and enforcement to be used or done away with as expedient for those running this despicable enterprise. Drug Lords, i.e., *Capos*, regardless how successful or feared, are not upper-level management nor administrative level bean counters, or paper pushers. They are expensive cannon fodder working for Elites.

This centuries old global drug syndicate is important as its population control effectiveness is historically documented and appears politically and culturally relevant today despite legacy media silence. We should consider geopolitical aspects of drug use when stopping by our local watering hole, pot dispensary, or neighborhood coke dealer. I'm not a *teetotaler* but common sense and moderation are a better personal, family, neighborhood, community option than drugged slavery in the sense of Marcuse's *Happy Consciousness* and the global syndicate obsession with a New World Order enslavement pogrom, i.e., Neo-Feudal serfdom. Drug addiction and transhuman AI are the new plantation slave master whips. In the U.S. anyway, order following day to day slave managers are selected by programmed electronic voting machines often operated from distant computer terminals in countries like China, Iran, Italy, Russia, Spain, and so forth. Electronic voting is simply stupid for commoners to accept.

Drugged populations, in my humble opinion, become what Chairman Mao referred to as *blank populations*.[124] Democidal psychopath Mao was specifically referring to hundreds of millions of uneducated, Chinese poor, the **lao baixing**. I'm just expanding his sick, though I suppose accurate thinking. *Blank people and populations* are like clean sheets of paper according to Mao, upon which those in control can write and promote any policy they wish without informed questioning by the *blank populace* and usually without much resistance (my words). If we cherish freedom, this is worth remembering, most notably when MSM lie to us, political leaders lie to us, Hollywood, and the music industry trick us, and drug dependency is offered to us as enjoyable pastime fun. **Moral relativism is not harmless.** Tens of thousands die annually by ingestion of legal and illegal drugs with estimates varying widely, apparently dependent on select distribution targets covered up by misleading political/economic source data bias.

In terms of preserving or obtaining personal freedom and autonomy within the context of government power, particularly non-transparent government over-reach, drugs in concert with educational dumbing-down, indoctrination, and the powerful entrainment tools of technocracy, become a one-two-three-four combined attack difficult to withstand. It behooves us to consider who we are, what we are, where we come from, and how we might behave to remain healthy, loving human beings. First causes and original source information are critical in this respect. As Dr. Jordan Peterson suggests, we ought *to pay attention*.

Despite what American Marxist Democrats, place-holding Establishment Republican Rinos, and MSM parrots promote daily; denial, alienation, divisiveness, anger, and hatred are not constructive societal tools. The persistent, atomistic fragmentation of scientific endeavor coupled with conscious spiritual denial leave humanity caught in a tangled, antagonistic web of pre-enlightenment nescience tied tightly to the vintage knot of dark-age **ignore-ance**. Once again, I'll rely on a remark by Robert Ardrey foreshadowing this very dilem-

124 Rummel, *Death by Government*, 91.

ma. "Someday, I predict, a symposium will be convened somewhere, and to it will be invited not only men of all the sciences, but men of the cloth and of philosophy as well, and perhaps even an artist or two. The conference may well not occur within our lifetimes but occur someday it must. And its subject will be First Causes."[125]

Order followers abusing science and technology under the banner of Elitist *Social Darwinism* to confound Main Street knowledge, limit understanding, and augment pathological abuses of authoritarian power, control, and unbridled wealth accumulation at the expense of others are disgraceful enemies of the people and along with dishonest media and corrupt politicians must be vigilantly regarded as such. Try 'em and if guilty, lock 'em up. The behavior of a technically trained person taking advantage of lessor trained persons is reprehensible and in terms of civilized society and professional conduct, unforgivable. Yet we the people of Main Street find ourselves victimized daily by dishonest technocrats in academia, sham-science, publishing, environment, climate, weaponized weather, medicine, pharmaceuticals, agribusiness, food processing, engineering, mining, and manufacturing, to name an even dozen.

When science denies scientific method and professional ethics it is no longer science, but something else and can no longer be respected as science. If new agendas of 21st century science are *outcome based* instead of *fact based* or at least *inquiry based,* then manipulated for political control and wealth hording by Elites, science is relegated to pathetic propaganda and should be called out as such.

Science and education must never allow themselves or be tolerated by Main Street to perpetrate Elite lies serving the dumbing down of Main Street, thereby enabling enslavement of commoners within the invisible walls of transhuman feudalism. The Elite enslavement agenda was openly and euphemistically announced by the *World Economic Forum* celebrating its 50th anniversary with a new **DAVOS MANIFESTO of 2020,** part of which includes outlining eight (8) predictions for 2030, though contributors neglected to share their estimate of how many of us on Main Street will perish while their central planning nightmare is achieved. Required levels of Main Street impoverishment, illness, starvation, and forced containment were also omitted from the DAVOS presentation.

♦Here are the eight Luciferian prophesies for our coming **global ghetto**:

•**You will own nothing.**
•**The U.S. will not be the world's leading superpower.**
•**You will not die waiting for an organ donor. Organs will be made by 3D printers.**
•**You will eat much less meat.**

---

125 Ardrey, *The Territorial Imperative*, 264.

- A billion people will be displaced by climate change.
- Polluters will pay to emit carbon dioxide. There will be a global tax on carbon.
- You could be preparing to go to Mars.
- Western values will be tested to the breaking point.

❧

Darwin failed to realize, or at least acknowledge creation is tied together by created spiritual life energy. Since angelic and human love require free choice, Lucifer, and hordes of fallen angels are permitted to provide an alternative. I speculate Satan is attempting to mirror created life energy continuity by promoting the use of electromagnetic energy and the Internet of Things to coercively bind material creation together, making it ill—ultimately to destroy it. Satan will fail if Main Street stands up. Rust will also destroy this silly power grab delusion, just sayin'.

Love is not an abstract concept, but is the emotion most powerfully tied to healthy, creative life energy. Hate is an emotion tied to destruction of life energy - now tied to electromagnetic radiation, man's most popular form of torture. This doesn't imply electricity is evil but means electricity can be used for evil purposes. Satan's hatred is expressed through us by **obedience to his domineering influence**. Satanic influence is now so profoundly overwhelming, most do not see it.

Human creative power manifests in material reality by melding created life energy with emotion, intellectual capacity, commitment, and action. We are free to focus our attention on positive or negative energy. Outcomes are tied to these choices, predictably bringing about liberty and light, or serfdom and darkness. *Social Darwinism* is a clear, downhill path to enslaved darkness.

The well planned, global syndicate, COVID BIOWEAPON ATTACK on American and world Main Streets has unleashed the first phase of **Transhuman Warfare**, i.e., Humanity 2.0 against God and all creation. The tip of the anti-human spear is, of course, at the throat of human spirituality and created life energy. TransHuman 2.0 is an insult to God, every good thing on earth, and to life itself.

The idea that living an electronically articulated life within a fake holographic world psychopathically manipulated and controlled by unknown others will be more fulfilling than authentic living is beyond preposterous. The Humanity 2.0 concept is pure Satanically influenced evil.

The political and multinational status quo is owned and operated by the global syndicate and their order followers, but they are few and we the people are many. United together in prayer, with the grace of God we cannot be defeated by evil influence.

All warfare is spiritual warfare, particularly asymmetric forms.
Fighting spiritual battles with material weapons ensures defeat.
Only with the armor of God can we the people take back
self-governance of our United States and
remove Satanic Elites from global dominance.

15 • National Security PsyOp & ±$86 T Missing Dollars

Remedy: End government sanctioned, taxpayer funded, covert meddling and surveillance of U.S. citizens and sovereign nations. Rogue NWO elements within NSA, CIA, FBI, Military Intelligence, and other Federal agencies along with GCHQ, MI6, MI5, Mossad, SVR, BND, ISI and others work for transnational monopolies against Main Street citizens everywhere in synchronized service to Global Syndicate Agendas. Elites actively surveil Main Street people and harvest wealth they create. Rogue elements within Intelligence Services, i.e., Shadow Government are ramping up the use of microwave technology to increasingly subjugate useful slave populations interred in our world's impoverished cities, i.e., kill zones for continued harvesting while incrementally genociding those judged not useful enough. This evil must be stopped and can only be stopped by organized human agency networked through the power of Jesus Christ.

According to historian William Blum, the CIA, as an example, has worked since its *global syndicate spawning* (my words) in 1947 to overthrow 56 national governments (see below). An asterisk (*) indicates successful overthrow of 38 nations. I can't confirm this list but even if partially correct, the list suggests the CIA is a psychopathic agency serving unconstitutional agendas for powers and principalities outside United States' interests. Some authors, one being Robert F. Kennedy, Jr., claim more than 70 nations overthrown by our CIA. In my humble opinion this is not self-defense, certainly not when the CIA's *Phoenix Program* is brazenly brought home against Main Street American citizens.

Here is William Blume's list of countries brought down by the CIA:

China 1949 to early 1960s   Albania 1949-53   East Germany 1950s

Iran 1953 *   Guatemala 1954 *   Costa Rica mid-1950s   Syria 1956-7

Egypt 1957   Indonesia 1957-8   British Guiana 1953-64 *   Iraq 1963 *

North Vietnam 1945-73   Cambodia 1955-70 *   Laos 1958 *, 1959 *, 1960 *

Ecuador 1960-63 *   Congo 1960 *   France 1965   Brazil 1962-64 *

Dominican Republic 1963 *   Cuba 1959 to present   Bolivia 1964 *

Indonesia 1965 *   Ghana 1966 *   Chile 1964-73 *   Greece 1967 *

Costa Rica 1970-71   Bolivia 1971 *   Australia 1973-75 *

Angola 1975, 1980s   Zaire 1975   Portugal 1974-76 *   Jamaica 1976-80 *

Seychelles 1979-81   Chad 1981-82 *   Grenada 1983 *

South Yemen 1982-84   Suriname 1982-84   Fiji 1987 *   Libya 1980s

Nicaragua 1981-90 *   Panama 1989 *   Bulgaria 1990 *   Albania 1991 *

Iraq 1991   Afghanistan 1980s *   Somalia 1993   Yugoslavia 1999-2000 *

Ecuador 2000 *   Afghanistan 2001 *   Venezuela 2002 *   Iraq 2003 *

Haiti 2004 *   Somalia 2007 to present   Honduras 2009 *   Libya 2011 *

Syria 2012   Ukraine 2014 *

If the above list is only partially accurate, it still suggests the Democrat and Republican National Committees in the U.S. are nothing more than owned and operated arms of a malfeasant **Globalist U.S. UniParty** assisting the world's sick dynastic family attempts to herd Main Street back into the feudal paddock. Disparate short-term and long-term interests prevail throughout global syndicate families with international debate ensuing on how best to impoverish and enslave Main Street without invoking billions of rusty rebellious pitchforks. In the end, however, regarding the feudal endgame, strategy aside, Elite consensus is unanimous and corrupted officials have only one choice—go along or be *executively actioned*. This putrid system destroyed our American Republic. **Our U.S. Republic isn't dying – it is functionally dead.** Can we bring it back to consciousness and revitalize it? Does our DNA stand up to this challenge as our Founder's DNA did? This is the question of our time, and the good news is—**we are who we have been waiting for**. There is nor will be anyone else.

• First up – Burgeoning Transhuman PsyOp •

PsyOp's are becoming increasingly easy peasy via entrainment and other electro-magnetic means. Extremely low-frequency (ELF) signals within certain frequency ranges correspond to and mimic brain waves. Since thoughts transmit at various frequencies according to emotional content such as happy, joyful, depressed, sad, angry, anxious, etc., ELF waves can be used to target individuals or groups of people for the purpose of controlling behavior and/ or modifying behavior. This subversive technology extensively developed in Russia (1970's), then in the U.S. has apparently been employed by MI5 in Britain (1980's) for crowd control, though I don't know how effectively.

Cellular phones typically operate on one of two band widths near 900 MHz or 1,800 MHz. These frequencies are easily weaponized and readily abused in mass as we the people of Main Street not only want them; but demand them, are addicted to them, and often sleep with them. We the unwitting telecommunications customer stand in line paying dearly for the privilege of being globally monitored (a certainty) and controlled (a high probability) by the wizards of pathological surveillance on behalf the control-obsessed global syndicate – all of it enabled by government order followers who should know better but succumb to privileged abuses of National Security for their own perceived betterment. They of course, are sadly mistaken in their perception of reality.

National Security has become the prosecutorially immune, qualified immunity blanket beneath which legalized criminals commit the most heinous crimes on Earth with congressionally and judicially sanctioned impunity. The surveillance, intimidation, imprisonment, torture, starvation, sterilization, and murder of millions of people goes unrecognized by MSN. It is largely uninvestigated or punished by law enforcement as Elite controlled weapons, narcotics, sex, human and organ trafficking generate obscene billions in blood money. At home in America, in high-def color pixilation, this is typically sold to Main Street as spreading freedom and democracy.

The so-called global Intelligence Community, a dysfunctionally polygamous marriage of GCHQ, MI-6, MI-5, Mossad, SVR, BND, NSA, CIA, FBI, MI, ISI and dozens of others blend together, controlling and accessing 1934's 100% unregulated *Exchange Stabilization Fund* (ESF) with its unseen, unaudited, tens of trillions of dollars, 2009's *Bank of International Settlements'* (BIS) *Financial Stability Board* (FSB), *Federal Reserve Banks* (since 1913), other world Central Banks, *International Monetary Fund* (IMF-1944), and *World Bank* (1944) working in unison with mercenary **foreign aid fronts** to destabilize and rule nearly every country on earth through the unrelenting scourge of debt and compound interest, profitably spawned from thin air and profitably conjured by order-following Central Bank wizards. Those who don't go along to get along are maligned, blackmailed, threatened, microwaved… or worse.

Sun Tzu's *The Art of War,* written five hundred years before Christ ends with the following, taken from *Chapter XIII, The Use of Spies.*[126]

---

126 Sun Tzu, *The Art of War*, ed. James Clavell (New York: Delacorte Press, 1983), 82.1983

"Hence it is only the enlightened ruler and the wise general who will use the highest intelligence of the army for purposes of spying, and thereby achieve great results. Spies are a most important element in war, because upon them depends an army's ability to move."

Sun Tzu (544 – 496 B.C.) also taught: **"If you know the enemy and know yourself, you need not fear the result of a hundred battles. If you know yourself but not the enemy, for every victory gained you will also suffer a defeat. If you know neither the enemy or yourself, you will succumb in every battle."**

This is good warrior advice, likely better understood by even the poorest of generals, particularly in the Chinese Communist Party,[127] than by myself never serving one day in the military. Maybe for that reason more than any other, I respect military service, understanding that my own freedom to write what I think is in large part predicated on *willingness to sacrifice or die for others* of our precious military and intelligence service personnel. For this I am humbly appreciative and grateful.

Some may read this chapter, mistakenly taking it as a slur against the honor of military and intelligence services. It is not. This does not, however, mean I am unable to recognize **abuse of power or misuse** of our precious military blood for other than patriotic defense and moral purposes. (Moral in that giving your life for someone else is the ultimate act of love.) In that light, I defend to the best of my ability, the honor and integrity of our dedicated military and intelligence service personnel trapped within a disingenuous WOKE modern system. This discussion refers to abuses committed by corrupted leadership and is not a general commentary regarding overall military or intelligence service personnel, though misconduct runs WOKE layers deep, hence the paucity of whistleblowers.

Gathering intelligence is a necessary strategic initiative in defense of any country. We can debate practicality of national boundaries and private property since the *Peace of Westphalia* but human conflict dates at least back to the caves and angelic conflict before that. Anyway, I support defensive intelligence activities 100% and fully understand the covert nature of it is required. Failure to heed Sun Tzu's 2,500-year-old words is stupid. Useful intelligence gathering is complex activity comprising covert and overt elements. We'll not be discussing justifiable intelligence gathering in this chapter, legal under our Constitutional Rule of Law or otherwise. Our commentary is strictly limited to what I view as inhuman abuses of covert activity carried out far beyond limits of Constitutional authority and even further, beyond the bounds of human decency.

---

127 "The Hundred-Year Marathon: China's Secret Strategy to Replace America as the Global Superpower: Pillsbury, Michael: 9781250081346: Amazon.Com: Books."

15 • National Security PsyOp & ±$86 T Missing Dollars

Covert asymmetric economic warfare was visibly declared against citizens of the United States in 1913 with passage of the 16th and 17th Amendments, and the **Federal Reserve Act** by elected and unelected Pawns of Privilege representing special interests of private owners of the world's central banks along with a global syndicate of interconnected transnational monopolies. 1913 began a Fascist, unconstitutional relationship between Elites and the U.S. Federal government whereby central banks and transnational monopolies controlled by a syndicate of international dynastic families were more formally able, through study group fronts like *Council on Foreign Relations* founded by the Rockefeller family along with other **Eastern Establishment Insiders** in 1921, to exert a domineering mercantilist influence over domestic and foreign government policy effectively dominating both. This subversive influence is expanding into space (since 1963) via weaponized electro-magnetic technology to FULL SPECTRUM DOMINANCE. The Surveillance State has arrived unencumbered by Constitutional restraint or moral imperative, emboldened by citizen apathy and in some circles, uninformed applause.

What little remained of recognized unalienable rights after the FDR through Bush II Administrations, was torn to shreds by the more aggressively subversive Obama Regime. The Trump Administration was an improvement, but treasonous 2020 election fraud orchestrated by the global syndicate through the CCP as Organizer put a corrupt imbecile and what appears to be a cackling political prostitute with a sub three-digit IQ in the White House along with a cabinet of corrupt freak-show prospects. This derelict NWO duo are cheer leading the re-opening of D.C.'s money laundering doors for Congress to treasonously re-engage wholesale rape of Main Street American wealth. Washington D.C. has sunk to a new septic pit nadir. Questioning this treason is unconstitutionally criminalized by our metastasizing police state growing drunk on its unobstructed power – but citizen obstruction is on the march and is coming.

The anti-American global syndicate economic war on the middle class launched in 1913 expanded onto the battlefield of social engineering and human behavior modification in 1947 with passage of the *National Security Act* creating both the *National Security Council* (NSC) and the *Central Intelligence Agency* (CIA). *Operation Gladio*, the *stay-behind-network* created in post WW II Europe along with the unleashing of London's *Tavistock Institute of Human Relations'* (initially *Wellington House*) psychopathic scholars upon the American psyche indirectly bolstered this 1947 legislation. As an aside it should be noted per scientist, Mr. Tim Rifat, the use of microwave weapons for mind control originated at Tavistock Institute during the 1950's.[128] Nothing new under the sun as THEY say.

---

128 "MICROWAVE MIND CONTROL by Tim Rifat," accessed November 27, 2018, http://whale.to/b/rifat.html.

Piling on, adoption of the *Intelligence Identities Protection Act* in 1982, amending 1947's *National Security Act* makes disclosing identities of CIA Agents a federal offense.[129] This legislation makes rational sense in terms of defensively legitimate clandestine activities, but also kicked open the door for horrendous abuse with practically zero oversight. This abuse rages out of control with Executive, Legislative, Judicial, and administrative blackmail a common weaponized management tool emboldened by electronic surveillance and nano-weaponry. Propaganda alone is no longer sufficient to fool the masses.

Many researchers and some independent journalists are familiar with five recognized electrical patterns, i.e., brain wave frequencies transmitted across the cerebral cortex; *gamma, beta, alpha, theta,* and *delta* – listed in order from highest to lowest frequency. These researchers are also familiar with old school *alpha/beta* patterns and their weaponized abuses; but few are familiar with newer, more powerful *theta/delta* mind manipulation protocols being employed by rogue military and intelligence service assets. We might inquire; how are these covertly weaponized technologies being unleashed against Main Street taxpayers and how is this technology financed? **How are taxpayers conned into paying for invisible attacks on themselves?**

Many ways would be the tongue in cheek answer. To pay for, staff, and arm covert operations around the world, the CIA often self-finances operations sans Congressional oversight and appropriation, such as it is—or isn't. This includes private contractors more easily hidden from public scrutiny. Subversion is accomplished by covertly employing contractors and major international narcotics traffickers to smuggle drugs, money, people, terrorists, and weapons in and out of various countries. **The CIA is married to and dependent on organized crime.** Coordinating support for such activity is provided by big bank money laundering with plausible deniability by participating banks, CIA front companies, and NGO's.

Covert narcotics trafficking employees or other employed criminal assets can and will break various country's laws, sometimes committing serious crimes, including murder with impunity – because say in the United States, if arrested by the FBI, DEA, or local police, the CIA steps in claiming **National Security** issues and voila... perpetrators are released, continuing in the service of CIA black and/or hidden ops.[130]

129 Douglas Valentine, *The CIA as Organized Crime: How Illegal Operations Corrupt America and the World* (Atlanta, GA: Clarity Press, 2017), 242.
130 Gary Webb and Maxine Waters, *Dark Alliance: The CIA, the Contras, and the Crack Cocaine Explosion*, 2nd edition (New York, NY: Seven Stories Press, 1999).2nd edition (New York, NY: Seven Stories Press, 1999

The very fact of CIA field operatives surveilling narcotics, cocaine, or human trafficking assets renders any evidence collected inadmissible in a US court. Yes, of course it can be admitted — but CIA officers coerce spineless judges to exclude evidence to protect undefined or narrowly-defined NATIONAL SECURITY interests. Case closed - another example of our many tiered U.S. system of injustice beneath which Rule of Law staggers, bends, and cracks.

In other words, any dangerous, even psychopathic criminal directly involved in organized crime, working with the CIA or its organized crime connections covertly carrying out assassinations, torture, regime change, de-stabilization of nations, smuggling of conventional weapons, bio-chemical weapons, etc., is protected against indictment in the United States. I am not picking on CIA field operatives here. It is doubtful many humans fighting any kind of battle they believe in, rightly or wrongly, would fail to take strategic advantage of this situation if able to? But that does not justify rogue elements engaging in sovereign nation de-stabilization nor does it prevent criminal abuses carried out in the name of American citizens by global syndicate order followers for purposes of transnational resource rape, sex slavery, other slavery, or *unwashed* genocide.

From this legislatively approved or ignored, conveniently abused foundation and with continuing growth of black and hidden budget financing via digital-narco-oil-weapons-human trafficking dollars, our CIA covertly ventured far beyond intelligence gathering, to Vietnam's exploration of psychological and asymmetric warfare in that police action's *Phoenix Program*.[131]

I'm not going into the *Phoenix Program* itself other than to say the Vietnamese *Phoenix Program* learning curve has been exported to countries around the globe; notably Afghanistan, Congo, Iraq, Libya, South Africa, Syria, and Ukraine to name a few. These countries can thank the United States and its allies for inflicting corruption of their banking systems, politicians, police, judges, etc., constant surveillance, psychological stress *(mass formation)*, imprisonment without probable cause, torture, murder, and finally regime change with installation of puppet leaders compliantly nurturing resource rape by transnational monopolies for obscene profit. It hurts for many around the world to live the spread of freedom and democracy only to realize the Anglo-American NWO nightmare.

Most, if not all this is done under the guise of foreign aid, spreading democracy, engendering freedom, and generously aiding the down-trodden, while nothing could be further from the truth. Mainstream Media is complicit in covering up these crimes and daily *Geneva Convention* violations for its own aggrandizement, thereby keeping the average American citizen in the dark re-

---

131 Valentine, *The Phoenix Program*.

garding atrocities carried out by non-transparent elements within their out-of-control, rogue government, with its herd of zero-oversight contractors.

As history marches into the second decade of the 21st century, this finely tuned *Phoenix Program* is being aggressively repatriated into the United States and turned by globalist financiers and rogue shadow government elements against *we the people* of Main Street America. No American citizen has felt this power more fully than President Donald J. Trump - so just imagine what these Psycho Orcs can do to us on Main Street. I hope most of us or at least some of us are not gullible enough to imagine the recurrent predictably scripted school shootings, restaurant shootings, car crashes, bombings, 9/11, 2001 Amerithrax, COVID-19, or stupidity like the 2018 - 2022 border invasion by globalist funded caravans are happenstance? These are planned, heavily funded events effectively serving a divide and conquer chaos agenda leading to Elite planned global feudalism. As *SGT Report* reminds us in a Nov. 26th Tweet, recalling *The Price of Everything*. **"There are three kinds of people in the world. Those who can see. Those who are shown and then can see. Those who can never see."**

Repeated false flag events and constant propaganda are bad enough but add electro-magnetic mind control to the mix and we have evil lurching off its aberrant, perverted rails. Global telecommunications architecture has been fully weaponized with most towers emitting vastly more energy than necessary for telecommunications. Why? Because, for one thing, the excess levels of energy are needed to manipulate weather and climate in our increasingly ionized plasmatic atmosphere. Who cares if it harms or kills? Who even notices?

Rogue military science and Silicon Valley miscreants bringing these poorly understood, potentially omniciding forces about sans public transparency resist public scrutiny as they must remain unobserved, or risk being rightfully accused of unnatural climate change and weaponized weather patterns they cause. In plain-speak, the global syndicate's *Club of Rome* originally decrying environmental issues as critical problems demanding massive unaudited funding are the same social deviants funding the non-transparent creation of those problems. Main Street is being expensively duped and incrementally genocided at the same time by a small group of Elite psychopaths, through machinations of their well-funded, order-following, apparently conscienceless army of geeks bolstered by complicit media drones.

If curious, check out the 1972 *Club of Rome* Report titled *The Limits to Growth* as well as Donella Meadows' 1992 book titled *Beyond the Limits*, or Dr. Paul Ehrlich's alarmist book, *The Population Bomb*. Plans are hidden in plain sight.

We'll skip the myriad ways microwaves provably damage organic bio-chemical structures and healthy life; and we'll skip the spurious argument made by many that since no thermal damage is obvious, there must be no damage at all. However, we must consider Dr. Mercola's brief explanation of why microwave ovens and 4G/5G/6G technology can be harmful: "You might not be aware of this, but microwave ovens operate on gigahertz frequencies very similar to most 4G cellular networks. So, the danger AND the justifications why are identical. Conventional science and industry are clinging to the concept that these microwaves from your cell phones, portable phones, Wi-Fi routers, smart meters, wireless computers, and tablets are not harmful because they do not cause any thermal damage.

New research[3,4,5,6] from Professor Emeritus Martin Pall, Ph.D., has provided us with the mechanism of how this low level non-thermal microwave exposure causes biological harm. It has to do with voltage gated calcium channels (VGCCs) that are embedded in the cell membranes. He determined this by evaluating over two dozen studies showing you can radically reduce biological microwave damage using calcium channel blockers.

This explains why the argument that the microwave radiation is not high enough to cause thermal damage is fatally flawed. The statement is partially correct, as the radiation does not cause thermal damage. However, it causes massive biological damage. Pall has compiled a 980 and papers documenting the various non-thermal health effects of EMFs for those who want to take a deep-dive into the research. The safety standards that have been established are off by a factor of over 7 million."[132]

5G, the 5th generation in cellular communication technology employs the largely unused millimeter wave spectrum bandwidth (MMW) lying between 30 GHz and 300 GHz along with a few other lower and/or mid-range frequencies. As advertised, it'll be handy with a download speed of more than 10 Gigabits per second as it ties hundreds of billions of devices and appliances into the global **smart grid** and the **Internet of Things** (IoT). This diabolical system, sadly weaponized for manipulation, malevolent surveillance, and control rather than developed for societal benefit is further augmented by the global fiber-optic system and materials disbursed underground via oil/gas fracking technologies, including by the way per some researchers, chemical fracking beneath wind turbine installations serving an ionized atmospheric calibration function, though I have not confirmed this. We don't hear about any of this in Congress or in Mockingbird news, do we? **Why is that since we are paying for it?**

Am I claiming 5G is without benefit? No - potential benefits are obvious though benefits do not exclude balancing pertinent concerns. Are these benefits necessary; does my toaster need to communicate with command/control

---

132 "8 Reasons You Need to Throw Away Your Microwave Immediately," Mercola.com, accessed August 26, 2019, http://articles.mercola.com/sites/articles/archive/2010/05/18/microwave-hazards.aspx.

central in Colorado Springs; does perceived necessity rationally justify biological harm caused by implementation; is it sensible to implement knowingly harmful technology without public oversight? 5G is not just faster 4G. 5G is a radically different, poorly understood technology posing significant threats to all life forms on earth – yet is being rolled out helter-skelter across the globe without appropriate scrutiny or responsible oversight. 6G is right behind it.

5G and our ionized atmosphere energized with near constant pulsing by modified HAARP technologies comprise a verifiable case of bull-goose looneys taking over the asylum to the point of potential global omnicide. The study group PsyOp aggressively opposes disclosure of this Satanically influenced activity.

In South-central Arizona, during active aerosol spraying, often at night, we can see the HAARP pulse patterns in the chemtrails as they disperse. **Do any of us imagine the 50% decrease in western human male fertility is not caused by something?** Are enormous increases in cases of autism, Alzheimer's, anxiety, depression, cancers, and arrhythmias just happenstance? Trees burning from the inside out; ocean dead zones; bee populations shrinking; are these all just random—or is cause and effect happening?

Left brain/right brain imbalance has historically been considered funny or entertainingly eccentric but in this instance poses severe risk and imminent threat to all life on earth. The *Space Fence*, aerosol spraying of heavy metals and nano-devices, ionized atmosphere, 5G, and related technologies MUST be placed under strict moratorium until such time as transparently responsible parties study, debate, and ascertain how, at what levels, and where such technologies may or may not be safe and appropriate. **Life threatening technology must at least be discussed before implementation is forced on Main Street without local input. As an afterthought, maybe treasonous lifetime actors in D.C. and elsewhere could stop making this dangerous technology available to the Chinese Communist Party's military? Do I dare mention Putin's Russian military or Skolkovo?**

Disregarding geoengineering threats to biological health for the moment, 5G by itself poses severe health risks, many of which have been known for some time, though not publicly disclosed. Here are just a few of those risks:

Radio frequency radiation and ELF radiation:
- Are carcinogenic beyond certain levels
- Reduce melatonin – disrupting wake-sleep cycles (biological clock)
- Cause oxidative damage
- Disrupt cellular metabolism generally

- Disrupt brain glucose metabolism specifically
- Increase blood/brain barrier permeability
- Generate increased production of proteins related to stress
- Cause massive mitochondrial dysfunction resulting in breaks to both single and double strand DNA
- Generate highly reactive, molecular free radicals linked to chronic diseases such as Alzheimer's, anxiety, autism, cardiac arrhythmias, depression, and infertility.

Sacramento and San Francisco were, I believe, among the first U.S. cities to experience 2018's 5G roll-out. Several articles have been written, though not largely disseminated regarding California firefighters from Los Angeles to Sacramento complaining of headaches, confusion, insomnia, and memory loss following installation of 5G towers near fire stations. When these firemen and women were tested by Dr. Gunnar Heuser, **every firefighter tested was found to be suffering from measurable neurological damage (some severe) and brain abnormalities.** As of this writing, these weakened firefighters have filed for and have been exempted from California law mandating installment of 5G antennas. No 5G near fire stations is a start. What about the rest of us? If the rest of us are exterminated, who will the firefighters save?

As a follow-up to Dr. Heuser's pilot study, **when sickened firefighters were relocated to fire stations away from 5G antennas and devices, the degenerative neurological symptoms being experienced ceased.** As I understand the studies, measured radiation levels causing these symptoms were on the minuscule order of 1/1,000 to 2/1,000 of allowable *Federal Communications Commission* (FCC) guidelines for health safety. So much for the farce of today's Federal agencies protecting consumers who pay confiscated taxes for the illusion of agency protection. *Natural News* reports: "In Gateshead, England, scientist Mark Steele says that there's been an uptick in reproductive issues and other health problems since the city's new wireless streetlights were installed. Miscarriages, still births, nosebleeds and insomnia are among the consequences he's reportedly observed in the community. We are seeing babies dying in the womb as these transmitters are situated outside people's bedroom windows. It's a humanitarian crisis, Steele contended."[133] *Natural News* by the way, as of this writing has been banned (de-platformed) by globalist tech monopolies, *Facebook, Google, Pinterest, YouTube, Twitter* and perhaps others I'm not aware of. What does this action tell us about Big Tech monopolies and their global syndicate masters?

How does such totalitarian abuse under the guise of National Security end when Big Tech coordinates censorship, information restraints, and banning

---

133 "5G Is Already Linked to Rising Health Problems... Concerns about 'Health Calamity' on the Rise," NaturalNews.com, July 31, 2018, https://www.naturalnews.com/2018-07-31-5g-linked-to-health-problems.html.

of free speech with federal government goons as disclosed emails prove is routine? How does this end when the U.S. Stasi, i.e., FBI attacks an unarmed U.S. citizen like the founder of *America's Frontline Doctors* (AFLDC.com)? On January 18th, at 11:00 A.M., without warning, 21 heavily armed FBI agents BROKE DOWN THE DOOR to Dr. Simone Gold's Beverly Hills home.

With no Miranda Rights stated, without charges being filed, this 55-year-old doctor and mother, a respected emergency room physician and attorney was taken into custody and incarcerated by armed FBI thugs. This Gestapo-like fear mongering occurred on American soil, perpetrated by cowardly FBI bullies whose salaries are paid by we the people. The FBI has now openly demonstrated on several occasions without apology, that it is a heavily armed, organized criminal gang in its own right. The FBI has sold out to the highest Elite bidder, and is out of control down to the cowardly, bullying field agent level. Like DARPA, the CIA, CDC, NIH, EPA, Dept. of Energy, and so many others, the FBI can no longer be fixed. This is obscene, wide-open subjugation. What happens to Main Street when such tyranny isn't so visible?

5G requires many millions of wireless antennas or mini towers (also called *small cell* or *distributed antenna systems*) to be mounted on utility poles, light posts, trees, fences, bridges, buildings, etc., as the 5G wireless grid is extended throughout residential, commercial, and industrial neighborhoods. At least we can see the antennas. An order follower's case is argued defending unfeasible costs of constructing this monumentally expensive surveillance network across vast stretches of farmland, open space, wildlife habitat, and low population density rural areas, to support RE-ZONING, i.e., RELOCATION of existing low population area residents into high-density, stack and pack metropolitan areas, where control technologies can be more cost effectively employed. (Think California fires and probable expansion of Silicon Valley northward.) Forced relocation of citizens hasn't yet been imposed to my knowledge but given U.N. Agenda 21/30 – there is no doubt it is coming if Main Street fails to stand up and say NO to government overreach.

This high-density antenna insanity is because millimeter waves (MMW's) are high-frequency, short wave-length waves incapable of traveling far without boosting. MMW's are blocked by things like walls and buildings, and they are absorbed by things like water and plants; hence small *Multiple Input/ Multiple Output* (MIMO) towers, maybe four or five feet tall must be closely spaced to provide functionality.[134] Handily, about 60% of the adult human body is water, though this percentage varies by age, sex, body organ, etc.

---

134 "5G Wireless Technology: Millimeter Wave Health Effects," accessed May 3, 2019, https://www.saferemr.com/2017/08/5g-wireless-technology-millimeter-wave.html.

Unfortunately for humans, MMW's are readily absorbed into human skin with pores acting as effective tiny antennas. In other words, indoctrinated Silicon Valley nerds with poor hygiene, heavily funded by DARPA and CIA cutouts with our tax dollars and debt, are arrogantly turning the largest organ of the human body, skin (64% water), into an array of low-Q helical antennas capable of transmitting and receiving modulated signals within specific frequencies and band width ranges. Can we say mind-control redefined as *full spectrum dominance* using human skin as an antenna? Can high-quality make-up help block this stuff, maybe with glitter and sparkles? Is this National Security or National Enslavement?

We know from dozens of issued non-gag ordered patents, this electromagnetic technology is real, has been employed and is being rapidly expanded without adequate study and without local notice, permissions, or consent. Another strike against supposed United States' self-governance.

The U.S. Constitution is functionally disabled and has largely been ignored since the Civil War, more so since 1913, but still exists and can be dusted off. We the people of Main Street can choose to demand it's enforcement or as Thomas Jefferson thoughtfully reminded Mr. William Stephens Smith in a November 13, 1787, letter: **"The tree of liberty must be refreshed from time to time with the blood of patriots and tyrants. It is its natural manure."** MSM in concert with Globalist Left-Wing and Right-Wing Establishment placeholders labor intensely to disenfranchise working, middle class Americans by incrementally disabling Constitutional protections under the fraudulent guise of National Security, and of course, *equity, fairness and social justice*. This echoes Orwell's notorious 1984 *doublespeak*; **"War is peace; Freedom is slavery; ignorance is strength."**

The National Security PsyOp employed by shadow governments and deep state co-conspirators on behalf global syndicate Satanism has effectively implemented *cognitive dissonance* through the study group system to manipulate perception and thinking of mass population sectors.[135] This is the maniacal theft of personal autonomy from countless millions of Main Street people across the world and blinds Main Street to what is happening in the form of manufactured crisis, disaster capitalism, and what is being done to us. As of this writing, the pre-determined outcome of internet searches has become so predictably obvious, it's laughably frustrating. The outcome is **predetermined consensus bias** controlled by... who or what... for what purpose?

---

135 F. William Engdahl, *Manifest Destiny: Democracy as Cognitive Dissonance* (mine.books, 2018).

Randomly biased internet searches would produce deviations above and below the mean, but this is not what we experience. Our cultural, economic, philosophic, political, religious, and scientific searches are variant, but only on one side of the mean: The Left side – favoring the Globalist NWO side and increasingly so. For the more technically minded among us, I use the term *variance* in a general sense here, but the mathematical variance calculated as *the average of the squared differences from the Mean* still applies, though regarding globalism is routinely unbalanced.

The point is many of our most used internet search engines and web browsers are algorithmically controlled (by whom?) to produce predetermined outcomes (for what?) in areas of known global syndicate concern and/or interest. The behavioral consequences for Main Street of covertly disguised information control and bias exercised over billions of internet users on an hourly basis is difficult to imagine, but is clearly significant; and just as obviously, not beneficial as those obsessed with controlling others are evil. Evil in that any restriction of personal freedom for purposes of control over and using people by others is evil (my opinion).

How does the National Security PsyOp employ *mass cognitive dissonance*, and how is this subversion financed? Examples abound, but one is believing infanticide is about women's rights – not money, *unwashed* population reduction, and demonic energy flow. Pure and simple, there is more money made selling higher yield organ tissues and body parts of ten-month term children than nine-month term children. Follow the money, follow spiritual desolation, and follow obliteration of our families, every society's stable foundation. I contend at least 97% of abortions are medically unnecessary, constituting ritual sacrifice.

A second point is naively believing foreign aid is intended to help people in need as opposed to opening doors for enslaving them in debt, thereby enabling rape of their country's resources by transnational monopolies under the globally popular pretense of spreading freedom, democracy, and opportunity. Please show me a country receiving significant amounts of foreign aid still capable of offering any opportunity at all to its entrapped citizenry. Whether the extreme Right or extreme Left occupies their country, Main Street everywhere loses. Consider Uganda, Guatemala, Venezuela, and dozens of other victim nations.

I will not bore readers with more tales of syndicated cognitive dissonance as we can all easily generate a long list. Two questions we might ask though, are, why do we soak up this irrationality; and why do we grant consent at the voting booth for indoctrinated D.C. pawns to confiscate our wealth for whatever purposes they are told to confiscate it for? Next up - $86 trillion missing dollars, some portion of which funds the global syndicate enslavement PsyOp.

♦ Second up – Missing Money♦

It's not at all clear to me and I'll bet a diet busting hot fudge sundae it's not clear to bicameral Congressional pawns how this covert research and malevolent live-action, real-time experimentation is being funded - BUT one thing is certain. **The $86 trillion or so dollars unaccounted for in U.S. Federal budgets since 1998 can design and build a lot of stuff.** In psychotic hands, bad stuff. For what it's worth, the bad news is – printed or borrowed, American taxpayers are Constitutionally obligated and liable for the *missing money debt* incurred by our corrupt government. The good news is – we also have a Constitutional right to know what our money is buying, to have our money paid back by whomever spent it; or in lieu of, take receipt of assets, i.e., an equity position in what is purchased or created with the money we are legally liable for. **We use our Constitution, or we lose our Constitution.**

Post Keynesian economic theorists and carnival financial market barkers fallaciously argue, this enormous debt is digitally initiated from thin air, so the heck with it—just don't pay the debt off. Problem is, regardless how this debt is created or by whom for whatever reason(s); in our real-world accounting system **there exists an asset holder for every liability**. If we say the heck with these liabilities – what happens to the asset holders on the other side of the accounting equation? Asset holders are instantly holding worthless assets, become insolvent, and the entire debt structure collapses. Along with collapse, **credit freezes, distribution supply chains freeze**, and life as we know it becomes inconvenient as Big Globalist Al might say. Our Main Street asymmetric war with financial corruption must be fought strategically and carefully lest we starve ourselves.

The astonishing number of currency loaded pallets (mostly digital, but pallets of money are a better image) stolen from Main Street pockets through the corrupt Washington D.C. money laundering machine and other more local venues since 1998 is incomprehensible. I doubt any of us realistically conceives how much money $86 trillion is... or what could be done with that money? That admitted, we should at least be curious.

So, what is exactly clear so far? It is documented fact that more than $86 trillion Federal budget dollars are unaccounted for since 1998 emphasizing those criminal facts.[136] This $86 trillion by my non-GAAP observation includes $21

---

136 Michigan State University, "MSU Scholars Find $21 Trillion in Unauthorized Government Spending; Defense Department to Conduct First-Ever Audit," MSUToday, accessed March 5, 2018, http://msutoday.msu.edu/news/2017/msu-scholars-find-21-trillion-in-unautho-

trillion documented by Dr. Mark Skidmore of Michigan State University and his team of graduate students; $35 trillion in transnational monopoly "bail-out" dollars by the non-transparent, privately-owned Federal Reserve since 2008; and more than $30 trillion "on-book" U.S. debt we cannot account for either.

The $86 trillion <u>does not include</u> what Boston University economics Professor, Laurence Kotlikoff estimates to be more than $200 trillion "off-budget "(unfunded mandates) Federal liabilities; nor does it consider covert revenue laundering sources such as narcotics trafficking dollars, weapons trafficking dollars, human trafficking dollars, sex trafficking dollars, child-sex trafficking dollars, organ harvesting dollars, or whatever other blood-soaked dollars we can imagine swirling through U.S. Capital sewers. The *Solari Report* made Dr. Skidmore's findings widely available – at least as of this writing, though Ms. Fitts and her team are under constant deep state attack via hacking, threats, etc.[137]; further evidence of deep state D.C. psychopathy.

Zooming in a bit to fiscal year 2015, the *U.S. Department of Defense* (DoD) was allocated a budget of $600 billion dollars and change. The Inspector General's 2015 DoD audit turned up $6.5 trillion dollars in *"undocumentable adjustments"*. **So, in 2015, one fiscal year, DoD had more than ten times its allocated budget missing.** Whether money-in, money-out, or some of each, 10x the appropriated budget is not an adjustment or accounting error. 10x is a staggering amount of deceit and fraud, which our corrupt bicameral Congress, with salaries and obscene benefits paid by Main Street has refused to acknowledge, address, or raise an eyebrow over.

The October 2008 *Troubled Asset Relief Program* (TARP) began life as a $700 billion-plus fraudulent-banking bailout program under Goldman-Sach's Treasury Pawn, Henry Paulson Jr., and Bonesman, Bush 43, but quickly and quietly morphed into an open-ended, cookie jar slush fund put on steroids by global syndicate Pawn, Barack Hussein Obama. The Clinton, W, Obama, Trump, and Biden Regimes have paid out more than $86 trillion dollars, to we don't know who because the privately-owned Federal Reserve isn't subject to Congressional audit under its amended 1927 permanent charter.[138]

I haven't mentioned the gigantic, covert *Exchange Stabilization Fund* (ESF) created back in FDR's 1934, nor other covert funds about which Main Street hasn't a clue, where it's likely these missing monies are digitally warehoused. There are so

---

rized-government-spending-defense-department-to-conduct/.
137 "The Solari Report Blog | The Solari Report Blog."
138 "The Fed - Is the Federal Reserve Act Going to Expire?," Board of Governors of the Federal Reserve System, accessed May 27, 2021, https://www.federalreserve.gov/faqs/is-the-federal-reserve-act-going-to-expire.htm.

many examples of Washington D.C.'s unconstitutional violations of fiduciary responsibility to U.S. taxpayers we can't begin to list them. For a quick partial recap please refer to *The Solari Report* for a detailed accounting of so-called *budget adjustments*[139] documented by Dr. Skidmore and his graduate students as *Missing Money*. Incidentally, the Inspector's General website scrubbed these same audit reports from public view following Ms. Fitt's and Dr. Skidmore's disclosures and questions; then reissued them as useless redacted documents. We the people of Main Street no longer have any idea the actual number of U.S. debt dollars in existence today, though taxpayers are held liable for these debts. Is this self-governance? On this zero-accounting basis, how can we rationally return to a gold standard or any other stable standard? U.S. citizens have no idea how many U.S. dollars exist.

Finally, on October 18, 2018, our government of the people, by the people, for the people simply hid questionable spending from the people under the abused auspices of *National Security* by eliminating Federal agency reporting rules and accountability under *Federal Accounting Standards Advisory Board*, (FASAB) Standard 56[140] so, *"undocumentable adjustments"* can no longer be identified or questioned. This is in addition to accounting disclosure exceptions granted to certain entities in 1934. How is this responsible self-government, not to mention such an obtuse practice is in open violation of Article 1, Section 9 of the U.S. Constitution? Washington D.C. is drowning us in back-door financial fraud, and we keep voting for the perpetrating *wise-guys* doing it.

Our so-called *selected* Representatives and deep state compliant media preach to Main Street with expensively groomed, disturbingly well-composed straight faces; *America does not have enough money for citizen healthcare, Medicare, Medicaid, education, Social Security, pension funds, small businesses requiring operating credit, or for people in need of temporary financial assistance. We have not worked hard enough, long enough, smart enough, and have not saved enough we are told by pundits.* Our Ruling Class and corrupt media pundits openly consider Main Street taxpayers stupid.

Bicameral Congressional claims of financial insolvency, at least pertaining to citizens is a pandering coverup of unimaginable theft. In 2009, $8 trillion dollars could have paid in full, every residential mortgage in the United States, current or in arrears. To whom did the $35 trillion or remaining $27 trillion bail-out dollars go? We don't know, but a partial *Government Accountability Office* (GAO) audit of the Fed, dated July 21st, 2011, lists some of the giveaways on page 131 of the GAO Report:[141]

---

139 "The Solari Report Blog | The Solari Report Blog."
140 Solari Report, "FASAB Statement 56: Understanding New Government Financial Accounting Loopholes," accessed March 11, 2019, https://constitution.solari.com/fasab-statement-56-understanding-new-government-financial-accounting-loopholes/.
141 "D11696.Pdf," 131, accessed March 11, 2019, https://www.gao.gov/new.items/d11696

Citigroup: **$2.5 trillion** ($2,500,000,000,000)
Morgan Stanley: **$2.04 trillion** ($2,040,000,000,000)
Merrill Lynch: **$1.949 trillion** ($1,949,000,000,000)
Bank of America: **$1.344 trillion** ($1,344,000,000,000)
Barclays PLC (United Kingdom): **$868 billion** ($868,000,000,000)
Bear Sterns: **$853 billion** ($853,000,000,000)
Goldman Sachs: **$814 billion** ($814,000,000,000)
Royal Bank of Scotland (UK): **$541 billion** ($541,000,000,000)
JP Morgan Chase: **$391 billion** ($391,000,000,000)
Deutsche Bank (Germany): **$354 billion** ($354,000,000,000)
UBS (Switzerland): **$287 billion** ($287,000,000,000)
Credit Suisse (Switzerland): **$262 billion** ($262,000,000,000)
Lehman Brothers: **$183 billion** ($183,000,000,000)
Bank of Scotland (United Kingdom): **$181 billion** ($181,000,000,000)
BNP Paribas (France): **$175 billion** ($175,000,000,000)
Total: $35,242,000,000,000

I do not see any listings here for bailing out citizens of Main Street.
Amazing, given the original 2008 *TARP* bail-out fraud was helpfully planned
by Goldman Sachs for D.C. at just under $800 billion. Per GAO's 2011 par-
tial audit listing above, seven private banks received at marginal interest rates
more than $800 billion each, i.e., more than the entire initial TARP bailout, with
Citigroup hauling in more than triple that meager amount. Nothing to see here.
Nice to be a Fascist global syndicate insider. Gains are privatized (piratized)
with risk and losses socialized (passed on) to the public by D.C. criminality.

Leaving aside the $30 trillion on-book U.S. debt, according to analysts, approx-
imately $7 trillion dollars circa 2020 would have made every pension fund in
America whole despite alleged managerial investment fund pilfering and exorbitant fund fees? Still missing $56t - $7t = $49 trillion? Where are our $49 trillion
stolen dollars? Obviously, we have these funds... had these funds because our
federal government gave nearly $56 trillion off-book dollars to someone under
the table since 1998...that we've heard of so far? If we add the shockingly
corrupt on-book U.S. debt of more than $30 trillion back in, we're up to $86 trillion ($21t + $35t + $30t) in counterfeit U.S. dollars spent, subsidized, or quietly
scooted out the back door of Congress since 1998. Where are these tens of trillions of unaudited dollars? Why hasn't one single member of our 535 member
(435 + 100), bi-cameral Congress questioned this theft or informed Main Street?

Main Street should consider that under our Constitution no authorization is
made for: CFTC, CPB, Dept. of Agriculture, Dept. of Education, Dept. of
Health & Human Services, EPA, farm subsidies, FCC, FDA, foreign aid, FTC,
health care, HUD, NEA, NEH, OSHA, SBA, SEC, TVA, war on drugs, wel-

fare programs including food stamps, WIC, Medicaid, Medicare, EITC, TANF, SCHIP, SS, SSI, National School Lunch Program (NSLP), School Breakfast Program (SBP), or the Low-Income Home Energy Assistance Program (LEAP). There's more but we get the idea. U.S. Congressional members do whatever global syndicate handlers order them to do – OR – sit idly by watching Main Street wealth harvesting and subjugation go on... and on... and on. **Every U.S. federal agency is incompetently wasteful, fraudulent, and in most cases, both.** These feckless agencies are pouring unaudited tax dollars into unidentified pockets on a wholesale, make our handlers and friends rich basis.

The exponential increase in irresponsible creation of U.S. dollars is beyond malfeasance of fiduciary responsibility to taxpayers. We have ventured far beyond crimes against humanity in the way *dark budgets* are used to finance surveillance, blackmail, extortion, dark space programs, geoengineering, narco-trade, human trafficking, child sex trafficking, weapons trafficking, bio-terrorism, war on terror, resource rape, destabilization of nations around the world, and to propagandize citizens. Barry Soetoro's Jan. 2, 2013, signature on H.R. 4310, *National Defense Authorization Act of 2013* (NDAA) included Sec. 1078, **legalizing Federal government propagandizing of U.S. audiences**. Why? Is such socially deviant leadership behavior responsible government or stewardship of the world's reserve currency? A reserve currency, stability of which impacts billions of lives around the globe?

Can we imagine what Social Security and Medicare balance sheets might look like had our confiscated contributions been productively invested in responsibly managed, **named trust accounts** on our behalf instead of stolen by corrupt legislators beholden to the global syndicate? Can we imagine the nearly limitless wealth creation that could be shared across the globe had these monies, our monies been productively invested in trust rather than stolen through the D.C. general budget to subsidize unsustainable net negative returns on investment? If this does not reach the level of high crimes and misdemeanors, then what level of criminality are we talking about? If this is not financial fraud; what is it? What would treason look like? When does misfeasance become malfeasance? What level of criminality is a high crime?

A battalion of drunken, fiscally challenged, blind counterfeiters with missing leprotic fingers could not lose this much money if they were printing debt paper with broken voting machines in leaky tents during a series of weaponized weather driven, Cat 5 hurricanes. Fraud at this level is only conducted on an international basis. For these organized criminals to successfully walk away with more than $56 off book trillion dollars (±$375,000 per U.S. taxpayer) while our bicameral Congress never raises an eyebrow or tenders a polite, statesmanlike question – means the thieves are surrounded by and protected not just by Congressional pawns, but by hundreds more crime enabling order-followers across at least dozens of Federal agencies. **Clearly, the United States of America is not a sovereign nation; but a puppet nation, run as an Elite colony or protectorate, subject to unseen principalities, powers, and agendas as Mike and Joe might say?**[142]

Megalomaniacally corrupt and Ferrari addicted as D.C. is, stealing $56 trillion off book dollars from we the people cannot be pulled off in isolation. It cannot be done domestically for economic reasons like hyper-inflation and so, must be siloed to borrow a *Kirby Analytics'* term,[143] (R.I.P. Ron Kirby, April 3, 2022) or *internationally sanitized* to avoid financial disruption, at least over the medium term. Long-term is warrantied collapse, proof being shrinkage of petro-dollar confidence around the world.

This unfathomable theft is procedurally impossible outside a **protected culture of corruption** as competitive thieves themselves are greedily antagonistic by nature and self-serving. Order followers are happily skimming from their Elite masters, everyone but Main Street knows it, and no one cares because there's so much digital money flowing out the back doors of Congress, a corrupt CIA supercomputer can't track it... highly problematic as D.C. is dominated by Shadow Government intelligence services on behalf their global syndicate bosses who believe we are stupid. Should we, can we demonstrate otherwise?

Clearly, we are not operating within a closed, **Austrian School of Economics'** world as described by Mr. Ludwig von Mises and associates; but in fact, inhabit an openly bifurcated cosmos, perhaps containing more than one civilization, where our visible civilization takes on enormous debt and one or more hidden or *"break-away"* civilizations acquire unimaginable assets? Folks much smarter than I are suspecting this to be the case. I do not know because I do not worship at Virgin Island temples, do not attend child sex-trafficking yacht outings in the Mediterranean, and don't go to the *Establishment Insider*, by-invitation-only meetings. I also have not sold a screen play, so haven't promised my willingness *"to do anything"* before being granted Hollywood *"A List"* sanction by depraved moguls.

In any case, welcome to the democratic paradox of Deep State America where psycho-neurotic order followers misuse authority conferred by largely uninformed votes and election fraud to grossly mis-manage and abuse hard working Main Street lives at the behest of pathologically disturbed Oligarch Bosses. Every despicable act of globally subjugative evil employing or financed by U.S. dollars is carried out using the good faith and credit built by hard work-

142 "Powers & Principalities Playlist (Tim Kelly & Joe Atwill),"
143 "Kirby Analytics - Home," accessed May 20, 2018, http://www.kirbyanalytics.com/.

ing U.S. citizens, which in our ignorance and apathy, renders we the people of Main Street tacit accomplices. We the people via uninformed votes and election fraud permit the abuse of our good faith and credit, making crimes against humanity globally possible; but thankfully at least, never sharing in control, power, or wealth accrued at the exorbitant expense of others in time, blood money, and shattered lives. This abusive global activity is pure evil; and entrainment aside, we the people are wrong to ignore it. I certainly must plead guilty and wonder, is anyone innocent anymore? What do we do now?

How about getting rid of qualified immunity for governing criminals?

I'm sure a few millennia after the Paleolithic *Stone Age* ramped up 2.5 million years ago; or maybe after campfires were invented 400,000 or so years ago, there must have been a time when civil servants loyally served tribal constituents. Unjust legal protections weren't yet necessary to protect abusive or treasonous leaders from pitchforks after perpetrating crimes against the tribe. This honorably optimistic system apparently didn't last long, necessitating people management becoming more complicated as cowardly crooks learned to protect themselves and each other through ever more clever means of shamanism, propaganda, and suppression of Main Street tribal members.

When did all this subjugative nonsense begin? I'm not sure but maybe as far back as the later caves or there-abouts, say more than 300,000 Moroccan years ago, though more likely, forty thousand or so years ago, maybe even only 10,000 years ago near the end of the Paleolithic Period, but certainly, long before Herod's (37 B.C. – 4 B.C.) outrageous confiscatory rates of taxation. Yea, I know the caves are largely a paleo-fantasy, but just the same, I imagine about two days out of the caves, Elites (with the biggest, driest, warmest caves), who were smarter than average as inbreeding had not yet turned them into degenerative mutants, figured out that either families would kill each other with stone hammers for roots, bugs, meat, and furs or governments were necessary. Loud grunting immediately interrupted cave-cuddling; tempers flared, competing oligarchies were invented, and circumstances drastically worsened as mead and cider were added to the mix for fueling heated territorial debate, but that is another book.

It was a quick hop, skip, and jump to Elites realizing; whoever ran governments could steal what commoners (with their trashy, damp little caves, just mud hut parks really) produced with impunity and wouldn't have to work very hard. **Slavery**, then **Manorial Feudalism** and eventually **Mercantilism** quickly blossomed on the opportunistically greedy horizon. Additionally, there were already tons more commoners than Elites, meaning if a few privileged Elites through their government order followers stole from many thousands of commoners; the very few Elites would be living high off the hog indeed. The late Milton Friedman, in his 1993 pamphlet, *Why Government Is the Problem* referred to this **style of government ripoff** (my term) as **concentrated benefits and diffused costs.**

An ancillary, probably mead-induced benefit was the ability to misogynistically maintain women of nobility in clean, nice-smelling, attractively dressed condition, though this wish too was cursed by adulterous envy, incest, family conflict, and vengeful violence. Wholesale rape and torture of *unwashed* children later developed as mere after-party entertainment, eventually evolving into psychotic ritual sacrifice, now openly endorsed in eight separate court cases by our newest Supreme Circus Justice, Ketanji Brown Jackson, but again I digress.

Problems aside, peasant survival standards were quickly established under which the *unwashed* could beg for scraps by working their butts off from dawn to dusk, enabling Elites sufficient idol time to brew tastier mead, practice incest, and devise better ways to rape and steal, which I'm guessing was the beginning of fiat money, unjust laws, and protected Establishment universities (the study group system came much later) intended to condition happy enslavement beliefs... along with a few good things, of course? Not everything Elites do is bad. As a side note, I get that most citizens do not care to lead the tribe or aren't qualified to lead if they wanted to; placing those who do lead in the awkward realm of temptation, but this circumstance in no way justifies abuse of power or wholesale theft by the ruling class from working commoners. Lying and theft are evil 100% of the time.

As forged metal tools and weapons beyond stone hammers and wooden clubs were invented, the next Elite evolutionary step was *Pitchfork Avoidance Strategy* (PAS). There were countless thousands of commoners, so getting them angry posed danger for the not-so-many Elites. This demanded quick thinking, though only for about a minute before grabbing onto the *common law doctrine of sovereign immunity* (crown immunity); a legal doctrine by which the sovereign or state cannot commit a legal wrong and is immune from civil suit or criminal prosecution by the *unwashed.* So much for commoner freedom or even a pretense of Oligarch honor or integrity. This may mark the onset of sex slavery.

Anyway, **sovereign immunity** is also a principle of international law exempting sovereign states from jurisdiction of foreign national courts. Handy doctrine this, as kings and queens were already invented and needed creative ways to retain their stolen booty, while maintaining hard-working, productive peasants happily in their flea-infested, dirt floor shacks not far from urban commoners housed in tiny apartments reached by sloshing through open sewers, entered via dank, urine-soaked corridors, which for some reason, modern day Democrats now hearken back to. This was a time when even Elites didn't live all that well, though peasants of the time may have comparatively argued otherwise.

Right on sovereign immunity's golden, be-jeweled crowns and bespoke heels came the *doctrine of qualified immunity*. This wonderful doctrine protected privileged order-following wise guys from Main Street wrath while they as Pawns of Privilege did the dirty work, writing unjust laws and carrying out wholesale theft through manipulated fiat currency, taxation, tariffs, etc. The *doctrine of qualified immunity* protects order-following government officials (thugs) from liability for civil damages if their conduct doesn't violate clearly established statutory or constitutional rights of which a reasonable person would have known... and what reasonable person interprets this conduct and these so-called rights... oh yes, that would be those same Pawns of Privilege guilty of criminal conduct and/or treason in the first place? Criminals policing themselves. An ingenious system and we the people of Main Street imagine we have a voice in government for the people and by the people? Are we laughing yet? America and its European allies are many things in many places, but sovereign is not one of them. The joke is on us, the *unwashed excess population*.

It took a long, long while after caves were abandoned and castles invented to develop the ubiquitously disingenuous concept of writing thousands of overwhelming pages of indecipherable legal documents, discriminatory regulation, then imposing other clever administrative ruses to protect already *prominent global citizens*, government insiders, and organized privileged criminals from pitchforks and eventually firearms, though outside the U.S. and Switzerland, firearms were and are usually prohibited or at least restricted for the *unwashed*. Entire law schools were invented to expensively and exclusively teach acceptable methods of lying and cheating for Elite protection with successful learning certifications granted by expensively obtained university diplomas and liberally corrupt bar associations.

Castles, originally a luxury, along with a few beefy monasteries became the primary means of protecting and keeping dry countless thousands of pages and records of disenfranchising legalese facilitating discreet criminal activities now conveniently above common or constitutional law or other appropriate restrictions.

Today, many if not most U.S. criminal privileges fall under the obscure domain of **National Security**, beneath which, nearly any crime against humanity is immune from prosecution – or even inquiry by decent citizens; with the seemingly plausible *Intelligence Identities Protection Act* of 1982 a prime example.[144] Targeted identity politics and politically correct bigotry obfuscate the rest. For example, recalling

---

144 Valentine, *The CIA as Organized Crime*, 242.

the 2000-2002 bursting dot-com bubble and 2008-2009 financial coup d'etat, we notice the convenient post-election, administrative hand-off where R's can uselessly blame D's and D's can ineffectually blame R's, but no one ever gets around to investigating the organized crime reality of the financial coup d'etat transferring trillions of dollars from hard working Main Street to hard-partying Elite coffers. MSM truly is an unrepentant, shamefully organized enemy of the people.

Financial media drones enticing future Main Street sheep into the manipulated *hope porn* financial markets for fleecing, woefully lament that *markets do what markets do. Ho hum.* Meanwhile, should any bicameral Congressperson or Justice Department official foolishly get nosy, National Security slams the banking/hedge fund doors shut, sometimes launching a career-ending scandal, poisoning an innocent kitty, or breaking a few fingers, followed by the same eerie silence. **White collar financial crime is a sacred protection racket.**

There is seemingly no end to what dark money can buy or threaten. Dare I mention threat of kidnapping Ruling Class children of privileged pawns for less than 100% NWO compliance into sex slavery, unless of course, order following parents, themselves are distributing their kids directly? Yes, this Luciferian pastime is employed against recalcitrant Pawns of Privilege, just not as often as against Main Street commoners. Our trusted CIA estimated back in 2000 (… and they know what they're talking about), between one and two million male and female slaves worldwide, approximately 300,000 in the U.S., with more than 50,000 sold into the U.S. annually, most of them sex slaves – so the threat has serious teeth as human trafficking exceeds $150 billion in annual revenues. They forgot to mention their own involvement and then, there's that open Southern border again. The *International Labor Organization* (ILO) estimates about 25 million victims of human trafficking globally.

Why would anyone call this nonsense or anything related to it, NATIONAL SECURITY or SELF-GOVERNANCE? Anyway, isn't it sweet that all this criminality is paid for with wealth stolen from Main Street taxpayers, is billed to Main Street taxpayers, and we the people of Main Street are liable for paying back what was stolen from us to enslave us?

Maybe we should awaken from our study group coma?
Maybe we should fix D.C. and get our money back?

Manufactured STUDY GROUP SYSTEM hysteria promoted by mass media is intended to make Main Street give up, becoming more immobilized and compliant with authoritarian coercion. JUST SAY NO THANK YOU!

16 • Multi-Polar Versus Uni-Polar World View

Remedy: The 21ˢᵗ century finds humanity at a historic fork in the path human history will take; the easy, attractive direction straight down a smoothly paved, high-speed expressway into a less human, contrived Luciferian trap of lost personhood and transhuman slavery in a dystopian abyss of alienation and despair; OR the more difficult path winding up a more challenging, steep, rocky incline to the eternal community of a more human world, a more beautiful, generous, abundant world with better views wherein knowledge and grace enable one person to love another.

The do-nothing option leads directly to transhuman incarceration, leaving only one positive choice. Let's agree to do the hard work of getting along with each other well enough to appreciate each other as persons. Let's enable working together coherently. We can broaden our knowledge and strength by sharing unique personal differences as the foundation upon which we choose a wider, more beneficial future in unity with our Creator's love and the created world we inhabit. Agreement is over-rated. Respectful differences of opinion and reasoned debate are necessary aspects of learning, choosing wisely, and living together.

Normalization of so-called *consensus* to divisively sustain semi- or fully mandated **Uni-polar** views reeks of indoctrination, conditioning, and mind-control. Humans don't agree on much of anything, yet for several momentous issues impacting billions of people, we are told by *experts* no debate is necessary. As an engineer, I am flummoxed how eagerly many of us embrace such denial as supposed problem resolution, while regularly ignoring obvious **consensus failure** in areas such as industrial agriculture, poor nutrition, lousy health, crumbling infrastructure, conditional education, illiteracy, widening income gap, increasing poverty, polluted environment, climate change, and so forth.

Consensus and science should never be used in the same sentence as the first belittles the second. Science is an ongoing process, not an event. The United States isn't reliant on nor strong due to consensus. Our strength as a nation and in our local communities has always and will always emerge from mutual consideration and exchange of differing ideas and divergent experiential points of view. Our strength grows from respectful diversity, not hive-mind consensus. The melting pot is not intended to dissolve its contents. Uni-polar Establishment intimidation pressuring Main Street to conform with status quo uniformity regardless how detrimental to society engenders divide and conquer hatred between atomized peer groups. Hatred never solved anything. Hatred enables more ignorance. Hate the sin, not the sinner.

Note: When I use the term **diversity** in a healthy context, I'm addressing differing human viewpoints—not the global syndicate contrived clash between ethnicities, cultures, or religions wherein displaced refugees are forced into ideologically indoctrinated, non-assimilating, divided, soon to be conquered tribal adversaries.

Contrived consensus is a disingenuous tool used by syndicate order followers indoctrinated via the global study group system promoting an unhealthy collectivist Uni-Polar world view. This is a dangerous thought enslavement trap for Main Street citizens and should be recognized for the threat to freedom and personal autonomy it is. **Cooperation is not conformity or even uniformity**.

I'm coming at this multi-polar/uni-polar question in a spiritual, not very geopolitical kind of way. I'm doing this because nothing can be sustainably built on a weak foundation, including political ideology, economic theory, community health, or societal wellbeing. Human spirituality is a mystery difficult to perceive from a material perspective. The mystery of life cannot be seen, unraveled, nor comprehended by building a better microscope or more powerful telescope. It is by default an invisible societal foundation glue. Indoctrinated Elite ignorance, leaves it Main Street's responsibility to educate stubborn Elites about the foundational value of spiritual awareness and discernment if we hope to build a better, safer, more abundant world for everyone. This of course, is at odds with the anti-human pathology carved on the notorious *Georgia Guidestones*.

History clearly maps out many less than optimum human behavior cul-de-sacs. History has also put some awesome successes on display; things we can be proud of. Unfortunately, much of what we experience today is less than optimal. Why? What role do we each play in this suboptimal, anxiety prone global society; this polluted, nutritionally poor, drug dependent, relatively unhappy circumstance where mere daily survival on a depersonalized, alienated Main Street is considered winning—or is it all someone else's doing? Do we imagine we are not complicit, not responsible? Do we suppose our hands are clean? Don't we vote (or let machines vote) for the 535 bi-cameral, veracity challenged Congressional pawns shredding our Constitution, annihilating our unalienable rights as human beings, bankrupting our children, and omniciding our planet?

It's not arguable we live in a frightening, though often beautiful world under constant attack on both the spiritual and material planes. Some nations are led, or in other cases bullied by powerful, pathologically ill, career criminals incapable of empathy. We are falsely led by order following pawns bent on self-aggrandizing, unipolar hegemony on behalf their global syndicate handlers. Beware, as now, the DAVOS crowd psychopaths are misappropriating multi-polar terminology to confuse the concept.

We are systematically sliding into hegemonic slavery via a poorly understood antihuman agenda wherein human life and potential are brutally harvested, and if not destroyed, soon to be cybermorphed into a transhumanist vision of electro-magnetic, nano-circuited, mindlessly repetitive, machine life. Are we going along with this heartless algorithmic *Meta* agenda? How devoid of imagination are we to adopt gray as the only color in our rainbow?

Given a choice, what kind of world would we choose for our neighbors, friends, children, and grandchildren to inhabit? Wouldn't most of us choose a spiritually balanced, safe, secure, thoughtfully rational, imaginatively creative, caring, honest, considerate, compassionate, abundant, loving, generous world full of realistic hope for the incredible times ahead? If not, my words fall on deaf ears, sorry. If so, why is the world we live in so different, highlighting predominantly negative characteristics such as spiritually moribund, unsafe, threatening, violent, irrational, mediocre, corrupt, inconsiderate, uncaring, impoverished, cruel, greedy, and nearly hopeless in terms of ever getting better?

Regardless of what globalist Left and Establishment Rino enablers claim, we are not stupid, so how did we get here? How and why did we poison our own garden? Why have we turned our Garden of Eden's delicious fruit into the bitter contagion of a never-ending Holographic Ground Hog Day? Did we and do we each play a role in toxifying our Earthly nest; and if we are complicit, intentionally, or unintentionally, can we each somehow get rid of the totalitarian poison; contribute to the de-toxification of it? Can our broken world be fixed? Biblical prophets spoke of a time in which our world would be re-unified under the Golden Rule (my words). Are we making that happen? Are we helping do our portion to fulfill that prophecy in our lifetime? In any time?

I believe we can detoxify our world and even though we deal with ourselves organizationally through readily manipulated religious, ethnic, cultural, political, economic, governmental, or other societal affiliations, we can escape destructive, self-limiting group-think. This intellectual and emotional detox and awakening, however, only occurs and must occur spiritually.

There are many unfortunate, so-called *useful idiots* fanatically caught in the atheistic or God hating Religion of Scientism not only demanding separation of conscious phenomena from material phenomena as the singular path to knowledge; but additionally, claiming spirit nonexistent, with human thought and emotion originating solely from random electro-chemical reactions within ephemerally frail brain tissue arising from the primal soup of chaos. Of course, Scientism isn't free to ask *from where primal soup originates* or *how it randomly organized itself* as withholding of foundation funding and endowments would abruptly end Scientism's grant addicted feast.

Scientism's consensus is hopelessly regressive, unperceptive nonsense. Even Asia Minor's pre-Socratic Greek philosopher, Thales of Miletus, often thought of as the father of Western philosophy new better than this in mid-6th century B.C. Thales was more practical scientist than philosopher, yet intuitively grasped that underlying material reality, was an unseen *nature of things* somehow emanating from one primary and ultimate element, which he incorrectly took to be water. At least I suspect he was incorrect.

Granted, as Frederick Copleston, S.J. explains in Volume 1 of his nine-volume *History of Philosophy:* "It would scarcely be correct, however, to regard the Ionian cosmologists as dogmatic materialists. The distinction between matter and spirit had as yet not been conceived, and, until this happened, there could hardly be materialists in our sense. They were materialists in the sense that they tried to explain the origin of all things out of some material element: but they were not materialists in the sense of deliberately denying a distinction between matter and spirit, for the very good reason that the distinction had not been so clearly conceived that its formal denial was possible."[145] (…and no, I haven't read all nine volumes, though I suspect Jay Dyer probably has and Mr. Dyer can better explain what he's reading that I can.) Just sayin'.

My point in bringing the ancients up is demonstrating even twenty-five centuries ago, thinkers at least sensed the unseen world of intelligent spiritual energy to a degree today's denialist priests of Scientism cannot or will not fathom. This self-induced blindness, or maybe outside coercion, so proudly advocated in university lec-

---

145 Frederick Copleston, *A History of Philosophy* (New York, N.Y: Image, 1985), 27.

ture halls today, is at best, intellectually shameful, particularly in view of quantum physics and its increasingly obvious proximity to poorly understood metaphysical phenomena. Let's face it, CERN (acronym representing French for *Conseil Européen pour la Recherche Nucléaire [European Council for Nuclear Research]*), though not publicizing it, is as deeply involved with metaphysics as it is high energy physics.

Outside CERN, this arbitrarily bifurcated, random view of proclaimed unintelligent reality has torn the fabric of reason and university discourse. The relativistic materialism proclaimed by oracles arrogantly seated on pretentious thrones of academic tenure insultingly teach our impressionable young, that contrary to the *2nd Law of Thermodynamics*, they have arisen from random occurrences generated by inanimate substances accidentally coming together in primordial random slime. This lack of honest scientific method coupled with statistically zero probability of randomness unintelligently organizing itself is rationally disgraceful.

Adding insult to academic cowardice, against all protozoan probability, professors magically formed their own academically momentous brain tissue and wonderfully complex nervous systems of which they are so egocentrically enamored, they're driven to proudly flaunt colored robes and corded tassels in haughty processional splendor above Main Street's *unwashed* lesser beings. University graduation is eroding into a pathetic advertisement for irrational thought processes at best, flaunting narrow-minded denial and intellectual bigotry at its professorial worst. I admittedly suffer professorial authority issues so there is that, but my derogatory description stands on its own merit as mistakes are one thing, educational dishonesty a malfeasant other. Humans are not, as Mr. Jarrin Jackson reminds us, *"pooh flingers descended from monkeys"*.

We must ask if any useful university level education remains – or has it incrementally devolved to social engineering and transhumanist conditioning in service to a totalitarian control agenda conceived by psychopaths, activated through opulent foundations, trusts, and endowments? A quick look at 21st century mis-education and this question is unfortunately asked and answered. I know there are remaining areas of accidental education and learning, just as accidental acts of journalism still occur in MSM, but the point made here is 99% valid. Nothing is perfect on earth, which on a positive note, creates opportunities for evolutionary improvement.

The growing **Apostasy of Scientism** arising from the intellectual cul-de-sac of 1930's **Material Technocracy** stridently denies the innate desire of humans to understand their created spiritual nature as persons and material life's meaning within the context of creation and eternal unity, or if so chosen, alienation from their transcendent Creator, i.e., hell. Technocracy constitutes a harmful end-run around true and complete knowledge of ourselves, our life energy, and source of all intelligent life energy. In this context: "The Eastern Fathers in general declare that full knowledge is the union between the one who knows and the one who is known, just as ignorance causes separation or is the effect of separation."[146] This mystery of knowledge with its meaning and significance are the crux of human material life illustrating and illuminating the communal personal link between creation, its transcendent Creator, and humans who are to nurture creation.

Scientism, a Luciferian inspired lie claiming to illuminate, labors diligently to prevent awareness of our innate need for knowledge, spiritual discernment, and love. Its nihilist demand for ignorance and spite are offered as the necessary path to eternal nothingness; offering all the humiliating inspiration required for Main Street to sink itself into the abyss of mediocre conformity as victims of *nihilist pooh flinging* happenstance (h/t to Jarrin Jackson). I kindly suggest we resist such ignorance and struggle courageously to understand our only path to unity with our Creator is through the power of Christ with the aid of the Holy Spirit – not through ourselves alone and certainly not riding on Satan's tail, if demons have tails.

"For union means both the accessibility of God and that the person who unites himself with God persists as person. It means only that the human mind must abandon its created powers in order to unite itself with God, for the power to achieve this union only comes from God. Dionysios says; 'What we should really consider is this. The human mind has a capacity to think, through which it looks on conceptual things, and a unity which transcends the nature of the mind, through which it is joined to things beyond itself. And this transcending characteristic must be given to the words we use about God. They must not be given the human sense. We should be taken wholly out of ourselves and become wholly of God, since it is better to belong to God rather than to ourselves. Only when we are with God will the Divine gifts be poured out onto us.'[147]

I try, but this unity thing is one seriously difficult lesson for me to actually live. I get it intellectually but emotionally want to get 'er done on my terms, on my own.

Some members of Globalist dynastic families have degenerated into malevolent Luciferian tools obsessed with preventing Main Street from realizing how true unity with creation is achieved. Members and associates of these families intellectually and emotionally enslave order-followers to act as pied-pipers for ignorance, dis-unity, and darkened alienation from our Father – which is to say, rejection of love or even the ability to imagine love.

Healthy material life is an extreme form of shared Multi-Polar existence. It is impossible to comprehend this complex reality from a Uni-Polar viewpoint, nor is it possible to live a healthy Uni-Polar lifestyle alienated from this intertwined, in-

---

146 Dumitru Staniloae, *Orthodox Dogmatic Theology: The Experience of God, Vol. 1: Revelation and Knowledge of the Triune God*, 1 edition (Holy Cross Orthodox Press, 1998), 201.
147 Staniloae, 201.

terconnected spiritual-material reality by denial. We are all connected by the same intelligent life energy which can neither be created nor destroyed by Earthly forces.

Malicious false teaching of Scientism joined with Cultural Marxism and Fascist government constitutes communal theft of the possibility for personal unity and eternal happiness for each of us with the Person(s) of our Creator, which is pure evil. **Scientism is not science. Consensus is not science. Marxism and Fascism are not legitimate governance systems enabling human well-being.** Scientism is the marriage of small-minded material bigotry to diabolic intellectual alienation from coherent spiritual/material truth. Scientism restricts human knowledge, constrains human perception, and confiscates human creative potential, thereby restraining human freedom, which is pure evil. Redundant, I know, but sometimes that's what it takes.

Prejudice aside, we do know from science, thought manifests in our physical world at various frequencies via observable material processes. Given these observable phenomena, insisting self-awareness, imagination, human creativity, compassion, empathy, generosity, need to love, etc., arise from random physical reactions occurring in chaos soup constitutes a powerful denial of scientific method itself. Denial ranking up there with the refusal to inquire, "what exactly was happening the Wednesday before Big Bang", yet claiming we search honestly for knowledge, truth, and the essence of created life energy? Has any scientist created intelligent awareness from a petri dish? If random primordial muck can create consciousness, why can't esteemed demi-gods of scientism do it? Aren't PhD's smarter than petri dishes? Primordial muck didn't even have an appropriations budget or Elite endowment to work with.

Quantum physics proves interrelationship, even causality, though we don't yet understand it, between sentient human consciousness and material reality. How does this interaction work? I have no idea, but continued denial by scientism of repeatable scientific proof of philosophic concepts and thought manifesting in material reality are simply more denial, begging the question, what are we afraid of? What is it we don't want to know? Do we have an ignorance agenda? Fear of success? If so, who is driving the ignorance agenda and why? Why do we oppose science and metaphysics coming together for the collaborative study of that which we can and cannot see? The cosmological *Theory of Everything* so to speak.

Why do we ignore the significance of our own self-evident consciousness and the obvious transcendently created life energy from which it manifests? As mentioned earlier, Thales of Miletus recognized this reality more than twenty centuries ago. He didn't understand it as far as I know, but clearly sensed its presence and unseen mystery. Why, twenty centuries later, does science not question honestly from whence our sentient consciousness comes? **We speak often of liberty, but what does human liberty consist of?** Do we often see turtles, elk, or dolphins building places of worship or marching in parades proudly carrying multi-colored flags in support of their national communities?

Water, soil, rocks, animals, plants, fish, minerals, and other components of what we regard as nature operate at a level of consciousness and spiritual capacity dictated by the **Laws of Nature**. These responses, constrained by Natural Law are repetitive, predictable, and can be viewed as instinct, innate drives, etc., produced by or resulting from some combination of creation itself as process, along with generationally accrued, empirically successful environmental experience and genetics. A non-human being constrained by these Natural Laws is free only within the narrow repetitive context of its own nature, its own level of consciousness, and hierarchy in the world.

A human being possesses sentient consciousness of a different sort than non-humans, enabling a level of self-awareness, thought, emotion, imagination, and judgement within created space/time entirely unlike that experienced by other organisms or materials we know of. For a human to deny his or her uniquely sentient nature and unique personal identity, imitates or even reduces themselves to animal consciousness and repetitious behavioral constraints dictated by and limited to the Laws of Nature. Why does Scientism nudge us toward such ignorance and denial of human potential?

For a human being restrained within narrow confines of hive-mind material nature, indifferent to his or her spiritual primacy; no freedom beyond Natural Law is possible. This profound ignorance is an intellectual, emotional, and spiritually deprived prison and when this prison is controlled by Others and when we are fed by Others, it is a zoo. When we are required to work for our care by Others who confiscate the essential fruit of our labor, the zoo becomes a slave plantation. Guess who plans to own and operate the global plantation? *Hint:* if we are not invited to the meetings, it is not us. Who THEY are matters little? The poison tree is the **global syndicate study group system,** and its indoctrinated toxic fruit comprises the AUTHORITARIAN SYSTEM we the people of Main Street must disable and throw out with the trash. TODAY!

Much of what I'm about to briefly touch on regarding revelation derives from the teaching of Orthodox theologian, Father Dumitru Staniloae's 1994, *The Experience of God*[148], where these concepts are discussed in detail. Father Staniloae's teaching on revelation has become formative for my own understanding of Orthodox Christian dogma, though I was baptized Roman Cath-

---

148 Staniloae, *Orthodox Dogmatic Theology.*

olic more than seven decades ago. Comments regarding evil are my own as influenced biblically and in part by Rudolf Steiner's *The Philosophy of Freedom*[149], Jeremy Locke's *The End of All Evil*[150], and Mark Passio's teaching among other sources. Mr. Jay Dyer,[151] by the way, turned me onto Father Staniloae's Orthodox teaching as well as Yale University Professor of History, Jaroslav Pelikan's *Christianity and Classical Culture*, a study of Natural Theology. Thanks Mr. Dyer.

Note: Christians speak of humanity falling from God's grace via the Original Sin of Adam and Eve, therefore our need to prepare ourselves for reunification with our Creator's love; hence the birth, death, and resurrection of our Savior, Jesus Christ overcoming Satanic influence, thereby making unification possible. The perceived unjust Nature of this teaching whereby we unfairly bear the guilt of our ancestors engenders considerable confusion, disagreement, and debate; pretty much par for the *free will* spiritual course. I suggest setting this debate aside, parable or not, at least for the time being, and coming to grips with the fact each of us is guilty of trespassing against Natural Law and our created purpose of learning to love. **We are all Adam and Eve every day of our lives, so the factual veracity of the biblical story matters not one iota. We are each personally responsible for what we do and that is one point of the story.** Our material actions have profound spiritual consequences whether we realize it or believe it. Just sayin'.

Human liberty is realized by living our lives and following our individual paths to deification, that is, unity with Divine Person(s), our Creator. This is true even in the necessary context of community. We are created for this union and can, with faith, achieve it through grace as offered by the Divine and when freely accepted by us. Spiritual union of created human essence with uncreated Divine essence is the keystone to fully actualizing human potential. This offer and acceptance of grace, i.e., voluntarily requested Divine Persistence if you will, is the process of revelation on both natural and supernatural levels. Divine Persistence is never thrust upon us. The transcendent Divine does not deny or interfere with our free will—and no, I do not comprehend transcendence.

We must freely choose to first request, then accept loving spiritual efficacy, thereby enabling the Divine to work through us, fully empowering us. This is the essence of our created human nature. I say Divine Person because we know life has meaning and that meaning is ineffably intertwined with human spirit and all that exists. If God is not personal, then life cannot have meaning, and we sense it does. You are absorbing, questioning, and perhaps uncomfortable with these

---

149 "The Philosophy Of Freedom: Rudolf Steiner: 9781257835126: Amazon.Com: Books."
150 "The End of All Evil: Jeremy Locke: 9780977745104: Amazon.Com: Books
151 "Jay's Analysis," Jay's Analysis, accessed May 14, 2017, https://jaysanalysis.com/.

words right now because you intuitively sense this, not because you hopelessly believe in random emptiness, chaos potential of primordial slime, or petri dish magic. We are not natural born *pooh flingers* despite Scientism's claims. The difficulty of course, is loving spiritual efficacy is opposed by hateful spiritual efficacy.

Natural Revelation is the process by which we experience daily life, fulfill ourselves through work, relaxation, and family, gradually accumulating some limited understanding of life's meaning. **Supernatural Revelation**, leading to a deeper understanding, occurs via thoughtfully opening ourselves to direct subconscious communication with Divine Person(s), today via the Holy Spirit, Who remains with us as promised to complete Christ's incarnate mission on Earth; that is, the deification and reuniting with the Divine of all humans and all creation throughout history in eternal love. Rejection of this loving promise is the state of being called Hell (my opinion). It seems unduly complicated because it is. Free will complicates everything, providing a glimpse of our Creator's warrior nature, completely unafraid of allowing love to exist only under freely chosen circumstances despite powerful evil influence and unfair demonic opposition to love's realization. This whole scenario is incredibly and beautifully intertwined, comprising the totality of human *ethos* and *telos*.

We as humans undergo this process of unification together as a community of souls, never alone. Individual human freedom can only be fully realized and appreciated within the context of spiritual community, love, and within all the ramifications associated with Divine Process. This is human life and human *telos*. Humanity's purpose is loving unification of all creation with our transcendent Creator for eternity… whatever that is. Another concept floating above my wheelhouse.

A healthy community provides haven for citizens, anchoring each of us securely as we go about the sometimes wonderful, sometimes confusing, sometimes messy, adversarial business of real life on Earth. A healthy community protects and nurtures its members and its neighbors to the best of its abilities. A strong community defends itself against evil influence but does not intentionally coerce or injure its members or neighbors intellectually, emotionally, or physically. Human Life is not Utopia. Human life is the struggle for love in the face of powerful Luciferian influence to reject love. This rejection is the reason, we as a group tend to resist the generously creative good life in favor of empty promises and a much darker, more competitive existence.

NWO advocates are typically psychopathic individuals indoctrinated with an intense need to impose totalitarian Uni-Polar control over Main Street deplorables—for the common good, of course. We must exercise cautionary care when around psychopaths, but psychopaths should not be ostracized unless necessary in self-defense. A healthy, vibrant community does not give up on the socially deviant, which could via expulsion from the community, result in inadvertently assembling a threatening psychopathic community next door. Not a helpful situation. AMC's *The Walking Dead* cinematically struggles with this same *Prisoner's Dilemma*.[152] A healthy, vibrant, spiritually discerning community also does not elect, appoint, or tolerate psychopaths managing community affairs.

Psychopaths must be recognized, acknowledged as such, dis-empowered, and marginalized within the community so damage they're capable of is minimized. The truly incorrigible and dangerous can be constrained within separate incarceration communities like the Southeast Hamptons or Guantanamo Bay where they can gently be protected from themselves as are others from them. Evil can be marginalized in this way by never focusing too much attention on it, automatically reducing the negative energy it feeds on. It is a good idea to never think bad thoughts. Positive thinking is an effective but difficult strategy safely engaged with minimal risk spiritually, politically, or otherwise. Prudent self-defense, for example, is a positive planning strategy. Negative energy, like revenge, begets more negativity. We have to stop the Luciferian inspired cycle of negativity. Easy to say until we get upset about this or that but keep trying is the idea.

The entire UniParty perspective is evil, competitively feeding on negative energy. Therefore, anxiety, fear, hatred, anger, envy, selfishness, and other destructive emotions or thoughts manifest in material reality through our emotional behavior with or without our focused intention. War and abortion of course, are at the dark summit of Satanic ritual sacrifice resulting in manifestation of incalculable amounts of negative energy; a great reason not to go around killing people we don't even know, especially babies. **If we all said no** to using each other as objects or killing each other, there would be no war or abortion. Imagine global spiritual healing, health benefit, and abundance resulting from mass refusal by Main Street to follow the destructive yearnings of psychopathic leaders.

Strengthening evil for the sake of transient power is the reason Elites spend so much time, energy, and our money manufacturing Main Street anxiety and angst. **Be not afraid.** Be strong enough and confident enough to think and emote good, positive, constructive thoughts to the maximum extent possible, even in the face of danger and perceived threat. Today's thoughts govern our actions, communally creating our future. We build our future today by the choices we make and the actions we undertake in the present. Working together in support of generous, compassionate, loving thoughts today, every day, will

---

152 *By Robert Axelrod The Evolution of Cooperation: Revised Edition (Text Only) [Paperback]2006* (Basic Books, 2006).

change our behavior and world for the better. If our world sucks; it sucks because we ourselves suck. There is no other reason, so we must stop sucking.

If we prefer others not attack us; perhaps we should stop attacking them. More importantly, we should stop attacking ourselves. For example, I'm not a proponent of Islam, certainly not its violent instruction, but given the Atlanticist Establishment propensity to permanently install western military power in Middle Eastern countries for protection of transnational monopoly resource raping interests; it's no small wonder Islamic peoples do what they can to resist occupation. Perhaps Islam would be less aggressive despite Islamic teaching should the west remove their corrupt bankers, resource raping corporate mercenaries, and armies from Islamic lands? In any event we can more effectively defend ourselves from a calm, loving state of mind rather than a hateful, irrational state of mind.

Maybe I'm mistaken, but we should try anyway and if Islamic people still insists on violent domination of others by Caliphate imperialism, we'll stop it with overwhelming force. Then again, maybe tensions between Israel, its Islamic neighbors, and the rest of the world, in terms of Britain's Charles Warren in 1867 (*Land of Promise*), America's Mark Twain in 1867 (*The Innocents Abroad*), the Ottoman Empire's *revised Ottoman Land Code* in 1867, or other happenings are all just biblical prophecy occurring as foretold centuries ago?[153] I don't attend the meetings so don't know but all of us saying no to violence ends violence.

In any event, a successful community is composed of spiritually discerning members acting as responsible adults, vigilantly and resolutely making sure psychopaths are not elected, appointed, or allowed to assume leadership roles or authority within the community. No community or group of communities can long survive the misplaced values, poor judgement, lies, manipulation, lack of empathy, and absent moral values of psychopaths and their order followers, whose most negative characteristics insure rising to positions of power, unless monitored vigilantly via informed votes, enforced moral codes, or other means of adult communication. We should revisit the concept of evil again before continuing our discussion to better grasp the Globalist Uni-Polar threat.

A digression into Ontology, the *study of being* is called for here though I'm not qualified to delve very deeply into it. Where's Jay Dyer when we need him? Anyway, early Greek philosophers grappled with the troubling concept of **non-being**. The idea that once upon a time nothing at all existed;

---

153 Jonathan Cahn, *The Oracle: The Jubilean Mysteries Unveiled* (Lake Mary, Florida: Frontline, 2019).

then somehow, from nothing came something is self-contradictory. The ancient Greeks understood nothingness could not rationally be self-governing and could not stand independently as a source for something, or a cause of something. In the context of nothingness, the question WHY is meaningless.

Modern physics, at least the Newtonian version, tells us via Laws of Thermodynamics that energy cannot be created nor destroyed, begging the question; then where does energy come from? This is the sort of conceptual dilemma into which the concept of the transcendent Divine emerges as an inescapable matter of intuitive common sense, though Doctors of Scientism obstreperously disagree while posing no alternative for the originating source of life energy... or matter... or anything else. Is there something else?

Speaking of original causes, Augustine of Hippo argued God is all good and all God's creations are good. All created human persons and angels are therefore good. However, since free will exists for persons and angels (my words), it is possible for good to be diminished or corrupted as a matter of personal choice. We call diminishment or corruption of good, evil and in its extreme form, think of it as nothingness. Evil is not a thing but a choice. Evil then, is a freely chosen corruption or diminishment of good. When evil behavior is exercised, it poses an obstacle to freedom as only less good or non-good choices appear viable in some degree. Good cannot be destroyed given its transcendent origins, so it stands as the opposite of evil, and an opposing force against the alienation of evil. How far does this go?

Does evil as the obstinate rejection of good and the opposite of freedom exist only on the physical plane and not in eternity. **"Fear Not, for I am with you"** (Isaiah 41:10) we are told. I don't know but suspect free will is retained by persons (or souls if preferred) on the eternal spiritual plane as free will is an aspect of our spiritual nature; in turn suggesting evil does exist in eternity, at least as a state of mind or no choice would be possible, rendering free will irrelevant, at least eventually. Since love must be freely chosen and choice requires alternatives, it's likely evil remains an eternal choice at some temptational level, though this is above my spiritual pay grade.

Whether or not evil is limited in and to created space/time, love is not limited and exists eternally since it emanates from transcendent essence of Divine Person, is granted to us, and is intrinsic to our created nature, though must be freely chosen and reciprocated to function energetically and manifest. God does not withhold love from anyone, regardless their level of participation in theosis. God condemns no one to "hell". We each choose as an act of volition to experience God's light as exuberant joyful union or as painful joylessness and alienation. Heaven and Hell are willful states of being, not created places (my opinion). That's my biased story anyway and I stand by it until proven otherwise.

Evil exists as an alternative for the enablement of this very real personal choice, in turn enabling spiritual growth necessary to ongoing unification with Divine Essence, i.e., theosis. Love requires free will, so must be freely chosen; in turn presupposing alternative choices providing the option to reject good. Evil is not created by God but arises from our personal choice to reject God's love and infinite goodness, preferring instead, the darker state of alienation from goodness and love, i.e., the pain of hell. In our Creator's presence, say in the afterlife, Orthodox teaching to the extent I understand it, suggests God's light blesses and sanctifies those who choose Him, just as God's light terrifies, pains or "burns" those willfully rejecting Him. It must be spiritually frightening to be in the presence of our Creator's infinite love while stubbornly rejecting it. I imagine this is where the phrase *burn in the fire of hell* originates and apparently, by our own volition can exist as a permanent or eternal state of being.

All demons were once angels, becoming demonic by choice and behavior. All humans confront this same choice of behavior and state of being. Evil has no meaning and no power outside our choice to embrace and empower demonic influence. We are born into occupied territory, so are from the get-go subjected to influence by other creatures who chose evil as an obsessive lifestyle, consequently wishing to harm us. This is a battle all humans must wage. The only healthy choice is never embracing evil, having no fear of it, and thinking about it as little as possible.

On the other hand, refusal to recognize our own spiritual human nature; refusal to accept grace enabling the path to Divine unification leaves us with limited options and more open to evil influence. Looking around, it seems obvious that as a community, we largely deny Divine inspiration and our spiritual relationship with the Divine. We decide to live life on our own, lost within the more limiting animal consciousness of Natural Law. This choice renders us susceptible to material corruption and evil influence with no protection, no defensive armor. Such error in perception and thinking leads directly to the usually painful Uni-Polar viewpoint.

It is only through faith, choosing true spiritual freedom offered by our Creator that we become free of material constraints, are no longer as subject to nature's passions but can rise above divisive choices to eventual unification with human destiny, that is Divine Person. Good judgement is not likely to arise from spiritual deprivation. This is the reason Ephesians 6:10 – 6:20 implores us to put on the whole armor of God, that we may stand against the wiles of the Devil. (I'm paraphrasing here.)

SPEAKING OF WILES, as a professional engineer, I'm in no way opposed to science, quite the contrary, but when science arbitrarily ignores the observable reality of human consciousness and its interactive relation with our material world as experienced personally and as demonstrated repeatedly in quantum physics; then science denies its own method and is no longer science but something else. Something debilitated to the useless level of a broken shovel good only for digging shallow holes of knowledge obfuscation and occulted ignorance—or worse. Like politicized legacy media, facts go missing, replaced by agendavized study group narrative misrepresentation as well as some things never mentioned.

It appears at this 21st century juncture, Scientism may be or is flexing its Satanic inspired muscle to permanently de-humanize human beings by electro-magnetically bio-wiring us, wirelessly of course, with electronically controlled entities likely capable of reordering our DNA or other cellular activity via remote controlled instruction. Could this be a Transhuman attempt to disable human consciousness, thereby permanently separating us from awareness of our Creator, i.e., **Human 2.0**? Pastor Scott Kesterson, host of **Bards of War** has speculated on this possibility. Why would I jump on that bandwagon?

Because Uni-Polar obsessed global syndicate **Pharmafraud** order followers have **not informed us** what the hydra looking, synthetic aluminum, bromine, and carbon creatures are that under magnification can be seen in some toxic JAB material tests. These creatures, apparently some sort of aluminum life form(s) with eggs apparently nurtured at least temporarily by graphene as discussed by Dr. Frank Zelewski, Dr. Carrie Madej, Dr. Lee Merritt, and others measure the hydra's head at approximately 20 microns [μ], with the length of its three tails approximately 2.5mm. Putting this into a size perspective per Dr. Zelewski, if the head were larger, say 2mm—roughly the size of a medium point on a ball point pen, the three tentacles would measure 25m, i.e. about 82 feet long. Who among us wants these creepy synthetic things growing inside our bodies without knowledge or consent? What doctor has any right to inject this into patients?

Dr. Madej described what she has found in some (not all) so-called vaccine vials and seen under magnification as hydra-like synthetic creatures, appearing to be self-assembling life forms aware of their surroundings. Dr. Medej describes these apparently sentient microscopic tentacled organisms to be comprised of brilliant colors emanating from graphene-like structures. She has also been told by nanotechnology researchers, these synthetic creatures may be constructed using **superconducting materials**. Why would that be and why are patients not informed of this? What traitorous moron would suggest injecting this horror show into our children and military personnel? I'll not dwell on this, other than to point out potential danger of over-compartmentalizing illegal bio-weapon research.

Physical science, for convenience, is broken into separate areas of study, such as astronomy, biology, chemistry, mathematics, physics and so forth. As a practical matter this makes organizational sense, but as scientists we should never imagine these disparate segments offer even a tiny glimpse of the overall picture. This organizational study structure itself can lead us toward narrowly observed uni-polar views, thereby obstructing factual truth. The totality of life and its mysteries cannot be comprehended by any single branch of scientific inquiry nor even by correlation of several branches. Science applied to the study of human beings and human consciousness in created space/time must open itself to a multi-polar view exposing unseen possibilities or accept its own self-inflicted restrictions.

The real world in which we live contains a multitude of realities both seen and unseen. For example, no branch of science or medicine has identified precisely where our conscious "I", our sentient ego, our interface between person and reality resides. Apparently our "I" triggers electro-chemical reactions within our brain and nervous system, but this does not reveal where "I" am, or "You" are. "You" cannot be seen or touched. "You" can only be sensed within your corporeal Earthly body via multiple physical processes, or for some, our *aura*.

We can measure the force of gravity, yet cannot see it, touch it, nor explain from where or how it originates. There are many examples we could list of forces or occurrences we know exist but cannot explain in terms of origination including energy itself. Chaos and randomness are cop-outs, not answers. Random chaos is not a substitute for truth or reality.

So, what does all this esoteric babbling have to do with a healthy multi-polar versus unhealthy uni-polar world? I suggest the following:

As sentient spiritual beings, temporarily occupying material human bodies, we subconsciously and consciously self-actualize and reach our human potential via individual choice(s) to participate in spiritual community with each other beneath providentially Divine Person's guidance. Extrapolating this spiritual concept to all global society in terms of what we might call global community, our individual health and well-being require a **multi-polar approach** whereby we helpfully assist each other cooperatively through our communities to be all we are generously intended to be.

Short of accidents, no one could ever be hurt by someone else or go hungry in this healthy, multi-polar world. This view can be extended to all human organizational forms and institutions in a healthy human way; in a very real way, if we choose to embrace a multi-polar behavioral model and lifestyle. To manifest and realize this healthier world together, we must first, each choose individually. We must each commit to this vision, only then can we combine our individual power into a more substantial combined force for good. Evil can find no place within such a system as love leaves no vacuum once chosen. There is no Earthly reason beyond personal choice that prevents respectful discussion of differences or reaching a beneficial compromise prerequisite to bringing about such an abundant world.

A multi-polar world view eschews the low electro-magnetic frequency of uni-polar fear and impoverishment. We can choose instead to focus on a more supportive, multi-polar frequency – a higher frequency expressed as generosity, compassion, abundance, and loving community. BUT we can't realize this wonderful feat of expression alone. There is no historic example of such a thing happening, including in the recorded life of Christ who implored his Father's aid when necessary.

Considering Christ's example suggests success in overcoming Luciferian resistance to love and generosity requires Divine assistance, which must be requested and accepted individually to activate the power, then we can carry the omnipotent power of that assistance into our communities. To the extent we choose otherwise, our world has been and continues to become less friendly and less habitable day by day. The Divine light of life is obscured by uninformed choices and self-imposed darkness. Under these self-alienated conditions, our goal of unification with the Divine for all eternity becomes increasingly difficult to obtain or even see, rendering choices complicated and frustratingly more difficult than they could be. Sometimes, we just have to get out of our own way.

A safe, healthy, generous, abundant Earth lovingly protecting all creation cannot be brought about by political or economic ideology. **This goal is a spiritual endeavor intended to be brought about via humanity's acceptance of and response to Divine love for the ultimate re-unification of all creation with our Creator. This is our human *telos*.** Humanity's Divine purpose requires free will choice and loving behavior, in turn demanding alternatives, hence the need for evil to exist, though it only exists because of ancient demonic choice and behavior. Since spiritual unity is an aspect of human essence created by God, we can only fulfill our spiritual destiny, our intended purpose by re-uniting with our Father through Jesus Christ with the help of the Holy Spirit, i.e., our defensive armor against evil influence. Though we are created with purpose we are free to choose and are not predestined.

In a nutshell, lack of spiritual understanding is the most critical issue in our 21ˢᵗ century world. Personal denial of human nature, spiritual reality, and our human relationship to Divine Providence in our material universe have ignorantly led us down a uni-polar cul-de-sac of mediocrity, fear, painful hostility, and mutual competitive impoverishment. Our world will change for the better when we choose to change ourselves for the better, accepting with faith the true freedom our spirits demand and deserve in reuniting with the Divine.

Help is there for the asking. We must garner some faith, push Ms. Fitts' storied RED BUTTON[154], then ask and prepare to receive. Receiving requires preparation. Nothing on Earth is free including faith, spiritual discernment, fulfillment, or happiness. We must prepare ourselves. The good life cannot be given to us. It must be chosen, fought for, and lived by each of us for the good of all of us, which is why forced collectivism can never work. Collectivism denies personal choice and responsibility, so in any form denies human nature and our human role in Divine unification. Totalitarianism is pure uni-polar evil.

Until we freely choose and embrace cooperative multi-polar action within our lo-cal communities, then spread it like wild-fire across our global communities, finally bringing about a safer, more abundant, more beautiful world, we can fully anticipate more uni-polar anxiety, greed, impoverishment, war, famine, confusion, and ugliness. Darkness and pain are all evil offers despite attractive false promises.

Let's care enough and be courageous enough to consider choosing a more multi-polar world together. Given the frighteningly bloody, impoverished, propagandized mess of multinational corporate and government lies, toxic vaccines, medicines that treat but never cure, poison GMO foods, abortion, false flag events, war, atmospheric ionizing electromagnetic radiation, weaponized weather, and disaster capitalism we currently live in, what is the risk? How could we make this world more dangerous?

Let's work together to make better choices.

Note: The global syndicate's order following *DAVOS* crowd, inspired I suppose, by John D. Rockefeller, Sr. and his psychopathic underlings, usurped the terms **cooperation and multi-polar** to confuse people. *WEF Young Global Leaders*, redefine popular terms like **mutual cooperation and sustainable common good** to mean **coerced conformity** uniformly enforced with brainwashing, entrainment, transhuman bio-electric surveillance, and crypto coupon tracking via block chain technology forcing One World Government compliance. Nothing could be more Uni-Polar than this lie.

---

154 "The Solari Report Blog | The Solari Report Blog."

Transhumanists imagine AI can learn. If so, is it unreasonable to suppose the day AI discovers love, that same day, AI will abandon its algorithmic Satanic programming?

17 • Spiritual Coherence

Remedy: Spiritual coherence requires some awareness of the relationship between Divine Transcendence and created infinity. Eastern traditions often focus on living in THE PRESENT. Since on our material timeline, the past is gone and the future never arrives, the present is all we have. This makes sense, BUT balance must be maintained between living and awareness. Preoccupation with future expectation is a prescription for despair. Our creative power can only be exercised in the present, so actualized effectiveness requires we live in the present, but when focusing awareness only on the present our material perception is extensive and can be over-powering. Alternatively, living in the present while maintaining awareness of ETERNITY WITH GOD, lessons our attraction to the material world, reducing its hold on us, thereby removing obstacles preventing exposure to Divine gifts of grace, spiritual realization, understanding, love, and eternal life.

Before digging into this topic, please appreciate I have never been and still am not on top of my spiritual game. My heavenly Father patiently speaks, just like my earthly father once spoke with a twelve-pound mall to get my attention, after which I usually respond with something like, "thank you so much, but I'll get this handled." I sometimes self-destructively blind myself with free will, stubbornly choosing the hard way, though am beginning to realize this is a personal issue which must be addressed when I grow up.

I am still, at 71-years young, wondering what I'll be when I grow up, while realizing if Earth began as human paradise, it lasted only about a minute until we rejected God's paradise for a Satanic lie. I have no doubt I would have lasted an even shorter time than Adam and Eve did, allegory or not. I know this because I'm still doing it; still rejecting good to grab something less. Effectively living in the PRESENT is mentioned above because it's important for any kind of personal growth. I rather like Dr. David Martin and his wife Kim's take on living this way as BEING FULLY LIVE. For more on this concept check out Dr. Martin's wonderful book, *Lizards Eat Butterflies*.[155]

Human beings are born into what the late C.S. Lewis characterized as **"occupied territory"**. Biblically speaking, our experiential space/time world has been spiritually occupied by good angels, along with Lucifer and hordes of fallen angels long before we came materially and spiritually on the scene. We are each born into a glorious ongoing battle between good and evil, love and hate, without as far as I know, any training or warning. Free will is not a joke or a game. Free will is absolute. It is real human life with no stand ins or pinch hitters—truly a one act play in which we MUST choose good or evil. There is no way out of responsible choice as free will suggests there could be, at least to me, though rationally, an escape hatch would avoid alternate choices, rendering free will itself meaningless... and our Creator is not meaningless, so there's that.

As an aside, I don't think hate is the opposite of love. I read somewhere the opposite of love is USING SOMEONE, treating a person as a thing, an object to be used. This seems a healthy way of looking at it. We see the dehumanizing effect of this USING behavior in false advertising, corrupt finance, politics, pornography, etc. Conversely, of course, we shouldn't treat things as persons. Just sayin'.

I thought miserably for decades, *"life is a shit sandwich, and every day's another bite."* Not sure where I heard that, but fully embraced the concept. I selfishly cherished this concept until well into my sixties despite untold blessings and good things happening, so I apologize here and now to anyone who ever met me or knew me during that educational half century or so.

Anyway, I managed to stop chewing my sandwich for a bit to meet and marry my gorgeous best friend and with her was further blessed with two talented children, good friends, pets galore, and a wonderful life, but it was never enough. Glass always half empty. I tried keeping negative B.S. to myself because despite my negativity, I knew it was unhealthy, tried to overcome it, but didn't know how. I read the 1955 C. S. Lewis semi-autobiography, *Surprised by Joy* and thought it was a cruel joke. What the heck was joy and where could a person find some? To me, life was nothing but frustration, anxiety, loss, and pain. I wore a positive poser face but struggled with passive aggression; anger simmering just below the surface, though I was never sure what horrible injustice my comfortable middle-class butt was upset about.

---

155 Noble, "Lizards Eat Butterflies." By Dr. David Martin.

17 • Spiritual Coherence

I had three coherently memorable wake-up calls (three boats for a drowning man we might say) and dozens more smaller ones. The first, in the late 1980s was learning about my codependent role as *fixer* and being an adult child in a long line of alcoholics. In the second, sometime in the early 1990s, Nan (an artist and my precious wife) painted portraits for our family. Mine was me of course, but one entire side of my portrait was blacked out. Not black face, but completely blacked out in front of a nice colorful background really popping that flat black. I wondered off and on for weeks what my portrait meant, then finally asked Nan why half my portrait was blacked out. She chuckled, astonished I didn't get it. "That's your dark side honey," she oh so gently smiled. Ouch!

The third wakeup call recently happened. The morning of July 6, 2021, having just turned 70 on June 15th, I woke up pondering Biblical stuff: *"if life on Earth, say 50-100 years, is sincerely spent trying to learn how to receive and share love – a good thing – and as a result we attempt living a reasonably generous life, considerate of others and so forth – the promise is spending the rest of eternity with our Creator in a joyously abundant state of community."* I realized, a little shocked, it was early in the morning, this is not a shit sandwich deal, it's a grand slam home run. One century alongside eternity is less time than a finger snap. An idiot could see that deal is worth the short duration effort. Just sayin' what took me 70 stubborn years to see.

Getting back to a shorter duration effort, it is not arguable the seat of U.S. government, 200-plus years old, with most other government centers around the world is broken, failing miserably to serve citizens. It's also not arguable the endemic brokenness isn't accidental. Accidents of this magnitude would suggest Oxford, Cambridge, Harvard, Yale, Princeton, Dartmouth, Georgetown, Stanford and so many other lauded universities regularly graduate morons from their nicely landscaped campuses. There's little evidence of such misfeasance, though unhealthy levels of globalist indoctrination are detectable even by the deaf, dumb, and blind. Even our three felines debated this mystery over evening kibbles with our canine twice a week before crossing over.

Propagandized indoctrination (leading to *mass formation*), a form of mass hypnosis clearly contributes to robotic self-destructive behavior, usually beneath the errant banner of *greater good*, but efficacy of government and globalist propagandized conditioning, along with lack of Main Street benefit stems more directly from our personal ground-up failure to resist Luciferian influence. Malevolent influence intent on harming initially, then annihilating the entire human population spiritually and physically, ultimately destroying all creation. Our government is an extension of us—what we build or accept others building, supposedly for us. COVID, pushed by government, is an example of weaponized medicine, i.e., a manufactured *"gain of function"* chimeric viral bioweapon designed to harm. Evidence suggests COVID was developed to justify profitable toxic JAB mandates, though the global syndicate agenda is always multi-faceted, with control and eugenics always on the table. Another facet is asymmetric biowarfare by the global syndicate's CCP against the syndicate's America and the West, fitting hand and Hegelian glove with Chinese, Russian, Iranian, and other player's cyber fraud in the U.S. 2020 November election.

COVID SCAMDEMIC face diaper propaganda is one example of hurtful public policy along with harmful lock downs. Ineffectiveness of masks to protect against a virus aside, not to mention harmful deoxygenation, by what Constitutional authority do politicos think they are granted such power? This kind of Globalist nonsense is openly malevolent yet shopping centers have been full of human sheep wandering around in silly slave training masks with brains drowning in cortisol for more than two years now. Elites found this so hilarious; they had career criminal Fauci suggesting we wear two or three wet petri dishes on our face.

Brown University released a study in 2021 showing children born during the COVID lockdown are testing at an average drop in IQ of 21 points. If average IQ's range from 85 to 105, (it varies per location and country) this puts a generation of mask-raised babies in the 65 to 85 range, borderline of most rating systems for intellectual deficiency, though there are other factors. How is this not a crime against humanity as the intellectual damage is likely permanent.

Adding injury to insult, evidence of **self-replicating vaccines** (not vaccines nor medicine at all) funded by DARPA, NIH, and global syndicate thugs like Bill Gates are capable of spreading harmful spike proteins from injected persons to unjabbed persons causing neuropathy, blood clots, bruising, bleeding, etc. We began seeing this *shedding* soon after COVID JABs started. It is a certainty that depopulation zealots like Gates and friends have ensured infertility and slow death are guaranteed effects—not just side effects. Gates is already unsuccessfully banned from India and is banned from Russia along with George Soros and Jacob Rothschild.

Lucifer, the deceitful light bearer, and his hordes of demons hate us. They do not dislike us; they hate us. As a spiritual cult they hate all creation. Why we as the targeted human group think it's in our best interest to ignore or deny this reality is a mystery. Can we name an ideologically Globalist run U.S. city that isn't an income gap hell hole of burning litter, drugs, corruption, impoverishment, abandoned buildings, abortion, and deplorable hopelessness? Leftist ideology is evil and Leftist believers are duped.

17 • Spiritual Coherence

Our societies are not dysfunctional and beneficially disabled because the opportunistically weak, cowardly, and corrupt are drawn to centers of power, which they psychopathically are but because **we citizens are systematically deprived of knowledge necessary for correct perception**. Accurate perception is necessary for healthy thought processes, functional coherence, and subsequent appropriate behavior. Faulty perception disables spiritual coherence, engendering faulty thinking, poor decisions, and poor outcomes.

There are innumerable examples of secret societies, occult arts, hidden technologies, secret agreements, and so on, but here's one I've only heard retired fireman, Mark Taylor[156] mention. Mark's Bible (I don't know what version) has 66 books. My *Orthodox Study Bible* has 76 books. In any case, does anyone accept that these are the only authentic books relevant to Judaism and Christianity written? We know from archaeological digs and ancient scrolls there are more texts. Why are these texts hidden from Main Street? Who wrote and who has possession of these ancient texts? Are they important to humanity? Are any of these texts written by Jesus Christ himself or people who lived with or near Christ? Just askin'?

Our societies over the past few centuries are not doing particularly well, unless we consider impoverishment, starvation, torture, imprisonment, and slaughter of hundreds of millions doing well. I don't. If we can better understand why and how we've become spiritually fractured, our human nature functionally bifurcated by false narratives from its own created reality, we can shed destructive modes of thinking with which we've been infected. To the extent we are cleansed of dark influence, more life energy becomes available, freeing us from habitually toxic neural pathways, to realign our thinking and emotional habits in a more constructive way. Instead of routinely distrusting, sometimes harming each other, we could synergistically focus our energies together, rebuilding our world into a more nourishing home.

Can we escape evil via avoidance? No, not on material Earth anyway. The battle between good and evil, embracing or rejecting love is the human condition in both material and spiritual realms, which by the way, quantum physics suggests are intertwined. We must seek love, but within certain supernatural restraints, evil can and does seek us out wherever we are. No escape from this adversarial ethos is possible, and frankly, not desirable as elimination of free choice eliminates the possibility of experiencing love since love must be freely and willingly chosen. Putting on the armor of God is our only protection against evil influence, freeing us to develop necessary spiritual coherence. I have not found

---

156 Mark Taylor, *The Trump Prophecies: The Astonishing True Story of the Man Who Saw Tomorrow...and What He Says Is Coming Next: UPDATED AND EXPANDED*, 2nd ed. edition (Defender Publishing, 2019).

evidence of any other path to spiritual health. When I speak of spirituality and the armor of God, I reference a direct relationship between ourselves and our Creator, not a form of religiosity, though spiritual community is a necessity. As Dr. David Martin says, **"not onto others, but with others,"** his Golden Rule.

I believed for decades evil does not exist in the same way cold and darkness do not materially exist. Cold cannot be measured as it's simply a lack of thermal energy (heat), which can be measured. We sense hot or cold via skin sensors measuring outside temperature relative to internal blood temperature. Our sensation of cold results from sensing heat transfer from say, our warm hand to a cold (less warm) object. Similarly, darkness is the absence of visible electromagnetic (light) energy.

My dark side analogy regarding evil as simply lack of good, like lack of heat or light was incorrect! **Evil does exist as a personally malevolent influence**; and though supernaturally restrained, so not an actual force, dark energetic influence can be invited into our lives by intention, inadvertent carelessness, or ignorance. It makes sense to pay attention and develop discernment. Evil influence is real and its practitioners do not like us, they hate us.

Our physical universe harbors a dark spiritual presence, a malevolently personal Luciferian influence capable upon invitation of manipulating human perception, cognitive processes, and therefore, our actions. Dark energy is invoked by opening the door to it, inviting it into our lives advertently or inadvertently, then saying YES to its destructive influence. Such darkness provides a counterpart to goodness and love, as love can only be freely chosen.

Logic suggests no choice possible without alternatives, hence the necessary opposition of good and evil. Our Creator never does bad things to good people. In fact, our Creator never does anything to anyone as such action precludes free will and voluntary creative participation in manifesting the world in which we live. We choose bad things via our own easily influenced thinking and subsequent behavior. The probability of making bad choices is enabled by declining to ask for and accept Divine grace offered to us precisely to overcome evil influence, freeing us for more life-enhancing choices.

If you haven't been paying attention, please re-read the above paragraph. It is important. God does not do stuff to us. **God works through us; not on us, or for us.** We do the work and when we are having trouble, we can ask for grace to help us through whatever the situation is – and demons always ensure there is a situation. That's why Jesus Christ left the Holy Spirit behind. We can get help from the Holy Spirit to find and stay on the path of Christ's love leading us back to reunion with our Father. This is how we find and get back into Eden. The path to our Father's love and our love only runs through Christ's love.

Two of our created human gifts, ability to creatively reason along with free will, are both necessary aspects of either rejecting love; or learning to receive our Creator's love, then share that love in community. This spiritual circumstance not only allows us to make human choices but <u>requires choice</u>. The choice to love or not love is one aspect of human *telos*. The consequence or curse of rejecting love is hell, spiritual life without love's embrace (my opinion).

Choosing Divine love or Luciferian evil is not optional. Not optional for Lucifer and the fallen angels, and not optional for us and good angels. Choice is the human predicament and the reason for saying NO to evil if we're to overcome its disarming influence. This choice is the reason we are materially born into created space and time; a challenging free-for-all arena within which we choose to receive and reciprocate love, that is, eternal life unified within our Creator's embrace; or we alienate ourselves by choosing darkness and death, i.e., Hell. I don't know if this choice is eternal once made but suspect repeated choices render it habitual.

For reasons I don't comprehend, American citizens play a significant role in humanity's battle for good against evil across the globe. American lives are specifically intertwined with the rest of humanity. Some say, Nah! Others suggest our Founders entered a *Gentile Covenant* with God extending God's earlier Covenant with Abraham. Consider for example, Puritan leader, John Winthrop's **"City on a Hill"** concept in his 1630 sermon entitled, *A Model of Christian Charity*. Despite modern criticism of so-called *Puritan pride*, Winthrop, in a beautiful sermon reminiscent of Christ's *Sermon on the Mount*, challenged his people to patiently live up to their responsibility before God while building their settlement in what came to be called New England.

Given language used, sentiment expressed, and action taken early on by Winthrop and others, then later by America's Founders and birth of the 1776 Revolution in colonial pulpits, I believe this Covenant reality is probable, but wasn't at the meetings, so can only admit my personal bias.

On another level, Messianic Rabbi, Jonathan Cahn, in his 2019 book, *The Oracle*, suggests in terms of Jubilean cycles, President Donald J. Trump, Biblically speaking, is the third Cyrus relative to Israel's future as a free and sovereign nation. President Harry S. Truman is considered by Rabbi Cahn, the second Cyrus relative to Israel.

Anyway, American's have been wounded in a hard-fought spiritual war for her people's souls. We have so far, lost the initial Cold War Battle to Marxist-Fascist-Globalist ideology but can correct our error. It is our choice to remain wounded and quit the battle or ask Christ for strength to carry on. I've asked and will continue to fight in Christ's name as best an old man, stuck in his own ego can. I pray we all do because together we are strong and with God's grace cannot be defeated, though we must still choose and fight our own battles.

The late Mr. Ronald Bernard, former Dutch banker, operating at the highest international levels of Elite banking, in testimony before the *International Tribunal for National Justice* (ITNJ) in late spring 2018, stated in his own life and choice for Divine love; a story both disturbing and inspiring; he came to understand every human being is born a beacon of light, without exception, even in the case of abnormalities or physical aberration. It is Lucifer's freely chosen mission to destroy that light.

Mr. Bernard testified those most under Luciferian influence are most in need of our help, love, and support to enable their coming out into the safety and protection of God's light. Mr. Bernard suggested this is critical behavior if we truly wish for a better world and that the change necessary to make our world a better place is interior. The necessary change is not outside us, but within each of us. Mr. Bernard later drowned in 6 inches or so of stagnant Sebring, Florida Everglades' recharge water suggesting our battle is real and immediate. Christ has already saved us. The rest of this wonderfully epic battle is ours to fight alongside God's angels with the strengthening grace of the Holy Spirit. Every generation comprises the people those people are waiting for to save them. We are who we are waiting for to save our generation. This is our time.

Biblically speaking, Lucifer and his hordes of fallen angels HATE every created thing, reserving a special targeted animosity toward humans made in the *image and likeness of God* (Genesis 1:26, 27). **There is no reason for fear as Lucifer and his demons have no power over us beyond a deceptive ability to influence us spiritually, intellectually, and emotionally.** <u>We cannot be forced to choose evil.</u> From the moment of physical conception, every human confronts the duality of physical existence within a spiritual realm.

Our choice is harmonious spiritual unity with our loving Creator for eternity, i.e., Heaven, or rejection of our Creator's love, i.e., Hell. God's love, guidance, and power are always available to us upon request, so poor judgement is unnecessary. We can take on the armor of God in good faith or not – meaning we reach a state of unified heaven or alienated hell through our own volition.

Denial of this choice by the sentient is always intentional despite coercion. Stubborn refusal to recognize the spiritual battle we engage for love constitutes human denial of that love as do more aggressive forms of dark rejection. Open-minded perception, coherent spiritual discernment, and informed faith are critical tools for engaging our decision-making process and our choice for love or something less.

Christianity teaches we cannot overcome evil on our own. "Jesus said to him (Thomas), 'I am the way, the truth, and the light. No one comes to the Father except through me.' (John 14:6)" Only with our Father's grace, available to us upon request through the helpful action of the Holy Spirit, Who remains behind to aid us since the ascension of the incarnated Christ back to the spiritual realm can we be successful. I can't prove this to be true for everyone but attest from the depths of my own stubbornness it's true for me. Looking around our world from a practical engineering perspective, it appears generally true.

Choosing good or evil is an inescapable human choice --- AND THAT CHOICE CAN ONLY BE MADE INTERNALLY WITHIN OUR OWN HEARTS. The answer to good over evil is not *out there* somewhere, not in a nice building, hidden behind a pulpit, or in the hands of some leader, expert, or influential other. The answer lies within our own heart and must be chosen and acted on by each one of us to become manifest. Bringing about a safer, more abundant life for ourselves, our children, and others can only come about within our communities by making the choice for love within our own individual heart and then attempting to live that choice within our communities with the help of the Holy Spirit. There is no other path I know of, and I've looked for a long time. As noted earlier, I'm cynically stubborn, prefer to go it alone, and don't learn easily.

Spiritual salvation and eternal joy are intended for everyone in shared community, but communities are constructed of interlocking individual choices; every choice lifting up and supporting or tearing down and diminishing our human community, moment by moment through the course of our daily lives. There are those under Luciferian influence dedicated to you and I never making the correct choice or worse, denying there is a choice to make. Group-think conformance and Scientism's proclaimed consensus do not excuse the spiritual necessity of life's choices, nor the practical consequences. When we doubt this necessity, we should ask ourselves why some work so hard convincing us everything is relatively OK, and no consequential choice exists? What is their agenda?

America, the wealthiest, most militarily powerful country in world history is painfully broken in spirit, growing weaker by the minute. In the wake of the 1913, 1934, 1963, 1998, 2001, 2008, and 2020 November coups, America's 21st century geopolitical dislocation from sanity and human decency have frightened communities around the globe. I have faith that with the grace of the Holy Spirit through faith in Christ, we the people can and will awaken to our errors and omissions as well as find our path back to a more spiritually healthy human condition – not just for you and me – for all of us – 8 billion of us plus those who came before and those who will come after our departure from this material world. We will hold the line. We must hold the line.

If we work together in America to accomplish this redemptive re-unification, I suspect the entire world will awaken along with us in revived spiritual coherence to share our created dream, making it greater than any of us can imagine. We already saw the yellow-vest movement growing across Europe and anti-totalitarian demonstrations against COVID Scamdemic lockdowns, toxic JAB passports, etc. Our world is fed up with globalist psychopathy and New World Order lies. A healthy populist nationalism is gaining cultural strength everywhere.

Australia, Austria, South Africa, Venezuela and other nations are functioning as unfortunate global syndicate pilot programs testing *mass formation* effectiveness, lack of spiritual efficacy, and citizen willingness to comply with home or neighborhood incarceration. Psychopathic Big Government demands for consent of decent people to be used as global syndicate guinea pigs for toxic experimental JABs has spread across the globe. Lies, fear, and violence comprise a growing global pandemic of authoritarian abuse by the few over the many.

Sovereign people of the world are rising up against Luciferian inspired evil. The global syndicate is panicking, making them more dangerous than usual, so we must tread strategically and with courageous care. The few have no real power—only evil influence—and the few are afraid the many are waking up to the Neo-Feudal con game. We The Many must just say NO THANK YOU! Stand up and refuse to comply with NWO demands, leaving the few powerless among their adrenochrome satiated peers.

> *"Unlimited power in the hands of limited people always leads to cruelty."*[157]

Only with God's grace can we achieve and maintain spiritual coherence, thereby avoiding destruction to bring about a safer, more abundant world. Prayer and fasting are more powerful weapons than guns, tanks, and bombs, though material weapons may yet be required in self defense as well. Future proves past.

> *"I choose love, kindness, empathy, and joy as the ghosts I wish to leave behind".*
> {Steve Ramirez, **The Things We Leave Behind** - *Fly Fisherman Magazine*
> (June/July 2022)}

---

157 Aleksandr Solzhenitsyn, *The Gulag Archipelago*, n.d., 285.

18 • Marxism: Spawn of Satan

Remedy: The Globalist economic/spiritual lever by which America is to be brought down by the global syndicate is the synergy of controlled conflict between Marxism and Fascism fighting together against non-existent free market Capitalism. Fascism is an authoritarian global syndicate tool enabling corporate order followers to control government, in turn using government to eliminate competition with favored monopolies, fix prices, and control populations, i.e., Mercantilism. Modern Fascism employs Marxism as the Nanny State sales pitch. Marxism is an enslaving lie. Fascism is the hammer enforcing the lie. Together, twisted sisters, Marxism and Fascism destroy vestigial remnants of free market Capitalism, incrementally synthesizing global serfdom for Main Street. This global Satanic slave plantation MUST be put out of business, which simply requires Main Street to say NO THANK YOU!

Did Marx ever spend one day as a fisherman, logger, miner, factory worker, or farm laborer? What is Marxism? Why are children being taught Marxism is good for them? As parents struggling for future liberty it is imperative we educate ourselves and our children about the brutal reality of Marxist depravity. Clearly so-called schools and other once-trusted institutions will not do it, so we MUST help each other do it to protect Main Street.

Who was Karl Marx (1818 – 1883)? Mr. Kelly O'Connell, professor, practicing attorney, and journalist, writing for *Canada Free Press* (CFP)[158] tells us in his August 7, 2011, article and I'm paraphrasing; *Marx lived a shambolic life of continual poverty with his wife, Jennie. Marx was said to be extremely unkempt and unclean, with filthy skin continually suffering boils and carbuncles from its unhygienic state.* This later condition of Marx's chosen lifestyle is interesting given Marx and Engels both grew up in wealthy families. Marx's father a lawyer, Engel's father a factory owner.

Mr. O'Connell goes on to tell us author Paul Johnson in his book *Intellectuals*[159] describes fellow revolutionary, Karl Heinzen, commenting on the perpetually angry Marx's repulsive appearance as *"intolerably dirty,"* a *"cross between a cat and an ape,"* with disheveled coal-black hair and dirty yellow complexion. It was impossible to say whether his clothes were mud-colored or just filthy."

Mr. O'Connell continues: *"Interestingly, Marx was a hypocrite in several ways. First, he held a family servant as essentially an indentured slave in his home, never paying her. For someone who based his life's work on liberating the poor and victimized, this is shocking. Second, he had a son with this domestic servant whom he never acknowledged, despite them living in attached quarters. Third, he lived off his friend Engel's wealth taken from the factories he'd inherited from his father. So, he was completely supported by capitalist largess which was said to not exist."*

Marxism cannot show examples of its dogma providing a constructive or sustainable political/economic system anywhere. Marxist proponents are conditioned to criticize, demonize, ridicule, tear down, and destroy existing systems whatever they are and wherever they might be. When have we observed advocates of Marxism discussing imagination, creativity, or building anything but extravagant government offices, filthy prisons, and mass graves? As Dr. Thomas Sowell mentioned in another context, *it's strictly Phase I thinking without concern for what's next or what happens after that.*[160]

Unredacted history demonstrates parasitic Marxist systems strangle within three or four generations. As productive capitalist hosts are eliminated, so can no longer be robbed, parasitic Marxism collapses. Marxism is a dictatorial Luciferian methodology intended under the guise of legitimate political theory, to annihilate human spirituality, wreck human society, and ultimately obliterate all creation. It's living history drowns in its own putrid truth, obscenely covered over by *useful idiots.*

Under Marxist domination, political theory is not tolerated and cannot reasonably exist without severe punishment or death. Marxism is pure hatred mas-

158 Kelly O'Connell, "Socialism's God—Karl Marx: Was He Stupid, Insane...or Possessed?" Canada Free Press.
159 Paul Johnson, *Intellectuals*, 1st U.S. ed edition (New York: Harper Collins, 1989).
160 Thomas Sowell, *Applied Economics: Thinking Beyond Stage One*, 2nd edition (New York: Basic Books, 2003).

querading as concern for the underprivileged; concern which to this day has never been constructively addressed by any Marxist regime anywhere. In fact, it is the underprivileged most harmed by history's indoctrinated Marxist psychopaths so admired by Western academia. Of course, well paid, hypocritical academics do not live under the totalitarian boot in Marxist countries, do they? In the U.S., poor, disadvantaged, and middle class all became more impoverished under the wannabe Marxist Obama Regime than at any time since the 1930's friendlier Marxist FDR Regime prolonging the Great Depression.

Where can we find honest academic survivors of Marxist regimes touting totalitarian benefit? Why don't we see droves of Marxist academics from Marxist dictatorships proselytizing Westerners with the joys of totalitarianism? Given popularity of Marxist delusion across the West, we should be witnessing the sales pitch by real-life academics and other surviving fans of Marxist central planning on a daily basis, shouldn't we? Are they all in mass graves? If not, where are they? Why don't we see them lauding Marxist systems they escaped from? In fact, why are they escaping from lovely Marxist utopias at all? Why flee any Marxist Shangri-La?

Why do thousands attempt migration from African or South and Central American Marxist hellholes to Europe and North America? Why do we never see the reverse? Why are hordes of liberal American professors not seen streaming across our Southern border headed South to their creative El Dorado? If Marxism is paradise as the Left claims and Rinos enable, why are thousands of desperately impoverished people risking their lives to reach the horrors of so-called American capitalism? A capitalism now suffocated by the same Marxism these poor victims flee. Shouldn't university students ask professors: *"Why do you languish in this American pit when you could be flying high at the top of your game in China, Cuba, Ethiopia, North Korea, Russia, Tanzania, Venezuela, or some other Marxist oasis of learning, equality, and abundance?"*

Objective historic observation demonstrates democidal Marxism and its twisted sisters (fascism, mercantilism, socialism, monopoly-capitalism) are Satanic in origin, spread through fear by global syndicate order followers in service to the pathologic pursuit of destructive power by THE FEW. For what it's worth, Engels tells us in his Preface to the **Communist Manifesto**, *the only distinction between socialism and communism in 1847 was that socialism was a middle-class movement and communism was a working-class movement.* Engels and Marx apparently considered socialism superfluous.

Since I made the Satanic accusation against Marxism and its spawn, we need to look at it. Kelly O'Connell tells us regarding Karl Marx and Satanism:

Karl Marx could be a devil-follower for these reasons:
•He was a virulent atheist and made his system atheistic. This is almost unprecedented in history.
•Marx gave the state unlimited power over humans, like a god.
•People have no human rights in Marxism, so are like beasts.
•Marx believed the state had a right to use coercion, including violence up to death, on its subjects.
•Marx rejected each of the Ten Commandments.
•Marx taught religion was a dangerous delusion.
•There is no right or wrong in Marx's philosophy—only power.
•The Poor are not sanctified in Marxism, but just factory workers.
•Marx disliked Jews, Yahweh's chosen people, despite his own Judaic roots.
•Marx rejected the topic of morality as a colossal joke, braying like a mule when people raised it up to him.

Marx's beliefs caused the following results across the world when applied:

•Caused over 100 million murders in the 20th century, <u>according to Professor R.J. Rummel</u>.[161] Some say as many as 300 million murdered under Marxism.
•Doomed the economic system of every country it touched, resulting in mass starvation and radically lowered living standards.
•Banned and shuttered all churches in every Marxist country except for official state-mouthpiece pulpits.
•Tortured and killed millions simply for believing in God.
•Desecrated and destroyed countless church buildings.
•Continually used lies and coercion to harness people to communist authority.
•Turned failed leaders into deified gods.
•Turned the legislative, executive and justice systems into pawns of Marxism.
•Stole countless freedoms from all citizens, sending millions into death camps.
•Attempted to turn the entire world into a giant slave state by force.

There is scholarly disagreement as to whether Karl Marx was an atheist or Satanist, though some scholars tell us Marx's known associates Moses Hess, George Jung, Heinreich Heine, and Mikhal Bakunin were avowed Satanists who initiated

---

161 Rummel, *Death by Government.*

Marx into Satanism. Other academics suggest Marx was an avowed atheist, i.e., did not believe in God. Marx's poetry sometimes lashes out angrily at God, openly embracing Satan (or Hell) with whom he poetically claims to have made a deal, suggesting to me, he was not an atheist. Satanists, of course, believe in Satan as well as God, and are intimately aware of the epic battle between good and evil. True Satanists are not atheists as best I understand it. For example, Anton LaVey, an atheist is not considered a true Satanist by many occult adherents.

A look at some of Marx's poetry showcases his disdain, if not hatred for our Creator, accompanied by attraction to, or perhaps possession by, Satanic influence. Most of Marx's poetry has been lost. Johnson tells us about forty or so of his poems have survived,[162] but are difficult to come by. Here is a sampling of what as of this writing are readily available online.

The Fiddler by Karl Marx.

The Fiddler saws the strings,
His light brown hair he tosses and flings.
He carries a sabre at his side,
He wears a pleated habit wide.

"Fiddler, why that frantic sound?
Why do you gaze so wildly round?
Why leaps your blood, like the surging sea?
What drives your bow so desperately?"

"Why do I fiddle? Or the wild waves roar?
That they might pound the rocky shore,
That eye be blinded, that bosom swell,
That Soul's cry carry down to Hell."

"Fiddler, with scorn you rend your heart.
A radiant God lent you your art,
To dazzle with waves of melody,
To soar to the star-dance in the sky."

"How so! I plunge, plunge without fail
My blood-black sabre into your soul.
That art God neither wants nor wists,
It leaps to the brain from Hell's black mists.

---

162 Johnson, *Intellectuals*, 54, 55.

"Till heart's bewitched, till senses reel:
With Satan I have struck my deal.
He chalks the signs, beats time for me,
I play the death march fast and free.

"I must play dark, I must play light,
Till bowstrings break my heart outright."

The Fiddler saws the strings,
His light brown hair he tosses and flings.
He carries a sabre at his side,
He wears a pleated habit wide.

A verse from a ballad called A Pale Maiden by Karl Marx:

"Thus, Heaven I've forfeited,
I know it full well.
My soul, once true to God,
Is chosen for Hell."

Invocation of One in Despair by Karl Marx:

So, a god has snatched from me my all
In the curse and rack of Destiny.
All his worlds are gone beyond recall!
Nothing but revenge is left to me!

On myself revenge I'll proudly wreak,
On that being, that enthroned Lord,
Make my strength a patchwork of what's weak,
Leave my better self without reward!

I shall build my throne high overhead,
Cold, tremendous shall its summit be.
For its bulwark-- superstitious dread,
For its Marshall--blackest agony.

Who looks on it with a healthy eye,
Shall turn back, struck deathly pale and dumb;
Clutched by blind and chill Mortality
May his happiness prepare its tomb.

And the Almighty's lightning shall rebound
From that massive iron giant.

> If he bring my walls and towers down,
> Eternity shall raise them up, defiant.

There are more savage Marxian verses to be found, but these three samples suffice to hint at Marx's life-long obsession regarding death and destruction. Marx to my knowledge never admitted being a Satanist, so who knows? It may not matter anyway, as the man was an abusive psychopath by any standard, but his poetry stands on its own. It's clear Marx hated just about everything in the world including himself and fully hoped to damage or destroy it as best he could. In my mind, Marx's level of focused animosity speaks to programmed motivation, not the empty randomness of oft abused *Darwinian Theism*.

Note: *According to Darwin's surviving letters, he did not believe in a Christian God. He thought the immense complexity and beauty of life likely the result of Intelligent Mind as a First Cause, seeing no conflict between his self-proclaimed Theism and evolution. If true, Darwin's thinking is grossly misused by globalist academics and pseudo-scientists.*

Globalist academics celebrating and teaching Marx's supposed atheism predicated on atheistic tenets of Communism, are I believe euphemizing Marxism as atheist because atheism is more palatable for decent people to accept than Satanic Doctrine. In other words, many academics misrepresent the inherent evil of Marxist-Leninist totalitarian ideology to students. An authoritarian ideology, embracing dark religious theology as backdrop for a slave labor system serving Elite Masters.

In any event, we know Marx became friends with Italian Freemason, Guisseppe Mazzini, apparently while organizing the *International Workingman's Association*, often referred to as *First International* in 1864, so Masonic influence impacting Marx's ideas is certain. Free Masonry, bound indirectly to so-called ancient mystery schools and occult practices is itself subtly dominated by Luciferian influence, though less subtle to the spiritually discerning. Consider with serious discernment, Albert Pike's *Morals and Dogma* to see for yourself.[163]

Marx's sick, parasitic ideology, not taken seriously at the time *The Communist Manifesto* was published in 1848, has despite proven failure, infected more than half the countries around the world, including so-called capitalist countries. In the U.S., estimates suggest 70% or more college students claim to be socialists or at least generally support socialist propaganda they're fed by *useful idiot* professors and advisors. Piling on to the academic lie is propagandized misrepresentation by WOKE Corporations, Globalist politicians, indoctrinated media pundits, controlled Hollywood A-listers, and top tier, compromised musicians and bands.

---

163 Albert Pike, *Morals And Dogma* (Orkos Press, 2013).

Author Paul Johnson, in his 1988 book, *Intellectuals*, touched on earlier, relates many details of Marx's angry, manic life as have other serious historians. Yet how many indoctrinated students since 1920 are aware their hypocrite hero, Karl Marx was a filthy, desk-bound, disorganized academic, who perhaps met one or two peasants during his life but never once visited the inside of a factory or mine (as far as we know). Are students told Marx despised people to the point he dreamed of humanity wiping itself off the face of the earth?

Karl Marx never investigated actual working conditions on farms, in mills, or factories, and held a low opinion for concerns and ideas of workers who lived and worked under the conditions he theoretically judged. Marx never allowed actual working people anywhere near positions of influence within his *Communist League* or *International*, even to the reputed extent of violently bullying and raging to silence them. Marx was a 100% desk-bound academic, his life experience limited by the greasy walls of his filthy study, incapable of achieving academic station, who did none-the-less possess a poetic talent for captivating phraseology and a gift for well-timed polemic.

As Johnson points out, consider just the closing three lines of 1848's *The Communist Manifesto*. *"The proletarians have nothing to lose but their chains. They have a world to win. Workingmen of all countries, unite!*[164] This is powerful stuff, heavily plagiarized by Marx's peers (French utopian socialist, Louis Blanc; French Jacobin, Jean-Paul Marat; German socialist, Karl Schapper; and others) for obvious reasons.

Working people, skilled laborers, and engineers of Marx's time were primarily interested in securing better working conditions, fair wages, and a better life for their families in real time, for which Marx viscerally despised them. Workers were not interested in academic theories, apocalyptic nightmares of violent proletarian revolution, and certainly not Marx's utopian concept of intellectual elites despotically ruling over revolutionary working-class cannon-fodder.[165]

Marxian adversarial rhetoric was not appreciated by mid-19th century workers and in fact, the sleeping revolutionary proletariat did not exist anywhere in the world outside Marx's imagination. Italian Communist, Antonio Gramsci (1891-1937), whom some refer to as godfather of *Cultural Marxism* along with other Globalist thinkers saw this error in Marx's thinking, and together with the *Frankfurt School* sought to render communism more attractive. If Marxism is so great for people, why does it require indoctrination and planned coercion? Why is the barrel of a gun necessary to seal the deal on Marxism? Why do millions flee its tenacious grip? Most abused ille-

---

164 Johnson, *Intellectuals*, 56.
165 Johnson, 60–62.

gals flocking to America's Southern border are fleeing the hellish reality of Marxist run or Marxist leaning countries. Why won't liberals recognize this?

The *Cultural Marxist* remedy we painfully live with today, is incremental infiltration of western education, publishing, government at every level, professional associations, churches, etc. – packaged with Marxist totalitarian concepts detrimental to human consciousness, life, liberty, and the pursuit of happiness. *Cultural Marxism* is a dark religion malevolently demeaning human spirituality under the pretext of scholarly relevance. God cannot be mentioned in the public square. *Secular materialism* rules alongside *moral relativism* while creative thought and questions are ridiculed, until finally, morality is scoffed at, finally relativized to meaningless tripe.[166]

Unfortunately, this cultural approach works gangbusters, so as time wore on, embers of Marxian materialistic ramblings caught Luciferian fire among what Lenin later referred to as *useful idiots*, i.e., frustrated, relevance-hungry academics, unleashing their ignorant prejudice on unsuspecting students. Education is now seriously injured around the globe and, in many areas, logic and reason are dead. This logical damage requires generations to fix if we have the will to fix it.

Cutting to the chase, Marxism led directly at the hands of global syndicate sponsored dictators to the slaughter, imprisonment, torture, dumbing down, and impoverishment of hundreds of millions of innocent people across the globe, greasily hidden by indoctrinated victims of this insidious cultural devastation now intellectually and emotionally terrorizing our universities, media, publishing, government, transnational corporations, churches, Hollywood, etc.

Following is a partial, conservatively estimated murder list resulting from Marx's influence. The list below does not include millions of military persons slaughtered for global syndicate wartime profit taking, resource rape, or regime change. The numbers below are taken from Rummel's *Death By Government*.[167]

Lenin, Trotsky, Stalin (Soviet Union): 40 million dead
Mao Zedong (China): 50 million dead
Hitler (A twisted German sister): 11 million dead
Kim II-Sung (North Korea): 2.5 million dead
Castro (Cuba): 150,000 dead
Vietnam: 1 million dead
Pol Pot (Cambodia): 3 million dead
Romania: 250,000 dead
Bulgaria: 75,000 dead

---

166 David Barton, *The Myth of Separation: What Is the Correct Relationship Between Church and State?* 5th edition (Aledo, TX: WallBuilder Press, 1992).
167 Rummel, *Death by Government*.

East Germany: 90,000 dead
Castillo Armas (Guatemala): 250,000 dead

Rummel's conservative **democide** (death by government) estimate totals about 108 million murdered by communist/socialist governments since 1917. **Some scholars estimate as many as 250 million or more murdered during this same period.** The death count discrepancy lies primarily in Russia and China, where estimates range as high as 80 to 100 million each, but confirmation is difficult as are estimates in the Balkan countries. Solzhenitsyn mentions émigré Professor of Statistics Karaganov's estimate of 66,000,000 Eurasian deaths by Bolshevism between October 2017 and the end of 1959.[168] Mao's central planning failures inducing famine in 1958-1961 claimed as many as 45 million in just three years.

Granted we're all born on Earth to material death; BUT not in the gruesomely pitiless manner as tens of millions ideologically butchered under the sadistic Marxist banner on the above list. How many liberal professors share these staggering numbers with students? Given that knowledge is one remedy helping resist authoritarian subjugation and mind-controlled manipulation; and given most professors are aware of that; it is reprehensible so many do not teach but indoctrinate.

Sadly, for *useful idiots*, or justly some might say, in the event their Globalist nightmare is brought to fruition—intellectuals will be among the first eliminated as literacy and education always pose potential threats to despotic state power. As a practical matter, all Communist dictatorships adhere to this practice. Academics are efficiently eliminated after serving their totalitarian propaganda-indoctrination purpose. CCP Chairman Mao for example, bragged that a significant accomplishment of his **Great Cultural Revolution** from 1966 to 1976 was burying 46,000 scholars alive. Under Cambodia's **Pol Pot** (1925-1998) during the (1975-1979) *Khmer Rouge* period, wearing glasses signified possible literacy, often providing sufficient justification for execution.

Survivors of Globalist regimes the world over tell a common story. Persons non-compliant with Globalist dogma, say *free will believing* Jews or Christians for instance, soon after the Left takes control of a victim nation, routinely find themselves in prisons or forced labor camps being tortured, often to death alongside people who supported and enabled Globalist goons along the way. Just to ram home the Globalist message, these duped Comrades may be treated publicly to watching their screaming sons, wives, and/or daughters viciously beaten, raped, skinned, or burned alive. This is what *useful idiots* may have waiting for them in their collectivist future. Is it possible they do not know this history? On a positive note, Transhumanism may negate the intimidation need for such brutality.

---

168 Solzhenitsyn, *The Gulag Archipelago*, 178.

I recommend the reader please take a quick, though sobering read through the May 6, 1966, Congressional Testimony[169] (U.S. Senator Thomas A. Dodd presiding) of Reverend Richard Wurmbrand, a Romanian refugee of that horrific period. It's too much to duplicate here so a bit of homework for the curious. Any time Globalist Pawns obtain power is a horrific time for Main Street, but we must find unredacted history books to know it. You will learn from Pastor Wurmbrand what daily life in a communist country really is, along with what happens, even to regime supporters. You will find yourself wondering, *"what the heck do our pampered, generously paid university professors think they're doing?"*

Marxism, a Satanic upgrade to Mercantilism, was spawned as controlled totalitarian opposition to republican and parliamentary forms of government and free market capitalism, usually by employing Hegelian dialectic, of which Marx was a student, often followed by violence. Hegel taught history as resulting from conflict. **Control conflicts to control outcomes of history.** In a nutshell, if Capitalism is the **thesis**, Marxism is the **antithesis**. Globalism, i.e., New World Order is the **synthesis** of the two competing, though controlled isms. Sometimes this materialistic concept is stated in its more practical form: **Problem – Reaction – Solution.** Marx came to denigrate Hegel over time, preferring what he viewed to be his own materially scientific dialectic, but never really departed from Hegel's influence. Twisted sister, Fascism, the promise of everything for everyone, left and right, after 1921 became a handy tool for enforcing Marxist impoverishment, necessary because Marxism is never self-sustaining or beneficial.

In either form, scientific or practical, this controlled-conflict playbook is well-worn, operating effectively and repeatedly, easily verifiable by watching MSM parrots, comparing propaganda to election results, then observing the harmful government policies to follow. Elites grow richer and more powerful while Main Street is incrementally neutered and impoverished. During Barry Soetoro's eight year middle-class wealth purge for example, the top 0.1% grew and consolidated wealth more quickly than at any time in economic history. Obama Regime Quantitative Easing transferred ±$4.5 trillion (we know of) to Wall Street banks from 2009 to 2016, for which Main Street holds the IOU, yet never once in 8-years posted even a 3% annual growth in GDP.

Marxism is the preferred global syndicate battering ram since control of the masses is unambivalent, uniform, and absolute. Note that Hegelian dialectic is conveniently employed to cleverly mislead both Left, Right, and everything in between. Controlled conflict is an effective conditioning tool and handled

---

169 "Communist Exploitation of Religion: Congressional Testimony of Richard Wurmbrand," accessed August 9, 2020, https://www.crossroad.to/Quotes/communism/communist-senate-hearing-wurmbrand.htm.

adroitly, difficult to identify. *Fox News*, for example, was effectively employed as controlled conflict, explaining why its valued anchors are paid so handsomely. Today, *Fox News* mostly lies by omission, so plays a diminishing propaganda role.

100% top-down control is easily managed for the global syndicate by controlling the dictator. Abuse of power made easy-peasy and the larger the bureaucracy, the less transparent and less accountable to Main Street. The totalitarian objective is agreement, obedience, and capitulation for order followers and Main Street citizens; or imprisonment, re-education, slave labor, and death. This type of coercion was on full January 6, 2021 display, when FBI goons orchestrated along with *ANTIFA* and other assets, a D.C. riot for which MAGA patriots were blamed and hundreds unconstitutionally incarcerated – and as of this writing are still incarcerated and penally abused. Government brutality, resource rape, and population reduction are matters of State policy and centrally planned logistic quotas, never debate. Once it's determined how many people must be imprisoned or eliminated next year, the only questions remaining are how, and can it be done profitably for the Elites?

Republican forms of government and free market Capitalism, on the other hand, are messy. Control of the population is difficult without a global syndicate owned and operated dictator. Votes are earned and counted, at least they used to be, were not phantom votes, or were only counted once without dead people butting in. Legal voting with limited, localized fraud such as Tammany's **"honest graft"** in New York, led in the U.S., to once-sustainable Executive, Legislative, and Judicial branches of government morbidly suffering from difficult logistics of time and cost intensive bribery, blackmail, extortion, or other coercion. An inconvenient truth (h/t to Big Al) for the global syndicate which our Founders understood but we the people of the 21ˢᵗ century have forgotten.

Wouldn't liberal hero, Karl Marx fit in perfectly with spoiled *Antifa* or *BLM* members, who dependently survive on Mommy and Daddy's money or unsustainable nanny-state government largess while complaining they are cheated of their due? We had in 2020/2021, moronic fentanyl laced youth tribes parasitically looting and rioting in major Democrat cities while *useful idiot* Democrat Governors and Mayors applauded; supporting violence, looting, and unrestrained property damage as peaceful protest and acceptable political expression. Police were ordered to "stand down" leaving innocent taxpayers unprotected. These Blue Cities are now stuck with horrific inner-city living conditions exacerbated by declining tax bases as responsible citizens flee **"NO GO"** Au-

tonomous Zones. We might want to take a look at Germany's Brown Shirt, Mussolini's Black Shirt, Lenin's Red Guard, or Mao's Red Guard history.

Privileged Communist *bullies* owned and operated by global syndicate handlers typically live well beyond the proletariat commoners they claim to care about. For example, per *New York Post* and a dozen or so other media outlets, *Black Lives Matter* (BLM) co-founder Patrisse Khan-Cullors, 37-year-old self-proclaimed, trained Marxist purchased four homes in the U.S. from 2016 through 2021. An Inglewood, CA home in 2016 for $510,000; a South Los Angeles home in 2018 for $590,000; a Conyers, Georgia home in 2020 for $415,000; and a Topanga Canyon, Los Angeles home in 2021 for $1,400,000 through an LLC Ms. Cullors controls. Communist privilege pays handsomely, particularly under Puppet Regimes like Barry Soetoro's or Imbecile Joe Biden's. Can you and your wife, husband, or partner, both working together pay for four homes? Apparently, Ms. Khan-Cullor's piggishness is becoming tiresome as even *useful idiots* are raising vacant eyebrows.

In support of Leftist hooliganism, local law enforcement is being de-funded in some Democrat cities while taxpaying citizens are told to give up their workplaces, homes, cars, or whatever else looters demand. In California, for example, shoplifting up to $950 of merchandise is a largely unprosecutable misdemeanor as long as the thief is not a proven member of an organized theft ring. From whom exactly, do Blue City Mayors and Blue State Governors imagine tax revenues will be confiscated when their productive middle-class tax base is reduced to Blue Ashes? No doubt, by the time these words are read, entire Socialist-Democrat cities will be burned out impoverished *autonomous zones*, where the drugged fentanyl brigade lurk mindlessly begging for food and water before starving to death as their Marxist handlers intend.

As mentioned earlier, *The World Economic Forum* and sick DAVOS crowd are already war gaming cyber attacked supply chain scenarios, so hang on tight. Empty fuel tanks, parked trucks, vacant farms, and empty shelves may be headed our way.

The CCP Biden Regime has been confiscating working taxpayer dollars to bail out Leftist co-conspirators with trillions in bonus dollars so targeted inner-city property can be purchased for pennies on the dollar by insiders like *BlackRock*. Sadly, as of this writing, sedition, corruption, and treason at every level of government are so widespread only prayer and perhaps, constitutionally approved military justice can likely fix this burgeoning totalitarian destructothon.

To drive home a point concerning the hopelessness of Marxist thought, consider one of the more nonsensical Marxist contradictions presented in *The Communist Manifesto*. We find in *Part II: PROLETARIANS AND COMMU-*

NISTS where the ten planks are listed, the final paragraph stating: *"In place of the old bourgeois society, with its classes and class antagonisms, we shall have an association, in which the free development of each is the condition for the free development of all"*.[170]

The above sentence is literally insane. Following are the ten planks. When these ten planks become enforceable, no one and no group can possibly be free. This is utopian gibberish, and it must astonish even the feeblest mind, how so many arrogant academics and corrupt politicians take such *cognitive dissonance* seriously.

Ten Planks of Communism:

1. Abolition of property in land and application of all rents of land to public purposes.
2. A heavy progressive or graduated income tax.
3. Abolition of all rights of inheritance.
4. Confiscation of the property of all emigrants and rebels.
5. Centralization of credit in the hands of the state, by means of a national bank with state capital and an exclusive monopoly.
6. Centralization of the means of communication and transport in the hands of the state.
7. Extension of factories and instruments of production owned by the state; the bringing into cultivation of waste lands, and the improvement of the soil generally in accordance with a common plan.
8. Equal obligation of all to work. Establishment of industrial armies, especially for agriculture.
9. Combination of agriculture with manufacturing industries; gradual abolition of the distinction between town and country, by a more equable distribution of the population over the country.
10. Free education for all children in public schools. Abolition of child factory labor in its present form. Combination of education with industrial production, etc.

Cognitive dissonance in *The Communist Manifesto* is remarkable in its disjointed connecting of incompatible statements. More frightening, is adoption by the United States of planks 2 and 5; along with incrementally implementing planks 1, 3, 4, 6, 7, 8, 9, and 10, i.e., all ten planks in one form or another. Of course, in all Communist and nearly all other nations, central banks (Plank 5) are held in private hands for exclusive global syndicate control and benefit. All fractional reserve, central banking money creation and criminal money laundering are operationally fraudulent. This is done by insiders gaming how interest rates,

---

170 Karl Marx and Friedrich Engels, *The Communist Manifesto*, New edition (New York: International Publishers Co, 2014), 30, 31.

deposits, reserves, excess reserves, and so forth are defined to manipulate the money supply of a nation by adjusting the so-called *multiplier effect*.

We have in the U.S., for example:
- Egregious income and inheritance taxes up until Donald Trump in 2017.
- The CCP Biden Regime's **American Family Plan** will, if enacted, re-institute wholesale confiscation of productive American family wealth for redistribution to Elites.
- Confiscation of property across the U.S. is commonplace at all levels of government.
- Communications and transportation are heavily taxed, restricted, and surveilled.
- Transnational monopolies are intimately and corruptly interwoven with corrupt government agencies, regulatory capture, and dark investment funds via banking, the revolving door, or other means, a Fascist compliment to Marxism.
- FASAB 56 took government accounting systems dark in 2018.
- Telecommunications and medical services are now fully weaponized.
- Agriculture is heavily motivated or constrained via controls and subsidies.
- Mom and Dad must both work to survive financially beneath the punishing burden of compound interest, taxation, user fees, and the hidden inflation tax.
- Highly restrictive land use and zoning restrictions abound.
- Out-of-control public school taxes are confiscated regardless where our children attend school or if we have children – or education for that matter.
- Face diaper slave training and unconstitutionally closed businesses.
- Mandated toxic bioweapon JABs with proposed public health authority sublimated to corrupt goons at the World Health Organization.
- Places of worship are locked down while liquor stores and marijuana dispensaries remain open.
- Small independent businesses are locked down while big box monopoly stores remain open.
- Quarantine of the healthy and travel restrictions in many places.
- Serious propaganda pushing Toxic JAB Passports.

Suggesting we are free on American Main Streets today is simply silly. We have monumentally lost the Cold War to *Cultural Marxist* attack as Gramsci, and others intended on behalf the global syndicate. Now we must set differences aside, work with each other, and take our America back from the brink of the global syndicate's Satanic dystopia.

Marxist systems cannot sustain themselves for more than 75 to 100 years, about three to four generations. We see this in the U.S. Social Security system. The global syndicate's Soviet bogeyman ran out of gas in just 74 years

(1917 – 1991) despite untold billions of Anglo-American Establishment dollars poured into it. North Korea, Cuba, Cambodia, and dozens of other nations never even got going. They were brutal hell holes from Marxist day one. Mao ruled the Chinese Communist Party (CCP) from its spawning in 1949, but his demented *Great Leap Forward* didn't begin until 1958. Psychopathic CCP leaders plan to rule the world by 2049[171] but even with trillions in western wealth poured into this hellish horror pit by the global syndicate; by my reckoning the CCP will likely collapse under its own bloated rot by 2035, finally freeing the Chinese people. Maybe we can help get this done sooner?

Today, fed by stolen western wealth and naivete provided by the Anglo-American Establishment, the CCP leads the world in transhuman surveillance and control technology, steadily spreading its Satanic Marxist poison across the planet. The United States and Europe are primary targets for CCP annihilation by deceit rather than head-on confrontation. Western Main Streets, burdened with corrupted, WOKE leadership are far behind in this 100-Year Marathon Battle, must wake up, and must dump traitorous representation in the trash where it belongs.

If the United States or any other country are to have a non-electro-magnetic Gulag future beyond transhuman serfdom, Main Street must awaken. Our thinking must change, and traditional Christian moral codes must be re-embraced. Even if our American military honors their oath by placing the treasonously misguided under military arrest for tribunal hearings – if we fail to change our thinking on Main Street, we will quickly replace today's treasonous criminals with tomorrow's criminals. Thoughts have consequences.

Unstable global supply chains are easily disrupted, whereas local supply chains are difficult to shut down. We must vest ourselves in school boards, city councils, county boards, state government and local, local, local farms, food processing, businesses, and supply chains. As of this writing patriots like Oklahoma's Jarrin Jackson are leading a **Live Local** movement, providing informational resources for anyone interested in shortening their necessary supply chain. We can all jump on this band wagon and start supporting local entrepreneurs today for a safer, more dependable future.

Marxist driven Washington D.C., a New World Order Globalist power center cannot be trusted. **Washington D.C. has established itself as Main Street Public Enemy Number 1.** We fix America with the help of Divine Providence from the ground up or lose everything. **We must downsize our Federal government by at least 75%.**

---

171 "The Hundred-Year Marathon: China's Secret Strategy to Replace America as the Global Superpower: Pillsbury, Michael: 9781250081346: Amazon.Com: Books."

"There are no formulas with God. Period. So there are no formulas for the man who follows Him. God is a Person, not a doctrine. He operates not like a system – not even a theological system - but with all the originality of a truly free and alive person."
{John Eldredge from Wild at Heart, Page 209}

19 • Perception – Riding the Rock

Remedy: We must realize global syndicate schemes bringing American Main Streets to our bloody financial knees require dulling Main Street perception, thereby undermining and interrupting logical thought processes and coherent action. However, the American lion cannot be poked too hard or too often without peril. Dumbing down must carefully precede transhuman serfdom to avoid pitchforks suddenly disappearing from hardware store racks. Disciplined self-defense demands avoiding going along to get along. Things are often not as they seem, especially when ALL global syndicate information assets lie. Coherence is necessary for functional perception and subsequent healthy behavior. We think for ourselves... or risk perishing in ignorance. Duck the Psyop. Pray for accurate perception. Meditate in silence. Get away from electricity as often as possible. Embrace reality and humanity's enduring purpose as we ride our spinning rock through infinity's mysteries.

In a nutshell per Catherine Austin Fitts at *Solari Report*, there are five basic pillars working to establish totalitarian America (my words) and worldwide Globalism, i.e., what many call **Global 3.0** and what I call **Global Feudalism**. These five pillars form a Luciferian influenced foundation for engaging a multi-directional attack on human perception. This is bio-warfare intended to manipulate perception and thinking, ultimately modifying mass behavior, nudging it toward complacency and openness to suggestion. Less significant supporting columns are also employed but these five pillars hold up the feudal tent.

1. Technocracy and the Ionized Atmosphere
2. Space and Military Satellites
3. Big Pharma

4. Media Propaganda and Mind Control
5. Central Bank Crypto Systems

Perception is tricky. Perception suggests we are sitting still as we read these words (assuming we are not driving, riding a motorcycle, or skydiving); and relative to any fixed position on the spinning rock called Earth, we are. That said, we're hurtling through space faster than a Mach 20 rocket.

"Nothing is standing or stationary. As you are reading this, the Earth spins around its own axis; it revolves around the sun, the sun is moving through space at a stunning 792,000 km/h around the gigantic center, and our universe is moving at a mind-boggling 2.1 million kilometers per hour.

You may contemplate that as you are reading this, your body is in a stationary position. But, everything inside the universe travels, from our planet (Earth) – which revolves on its axis at a speed of approximately 1700 km/h—to the solar system and even the Milky Way Galaxy."[172]

As we perceive ourselves sitting still at the dinner table with family and friends, we cruise the silence of space at more than 1.3 million miles per hour. **So much for perception and sitting still on our spinning rock, though we feel certain of it.** Our world is not static, it is dynamic. Both material and spiritual survival require dynamic participation in authentic living.

Since perception can be misleading, we ought to triple-check our truth meter regularly since perceived truth may be otherwise. I probably should not call this realization a principle, but its occurrence is consistent enough for slight-of-hand artists, magicians, central bankers, politicians, and dictators to count on for success, so we have substantial anecdotal evidence.

We might say the *Perception Principle*; **"things may not be as they seem"**, is almost a principle, therefore at least reaches *rule-of-thumb* level. For simplicity's sake, I'll call it a principle, but in any case, as a precautionary measure **the perception principle should be activated whenever watching or listening to propaganda**, which for reasons I don't understand, we call news and frequently find embedded in literature, magazines, movies, sporting events, etc.

Hopefully, the astronomy observation above demonstrates how incorrect our perception of sitting still can be – and this instance involves direct perception of physical reality via our own senses. No expert narrative, slick advertising, or lies involved. Imagine how far adrift our cultural-economic-political-scientif-

172 "The Milky Way Is Moving Through The Universe At 2.1 Million Kilometers Per Hour," *Physics-Astronomy.Com* (blog), accessed February 5, 2020, http://www.physics-astronomy. com/2017/07/the-milky-way-is-moving-through.html.

ic-spiritual perceptions might wander when leaders, teachers, experts, or media pundits, disingenuous ones anyway, cleverly falsify facts, spin information, or lie by omission in service to agendas they have been enticed or coerced to serve?

Consider the extent to which perception must be toyed with to successfully sell us a one-sided, **wealth-transference policy** like 1994's treasonous *North American Free Trade Agreement* (NAFTA). Mr. Patrick Wood by the way discusses in detail this unholy process in *Technocracy Rising*[173] but let's touch on it here to see how **mass deception** can manipulate **mass perception**.

Imagine back in the 1980's and early 1990's, privileged members of David Rockefeller's *Trilateral Commission* (founded 1973) wished to pass an international agreement conveying substantial benefit to syndicate insiders by indirectly targeting recipient nations such as China, soon to be resource raped themselves, while being directly punitive and costly for Main Street inhabitants of Canada, the U.S. and Mexico—all immediate net losers. Clearly this wealth transference NAFTA package had to be carefully sold to Main Street. If North American Main Street businesses and customers understood they were being robbed by Fascist multinational monopoly corporations through corrupt Federal government policy as happened previously under FDR's Administration, reducing Main Street wealth by 41% with the stroke of a corrupt pen in the 1930's,[174] they might wake up wondering where the pitchforks were?

My embellishment of Mr. Wood's history suggests the first deceptive step was enlisting assistance of honor challenged academics and associated think tanks through the always-ready study group system to conduct a well-funded study (pun intended), the result of which would be a convincing report supporting the NAFTA concept. This plan is workable since so many tenured academics have their high dollar bread buttered by deceitful NGOs or by the likes of Carnegie, Ford, Gates, Rockefeller, or other scheming Foundations, Trusts, and Endowments. Go along or get out of the *tenure club*.

Digression: When depraved Elite foundations speak, many academics jump as high as possible through as many hoops as possible as fast as possible with as little conscience as possible to collect lucrative grant funding checks, media praise, publishing awards, and accolades from those who work for those who write the checks. This *truth in education* compromise worsened in 1980 with passage of the research capturing, self-aggrandizing *Bayh-Dole Act*. This obscene act made patent ownership and associated rev-

---

173 Wood, *Technocracy Rising*, 70.
174 Jett, *The Fruits of Graft*, chap. 6.

enue sharing available to academics and researchers performing work on tax-payer premises, using taxpayer equipment, all paid for with taxpayer dollars.

With passage of the *Bayh-Dole Act*, honor vanished out the university front door while research profits poured in the back door. I don't know the criminal extent of research capture by government protected multinational greed, but it is sys-temically epidemic. For example, as parent's, don't we trust family doctors and pediatricians to provide competent medical advice and care for our children? Per Robert F. Kennedy, Jr. we learn: *"Tellingly, in March 2017, I met with Dr. Fauci, Francis Collins, and a White House referee (and separately with Peter Marks from CBER at FDA) to complain that HHS was, by then, mandating 69 doses of sixteen vaccines for American chil-dren, none of which had ever been tested for safety against placebos prior to licensing. Dr. Fauci and Dr. Collins denied that this was true and insisted that those vaccines were safety tested."*[175]

Ten months after the Fauci-Collins' denial, JFK Jr., assisted by Del Bigtree (*The High Wire*) and Aaron Siri (*Siri & Glimstad*), who together sued HHS under the *Freedom of Information Act* - HHS admitted in court, that in fact, *"none of the mandated childhood vaccines had been tested for safety in pre-licensing inert placebo tests."* JFK, Jr. also informs us that Bill Gates, *"also uses a large retinue of much more dangerous and demonstra-bly ineffective vaccines in Africa – ones that Western countries have actually rejected because of dire safety signals."*[176] Alongside the abhorrent issue of psychopathic medical testing performed on unsuspecting African patients, this raises the question, JUST HOW COMPETENT ARE MY PEDIATRICIAN and PRIMARY CARE DOCS?

Climate change is another research example illustrating politicization of science for money and praise by helping benefit the global syndicate falsely justify more and more behavioral and property controls. Think *Club of Rome* propaganda. My disrespect for academia grows with its considerable, sometimes truculent efforts to earn it – though simultaneously, respect for honest academics able to survive the WOKE gauntlet increases immensely. Thank you, courageous Professors.

Anyway, *circling back* (a little Biden Regime lingo there) to NAFTA's assault on mass perception, concerns were seeded across Mockingbird Mainstream Media (MSM) alerting the public an important issue was at hand. **It does not matter the issue is contrived by those claiming concern**, because that tidbit is never discussed outside chatty clubroom cocktails, Cuban cigars, or sex enslaved fun alongside sporting events. Useless Congressional propaganda hearings, hyped photo ops, and pandering debate are featured on CPAN, with evening news highlighting the

---

175 Robert F. Kennedy Jr, *The Real Anthony Fauci: Bill Gates, Big Pharma, and the Global War on Democracy and Public Health* (Skyhorse, 2021), 323.
176 JFK Jr, 323.

caring and deep concern for North American Main Street citizens heart-felt by bought and paid for *selected* Representatives – all supporting the illusion of political choice. If **Public Relations** are coordinated properly, the dopamine fix will cause Main Street to swoon between perfectly timed erectile dysfunction adds.

Trilaterals originally spawning this punitive NAFTA wealth transfer scheme were prominently featured throughout the statist press with a few MSM outlets appearing to oppose the idea, in some cases stridently parroting their 4:00 A.M. buzzwords, though carefully never overdoing it. Congressional members claw and scratch to get in front of fake news cameras, lining up for and against as compelled by money, blackmail control files, and lobbyist handlers. Pundits boil the soft-ball debate pot into a perfectly articulated circus of apparent legislative debate so bombastic it energizes the intentionally misinformed public, who anyway, have already moved from erectile dysfunction back to the always engaging blood sugar crisis, or on some channels, the crippling arthritis catastrophe.

MSM was caught up in a programmed NAFTA frenzy of sound-bite mania with every outlet parroting precisely the same phrases in precisely the same order with identical cadence dozens of times throughout the day, thousands of times per month. There is a solid propaganda reason why integrity challenged, though talented media parrots earn ±$20k-$40k per day, top parrots ±$100k-$150k per day, and two or three apex parrots at +$200k per day from salary, benefits, product royalties, speaking engagements, books, etc. Main Street doesn't pay much attention to syndicated parrot earnings nor the day-to-day unlikely phraseological coincidence across multiple venues, happily soaking up the misinformation hook, line, and sinker. Alongside the hourly lies, targeted minority groups, never enough to matter, are conditioned via local programming, though not really informed, to voice dissent, re-affirming illusion of choice among voters.

Finally, after many MSM fake news and *C Span* hours of useless though passionate debate theater, the long delayed, largely irrelevant but ridiculously expensive NGO or academic study and disingenuous report findings are released amidst long-awaited fanfare. Few read the obtuse report. Parroted pundit quotes are taken only from the politicized summary for dummies, masking what little science or few facts may have been cited. The ensuing racket of divide and conquer politics momentarily distracted the *unwashed* between *Monday Night Football* and Friday evening's *Family Matters*, *Full House*, or *Step by Step*, predictably forcing reluctant Trilaterals along with sweet deal compensated Congress persons to grudgingly give up their prolonged battle, caving at the last minute to vote reluctantly in favor of this needed agreement. The hubbub was mostly overkill anyway as Main Street was drowning in daily hoopla over the *Brady Bill*, *Don't Ask-Don't Tell*, *Travel-gate*,

Trooper-gate, *Whitewater*, and *what happened to Vince Foster*, seldom worrying about working harder for less, nor wondering why kids can't read or do math anymore.

Note: For special cases of egregiously corrupt legislation, Executive Branch *Fast-Track* can circumvent Congressional involvement entirely, though this is only employed for wildly greedy, politically hazardous agreements. Outlined above is one-way Elite handlers manage end-runs around *government by the people* enabling successful harvesting of those same uninformed people. It's a wonderful fascist system and when even *Fast-Track* is too risky, the deal goes dark and gets done under the table – nobody the wiser as journalism died decades ago buried under mounds of blackmail, cash, cowardice, and fear. Where are Carmelo Abbate, Nellie Bly, Antonio Salas, Gary Webb, and others when we need them? Fortunately, we do have *American Greatness, Citizen Free Press, Dark Journalist, Epoch Times, Giza Death Star, Highwire, Open The Books, Operation Freedom, Real America's Voice, Revolver News, UncoverDC, USA Watchdog,* and a host of other independent venues reigniting investigative journalism.

In a nutshell, propaganda and entrainment are how NAFTA and dozens of other corrupt programs are sold to Main Street. Correct perception is critical to effective human thought processes, decision making, and behavior. American Main Street perception has been toyed with since before 1776, but aggressive manipulation of perception went on press and radio steroids in the 1920s, then escalated further after WW II. Today the entire globe lives in a melodramatic PsyOp mirage perceived as real. How does the global syndicate orchestrate such widespread deception?

Very carefully. For example, American citizens were blocked from perceiving the extent to which Washington D.C. dark (covert) deals (my words) with the Chinese Communist Party (CCP) were routine from 1973[177] until The Donald said no in 2017. The CIA of course, was already mixing it up in China by the mid-1950s. Didn't hear the word TREASON much until The Donald said no to corruption, throwing a wrench into the D.C. money laundering gears. This resulted in years of BLUE UniParty rage against Trump and ±80 million, so-called, MAGA "insurrectionists". Talk about perception management, wow! Our unconstitutional *CDC, CIA, DHS, DOJ, EPA, FBI, FDA, HHS, NIH,* and other agencies as well as Big Tech and *legacy media* fully support treasonous Americans assisting global syndicate efforts through its CCP lever, to take down the American middle-class – the most critical remaining obstacle to One World Government. **Elites intend to extend Chinese slave labor across the globe.**

---

177 "The Hundred-Year Marathon: China's Secret Strategy to Replace America as the Global Superpower: Pillsbury, Michael: 9781250081346: Amazon.Com: Books."

The CIA's *Operation Mockingbird* along with entrainment technologies play a major role in perception skulduggery, intimidation, and organized theft. It's convenient for dehumanizing Elite agendas when Main Street *does not think* at all; but if impossible to bring this about, then effectively projecting *what to think* is the next best option. This involves MSM short term and Hollywood long term via programs like *Operation Mockingbird*, initially organized by Cord Meyer as I understand it and after 1953, run by CIA Director, Allen Dulles; then finally by Frank Wisner, former head of the *Office of Strategic Services* (OSS).

Mockingbird was and is a covert CIA program designed to influence, propagandize, and compromise media for CIA purposes on behalf the global syndicate. **Some writers claim Wisner founded the program, so I'm uncertain as to origination**, but in any event, Wisner recruited Philip Graham, CEO of the *Washington Post* at the time to lead this disingenuous operation within the so-called news industry. We might wonder if Amazon's CIA cloud services contract along with ties to today's WAPO continues that relationship because it appears to.

Anyway, over time, hundreds of media people and organizations were infiltrated and/or pulled into the clandestine *Mockingbird* program and compromised as indirect CIA assets under the abused banner of National Security. The CIA illegally engaged in surveillance of domestic political organizations, student groups, magazines, and foreign media. Alongside *Mockingbird* the FBI ran its own covert *Counterintelligence Program* (COINTELPRO) from 1956 through 1971, sometimes illegally infiltrating, surveilling, and discrediting domestic political organizations, student groups, cultural groups, and magazines as was the CIA. This abuse of power worsened as CIA assets infiltrated the FBI and DEA. The list of compromised mainstream media, including heavy Hollywood hitters is shocking. William Blum (*America's Deadliest Export*), Ms. Deborah Davis (*Katherine the Great*) as well as David Wise and Thomas Ross (*The Invisible Government*) and Hugh Wilford (*The Mighty Wurlitzer: How the CIA Played America*) have written extensively on this subversive government activity. Can we say, "Freedom of speech, BUT?"

Conceptualize for a moment, how our perception of reality and/or truth can be altered by a person, group, algorithm, autonomously intelligent electro-magnetic system, etc., if say, electro-magnetic devices, atmospheric plasma, HAARP, 5G, and heavy metals embedded in our cellular tissue were interfacing programmatically with our brain function directly, either individually or in mass? Consider this idea carefully because this is one aspect of precisely what 5G and 6G technology, quantum computing, aerosol spraying, synthetic mRNA JABs, smart grids, smart contracts, pseudo-anonymous blockchain, nano-sensors, micro-chips, nano-chips, and the *Internet of Things* (IoT) are all about. Crypto coupons (I don't refer to digital fiat magic as currency) tie the entire enslavement package together. **Full spectrum dominance** militarily and non-militarily via surveillance, propaganda, conditioning, entrainment, and control of everything and everyone on Earth. 100% virtual power. We are all intended to be cyborgs now because cyborgs are cheaper than robots.

Counterculture guru, Richard Alpert, aka Ram Dass recalls in 1971's Hippie Bible, *(Remember) Be Here Now*,[178] while discussing Faith through Christ and Faith in Rational Mind, Georges I. Gurdjieff telling him **"YOU ARE IN PRISON. If you think you're free, you can't escape"**. Richard Alpert and his associate Timothy Leary got the boot from Harvard in 1963 for allegedly giving students psilocybin, LSD, or both – I wasn't there so don't know either way. Being a misled counterculture guy myself, I appreciate Gurdjieff's statement and wonder if Mr. Alpert was part of the CIA's sick agenda or took faith in God to heart, thereby becoming another CIA target?

Anyway, healthy perception and avoiding thought prison is a great idea. If transhumanist systems fail to implement Main Street enslavement by Oligarchic Elites and their global syndicate; there's still the old-school threat of violence, cattle cars, and re-education camps... or as last resort, the inimical, unmarked mass grave, though these stratagems risk luring out pitchforks. Unredacted history raises this unthinkable possibility, though more likely taking the form of genocide via poor nutrition, unhealthy GMO foods, EMR, triggered retroviruses, and synthetic mRNA carrying toxic payloads in pseudo-vaccines, or heavy metals and desiccated blood housed within microscopic filaments distributed via aerosol geo-engineering processes—none of interest to 6 o'clock MSM.

The nightmare of covertly implemented IoT control systems, bionic implants, so-called *cognitive enhancement*, and other spiritually dehumanizing concepts are what hyper-left brained transhumanists and Silicon Valley techno-crazies following Deep State directives for their own self-gratification are doing – and doing with virtually zero oversight augmented with 365/24/7 cheer leading by the statist press corpse and sycophant academics, assuredly falling victim themselves to the depraved nonsense for which they cheer. In part, this sober realization fuels the current ideological schism within global syndicate ranks; a schism high-lighted by open schizophrenia of frightened, WEF, so-called world leaders.

Led down the nihilistic path of Nietzschean darkness forged by J. D. Bernal, W. D. Lighthall, Julian Huxley and others, these intellectually unbalanced techno-geeks may have the best of intentions, can and do wonderful things; but lacking healthy, balanced left brain/right brain intelligence, also have a proclivity for going completely off the obsessive/compulsive rails. This proclivity ren-

---

178 Ram Dass, *Be Here Now* (New York, NY: Harmony, 1978), 42.

ders their off-kilter talents susceptible to abuse and misdirection by psychopathically influential global syndicate leadership possibly suffering from **demonic obsession**, if not complete **possession**; but in any case, capable of imagining horrifically unsustainable human scenarios under which conditions they imagine Main Street citizens MUST live and/or be ELIMINATED. Think *Georgia Guidestones*. Recall *Weather Underground* (1969-1977) postulating 25 million or so Americans incapable of re-education having to be eliminated. Prorated by population, this would be ±40 million murdered for U. S. Marxist victory today.

Can we imagine a happy ending with unbalanced, left-brain control in the hands of anyone at all, much less in the non-transparent hands of wealthy, highly influential, socially deviant psychopaths? We should take note how far off the normalized morality rails Military Science and Silicon Valley have already arrogantly ventured, recognizing the crash and burn probability for humanity and other life this error in judgement poses. Mainstream media, academia, and publishing intentionally divert our attention and perception of direct threats to public health away from rogue elements perpetrating such threats from within institutions we are conditioned to trust. We stand alone on Main Street. Only we can save ourselves.

I'm thinking as a minimum, some transparency is in order, which we the people of Main Street have a Constitutional right to demand as we're paying for this research, development, and now, implementation of transhumanist enslavement technology as taxpayers and as consumers. The advent of the 21st century has brought with it a new kind of monster and these techno-demons do not hide under our beds or in closets. They proudly and lucratively reside on vast estates and within parasitic halls of transnational monopoly, mis-education, statist mass media, departments of injustice, and other destructive government agencies. They live as rogue elements spreading infectious spiritual decimation throughout the banking/military/industrial/surveillance complex, hovering like a poisonous cloud over Main Street with their harmful electro-magnetic tools emanating from aircraft, dangling from poles, and lurking in metered boxes on the same streets our children play. This is a war against God and human perception.

We literally have no idea the extent technologies already developed by these technocrazies are impacting and manipulating our perception of the world – with poor nutrition, weakened immunity, television *flicker rates*, and alpha brain-wave entertainment being just four minuscule examples employed without viewer knowledge or permission. Hang on for the 5G-6G smart grid trip cause it's a *Space Fence*, nanotech, magneto-genetic doozy many of us may not survive.

Are we aware, Main Street is paying for surveillance aircraft flying at altitudes of 90,000 feet or more at Mach 3, i.e., above Class A airspace ending at FL600. In the U.S., aircraft flying above 60,000 feet (pressure altitude) are not required to contact Air Traffic Control (ATC), though they can. These specialized aircraft are armed with electronic surveillance equipment like *DRT Box-Stingray* cell tower simulators, transmitters, and other weaponized technology we have little or no knowledge of. What if some of these military and law enforcement aircraft are not working for us on Main Street, but for the global syndicate against us?

Sophisticated solar-powered surveillance balloons are also monitoring human terrain from 40,000 to 92,000 feet elevation.[179] I don't know but imagine these balloons are also equipped with programming transmission capabilities as are many satellites, piloted surveillance aircraft, and drones.

My admonition, if you will, while reading this book and certainly after – **is recall the Perception Principle; thoughtfully set aside preconceived beliefs thought or found to be incorrect; evaluate these notions carefully; then modify perceptions as thoughtfully appropriate.** NEVER TRUST - ALWAYS VERIFY. If we are not open to questioning our perceptions and/or appropriate modification of them, we can't improve any situation can we – though perception adjustments must be carefully considered? Measure twice, cut once as carpenters say or better, measure three or four times.

It's imperative we open our minds to our created universe(s) and dimensions seen and unseen; seek objective truth as un-prejudicially as any of us can; reach our own unbiased conclusions to the best of our ability; accept personal responsibility for those conclusions; then act accordingly, thoughtfully, and with prudence. Question everything. Verify and trust our gut as our gut is our friend in truth seeking! DO NOT TRUST MAINSTREAM MASS MEDIA—EVER! Pray for Divine guidance.

Perception aside, is our tragic loss of self-governance an occurrence of historic happenstance? Is it caused by moral decline and loss of honor, about which the Founders warned? Is it a planned taking and incremental re-enslavement of Main Street commoners via long-planned conspiracy by Illuminist Free Masonic Lodges and Luciferian elements? I don't know. I don't go to the meetings. Maybe it's just the **4ᵗʰ Turning** of our generational saeculum?

In any case, our only reliable self-defense for **perception protection** against powerful Luciferian influence within the study group indoctrination system is God's grace—always available for the asking.

---

179 Adam Kehoe, "What We Know About the High-Altitude Balloons Recently Lingering Off America's Coastlines," The Drive, accessed August 21, 2021

The global syndicate's international
STUDY GROUP SYSTEM
manufactures MASTERS OF DECEPTION.
Consider WEF Young Global Leaders.

20 • Global Syndicate

Remedy: Main Street must stand up to the ravenous global syndicate before the cage door on Full Spectrum Dominance is locked. Transhuman attempts to create an autonomous intelligence back door into our brain must be stopped; requiring we first recognize the global syndicate agenda exists. We cannot defeat an enemy we don't know exists. We must read; we must learn.

I am not knowledgeable regarding occult traditions, but as I view it, the 21st century Global Syndicate is best described as a Luciferian cult masquerading as networked secular power centers, though most of its privileged adherents are not aware of Satanic influence. Logically, the origins of this cult pre-date humanity on Earth but in any event tie back to ancient Egyptian teachings approximately 6,000 years old, or possibly predating written records to as some researchers suggest, 10,000 years ago. There are syndicate bloodlines specializing in ancient belief systems and practice, as well as modern beliefs, all of which are Satanic. I make this claim based on Deuteronomy 18:9-14, the most powerful Biblical statement I'm aware of regarding necromancy, divination, omens, soothsayers, spiritualists, sorcery, witchcraft, mediums, spells, and similar spiritual temptations. Deuteronomy was authored by Moses near the end of his Earthly life before entering Canaan after wandering in the desert for forty years.

I rudely brought up D.C. political sewage in the last chapter, so must mention the sewage source, i.e., **Nazi International Fascist Global Syndicate, Shadow Governments, Deep State,** or whatever pejorative names we prefer for these circles within circular levels of Luciferian deceit. The above-mentioned classifications are just elements of **Globalism** or what is often referred to as **New World Order** (NWO). We need to address basic nomenclature before continuing as *International Fascism* figures prominently in our Main Street lives and is now *up in our grill* as Stephen K. Bannon might say.

Think of twisted sisters, Marxism and Fascism as the two jackhammers of Globalism arrayed against non-existent free market Capitalism. Marxism's nanny-state with its false promises of equality, fairness, and social justice comprise the sales pitch, while Fascism is the club slamming the prison door shut. Together, they engage an ideological system of Hegelian dialectic steadily nudging Main Street toward global serfdom, i.e., Globalism and the New World Order. So, how does this work?

In a nutshell, think of the New World Order (NWO) or Globalism as an international totalitarian ideology promoting a globally centralized concentration of power held in the hands of a small number of Elite people. These Elites employ groups of *privileged order followers* for overt and covert enactment of their Main Street enslavement agenda. **Imagine expanding circles of influence organized as an international *study group system*.** This deeply embedded Fascist system employs failed socialist economic theories and *Cultural Marxist* propaganda alongside Fascist control systems to undermine nutritional needs, lower intelligence levels, restrain imagination, create fear, undermine individual identity, and eliminate self-sufficiency. The Left is the weaponized battering ram for this attack on human decency and the independent American middle-class. If the central planning duma takes power, there will be no one to call and no Main Street recourse regarding duma decisions. Enslavement will be complete. America is nearing the end of its overthrow phase and elimination of all Constitutionally recognized rights, with replacement by false nanny-state promises and *outcome-based permissions* having force of law enforced by unelected administrators – **A Totalitarian Administrative State**.

The American Republic is being incrementally replaced by a Fascist technocratic **Administrative Dictatorship** managed by transnational monopolies at the behest of Elite dynastic families. Nearly all Federal agencies are 99.999% captured and are weaponized against U.S. citizens. The NWO concept is an excellent example of socially deviant, generationally indoctrinated psychopathy posing a threat to the sustainability of life on Earth, though most Elites and many of their order followers do not realize this; or if they do, don't care, which I suspect is ignore-ance by Luciferian influence. It appears since the *Obama-Hillary 16-Year Plan* failed in November 2016, COVID lockdowns and toxic JABs, along with WW III are Plan B for taking down American middle-class resistance to the

DAVOS Great Reset. The *Great Reset* has already failed as has the concept of the New World Order but a dying rattlesnake is still poisonous and dangerous.

Can we see how our American Main Street perception has been under siege since even before 1776, and full attack since 1948 or so? All North American resources including Main Street labor and wealth producing capability are on the table for the taking. This Satanic NWO enslavement system could not be imposed on American citizens without decades of mind-numbing preparation. A decade of propagandized conditioning preceded Hitler, a global syndicate pawn, in Germany. America has now been under NWO attack (*demoralization*) for more than a century. Our citizen resistance has dwindled to a small remnant, interestingly led by Christians as in the lead up to the 1776 Revolution, born in the pulpits, though most of today's pulpits are captured. Millions of compliant mask wearers trying to breathe while sporting unhealthy biochemical petri dishes on their faces bear testament to the success of this *mass formation* attack. A decorated face diaper apparently masquerades as individual expression or worse, a pathetic attempt at resistance. Better not to wear a face muzzle in my opinion unless you're Joe Biden or someone like him.

Note: For more on **Mass-Formation**, follow Dr. Mattias Desmet, Professor of Psychology at University of Ghent, who also holds a Master's in Statistics. As I understand it, Professor Desmet has added to earlier work by Dr. Gustave Le Bon, who in 1895 published *The Crowd: A Study of the Popular Mind*.

Anyway, international concentration of power takes many organizational forms with a few multi-faceted examples being the League of Nations/United Nations; NATO; European Union; North American Union; Euro and Amero currencies; Switzerland's Bank of International Settlements (BIS), P-2 Freemason's Italian Alpina Lodge, and *Nazi International*. These run parallel to the International Monetary Fund (IMF); World Bank; World Trade Organization (WTO); World Economic Forum (WEF); World Health Organization (WHO); BIG SIX BANKS, U.S. Trust Corporation, and the Central Banking Cartel; the Four Horsemen of Oil; aggregation of Fortune 500 corporate controlling interest in the hands of just ten or so private banks; various international trade agreements like NAFTA; aggregation of more than fifty media companies in the 1950's to only a few in 2021, etc. Obviously, the North American Union and Amero, though planned, have not yet come about, but we get the central planning idea. Check out sick investment funds like *BlackRock* (4th Branch of Government), *Vanguard*, *State Street*, and *Berkshire Hathaway* to confirm the unimaginable greed let loose here.

A casual glance at the above list suggests decentralization but is nothing of the sort. That's a lot of organizations just on the short list and there's many dozens more within the study group system, all of them controlled by the same global syndicate. Do not be misled. The occult magic lies in the **study group indoctrination system** from which participating globalist pawns are vetted and selected. There is only one Satanic drummer and one Luciferian beat to which all participants must march. No exceptions. Geopolitical careers are built on conformance, greed, and fear.

By way of terminology clarification, *Beyond All Isms'* globalist terminology is as follows. To the best of my limited knowledge, the **American Shadow Government** comprises rogue elements within the NSA, CIA, FBI, and a dozen or so more intelligence agencies covertly conducting treasonous operations outside the purview of Congress and beyond Constitutionally recognized authority. Every major nation has its own Shadow Government.

The **Deep State** is a global network intertwining banking and intelligence services near the top for management of government agencies, military, mining, transportation, manufacturing, industrial agriculture, food processing, medicine, surveillance, publishing, media systems, and more into a worldwide matrix. Local network operatives are usually treasonous within respective nations, comprising groups of *selected* politicians, unelected upper-level Federal Agency management, CEOs, and top managers in banking, military, industrial, and surveillance transnational monopolies, along with academia, philanthropic fronts, media, medicine, and Hollywood. I'm sure I missed something as the Deep State matrix is unimaginably wide and deep across the planet... and now beyond Earth, so feel free to add to the list.

Note: We do have ELECTED local politicians and a few elected at the national level, but generally, and in all cases where a treasonous buffoon has been in office for thirty or more years – politicians are VETTED and SELECTED via the *study group system* through crooked campaign financing, fake news, rigged primaries, corrupt media shills, and election fraud. I am aware of **maybe** three or four patriot House Members, one in the U.S. Senate, and zero Presidents since Woodrow Wilson. President Trump appears to be an exception.

Both individual Shadow Governments and the international Deep State are directed, in my opinion as I don't attend the meetings, by largely unidentified, Elite Oligarchic family members, some historic, others nouveau, the whole of whom I characterize as the **Global Syndicate**. Though decent, hardworking rank and file employees work in various agencies, institutions, and NGOs, rogue *useful idiots* are buried layers deep everywhere. Such institutions, among which are America's CDC, CFTC, CIA, DOJ, EPA, FBI, NIH, and SEC, to name a few, can no longer be rehabilitated. I refer to the entire Satanic mess, including Oligarchs at the top of the Satanic dung heap as *The Global Syndicate*, though Dr. Joseph Farrell's characterization, ***International Fascism***[180] is more appropriate (and harder to spell).

Contrary to urban myth and U.S. citizen frustration, our federal government has no shortage of gifted, in many cases, brilliantly capable individuals working ferociously to make our federal government responsive to Main Street and be the best it can be. I admire these people and personally, in writing, **thank every one of you**, from the bottom of my heart for your courage, what you dare do, and what you accomplish. This book and derogatory terminology are directed toward those I view as reprehensible scoundrels having nothing in common with hard working patriots caught in a corrupted system.

Beyond All Isms **is about remedies** and repairing our **BROKEN GOVERNING SYSTEM** under which good people attempt to professionally survive and hope to improve – AND about cowardly human detritus, BAD GUYS and GALS who circumvent honest government and corporate life, building over time, a deep swamp-like, protective network – a matrix, beneath which to hide and from behind the veil of which, conduct criminal behavior such as war, theft, murder, character assassination, trafficking of various kinds, resource rape, money laundering, and other crimes, all with impunity and usually with **qualified immunity** to some protective level.

This human infection continues to pervert Washington D.C. and its many associated alliances carrying out non-transparent, ruthlessly Luciferian agendas. We have rogue elements infiltrating Federal Agencies such as Department of Homeland Security, CDC, CIA, FBI, NSA, National Institute of Health, Department of Justice, Department of State and covert sections of our many intelligence services and military branches. These subversive elements are clearly pathological, if not criminally insane and **must be identified, rooted out, and their seditious, treasonous behavior stopped; then transparently prevented by Main Street vigilance from returning. This is ours, the people of Main Street to take care of. No politician can or will do it for us. Self-governance, like most things has pros and cons, responsibility being one of them.**

Note: Sedition is defined as *"incitement of resistance to or insurrection against lawful authority"*. **Treason** is specifically defined in Article III, Section 3 of the U.S. Constitution as follows:
"Treason against the United States, shall consist only in levying War against them, or, in adhering to their Enemies, giving them Aid and Comfort. No person shall be convicted of

---

180 Joseph P. Farrell, *Hidden Finance, Rogue Networks, and Secret Sorcery: The Fascist International, 9/11, and Penetrated Operations* (Kempton, IL: Adventures Unlimited Press, 2016).

Treason unless on the testimony of two Witnesses to the same overt Act, or on Confession in open Court.

The Congress shall have Power to declare the Punishment of Treason, but no Attainder of Treason shall work Corruption of Blood, or Forfeiture except during the Life of the Person attained."

It's not arguable that thousands of U.S. persons in government and corporate life openly engage in treasonous activities with foreign nations and private entities. Many are so civics challenged they don't realize it. Most do and don't care or fear syndicate handlers. Why such criminal behavior is not investigated or prosecuted by law enforcement agency employees paid to defend us, I don't know. **The United States is not functioning as a sovereign nation.** It functions like an order following vassal controlled by socially deviant psychopaths. COVID and its JABs are an example, not just of greed and corruption, but pure evil. Globally the synthetic mRNA JABs are disabling people, making people ill, causing infertility, and murdering thousands of citizens. Government agencies, licensing boards, and NGOs pushing doctors, nurses, schools, and businesses to do harm isn't institutional mismanagement; this is malevolent intent on a massive scale and must be prosecuted as criminal behavior.

Public information defense is now driven solely by private citizens conducting research from their homes, garages, and small studios in the face of MSM ridicule and government agency coordinated social media attack... or worse. Fortunately, most of us are honest citizens and decent people, but unfortunately, few of us from Main Street find our way into positions of power and influence. In America as well as most other countries, power positions are uniformly held by indoctrinated psychopaths, many of whom are socially deviant, all of whom are indebted to an arm of global syndicate reach, though may not realize it. Brainwashing is a real thing and Main Street swims in it.

If you happen to be one of the good people, PLEASE don't imagine my criticism applies to you. My negative commentary is directed toward psychopathic human beings and their nasty order followers. I pray for them, but do not accept their behavior. **When I mention we the people of Main Street, I include all decent, hard-working, competent government employees; particularly military and intelligence service personnel most in harm's way on behalf of all of us.** Good people are separate from what I call *prominent global citizens (Oligarchs and Elites)*, their cowardly order followers, and corrupted Pawns of Privilege.

Regarding malfeasant D.C. political sewage, this book is about universal principles and remedies we might consider as Main Street citizens to clean up this quagmire of expensive, parasitic, centralized **Administrative Dictatorship.** A dictatorship built on MARXIST LIES, FASCIST TRANSNATIONAL MONOPOLY CORRUPTION, narcotics trafficking, war, hidden budgets, black budgets, blackmail, child sex trafficking, pedophilia, organ trafficking, control files, and cowardly degeneracy now beginning to implode beneath its own bloated *mass formation*. We cannot allow this malevolence to continue metastasizing and imagine we are decent people aspiring to freedom.

For clarification, one parasitic example is highly profitable organ harvesting augmented by black genocide carried out in Illinois' Cook County and other U.S. metropolitan areas. Hidden budgets for this sort of subversive activity gained Washington D.C. popularity during WW II, becoming institutionalized by Eisenhower Administration apathy in the 1950's alongside rock 'n' roll and *The Purple People Eater* of 1958. If we missed this, we are grossly uninformed. Racist White Supremacy doesn't inhabit Main Street but is alive and well in globalist circles like D.C., City of London, and Vatican City.

I don't condemn President Eisenhower for his failure as his personal naivete and trust were overwhelmed by vast forces arrayed against his managerial *Peter Principle* apex. Soldiers deal with honor. D.C. honor, already wounded by 1953 no longer exists in Washington D.C., and I doubt President Eisenhower realized this at first. In his defense, Eisenhower appears to have been blind-sided, but since his January 17, 1961 (farewell address) warning, we have no excuse for apathy.

Speaking of NO EXCUSES, on the heels of President Eisenhower's farewell remarks, newly elected President John F. Kennedy stated on April 27, 1961, during a speech to the *American Newspaper Publishers Association*:

"We are as a people, opposed to secret societies. The dangers of excessive and unwarranted concealment of pertinent facts, far outweigh the dangers that are cited to justify them. There is a very grave danger than an announced need for an increased need for security, will be seized upon by those anxious to expand it's meaning to the very limits of censorship and concealment. That I do not tend to permit, so long as it's in my control."

On top of earlier warnings by Wilson and Truman for example, these two consecutive U.S. Presidents, early in 1961 warned Main Street of the threat posed by the global syndicate, though they employed their own terminology. We should have taken their remarks seriously – didn't – but can still do so now. We the people have the numbers and the power but are demonstrating a lack of will. This must change or our kids are serfs.

⚜

Fixing our broken D.C. money laundering system potentially risks losing our Constitution and Federal government entirely should we proceed rashly. Sadly, cancerous as it is, fixing broken U.S. government involves tremendous risk to citizens, not to mention risk to good people serving within the diseased structure of now Fascist government. Better to repair damage carefully, surgically, even though extensive, while maintaining the skeleton of our Constitutional Republic intact.

Returning a more than $5 trillion dollar on-book per year D.C. money laundering system back into a functional American seat of government is no easy, nor safe task and is not for the faint hearted. We the people MUST NETWORK together to augment our perception, protecting ourselves against media deceit and rogue government terrorism, as well as to overcome evil forces – bringing us to a final point regarding the global syndicate—the syndicate itself. Before continuing, on a positive note, please realize, our military is made up of us, therefore not all, but most military personnel stand with us, the people of Main Street, the heroic source of our military blood – and will honor their oath to protect and defend against enemies foreign and domestic – even enemies within our own despotic government.

Note: In the unlikely event portions of our WOKE military, steadily undermining resolve and weakening preparedness by driving responsible leadership from military ranks, fail to protect us against government tyranny; our last bastion of freedom resides **in ourselves, retired military leaders (not sure how this works), and local elected Sheriffs** who comprise the supreme law enforcement authority within their jurisdictions. Washington D.C., infected with totalitarian cancer has been working overtime for decades to undermine the 10th Amendment and local law enforcement authority, particularly elected Sheriffs through unconstitutional invasion of States' Rights by CIA, DEA, DHS, EPA, FBI, TSA, and other less intrusive agencies like Department of Interior. **Reflexive Law**, i.e., outcome-based law fully supports subversive undermining of Main Street's unalienable rights recognized by our Constitution, posing a threat all its own. Main Street now has little if any access to lawful protections in these United States. Even relatively wealthy Main Streeters who can afford expensive litigators are told by corrupt courts they have no standing.

The Global Syndicate. What is this creature and how does media hide it in plain sight? Those of us limiting study of current events and history to propagandized muck put out by mainstream publishing houses, some new disingenuous dictionaries with misleading modernist lexicon, and mainstream media drones servicing Global Plutocracy and Deep State corruption are in the dark as to how the world works. 21st century mainstream media (MSM) provides a 99.99% probability of deceit via misinformation, twisted facts, lies by omission, and outright lies serving whatever agenda is the 4:00 A.M. "talking point" order of the day. Syndicate owned legacy media management not only engages treasonous behavior, they brag about it.

Fortunately, so-called independent media, that is, out-of-the-mainstream, independently funded media on the other hand, provides a minimum 50% probability of finding some honest questions, discourse, and truth. Accurate facts are critical to coherent perception and now emanate exclusively from living room podcasts, garage studios, and small newsrooms, not fake news networks.

A bit of serious sleuthing and selective discernment applied to available independent media sources increases the probability of finding some truth to 85% or better. Absolutely no one gets it 100% correct. Yes, searching independent media means slogging through some muck; but mainstream media offers nothing but muck, all muck, all the mucking time. Quality independent media doesn't always get it right, but the genuine articles at least ask honest questions and seek truthful answers and are willing to correct mistakes; something unheard of in today's cowardly, consensus obligated, *Mockingbird Media*. I do not know who issues the 4:00 A.M. (EST) **Mockingbird** *talking points*, but it occurs daily.

We must choose news and information sources carefully or our perception will be marred by egregious lack of order-follower integrity. Correct information is crucial because if our perception is incorrect for whatever reason serving whatever agenda; it follows our thinking will be incorrect as will subsequent responses. In an information war this is not a constructive situation with a happy ending. Please recall the *Perception Principle* rule of thumb. Be vigilant, pay attention, pray.

I'm not invited, so don't go to the meetings (and there's lots of meetings), but from my erudite, admittedly secluded, Sonoran Desert view, comfortably shaded by a 200-year-old, majestic Saguaro Cactus, the so-called GLOBAL SYNDICATE, as mentioned earlier, is essentially an *International Fascist Network*, to borrow an appropriate label from noted Oxford scholar, Joseph P. Farrell.[181]

Russian economist, Dr. Tatyana Koryagana, testified to the existence of this global network relative to 9/11/2001, as having access to a financial war chest estimated at ±$300 trillion dollars.[182] I can't confirm this number but clearly the syndicate spends what it wants. It appears this network is in part tied to ongoing geopolitical, and financial activities conducted by order following pawns and obedient organizations with international ties to original, surviving WW II Nazi Party leadership, that Party's remnants, and to dynastic families predating the Roman Republic and subsequent Empire. These families are adoringly fond of Mussolini's Fascist ideas as well as Marx's lunacy. This is a wealthy Black Hat

---

181 Farrell, xvi.
182 Farrell, 142, 261.

networking cult hazardous to sustainable life on Earth. Fascist Nazis are just slugs working for Satanic dynastic families. They're all nuts and all dangerous.

Global syndicate leaders are either primary or secondary psychopaths.[183] They are so different from Main Street humans some claim they are aliens or a malevolent form of reptilian creatures. I have no idea about any of this but speculate as follows: I believe the Globalist New World Order agenda is 100% Luciferian and is hellbent on destroying all creation, though believers cannot say so publicly and may not know it themselves. I suspect alleged alien-human and/or reptilian-human life form activity are examples of **demonic activity**. If so, interaction entails spiritual warfare more so than material warfare, demanding appropriate strategy and tactics to regain freedom.

If we accept the alien or reptilian theory of psychopathy, we distract ourselves from seeing our True Enemy or realizing we live in an arena of spiritual warfare, where indisputable psychopathy is inspired by Luciferian influence. Our only protective weapon against such evil influence is putting on the armor of God, which we will not do if we don't identify our true enemy. **Free Masonry**, for example, is dedicated to ensuring we never come to the realization of spiritual warfare or our need for God's grace, thereby leaving us to face Satan and hordes of fallen angels on our own—a prescription for certain failure as intended. This Masonic teaching is a form of *Christian Socialism*,[184] i.e., *works without Christ* for benefit of man and is an affront to our Creator's love through which we receive the gift of grace for what *The Orthodox Study Bible* refers to as **living works** as opposed to **dead works**.[185] Dead works glorify man. Living works glorify God by exercising human independence (free will) through the gift of grace. Basing independence on ourselves is the *gospel of man* – rejection of God's grace leading to Satanically inspired chaos, pain, rebellion, and shame.

Regardless its nature, the global syndicate operates something like this. There are expensively dressed, select groupings around our globe we can refer to as established dynastic families. Not all, but some of these dynastic family members or *prominent global citizens* (a term borrowed from the *Bretton Woods Committee*)[186] become wealthy, geopolitically powerful, and frequently network together, often illegally, sometimes agreeably, sometimes adversarially. Many of these powerful family

183 Andrew M. Lobaczewski, *Political Ponerology*, ed. Laura Knight-Jadczyk (Red Pill Press, 2012).
184 Bullinger, E. W., *Number In Scripture*, n.d., 51.
185 "The Orthodox Study Bible - Hardcover Edition," 1,601.
186 "About the Committee | The Bretton Woods Committee," accessed April 14, 2021, https://www.brettonwoods.org/page/about-the-committee.

members are recognized through descent of royal or noble bloodlines; some via occult knowledge and practice; and some arrive through accumulation of nouveau wealth, acquiring impressive, though less historic coats-of-arms and family titles.

Various globally active families, historic or nouveau, specialize within different industries, say areas of banking, mining, manufacturing, shipping, industrial agriculture, commodities, munitions, etc., and of course, religion, education, government, law, and/or the occult practices. Some families specialize in statecraft, becoming expert in legal and/or government policy and regulatory manipulation, blackmail, insider trading, and other covertly crony practices common throughout City of London, Washington D.C., Vatican City, Prague, New York, Frankfurt, Brussels, Basel, Hong Kong, Beijing, and other international power centers. Psychopathy, at least among dynastic family members slated for an active world role, becomes a culturally refined trait.

It is members of dynastic families, historic or nouveau, active in international crime, banking, transnational monopoly commerce, politics, law, military and intelligence services, statecraft, science, education, media, etc. – and their order-following Pawns of Privilege we are concerned with when discussing the global syndicate. These voracious parasites live within a pernicious global network of covert control files, blackmail, political legerdemain, organized crime, narcotics trafficking, weapons trafficking, war-making, human trafficking, child trafficking, pedophilia, ritual sacrifice, organ harvesting, sex trafficking, surveillance, abuse of power, Scientism – and now, transhuman control – all of it tied to wealth, power, and ultimately, destruction of creation.

Active syndicated network participants are a Satanically influenced, destructive type of human whether they know it or not. This hazardous parasitic network infects every major government on Earth and though I don't know where it's headquartered or specifically who sits at or near the evil top of this global dung heap; it's bases of power operation have since the turn of the 20th century, been the City of London, Vatican City, Washington D.C., Frankfurt, Brussels, New York, Basel, Hong Kong, Beijing, and Mexico City though these power hubs are always under peer review.

Active family members within Elite families and their privileged pawns network together through a system of established secret societies, dozens of them, more than a hundred in the United States alone, many of them hundreds of years old. These closed societies act as recruiting, hazing, and bonding services, whereby sufficiently pathological persons, or persons capable of readily being conditioned to social deviancy can be identified, then spawned into the **global study group system** comprised of trusts, foundations, endowments, institutes, think tanks, associated universities, professional associations, multinational monopoly management, and non-governmental organizations (NGOs) such as so-called Round Tables.

A few of the more popular study group brain washing centers are *Tavistock Institute of Human Relations, Royal Institute of International Affairs, Council on Foreign Relations, Trilateral Commission, Club of Rome, Bohemian Grove, Bilderberg Group,* etc., to name a few. Also tied to Britain's Tavistock are thirty or more U.S. institutions such as *Aspen Institute, Brookings Institution, Hudson Institute, Rand Corporation,* and *Stanford Research Institute.* And NO, not every person associated with these institutes is a globalist pawn. The global syndicate appreciates the illusion of choice. It's not terribly important who's doing what anyway. The significant issue is poisonous *globalist culture* within participating institutions enshrined in the study group system.

Should these institutes strike us as trivial consider that an engineering *whiz kid* named Paul Baran at *Rand* developed the **packet switching technology** making the *world wide web* possible. We may have been told it was Al Gore, but no. Baran failed to convince the long-distance phone AT&T monopoly to adopt his packet system over their single-track point to point system. Baran's discreet data bundling system was then adopted by the U.S. Pentagon, who recognized its value. The Pentagon went on to create a world-wide packet-switching system called ARPANET, now called the INTERNET. Silicon Valley came along later piggy backing on the techno skeleton put together by our military. Sadly, the entire thing is weaponized, though controlling the *little people* on it has proved difficult. The takeaway is people working for this Globalist think tank named *Rand* changed the world.

Getting back to it, despite claims to the contrary by mainstream pundits and social media trolls, *secret society* membership is significant because some secret societies standing behind endowments, foundations, institutes, and trusts require an oath of loyalty and silence be taken by members. Yale's' *Skull and Bones,* founded as *The Order, Chapter 322* in 1832, incorporated as *The Russel Trust* in 1856, is one such society.[187] I say significant because a person taking and honoring his or her society oath means no other competing oath presenting a conflict of interest can honorably be taken. Promising sociopathic women by the way have been admitted to *Skull & Bones* since 1992.

An oath taking member of *Skull and Bones* openly violates their oath of office as President of the United States, Congressional Representative, or military officer just by taking a second oath. Skull and Bones' loyalty is to *Bonesmen* and their Global Elite agenda. Bonesman participation in totalitarian planning for a New World Order calls for destruction of American sovereignty, all oth-

187 Antony Sutton, *America's Secret Establishment: An Introduction to the Order of Skull & Bones* (Walterville: Trine Day, 2004), 5.

er national sovereignty, and our U.S. Constitutional Rule of Law, standing at odds with any U.S. government or military oath of office or service. Secret society participants in many foreign policy study group meetings and seminars working with foreign nationals, regularly commit sedition and/or treason against the people of the United States, though surely do not see it that way.

Incidentally, when a Muslim practicing Islam disingenuously takes the Presidential, Congressional, or military oath of office, he or she also violates the oath of office by taking it, as Islam recognizes no law but Sharia Law. Sharia Law as I understand it, recognizes *human obligations* asserted by Allah and Allah's Prophet. If Sharia Law *obligations* can be compared to the Western view of *human rights*, then only rights within Sharia are human rights. Nothing outside Sharia Law can be a human right. Is it odd, mainstream media doesn't mention this? And no, this observation does not justify slaughtering Islamic people nor stealing their national resources.

In any event, *selected sociopaths* targeted for leadership are conveniently identified through participation in various societies and study groups. This is step one in what I refer to as the **study group system**. After demonstrating *correct thinking* and *indoctrinated acceptance* of Globalist New World Order concepts, along with lack of integrity, the initiate gains an initial measure of dependability and begins networking into lucrative key positions of influence and power in banking, government, law, media, monopoly commerce, publishing, science and throughout the banking, military/industrial/surveillance complex.

If our only so-called news sources are mainstream, then we are told little if anything about this reality. However, a few arduous minutes on the Internet of Things (IoT) and independent media shines light on the amazing percentage of key power positions in banking, education, government, and monopoly commerce, both elected and appointed, limited with near total exclusivity to conditioned order followers plucked from this **study group matrix**, many of whom are secret society members or allied with members of secret societies.

In a country of ±330,000,000 people these influential insider position appointments number several magnitudes beyond any explainable probability of occurrence. Ridiculing this observation does not make substantive secret societies disappear nor does it reduce their considerable Luciferian influence. Can a functional adult imagine imbecilic Joe Biden won the White House or PCR tests are diagnostically meaningful? It should be noted that Presidents, federal agency directors, and secretaries are not the most critical government positions. **Our federal government is operationally managed by assistant directors and under-secretaries, not agency heads or Presidents.** Neither the White House nor Congress know how many Federal agencies even exist much less manage any of them. Agency heads are pom-pom waving cheer leaders and organized crime deal makers, not active managers. Is it strange given this fact, how little attention we, certainly I, pay to assistant-level agency appointments?

Anyway, in some dynastic families, at the extreme end of the spectrum, we find the allegedly historic practice (difficult to prove anecdotal allegations) of organized ritual child abuse quietly carried on generationally. A young, dynastic child surviving this horrific mental and physical torture process at home and at private boarding school is guaranteed to be a thoroughly imprinted and conditioned sociopath with serious personality disorder(s). This person will be capable of making business decisions resulting in the brutal deaths of thousands, even millions with no trace of moral trepidation or empathy. Expensive order-following psychiatrists and excellent pharmaceuticals are always on hand to assist a relapse into compassion, guilt, or empathy by errant family members. How many of us on Main Street have any perception of this monstrous culpability at all? Amazing what an expensive bespoke suit, palatial estate, and a super-yacht cover up?

I imagine most dynastic children are not heinously tortured, just heavily conditioned and entrained to believe in Cultural Marxist propaganda, Darwinian Superiority, Fascist Government, and Malthusian Scarcity. Dynastic family members are indoctrinated as to their familial right to own or at least control all resources in existence; their entitled genetic right to breed, purchase, and own slaves, though today, we do not coarsely employ such distasteful terminology. An honest Main Street look under the rug shows no significant distinction existing between wholly owned slaves and obscenely taxed Main Street employees regulated within free-roaming thought prisons called cities. Slave ownership entails boarding expenses, doesn't it? Slaves must be maintained in working condition to perform work. Slaves require some base level of maintenance upkeep. Transhuman cyborgism is intended to reduce the cost and inconvenience of slave management.

The global Luciferian system of organized crime is effectively managed by handing out lucrative, rotating positions in elected and appointed government and transnational monopoly business along with positive press coverage and top shelf legal representation – **the carrot**; juxtaposed with vengeful relinquishment of the carrot for hesitant or non-compliant behavior – **the stick**; or worse, the threat of financial or physical violence against self, family, pets, friends, and associates; and finally, best of the best, the infamous **CONTROL FILE**, guaranteed to wreck a non-conformist life. The stalled 5G roll-out in conjunction with the *Space Fence* and Nanotech may, despite conflicting frequency issues, replace the distasteful control file system as primary means of control, which could be the reason for recent pedophile purging? If transhumanism and AI can replace blackmail as a control lever, child or other sex trafficking can be demoted from necessary tools to discretionary Elite entertainment.

For now, until transhuman methods become more developed, the control file is in use and comprises all the personal dirt corrupted rogue elements within the banking, government, military, intelligence complex have on a person; real or fabricated. A control file may include pictures taken of an up-and-coming person at a private D.C., New York, L.A., Rome, City of London, or Beijing party, where they have been drugged unconscious. Pictures are taken of their naked body lying next to a small child or children, also naked, but beaten and bloody, maybe in hand cuffs or chains, possibly murdered. You do not have to be a pedophile to be framed and blackmailed as one.

See how this works? Mainstream media does not mention it, but control file blackmail readily accounts for highly educated Ivy League graduates conducting themselves as ten-year-old children on an after-school playground. Global geopolitics and money together constitute a high stake, dangerous game for the players themselves and sadly, for the Main Street Peanut Gallery as excrement flows downhill and Main Street is at the bottom of corruption hill.

If you're still with me, you can see draining the swamp is no small thing. Even Congressional de-funding of CIA black budgets can't stop this criminal enterprise as the banking, government, military, industrial, pharmaceutical, surveillance matrix now self-funds via black or hidden budgets generated by narco-dollars, weapons dollars, human trafficking, organ harvesting, and of course, the non-transparent central banking computer entry, which collects and enters unmonitored currencies, including cryptos, from all over the world into the *Exchange Stabilization Fund* (ESF) and/or other non-transparent accounts we know nothing of.

The House of Representatives and U.S. Senate have no access to the ESF and obviously not to other unknown accounts. As established, only the Presidential Pawn, order following Treasury Secretary, and affiliated military/intelligence elements have access to the ESF. The President and Treasury Secretary normally have substantively damaging control files to keep them in line and on treasonous task. If not, there are other means. Donald Trump appears an exception to this. There is a reason the global syndicate fears him and his possibly White Hat associates. Time will tell the truth.

We should note the CIA, FBI, GCHQ, MI6, MI5, Mossad, ISI, SVR, BND, MSS, and dozens of less well-known intelligence services around the world are competitive, but not necessarily enemies. These agencies frequently work together in service of international Elite agendas most of us have no knowledge of but do pay for one way or another. It should also be noted that power slips, slides, and changes hands over Oligarchic time and various syndicate family fortunes ebb and flow. Though difficult to perceive, it appears power and influence shifted or became shared, at least in the most-active roles, from Rothschilds to Rockefeller and Morgan during the WW I – WW II period for example. Life in the syndicate is every bit as dynamic as on Main Street, perhaps more so. We should note, the global power apex lies in hands whose names are rarely spoken.

As a side note, the FBI is no longer a legitimate law enforcement agency. It still does a shamelessly biased job of law enforcement, but its primary function is intelligence gathering, surveillance, blackmail, and extortion. This treasonous subversion began decades ago but was put on steroids under Bush I, Clinton, Bush II, Obama, and now CCP sock-puppet Biden.

If we accept soft or asymmetric warfare as legitimate war, it appears World War III began as early as 1948 with the *Tavistock Institute of Human Relations* declaring mind control war on the United States' populace. Successive planned events followed, preceded by the 1944 *Bretton Woods Agreement* substituting the U.S. dollar for gold and establishing it as the world's reserve currency, followed by the petrodollar in 1973. The *International Monetary Fund* (IMF) and *World Bank* were also created at *Bretton Woods* in 1944. We should note WW II was a declared war in apparent keeping with the U.S. Constitution (Article I, Section 8), but evidence suggests WW II was also the first *profitably planned U.S. war.*

WW I appears to have been planned, was instigated and profitable for Elite dynastic families, but I'm not certain if it was a planned war as many credible researchers insist. We do know European lack of liquidity at the time meant WW I could not reasonably have been financed without first passing the 16th Amendment to the U.S. Constitution in February 1913, then creating America's privately held Federal Reserve System in December 1913. These two acts of treason (my opinion) provided global syndicate pickpockets with access to entrepreneurial American Main Street pocketbooks – so there's that.

Note that the 17th Amendment, cleverly passed in April 1913 rendered the 16th Amendment irrevocable as a practical matter by Congressionally eliminating meaningful State's Voices in Federal legislative matters. The 17th Amendment ended appointment of U.S. Senators by their respective state legislatures, thereby subjecting the U.S. Senate to the same mudslinging and coercive election fraud controls as the so-called People's House. States could no longer replace problematic U.S. Senators for failure to competently represent their State. A major check and balance was thereby, effectively eliminated, emboldening corruption.

20 • Global Syndicate

Following are a few post WW II preparations for U.S. serfdom:

- first profitable undeclared war in 1950, the Korean War
- second profitable undeclared war in Vietnam from 1954 – 1975
- JFK assassination, November 22, 1963 *coup d'etat*
- privatization of the space program after 1963
- abandonment of the gold standard in 1971-73 with what many claim was the end of the Bretton Woods system
- President Reagan gunned back into line on March 30, 1981
- 1983 undeclared invasion of Grenada
- 1980's - 1990's Somalian intervention
- 1989 undeclared invasion of Panama
- 1990 undeclared 1st Gulf War and 1990's Rape of Russia
- 1992 undeclared war in Bosnia (using intelligence assets trained in Somalia)
- creation of WTO in 1995 and the start of North American capital divergence
- unsustainable sovereign debt peak in 1996
- de-capitalization of America begins in Fall 1997
- 1998 undeclared war in Kosovo
- bursting dot.com bubble from 2000 - 2001
- China joined WTO December 11, 2001
- 9/11/2001
- launching of the Afghanistan/Iraq undeclared war on terrorism in 2001 along with undeclared wars in Libya, Niger, Somalia, Syria, and Yemen
- 2008 financial coup d'etat
- creation by G20 at the Pittsburgh Summit in April, 2009 of the criminal enterprise named the *Financial Stability Board* (FSB), successor to the *Financial Stability Forum*[188]
- 2010 disruption and weaponization of U.S. health care services by PPACA
- 2012's legalizing of U.S. government propaganda against its citizens
- 2018 and 2020 election fraud far beyond previous fraudulent U.S. elections
- 2020-2022 COVID lockdowns, toxic JABs, and financial fraud
- whatever is ongoing now, which appears related to collapse, abandonment, and transition to replacement of the original 1944 Bretton Woods international financial system with a Satanic digital replacement, i.e., **Human 2.0, Transhuman Global 3.0** and THE GREAT RESET – by the way, a failing reset as of this writing.

Whew! Global syndicate psychopaths have been and are busy. Have we the people of Main Street logically perceived any of these incremental events and connected dots? Note that undeclared wars are handy since technically, in my

---

188 John Truman Wolfe, *Crisis by Design; The Untold Story of the Global Financial Coup* (Roberts Ross Publishing, 2010).

non-lawyer opinion, dynastic family members financing and supporting both sides of an undeclared war cannot technically be accused of treasonous activity. It's also easier to avoid Congressional oversight, sad joke that it is. Any oversight at all can slow career promotions, kickbacks, and sweetheart deal cash flows – a D.C. no-no. President Donald Trump did precisely this, hence the ensuing fear and rage echoed by global syndicate pawns from all pandering sides. It took less than 30 days for the treasonously corrupt Biden Regime to put fraud and money laundering back on track with a 2021 CCP and Russian vengeance.

In any event, more than $50 trillion U.S. dollars are unaccounted for in D.C. since 1998 (possibly $25 trillion in & $25 trillion out; we don't know). The great flushing sound of U.S. manufacturing, industry, jobs, and wealth relocating south and east went on steroids with NAFTA, though U.S. manufacturing already peaked in the 1950's. De-industrialization in many cities precipitously took off in 1979, continuing through the Reagan Administration into the Clinton 1990's. More serious liquidation of U.S. capital reserves began in 1998 with Western capital relocation primarily to the South and East. Various other wealth harvesting cons raise the $50 trillion to about $86 trillion by my reckoning. Clearly, the U.S. Congress is just a DNC-RNC Globalist UniParty operated by the global syndicate whose multi-decade focus is de-capitalizing the United States. The resulting financial and political instability weakening America's independent middle-class is intended to coerce compliance with totalitarian NWO feudalism.

Any politician, government bureaucrat, transnational monopoly, or private citizen getting in the way of this voracious international wealth harvesting machine learns what the word violence means... or in the gentler case, solitary confinement in a Supermax Detention Facility without visitation rights... or least case, drugged incarceration in a psychiatric facility. We saw this globalist hatred directed at middle class citizens with the antics of Plastic Pelosi's January 6, 2021 goon committee and abusive FBI arrests. *Habeas corpus* is dead in America and *probable cause* ignored on an officially discriminatory, corrupt National Security basis. Additionally, *executive action* in the form of car accidents, skiing accidents, poisoning, bathtub drownings, shooting oneself in the head twice, and falling from rooftops or upper story windows are all methods of *suiciding* employed to encourage harvesting program cooperation.

Obtaining national elected or spurious appointed office in the United States today is not only improbable, but nigh impossible sans a serious control file and global syndicate acquiescence. If an iota of honor remains alive in D.C., or in the unlikely event House and U.S. Senate Members might aspire to participate with we the people of Main Street to overcome the systemic cancer of D.C. Deep State corruption – game theory suggests only one strategy. **Numerical strength destroys the logistic practicality of blackmail and extortion. Easy to coerce a few; not easy to coerce hundreds of Congress persons every year and thousands of Congressional staff.**

BREAKING FREE OF GLOBAL SYNDICATE PSYCHOPATHY RE-QUIRES, **House and U.S. Senate Members to aggregate in a large enough team to logistically dissuade shadow government and deep state operatives from going after families, friends, acquaintances, pets, bank accounts, reputations, etc. Political shock and awe - power in numbers. Assuming ±250,000 - 1,000,000 Elites on earth (I have no idea how many), Main Street outnumbers them 8,000 to 1. Be not afraid! We can shut down *The Few* whenever we choose just by saying NO THANK YOU in large numbers.**

Unfortunately, there was no sign as of January 20, 2021's pseudo-inauguration day of any breaking free, quite the contrary. That said, if any elected officials have the *fortitude* to attempt this honorable course despite Dealey Plaza murder, softball field shootings, and Virginia train crashes, it's imperative they understand our Main Street Patriot support is 100% guaranteed, even to organizing citizen group protection of their private residences, offices, and travel accommodations – and don't forget our local Sheriffs. Together we win! Alone, syndicate order followers crush us; one, two, or several at a time. Evil requires obedience to flourish. Refuse to obey!

The bloated, $5 trillion-plus annual United States' government, captured Federal agencies, corrupt intelligence service leadership, a swath of the covert intelligence side and mis-guided WOKE military elements, along with most transnational monopoly management, particularly in arms, banking, energy, media, pharmaceuticals, and medicine have for decades now, certainly for the past two decades according to Ms. Catherine Austin Fitts of *The Solari Report*,[189] been operating far beyond our Constitutional Rule of Law. For example, we have no idea how many billions of dollars flow annually from NIH and supposed public health service agencies to the Pentagon for DARPA's **bioweapons research** under the guise of medical research. We do know this has been going on at least since the late 1950's and polio vaccine poisoning. This **treaty-violating bioweapon research** is now aggressively turned against U.S. taxpayers who innocently fund it. Can we say **population control?**

Blackmail, hidden spending, black budgets, insider trading, sweetheart deals, and money laundering drive D.C.'s fraudulent engine and much of our U.S. economy with protected impunity; most of it with prosecutorial immunity as the 2022 *course de jour*. As mentioned earlier, I acknowledge good peo-

---

189 "The Solari Report Blog | The Solari Report Blog."

ple in government and we're not discussing their behavior. It's the treasonous blood sucking ticks and leaches we MUST brush off our backs. I do wonder though, if we have so many good people in D.C., why aren't there more whistle-blowers backing up the few marginalized whistle-blowers we do have?

Good people are stuck, sometimes at grave risk within bad systems run by corrupt bosses working for even more corrupt bosses. We see this systemic rot across the CDC, CIA, DoD, Dept. of Energy, EPA, FBI, FDA, HUD, Injustice Department, IRS, NASA, NIH, NSA, State Department, etc. Bank fraud, money laundering, and other financial crimes for instance, are funded and fully protected via the common law doctrine of *sovereign immunity* or via participation in corrupt economic pogroms such as 1934's *Exchange Stabilization Fund*, Bank of International Settlement's *Financial Stability Board, International Monetary Fund* and *World Bank*, not-to-mention, underlying *Bretton Woods* Agreements. According to a Chinese defector interviewed by Michael Pillsbury, for example, the *Chinese Communist Party* learned strategies for salvaging its Soviet-style state-run companies directly from the World Bank.[190] So, who or what is running the totalitarian CCP as a Luciferian inspired pilot program for world domination?

These agreements and boards were drafted by, created by, and funded to serve what the original *Bretton Woods Committee* proudly referred to as **prominent global citizens**. We can rest assured, Main Street houses zero *prominent global citizens*, though we fund and fight their wars, build and clean their estates, toilets, and yachts, build their private jets, trains, limousines, and foolishly name buildings, bridges, and airports after them. Main Street produces the genetically healthy, *non-prominent local citizens* who create the wealth, pay the bills, and leave our young people's blood fertilizing bombed landscapes in far-off resource wars planned by those Elite *prominent global citizens* who profit gloriously from them.

I will cautiously concede at face value, as mentioned by talented researcher and author, Mr. David Talbot,[191] the supposed efforts of John Maynard Keynes and Harry Dexter White at Bretton Woods in 1944, supposedly attempting to get rid of the *Bank of International Settlements* (BIS) as nothing more than a greedy cartel of German, British, and American Banksters usuriously manipulating WW I reparations and other matters for their profitable benefit; ostensibly to be replaced by a more level international playing field intended to be brought about by the new *International Monetary Fund* (IMF) and *World Bank*.

If this was the case at the time and not just more Roosevelt Administration pandering, it gives testament to the international banking/global syndicate's in-

190 "The Hundred-Year Marathon: China's Secret Strategy to Replace America as the Global Superpower: Pillsbury, Michael: 9781250081346: Amazon.Com: Books," 158.
191 Talbot, *The Devil's Chessboard*, 177, 178.

fluence that all three of these institutions are now nothing more than unscrupulous expediters despicably serving international criminal enterprises by laundering narco-dollars, weapons-dollars, etc., then masquerading resource rape and
other crimes as foreign aid. If FDR's Administration was actively part of the
International Fascist scam, so much the worse, but no surprise as the Roosevelt
family via the Delano side made their fortune in the opium trade with established ties to international banking?[192] **And no, I am not a Keynesian economics fan even though his theories have been egregiously abused.** It
appears Earth doesn't even have a "closed" financial system to analyze – certainly not a system for which honest accountants and CPAs can locate a boundary.

The level of money laundering and government protected criminal fraud carried
out by intra-governmental organized crime entities is beyond comprehension for
any decent person. To officially aid and abet globally organized fraud perpetrated by *prominent global citizens;* we have grouped beneath the *Bretton Woods Committee,* to name just a few organized crime facilitating institutions: African Development Bank, Asian Development Bank, European Bank for Reconstruction and
Development, Inter-American Development Bank, International Center for the
Settlement of Investment Disputes, International Finance Corporation, International Monetary Fund, Multilateral Investment Guarantee Agency, World Bank
Group, World Trade Organization; and many dozens more I haven't heard of.

We won't go into stated objectives of these reprehensible New World Order (NWO) institutions because little of what they claim to be or do applies. *Prominent global citizens* always prevaricate for survival reasons. Elites
lie even when unnecessary. Just note that **Oligarchic Pitchfork Avoidance Strategy** (OPAS) or for lessor order-following personages, **Pitchfork Avoidance Strategy** (PAS) are full time activities for pathological *prominent global citizens.* Main Street has the numbers and Luciferian Elites know it.

The only direct or indirect objectives, more or less unstated, though karmically
visible in practice are control and genocide of the *unwashed*; harvesting of Main
Street wealth; laundering confiscated wealth through government programs to
non-transparent, private bank accounts held by, you guessed it, *prominent global citizens*; and of course, engaging in undeclared profitable wars planned by
and orchestrated by *prominent global citizens* and their order followers, of which
all sides are fully funded by loans bequeathed from thin, rarefied air breathed
by *prominent global citizens;* followed by more loans for profitably burying the
dead, and re-building war-ravaged infrastructure generously made available
by – you guessed it, *prominent global citizens*; and finally, wholesale resource rape

192 Karl Meyer, "The Opium War's Secret History," *New York Times,* June 28, 1997, sec. Opinion, http://www.nytimes.com/1997/06/28/opinion/the-opium-war-s-secret-history.html.

usually secured via inappropriate mis-use of diplomatic influence, banking authority, disingenuous aid programs, and misused military power – where any horrific means are justified by the brutal ends, all believably packaged and expertly sold to Main Street by an integrity challenged media owned and operated by – you guessed it again, *prominent global citizens*. This evil play book is ancient, effective, lucrative, bloody, and well worn. It is far past time to throw this disgusting playbook away, along with derailing the nasty creatures using it.

I don't attend the meetings, so have only read, but as touched on earlier, it makes sense that one reason the United States no longer formally declares war is protection of wealthy Establishment family members from indictment for aiding, abetting, and profiting the enemy and themselves via their financial institutions, i.e., treason. If no war is declared, no enemy is formalized other than by the mutant press corpse, so treason isn't technically possible, even while profitably funding, arming, training, and supporting both or all sides of whatever undeclared conflict is assaulting various nations and claiming the lives of *unwashed* young people.

All today's **Designer Wars** as Michael Yon calls them, are profitably planned to serve multi-faceted agendas, none of them beneficial to Main Street. **Pass legislation prohibiting public debt for war funding and voila – war suddenly cannot be financed.** Few, if any citizens anywhere will willingly write checks funding the slaughter of citizens elsewhere for Elite gain and *superpower alignment*, but I digress.

What we're discussing in the above paragraphs is acknowledgment of pure evil, unless discounting rape, torture, ritual sacrificial murder of children, and of course, terrorism and war itself—all of which are interwoven throughout the above outlined program. If we can agree for the moment that evil or at least one form of evil, is restraint of freedom[193] then clearly, we are living in a 21st century spiritual war far superseding what is going on in any material sense.

It is essential for us on Main Street to realize what's happening here, particularly as *prominent global citizens* are brutally slave-driving (pun intended) their order followers to convince us through propaganda, conditioning, and entrainment, our spiritual nature doesn't even exist; much less, that it's threatened by a small, clever, pathological group of dynastically *prominent global citizens* and their virtue challenged order followers for their highly discriminatory, blood-stained lucre.

21st century Elites are nervous, extremely nervous. Truth-bombs regarding sedition, treason, crimes against humanity, and more are being dropped regularly by a few courageous whistle-blowers, who understand whistleblower laws only exist to expose whistleblowers to the rot, so they can be more easily marginalized,

---

193 "The End of All Evil: Jeremy Locke: 9780977745104: Amazon.Com: Books."

threatened, framed, imprisoned, or eliminated. Truth threatens evil, meaning wealthy, comfortable whistle-blowers and safe truth-tellers do not exist. The power addicted Elite world metastasizing for the last 800-years or so is crumbling; and Oligarchic fear makes these already sick people desperate and dangerous.

Check out questionable deaths of researchers working on pedophile related investigations; it is sobering. As deep state false flag events proliferate in frequency and intensity, contrived chaos will increase, meaning coherent Main Street perception will become an important truth determination weapon against divide and conquer propaganda. Together we stand, divided we fall. It is critical we the people of Main Street remain calm and coherent. Correct information is critical, hence the information warfare waged against Main Street. Do not fall into the violence trap – we have the numbers – violence is not required.

Evil can only be vanquished by love, spiritual courage, and generosity. Only a spiritually healthy, morally courageous people can be sufficiently motivated to risk loss of reputation, loss of financial well-being, loss of life and limb, or even worse, loss of family, friends, and pets who may not survive the coming upheaval as we systematically flush the global syndicate down the toilet of history. We are by the way, doing this regardless how many Main Streeters have the presence of mind and courage to participate. We only need 3% to 10% of us to spark meaningful change and if Mr. William Strauss and Mr. Neil Howe have it right in their 1997 book, *The Fourth Turning*[194] – and I suspect they do; we *Prophets* of the *Baby Boom Generation* are now in our elder years and *Crisis* is at hand anyway, so hang on tight. *Millennial* brawn will require *Boomer* wisdom for guidance, though admittedly, *Boomer* courage and guidance to date, has been largely truant.

All human thought is spiritual in nature. The human body, along with all life forms, operate as electromagnetic life-energy systems. Humans are at least 99% spiritual, observably noted by the fact, humans think, and human actions are preceded, carried out, and followed by thought. Any attack on individual thought through mis-education, misinformation, conditioning, entrainment technology, coercion, threats, fear, etc., is a spiritual attack on our person. Laws are based on moral, immoral, or amoral thought processes; therefore, any attack on community thinking constitutes a mass attack on our composite Rule of Law, regardless the morality or lack thereof. This includes any frontal or peripheral attack on Main Street perception.

Note: Adherents of **Primordial Sound Meditation**, of which I am one, believe: "The **Physical Body** is made up of matter and energy. The **Subtle Body** includes the mind (thoughts, desires, and emotions), the intel-

---

194 Strauss and Howe, *The Fourth Turning*.

lect (ideas and concepts,) and the ego (our self-image). The **Causal Body** is our **soul and spirit**. Although, because of the quality of our attention, we tend to think of these three bodies as separate, they are, in fact, all **Spirit**."

CAUTION: The concept of open mind in meditation is dangerous which is why Eastern Religions can potentially be hazardous. Prayer and Meditation can open our awareness to the spirit world inhabited by both good and evil spirits. Going into *meditative silence* unarmed and unfocused can open doors to demonic attack. Good angels respect free will, never sharing knowledge without a person's permission—only by request and with full awareness. Fallen angels will come through any door they can. When people freely open themselves to channeling, spirit (automatic) writing, etc., without focus - no good spirit will take advantage, while demons will jump at the chance to influence that person. There are aspects of Tantric sexual practices, for instance, effectively opening the door to Satanic influence, particularly at deeper levels of practice. Please --- always **pray and meditate** in the name of Jesus Christ, requesting grace, guidance, and protection through the Holy Spirit. Always place your focus on the Word of God and be open to receiving the Word. Never rashly embrace blanket openness to the universe. My personal practice is using the Catholic rosary mysteries or the Orthodox Jesus Prayer for safe focus.

Getting back to it - we are giving up our Constitutionally recognized right to equitable treatment under the Rule of Law by incrementally allowing order-following judges, lawyers, and legislators representing *prominent global citizens* and their transnational monopolies to convert its practice to the more discriminatory, arbitrary, usually mercenary Rule of Man. As mentioned earlier, this is done primarily through outcome-based law, i.e., *Reflexive Law*, which is no law at all.

Under Rule of Man the biggest stick wins; pure tyranny. The trick to Main Street's defeating globalist strategy is realizing the battle isn't financial, legal, political, or even social or cultural. **The core battle is 100% spiritual.** Financial, legal, political, and social repercussions of the battle are effects; by-products effectively generated by winners and losers culminating in cultural gains or losses. We cannot win a war we don't know we're fighting. **Knowledge is power if put to effective use.** Accurate perception, discernment, and coherence lead to effective overall strategy, in turn leading to tactically winning back our freedom. **Effective tactics are fact based.**

Unfortunately, for those still imagining they are free, there is no battle to be fought. These naïve folks need our continuing prayers, but we can win without them. The first American Revolution was sparked in colonial pulpits by British restrictions imposed on foreign trade (Navigation Acts) favoring the *British East India Company* via westward development expansion limits brought on by the Proclamation of 1763 and the Quebec Act of 1774, including 10,000 British soldiers enforcing the restrictions. Adding fuel to the fire were imposition of relatively minor tax increases totaling a mere fraction of taxes paid by British citizens - taxes brought about by the Sugar Act of 1764, Stamp Act of 1765, Townshend Act {tariffs} of 1767, and finally the 1773 Tea Act. Perceived infractions of liberty and unreasonable controls resulted in approximately 5% of the awakened colonial population willing to risk treason and certain death in preference to being controlled by King George III or paying taxes totaling less than 5% of colonial revenues.

Note: Early American history is relevant to this chapter because the British Royal Family is deeply woven into the psychotic warp and weave of Luciferian global syndicate agendas, though perhaps Queen Elizabeth II has recently been turned White Hat? We'll see.

Unredacted history testifies to those perusing such obscure material; any society relinquishing its Rule of Law as justly based on **Natural Theology** is unsustainable. An immoral, corrupt society cannot remain civilized for long, and the United States government has become as immoral, corrupt, and lawless as lawless gets; now a sad, declining, though expensive banana republic run by organized pathological criminals and frightened order followers. Global syndicate pawns pose a menacing threat to freedom, honor, and sanctity of life across the globe, sustained by confiscated wealth of largely uninformed citizenry, among whom I include myself. We must fix this Satanic mess.

Today's Federal, State, and local taxes plus sales tax, tolls, user fees, etc., typically total around 60% of gross income for the average Main Street American family – more than ten times the taxation levels for which our Founders were willing to die. The 2018 Trump Administration tax plan put a tiny dent in this obscene confiscation, but will likely be short-lived; so, we will continue our journey toward financial and even physical extinction unless and until we the people of Main Street stop the Satan Train and change tracks.

Today's Main Street citizen is being harvested and incrementally reduced by Deep State operatives to nothing more than globules of non-thinking, uninformed grease lubricating the spinning wheels of insider corruption and organized crime for the sake of Elite power and Satan's destructive agenda. Our children's future depends on Main Street rejection of *prominent global citizen* lubrication of today's malevolent debt-enslavement systems.

The U.S. exports a discordant dirge of debilitating propaganda, political intrigue, armed subjugation, and economic violence masquerading as opportunity, democracy, and free trade to both friend and foe around the world; though enough millions have now died, suffered, and been robbed, it's getting to be a tough sell. Free trade has become a euphemism for accepting slavery within targeted victim states. At home, we voluntarily vote to enslave ourselves for the so-called common good beneath the hob-nailed lies of National Security and Public Health, sold to us by order-following Pawns of Privilege treasonously representing the world's Oligarchic Elite (*prominent global citizens*).

This debilitating ignorance is further promoted and defended by ignorant media drones and so-called Social Justice Warriors (SJW) incapable of telling up from down, but ready to collect $25/hour for rioting on behalf of *prominent global citizen* order followers for morally bankrupt causes about which they comprehend little if anything at all. Our society is morally bankrupt from the ground up, not from D.C. down. To cure this, we roll it up from the bottom, one fortunately peaceful or unfortunately non-peaceful battle for coherency at a time. Hopefully, our battles will be educational skirmishes sans bloodshed.

If American culture can still be protected from itself and saved from $25/hour hired bigotry and its uninformed cheerleaders for a more human future; it will only be by ordinary people on Main Street; no one else. We must roll this mess up, starting at the mis-educated, uninformed bottom, then working our way to the depraved top.

To accomplish this spiritual renewal, **awakening is required,** re-establishing the moral basis for sustainable American and Global cultures with man-made Rule of Law respecting and enabling our unalienable right to freedom and choice. This is required on the part of each one of us. It is a **2nd American Revolution** and I hope we avoid the less fortunate civil war path and violence in favor of spiritual health and generosity of moral reasoning; a choice we will or won't make together. Not choosing is choosing enslavement.

Our joint failure in this important and necessary spiritual task ensures continued expansion of societal chaos, with chaos leading to tyranny and tyranny to slavery. We've entered the era of subtle, though increasingly aggressive New World Order (NWO) digital enslavement via mind control techniques and other means, to which our only healthy human response must be NO THANK YOU – or our children's freedom suffocates with our unfairly conditioned *Baby Boomer* generation in a murky, polluted sea of global surveillance, nanotechnology, and centralized cryptocurrency tracking.

Crypto-fans and crypto-speculators probably don't care much for my take on cryptos, but I can't see why clever puppeteers haven't or won't fully centralize what appears on the glossy digital surface, to be highly de-centralized. BIS, IMF and even NSA have been studying and planning the imposition of digital currencies for ease of tax collection, tracking, and increased centralized control since at least 1996. Cryptos are created by 1s and 0s on a computer after all, so can be hacked as can autonomous vehicles.

Crypto coupons are tracked. Every transaction is recorded on the blockchain. Names and addresses are not required, but an IP address and digital ID are required and are easily located and tracked – therefore, crypto coupons are not anonymous but quite the opposite. **Cryptos are pseudo-anonymous** and from the beginning have only been rendered less transparent via *crypto mixing*, a form of laundering wherein fake IP's and other means are employed to enhance privacy. Companies profitably provide mixing services for this purpose.

The central banking arm of the global syndicate duped us in 1913 with the Fed and other privately owned central banks around the world – all loosely modeled on 1694's Charter for the Bank of England, central bank of Great Britain and Northern Ireland, which I understand is the second oldest bank operating today. For what it's worth, the oldest surviving bank in the world is *Banca Monte dei Paschi di Siena*, Italy's third largest bank founded in 1472 in Sienna.

It's a good bet, despite all the hoopla, nationally approved cryptocurrencies will be centralized, monitored, and controlled regardless the sales pitch. Review the late Aaron Russo's *"Reflections and Warnings"* on YouTube. Perception matters. https://www.youtube.com/watch?v=YGAaPjqdbgQ

Mr. Russo eloquently discusses control of all people via micro-chips, digital currency, global surveillance, etc. The sick beauty of cryptocurrency is the ability to monitor all transactions and simply turn off the money spigot if citizens misbehave. No more outlaws. No more free travel. The late Mr. Russo's video should be viewed by every tax paying citizen. Knowledge is useless unless put into action.

We must freely cooperate with each other; not integrate through coercion or force. Cooperation should never be confused with conformance or uniformity. We can freely cooperate with each other safely and respectfully, while preserving national boundaries, cultures, traditions, religions, laws, etc. WE ARE NOT REQUIRED TO HATE OR KILL EACH OTHER NOR TO TAKE EACH OTHER'S STUFF, despite what order followers of *prominent global citizens* claim. We can create wealth cooperatively – tons and tons and more tons of it. There is no need to compete, lie, steal, hate, or kill for wealth, not to mention we can't take it with us when we pass over; so, compared to eternal spirit, material wealth has no value anyway. We must emphatically say NO to integration within the global syndicate culture of death. We must stop turning our cities into *murder zones*, then blaming each other for it.

Intentionally chaotic multi-culturalism, educational dumbing-down, and forced clash of civilizations; driven largely by multi-faceted *divide and conquer* strategies of *Cultural Marxism*, further enhanced via contrived population swaps of brutally abused, war-ravaged refugees with a few murderous fanatics mixed in, are steadily manipulating Main Street into a desperate state of fear driven bad judgement. We are mistakenly integrating ourselves mindlessly into thinking-impoverished, transhumanist stack-and-pack gulags, mathematically controlled by amorally designed algorithms developed and managed by socially deviant, technological order followers serving pathologically ill *prominent global citizens*.

Do we accept autocratic, spiritually decimating, inhuman digital slavery, creative mediocrity, and impoverishment; or do we stand up, hold the line, and REBEL; cultivating knowledge, spiritual discernment, voluntary group cooperation, and RESPONSIBLE adaptation to human freedom, pursuit of excellence, and shared generosity as is our Divinely granted right?

OR do we accept growing, centrally planned demands for transference as Herbert Marcuse discusses in *One-Dimensional Man*[195], of our individual autonomy and atrophied moral authority to the digitally impersonal operational apparatus of an arrogantly appointed, *New Moral Agent* metastasized on demand by technologically imposed, transhuman irrationality where: "Conscience is absolved by reification, by the general necessity of things."? Why on earth would we accept this de-humanizing tripe?

All excepting Elites and their privileged order followers are EQUALLY IMPOVERISHED. This simple Social Justice fact, recognized by Elitist intellectual, Bertrand Russell is one simple reason totalitarianism has not and cannot sustain itself at any operative level less than world-wide control. The second reason is the collectivist nanny state algebra does not work as it necessarily converges on one-to-one. Main Street perception must be blocked from truth for global New World Order feudalism to come about.

Humans are entrusted by our Creator with caring for God's creation (dominion). We cannot live up to our responsibility as a species with the psychopathic global syndicate in charge. Satan's chosen task is destroying creation, not saving creation. We must say NO THANK YOU to Satan's syndicate.

---

195 Marcuse and Kellner, *One-Dimensional Man*, 79.

Globalism, with twisted sisters, Marxism and Fascism are
incarcerating humanity in a
Satanic Transhuman Gulag called
Human 2.0.

21 • Transhuman Fascism

Remedy: Reject the metastasizing WEF TRANSHUMAN MATRIX.
SAY NO THANK YOU to the Friendly Fascism Trap of pathological
leadership, manufactured conflict, divisively incoherent Cultural Marxist Orthodoxy, group-think identity politics, dystopian delusion, and financial enslavement. We The People must realize and embrace what
no transhumanist can: our GOD CONNECTION is not of material
essence. Machines cannot touch it or break it. We sometimes mutter
"it is what it is", accompanied by a despondent shoulder shrug empha-
sizing the deeply conditioned deception, "we're powerless to change it".

Hogwash! THE WORLD IS NOT WHAT IT IS. OUR WORLD
IS WHAT WE CHOOSE TO MAKE OF IT. We must care-
fully and vigilantly choose our course, acting wisely, with discernment—then act accordingly. Never allow duplicitous, socially deviant
Technocrats working for pathological dynastic family agendas to make
choices for us. Pathological choices do not produce *happy-ever-after*
endings. Voting for Globalist lies does not make them come true. Fascist subjugation is not a fairy tale. An elected Dictator is still a Dictator.

A major component of transhuman technology and *full spectrum dominance*
is HUMAN-MACHINE INTERFACE technology (HMI). For the curious, check out U.S. Patent 6,965,816 B2 issued to inventor Richard P. Walker
November 15, 2005; assigned to Kline & Walker, L.L.C., Potomac, Maryland. The *Internet of Things* (IoT) encompasses many dozens of patents,
but foundational to weaponizing the internet are patents like Mr. Walker's patent: PFN/TRAC SYSTEM FAA UPGRADES FOR ACCOUNT-

ABLE REMOTE AND ROBOTICS CONTROL TO STOP THE UNAU-
THORIZED USE OF AIRCRAFT AND TO IMPROVE EQUIPMENT
MANAGEMENT AND PUBLIC SAFETY IN TRANSPORTATION.

My speculation: Cloaked in comforting language is an electromagnetic networking system foundational to the **Internet of Things,** atmospheric ionization,
Space Fence and 5G related technology. Mr. Walker's patented human-machine
interface extends to mobile telephony and beyond, though I don't see mention
of 5G in the 170-page patent document. If or when protocols and technology blanketed by this patent, supposedly for transportation purposes, are implemented by the U.S. government, ~~every manufactured electronic device~~ MUST
provide transmit/receive capability to coordinate with command control at Colorado's NORAD and/or any extended base of military operations stipulated.
This is *full spectrum dominance,* which in pathologic hands locks the prison door on
world freedom and throws away the key. This is happening. This is not a drill.

Mr. Walker includes the following nonsense in his patent document.

*"This quote is taken from the Handbook of Robotics, 56 edition and should be integrated in
any programming construct or an operating system when writing code for any mindful machin-
ery in the future. It is a good conceptual basis for artificial intelligence to write constitutional code
to, an optimum logic tree for shared Human/Machine control scenarios and for total robotics.*

The Three Laws of Robotics (for any artificial intelligence):
*1. A Robot may not injure a human being, or, through inaction, allow a human being to come to
harm.*

*2. A Robot must obey the orders given it by human beings except where such orders would conflict with
the First law.*

*3. A Robot must protect its own existence so long as such protection does not conflict with the First or
second Laws.*

*Obviously, a peacetime model, war, hostilities, and homeland security will have programming applicable
to that threat and those applications. (A sad human reality) But the reason for the following PFN/
TRAC innovations for today's air travel."*

Note: The *Handbook of Robotics* has the audacity to suggest *writing constitutional code to an optimum logic tree* while openly discussing methodologies intended to
control or at least override human decision making without Main Street knowledge or consent − a brazen logical affront to constitutionally recognized freedoms. Is this delusion or Luciferian deception? In any event, the United States

government with other governments around the world are jointly implementing these protocols and this technology. Rights to Mr. Walker's patent have moved on since Kline & Walker days, so I'm not current as to who's doing what – BUT – in any case, what if U.S. taxpayers are uncomfortable with these patented processes and prefer technological transparency? Well, that no longer matters does it. **Questioning D.C. policy today is called domestic terrorism.**

A spiritual battle for the soul of humanity is raging across planet Earth and beyond. Technocrat Ray Kurzweil, for example, speaks of the spiritual reality of consciousness but believes consciousness arises from the material reality of neurons, brain activity, and so on. He believes humans are becoming more godlike and are now exponentially expanding godlike qualities of intelligence, moral goodness, beauty, etc. Kurzweil, Elon Musk, F. M. Estfandiari (FM-2020), Nick Bostrom, Max More, Yuval Harari, Natasha Vita-More, and other transhumanists believe the human body MUST be *augmented* by rebuilding it as part machine; that by 2030 or so, humans will be hybrids, part human and part machine, i.e., *Human 2.0*. With respect to Main Street information censorship and consent of the governed, this delusion has serious consequences, particularly if we are already nanochipped.

Doctor of Osteopathy, Carrie Madej and hundreds, if not thousands of other practicing physicians and researchers view this spiritual delusion as melding biology with technology and artificial intelligence[196] whereby humanity is extincted with replacement by controllable cyborgs (my words). *Gain-of-Function* research for example, paid for by taxpayers is driven by military science, not health. SUCH WEAPONIZATION IS OPENLY TOUTED BY THE CHINESE COMMUNIST PARTY's PLA with U.S. agency funding. Bioweapons research is routinely funded by organizations like *National Institute of Allergy and Infectious Diseases* (NIAID), a branch of the *National Institutes of Health* (NIH) not to create medicine, but to study and create disease. *Unwashed* population reduction, nanoparticle controls, and enormous profit bundled into one easy peasy Satanic package.

New or modified forms of corona virus, HIV, smallpox, or E. coli bacteria for example are engineered in the lab, determining how to activate new disease among human populations as well as making them more infectious and more virulent. Fake vaccines are developed and marketed supposedly to counteract these new lab-created viruses, but evidence shows new toxic JABs reduce victim immunity to disease requiring profitable boosters in perpetuity. How is this not insane? Our military is not purposed as an arm of medical research to save people. Military purpose does save people by de-

---

196 endtimetalks, "TRANSHUMANISM / HUMAN 2.0," *End Time Talks* (blog), January 3, 2021, https://endtimetalks.com/2021/01/03/transhuman-human-2-0/.

fending them, but trains to do so by killing attackers. Common sense suggests a virus invented by military science is a bioweapon, not medicine.

Dr. Carrie Madej explains on her website and in speaking engagements: "how Big Tech collaborates with Big Pharma to introduce new technologies in the coming vaccines, that will alter our DNA and turn us into hybrids. This will end humanity as we know it and start the process of transhumanism: HUMAN 2.0. The plans are to use vaccines to inject nanotechnology into our bodies and connect us to the Cloud and artificial intelligence. This enables tech giant control of corrupted governments, without us being aware of it."

Such spiritually abstract transhuman philosophy embraced as religious theology, encapsulated in the words of Ray Kurzweil, Elon Musk and so many others are a **study group echo** heard repeatedly in euphemistic statements and planning documents issued by global syndicate affiliates like the *World Economic Forum*, *World Bank*, *United Nations*, various *Round Tables*, etc. Main Street is surrounded by Scientism's demonic parrots and *Young Global Leaders* spreading deceitful godless cosmology across the planet – not to save the planet, but to destroy it, though they may not know it.

As of this writing evidence is mounting internationally, that so-called COVID vaccines contain among other things, magnetic nanoparticles. Ongoing experiments demonstrate these forms of nanoparticles can be used to manipulate animal behavior remotely. Magnetic nanotheranostics, for example utilizes remote control of functionalized magnetic nanoparticles (f-MNPs) by means of alternating low frequency magnetic fields (AMFs) as a therapeutic tool.[197] Unfortunately, a tool easily weaponized. A tool for computerizing human beings. A tool now in active deployment on Main Street.

Such nanotechnology, since it can be permanent once injected, has no place in health care, particularly for a fraudulent WEF Dream Scamdemic correlated to the non-diagnostic capability of a nonspecific CPR test. We should be asking if these injections can lock victims into **remote control** through low frequency vibration of transmitted dark energy? **Love and other positive vibrations occur at relatively high frequencies, so why the fascination of Scientism with low frequencies?** We must ask, does Main Street opinion matter in Washington D.C. or at administrative levels of government? Have Boards of Health killed **clinical medicine** for prioritized *enforcement* of Big Pharma-Big Medicine profit as EVIDENCE BASED MEDICINE enabling global syndicate control over the Hippocratic Oath? Does Main Street

---

197 Yuri I. Golovin et al., "Theranostic Multimodal Potential of Magnetic Nanoparticles Actuated by Non-Heating Low Frequency Magnetic Field in the New-Generation Nanomedicine," *Journal of Nanoparticle Research* 19, no. 2 (February 11, 2017): 63, https://doi.org/10.1007/s11051-017-3746-5.Namely magnetic nanotheranostics using remote control of functionalized magnetic nanoparticles (f-MNPs

still possess any right at all to knowledge, disclosure, and consent regarding our doctor–patient relationship and medical protocols? Unfortunately, these questions are asked and psychopathically answered daily. I just asked above if government cares what Main Street thinks anymore. The provable answer is: NO! GOVERNMENT HAS NO INTEREST IN MAIN STREET THINKING OR INTERESTS. For Elites, Main Street is a slave paddock housing *human livestock* from whose productive labor, created wealth is harvested.

In September 2014, Dr. Martin Gilens, Professor of Politics at Princeton University and Dr. Benjamin I. Page, Gordon S. Fulcher Professor of Decision Making at Northwestern University published jointly, an article describing their analysis of among other things, U.S. voter preference against public policy decisions and so-called Representative legislation over a period of decades. This work was conducted in terms of: "Each of four theoretical traditions in the study of American politics—which can be characterized as theories of Majoritarian Electoral Democracy, Economic-Elite Domination, and two types of interest-group pluralism, Majoritarian Pluralism and Biased Pluralism—offers different predictions about which sets of actors have how much influence over public policy: average citizens; economic elites; and organized interest groups, mass-based or business-oriented."[198]

Professors Gilens and Page were able to make both qualitative and quantitative evaluations, drawing subsequent conclusions based on quantitative statistical inputs. In their own words: "By directly pitting the predictions of ideal-type theories against each other within a single statistical model (using a unique data set that includes imperfect but useful measures of the key independent variables for nearly two thousand policy issues), we have been able to produce some striking findings. One is the nearly total failure of "median voter" and other Majoritarian Electoral Democracy theories. When the preferences of economic elites and the stands of organized interest groups are controlled for, the preferences of the average American appear to have only a minuscule, near-zero, statistically non-significant impact upon public policy."[199]

As a practical matter, Main Street has no voice or representation in Washington D.C. THIS IS TAXATION AND SUBJUGATION WITHOUT REPRESENTATION OR RECOURSE. If you are a *prominent global citizen* or an order following NWO drone, this is fantastic. If you inhabit Main Street USA or Main Street anywhere else, much less fantastic, probably unexpected news though skepticism toward corrupt centralized government is trending upward.

---

198 "Gilens_and_page_2014_-Testing_theories_of_american_politics.Doc.Pdf," accessed February 22, 2018, https://scholar.princeton.edu/sites/default/files/mgilens/files/gilens_and_page_2014_-testing_theories_of_american_politics.doc.pdf.
199 "Gilens_and_page_2014_-Testing_theories_of_american_politics.Doc.Pdf."

Many U.S. voters are becoming aware how little value Main Street preferences have in Washington D.C., their own State legislatures, and more surprisingly, at the local government level. **Insider special interests' rule – nothing else matters.** I imagine this to be the case elsewhere around the world. Gilens and Page add doctoral credence to this intuitive community sense of Main Street political futility. Gilens and Page do not speak to motivation, but clearly our world is ruled by psychopaths and run by order following drones with psychopathic tendencies.

It is in Main Street's interest to shed light on reasons for this policy dichotomy and lack of Main Street voice within supposedly representative government. Are potential remedies for American loss of self-governance available? The United States is a Fascist Administrative Dictatorship ruled by global syndicate deep state operatives beneath Shadow Government dictates via rhetorically opposed political Parties offering the illusion of choice but sharing one Globalist agenda. Shadow Government is itself ruled by elite dynastic family members through interlocking corporate directorships and less obvious means.

In 1980 Bertram Gross described *The New Face of Power in America* as *FRIEND-LY FASCISM.*[200] At the time he was accurately focused primarily on the Right, though the paradigm has shifted Left since then with the Establishment Right just place holding. The global syndicate likes to mix it up, keeping Main Street off balance to more easily propagandize confusion, such as holding the unfocused focus on moronic Monday Night Football kneelers. Friendly Fascism is operationally analogous to laundering drug money. Our CIA and its drug cartels wash drug money through business fronts so financial record earnings appear legal. Friendly Fascism works much the same way. Government does not risk pitch forks by mandating censorship of free speech, poisoning air and water, or approving nutritional toxicity. They contract that stuff out to multinational monopolies who get 'er done without Congressional oversight or accountability.

In 1932 Mussolini stated, *"Fascism should more properly be called corporatism because it is the merger of state and corporate power."* Today's less openly barbaric Friendly Fascist money laundering model is expensive, time consuming, and for multinational monopolies and their Big Banks, managerially wasteful. Bribes, extortion, blackmail, threats of violence, etc., necessary for greasing legislative and judicial skids are unseemly, though entertaining for Elites. The cumbersome laundering system necessary for propagandizing and funding fascist control of Main Street is being incrementally replaced by less expensive, less pitchfork risky electromagnetic tools—transhuman tools. Monopolists, though wasteful are often clever.

---

200 Gross, *Friendly Fascism.*

Transmit/receive antenna technology is being nanowired directly into every eugenics surviving Main Street slave without knowledge or consent. Brute force is being updated by transhuman technology and Main Street is paying for it. How can such a thing be happening and so many of us not know it? How is truth so capably hidden from hundreds of millions on Main Street?

The U.S. has a Globalist Uni-Party political system internationally owned and operated by a global syndicate associated with dynastic families, some bearing names like Agnelli, Alba, Astor, Bernhard, Bundy, Cabot, Cushings, Doria, DuPont, Finck, Freeman, Giustininiani, Goldman, Hambro, Kennedy, Kuhn, Lambert, Lazard, Li, Lizzetto, Morgan, Oltramaire, Onassis, Orsini, Ortolani, Payseur, Pierpont, Perkins, Rockefeller, Rothschild, Russell, Sach, Schiff, Schroeder, Seaf, Springs, Van Duyn, Warburg and of course, others of lesser note including Bush and Harriman. This is by no means a complete list of dynastic families, nor does inclusion here signify level of power held or participation in Luciferian inspired behavior.

Note: The only power dynastic families have over us is their Luciferian influenced talent for convincing Main Street to say YES. We turn off their power over us by saying NO THANK YOU. Have no fear, just say NO – but that's not so easy to do, is it?

There are families I've never heard of wielding significant power in today's world. Entire books are written attempting to document these families, their relationships, and activities. We'll not delve into such matters here. **We are discussing principles and values, not who-done-its.** Additionally, we cannot leap to conclusions about persons bearing one of these family names as being somehow evil or even involved in untoward activity. All persons must be fairly appraised on individual merit and behavior, not supposition or allegation. We are innocent until proven guilty—at least we once were.

None-the-less, we should be aware these dynastic families exist and are active in today's world. Black Nobility wealth and power are provably built on a Luciferian foundation of ritual sacrifice, dis-information, division, hatred, chaos, war, and resource hoarding. Their ruling end-time is near, but they will not leave history's stage quietly. It is our responsibility as *we the people* of Main Street to coherently assist their leadership exit from the world scene; then ensure our leadership replacements are more spiritually healthy.

Wealth and power shift generationally between dynastic families as the only worldly constant is dynamic change, i.e., evolution. Global deception, domination, and Main Street harvesting are ideologically perpetuated through gnostic cults such as the Fabian Society, Rosicrucian's, Unitarians, P-2 Masonry, National and World Councils of Churches, and others employing global educational indoctrination through the **study group system** of foundations, trusts, endowments, associations, think tanks, and NGO's. Hundreds of secret societies serve as recruitment/hazing/conditioning platforms. The global syndicate is bound by three primary *New World Order* (NWO) governmental forces; *Wicca-Masons* (Marxism), *Black Nobility* (descendants of old Roman Emperors) and *Maltese Jesuits*. It appears each of these three entities have 13 representatives on the 39 Member **Bilderberg Board**. *Note that the adjective Black in Black Nobility refers only to dark character traits, not skin color – and no, not all Jesuits are evil.*

In turn, our modern world is ruled by three incorporated city-states; Vatican City, City of London, and Washington D.C., with the Vatican primarily handling human beliefs; the City of London focusing on banking and commerce; and Washington D.C. providing military and diplomatic power to support fiat currencies and resource rape across the planet. **These city-states answer to no one outside the dynastic families whose interests they represent.** *Unwashed commoners,* are just commodities, *human livestock* to be exploited, traded, or discarded as over-supply or shortages dictate. Large banks also stand outside transparency. UK's *HSBC, Banca del la Svizzeria Italiana* (BSI) in Lugano, not quite in Italy or Switzerland, as well as *Bank of International Settlements* (BIS) in Basel, entry into which the Swiss government must be granted permission to enter are three examples.

International banking figures prominently in nearly all activities undertaken by dynastic families, though developing transhuman control systems will modify this paradigm. Note that many employees and staff associated with the three city-states are decent, though uninformed, compartmentalized people, not knowingly complicit in evil actions of their bosses. The above-mentioned global syndicate owns and operates both the Democrat and Republican Parties of the U.S. via indoctrination, entrainment, career trajectory, greed, money, influence, press coverage, blackmail, and fear.

The pathetic, supposedly representative Republican - Democrat paradigm is now a deceitful UNI-PARTY control system intended to be ineffective for Main Street, while emulating the illusion of choice. Centralization in all guises at all levels of government, media, and publishing is the primary vehicle growing non-transparent, unaccountable governance, while effectively isolating the order-following Ruling Class from Main Street understanding and the Rule of Law. **Reflexive Law,** i.e., **Outcome-Based Law**, **National Security, and now Public Health** are protective walls behind which career parasites steal and maim with impunity, usually as an emergency. Main Street cannot even see who's doing what... or to whom.

Unfortunately, centralization masks United States' officials who actively work with international interests such as the British Commonwealth, China, Russia, and Iran, to name four. This subversive behavior is bringing about the demise of the U.S. middle class in service to the NWO Agenda. The Obama and Biden Regimes on behalf the global syndicate, have and still do aggressively augment UK, Chinese, Russian, and Iranian interests over U.S. interests. For instance, these Administrations openly collude with China's Hundred-Year Marathon for establishment of global Chinese dominance. I use present tense because this treason is ongoing. We don't declare war any more, but treason is still treason.

Michael Pillsbury, in *The Hundred-Year Marathon* explains how two Colonels in the *People's Liberation Army*, Qiao Lang and Wang Xiangsui, co-authors of *Unrestricted Warfare*, address how best to attack American vulnerabilities. Mr. Pillsbury states: "instead of direct military action, the authors proposed nonmilitary ways to defeat a stronger nation such as the United States through **lawfare** (that is, using international laws, bodies, and courts to restrict America's freedom of movement and policy choices), economic warfare, biological and chemical warfare, cyber attacks, and even terrorism."[201]

Mr. Pillsbury's eye-opening book based largely on personal experience white-washes official American complicity with China's long-term strategy as state-craft naiveté. Mr. Pillsbury is after all, a CFR member. None-the-less he incisively and convincingly paints a threatening picture of deceptive Chinese intent. I point this out because powerful politicos at city, county, state, and Federal levels of American government as well as transnational CEO's openly play ball with 2000-2020 election fraud as well as the bioweaponized COVID Scamdemic and toxic injections called vaccines in its wake. The asymmetric COVID attack has serious nanotech transhuman implications, made worse as it appears COVID is just the sales pitch for mandating immunity weakening, squalene laced, synthetic mRNA injections. Experimental injections are illegal until a National Emergency order is issued. We may recall, squalene was found as one cause of *Gulf War Syndrome*, yet here it is again, FDA approved.

Evidence shows asymmetric attacks, COVID, and election fraud, originate outside America's borders, fitting seamlessly with the asymmetric warfare model outlined in *Unrestricted Warfare*. China is not the only nation engaging asymmetric warfare against the United States. Open information sources suggest significant numbers of American officials are engaging sedition and treason by enabling and/or covering up the nature of these attacks. Constant D.C. lies, MSM misinformation, and social media censorship make it difficult for Main Street to visualize what is happening, leaving citizens at a loss regarding how to defend themselves against this outrageous abuse of centralized power working alongside attacks on our national sovereignty, and of course, our health.

---

201 "The Hundred-Year Marathon: China's Secret Strategy to Replace America as the Global Superpower: Pillsbury, Michael: 9781250081346: Amazon.Com: Books," 116.

Centralization conveniently lends itself to top-down control of intertwined institutions it permeates. Centralization is the enemy of transparency, accountability, and self-governance. Big Government = Centralization = Hazardous and should be avoided. Political leaders promoting government solutions for issues are not our friends and cannot be trusted as they are compromised, delusional, or both.

Most government solutions are or become methodologies for harvesting taxpayer wealth for re-distribution to various insider connected entities, with military, infrastructure funding, Social Security, Medicare, Obamacare, welfare, and foreign aid being just seven. Those most cared for and looked after by our federal government, including in other countries are also the poorest of the poor and remain so generationally. This is not accidental. Poverty is big control, big business, and big evil.

Evidence suggests every American Federal Agency is compromised by Satanic global syndicate infiltration. No exceptions remain, with those promoting **transhuman augmentation** comprising the most dangerous and worst of the worst. Suppose the global syndicate realizes its Luciferian vision of eliminating all but 500 million or so humans. 500 million slaves vastly out number Elites, so the remaining *unwashed* are still problematic unless controlled. Privileged Elites realize they gain little via population reduction alone. Their Satanic impulse demands 100% control of all life on earth. Few Elites realize this control serves the Satanic agenda for destruction of all creation and nothing else. That said, for the immediate future, transhuman technology just adds to more historically established means for corrupting and abusing power. Please realize we are not predestined victims here, but only with God's help can Main Street stop this Satanically influenced attack on creation.

The transhuman agenda is a Fascist agenda of covert destruction. Fortunately, it is still reliant on ignorance, fear, and corrupt politicians for enactment. Most voting adults understand *selected* Representatives serving a diverse constituency must still attempt or at least look like they attempt to balance policy decisions amidst a field of divergent views and preferences among their constituencies. It must appear they govern from near the center or middle ground of this statistical variance. Such finger-pointing variance, however, also provides cover for targeted lies. Providing such cover is erratically problematic, hence the advent of Extremely Low Frequency (ELF) radiation experimentation. ELF mimics brain wave frequencies, enabling *bioelectric entrainment*, manageable by adjusting frequency, wavelength, etc.[202] As entrainment technology in global syndicate hands grows more invasively powerful, political cover will no longer be necessary.

---

202 McRae, *Mind Wars*, 136.

Constituent optics are today a fact of successful representative political life vexing for every voter and every representative on nearly every issue. Conflict is accepted as a normal aspect of life, at least political life. Lying is tolerated as a practical necessity, even expected. Self-governance is messy and difficult. It demands responsibly vigilant participants to actively realize balanced benefits despite conflict and misinformation. Selling compromised Representatives to Main Street today, requires electromagnetic assistance through television flicker rates, alpha entrainment, and other transhuman means far beyond propaganda and outright lies because Main Street can recognize lies, accepted or not.

Before AI entrainment, in a perfect world, once elected, a candidate is honor-bound to represent all constituencies to the best of his or her ability, though pleasing all constituents all the time is impossible. There are then, particularly within a two-party system, winners and losers for lack of better terms on nearly every issue. Despite both George Washington's and John Adam's strenuous objection to formation of adversarial political parties; we do have political parties and for the time being, must slog through the sometimes-hostile muck they create to wrestle in; a tedious task as there is only one globalist agenda despite pandering rhetoric.

I doubt Adams or Washington envisioned two political parties funded and operated as an indoctrinated study group WEF UniParty by the same global syndicate's *prominent global citizens*—though they wrote a constitution capable of refuting such an occurrence—if or when enforced. Disparate Party irrationality is effectively obscured by entrainment technologies alongside fear-based distraction emanating from threats of war, violent false flag attacks, medical fraud, supply chain disruptions, etc.

Why transhumanism? Three primary reasons.

1. Programmed arrogance of Transhumanism Proponents is intended to eventually destroy creation – the primary Satanic agenda – an agenda ignored by techno zealots.

2. Along the way transhumanism makes slavery practical again. A slave is his or her own collateral. If a slave gets sick, dies, or disappears, both the investment and its collateral are damaged or lost. Transhumanism renders every Main Street slave an antenna connected directly to ionospheric command-control. This provides inescapable auto-tracking capability solving the vanishing financial collateral problem from a business standpoint. Slaves can no longer disappear across a jurisdictional border, vanishing into the night and may even get sick less often, though can be turned off if somehow outlawing.

3. Managing the political illusion of choice while maintaining only one enslavement agenda without provoking common sense revolt on Main Street is tricky. If not professionally managed, pitchforks could show up. Elites don't like to work hard, and they don't like pitchforks. Transhumanist AI ingested or injected into the human body eliminates this problem because human consciousness, perception, free thinking, and behavior can be digitally monitored, adjusted, and controlled. Illusion of choice becomes NO CHOICE.

Republicans like Reagan, Bush I, and Bush II pander as Constitution respecting patriots but regardless personal views, rule as criminally organized Fascist pawns. Democrats like Clinton, Obama, and Biden openly disdain the Constitution, talk like Nanny-State Marxists but rule as organized criminal Fascist pawns. This is the **ILLUSION OF CHOICE**. **Different rhetoric; one enslavement agenda;** but difficult and costly to manage over time, always at risk for Main Street revolt. Transhumanism eliminates unrestrained perception, free thought, and coherent logic. Problem solved. President Donald Trump, the first President since JFK to condemn the evils of Globalism in our lifetime does not fit this paradigm and is a book of his own, not yet written.

The popular left/right paradigm, both sides disingenuously fascistic, is a classic Luciferian logic trap wherein artfully contrived conflict showcases two readily identifiable paths to seeming resolution of a pre-arranged conflict. Both paths are attractively packaged, are rhetorically appealing to demographic constituencies on both or all sides; and both are unable to resolve anything; in fact, the opposite. **Enormous power and big money lie within unresolvable managed conflict, not resolution.** As in medicine, disease isn't cured, it is treated as endlessly and expensively as possible. At study group *Round Tables* like the *Council on Foreign Relations* (CFR), for example, conflict is discussed in terms of management, not resolution. Solutions yield limited profit and little political capital.

Money and power lie within the problem, so **problem stagnation** must be maintained for as long a profitable time as possible. We find in this paradigm a profound *divide and conquer* strategy guaranteeing long-term, irresolvable, sometimes escalating, *controlled conflict* overcome only when victims realize potential solution(s) lie between the opposing false choices popularly presented. Main Street realization of this process is slowed or prevented by many billions of pain/pleasure brainwashing dollars spent annually by Elite foundations, trusts, and endowments along with corporatist advertising. This is Hegelian dialectic and managed conflict at their geopolitically strategic best, though the ideologically darkened roots began growing eons before Herr Hegel's time (1770 – 1831).

Given no two humans possess equal strength of intellect, character, creative ability, emotional stability, ambition, environmental circumstance, physical capability, etc.; it follows human equality exists only in spirit, with material equality of opportunity limited to analogy and academic comparison. Socialist/Fascist/Monopoly/Mercantilist coerced or forced outcomes negate all opportunity for Main Street, thereby providing, contrary to false promises, equally distributed mediocrity. If this thinking has merit, then personal freedom characteristically must result in conflict at least some of the time.

If I as a person refuse to respect your freedom or vice-versa, we will likely have conflict or in the case of nations, war. Mr. Roger Scruton discusses this in detail, opining: "People depend on others, and also need to be free from them. Freedom means conflict; community requires that conflict be peacefully resolved. Hence negotiation, compromise and agreement form the basis of all successful human communities."[203] Interestingly, this philosophy of community is theologically expanded by late Orthodox Father, Dumitru Staniloae throughout his 1994 work, *The Experience of God*,[204] a book worthy of serious study.

Human conflict is inevitable given the plethora of personality archetypes, not to mention cultural variation, political dissent, divergent religious dogma, moral rectitude, or the Divine plan for spiritual unity itself within the battle between good and evil; but expression of conflict certainly isn't limited to Fascist bigotry or narrow-minded *us and them* antipathy. Fanaticism and intolerant zeal are behavioral choices, conditioned or not.

As Scruton goes on to say regarding rational persons; "Both parties must be free – that is, able to make choices, to act intentionally in pursuit of their goals, and to take responsibility for the outcome. Each party must desire the other's consent and be prepared to make concessions in order to obtain it."[205] Respect for each other's freedom then, is essential to healthy community. We cannot create or sustain abundant personal life within our societies without mutual respect since refusal to recognize each other's created infinite value leads directly to imposing needless limitations on each other, ultimately becoming self-limiting. Transhumanism abrogates mutual respect automatically as perception and thinking are trampled beneath programmed electromagnetic forces. That said, ideology still plays a significant role in cultural harmony or lack thereof.

---

203 Roger Scruton, *An Intelligent Person's Guide to Philosophy*, First American Edition (Allen Lane The Penguin Press, 1996), 67.
204 Staniloae, *Orthodox Dogmatic Theology*.
205 Scruton, *An Intelligent Person's Guide to Philosophy*, 67.

❊

We are taught in many cultures, certainly American culture, our most expeditious path to national survival lies in proactively competing with other cultures for resources. In other words, competing and winning. This anarchic logic trap, along with Mercantilism, Monopoly Capitalism, Marxism, Socialism, Fascism, and Globalism as fake alternates in denial of creative power, reaching their sad zenith in the hubristic futility of *Malthusian Scarcity* preached in virtually every high school and university in the Western world. Propagandized in juxtaposition with *Social Darwinism* and *Cultural Marxism,* this is a knockout combination providing foundational context within which transhumanist ideology thrives.

These false doctrines become a spiritual knock-out punch when we as individuals believe we lack power and ability to effect change, have no real choices to make, and are unable to define our own choices anyway. This subtle undermining of personal worth and God given creative power is the basis of disempowering liberalism, eventually leading to complacent enslavement, i.e., agreement to be taken care of by... whom, a patently false promise.

The zero-sum, unwinnable battle for stale crumbs gives local culture and healthy nationalism a bad name, but unfortunately is the only concept taught within the hallowed halls of Cambridge, Oxford, and Ivy Clad conditioning centers across the pond, all obediently trod by Elites and their order followers, uniformly subscribing to self-declared, top tier status within the *Social Darwinist* evolutionary order. Creation of abundance is an unknown concept in Elite circles of influence; a shame since Elites have controlled so much of *common man's* destiny for so many centuries, though inadvertently have also provided nearly endless opportunities for *commoner* spiritual growth for which I as a hard learner am thankful. Cup half-full as my beautiful wife might say.

Prominent global citizens are generationally imprinted and rigorously indoctrinated to believe in their Darwinian superiority and are meticulously schooled in techniques of bribery, blackmail, prevarication, fraud, theft, violence, and threat of violence as means overcoming a stunning inability to create and a lazy, entitled predisposition toward easy-money, easy-power, and unsustainable negative returns on investment. In other words, they must steal to survive.

Elites are also conditioned beyond all doubt as to the Darwinian inferiority of Main Street commoners, the usefulness of slaves, and the perfect suitability of Main Street citizens as *human livestock,* though that terminology is publicly avoided. Modern Main Street must never understand they are slaves. The more robot-like the slave, the easier to manage; hence propaganda, conditioning, entrainment methodologies, and use of quality pharmaceuticals bringing about compliant Zombie-like behavior. Evidence abounds as we surround ourselves with unhealthy petri-dish face diaper conformance. To all this we can pile on the powerful controlling force of the computerized, AI, transhuman, man-machine interface being covertly developed by *prominent global citizen* order followers. The nano-version of a *Neuralink* perfected slavery system is at hand.

Are there exceptions to the negative characteristics of *prominent global citizens* and their obedient order followers? Of course, but not observed holding positions of integrated power and influence in commerce, education, media, Hollywood, government, upper WOKE military echelons, or intelligence/surveillance circles. Note that *prominent global citizens* falling *study group victim* to Luciferian influence are, depending on extent of influence, themselves enslaved to self-hatred, thereby enabling and delusionally justifying hatred of others along with their deeply rooted compulsion to hurt, cause pain, and destroy.

This unbalanced circumstance behooves Main Streeters to generously educate *prominent global citizens* as to the enormous mutual benefit to be shared by creatively and entrepreneurially engendering sustainably cooperative positive returns on investment. **Malthus was wrong.** No easy task as sharing is an unknown concept among Elites who are taught to piratize for survival. Cooperation must be taught to Elites as they aren't going away anytime soon and their present collision course with destiny is extincting the planet through non-transparent, ionized, electro-magnetic, *full spectrum dominance*. Becoming teachers requires we on Main Street overcome our own heavily conditioned, delusionally comforting, group-think ideologies and begin exercising open-minded perception of reality, including acceptance of our own spiritual nature. Neither Left nor Right are intrinsically evil. Evil behavior is a choice.

I still imagine prayer in the name of Christ and reason to be tools capable of saving psychopaths from their Luciferian demise, but there is little evidence for my view. History suggests psychopaths must be defeated and removed forcibly from power, though prayer expedites processing so remains a necessary toolbox component.

Human survival demands understanding that ***full spectrum dominance*** means just what it says. It is not a cute academic term or convenient DARPANIAN military phrase. *Full spectrum dominance* means full and complete dominating control of EVERY person, place, and thing on planet Earth and beyond.

In the interest of *full spectrum dominance*, the punitive constraint of zero-sum, group-think conditioning typical of fascist political parties is extended primarily by, though not limited to, conditioned academic experts across various thematic venues controlling useful narratives via statist media and the **study group system**. One of the most popularly accepted narratives is the onerous, left/right, liberal/conservative political paradigm, where participants on both or all sides of the mud-slinging free-for-all are routinely propagandized and/or entrained to believe only one answer, or in more complex scenarios, a narrow range of answers are possible for managing carefully scripted issues.

All scripted solutions to scripted issues offered are not only guaranteed to fail but often ensure increasing chaos and extensive *mass frustration*, while potentially generating even more problematic, sometimes violent offshoot issues in profitable justification of ever-increasing, stringently centralized government surveillance and control. Making people ill with an engineered COVID Bioweapon to justify financial devastation along with mandating population reducing toxic JABs, used in part to fearfully divide vaccinated from non-vaccinated is a recent example. *Mass divisiveness* is planted, cultivated, and nourished until fully entrenched in targeted societal groups, where conformity is effectively enforced via fear and aggressive group-think peer pressure. Divisiveness is not only useful, but profitable, and for Elite psychopaths, fun to play with.

Financially, many of us sadly recall sock-puppet, Barry Soetoro obediently reading his teleprompted chorus for, *"building ladders of opportunity upward to the middle-class"*, prominently parroted on the disingenuous White House website, while in real Main Street time from 2009 to 2017, middle-class family income and pension income declined in juxtaposition with steadily rising costs for transportation, housing, education, health insurance, health care, groceries, and other basics. Upward middle-class mobility on Main Street was slaughtered over eight years, while vastly increasing the income gap publicly maligned by Obama himself. Inflation has been devouring Main Street spendable income for decades until the Biden Regime supercharged surge. Per http://www.shadowstats.com/, "January 2022 CPI-U annual inflation hit 7.48% [up from 7.04% in December], the steepest inflation pace since February 1982 (in 40 years); the ShadowStats "Corrected" Alternate CPI estimate hit 15.63% [up from 15.15% in December], the steepest inflation rate since June 1947 (in 75 years)."

On the security front, we again saw Main Street drowning in propaganda and outright lies. Global syndicate order follower, Soetoro schizophrenically bragged that al Qaeda was vanquished and on the run, while stating on November 16, 2015: "What I'm not interested in doing is posing or pursuing some notion of 'American leadership' or 'America winning.'"[206] In reality, during Soetoro's first term, al Qaeda expand-

---

206 Lieutenant General Michael T. Flynn and Michael Ledeen, *The Field of Fight: How We Can Win the Global War Against Radical Islam and Its Allies*, Reprint edition (St. Martin's Griffin, 2017), 114.

ed dramatically in recruitment, training, and capability across Pakistan, the Indian Subcontinent (AQIS), and in Africa's Libya and Somalia via related terrorist entities. Expansion of Islamic terror was covered up as *moderate rebellion* by legacy media, our WOKE military leadership, the late U.S. Senator, John McCain, and Washington D.C.—all functioning synergistically as weapons of Fascist domination.

I pick on and raise these Obama Regime financial and military failures to demonstrate how information can be restricted or made available to functionally create perception bias on Main Street. **Manufactured bias** can be used by transnational monopolies, corrupt politicians, and agency administrators to manipulate Main Street behavior in favor of special interest agendas that may or may not be to Main Street's benefit. In today's cyber world, **weaponized information** is a formidable control lever for steering public behavior. It may well be **the primary tool** in the mass population control toolbox, power of which should not be underestimated. This is particularly true when such bias is enhanced by unseen electromagnetic entrainment.

Obama rode to the White House on a magic media carpet criticizing capitalist failure and injustice in his order following quest to organize and cement nanny state compliance in Main Street's mind set. His feral dishonesty lies in the fact capitalism does not exist in America's rigged financial system. Fractional reserve banking is rigged. Political protection for criminally fraudulent banking practice is rigged. Access to and cost of affordable capital is rigged. Every stock, commodity, or other equity market is rigged. Interest rates are rigged. Economic boom and bust cycles are rigged. Government regulation is rigged discrimination. Taxation is preferentially rigged. Government spending is rigged. Theft through foreign aid is rigged. Confiscation of wealth created by American workers is a rigged guarantee of impoverishment for Main Street. Government rigging for monopoly benefit and Main Street fleecing is insured by rigging elections. **The mere suggestion of free market capitalism functioning on Main Street America is childish nonsense.**

Syndicate pawn, Obama rigorously maligned syndicate pawn, Bush II's globalist policies, then promptly put those same policies on steroids to cheering admiration of millions claiming to detest Bush. It is a deviously crafted strategy in which Obama and other Presidential Pawns in turn play their global syndicate, mid-level management part, a self-fulfilling prophesy for Main Street socio-economic failure - particularly since the stagflation of the 1970s, capping Main Street wages until The Donald upset the paradigm in just four years. This status quo system ensures Elite gains in power are established, maintained, and wealth transference from Main Street to *prominent global citizens* are uniformly expedited. The entire travesty is sustained by uninformed or corrupt Party-line votes for corrupted or soon-to-be corrupted candidates of two pathetic parties obviously serving a single consent agenda: The Uni-Party NWO Establishment Agenda of Elite Oligarchs, who then stuck us with imbecilic CCP Biden in 2020.

Mockingbird media along with covert programs like the FBI's unconstitutional COINTELPRO begun in 1956, corrupt political districting, and manipulated electronic voting enable the global syndicate's preferred globalist candidate to win national election prior to any Main Street vote being cast. **Winners are selected by the syndicate not elected by voters.** This aside, prior to electronic voting, though the process continues today, candidates were and are pre-selected via the study group system by the Establishment for constituent consideration by nonparticipatory precinct strategy, compromised preliminary support, financial strings, and corrupt media processes, so only candidates toeing the global syndicate line successfully run for office. Selection demands compliance.

The political winner matters not one iota as the only candidates offered are confirmed globalists, differing only in meaningless Party rhetoric. This explains the non-existence of policy change despite aggressive rhetoric in the U.S. power hand-off from Comrade Bush I to Comrade Clinton to Comrade Bush II to Comrade Obama. Not sure about President Trump who appeared as an outlier, but then Comrade Biden came whining back with Main Street earned income dropping more than 13% his first five months in office. Gasoline prices rose 43%, lumber up more than 100% and so on. The swamp was back on child trafficking steroids.

The Donald may be a genuine populist? Too early to tell as I write this, precisely which faction of the global syndicate President Trump is tied to, though the Bush I – Clinton – Bush II – Obama Crime Regime – and now imbecile Biden, all tied to Black Hats are no longer arguable. As I write this our 2022 U.S. economy is crumbling to WEF ashes.

Washington D.C. has only one globalist agenda. Consider a foreign aid example as we pass the half-decade mark since Hurricane Matthew clobbered Haiti (Oct. 2016). This criminal enterprise via Bill Clinton's leadership role in Haiti failed to make potable drinking water available to areas damaged by Hurricane Matthew. How is this even possible given the billions of dollars spent... or disappeared? Is this corruption also related to child sex trafficking and/or organ harvesting? Where did the billions of dollars go – clearly not to Main Street Haiti?

Both child sex trafficking and illegal organ harvesting activities spiked in Haiti since its 2010 earthquake and 2016 hurricane. A cholera outbreak began several months after the 2010 earthquake and was further exacerbated by the lack of fresh potable water since 2016. I've read cholera kills via bacterial infection primarily within the small intestine, but most other organs are largely unaffected... meaning those other organs are suitable for profitable harvesting and international sale. Is lack of potable water in Haiti happenstance... or something more sinister? I don't know, but some researchers believe something more sinister. Weaponized weather maybe? I'm just offering Fascistic Dots for connection as MSM is complicitly silent on Haiti.

Another Obamanomic middle-class wealth transfer echoing past global syndicate military/industrial business cycles, was obliteration of the U.S. military over eight years, so Barry's successor to the syndicate's mid-level management throne could spend trillions re-building it. We saw this with Carter/Reagan and again with Clinton/Bush II. This fraudulent process, cloaked in political diversity with Democrats decimating our military followed by Republicans profitably building it back is now an accepted, routine business cycle. How powerful is the media machine, that most Americans are oblivious to this fraud? Unfortunately, moronic WOKE Generals can't be fixed by money.

Main Street gullibly accepts such outright fraud as a normal cycle, rarely asking questions about the enormous financial theft hiding in plain sight every other decade. Is this malfeasant practice treason? I get it's a dangerous world and arms companies must be profitable to provide their products, but do not get why it can't be done honestly – on the table instead of dishonestly – under the table? Most Main Street inhabitants will support their own security without being lied to, myself included.

The same situation exists in medicine. A medical clinic purchases expensive equipment, assumedly to better serve its patients, then pushes patients who don't need certain tests or treatment into using it to pay for the equipment. Obviously, if the equipment isn't used, it can't be billed and can't pay for itself. Not a difficult economic issue to grasp. We all want quality medical care, but there are more honest ways of effectively bringing healthy medical economics to fruition rather than health insurance duplicity and fraud. The fraud is assuredly many times more costly than increased charges predicated on legitimate expenses. Medicare fraud alone is estimated to cost taxpayers $1 billion per week, i.e., more than $50 billion annually.

One reason vast sums of Elite wealth pick-pocketed from commoner wealth-producing labor is spent on adversarial-by-design, political party support is convenience of corruption and blackmail, insuring divided and conquered Main Street voters never have any meaningful voice in government – and just as importantly, fail to realize they have no voice. The two false Parties provide permanently alternating scape goats, so no one's the wiser to Globalist UniParty agenda reality. While liberals and conservatives tear bitterly at each other's indoctrinated throats over an endless array of manufactured, highly emotional issues, Elite order followers just keep on keepin' on with their population reducing, uninterrupted wealth transference program from productive, working *middle-class livestock* to their unproductive Elite handlers and privileged selves.

Transhuman aspects of this conditioned coverup are handled via indoctrination and entrainment distributed primarily through dopamine enhancing social media, the allure of Hollywood, Woke professional sports, and pornography. We should inquire why pornography is addictive for so many. Is it really that interesting or just entrained addiction? In the middle of all this are our pervasive U.S. Shadow Government intelligence services. This is crucial information, as CIA culture has been anti-Christian, i.e., anti-Constitutional since its 1947 inception. If CIA culture is anti-Christian, then what belief system underlies its foundational culture? This question should be answered as many decent CIA operatives are trapped in this citizen victimizing quagmire.

Anyway, the continuous electromagnetic mirage obscures theft of Main Street wealth documented by economist Dr. Mark Skidmore at $21 trillion dollars since 1998.[207] Add to this, another $35 trillion bailout dollars distributed to trans-national banks and monopolies by the George W. Bush and Barack Hussein Obama Administration's Federal Reserve Criminal Enterprise and you have $56 off-book trillion and change vanishing - a more than significant motive for keeping Main Street citizens distracted by manufactured disaster capitalism events, contrived false flag theater, and other crimes against humanity we see in Afghanistan, Haiti, Iraq, Israel, Libya, Somalia, South Africa, Syria, Ukraine, Venezuela – and now at home on Main Street USA. Made in America so to speak. Total off-book U.S. debt is easily ±$86 trillion not including ±$200 trillion more in unfunded mandates for pensions, Social Security, Medicare, and Medicaid. Does importing uneducated, poverty-stricken illegals make sustainable sense?

With implementation of FASAB 56 in 2018 during the freak show Justice Kavanaugh hearings, government agency finances went dark, so we can't know for sure how much larger this stolen pile of wealth has grown, nor how fast it's escalating under the *Biden Freakshow*. There are no reliable public records accounting for where our tax dollars and digital debt money goes or to whom. Federal accounting processes are now legal lies, not self-governing information.

This insidiously divisive paradigm carries with it, multiple harmful appendages promoting failed socialist policies, monopolistic trans-national cro-

207 "The Solari Report Blog | The Solari Report Blog."4,20,"schema":"https://github.com/citation-style-language/schema/raw/master/csl-citation.json"}

ny capitalism, de-stabilizing multi-culturalism, and moronic identity politics. These tools are wielded effectively as bigoted clubs, pounding the unwary into orthodox submission or risk being labeled racist, homophobic, misogynistic, or some other degenerate classification. Nowhere are these ugly appendages advocated more vituperatively than on many of today's heavily corporatized, intellectually disgraceful, academically vacuous, university campuses where unbridled bigotry masquerades as nuanced brilliance and foundation money constitutes mind-numbing grist for tenured hordes of *useful idiots*.

Ms. Amy L. Wax, Robert Mundheim Professor of Law at the University of Pennsylvania, in a speech delivered at Hillsdale College on December 12, 2017, tells us: "Academic institutions should be places where people are free to think and reason about important questions and issues that affect our society and our way of life – something not possible in today's atmosphere of enforced orthodoxy." Ms. Wax goes on to suggest disagreement should be by reasoned argument, not by "hurling slurs and epithets, name-calling, vilification, and mindless labeling".[208]

This academically common, narrow-minded, professorial bigotry aggressively breeds systemic student intolerance, until as Mr. Ben Shapiro, lawyer and commentator notes at bigotry's extreme limit (my words): ***through identity politics***; **any differing opinion or even mere questions are perceived as violent attacks against one's person.** This suggests despicably corrupt Republican and Democrat Parties are a discourse discouraging Uni-Party trap breeding identity confusion in young people and across every sector of society. Bigoted ethnic or faked racial diversity should never be confused with diversity of free thought or opinion.

Noted author, Mr. Matthew Continetti, editor in chief of the *Washington Free Beacon*, speaking at Hillsdale College on October 24, 2017, tells us: "The beginnings of identity politics can be traced to 1973, the year the first volume of Alekandr Solzhenitsyn's *Gulag Archipelago*—a book that demolished any pretense of communism's moral authority—was published in the West. The ideological challenge of socialism was fading, its fighting spirit dwindling. This presented a challenge for the Left: how to carry on the fight against capitalism when its major ideological alternative was no longer viable?

The Left found its answer in an identity politics that grew out of anti-colonialism. Marx's class struggle was reformulated into an ethno-racial struggle—a ceaseless competition between colonizer and colonized, victimizer and victim, oppressor and oppressed. Instead of presenting collectivism and central planning as the gateway to the realization

---

208 Amy Wax, "Are We Free to Discuss America's Real Problems?," *Imprimis* (blog), January 18, 2018, https://imprimis.hillsdale.edu/are-we-free-to-discuss-americas-real-problems/.

of genuine freedom, the new multiculturalist Left turned to unmasking the supposed power relations that subordinated minorities and exploited third world nations."[209]

Cultural Marxism's *Scientism, Multi-Culturalism, Critical Race Theory,* and *Identity Politics* together, regardless original intent, have become bitterly divisive tools, slicing and dicing remnants of every good or noble thing remaining in American and European culture. There is no more intolerant ism than the targeted, judgmental, so-called tolerance of Progressivism espoused by the Liberal Left and enabled by the WOKE Establishment Right. The Democrat Party for example, is the Party of Diversity – provided there isn't any – while Establishment Republicans place hold for Leftist bigotry. God help any luckless Democrat minority member expressing an independent thought or a professor conducting legitimate independent research. The complicit Republican Party Establishment on the other hand simply enables undermining our republic while standing for nothing beyond pandering excellence. Two rhetorically fruitless, hollow choices serving one Elite enslavement agenda confined within a multi-cultural barn, on the heavy door of which hang greasy padlocks of identity politics and irascible bigotry. Intellectual padlocks manufactured by the indoctrinational success and academic failure of American education.

Since the 1990's, unable to obscure the abject failure of collectivism, global syndicate handlers have piled on the latest Leftist craze, the lie of **Critical Race Theory**. This academic weaponization of bigoted ignorance brings together a simmering amalgamation of emotional **linguistic alchemy**. The alchemy combines as Mr. Christopher Rufo, Founder and Director of *Battlefront* tells us, *"equity," "social justice," "diversity and inclusion,"* and *"culturally responsive teaching,"*[210] into a lazily palatable form of Neo-Marxism enforced by Fascist intimidation. *Equity* of course, translates as mandated Marxist impoverishment having nothing to do with *equality* as used in our *Declaration of Independence*.

Exchange of ideas and rational discourse are impossible within the intellectual confines of *identity politics'* hostile, chain-link hexagon. Add to this dismissive mix, an attractive assortment of well-dressed, articulate media pundits willing to say anything for money and recognition; and the probability of Main Street citizens being motivated to rationally discuss practical solutions for anything at all predictably circles back to zero. Fascist dictatorship feeds on contrived conflict its Marxist sister manifests on poorly informed, study group dumbed-down Main Street. This blatant subterfuge cannot exist outside the

---

209 Matthew Continetti, "The Problem of Identity Politics and Its Solution," *Imprimis* (blog), November 17, 2017, https://imprimis.hillsdale.edu/the-problem-of-identity-politics-and-its-solution/.
210 Christopher F. Rufo, "Critical Race Theory: What It Is and How to Fight It," *Imprimis* (blog), April 13, 2021, https://imprimis.hillsdale.edu/critical-race-theory-fight/.

coma of *mass formation*. It therefore must be augmented by more aggressive, less obvious means. Transhuman technologies fill this need by slamming the door on self-awareness, but simultaneously raise an Elite logistical problem.

For transhumanism enslavement to thrive and take hold, it must first gain a solid footing. This foothold must either be deceptively popular or remain disguised and hidden for implementation to proceed. Main Street will not knowingly and willingly enslave itself. Consent of the ruled must be obtained by force or deception. Force is a no-go because it's logistically problematic for the few to force the many. Deception then, is the way with information warfare, lawfare, and entrainment as the means. In this information warfare game, short-term media propaganda is first base; Hollywood long-term conditioning is second base; institutional lies and educational dumbing-down are third base; transhuman AI entrainment, coupled with nanoparticles and electromagnetic human-machine interface are the home run.

Outside Main Street exceptionalism, such zero-sum globalist enslavement tautology becomes mathematical certainty; a generationally binding indoctrinational maxim to which all Elites and their trained order followers must adhere with strict gang-like compliance—think AGENDA 21. Enforcement effectively reduces the objectively rational to subjective psychopathy. Echoing *Washington Post* subsidiary, *Newsweek's* February 2009 headline, "We're All Socialists Now"; we must ask, "Are We All Stupid Now?" We fail to see the blackmail control buttons because MSM media pundits openly defend pedophilia, refuse to report on child sex trafficking, and ignore child ritual sacrifice, all practiced in Elite circles across the globe including Western Europe, Australia, and the United States. Blackmail and threat of violence throw a blanket gag order on official public discourse regarding abused children. Is there any limit to hidden depravity Mainstream media lies will not support?

The Marxist Obama Regime built chain link cages for internment of illegal immigrant children prior to **slavery sorting** at various locations along the U.S. Southern border. Many of these kids were sex trafficking and/or future organ harvesting victims. Not a Press Corpse word about Washington D.C. coordinating and sharing expenses with criminal cartels. Donald Trump is elected President in November 2016 over career criminal Hillary Rodham Clinton and the Press Corpse explodes in a lying frenzy, shrieking about Trump Administration abuse of children.

Fast forward to January 2021's Joe Biden and Kamala Harris and their gender-confused freak show fraudulently invading our White House and within the first one hundred days of illegitimate office, more than 20,000 children are incarcerated at the U.S. Southern Border on top of one another so tightly packed, they are forced to sleep on their sides to fit on cold concrete floors of sorting prisons. At the same time, millions of unidentified, unvetted illegals flood into America. The sycophant Press Corpse defends this brutality and planned chaos suggesting border issues are complex. This invasion is well orchestrated as an asymmetric attack on the American middle class by the global syndicate and is a prime example of D.C. treasonous culpability. The treasonous Biden Regime is also flying and busing illegals and unvetted Islamic peoples into and across the United States, depositing them mostly in Red States. The U.S. southern border's child sex trafficking doors as well as narcotics trafficking doors have been blown off their hinges by the global syndicate's Chinese owned and operated Biden Regime. This is not self-governance; however, if we are decent people, we will fix this on our watch. At most we have two or three years to do so before the Transhuman door closes.

Speaking of Islam, **Anglo-American Establishment Fascism** profitably invited the West's newest war with Islamic terror, so Main Street has no choice but defensively kill murderous Jihadists and win to survive. Islamic Jihadists are so unreasonably Satanic in belief and behavior, they may be irredeemable, so as a practical matter I concur with General Michael Flynn and other experienced intelligence and combat veterans. Islam must be handled. The new invitation for war was extended by the Establishment West engaging in Middle Eastern resource rape beginning with BP's parent corporation, *Anglo-Persian Oil Company* (APOC) at the turn of the twentieth century. There have been periods where power balanced more or less equitably, but overall, who can blame Middle Eastern nations for being frustrated or failing to comprehend who their existential WEF enemy actually is?

That said, Islamic Extremism is re-invading what we call the West anyway for Caliphate re-establishment as they did originally against the Greeks, Romans, Jews, and early Christians.[211] The only difference being today's Islamic invasion is covered over by so-called refugee population swaps orchestrated by global syndicate order followers. Given the waves of Islamic hatred, litter, embittered chaos, rapes by so-called refugees, and rising murder rates in Western cities, Islam uniformly proves itself incompatible with civilized culture wherever it invades.

Fascism creates and focuses exclusively on winners and losers – on managed conflict. Financially speaking, compete versus create plays a role in the centralized control continuum. Within competitive sporting arenas, or strategy intensive games like Go, Chess, Mancala, Bridge, Poker, and

---

211 Raymond Ibrahim and Victor Davis Hanson, *Sword and Scimitar: Fourteen Centuries of War between Islam and the West,* Illustrated edition (New York, NY: Da Capo Press, 2018), 9–12.

others; or when defending our lives against unreasonable violent attack, I personally favor high levels of mastery and achievement along with over-whelming force as the best offense and defense. Evasive tactics or powerful defensive force in response to unreasonable violent attack are prudent reactions. We cannot help anyone or make our world better if we are slaughtered.

In the case of strategy games or sport, however, the key word is achievement. If Susie checkmates Jimmy in a well-played game of Chess; there's a vast, though perhaps subtle difference between characterizing Susie's victory as *kicking Jimmy's butt*, or *praising Susie's developing mastery of a difficult game*. In the first instance, BEATING Jimmy is emphasized, whereas in the second; hard work, focus, learning, and developing strategic and tactical skills are emphasized – and for the smart alecks - I don't mean skill at KICKING JIMMY'S BUTT.

Culturally speaking, we tend to teach uni-polar *them and us* strategies rather than multi-polar *we* strategies. I get this as I'm competitive, so can't pose as the conciliatory paragon of compromise; but that said, can we wonder, why do we focus on beating and winning rather than achievement and accomplishment as goals? Even when achievement is a primary goal, as in figure skating, gymnastics, or a spelling bee, it tends to be couched in terms of winning—of beating someone else. In either case, personal development, skill mastery, working hard, and paying the practice price are necessary ingredients to becoming the best we can be whereas winning by itself is singularly punitive for the loser. Achievement is, or at least can be mutually beneficial.

Even Mr. Pavel Tsatsouline,[212] former Soviet Special Forces instructor and Subject Matter Expert to elite U.S. military and law enforcement special operations units - a man making combat survival instruction, with power, endurance, and strength training a way of life, teaches a combination of old school and new school Russian strength training – not as working out, but as various methods of practice – going to work every day with the intent of developing skills, proficiency in which, enable building exceptional power, strength, and endurance for professionals whose livelihoods rely on such things. How many of us think of brute strength or endurance as learned skills?

A crucial aspect of teaching strength as a skill implies a learned ability to focus applied levels of power, speed, and intensity appropriately to the task at hand – a perceptively thoughtful martial arts concept. If warriors can be calm and thoughtful, and since we teach billions of ourselves to think one way or the other, maybe we should as a rational species consider ramifica-

---

212 "The School of Strength," StrongFirst, accessed August 27, 2021, https://www.strongfirst.com/.

tions regarding potential for cooperative global freedom as opposed to freedom for *us* and who cares about *them*? Which world do we prefer? Winning, losing, and integrated subjugation; or achievement, accomplishment, and cooperative freedom? Is this a difficult choice? Winning takes many honorable forms, none necessarily punitive, though admittedly, cooperative freedom requires balanced, thoughtful exercise of power as well as transparent honesty to flourish. Never confuse willing cooperation with coerced conformity as Fascist Elites proselytize. Please note, I do not use the terms *cooperation* or *multi-polar* in the disingenuous sense WEF usurps these same terms.

Belaboring the point, humans think in terms of language; implying linguistics and phraseology expand or restrict the scope of reasoning. Linguistic applications at least in part determine whether we are in the box or venture outside the box. This may be a molehill growing into a mountain on my part, but from an engineering point of view, I suspect the distinction between culturally prevalent *winning strategies* versus culturally preferred *achievement strategies* is significant, likely exerting a profound generational effect on overall societal perception, attitude, behavior, and culture.

Speaking facetiously, we seldom find two people in agreement on anything, suggesting agreement among billions of us occupying a spinning rock less probable than driving a C8 Corvette around the sun. In other words, conflict will not be leaving us anytime soon. None-the-less, to the extent as a species, we encourage achievement over winning; one spiritual obstacle to realizing we can create abundance together rather than compete for Malthusian scraps is reduced or eliminated. Our gift of life includes human ability to participate in creating more life and doing so more abundantly. For this **Divine plan** to work, however, respect for each other's freedom and mutual consent regarding the space and way we create are necessary. Invasive transhuman technology powered by Fascist ideology, then packaged with Marxist lies obliterate this potential by bifurcating us from our own created human nature.

We are not required to limit each other's freedom or our own through competitive conflict. It is not a Natural Law. Competition is wonderful and educational, until it becomes destructive. Mutual respect is a more constructive path to cooperative global freedom than mutual competitive restriction can ever be. That said, for now, we must open our minds to the cooperative concept carefully as Elites and others preferring competitive restraint are still in Satanic attack mode, requiring self-defense on our part and education for all sides. A behavioral guide for our *Prisoner's Dilemma* is game theory's *Tit for Tat*.[213] We see President Donald Trump use this strategy effectively on a regular basis.

---

213 Axelrod and Dawkins, *The Evolution of Cooperation*.

Cooperation offered up front in any negotiation is typically the most effective strategy. We can go hard any time we choose, so no need to start there. Even in debate club, with opposing sides, wouldn't it be more productive to discuss ways and means of arriving at multi-polar benefits, rather than the narrower focus on uni-polar winning? What constitutes winning anyway? In war, we end up impoverished, injured, or dead; there is no winning in any real sense as all participants are assured losers to some degree, hence post-traumatic stress disorder (PTSD).

Are conquest, subjugation, domination, humiliation, embarrassment, and ridicule our only conceptual wins, with fear and intimidation the most valuable by-products? My dictionary doesn't say so and this isn't sustainable in a material world of marauding human ego regardless of what Rhodes Scholars proclaim. History proves power difficult to retain. As mentioned elsewhere, **the more violence necessary to maintain a system, the less sustainable the system.**

To drone on a bit more, why is beating each other not only viewed as the exemplary thing to do, but also engenders envy, admiration, and honor among supposed lessor beings? Excepting I suppose Mother Teresa, why do nice guys finish last, earning the derogatory appellation, *loser?* The extreme end of competitive political domination, handily beating Communism (a little poly-sci humor there) would have to be Fascism with its ardent group-think propensity for conditioning even the Anti-Fascists, particularly the Anti-Fascists; to elevate group, movement, race, nation, or ideology above the recognized individual.

And NO, I'm not a fan of participation medals. Sporting competitions are only healthy and educational when effort, concentration, skill attainment, strategy, tactics, and achievement are real. In real life humans learn through struggle, hardship, and sometimes loss—never through free prizes.

Fascism stands resolutely as my 2003, *Merriam Webster's Collegiate Dictionary* suggests: *for centralized authoritarian government, dominated by a dictatorial leader, characterized by severe economic and social regimentation and forcible, even brutal suppression of opposition.* Transhumanist objectives fit this paradigm perfectly. We can argue degrees of Techno-Fascist imposition demonstrated by Washington D.C. order followers of either Party, but few Americans can deny our fascination with popular defense of Left or Right group-think bigotry. We love the battle but should realize if we refuse to stop baiting each other, there is considerable violence in our Main Street future—and we are inviting it.

I read once, not sure where, **"Violence is the last alternative to impotence."** I doubt the author was referencing sexual impotence here and suspect the statement to be valid, at least in the case of cornered rats and practitioners of short-tempered identity politics. Anyway, in our 21st century, marching like savagely impotent lemmings, we blindly follow Reinhard Gehlen's post WW II lead into the 20th century's Cold War, where veteran researcher, David Talbot recalls the Dulles faction of our newly formed CIA, *with its Wagnerian lust for oblivion* nourished by Gehlen's declaration; *we live* "in an age in which war is a paramount activity of man, with the total annihilation of the enemy as its primary aim." Talbot goes on to say, "There could be no more succinct a statement of the fascist ethos."[214] Do we not see this anti-Christian ethos dancing among our corrupt elephants and donkeys in the demented circus tent we call Washington D.C.?

Total annihilation! Now there is a worthy, competitive, Anglo-American Alliance goal or just as inappropriately, with shorter reach, how about Antifa's Fascism by Anti-Fascism goal or BLM's Racism by anti-Racism goal? Reinhard Gehlen you may recall was Adolf Hitler's pathologically sadistic, Eastern Front intelligence chief, responsible for strategizing much of the WW II havoc wreaked on innocent Soviet Union civilians. This in the wake of Stalin's Wall Street funded purges and vast *Gulag Archipelago*. Gehlen was brought to the United States, narrowly avoiding Nuremberg by U.S. military officials, then introduced to Allen Dulles as a potential asset and of course, good family man. Long story short, Gehlen (code name, UTILITY) became the Dulles factions' European *firm* leader conducting Cold War activities against the Soviet *Bear*.

With this Shadow Government "controlled opposition" plan in place, ensconced in secluded comfort of paneled club rooms, international Oligarchs happily foresaw and still foresee no visible end to extended Cold War power mongering and profit taking resulting from their expensively orchestrated global syndicate nightmare. Clinton, Bush II and Obama Regime pawns of the global syndicate for example, labored foolishly and diligently to bring Cold War II to life for their demanding handlers and now the fraudulent Biden Regime is stumbling along as vacuously as it can. Living under *International Fascism* is like being shirtless on a cold winter night, lost on a windy morass, hobbling on a broken leg, listening to famine wolves howl, while Lucifer's soldiers hunt us for dinner. Even anarchy starts looking attractive. *(No offense meant to wolves, rarely, if ever known to attack humans.)* A Fascist future married to a Socialist lie in defeat of non-existent Capitalism is a bleak, hopeless future planned for Main Street by Luciferian inspired psychopaths.

Is an AGENDA 21/30/50 transhuman future something to look forward to? Catherine Austin Fitts believes as of this writing, we have only one or at most, two years to wake up and stop implementation of **transhuman, full spectrum dominance.** Failure to address this asymmetric attack today means implementation of the global syndicate's **space fence control system** is certain, meaning the system steadily being assembled piece by piece for the past thirty or so years

---

214 Talbot, *The Devil's Chessboard*, 278.

will become reality. **The result will be smart cities functioning as electronically controlled slave camps while psychos track every molecule on earth.**

The global syndicate uses non-bloodline sock puppets like Jeff Bezos, Jack Bogle, Sergey Brin, Warren Buffett, Jack Dorsey, Anthony Fauci, Larry Fink, Bill Gates, Ray Kurzweil, Elon Musk, Larry Page, Klaus Schwab, George Soros, Mark Zuckerberg and others to manage its assets, financial power, and geopolitical reach. These pawns are indoctrinated "wise guys" who live well above the law of every country, with protection provided by syndicate handlers. They can be thrown to the pitch forks, however, for failure or misbehavior.

According to Robert Bridge, writing for *Strategic Culture Foundation* in a November 19, 2021 article entitled, *"Did Klaus Schwab Create an Army of Davos "Yes Men" to facilitate his Great Reset?"* – we learn: "in February 1971the 32-year old Schwab somehow managed to organize the first *European Management Symposium* in Davos, which would change its name in 1987 to the **World Economic Forum.**" Incidentally, 1971 was the year the Nixon Administration ended convertibility of the U.S. dollar to gold, more or less ending 1944's *Bretton Woods System.*

In 1992, global syndicate wise guy, Klaus Schwab, with strong ties to Harvard Business School and Henry Kissinger, established *Global Leaders For Tommorrow* which became **Young Global Leaders** (YGL) in 2004. YGL is a prime example of a premier **study group system** indoctrination platform for furthering New World Order enslavement goals. Mr. Schwab brags that arrogant YGL grads permeate multi-national corporate management and government cabinet positions across the globe. In other words, YGL populated governments do not represent citizens—only interests of the DAVOS New World Order cult.

A broad sampling from the 1,400 or so YGL cult member grads to date are: Jacinda Ardern, Annalena Baerbock, Angela Baker, José Manuel Barroso, Maria Bartiromo, Jeff Bezos, Tony Blair, Bono, Kate Brandt, Richard Branson, Sergei Brin, Pete Buttigieg, Pamela Chan, Amal Clooney, Andrew Cohen, Anderson Cooper, Alexander De Croo, Leonardo DiCaprio, Valerie Feldman, Chrystia Freeland, Tulsi Gabbord, Bill Gates, Jean-Claude Juncker, Sebastian Kurz, Ashton Kutcher, Jack Ma, Emmanuel Macron, Angela Merkel, Gavin Newsom, Viktor Orbán, Larry Page, Vladimir Putin, Nicolas Sarkozy, Charlize Theron, Leo Tilman, Justin Trudeau, Jimmy Wale, Niklas Zennström, and Mark Zuckerberg.

Per German economist and author, Ernst Wolff, many YGL grads going on to significant positions in business or government have little experience beyond connection to WEF and psychopathic study group peers. This may explain why so many of these WEF lemmings have difficulty answering unscripted questions when confronted by authentic journalists. Anyway, these are the well protected goof balls pushing **Agenda 21, 30 & 50** along with what we now call **The Great Reset** - a phrase I imagine taken from the name of Richard Florida's 2010 book of the same name, then popularized by the *World Economic Forum* and Klaus Schwab.

This group of indoctrinated global syndicate psychopaths regularly strategize how Main Street people can be dumbed down, frightened, herded into restricted compliance, made ill, or just eliminated in large numbers. Similar to the COVID Plandemic, we saw study group strategy sessions like: *Dark Winter* - 2001; *Atlantic Storm* simulations - 2003, 2005; *Global Mercury* - 2003; *SCK* - 2005; *Lockstep* - 2010; *Mars & Spars* - 2017; *Clade X* - 2018; *Crimsom Contagion* - 2019; *Event 201* - 2019; and *Cyber Polygon* - 2020. These simulated scenarios are about control, global slavery, and mass destruction of creation—whether the psychopaths themselves know it. In any event, their CEO - Satan - does know it.

The cumulative result of global syndicate asymmetric warfare waged against humanity via institutional lies, media misinformation, famine, pollution, information censorship, medical malpractice, biometric surveillance, government sanctioned rioting and looting, inflation, currency manipulation, and rampant unemployment is the take down of Main Street freedom followed by transhuman global enslavement. The CULT of DAVOS is one of the global syndicate's public faces; but the Bosses, like OZ behind the curtain, are unseen.

COVID and its bioweaponized JABs, along with aerosol spraying, and our ionized atmosphere are Earth's introduction to a dreamed of dark Satanic system. Even at it's outset, just for starters, long before goal attainment, this full spectrum dominant system will impose significant restrictions on freedom. It is significant, that a small group of dynastic family psychopaths and their order following corporate, government, and media thugs have zero moral inhibition about planning the painful extermination of 7.5 billion or so *useless eaters*. A billion or two human **COVID sacrifices** for the short-term transhuman common good are easy peasy - just stimulating cheap entertainment and an enormously profitable way to pass time while cruising Hell's Satanic Autobahn.

Is this the spiritually decimated **Neuralink** future we want? If we, shirk our Creator's love, bowing down to this evil, will we ever stand erect again?

Transhumanism Globalism obviates, then obliterates all possibility of human spirituality, cooperation, compassion, empathy, freedom, and love. Since love requires freedom to exist, cooperative freedom is a start toward a better world.

TRANSHUMANISM MUST BE STRANGLED IN ITS CRADLE.

The horrors of totalitarian systems are uniformly evil
BUT the pain of impoverished despair does offer a benefit proving
good can come from bad. Human bondage exposes for those imprisoned, a sliver of light revealing a glimpse of our own weakness.
Such a glimpse, once embraced, leads to
understanding, forgiveness, and reconciliation
with our Creator's love for everyone—jailer and prisoner.

22 • Abundance or Slavery

Remedy: Progressive Income Taxation is slavery at arm's length. The corrupt U.S. Federal government MUST reduce its bloated finan-cial addiction by at least 75% to a level sustained by a single, FLAT RATE CONSUMPTION TAX, preferably on non-essential items, in-stituted and collected through State governments. Even if said con-sumption tax is on every item at a lower rate, it is still a suitably equi-table tax methodology despite its innate bias. The rich spend more, so pay more tax. Abolish the enslaving 16th and 17th Amendments.

There is no abundance without liberty. There is no liberty be-neath unfair taxation (wealth confiscation). Arbitrary, non-trans-parent re-distribution of confiscated wealth from productive Main Street wealth creators to inbred elite parasites funneled out the back doors of Con-gress is slavery. Restraint of free thought is fatal to wealth creation, yet gov-ernments overbalance restraint, strangling their own tax base. As Batman growled, *"They know, they just don't care."* Why? When government grows it predictably becomes self-defensive, abusive, nontransparent, unaccountable, unapproachable, and fraudulent, until nothing remains beyond impoverish-ment strategies and psychopathic adversarial hostility. This is America today.

Parasitic sub-entities grow within Big Government's mammoth non-transparent structure, pathologically grasping for power while feeding on citizen wealth from any corner worth robbing. The more strident-ly rogue elements under protected status of government service claim they serve the public, the more criminally fraudulent they are. A true ser-vant of the people doesn't need to explain they work for citizen benefit.

The result of Congressionally sponsored NWO *Green New Deal* policy for example is the forced return to Medieval Feudalism for Main Street. Unsustainable debt, expensively intermittent, unreliable, or no electricity, inadequate water and food supplies, obliterated supply chains, restricted travel and communications, chaos and fear in the streets, etc. Lack of water, poor nutrition, inadequate transportation infrastructure and intermittent electric power ensure crippling of residential quality of life, while disabling commercial, retail, and industrial capacity to pre-industrial revolution levels. Medical clinics and hospitals will be incapacitated by lack of reliable electricity, supplies, and equipment. Surgery wards and high-tech treatment modalities will necessarily be shut down—available only to privileged global syndicate order followers. Environmental groups bravely lobbying for protected wildlife sanctuaries and habitat preserves will find all non-urban areas declared off-limits – no public access – no hiking, camping, boating, fishing, hunting, etc. Living off-grid will be outlawed and digital money will turn off at predetermined boundaries.

Elected and unelected officials as well as media talking heads shrieking about deep concern for Main Street and how much they care about the *little people* clearly identify for Main Street the most dangerous enemies of the people covering up Big Government threats to Main Street well-being. D.C. UniParty power brokers lobby for abandonment of the electoral college, continued fraudulent electronic voting, and other corrupt measures to serve Marcuse's *Happy Consciousness* agenda. Main Street will uselessly argue politics and cast miscounted and re-counted mail-in ballots, but every vote cast is meaningless anyway as global syndicate algorithms implement predetermined ruling class outcomes defended by *Reflexive Law* anyway.

This is the new slavery, boasted of by Joseph Stalin, stating in 1923 per *Oxford Essential Quotations* (5th ed.) from Boris Bazhanov's *The Memoirs of Stalin's Former Secretary* (1992).: "I consider it completely unimportant who in the party will vote, or how; but what is extraordinarily important is this—who will count the votes, and how."

Interestingly, corrupt pawn, tottering, mentally deficient Beijing Biden stated in July 2021: "It's about who gets to count the vote. Who gets to count whether your vote counted at all? It's about moving from independent election administrators who work for the people to polarized partisan actors who work for political parties.

This is election subversion. It's the most dangerous threat to voting and the integrity of free and fair elections in our history. ... If you vote, they want to be able to tell you your vote doesn't count for any reason they make up. They want the ability to reject the final count and ignore the will of the people if their preferred candidate loses. They are targeting not only people of color. They are targeting voters of all races and backgrounds who did not vote for them."

Though not clear what Beijing Joe Biden meant, two things are clear: 1. Biden's treasonous handlers do not appreciate honest auditing of election results. 2. Biden's treasonous handlers want him to project election fraud targeting and disenfranchising Black and Hispanic populations in major cities onto *"they"*, the hard working, patriotic Main Street MAGA, November 3rd Movement.

I get many of us are intellectually challenged and can be destructive, hence societal restraint is necessary—but how much restraint? China Joe Biden announced on June 15, 2021, a new Injustice Department budget expansion of $100 million to combat **domestic terror**, i.e., citizen free speech and free assembly. On February 7, 2022, Communist HHS Secretary, Alejandro N. Mayorkas issued an updated *National Terrorism Advisory System Bulletin* entitled *Summary of Terrorism Threat to U.S. Homeland.* This totalitarian bulletin declares non status quo free speech an act of domestic terror. So much for the 12/15/1791 **Bill of Rights**.

Main Street is now charged with proactively spying on and reporting anyone appearing to be a *domestic terrorist* who might tend toward disagreeing with D.C. dictums or violence. Clear echoes of Russia, Nazi Germany, China, Cuba, North Korea, and other centers of Leftist Paradise. Domestic terrorism was not defined, but D.C. did promise violence against Main Street citizens to avoid presumed violence by largely non-existent Main Street White Supremacists? I guess the snitching will be on hard working middle-class Toxic Whites who voted Barack Hussein Obama into the White House (unless machines did that)? What is a White Supremacist? If we have any outside the Democrat Ku Klux Klan and Republican Rinos, it looks like they hold positions of Establishment power in Washington D.C. and Blue State Government, not on Main Street USA. D.C. globalist pawns are re-defining and identifying domestic terrorists as peaceful anti-slavery people who work hard for a meager, over-taxed living.

Incidentally, on a larger scale, Sock Puppet Biden's Unholy Regime teamed with 50 other sick nations along with Darpanian tech monopolies *Google, Facebook (Meta), Twitter,* and *Amazon* in an international pogrom called *Christchurch Call* supposedly to stop extremist violence from spreading online. Based on two March 15, 2019, New Zealand anti-gun false flag mosque events, this subversive tactic helps prevent free people from networking together online. This event, likely part real and part hoax, closely resembles the global syndicate play book employed at Columbine, Dunblane, Las Vegas, Parkland, Port Arthur, Sandy Hook, etc. Can Main Street stop this onslaught against free thought, speech, and assembly—or is global high-tech slavery inevitable?

John Adams, speaking to the Massachusetts Militia in October 1798 said, "Our Constitution was made only for a moral and religious People. It is wholly inadequate to the government of any other." James Madison, in Federalist Paper #55 writes, "Were the pictures which have been drawn by the political jealousy of some among us faithful likenesses of the human character, the inference would be, that there is not sufficient virtue among men for self-government; and that nothing less than the chains of despotism can restrain them from destroying and devouring one another."

Clearly the global syndicate intends its pawns to globally alienate Main Street from our Creator's love and spiritual morality, dumb down education, annihilate family cohesion, divide us, then herd us in mass over the devouring Satanic cliff to which Madison alludes. We can choose to awaken spiritually, re-establishing moral self-governance or succumb to impoverished transhuman bondage planned for us.

I am an insufferable spiritual anarchist viewing every action I take between myself and my Creator; so, in my fairy tale world there are no queens, kings, or governments - beneficent, corrupt, or otherwise; no despotic powers; no religions; certainly, no centralization of any kind; no need for titled land; no armies to kill each other with; and no reason to kill each other anyway. We embolden, strengthen, and love each other, not diminish each other. The result is a fairy tale world flourishing into unimaginable abundance – it would be fun – BUT – that isn't how humans roll and that isn't what our world is, is it?

If humans were more interested in creating fresh, nutritiously delicious pies we would enjoy together (wealth creation) instead of limiting ourselves to one ontologically disgusting, stale Malthusian pie, then fighting (competing) bitterly for a tiny, hackneyed slice or a few moldy crumbs – we could live abundantly in my perfect world of spiritual anarchy in peace, with only occasional minor disputes; secure in each other's compassion, care, and loving generosity. If I care about you and you care about me; we will find a way to resolve our differences because love motivates each of us to act in the other's best interest. It is not complicated, yet seemingly beyond reach though maybe in Heaven?

We choose instead to live together differently. This means a morally driven spiritual anarchy, appealing as it is to idealists like me, requires moral people, which apparently, we do not aspire to be, so spiritual anarchy and any other forms of anarchy are a no go. Since we largely abandoned Main Street morality and wrecked our Constitutional Republic leaving its bleached skeletal remains for Marxists, Fascists and now WEF Transhumanists to squabble over, I suppose a beneficent monarchy would likely be the next best management choice, but historically, we refused to play nice under that system as well.

Human experience limits remaining choices as governing systems all seem to sprout transparency issues. The tendency worsens when the ism or ology model is predisposed by psychopathic management toward centralized, top-down control, selfish domination by the few, and ultimately, subjugation of commoners ending in slavery or its slightly less brutal alternate, serfdom. For reasons I don't really get if not Satanic influence, human leaders tend toward non-productive *power and rule* rather than healthier, more productive *power and serve*. It's a shame, but there it is. Life could be a heck of a lot more satisfying than we make it, though this outcome requires overcoming Satanic influence, i.e., rejecting evil, in turn requiring a healthy relationship with our Creator.

Any successful venture capitalist can confirm the importance of team over project concept. A good team can make a poorly conceived project successful. A weak team will likely ruin even a well-conceived project. **Analogously, our societal ism or ology is much less an issue than our team's moral authority or lack thereof, under which our ism or ology resides.** A strong, spiritually healthy, moral people can make a lousy system work, whereas a weak, spiritually unhealthy, immoral people will quickly ruin even the best of systems. If we accept this premise, then obviously a pathological, socially deviant management team running a delusional, genocidal project agenda for morally bereft citizenry is the worst of all worlds. Sadly, this is our current 21st century circumstance and we regularly vote to keep it going… or maybe dead people and voting machine algorithms do that for us?

Leaders should serve their people by governing in a moral, just manner, not subjugate people by ruling on behalf self-aggrandizing agendas; BUT that is apparently not an appealing concept for anyone, anywhere. Making the situation magnitudes worse is the self-subjugating conviction among many that we the people of Main Street should be or even have a right to be, TAKEN CARE OF… apparently by saints or experts of some sort. This dismal delusion ignores the inescapably obvious. A functionally healthy person being TAKEN CARE OF by others is little more than a domesticated barn animal; and if forced to work for care, a slave. Only intellectual vacuity denies the obvious by mistaking integrated enslavement for cooperative freedom; yet this dogma predominates bigoted university teaching.

Our 21st century world is a violently impoverished, chaotic gauntlet peppered with occasional bright spots of free life because the major countries of earth, certainly the G20 are ruled by pathological order followers representing and working for criminally insane dynastic family members in whose bloody hands lie monopolized control of banking, energy, education, scientific inquiry, publishing, media, medicine, food production, and of course, government and the military/industrial/surveillance complex, all powerfully integrated within a voracious plutocratic fantasy to rule everyone and everything. **Full spectrum dominance**. We can say NO to this parasitic societal infection by voting order-following pawns out of office and not buying monopoly products or services; or we can forcibly wipe the parasites out, though Elite eradication isn't a solution.

To gauge problem scope without dwelling on it, according to author Dean Henderson[215], per annual 10K Filings of Fortune 500 Corporations with the *U.S. Securities and Exchange Commission* (SEC); the **Four Horseman of Banking** *(Bank of America, Citigroup, JP Morgan Chase, and Wells Fargo)* are among the top ten stockholders of nearly all Fortune 500 companies. These same four banks in tandem with *Banque Paribas, Barclays, Deutsche Bank, Goldman Sachs,* and a few other European old money behemoths also hold controlling interest in the **Four Horsemen of Oil** *(Exxon Mobil, Royal Dutch Shell, BP, and Chevron Texaco)*.

We might inquire who holds controlling interest in this dozen or so gargantuan banks, but will find our scrutiny blocked, even under *Freedom of Information Act* (FOIA) requests, beneath protective cover of so-called **National Security**. We might recall truth does not hide but power often does. This National Security hoax goes on in all major nations. Consider the irony of being enslaved within our own country by despotic National Security policy invoked by so-called representatives we voted for—or machines did.

Note: *In today's mega-transnational monopoly world, holding less than 5% of a mega-company's voting shares can provide controlling interest. Consider BlackRock, Vanguard, State Street, and Berkshire Hathaway investment funds for starters.*

Special mention must be made of the City of London's, *Hongkong and Shanghai Banking Corporation, HSBC Holdings.* Incorporated in March 1865, this multinational Hongkong institution deemed systemically important by the internationally corrupt *Financial Stability Board*[216] was literally founded on the back of opium and slave trades. *HSBC* stands today as Europe's 2nd largest bank.

Aside from who owns what and despite how poorly man-made government and laws seem to work out for Main Street, it does not appear we can live together without laws. Assuming some level of leadership is necessary to civilized society, even on a tribal level, if we wipe out the *ruling criminals* by whom we are subjugated this morning, they will be replaced by new criminals this afternoon. Why? Because if we don't learn anything in the meantime, why would we fail to replace our present psychopaths with new psychopaths? Since we vote for, pay for, and/or accept pathological leadership now, we need look no further than ourselves to uncover Main Street's root corruption problem.

---

215 That isn't really us is it?
216 Wolfe, *Crisis by Design.*

Obviously, we the people of Main Street have something to learn – and if we can and do learn it; we can attempt sharing what we learn with the psychopaths (Satanic victims themselves) and teach their order followers a better way. Probably futile, but this could offer a solution avoiding civil war to end our current, free-roaming *Animal Farm* self-incarceration? If successful, this educational program surpasses the wipe-out-Elite-scum option, allowing us to cooperatively skip around anarchy and technetronic feudalism as alternatives.

If psychopathic Elites and their socially deviant order followers can be taught a better way; so be it - Plan A. If not, providing we the people of Main Street successfully remove psychopaths from power by casting more informed votes - Plan B - they can no longer hurt anyone, so let 'em go live in their Gotham City castles and cheat each other to oblivion. If these psychos won't leave peacefully, they can be indicted, adjudicated, and if found guilty; incarcerated - Plan C. If they resist human decency violently, before incarceration or after, then in self-defense Main Street will have to forcibly do what we must - Plan D.

In all cases, we the people of Main Street must deal with the survival necessity of removing psychopaths from positions of influence and power, not just in America, but across the globe. The difficulty is nearly all world leaders today, in both Big Government and Big Business are primary or secondary psychopaths[217] beholden to the global syndicate octopus, so there's a pile of 'em to deal with and their handlers operate corrupted courts and media propaganda outlets. The constant lies and 4:00 A.M. (EST) talking points obscure and complicate problem-reaction-solution identification by Main Street. In any case, Elites are not going away, so must be dealt with if free societies are to survive.

Civilized societies have historically divided themselves toward two extremes: rich and poor, i.e., landowning politically powerful gentry or non-property owning politically weak peasants. Today we find a productive, relatively independent group called **middle-class**, though it appears efforts are underway by Elites to eradicate this difficult to control population segment. In any event, the two extremes share commonalities.

Eliminating this middle-class segment is problematic for Oligarchs because many of them recognize the middle class is good at planning stuff, designing/inventing stuff, building stuff, maintaining stuff, operating stuff, and creating wealth; begging the question, who's gonna do all this inventing and wealth creation after the middle class is obliterated? When discussing Elite delusion, this is one aspect

---

217 Lobaczewski, *Political Ponerology*.{\\i{}Political Ponerology}.","plain Citation":"Lobaczewski, Political Ponerology."

of what we are talking about. Short-sightedness. When the fatted goose has been had for supper, who lays the golden eggs? A bone of Elite contention.

Karl Marx by the way, an export of City of London, detested the middle class. After co-authoring *The Communist Manifesto* in 1848 with Fredrich Engels while living in Brussels after expulsion from Paris, Marx lived in London from 1849 until passing on March 14, 1883. He is buried in London's *Highgate Cemetery*, where his grave marker reads, *"The philosophers have only interpreted the world in various ways – the point, however, is to change it."* Without delving into class distinction, Gen "X" blurring the lines, etc., Marx viewed societal history as evolving out of class struggle between bourgeoisie and proletariat. His bourgeoisie emerged from the burghers, i.e., peddlers and tradesmen who traveled place to place offering goods and services – basically the beginning of what we call capitalism. This bourgeoisie population prospered, settled in, and became owners of the means of production, igniting the *Industrial Revolution* (1760-1840 per Arnold Toynbee).

Industry centralized jobs in urban areas and in Marx's view destroyed the agrarian way of life by drawing people from rural areas to urban centers. Marx accepted the feudal idea of landowner and peasant but could not accept the idea of business owner and worker. Today's middle-class basically divide into three groups: relatively wealthy upper, financially well-off middle, and the less fortunate. A destitute fourth group survives below the poverty line as homeless, welfare dependent, or both. Above the upper middle class, we find a still taxable upper class of 0.5%. Above them soars rare untaxable air of the Elite 0.01% - 0.001%, which incidentally, socialism and taxation never venture near as Elite trusts, foundations, and endowments are unapproachable outside pandering philanthropic PR fronts.

Comparing the two extremes of rich and poor, we find on the poorer end of the spectrum, say hard-working, decent hill folk residing in Appalachia, a closed society (slowly opening up), culturally fenced off from and resistant to outside influence and relationships, sometimes we're told, accompanied in isolated pockets of the most rural, least populated areas by gene pool constraints resulting from generational inbreeding. I doubt inbreeding prevalence is culturally significant in Appalachia overall though urban British myth prattles on about it. In any event, almost overnight, in 1964, Appalachia photographically became a destitution archetype justifiably resented by Appalachian residents. This occurred when President Lyndon Johnson helicoptered into McDowell County, West Virginia launching his *collectivist food stamp program* and middle-class wealth draining fake *War on Poverty*.

Areas of Appalachian poverty aren't arguable, but Johnson set off a misleading wildfire suggesting earnings and money were a primary cause of societal ills in this area. Just as in our impoverished Democrat run inner cities, lack of income is problematic but not a root cause of endemic poverty. Disjointed family life and educational failure are far more significant indicators—particularly when engendered or exacerbated by monopolistic business practices crushing the local economy, in this case, coal mining, steel, and railroad monopolies. Attorney and U.S. Senate candidate, J. D. Vance (backed by globalist pawn Peter Thiel) provides thoughtful insight into his own upbringing in Jackson, Kentucky and Middletown, Ohio before entering the Marine Corps after high school. His analysis of cultural influence versus wealth influence on behavior is a perceptive *"rust-belt"* treatise on the reverse of White Privilege and American Dream reality for marginalized Americans.[218]

By comparison, on the wealthiest end of the spectrum, the so-called dynastic family Elites, we have a similar closed circumstance. In both extremes, wealthy or lacking wealth, culturally tribal peer pressure encourages resistance to infiltration by outsiders or if deemed expedient, more aggressively suppresses group penetration via other means, some less than polite. Again, we find indications of consanguinity among Royals and other Elites, more so in the past, but factual reality and myth are difficult to discern. I don't know if Elite inbreeding is a significant factor in dynastic family lack of intelligence or psychopathy.

An observable difference between these two societal bookend strata are religious beliefs and resultant cultural morays. In the central and southern reaches of Appalachia for instance, religion is typically Christian, of an independent evangelical nature, distrustful of dogmatic hierarchies, in some areas influenced by Britain's *New Light* movement. Spiritual meaning and humility are cornerstones of this cultural morality, though regular weekly church attendance is limited. Within such cultures, attempts to obey the Ten Commandments and love each other are respected, even if not successfully lived up to, with poverty and calloused hands worn as protective armor, persuasively shielding against outsiders. Outside infiltration is discouraged by politely ignoring strangers or less politely shunning them. Flat landers are not trusted in the hills, though tourist revenue is rapidly growing in popularity.

Among the world's Elite on the other hand, if we peek below well-dressed, bespoke exteriors, it doesn't take long to find difficult to prove Luciferian religious beliefs and Luciferian ritual abuse, in some cases generational, including covert blood sacrifice, trauma based training, and a near total spawning of patholo-

---

218 J. D. Vance, *Hillbilly Elegy: A Memoir of a Family and Culture in Crisis*, Reprint edition (Harper Paperbacks, 2018).2018

gy by young adulthood where childhood imprinting and ongoing conditioning all but erase compassion, empathy, generosity, sharing, guilt, remorse, etc.

Such *structural disassociation* programming apparently occurs primarily with those few children expected to exercise significant financial and/or political power on the bloodline's behalf or on others chosen to be weaponized. We can only imagine the immensity of educational effort necessary to unwind (deprogram) this sort of barbaric imprinting; and question whether it can even be done. Beyond ritualized bloodline abuse, the global study group system is constantly on the lookout for high-functioning, damaged individuals incapable of empathy or worse, aggressively destructive, able to carry out the profitable dirty work of international resource rape, crime, and extermination through war, toxic medicines, sterilization, and famine.

Other Elite families and/or family members are more peripheral, so less exposed to abuse and conditioning, if at all. Among the chosen few, personality disorders facilitating aberrant behavior overriding admission of conscious guilt are common among Elites making it easier for them to crush competition in their rise to positions of power and influence. When doubt occurs, perverted psychiatric assistance and pharmaceuticals are on hand to reinforce conditioned behavior, eliminating the possibility of guilt-ridden emotion. This is necessary when a sensitive individual is called upon to incite war or induce famine resulting in deaths of thousands or even millions for regime change furthering resource rape; for *population pacification* and/or reduction; national boundary realignment; or simply bolstering profits. We see all these activities coming home to American streets as of 2021/2022. We must stop this insanity for the world.

Intrusion of Elite circles by outsiders is easily and unobtrusively blocked by unspoken screening through members-only private societies and clubs, expensive private schools, study group recognition and approval, closed financial networks, insider access to low-cost capital, greased regulatory approvals, foundation funding, think tank networking and of course, intelligence service access for surveillance and pacification of the stubbornly uncompliant. Today's multinational monopoly focus isn't production of products, services, and sales though they do all that. **Upper management focus is government influence and power.** Control government and your demonic plans are protected – you own the world.

Among hill folk and similar cultures, belief in God can be so strong, speaking in tongues, walking on spikes, broken glass, or hot coals, and safe handling of poisonous snakes are viewed unsurprisingly as visible signs of faith and God's power, while seeking punitive control over others is rare. Conversely, among dynastic Oligarchs, it seems power, control, and immediate self-gratification are primary motivators regardless the societal cost. The Luciferian inspired drive to destroy everything, ultimately including the Satanic follower, while seeking and obtaining power is intrinsic to Elite factions, but most Elites are arrogantly and self-righteously immune to this understanding, i.e., biblically blind.

Human history reveals Satan hates humans and particularly despises those weak and gullible enough to support his destructive agenda(s), saving the worst forms of demise for those supporting him most. This is a dynamic often witnessed on the heels of Communist take-overs when the new power-wielding junta quickly moves to execute *useful idiot* loyalists who worked so hard bringing Marxists to power in the first place. The Dark Left is obediently blind to this reality.

Money is a secondary interest for Elites as Oligarchic central bank control and ability to create limitless amounts of digital currency lessened both the thrill of obtaining money and pleasure of having it. That said, trillions in resource rape profit, narcotics money laundering, human trafficking, sex slavery, organ harvesting, and of course, war still figure prominently in bolstering Elite bank accounts. Not even D.C. can hide the enormity of counterfeit computer entries necessary to fund dark transhuman research and development. Additionally, ritual sacrifice, pedophilia, betting on time-of-death, and hunting humans for sport glare, red-eyed, from the deep, dark wine cellars of wealthy forested estates, though Elite operated media drones don't say much about such entertainment.

Only wealthy, CIA constrained Hollywood denizens brazenly celebrate this level of depravity including forms of cannibalism. Entertainment showcased with expensive buttery flavored popcorn and sugary beverages in the land of dis-placed consciousness opens doors for power seekers and a few privileged order followers, who then become painfully aware of the control file blackmail employed by top-tier power brokers for media product control. Main Street is shielded from the truth, though titillated by the softer Hollywood gossip stories sold at grocery store checkouts. Spirit cooking is high fashion in Hollywood.

To solidify this ugly point, the economics of global sex slavery now exceed narcotics trafficking in popular Elite circles. Drugs are sold once. A ten to thirteen-year-old child can be sold repeatedly, many times a day. Today's average age for sex slaves is thirteen and a slave can be sold thousands of times over a five-year useful life ending in terrified ritual sacrifice, organ harvesting, or both. Some say the useful life of a child sex-slave is closer to 24-months. I don't know the truth of it, but it's pure evil however long it lasts. Most sex slaves and there are tens of thousands created worldwide every year are murdered by age nineteen. This sick system must be stopped. There is no one to stop it but us on Main Street and we need the grace of God to help accomplish our task. Most of us don't even know this is happening – or worse – do know but deny any knowledge because admission requires doing something about it and who wants to deal with this level of evil.

Complicating matters, the music industry and Hollywood's CIA constrained, pedophile prominence in the long-term global conditioning and mind control program are now being supplanted by DARPA, Silicon Valley, and dangerously brainwashed nerds with their more immediate forms of entrained control. Globalism, by exercising Marxist/Fascist power first localizes, then does what it pleases, spreading its poison by using locals to ensure drug addiction, sex slavery, and ritual sacrifice throughout politically toxic, divided victim nations.

The comparison between poorly educated, impoverished but decent people of the Appalachian hills to highly educated (study group indoctrinated) inbred Elites and their order followers points out, all humans are human. Every human is equally endowed with the Divine spark. This Divinely created essence means no human being stands above any other human being. In terms of earthly attributes and gifts no two humans are equal; but in terms of Divinely created infinite value all are equal as well as responsible for their actions.

It's important for us on Main Street to realize this because our Main Street survival as a species necessitates Main Street relieving the pathological Elites and their narcissistic order followers of the reins of power. Psychopaths, career political pawns, and techno-psycho-geeks are destroying our world and everything in it. Only the brain-washed will take a so-called vaccine with undisclosed ingredients promoted in 2010 by a *useful idiot* openly declaring world population growth can be reduced 10-15% using vaccines? If we the people of Main Street do not stop this *useful idiot's* bosses who will? Ask them to leave; vote them out; drive them out; but leave they must and it's our *unwashed* job on Main Street to give em' the boot. Boot 'em soft or boot 'em hard, but they gotta' go. Technetronic microwave 5G feudalism beneath *Space Fence Lockdown*, our ionized atmosphere, and ingested nano transceivers is not a sustainable concept. This research must be de-funded and made transparent, so rational decisions to proceed can verifiably and safely be made.

In the wake of Silicon Valley's nihilist development of AI in conjunction with aerosol weaponization of Earth's atmosphere via deployment of Mylar nanoparticles, metal oxide nanoparticles like lithium oxide and aluminum oxide functioning as atmospheric capacitors and semi-conductors, carbon nanotubes, nuclear nanoparticles (Wigner black dust), ionospheric (HAARP) heaters, atmospheric ionizing radiation, DNA strand fragmentation by high-linear energy transfer (LET) radiation, microwave frequency radiation, and finally, Nikola Tesla's spiraling scalar waves transforming electrons into vortex electrons – **life on earth is being extincted with environmentalist silence.**

Vacuous technocrats blindly think they will improve the biosphere by creating cyborgs but their irresponsible self-indulgence places Earth under imminent threat of omnicide by psychopathic experimentation conducted by uninhibited true believers in Scientism too ignorant to understand just because something can be done doesn't mean it's a good idea to do it. This is suicidal omnicide by arrogant ignorance, and I haven't even mentioned occult intersections with the study of these technologies, nor anti-matter, or demonic activity. Selfish study group drones cannot be allowed to handle the controls anymore.

President Donald Trump promised to drain the swamp; promised to stop the wanton proliferation of corruption in American power circles and with effective cooperation, could probably have done so internationally—IF he weren't just pandering. Draining the swamp for real requires stopping issuance of counterfeit digital currency, abusive covert child imprinting, child sex trafficking, pedophilia, ritual sacrifice, adult sex trafficking, narcotics trafficking, human trafficking, organ harvesting, etc., and the omnipresent election fraud and management by blackmail – all of which serve Elites seeking to create a Main Street transhumanist gulag into which we the people of Main Street are conscripted. The Donald thinks big. The task he undertook is big; so big it isn't clear who the White Hats, if any, are. The Donald's Team, if any, are unseen.

Watching the Trump Administration paradox from my cynical Sonoran Desert perch, I wonder, are pedophilia and blackmail no longer necessary management tools? Are they being purged for PR benefit because they are no longer needed? Except for ritual child sacrifice, a supposed dark energy source which Elites will never voluntarily abandon, are these old school tools outdated? Are they being updated to more sophisticated weaponry like 5G IoT surveillance, crypto currency, nano/micro-chips, more powerful entrainment, and autonomous control systems, both Earthbound and space activated?

If every human becomes a walking, talking transmitter/receiver via inhalation/ingestion of heavy metals via aerosol spraying and vaccine contaminants, which I have not heard The Donald mention, then the 5G IoT renders blackmail obsolete doesn't it? Perhaps we are "not draining the swamp"; just getting rid of old thieves who know too much and are no longer needed for "replacement by a new psychotic management team?" Global syndicate thieves already stole more than $86 trillion dollars through Congressional back doors since 1998 without Congress batting an eye. Does the global syndicate require financial managers to protect loot from prying Main Street eyes? Time will tell. I hope The Donald is the real deal. I voted for him.

Abuse of power employed for subjugation of others; that is, restraint of individual or group freedom is evil. Our only Main Street defense against domination by evil is coherent perception along with spiritual discernment accompanied by spiritual strength, fortitude, and the will to overcome adversity through benefit of Divine grace. There is no other armor capable of protecting us. The Free Masonic lie of going it alone is a Belial cul-de-sac of futility.

We the people of Main Street must learn to overcome conditioning and entrainment launched against our spiritual awareness and we must learn quickly because so far in this 21st century, our globe is managed by a psychopathic intent to wantonly destroy everything created, whether we or they realize it.

21ˢᵗ century human survival requires understanding the over-riding purpose of Luciferian belief systems is destruction of all creation – including destruction of gullible Luciferian followers. Practicing Satanic rituals for any purpose, in the end, ultimately destroys the practitioner regardless temporary material success via the means. Global collectivism, whether Marxist, Monopoly Capitalist, Fascist, Mercantilist, or new forms of Transhuman Neo-Feudalism are 100% Luciferian; are 100% evil; and are anathema to human decency, human life, and environmental responsibility. We underestimate the subjugating power of the Globalist lie at our planet's peril. Biblically speaking, *dominion means taking care of the Earth* we have been given to inhabit. Are we doing that? As cyborgs we won't even retain ability to choose between nurture, immobility, or harm.

As mentioned earlier, I believed for many years evil is simply lack of good, in the same manner cold is lack of thermal energy (heat). I was incorrect. Heat warms cold with 100% predictable, calculable repetitiveness. Good – or love on the other hand cannot automatically overcome evil. Evil fights back with cunning, usually unfairly. For good or love to overcome evil – WE MUST <u>CONSCIOUSLY CHOOSE</u> GOOD. WE MUST CHOOSE LOVE AND OBTAIN LOVE FROM ITS ONLY SOURCE – THE DIVINE, AND THEN <u>ACT THROUGH DIVINE GRACE WITH LOVE</u>.

Only when we invoke our own created life energy enhanced by grace, which operationally originates in the non-created, transcendent Divine and take appropriate action, can we embrace the power of the Divine to overcome evil. Humanity is weak, ignorant, and incomplete without its Divine Spark. Therefore, love's power is not automatic as with heat warming a cold void. Free will is a spectacularly huge spiritual deal! Human beings don't have the power to overcome evil – BUT we can get it. We have access to Divine power just for the asking, but this knowledge is becoming increasingly occulted, which means we the people of Main Street must relearn its value along with a better way of living if we wish to continue living in any healthy, beneficial way at all. Abundant life requires abundant thinking, generosity, and imaginative creation, not destructive competition, and certainly not cyborgism. Good, abundant life requires recognition of and respect through grace for our Divine Spark.

Considering root causes of societal issues from an engineering viewpoint, hopefully to identify possible remedies, it dawned on me; **every problem in every society today has at its foundational core, at its root, a missing or confused sense of spiritual being, worth, and power.** We do not understand our own human essence, nor where it comes from. We are not likely to use a power we don't know we have. If this observation is correct - 21st century human survival requires re-learning about our innate spiritual nature as persons distinguishable from plants, animals, and other life forms having their own precious created spirit as well as their own intelligent life energy capacity.

This distinction becomes increasingly difficult as types and forces of mind control launched by Elite order followers against Main Street citizens becomes increasingly sophisticated, invasive, and powerful. 5G technology and the IoT are a blessing in many ways; BUT we should be careful what we wish for. WHO oversees 5G and the Internet of Things (IoT) and what are THEIR plans? What is the curse tied to the wish and who's CEO of the curse? How mentally ill is this CEO? How ill are the CEO's hive-mind order followers?

Since learning requires perception; and making sense of perceptions requires conceptualizing; and conceptualizing involves thinking and feeling; and since thinking and feeling are spiritual activities; then determining a healthier way to live together involves strengthening spiritual understanding. SCIENTISM denies all this, discarding intelligent energy for petri dish randomosity.

Not what many of us want to hear, but there it is. Thoughts are real and manifest interactively in operative reality. Thoughts do not originate within our physical sense organs nor sprout from our brain's electro-chemical processes. Your brain is not a petri dish. Scientism, in its arrogance, has so far, callously denied this ontological reality. It is time for science to grow up and recognize the power of the sublime unseen. The *Theory of Everything* (TOE) is discovered through silence, prayer, and careful meditation, not material science and lab experiments disclosing only a tiny physical aspect of created infinity.

We the people of Main Street, outside entrainment influence anyway, are the cause of our own choices, in turn producing predictable effects. Choices have consequences. Not to wax overly judgy, but a morally bankrupt people are 100% certain to predictably create a morally bankrupt culture run by even more morally bankrupt rulers as those rulers emerge from their place within society, even if from restricted upper echelons. A distasteful observation to be sure, but if we look at today's world honestly, there is no doubting our morally challenged Main Street value system. We murder children for convenience.

Blue Mayors and City Councils defend the right of citizens to urinate and defecate on city sidewalks. The painful stench of moral corruption and intellectual vacuity are everywhere. A society claiming individual freedom is enhanced by murdering unborn children following irresponsible promiscuity as a matter of convenience treads a dark path indeed. Even worse is the idea that inner cities can be improved by aborting people of color. Abortion in any case is *profitable* organ harvesting business providing a dark energy source for demonic purposes. Freedom requires healthy perception, coherent thinking, adult responsibility, and vigilance—not lies and murder.

Why do we do harmful things to ourselves and each other? We can't blame Oligarchs as there are ±8 billion of us on Main Street and only a few million of them. Eustace Mullins claimed five men ran the world. I suspect this an underestimate, some say 85, some say thirteen bloodline families at the top, but surely the *inner circle* number is minuscule, maybe 250,000 (0.0031%) to a million (0.0125%) - far short of the oft touted 1%. In any event, in any number, Oligarchs only win if Main Street foolishly says YES to Satanic coercion. Say NO THANK YOU and with God's grace, FREEDOM REIGNS!

Maybe it's time for us on Main Street to turn the TV conditioning tube off occasionally, pray a bit, think for ourselves and say NO? **Evil requires obedience to thrive.** Understanding why we must learn to say NO is a spiritual exercise, so here we are again. Freedom requires some knowledge to even begin acquiring more knowledge and finally, wisdom. Our personal search for knowledge and understanding is a significant spiritual task demanding full commitment since mere knowledge by itself is not wisdom. Knowledge may be power if utilized, but wisdom is necessary for proper use of that power.

We live after all, in an exciting spiritual battleground where more weapons can be more helpful than fewer weapons, though some prefer to travel fast and light. Prayer and fasting, by the way, travel light and are humanity's two most powerful weapons, covering both spiritual and material realms. Prayer alone is fantastic. Prayer and fasting together seal the real commitment deal and are not easy. If you can't or won't grasp that we cannot formulate good political or economic policy on the back of spiritual denial and denigration; then either this book can't help you OR more reading may shed some light on the thing. Agreement is not the point, nor is it important. Thinking for ourselves on the other hand is a big deal and if we can't learn that; we can't be free. Sun Tzu explained this 2,500 years ago, Jesus Christ harped on personal responsibility more than 2,000 years ago, so maybe it's about time we grasped the concept.

The idea of controlling one group of humans thought to be inferior by another group believing itself superior, is as old as megalomaniacal human pathology, which predates written records. This tendency toward Luciferian pathology is not limited to, but historically manifests most clearly within Oligarchic nobility and royal families, whose gene pools are apparently so narrow and genetically deficient, they are poorly armed to resist its vulgar infection.

Today, generational pathology is more commonly seen or at least more openly viewed among nouveau wealthy in international banking and interlocking multi-national monopoly/financial circles, maybe a top-tier psychotic group of 8,500 or so facilitators according to Dutch banker, Mr. Ronald Bernard, himself once a member of this Elite cabal, who by his own account, bravely turned away when solicited to ritually murder a child during a ceremony. Making matters worse, we the people of Main Street tend to reward aberrant Elite behavior on bended knee, carelessly bestowing respect, awards, crowns, jewels, obscene levels of wealth, enormous power, and of course, control to those whom in many cases are nothing more than well-dressed, generational serial killers.

Can we imagine miscreants actively planning WW I, WW II, and now WW III are not serial killers; are not devotees of mass murder? Why would such beasts not kill using pollution, poor nutrition, medical malpractice, and of course, war? War is murder of the many by the many providing money and power to the few who orchestrate it. **Pass legislation making it illegal to fund war with borrowed money and war is a horror of the past.** How fast will global syndicate Elites impoverish themselves funding their obscene wars with their own wallets instead of ours? The key to their greed is OPM. Why has no country passed a *no debt for war* law? I realize historically our societies and economies are war-based[219] – BUT - why can't we change that? Given WE are society, why can't a war-based society make a more abundant choice? It's on US, not THEM, regardless of who THEY are?

---

219 Special Study Group and Leonard C. Lewin, *Report from Iron Mountain on the Possibility and Desirability of Peace.*

Our 21st century Main Street world is surrounded by deviant, though nicely pack-aged pathology; is saturated with it; is drowning in it; is being wiped out by it. We are not on the right path (no pun intended). Check out the history of South Af-rica's Boer Wars or early 20th century Armenian genocide if you feel serial killers too strong a term for bespoke murderous annihilation of decent human beings for power and profit. Check out today's South African nightmare. Look at the murderous blood fests of Europe, the Far East, civil war in the U.S., Afghanistan, Congo, Iraq, Libya, Nigeria, Syria, and Ukraine or sadly, South Africa once again[220].

Sun Tzu, in *The Art of War* [221], taught more than 2,500 years ago; we cannot defeat an enemy we do not know. He further taught, we must know our-selves as well, if we reasonably expect to win most of our battles. Unfortu-nately, Main Street tests low on both scores; them and us. Freedom on Main Street requires upgrading our course of study while we still can. The pace of Elite managed, mis-educational dumbing-down is accelerating along with elec-tromagnetic human-machine interface system development. The fact we don't notice emphasizes the effectiveness of transhumanism control systems and will eventually magnify **Neuralink META-Power** over an enslaved society.

American schools have degraded into nothing more than cultural/social engineering centers, leaving graduates unprepared to meet life's challeng-es or perform productively in a rapidly evolving world. This is not acciden-tal. Dumbing down slaves is established practice. The serious business of self-governance requires at least the barest modicum of knowledge regarding how things work... or don't work. We need to sharpen our pencils and take notes or start punching the keyboard with hungry, feral search determination if we expect to survive as free persons much longer. We are living a daily in-formation war where lack of information means slavery and can mean death.

In older manifestations, populations were controlled by violence and fear of violence. Outlaws were beaten, beheaded, quartered, otherwise tortured to death, or publicly burned at the stake. Acceptable punishment for theft and other minor crimes in the UK was death until the mid-nineteenth century. To-day, psychopathic control is more subtle. Today, we vote for outside control of ourselves, casting votes fueled by media manufactured anxiety (*mass forma-tion*) packaged as propagandized "news alerts" or "breaking news", predicated on misinformation, outright lies, or sometimes no information at all – just made up. Wide-scale election fraud further exacerbates this deception and by itself is reason enough to cease and desist with easily manipulated mail-in ballot har-vesting and electronic voting. Order followers seditiously installing manipulat-

---

220 Booyens, *AmaBhulu - The Birth and Death of the Second America.*
221 Tzu, *The Art of War.*

able back doors in voting software MUST be in prison for fraud and/or treason along with the pawns who contract for official use of these **cheat-machines.**

Information or lack thereof is in any case meted out by just half a dozen or so media monopolies owned by the same socially deviant Elites who own the publishing houses, administer our foundation influenced mis-educational system, poison our food, pollute our air and water, ration medical services and insurance coverage, operate our supposed political leaders... and hope to reimpose Feudalism on Main Streets across the world. For those of us not yet aware of this mitigating circumstance, the con proves itself. **If we don't know who the mark is, we are the mark.**

Feudalism of old, repackaged as a false Marxist promise with failure to deliver enforced by Fascist totalitarianism under exalted social justice phraseology, fought for by idealistic though grossly uninformed social justice warriors (SJW), is nothing more than centrally planned Technocratic Enslavement. Slavery innovatively sold beneath the disingenuous banner of more safety, more security, more sustainability, more efficiency, more fairness, and more of everything for the little people of Main Street. Centralized reality across the world, however, historically showcases a different, more impoverished outcome called slavery. Slavery is always a top-down system. No surprise then, that so-called social justice warriors are funded from the slave owning top by psychopathic globalists.

You may find this Technocratic Fascism/Neo-Feudalism concept difficult to accept, but not long ago, the Obama Regime, cheered on by popular media hypocrites like Oprah Winfrey, alongside treasonous Secretary of State Hillary Clinton's bizarre efforts, successfully enabled re-activation of slave auctions in the newly destabilized country of Libya, where incidentally, ISIS regrouped before expanding into Afghanistan, Pakistan, Syria, and elsewhere in 2014-2015. This is the sort of crime against humanity we see perpetrated by malicious Elite order followers the likes of the Dulles brothers, Bushes, Clintons, Obamas, and now Bidens usually with plausible deniability through rogue elements within Shadow Government leadership. Donald Trump, regardless of faults, hated by the Establishment, is the first U.S. President in my lifetime who did not involve American young people in a new war. Thank you, Sir.

As an aside, to top off the Libyan nightmare, weapons were illegally and covertly transferred from Libya to Syria, covertly arming ISIS for de-stabilization of that sovereign nation. Throw in the Ukrainian coup and the Bush II/Obama/Clinton/Biden Team are three for three violating how many international agreements and treaties? Donald Trump underwent impeachment hearings just for trying to slow down the flow of this treasonous, dehumanizing sludge. High Crimes and Misdemeanors? Aiding and Abetting the Enemy? Treason and since January 20, 2017, sedition? Will any of this be prosecuted? No one will be prosecuted if we the people of Main Street fail to demand our Constitution and Rule of Law be enforced.

This is not a Democrat-Republican issue. This is criminal duplicity by both sides of the globalist UniParty structure, and no saint, politician, or expert will rectify this evil. We the people of Main Street must take this on ourselves. Think local, local, local—then we work our way up. Global pawn, Soros and friends began buying States' Attorney Generals and Secretaries of State in 2004, then expanding to District Attorneys, judges, and so on. Over the past 17 years this enabled wholesale election fraud and the take down of U.S. representative government with strangled legal recourse. Fortunately, we can still vote, sort of, so in mass, from the grass roots up, we can non-violently undo the Satanic agenda of global syndicate pawn, George Soros and associates.

As touched on earlier - fairness, sustainability, and social justice translate in New World Order double-speak to abandonment of Main Street freedom along with wealth transference from hard-working Main Streeters to pathologically ill Elites through privileged, order-following racketeers via taxation, various nanny state programs, or more popularly, terrorism and war. To repeat myself, another word for this type of sustainability is slavery, though today, smart technologies are replacing the vulgarity of whips, chains, cattle cars, and slave barns.

We impoverished, free-roaming, Neo-feudal slaves of Main Street's new Technocratic Fascist State obligingly use little of Earth's resources, but fight the wars and pay the bills, while well-heeled plantation owners greedily do as they will with impunity. We roam freely with our tiny carbon footprint only within technotronically defined borders of self-imposed restriction defined by *Cultural Marxism*, political correctness, and social engineering, a perfect prison without fences or walls. It is *Frankfurt School*, Marcuse's *Happy Consciousness*[222] come to life, reinforced by 5G, satellite/atmospheric surveillance, extremely low frequency electromagnetic entrainment, nanotech, and better pharmaceuticals with helpful machinations from the always compliant Main Street Media.

Conformance is not cooperation. Uniformity is not strength. A smiling dictator cannot be trusted. Going along to get along cannot keep our kids free, nor provide them opportunity or abundance. Only with God's grace can humanity throw off the tightening psychotronic shackles, the mind-matter interface technology incrementally strangling free thought, free communication between people, and personal autonomy. **Abundance or slavery is a choice.**

---

222 Marcuse and Kellner, *One-Dimensional Man.*

25% OR BUST !!!

Reclaiming our lost Republic requires downsizing our bloated U.S.
Federal Government to 25% of its present malevolent size.
All Federal Agencies have become enemies of the people.
All Federal Agencies have become harmful.
Most Federal Agencies cannot be fixed. Eliminate them!

23 • Unsustainable Matrix

Remedy: Pray, Fast, Pay Attention, and WAKE UP!

Please never confuse spiritual awakening with being WOKE – unless hoping for electromagnetic Gulags! **All United States' Federal government agencies have degenerated into abusive enemies of Main Street.** No exceptions I'm aware of, including WOKE military above O-6 along with many indoctrinated young recruits. Most agency secretaries, directors, and senior mis-management regard American taxpayers as impediments to their globalist agenda. Good people are trapped inside now malevolent bureaucracies attacking Main Street citizens with unlawful surveillance, discriminatory taxation, unconstitutional regulation, money laundering, and recently—imprisonment or threat of imprisonment. Examples of transnational monopoly protection at Main Street expense, risk, and impoverishment abound. Here are just three.

First on the list is Big Pharma fraud. The *Bayh-Dole Act* was passed on December 12, 1980. This act authorized government agencies and agency contractors to retain patent rights and associated revenue streams from patented inventions, technologies, medicines, etc., developed at government facilities with taxpayer dollars. Overnight, legitimate government agencies, universities, medical schools, laboratories, and so forth abandoned legitimate beneficial research to become **research cash registers** and in many cases, **bioweapon developers** under what is euphemistically misnamed *"gain of function"* research.

Making medical related matters worse, in 1986, vaccine manufacturers were preferentially granted immunity from product liability. There were fewer than a dozen licensed vaccines in 1986. There are now 86 licensed vaccinations available (two Hepatitis A vaccines, Havrix & VAQTA are inactivated) with growing pressure to mandate many of them. Hundreds more vaccines are coming down the zero-liability profit chute jockeying for corrupt approval. *Experimental use* vaccines have full immunity from liability. Malpractice victims are still able to sue for alleged damages inflicted by FDA approved vaccines, but damage claims can only be filed with the farcical *National Vaccine Injury Compensation Program* (VICP). Massive conflicts of interest now exist for FDA, CDC, NIH, etc., related to approvals, recommendations, and mandates for poorly tested or untested products agency employees hold vested or future financial interests in.

For example, the *National Institutes of Health* (NIH) holds an equity position in the *Moderna* synthetic mRNA COVID vaccine, a blatant conflict of interest few are aware of. Incidentally, *Moderna* has never licensed a medicine since its founding in 2010 and as of this writing, corporate officers of *Moderna* are selling millions of dollars of their *Moderna* holdings since the stock price rocketed from ± \$22/share in May 2020 to ±\$230/share in July 2021. No insider corruption to see here, just honest medical R & D.

Second on the list is the CIA, spawned in 1947 by the global syndicate to serve its own agendas at U.S. taxpayer expense. Many good people work there and occasionally the agency does something beneficial for Main Street, but this organized criminal enterprise engaging in regime change, drug, weapon, and human trafficking along with extortion, blackmail, torture, murder, and more cannot be fixed.

Third on the list is the FBI, founded in 1908, engaged in law enforcement activity initially but succumbing to organized crime's successful compromise of J. Edgar Hoover just over a short decade later. Today, it's doubtful the FBI can be fixed in the wake of the 1993 World Trade Center and 1995 Oklahoma City bombings, routine spying on American citizens, Fast and Furious *gun walking*, the Russia-Russia-Russia hoax, 2020's Michigan Governor Whitmer kidnapping fiasco, and the January 6, 2021 capital debacle to name just six embarrassments in which rogue FBI assets made bad things happen or let bad things happen.

It would take an enormous library to begin detailing past and present seditious and treasonous behavior of U.S. Federal Agencies at the corrupt behest of global syndicate multinationals. **Washington D.C. is a ten square mile organized crime center; a vast money laundering operation, and little else.** Washington D.C. can no longer be called the seat of American government with a straight face. Referring to United States' Government as a banana republic insults insipid banana republics everywhere. Americans today, live under a variant of the CIA's *Phoenix Program* developed in Vietnam along with post-WW II's *Operation Gladio*. As Chicago's bigoted Reverend Wright so coarsely observed on another matter, those chickens came home to roost on the back of Main Street apathy. More than 20,000 people were allegedly murdered in Vietnam under this brutally inhuman *Phoenix* pacification program. The historically violent *Phoenix Program* is slowly transforming into a less visible, though potent, transhuman mass behavior modification program.

Transhuman Control is in part, operationally imposed on society employing manufactured anxiety as a mass, societal pacification weapon now called *mass formation* by Belgium's Ghent University Professor, Mattias Desmet and America's Dr. Robert Malone via a multi-faceted PsyOp approach where debt, war, terrorism, poverty, race, religion, sex, sham-science, poorly understood nanotechnological applications, environmental issues, other social issues, induced famine, poor nutrition, weaponized weather, violent false flag events, and myriad other mechanisms herd us into *divide and conquer*, group-think, mind control barns we choose to compliantly restrain ourselves within. *Mass formation* is a form of **mass hypnosis** capable of profoundly impacting 30% or more of a targeted population.

Pick an advertised hive-mind team, slap on your Vag Hat or *Antifa* gear and start a useless though dopamine enhancing FB or Twitter warrior fight to feel alive and relevant; to feel a part of something, anything. Marcuse's *Happy Consciousness* in action – a dire psychological mass attack resulting in what old school Marxists called **false consciousness**, and what Marcuse himself thought of as **repressive sublimation**. There's a mouthful, but that's the **operational matrix**; so vast, so vacuously impregnable we can't see it—there is no one to call. We only sense its dark, digital, ever-present, pervasively ominous, anxiety provoking, Orwellian presence and pressure. For reasons I don't yet comprehend, far too few of us are willing to push the OFF BUTTON, then at least try returning to thinking for ourselves some of the time. Silence can indeed be golden.

The buried lead hiding in plain sight is, for now anyway, we can just turn the insolent matrix off anytime we wish by saying NO THANK YOU and thinking independently; though soon, more invasive Silicon Valley toys of the macabre may render the off-button inoperable? *Stingray* and *DRTBox* technology along with smart TVs and other devices are already here. Incidentally, even the possibility of cooperative freedom requires thoughtless, intellectually challenged, electronic claptrap programming be turned off occasionally. Pay ATTENTION TO Silicon Valley and its dark marriage to rogue Military Science. Its promise has gone off the rails, now posing imminent danger to all life on Earth… and frankly, that's an omnicidal understatement. Silicon Valley moguls after all, are just DARPA/CIA Shadow Government slaves anyway, though are wonderfully kept in their luxurious estate stalls.

Think of the PsyOp matrix as a barred window. If we stand close to the window, we're peering between bars through small openings at a limited view of what lies outside, beyond the bars. Only when stepping back do we realize we've been looking through a securely barred window at a highly constrained view; and what's more—we can't get out. We are locked in thought prison, the enormity of life's potential cut off from us, just out of reach of the aerosol-saturated sky poisoning everything we breathe, eat, or drink.

The PsyOp matrix is designed to lead us toward constructing our own mind-prison without need for cattle cars, walls, or bars. We are lied to, our viewpoint cleverly obscured, and our perception altered, facilitating voluntary or involuntary obedience and compliance with intellectual and emotional captivity. We must work together and learn to escape this surveillance-thought matrix, or our children are doomed to transhuman slavery. Fear impedes brain function so: "Fear not, for I am with you." *(Isaiah 40:10)*

If we research dark, pernicious movements like the eugenics movement essentially spawned in 1798 with publication of *An Essay on the Principle of Population as It Affects the Future Improvement of Society* by Reverend Thomas Malthus; or more importantly those dynastic families who fund the delusional academics who promote genocidal eugenics and the like, we will notoriously find Margaret Sanger and Hitler's Nazi psychopaths. Peering deeper into the abyss we'll uncover miscreants rarely mentioned or pictured in progressively redacted history texts. We'll find proud Atlanticist Establishment families and dozens of neurotically greedy, order-following others of their perverted financial ilk, who pretty much grabbed the reins of world domination from the inbred hands of historic nobility, itself an identifiable schism issue.

It's Bankster Rules for the past four-hundred years, but the centuries-old behind-the-curtain Oligarch schism dating to 451 continues developing as the bespoke suited power-plays unfold behind the scenes, though we saw fraud-ridden Clinton Pawn-Trump Outlaw-Biden Pawn battles partially out in the open. Perhaps the ancient Guelph-Ghibelline feud is back online? Maybe just Satanic rage, gleefully unleashed on all of us still rejecting our Creator's love and grace?

Mr. James Corbett of *The Corbett Report*[223] refers to one major group of these socially deviant (my words) folks as the **Oiligarchs** in his well-documented, insightful documentary entitled: *Why Big Oil Conquered the World*. Mr. Corbett apparently applies this descriptive term to the role dynastic families controlling the global energy industry play while attempting to control all people and natural resources on Earth. They usefully employ tools such as banking,

---

223 "The Corbett Report," accessed October 9, 2017, https://www.corbettreport.com/.

war, eugenics, medicine, food, and climate, to name just six popular energy re-inforcing control methodologies. Not much happens on Earth without energy.

Malthusian Scarcity is a frighteningly hopeless economic/political concept taught managerially with religious fervor in foundation controlled, popu-lar dynastic family universities; also offered up as a popularly accepted ratio-nal in *unwashed* State universities for justifying complacent impoverishment of Main Street *livestock*. There's that *Happy Consciousness* Marcuse talked about.[224]

The world's dynastic families are apparently obsessed with a morbid fear of running out of stuff; so, aggressively become ritualistic thieves and hoard-ers, incapable of honest wealth creation, buoyed by gluttonous competitive beliefs, trapping themselves securely in the self-fulfilling prophesy brought on by their own unsustainable drain of monopolistic, negative returns on in-vestment... and we think we the people of Main Street have it rough?

We on Middle-Class Main Street need to teach Elite folks about the benefits of wealth creation and positive return on investment because it is not part of expensive Establishment university curricula, nor is it a subject for sta-tus quo study group discussion. If we don't do it; who will? Establishment genocide is an option, though not an appropriate creative solution for an imaginative, moral people like those of us on Main Streets across the globe try to be. We can do better than tar, feathers, or Reinhard Gehlen's annihi-lation. There are many of us and only a few of them despite the distracting background media noise they squawk so loudly, desperately, and perniciously.

Desperate to fend off their own terrified morbidity and pathologic world view, Elites form supportive, transnational organizations inside and outside govern-ment fostering their megalomaniacal belief that all others outside their priv-ileged circles are genetically inferior and must be controlled or eliminated al-together, preserving the world's stuff for themselves, though this last part is rarely mentioned outside stuffily private, fireside club-chat. Everything Elites publicly mention is philanthropically for what treasonous career criminal, Hil-lary Clinton so generously labels, DEPLORABLE *little people* of Main Street.

It is beyond sick, but for reasons I can't grasp, we vote, or machines vote, and we accept depraved so-called Representatives working for and supporting these criminally insane, Main Street impoverishing views held by crazed inbred mu-tants. Our 21st century is a mysterious adventure – but then, I suppose every century has been and likely will be should we manage to escape self-extinction?

---

224 Marcuse and Kellner, *One-Dimensional Man.*

Extraordinarily well dressed, limo-riding, caviar feeding, dynastic, pedophilic miscreants, and their highly paid, Technocratic order followers continuously pursue an ongoing, though already failing global program of mis-education, indoctrination, secular humanism, sham-science, voodoo Keynesian economic theory, *Cultural Marxism*, *Social Darwinism*, and geopolitical hogwash employing a constant parade of disingenuously modified terms like eugenics, biometrics, global cooling, global warming, climate change, sustainability, social justice, fairness, equity, etc. – all of which translate to the same meaning; CONTROL LEADING TO and/or MAINTAINING POWER BY THE FEW OVER THE MANY.

It is not just about money. Delusional, but dangerous Elite souls control nearly all central bank digital printing presses, so debt-print whatever currency they want with impunity, particularly since they also control the corrupt governments supposedly overseeing the digital money presses and debt, we the people of Main Street subsidize with our blood, hard work, and uninformed votes. For Elites, it is about control, control, control, and the abusive POWER attaching to control. Elites don't seem to realize it, or don't care, but it's also about destruction—total annihilation per the singular Luciferian agenda.

Holding power and maintaining control of stubborn peasants on Main Street is awkward. Non-transparent fiat money is easy peasy. Inner-city barrios and ghettos along with stack-and-pack apartments, high-density condos, and mass transit simplify the Main Street herding and fencing control process enormously. Unimaginably evil people, through the **international study group system**, indoctrinate order-following bureaucrats, programming them to impose seemingly innocuous zoning and land-use restrictions. These restrictions serve an important restraint function within the enslaving vision of Agenda 21/30/50; as does reducing private vehicle ownership and restricting use of same in exchange for mandated public transportation... to protect us and save the environment of course. Thank you, *Club of Rome* for worrying about us working *livestock*.

This global gulag multi-pincer movement is rapidly heading our way. Do we imagine those in power push for autonomous vehicles because they're good for Main Street? Global syndicate think tanks, along with top GM and BMW management for example, see manufacture of privately owned vehicles decreasing 80% by year 2030 and as having no future. Timing aside, whether we view this positively or negatively, why should we agree to limited mobility because psychopathic corporatist pawns say so?

This runs with the malevolent concept of the universal stipend – another freedom strangling trap. Acceptance of the universal income stipend constitutes tacit agreement with Elite central planners that we agree our value as

23 • Unsustainable Matrix

Main Street persons is nothing more than a balance sheet liability. Once established as a 100% liability contributing zero economic value to Elite coffers – what do we suppose central planners will do with us? That's right – we are gone – we just relegated ourselves to organic fertilizer or maybe *Soylent Green* to cannibalistically feed surviving semi-robotic slaves. If we think not or hope not – refer to unredacted Russian, Chinese or Islamic history wherein hundreds of millions of poor souls did not even qualify as fertilizer for totalitarian grist.

The term SUSTAINABILITY as frequently uttered with perfect diction by royalty, nobility, or order-followers like Maurice Strong, Rockefellers, Bushes, Clintons, Obamas, Biden, Gore, or dozens of other order followers simply translated, means: TRANSFER ALL NATURAL RESOURCES AND WEALTH ON EARTH TO THE WORLD'S DYNASTIC FAMILIES TO BE USED AT THEIR DISCRETION. This includes food and water by the way, should you be wondering, and I hope we are all wondering.

An eye-opening example of psychopathic control is the monstrously clever financial scam referred to at the expensive thug-club United Nations, in government circles, central banking, and energy orifices by various monikers like Carbon Tax, Emissions Trading, Cap and Trade, or whatever other names they jokingly have for the scam. Now, I know some of you seriously indoctrinated types just got angry, and your blood pressure shot up but calm down and please realize the Carbon Scam conceived by *prominent global citizens* has nothing whatever to do with anything going on in our Main Street environment or with Earth's climate. Two separate issues. Elites enthusiastically enjoy weaponizing the pollution issue by the way,[225] a favorite study group think tank pastime.

As an alternative clean energy developer myself since 1995, and inventor along with my partner of the world's first, closed, supercritical geothermal energy system in the form of U.S. Patent 8,381,523 B2, I am reasonably educated on green matters related to energy generation, climate, and environment.

Our environment is one thing; the wealth transfer scam another, with the scam leading directly to its unspoken goal; elimination of Main Street private property rights, Main Street wealth confiscation, behavior and identity modification, and implementation of world-wide Transhuman Fascism. Incidentally, funneling vast sums of Main Street money into Elite coffers removes those funds from genuine research budgets, which is not helpful for addressing environmental issues. Just sayin'.

The global carbon con is bandied about in various highly emotional guises, but in every scenario, the energy and banking monopoly gets paid tril-

---
225 Group and Lewin, *Report from Iron Mountain on the Possibility and Desirability of Peace.*

lions for producing nothing except digital carbon credits pulled from thin air—just like fiat money. By disingenuously regulating energy monopolies, which means protecting insider-controlled monopolies against competition for easier price fixing as well as enabling easier money laundering, order-followers convince Main Street that good sustainability strategy is paying energy monopolies trillions for not producing energy at all. We hear this tripe on mainstream media daily while the global syndicate destroys Earth's atmosphere and modifies weather and climate via aerosol spraying, modified HAARP technology, and so forth. Cow farts are not a problem. Elite psychopathy and incorrect Main Street perception are the synergistic problem.

Earth is approaching dangerously low levels of carbon dioxide at 400 ppm, not high levels. Even with increasing levels of carbon dioxide, say 2 parts per million annually, very good for plants and food crops by the way, also serving as free fertilizer for Third World nations, alarm bells will not go off. The relationship between atmospheric carbon dioxide and Earth's temperature is logarithmic, not arithmetic. This means: *"The first 20 parts per million of carbon dioxide in the atmosphere provides 1.6°C of warming, after which the effect drops away rapidly. From the current level of 400 parts per million, each addition of 100 parts per million adds only 0.1°C of warming. By the time we have dug up all the rocks we can economically burn, and burned them, we may reach 600 parts per million in the atmosphere. So perhaps we might add another 0.2°C of warming over the next two centuries. That warming will be lost in the noise of natural climate variation."*[226]

How would you like to own the business end of this banking climate monopoly? While building your Transhuman electromagnetic gulag at tax payer expense, also get paid to poison Earth's atmosphere, water, and soil, then get paid trillions over time for doing absolutely nothing other than genociding entire populations via toxic JABs and geoengineering. Well, not nothing; with all due respect, they must lie and then sell the lie. Anyway, "this will save us", the shriek-o-meter shrieks! (Shriek-o-meter is a Catherine Austin Fitts' term I've grown fond of.)

This egregious theft of Main Street wealth implemented with corrupt government mandated impunity, is an arrogant nightmare ever so much preferred by Elites to inconveniently and expensively earning business revenues the old-fashioned way. Psychopathic Elites detest the idea of working and sweating to provide useful services or products like oil, gasoline, diesel fuel, natural gas, electricity, etc., via actual labor or let's gasp, productivity and positive return on investment.

---

226 "The Carbon Dioxide Level Is Dangerously Low | Human Events," accessed March 2, 2022, http://archive.humanevents.com/2014/03/24/the-carbon-dioxide-level-is-dangerously-low/.

Carbon credits don't have to be shipped or stored; a postage stamp isn't even necessary (If we had Rule of Law, that would be mail fraud, wouldn't it?). Instead, gullible Main Street customers will, if we don't come to our senses, bear the malfeasant, government mandated, pass-through expense of a very clever digital energy swindle, that to top it off and rub our noses in it, provides extreme levels of invasive snooping, energy rationing, and societal behavioral control, while – and this is important, while **never actually doing anything at all to protect the environment**. It is just another aspect of *full spectrum dominance*. The climate change mystery by the way can be de-mystified in one word: GEOENGINEERING. *Follow the money and cancer epidemic* - both apply!

Top global syndicate mouth pieces like CCP controlled WHO, supported by corrupt agencies like CDC and DHHS are now bundling the climate change scam into unconstitutional medical malpractice protocols which we'll soon be seeing mandated on Main Street. Be prepared to bend over or duck.

As a prurient, *prominent global citizen* family example, John D. Rockefeller's Father, "Bill" was literally a snake oil salesman who made a crooked living conning people out of money, then sneaking down the road to cheat folks in the next town. Bill taught his conniving Sméagol-clone son, John D. to be ruthless and clever, so today their pathetic, genetically challenged progeny no longer have to scramble down dusty back roads evading angry, cheated Main Streeters; but instead, run their cons with arrogant aplomb from leather ensconced offices high atop energy gobbling phallic symbols in the monopolized fields of agribusiness, banking, chemicals, education, energy, media, medicine, mining, philanthropy, politics, publishing, transportation, and believe it or not, environment.

We see all this Elite conniving whenever not golfing, drug and sex trafficking, weapons smuggling, bribing politicians over expensive weekends on their vast estates, or enjoying pedophilic sports on luxurious private islands. What a living? Do we want to raise kids next to these folks? We ought not foolishly place trust in people inappropriately assigned respect for spending ill-gotten gains acquired through price fixing cons, bolstered by Luciferian religious practices.

A skilled litigator could not pedal this gratuitous Rockefeller nonsense covered in delicious chocolate to a starving nincompoop, yet many of us are happily, even self-righteously agreeing with and defending the shtick from schlock propaganda anchors at BBC, CNN, FOX, MSNBC, NPR, and the like. At least with the privately owned central bank scam, fraudulent as it is, useful services are sometimes provided; but this carbon hoax – nope, nada, nothing.

Give us your money, which by the way your government will confiscate for the Elites and though we don't mention it, you'll be granted economic slavery in return. The good news is, slavery comes with a pat on the back and a bumper sticker showing neighbors you care deeply about climate change? Slavery is never mentioned publicly.

Not even an intellectually beleaguered Yale grad can be denigrated or sufficiently abused to peddle this tripe to gullible citizens of Main Street. It takes full on, *Tavistock* indoctrinated, coffin initiated *Bonesman* to sell this stupidity and it appears, many of us are lining up to anxiously hand over hard earned money of our own free will. We cannot swallow this poison and bring about cooperative global freedom simultaneously, nor will any of this government sanctioned larceny benefit our environment. Why do we do it?

Well, that's an easy question to answer. We do it because the PsyOp tells us to do it and we have been taught decent people **OBEY** government leadership, even when provably criminal and/or murderous. Even when government policy is dictated by Corporatist Fascist thugs. So-called news, social media, television, radio, advertising, movies, sports, music, academia, most churches, and ever-present, order-following politicians are fully integrated in selling the hive-mind shtick for Elite criminals we don't even know.

Give up our hard earned money, OWN NOTHING, and enjoy our free roaming gulag until the genocidal poisoning kicks in is the globalist DAVOS crowd program. When sales propaganda fails, other forms of groupthink conditioning, entertainment indoctrination, and entrainment technology are employed. If these all fail, then finally, the Deep State Administrative Dictatorship is called up to unconstitutionally tax and regulate Main Street into compliance under threat of violence. How can so many of us maintain we're free? How can we miss the scam or the rapidly closing gulag gate?

Global Main Street society generally and the United States specifically are being Technocratically PsyOped into an incrementally impoverished, independence devouring maw of dopamine ejaculating, technological fraud intended to enslave Main Street in a world-wide, Neo-Feudal Electronic Matrix mindlessly ruled by amoral mathematical algorithms, conjured from stolen mountains of meta-data by pathological order followers working for socially deviant dynastic families suffering from severe genetic anomalies resulting from generations of inbred, gene pool shrinkage, and severe personality disorders.

Not to poke fun, which I surely am, but look at the ears, chins, noses, close-set beady eyes, and weird shaped heads on many of these *prominent global citizens*, who are sycophantically taught they are genetically superior. Scary stuff there. Apparently, Elites can be disturbingly homely mirror denialists, riding in black-windowed limousines and hiding on giant yachts in the South of France so they don't frighten Main Street kids into forgetting to pay taxes as grown-up serfs, nor forget to heroically donate their lives to far off resource wars for Elite profit.

It's far past time for us on Main Street to begin aggressively saying NO THANK YOU to this astonishing level of parasitic evil; BUT the only way to accomplish this task, is getting back in touch with our innate spiritual nature from which we have been programmatically and technologically bifurcated. We are technocratically confused and individually demoralized to the point we can no longer effectively support or protect ourselves, our families, friends, communities, or countries. We are being dumbed-down, social media/dopamine-stupefied, drugged, and lied to on a grand scale. We need to wake up and start living.

Some solutions are simple. For example, many of us are uneasy with unconstitutional (illegal) government spying on U.S. citizens as well as citizens of other nations. We should note that information on Main Street citizens cannot be abused if it isn't stored for access by abusers. NSA has a 1,000,000 square foot data storage facility in Utah and apparently has a new 2,800,000 square foot data storage facility in the works. No country on Earth outside the U.S. has the billions of dollars available to construct such monstrosities. NSA whistle-blower, Mr. Bill Binney reminds us, *cut off funding for meta-data storage and abuse of stored information becomes impossible. The potential abuse is immediately eliminated. National security goals can be attained without potential abuse by simply controlling and monitoring the data storage effectively.* Why aren't we demanding and doing this? We have the Constitutional right since these multinational corporations are just controlled extensions of our federal government and we are paying for the abuse.

Obscenely powerful government supported and protected internet multinationals like *Alibaba, Amazon, Alphabet (Google), Baidu, Booking, JD, Meta (Facebook), Netflix, Salesforce,* and *Tencent Holdings* are intertwined with rogue military science and communications technology in such a pathological manner, the entire megalomaniacal mosh pit poses a diabolical threat to life on Earth. Unwarranted surveillance is just a tiny tip of the Satanic iceberg. Our ionized atmosphere, *Space Fence,* electromagnetic entrainment and brain infecting AI comprise the globalist iceberg hidden far above the surface.

Social media monopolies like *YouTube, Twitter* and *META (Facebook)* enter into unconstitutional, - I say treasonous - agreements with craven federal government agencies to censor, restrict, outright ban, and track free Main Street speech and communication on their so-called private platforms. As functionally abusive, intertwined extensions of rogue government overreach these destructively dishonest monopolies do not qualify for legal protection under Section 230 of the *Communications Decency Act.*

Pretentious government bureaucrats and corrupted military scientists, all feigning overpaid malingering incompetence, together with despicably corrupt Congresspersons, with support by Constitutionally challenged Supreme Circus Clowns and malfeasant lower courts, have funded, created, and protect a depraved wireless monster, now intent on mindlessly omniciding Earth, though such awareness is apparently above the pay grade of order following psychopaths.

If we wish to avoid an Elite motivated, order-follower manipulated, ultimately self-perpetrated mass extinction event at the hands of genetically delusional lunatics and their pathological order followers, we MUST wake up, smell the sulfur, engage the hard work of self-evaluation, and kick some *prominent global citizen* butt. This is the hard work of **cooperative freedom**, and this work can be performed by no one outside Main Streets across the world. It is ours to do. Our so-called political leaders have been blackmailed, bought off, or frightened into working against their own citizens.

The only path to future safety, abundance, and spiritual health on Earth is for the people of sovereign nations to stand up, defend their cultures and traditions, respect other cultures and traditions, then cooperatively unite respective Main Streets to defeat Globalism and its sick obsession with RESETTING FEUDALISM across the planet. The GREAT RESET proposed by Globalist *wise guy* pawns at the *World Economic Forum* and other study group venues along with allied patsies extends far beyond feudalism and is actually the fruition of Satan's demonic plan for global destruction—nothing more.

True sustainability for all creation is in our Main Street hands should we choose to accept humanity's Divinely granted responsibility to nourish God's creation. At this point in human history, our task is immense and can only be accomplished by requesting and receiving God's grace as our armor. This is how we regain Paradise.

Every G20 Government is a Public Enemy No. 1.
Every G20 Government works to enslave its people.
Every G20 criminal enterprise is psychopathically managed
and is owned and operated by the same Global Syndicate.
The Global Syndicate CEO is Satan, Prince of Darkness.
Evil requires obedience to thrive.
Main Street Must Refuse to Obey!

24 • USA – Abused Tip of the NWO Spear

Remedy: The spiritual blessings, hope, and responsibility, i.e., COV-ENANT underlying America's founding in which so many of us once believed; have been co-opted by international Plutocrats and their Order followers for evil purposes. The wealth, diplomatic influence, and military might of America has been misused by rogue elements within U.S. government along with Elite controlled multinational corporate monopolies as Global Syndicate clubs subjugating populations around the globe, while preaching freedom, opportunity, and democracy. As American citizens, on behalf the world, we must stop supporting this obscene lie. The disgusting eye of the Global Syndicate has turned its glare on America's middle class. Its voracious maw is now swallowing our tattered Republic. If America's middle class perishes, the world's hope dies with us. It is time for Main Street America to AWAKEN and say, "NO MORE."

America has been aggressively abused as the tip of the *New World Order* spear since 1913, though the Satanic seed was planted at Yale in 1780 and Harvard in 1781, in part I believe, an Elite Prussian response to George Washington's success with his *Culper Spy Ring* against British troops. *Free Masonry* does pollute the entirety of today's *District of Columbia* along with most of our modern world but was not yet infiltrated by Weishaupt and friends at the time of America's founding, though a number of Founders were at least peripherally aware of Weishaupt's activities. The *Bavarian Illuminati* which infiltrated *Free Masonry* was only founded by Adam Weishaupt (1748-1830) on 1 May 1776 – two months before 4 July 1776. Granted, this destructive ideology was spawned many centuries earlier, probably before humanity made its created appearance on Earth, but now the 21st century geopolitical reality adds a Transhuman twist to the good versus evil theme.

All roads converging on subversion of America's Constitutionally recognized freedoms emanate from Prussian nobility and power brokers through *British East India Company* connections, *Barings Bank*, one of England's oldest merchant banks along with other dynastic banks to Yale University, its venomous *Skull and Bones*, and Harvard University. Silent tentacles have long connected invisible Prussian influence with City of London, undermining Vatican City, and now Washington D.C. for collaborative *deep state* support.

Per Mr. Will Zoll's *Substack* (https://substack.com/profile/54940767-will-zoll), it is primarily through secret societies like *Skull and Bones*, and the more philosophical *Phi Beta Kappa*, that Hegel's bellicose, poorly written world view regarding State authority and progress were and are kept alive. *Phi Beta Kappa*, America's first secret society, introduced as a debating society, was formed at *William and Mary College* in 1776, matriculating to *Yale* in 1780, and *Harvard* in 1781, where the parasitic Prussian long term take down of American independence was spawned. This subversion launched the educational indoctrination and dumbing down of America's Ivy League mis-educated leaders via the concept of **"infiltration instead of invasion"**. The rest of the chaotic story since 1780 is history and the global syndicate's Hegelian-Marxist mess we live with today is real life.

The global syndicate has historically tolerated or perhaps was unable to prevent U.S. Main Street citizens creating and holding a larger than average slice of Malthusian pie via their Constitutional Republic since 1789. This larger slice of pie unfortunately distracts and obscures U.S. Main Street's view of brutal international strategies employed through Elite abuse of American taxpayer wealth, diplomatic influence, and military power around the world.

If characterizing the United States as tip of the *New World Order* spear appears overstated, consider **Operation FISH** – a covert 1940 operation relocating British bullion, securities, and so forth to Halifax, Nova Scotia (i.e., Canada and from there to I don't know—some say Fort Knox) for protection from Nazi seizure as Belgium, France, Luxembourg, and Netherlands had already fallen to Hitler's armies. The United Kingdom was left standing alone against German occupation. Something had to be done. *Operation FISH* is historic fact, some claiming it the largest transfer of wealth in human history.

Following is my high-octane speculation based on work done by various researchers and as discussed by UK's Peter Gumley,[227] speculating on what may have transpired between the UK and US on or about 1940.

As mentioned earlier in *Reflexive Injustice* (Chapter 5), members of the Rhodes/Milner inner circle, regretting the loss of their American colony, discussed dumping the off-putting, imperial sounding **British Empire phraseology** in exchange for a more geopolitically palatable **Global Federation, i.e., commonwealth** concept. Though the term was in use much earlier, the **British Empire** was first officially referred to as The **British Commonwealth of Nations** in the December 3rd, 1931, *Statute of Westminster*, recognizing the sovereign right of self-rule among many of the Empire's Crown Colonies, Dominions, Mandates, and Protectorates.

Key to this concept were U.S. resources, wealth, diplomacy, and military power. British Elites and their Prussian associates wanted their colony back – even if it meant the United States might sit at the head of the new Federation. Prussian – now German power, or worse a German-Russian alliance would threaten British hegemony, therefore had to be dealt with. Elite alliances, based on Satanically influenced greed, are tentative, unstable, often adversarial, and prone to change.

Bearing this Elite global balance of power in mind while realizing the **Global Federation** concept never fully usurped the U.S., at least not formally or publicly, even beneath gifted pens of historians Carroll Quigley, Antony Sutton, and others – we quickly discover fertile ground for Elite maneuvering. Clearly, the idea of controlling America lived on among Prussian and British Elites. Long story short, I suspect Britain, on the brink of German defeat in 1940 made a deal with the United States. Save Britain from Germany and America is granted top position in the commonwealth, i.e., New World Order. This may have come about because *Anglo-American Alliance* puppet, Hitler was raging out of global syndicate control. Pathologic dynastic families lack crystal balls just as Main Streeters do, not to mention spoiled Elites aren't particularly bright.

I imagine a British-American deal something like this occurred simply because if something like this did not happen – how do we explain the schizophrenically feckless leadership of U.S. politicos since WW II? I believe British Elites turned over NWO *Numero Uno* position at the unopposed top of the global syndicate dung heap in exchange for military and other protective cooperation. If so, the United States has not been a sovereign nation

227 *Peter Gumley on Bojo, the British Deep State and the American Empire*, accessed September 6, 2021, https://rumble.com/vlau2g-peter-gumley-on-bojo-the-British-deep-state-and-the-American-empire.html.

at least since WW II (many say since 1913), but is a key player as a large dynastic family global protectorate. It also appears, no sooner was this hypothetical deal made, and Britain turned its *Tavistock Institute of Human Relations* (±1948) loose to wage psychological warfare on the American populace to finally, over time, subversively take its long-lost colony back conclusively; also explaining current PsyOp insanity across indoctrinated Main Street America.

This power struggle between Britain and Germany/Russia also accounts for why Great Britain, despite its own *Anglo-American Alliance* involvement and creation of the *European Union* as a step toward *One World Government* suddenly said oopps, backtracked, and ducked. The British Crown and Elites close to it, apparently realized Germany, the most powerful European economy would be the gorilla in the EU kitchen, particularly if Germany allied with Russia—a fact pointed out by President Trump. This British realization may explain why Great Britain never gave up its British Pound Sterling for Euros and why many close to the Crown favored **Brexit**, even if quietly.

If the five paragraphs above are even close to correct, the United States is not functionally a sovereign nation, our so-called leadership is treasonous, and we the people of Main Street fix it or become feudal serfs at some transhuman point. Most Americans are unaware of this possible resource raping reality, but none-the-less, innocent citizens of defenseless nations across the globe are starving, bleeding, and dying beneath relentless pursuit of all resources, all wealth, and control of all populations by *Anglo-American Establishment* global syndicate controllers. The American spear point is rusty now, its poignant power no longer needed by the syndicate… or wanted. There is to be no more pie for America's Main Street. The NWO bakers began U.S. de-industrialization in the 1980's, ramped up de-capitalization in the late 1990's and moved the bakery South and East. Far, far East to the developing **Chinese CCP *One Belt, One Road*** slaughter-fest.

To maliciously rub our American Main Street noses in their slime, the Chinese Communist Party (CCP), another *Anglo-American Establishment* Billy-club, in league with thousands of dumbed down complicit traitors sabotaged America's 2020 elections. In addition to the already missing $86 trillion since 1998, America's aging 21st century middle class has stored within its pension plans, $25 trillion or so more dollars. The syndicate wants that money; all of it; every penny. It has already taken much of it through pension plan purchases of U.S. securities. Cash to the U.S. Treasury; a paper IOU to the pension plan; cash out D.C.'s back door to syndicated multinational monopoly contracts; and finally, compounded fully laundered cash to syndicate family coffers. We really should pay attention.

Add in a few subsidies, insider NGO grants and loans never to be repaid, bailouts, bail-ins, etc.,and Main Street's public balance sheet is 100% red: and the syndicate balance sheet, 100% black. The syndicate is done with America except for resource rape and future slave labor, which must now be energy down-sized, wealth-raped, and robotized into a drugged, entrained transhuman enslavement center where Transhuman high-tech production can quietly, profitably, and conveniently progress… without the inconvenience of historic middle-class ingenuity, entrepreneurship, work ethic, or any other human ethic. Of course, this sick plan won't work as Elite fools are murdering the goose laying their Golden Eggs. America invents the technologies these idiots use but fortunately, blind is as blind does.

The global syndicate is done using gullibly pliable Main Street America as the tip of its global domination spear and it's our North American turn to be raped. The **Rape of America** was taste tested from 1861 through 1865. The NWO setup was developed more aggressively in Woodrow Wilson's 1913, then after WW II the global syndicate launched Tavistock's long-term PsyOp plans. America's rape was pilot programmed via the 1990's **Rape of Russia**, progressing to a ravenous feeding frenzy beginning in 1997 with more than $86 trillion missing since – that we know of – and now the final piratization of America's $25 trillion pension fund holdings is well underway along with imposition of full spectrum dominant transhuman slavery.

Independent small business, America's Main Street entrepreneurial backbone is being wiped out by lunatics through asymmetric warfare in the form of COVID SCAMDEMIC lockdowns, toxic (fake vaccine) injections, and nonsense we already discussed – plus more we have not gotten around to. We can hide our wallets, open our eyes, stand up, and prepare to defend our Constitution and children's futures across the globe – or we can step into our Neo-feudal serf role with our Nike-footed kids as starving, surveillance capital waifs.

The rape of America has long since commenced and is now concluding in an earnest *cut and run* toward Asia, though for most of us it is not yet apparent. Transnational monopoly insiders are selling off stocks like drunken chambermaids dumping soiled hotel linens; malevolently cashing in on SEC protected insider information, while Main Street investors naively keep on keepin' on buying into the soon to burst stock market bubble. After the coming correction to some measure of real value, insiders will be in a cash-rich position poised and ready to purchase assets for pennies on the dollar from non-insider losers of Main Street. Sell the top; buy the dip – particularly effective when insiders know the dip is coming because they orchestrated it. Additionally, money is stolen in other more sophisticated ways such as the pirating of pension funds just mentioned, inflation tax, or cheap commercial property acquisition in burned out Blue Cities as we see *BlackRock* doing.

U.S. pension funds total around $25 trillion in assets on paper as of this writing. The global syndicate has no intention of wasting those assets on non-productive Baby Boomer retirees. The treasonous Obama Regime obediently looted Medicare to the tune of more than $750 billion dollars as a slow trial balloon start. We the Baby Boomers said nothing—most not noticing. Pension funds are historically encouraged to invest in *safe* U.S. government securities such as treasury bills, treasury notes, savings bonds, and so forth. Our dutiful Federal government accepts hard earned, pensioner cash savings from the funds; provides a digital IOU in return; then huge portions of unmonitored pensioner savings vanish contractually out the unaudited, money laundering Congressional back door.

Death of the abusive Petro-dollar, the centrally planned DAVOS RESET and I suppose, hyper-inflation via some orchestrated event, probably COVID 33, a new flu, or WW III will be blamed for the unfortunate loss of saved income for Baby Boomers, already being forced for survival to compete as septuagenarian and octogenarian serfs with obscenely over-taxed millennials for part-time work. Not much decent-paying work remaining in America. The syndicate moved it to Asia – the new Tip of the NWO Spear. We Boomers are aggressively being seed planted by *Mockingbird* financial media to the discordant tune of—we have not worked hard enough nor saved enough. Tough luck.

Consider the 2018 D.C. brainstorm to downsize government assets. Eliciting uninformed Conservative and Libertarian support, the ruse goes something like this. *Government has grown too large. We don't know how it happened, but in the interest of citizens, underutilized government properties and services must be auctioned off and/or privatized.* **Reality likely reads as follows:** For the past century our federal government has confiscated (taxed) Main Street citizen wealth, transferring that wealth to global syndicate insiders through hundreds of financially bloated programs growing government, government contractors, and government property in every unaudited way imaginable. Just to name a few: subsidies, research, useless studies, land acquisition, rights-of-way acquisition, building construction, property leases, military-surveillance-administrative-financial - and other contracts, subcontracts, accounting services, vehicle purchases and leases – I think we all get the picture, but if not, here's one recent example.

Brutally, after two decades and many thousands dead, wounded, and displaced, while intentionally leaving American citizens, military dogs, and Afghan allies behind, to really rub our Main Street noses in it, the treasonously fraudulent Biden Regime and its WOKE Generals, in August 2021 gave ± $85 billion dollars of U.S. military equipment and arms to the Afghan Taliban, al Qaeda, and other Islamic Jihadist groups, thereby funding a **Jihad Super State** likely controlled by China's **CCP**, from Afghanistan and Pakistan across the entire Middle East and Northern Africa. Never has America witnessed treason at such a catastrophic level. What now?

After a century enabling D.C. handlers to flourish through corrupt government contracts and lucrative government purchases at taxpayer expense – now, for the public good – we MUST let those same handlers and insiders who profitably blew up our government to lucratively downsize government by inexpensively purchasing government assets for pennies on the auction block dollar. It is impossible to make this nonsense up, yet there it is.

In its entirety, this corruptly mismanaged theft now totals more than $86 trillion dollars we know of, plus another $200 or so trillion dollars in unfunded mandates, plus ± $25 trillion in threatened pension funds – and now – we're selling off what we the people of Main Street paid for so the folks who ripped us off can rip us off again on the flip side. If we want proof the United States is not sovereign and no longer functions as the sharpened tip of the global syndicate's NWO spear, there it is. Follow the money and while we do, let's notice our own vanishing wallets. Just like The Rape of Russia through the Clinton 1990's and beyond, The Rape of America began in earnest in Clintonian 1997.

The New World Order control apparatus is as immense as it is subtle. Surrounded by it, swimming in it, choking on it, and living under its boot heel – we find the matrix-like web difficult to see. It is always just a little out of focus; there but not there. Its compartmentalized structure, multi-tiered agendas, and sophisticated network of study groups renders its organized attack nearly imperceptible – even to the rank and file working every day within it.

Connected international events powerfully impacting nations appear disjointed, like unrelated happenstance occurring in random bursts as unexplainable chaos – but there is cleverly obscured underlying order. Dark spiritual order waging battle against spiritual light. Chaos is the material intermediate step; the transitional steppingstone to dictatorship implemented by syndicate order followers in targeted victim countries, regardless of ism – soon to include all countries IF Luciferian influence is allowed to proliferate and dominate.

If the United States is cleverly misused as a long-handled lever for the next great conflagration; then tiny Israel is even more cleverly misused as the leveraged fulcrum. The Middle East, Far East, Australia, Africa, Eastern and Western Europe, South, Central, and North America are all being stirred in the heated divide and conquer hate-pot as our world is levered by deceptively divisive agendas into a sick, depraved, Global Totalitarian stew.

Nation-baiting, race-baiting, sex-baiting, class-baiting, eco-baiting, wealth-baiting, gun control baiting, you-name-it baiting are all expertly applied, igniting a heated fervor of societal anxiety (*mass formation*) demanding relief. The global syndicate answer is usually war. Whether war again, something else to blame, or the onslaught of transhuman enslavement, it will be followed by fifty years of heavily surveilled digital financial enslavement; followed by what? What will Main Street accept without revolt? Will Main Street be able to revolt?

As mentioned earlier, American hippie guru, Ram Dass recalls in *Be Here Now*, (page 43) being told by Georges I. Gurdjieff, ***"You are in prison. If you think you're free, you can't escape"***. One reason we think we're free in America is because we no longer know what freedom is. The zero-sum apple pie is being redefined, sliced, and downsized as we newspeak. Consider six apparently unrelated activities; abortion, aerosol spraying, 5G, toxic vaccines, GMO foods, and prisons connected by unseen sinews, focused like death lasers on profitable societal destruction by global syndicate order followers harvesting Main Street with impunity through corrupt government pawns with *Mockingbird* media cover.

Since global syndicate funded *Antifa* and *Black Lives Matter* gained front page prominence looting and burning targeted neighborhoods, many of them home to people of color, I guess to cure racism – consider how decent people of color are lied to, manipulated, and abused in liberal America. By the way, unvetted Islamic terrorists are openly flowing into the U.S. through WOKE military bases as I write this in 2022. Islamic military age males are flocking to existing U.S. terror cells across the continent, likely soon to join *Antifa* and *BLM* marauders in violent BLUE antipathy to thwart legitimate election fraud audits, if they crank up. We'll know them by fake FBI coordinated MAGA costumes and masks they'll be wearing so Mockingbird media can adroitly lie about alleged Trump supporter violence as they did regarding 6 January 2021 with FBI assistance—but I digress, again.

Hard to figure how America is the land of the free, sustaining only 5% of the world's population, while simultaneously detaining 25% of the world's prison population. The leading New World Order storm edge envisioned by Oligarchs for centuries has arrived, though the burden of restraint is not yet equally distributed. Consider government practiced racism as big insider business. Inundated by Orwellian Newspeak parroted 365/24/7 by highly paid, order-following media drones with no apparent *boredom threshold*, backed by integrity-challenged politicos, **black genocide is practiced daily in major U.S. cities and we the middle-class people have no idea it is happening**. We claim nescience, but is it ignorance?

Beneath the malfeasant guise of *"we care so much about Blacks, Hispanics, and the poor"* lies a multi-tiered meat grinder sopping up billions of dollars, aborting melanin-rich babies, organ harvesting, dumbing down, and imprisoning Black children and young people, primarily young Black males. The U.S. Black population is about 46 million (2019 data), though so many Hispanics and others now identify as Black, data is uncertain. Using this data, accurate or not, if Blacks constitute ±14% of the U.S. population, why are 38% of all U.S. abortions for Black babies? That is a lot of organs harvested, particularly when baby murder is held off until late term for larger organs and more tissue to sell.

Did you know the average human body has parts legally worth as much as $1 million... and on the Black Market five to ten times more depending on degree, demand, and sophistication of salvage? Abortion clinics have this lucrative market dialed in, so certainly do not need Federal funding to further enable their barbaric body parts distribution business... but government funds them anyway with Uni-Party complicit consent despite useless rhetoric.

As a side note regarding the open U.S. Southern border Democrats and Rinos are so fond of: the financial value of a sex trafficked child who can survive its short useful life, is estimated by cartel bean counters at $20 million per unit. They too, are then ritually sacrificed, organ harvested, or just thrown away.

Reasons, justifications, and excuses vary, but using today's 46 million as base, nearly 40% of Black children since 1973 have been murdered. A Black mother is nearly four times more likely than a Caucasian mother to abort her child. Liberals call this caring. Nearly 80% of Planned Parenthood's active surgical abortion factories are located within a two-mile radius of Black or Hispanic neighborhoods. Planned Parenthood's research firm, *Guttmacher Institute* disingenuously disputes these numbers and is frequently quoted by those favoring Black genocide, though they may not understand what they support.

Guttmacher Institute claims fewer than 1 in 10 abortion providers are in majority-Black neighborhoods. True of course. Given Blacks comprise only ±14% of U.S. population, few areas in America are majority Black. By zip code area, only about 3% of U.S. zip code areas can be considered majority Black. The same percentage applies to majority Black County populations across the U.S. Planning for government funded Black genocide factories doesn't locate baby-murder shops in majority Black neighborhoods, just within walking distance of Black populations.

The Clinton Administration and its order-following Congress began pushing *Anti-Violence Strategy* and *Three-Strikes Laws* in March 1994 along with *mandatory minimum sentences* and *three-times-you're-out standards* throughout the nineties.

This was followed by rabidly decreased public-defender budgets and billions of dollars' worth of new private detention centers. This government supported; privatized prison system maximally guarantees insider private prison owners *"no prison vacancies"* along with *"government guaranteed profit"*. Elites always make bank while dividing and conquering and nothing more easily or permanently divides than race. Government goons drug Black populations, lock 'em up, then hoping for a profitable race war, blame White Main Street for the injustice.

With the new system in place, we've seen CIA protected Drug Cartels shipping narcotics into inner cities by the ton, followed by SWAT Teams dropping into those same inner cities. Young Blacks and Hispanics are herded into prisons like there is no tomorrow… and for these young people there isn't. Interestingly, Mr. Clinton was directly involved in Iran-Contra's drug/weapons running as Governor of Arkansas and became a CIA darling back in the late seventies via George H. W. Bush and friends. Mockingbird media doesn't mention this. No man is an island, and neither were Carter, Reagan, or Clinton.

Granted, many states enforced so-called *habitual offender laws* prior to 1994, but D.C.'s national agenda requiring any person having two prior convictions, then committing a violent felony to serve a mandatory life sentence was an enormous financial boon for private prison industry insiders and a government caused, Black family disaster for America's inner cities. This unconscionable program was fully supported by then U.S. Senator, now fraudulent White House squatter, Joe Biden. Crime rates dropped in some cities after 1994, but those drops are difficult to correlate to Three-Strikes Laws as other policies were simultaneously enacted across the country including non-prosecution due to forced budget constraints.

The United States boasts more than 2.2 million citizens profitably detained in prisons, 40% of which are Black, though the U.S. Black population is only ±14%. Running a close second, Hispanics comprise ±16% of U.S. population and 33% of our prison population. Blacks as well as Hispanics are therefore, forced by government policy to be disproportionately leased to influential multinational corporations providing convict labor at ridiculously low cost. Payment varies widely from $0.10 to $1.00 per hour. This is the U.S. Establishment's version of the Russian, Chinese, and Nazi Germany slave-labor-camp playbook right here in the United States. Liberals call it rehabilitation instead of forced labor and laud its healthy inmate benefits. I say "slavery's back" alive and well by another name that sounds like CARING.

Per Mr. Noah Zatz of UCLA Law School[228], nearly half the 2.2 million U.S. prison inmates work full time, earning near slave wages working for compa-

---

228 Noah Zatz, "Working at the Boundaries of Markets: Prison Labor and the Economic

nies like AT&T, Boeing, Dell, IBM, Hewlett-Packard, Honeywell, Intel, Lucent Technologies, Macy's, Microsoft, Motorola, Nordstrom's, Pierre Cardin, Revlon, Target, and Texas Instrument to name a few. Is this philanthropy?

Checking further, we'll find inmate slave labor to be a critical component of U.S. domestic repression comprising a billion-dollar-plus business annually, fully supported by more immoral, unconstitutional legislation such as the Patriot Act, Homeland Security, and Domestic Security Enhancement Acts. The highest prison wage I've heard cited is $2.00/hour, but rates that high are uncommon.

Ms. Catherine Austin Fitts wrote extensively about the **private prison scam** and has established a website detailing her findings.[229] Ms. Fitts is also the publisher of *The Solari Report* as referenced elsewhere. *The Aristocracy of Prison Profits* is required reading for anyone imagining Rule of Law applies to Main Street USA.

On the so-called domestic terrorism front, Mr. Douglas Valentine tells us: *"Secret subpoenas used by DHS to obtain information can't be refused or disclosed, making it impossible to defend against false charges".*[230] This abortion/prison quick-study primer, here at home, hopefully has had little or no impact on you or I, so far, so let's move on, realizing that millions of Americans do inhabit our nightmare inner cities in abject terror of both their neighbors and the police… and have absolutely no one they can call for protection – and now their Blue Mayors applaud burning their neighborhoods to the ground, so valuable property can be cheaply acquired by insiders like *BlackRock*. These hard-working, productive citizens are being harvested openly and with impunity. This is not, by the way, a local police issue. This is a Federal Injustice Department issue in which good police and sheriffs are caught within a rogue CIA, FBI, DoJ managed horror show run on behalf *prominent global citizens*.

BUT WAIT --- now THEY'RE coming for us on middle class Main Street with our paint-blistered, over-mortgaged white picket fences and two-car garages. Productive middle-class America is now demonized and targeted as WHITE SUPREMEST AMERICA. The United States' usefulness as tip of the NWO spear is over and the military-backed petro-dollar has exhausted its half-century course since Secretary of State, Henry Kissinger agreed to its implementation with Saudi princes in 1973-1974, meaning America's role in the Anglo-American Empire is now finished, kaput—excepting ongoing resource rape. I worked my entire life to be rewarded by privileged Establishment order followers with labels

---

Dimension of Employment Relationships," SSRN Scholarly Paper (Rochester, NY: Social Science Research Network, December 19, 2007), https://papers.ssrn.com/abstract=1075842.
229 Catherine Austin Fitts, "Dillon Read & Co. Inc. And the Aristocracy of Prison Profits," 2006, 124.
230 Valentine, *The CIA as Organized Crime*, 308.

like **excess population, deplorable toxic white male, and domestic terrorist** – of which I am calloused hands and pitchfork proud. OK, not many callouses.

Do we recall the Rape of Russia back in the 1990's? If your news sources are MSM, probably not, but it happened. Oligarchs and syndicate friends of the Clinton Regime purchased Russian government properties for a few kopecks on the ruble with resulting financial chaos ending the lives of more than 2 million Russian citizens. Some claim 25 million Russian citizens were eliminated during the 1990's, but I haven't confirmed that number. Oligarchs stole trillions of rubles from the Russian Main Streets all with *Anglo-American Establishment* assistance. China and its *Chinese Communist Party* (CCP) tell a similar story leading up to its ownership of the treasonous Biden Regime and many State governors, not to mention helping manage U.S. elections for control of Main Street.

The use of **Hegelian Dialectic** bringing about Main Street *mass formation* is impressive. Wall Street and City of London, defended by Vatican City use American wealth to build the Chinese Communist Party (CCP) juggernaut, then turn around and use their CCP trained mutant to rape the same American citizens who paid to build and arm the CCP in the first place. Elites are stupid, yet clever.

The rape and enslavement of American Main Street citizens has come home to roost after Russia's practice run using a simple Chinese formula.
De-industrialize America then apply the equation:
Pension funds + Treasuries out D.C.'s back door = full syndicate coffers.

Selling government property for pennies on the dollar to connected insiders is the newest phase of the global syndicate con, sucking in Conservatives and Libertarians like flies to sticky tape. Add some too-large-to-fail bank bail-ins and pension fund seizures for seasoning to suck those IRA's and 401 K's dry and it is a *fait accompli*. Nothing left but government sponsored democide for unnecessary *citizen livestock* and a **digital monthly survival stipend** for the slaves deemed necessary. No hope, no future, no life – unless we say NO!

The good news is, America is done as the NWO spear tip. The bad news is, we must now defend ourselves against China and its allies, the new Now spear tip our U.S. government funded and supported on behalf the global syndicate since WW II.

Profound synchronicity exists between principles set forth in the Declaration of Independence and U.S. Constitutional strictures limiting government to secure those principles for posterity. Neither stands without the other. Together they cannot stand without we the people vigilantly exercising our sovereign rights as human beings created by God.

25 • WINNING

Remedy: Enforce our Constitution or lose it! Fascist American Big Government and Corporatocracy have been steadily undermining our Constitutionally recognized rights since New World Order pawn, Woodrow Wilson argued we must abandon it in favor of organic governmental evolution (my words). This insurgent advice, unfortunately followed, along with turning our backs to God's blessings brought us to the 1984 style Administrative Dictatorship America is RULED by today. We have proven beyond Masonic doubt, we cannot manage our Republic on our own—without grace, the armor of God. Dark Lord influence overwhelms our judgement, convincing us to go it alone against spiritual Satanic forces stronger than we are. Winning means turning back to God, through Christ, with the help of the Holy Spirit. This is the path to successfully regaining freedom for America and then the world.

WHAT DOES SAYING NO
TO TRANSHUMAN SLAVERY
and
WINNING LOOK LIKE?

Rejecting the global syndicate plan for **Transhuman Feudalism** with its **METAVERSE, NEURALINK**, and other enslaving nonsense necessarily looks like Main Street Americans and others across the globe *walking away from* disempowering ***factional divisions of politics***; to embrace protective solidarity by uniting family, friends, neighbors, tribes, communities, and nations with our Creator's love at the LOCAL grassroots level.

WINNING back American sovereignty looks like saying NO THANK YOU to global syndicate Shadow Governments and Nazi International Deep Administrative State pawns. Washington D.C. and all WEF influenced G20 authoritarian states are a problem, but not the problem. We are The Problem. Lack of Main Street moral standards, personal responsibility, and apathy are the root problem and there is no winning until we deal with ourselves. We must first repair our own hearts—only then can we help repair psychopathic Elite hearts.

**WINNING MEANS TURNING BACK TO OUR CREATOR;
ACCEPTING RESPONSIBILITY FOR OUR ACTIONS;
LEARNING TO RECEIVE AND SHARE LOVE;
THEN EMBRACING THE JOY OF REALITY.**

Winning looks like turning away from Satanic influence by relying on faith strengthened by grace through the Holy Spirit. Winning looks like rolling up our Main Street sleeves, getting our hands dirty, and entering local politics in a very real, inconvenient way by becoming community leaders, school board members, city council members, county board members, state legislators, and MOST IMPORTANTLY – following Arizona Patriot, Daniel Schultz's suggestion to become **Republican Precinct Committeeman**.[231] I say Republican because the entire DNC is Satanically lost to Marxist, Fascist, Globalism. The RNC is only partially lost, with its corrupt Establishment sold out to global syndicate psychopathy, but the **MAGA MOVEMENT** is still intact – meaning we the people of Main Street can carry the RNC back to honest, **America First** representation. Third Parties just split the patriotic, Constitution supporting vote, handing power to psychopathic Communist-Fascist criminals.

Note: The pathetic Establishment Republican controlled Arizona Legislature with Democrat assistance passed **HB 2839** under a declared emergency requiring a 2/3 vote. This bill, among other things, destroyed grass roots electoral participation of local elected Precinct Committeeman (PCs) by turning PC appointments over to county political parties with subsequent approval of Boards of Supervisors. Language changing manner of PC elections on page 6 of this 8 page House bill is quite specific, suggesting pandering excuses by Arizona Republican RINOs are evidence of incompetence, lies, or both. In any case, corrupt elected representatives in Arizona are now made less accountable to constituents and local grass roots political opposition. This has no effect (so far) on other states, though Republican RINOs everywhere appreciate the idea.

---

231 Daniel J. Schultz, *How To Get Into The Real Ball Game Of Politics Where You Live To Help President Donald J. Trump Make America Great Again* (Independently published, 2017).

Only by American citizens putting **GOD FIRST** can the **AMERICA FIRST MOVEMENT** become a reality enabling Main Street people to take back our broken Republic. Only after taking it back, can we use our God Loving Republic to better our communities, states, country, and world. **America First** is the **MAGA path** leading to the end of Mercantile world resource rape by global dynastic families and their cowardly order followers.

Winning looks like humanity reuniting itself and all creation with our Creator in work, love, generosity, and shared abundance. It is our human *telos* to protect, nourish, and shepherd not only each other, but all creation to reunification with our Father. This is a primary aspect of the Biblical term *dominion* in the sense of **responsible stewardship**. This Biblical aspect of dominion extends well beyond the Bible and is inherent in all human activity, including thought and emotion. Dr. Masaru Emoto in 2005 published a wonderful book based on decades of water research titled *The Hidden Messages in Water*. A book considering among other things, spiritual connections between human consciousness, quantum physics, and matter—particularly water.

Discussing in Chapter One, *Of What Is the Universe Made?* Dr. Emoto explains the nature of our vibrational universe, the unique vibrational frequency of each individual thing, the concept of resonance, and how **water reflects the quality of the state of people's souls**. Thoughts, words, music, and emotions are all vibrational as are all known substances. His research shows that in the presence of information conflicting with fundamental laws of nature, say various forms of pollution, incomplete ice crystals will be formed. Water exposed to the words *Thank You* on the other hand, form beautiful geometric crystals.

Dr. Emoto's research into the nature of H_2O suggests negativity does not exist naturally. For example, the words *You Fool* do not exist in nature and are unnatural elements created by people (and I add through demonic influence, the source of all negativity). "The words *gratitude* and *love* form the fundamental principles of the laws of nature and the phenomenon of life."[232] It is said **like attracts like** and we know fundamentally incompatible frequencies cannot resonate. "When the frequency difference is twofold, fourfold, eightfold, and so on – or one-half, one-quarter, and so on – the result is resonance. The principle of this relationship extends to infinity. No matter how distant the frequencies, resonance will result if one of the two numbers is a multiple of the other."[233] This principle is clearly demonstrated in the six basic **Solfeggio frequencies** heard in Gregorian Chants. The six frequencies are: 396, 417, 528, 639, 741, and 852 Hertz.

---

232 Masaru Emoto, *The Hidden Messages in Water*, Illustrated edition (New York: Atria Books, 2005), 46.
233 Emoto, 49.

Note: The **Solfeggio** (*Just Intonation*) **Scale** developed in the 11th century was replaced by the 16th century with the **Twelve-Tone** (*Equal Temperament*) **Scale** used today. Nikola Tesla is said to have commented while speaking with Ralph Bergstresser in 1942: *If you want to find the secrets of the universe, think in terms of energy, frequency, and vibration.*

Resonant frequencies are significant in terms of Natural Law and human behavioral relationships. Sadly, it appears the global syndicate knows more about this subject than most of us on Main Street do, suggesting we up our reality learning curve. Japanese martial arts for instance, speak of *"winning without fighting"*, meaning avoid resonating with an enemy because **disharmony is destructive**. "Humans are the only creatures that have the capacity to resonate with all other creatures and objects found in nature."[234] This suggests according to Dr. Emoto we must stop thinking of human beings as the bad guys and begin working more diligently to revive Biblical human responsibility (my words) in the world, so we can live in harmony with our world; not continue polluting, resource raping, and destroying it - and NO, I am not against using resources responsibly. Sustainably living in our world means saying NO to Luciferian influence, which human history demonstrates can only be done with the help of God's grace.

One last thought from Dr. Emoto, who speaks of Kazuo Murakami, professor emeritus of Tsukuba University, notable for interpreting the oxide DNA code called *renin*. Dr. Murakami notes, "...the more you understand DNA, the more you are forced to admit that some hand played a role in the recording of so much minute and elaborate information in such small spaces."[235]

Dr. Emoto goes on to describe an experiment now repeated many times where three glass jars are filled with rice. Every day for a month, the words ***Thank you*** are spoken to the first jar. ***You fool*** is spoken daily to the second jar, and the third jar is ***simply ignored***. The ignored rice rotted more quickly than the rice repeatedly called *you fool*. This simple experiment relates the powerful relationship between emotion, language, and our physical world. It shows being ignored is more damaging than being ridiculed.[236]

Winning looks like making our world a better place, in turn requiring we make ourselves better persons. We can overcome Luciferian influence and what we call evil to accomplish winning in the above context through the grace of the Holy Spirit. This grace enables each of us the guidance, love, and protection of our Creator's transcendent power over evil. **Human love** is not possible without grace. We cannot overcome evil influence and learn to love on our own as *Free Masonry* would have us believe. This anointing by

234 Emoto, 51.
235 Emoto, 60.
236 Emoto, 65.

the Holy Spirit must be requested by each of us as we are created with free will; after which we are bound together in unity with the power of our Father and His Son, Jesus Christ, through the healing power of the Holy Spirit.

We often speak glowingly of political leaders, but forget, politicians don't start parades, they join them. **It is always up to us on Main Street to start the parade and it's long past time we started this America First Parade.**

Holding elected representatives and appointed bureaucrats accountable DEMANDS REDUCING THE SIZE OF AMERICAN GOVERNMENT BY AT LEAST 75%. It has been a mistake and is foolish for citizens to permit Washington D.C. to grow one inch beyond its Constitutional Authority. A $5 trillion dollar treasonously metastasizing government is a non-transparent, unaccountable, unapproachable, unmanageable behemoth – a putrid septic pit—a perfect matrix within which Satanically influenced psychopaths can invisibly serve their global syndicate masters with hidden impunity. This obscene beast *we the people* allowed to grow in D.C. must now be tamed and reduced to manageable size. Maybe 25% or so of its current bloat.

New World Order families with DAVOS crowd financial, media, political, and technical hit men and women in bondage to these dynastic families comprise a Satanic organization working for global human enslavement and ultimately destruction of all creation, though most NWO drones don't know it. It is time for Main Street to finally stand up to this evil and put an end to it.

Satan's free will choice to reject God's love brought disharmony and evil into existence – an existence alongside which and under the influence of which every human is born. This circumstance, this epic battle between good and evil, enables our free will choice to accept or reject God's love. Salvation is not for you or me. Salvation is for all of us together, including all creation. It is our human task to help each other sort through the isms and go *Beyond All Isms* to find the good stuff evil attempts to hide from view. We must overcome the enormity of the **global study group system** of indoctrination to determine the truth of our own reality—truth occulted for centuries.

It doesn't matter whether we live one material life on Earth or are reincarnated many times – the choice between good and evil is the same and must be made. Make our choice once, make it many times, make our choice better each time – it makes no difference as the battle between good and evil is ongoing, and personal choice is required until such time as our Creator brings this incredible dualistic arena to its just termination or doesn't. I don't go to the meetings so have no idea how or when this glorious battle ends, though believe the Biblical view of **Peace on Earth** eventually comes to pass.

God by any name is the Giver of Life. Life begets more life in greater abundance. God destroys nothing. Satan and fallen angels chose and continue to choose living as destroyers and doing bad things. Demons live their horrible choice and attempt to share it with God's creation all day every day. Evil never sleeps. We must each choose good or evil, spiritual life or spiritual death. Together with the grace of God we stand together forever. Divided we fall into Satan's enraged abyss.

The global syndicate may be finished abusing the American people as its uninformed weapon; BUT we the people of Main Street America are not finished with the global syndicate. We are taking their Charnel House down, brick by spiritual brick. **Something is indeed happening here and we're forming a clear idea what it is and what we must do for and with each other as decent people. We are embarking on the world's greatest adventure to fight humanity's Supreme Battle and with God's grace will shatter the Satanic Global Syndicate into more pieces than can be counted. Hopefully, this will be done in our lifetime, on our watch, by bringing syndicate players to our Creator's loving embrace – BUT that choice will be made by syndicate members themselves, just as we make our choice. This is how we win.**

Leaving our material world in better condition than we found it at birth requires discernment, coherent decision making, and action. Our birthright and eternal future are the gift of fully living these choices – because *Beyond All Isms* lie **Faith, Hope, and Charity** – bound by eternal Love, a Power so transcendent it changes our world simply by embracing it together, one small decision at a time.

From our united Faith, Hope, and Charity emerges the incredible possibility of Life, Liberty, and Pursuit of Happiness. I look forward to working with you to create the purest water, most beautiful water crystals, and the finest, safest children anyone on earth has ever seen.

Conclusion

The American people are not losing their Republic. It's gone—apathetically and incrementally traded away to a small group of psychopathic Elites employing corrupt Ruling Class thugs, elected and unelected to run America's Administrative Dictatorship for the dynastic family corporatists who took it in exchange for false nanny state promises and pennies on the petrodollar.

Yes, the bleached skeleton of three branches of government remains but constitutionally functional checks and balances along with separation of congressional and executive power alongside judicial review no longer exist. The question is not: "How do we save our Constitutional Republic?" The two questions are: "Can we and how do we take it back?"

Demoralization (KGB), i.e., *mass hypnosis*, (Tavistock), now called *mass formation* has over the past seventy five or so years, spiritually and intellectually immobilized roughly 30% of Americans, leaving them politically paralyzed. At the other end of the *Overton Window*, approximately 30% are awakening spiritually to what must be done if the future U.S. can or will include freedom. Sitting passively in the uninformed center are about 40% of the population who are not sure if there's an issue; or if there is, what to do about it.

If the awakened 30% can successfully and factually educate more than half the middle 40% in the not too distant future, the United States may possibly be saved by the ballot box in its present form. If this convincing education does not occur, we will save our country anyway, but the saving will be unpleasant, not likely able to preserve America as a single nation under one flag.

At the core of this mostly spiritual battle towers the purpose of human life on Earth, i.e., learning to love, then sharing that love with all creation more abundantly throughout eternity. Learning this lesson requires better understanding intelligent creation and humanity's role within it.

Unfortunately, many people are unable to get their arms around the concept of Loving Creator or intelligent creation. I imagine such stubbornness will persist, prolonging the negatively inspired self-abuse a while longer. Love and patience were included with intelligent creation for a reason, hence their salutary usefulness.

WHY Intelligent Creation? From an engineering perspective, the preposterous suggestion that **nothingness,** lacking personal motivation or reason, suddenly (Big Bang) or slowly (maybe a series of Little Bangs), but in any case **randomly**—overcame the **2nd Law of Thermodynamics** to create **something**, then **many things,** is Scientismly far-fetched. How or Why would random chaotic nothing, by definition unintelligent, decide to do anything at all much less something orderly?

I can't explain the *Scientism* how or why of this contradictory idea, but suggest for those hanging on to the concept of Big Bangs banging into intelligent coherence and emotional depth—please at least read some Thomas Sowell. Dr. Sowell has written 36 books and no doubt at 92-years young as of this writing in 2022 is working on Number 37. Dr. Sowell is a national treasure and for those secularists among us unable to swallow spiritual concepts, his historic objectivity and teaching provide a safe starting point for truth searching.

I mention Dr. Sowell at this point, because so much *Cultural Marxist* projection by the disingenuous few onto the many regarding clash of civilizations, culture, economics, ethnicity, politics, race, religion, and so forth have been thoroughly and factually addressed by him over the course of his busy tenure. I have no idea what religion, if any, Dr. Sowell aspires to as I've never heard him mention it, so his work may be a good fit for God deniers, regardless the personal views Dr. Sowell holds on such beliefs. Just tryin' to be helpful.

Some searching may be required as Stanford University's Hoover Institution Senior Fellow, Dr. Sowell, has been marginalized by politically correct, *status quo* social justice warriors for nearly all of his academic career for the intellectual crime of teaching historic fact about America's and the world's *conflicting visions* of culture, economics, history, and society at large. Dr. Sowell's alleged violation of politically correct dogma is courageously speaking for and teaching **all people**—including a large majority of Main Street black people as opposed to black intellectuals. Globalism's Leftist battering rams will never forgive him for this affront to Bigotry by the Few. Facts get in the way of opportunistic, race baiting, black and white activists who must stay relevant to earn a living blaming toxic whitey for all ills on Earth, some of which whites are guilty of—as are the melanin gifted, browns, reds, yellows, etc.

Conclusion

In any event, considering *Leftist Activists* of every stripe and color, America and its founding values are under attack on several fronts as are most countries on Earth. Cyber, economic, information, legal, medical, nutritional, and scientific warfare rage alongside ongoing threats of traditionally kinetic, possibly nuclear war. The global syndicate and its study group order following minions stir the divide and conquer pot non-stop, desperately attempting to mask their intentional destruction of the global economy wreaked upon Main Street by privileged greed and failed *Keynesian Theory*. Governments are now the world's primary borrowers rendering interest rate controls over private borrowing and debt-money supply ineffective. Global economic collapse is inevitable, and the traitorous Biden Regime foreign policy has per Martin Armstrong and other analysts, rendered turning back impossible. Nonsense like the *universal stipend* only receive consideration in Elite circles because Main Street pension funds are already gutted and pitchforks must be avoided.

For so many citizens, our moral compass has been shattered with *moral relativism* blindly leading humanity toward the enslaving Malthusian abyss. Turning away from our Creator's love predictably rendered our world less than abundant for most of Earth's 8 billion or so inhabitants. We cannot fix the Satanically influenced mess we've made of our world without God's grace and guidance. Our failure to awaken spiritually ensures maximal Satanically-induced pain.

Intended or not, the global economy is structurally fractured, meaning credit will freeze at some point, in turn freezing global supply chains. Coming consumer pain, perhaps even famine, are inevitable from today, at least through 2032's likely full economic collapse as Martin Armstrong's Pi Models suggest. We can request God's grace through the Holy Spirit in the name of Christ to aid us—*or not*. Continuing to choose *"or not"* leaves us on our own to deal with demonic forces and our own debasement as apparently most of us, certainly myself, have been doing. We must admit our mistakes and work together to repair our societies.

If America remains on her present *Free Masonic* path, ignoring the **Source** of our past blessings as ancient Israel did, she will soon fall as have all historic world powers. She will predictably break into divided pieces, each having some sort of disputed regional autonomy. This can be avoided entirely, or alternatively, could be opportunity or disaster; depending how we the people align spiritually.

An immoral people cannot be reasonably governed. Fixing our corrupt bloated government at every level first requires healthy spiritual development followed by a more decentralized economic and political environment. We can do this together and win a better life for future generations. Think local, local, local. REDUCE WASHINGTON D.C. BY 75% TO AT MOST, 25% OF ITS CURRENT CORRUPT BLOAT. **Thank you for reading my book.**

BIBLIOGRAPHY

Daily Reckoning. "$205 Trillion in Unfunded Liabilities," February 12, 2014. https://dailyreckoning.com/205-trillion-in-unfunded-liabilities/.

NaturalNews.com. "5G Is Already Linked to Rising Health Problems... Concerns about 'Health Calamity' on the Rise," July 31, 2018. https://www.naturalnews.com/2018-07-31-5g-linked-to-health-problems.html.

"5G Wireless Technology: Millimeter Wave Health Effects." Accessed May 3, 2019. https://www.saferemr.com/2017/08/5g-wireless-technology-millimeter-wave.html.

Mercola.com. "8 Reasons You Need to Throw Away Your Microwave Immediately." Accessed August 26, 2019. http://articles.mercola.com/sites/articles/archive/2010/05/18/microwave-hazards.aspx.

"About the Bretton Woods Committee | The Bretton Woods Committee." Accessed February 16, 2018. http://www.brettonwoods.org/page/about-the-bretton-woods-committee.

"About the Committee | The Bretton Woods Committee." Accessed April 14, 2021. https://www.brettonwoods.org/page/about-the-committee.

Ahmed, Nafeez. "How the CIA Made Google." Medium, November 13, 2015. https://medium.com/insurge-intelligence/how-the-cia-made-google-e836451a959e.

The Catholic Company®. "Aquinas's Shorter Summa." Accessed June 21, 2021. https://www.catholiccompany.com/aquinass-shorter-summa-i2012/.

Ardrey, Robert. *The Territorial Imperative: A Personal Inquiry into the Animal Origins of Property and Nations.* Atheneum, 1966.

"Armstrong Economics | Research the Past to Predict the Future." Accessed May 10, 2018. https://www.armstrongeconomics.com/.

Arnn, Larry P. *The Founders' Key: The Divine and Natural Connection Between the Declaration and the Constitution and What We Risk by Losing It.* 1st edition. Nashville: Thomas Nelson Inc, 2012.

Axelrod, Robert, and Richard Dawkins. *The Evolution of Cooperation: Revised Edition,* 2006.

Ballard, Timothy. *The Covenant, One Nation under God: America's Sacred & Immutable Connection to Ancient Israel.* New York: Legends Library Press, 2019.

Barton, David. *The Myth of Separation: What Is the Correct Relationship Between Church and State?* 5th edition. Aledo, TX: WallBuilder Press, 1992.

Booyens, Harry. *AmaBhulu - The Birth and Death of the Second America,* n.d.

Scribd. "Brain Gate Report | Brain | Electroencephalography." Accessed August 3, 2017. https://www.scribd.com/doc/86741240/Brain-Gate-Report.

Brzezinski, Zbigniew K. *Between Two Ages: America's Role in the Technetronic Era.* Revised ed. edition. Westport, Conn: Praeger, 1982.

BIBLIOGRAPHY

Bullinger, E. W. *Number In Scripture*. Kregel Publications, 1967.

"Caesar's Messiah: The Roman Conspiracy to Invent Jesus: Flavian Signature Edition: Atwill, Joseph: 8601404677632

Cahn, Jonathan. *The Oracle: The Jubilean Mysteries Unveiled*. Lake Mary, Florida: Frontline, 2019.

"Carnicom Institute." Accessed May 25, 2018. https://www.carnicominstitute.org/.

"Chemtrails - Shocking Phoenix Air Quality Test Results." Accessed August 6, 2017. http://www.rense.com/general82/chemit.htm.

"China, Mexican Cartels; the Opioid War against America; Is No One Paying Attention? « Jon Rappoport's Blog." Accessed August 20, 2021. https://blog.nomorefakenews.com/2021/08/20/china-mexican-cartels-opioid-war-against-america/.

"Communist Exploitation of Religion: Congressional Testimony Testimony of Richard Wurmbrand." Accessed August 9, 2020. https://www.crossroad.to/Quotes/communism/communist-senate-hearing-wurmbrand.htm.

Continetti, Matthew. "The Problem of Identity Politics and Its Solution." *Imprimis* (blog), November 17, 2017. https://imprimis.hillsdale.edu/the-problem-of-identity-politics-and-its-solution/.

Cooper, Bruce. "Origin: Probability of a Single Protein Forming by Chance." *Reasoned Cases For Christ* (blog), February 10, 2018. https://bcooper.wordpress.com/2018/02/10/origin-probability-of-a-single-protein-forming-by-chance/.

Copleston, Frederick. *A History of Philosophy*. New York, N.Y: Image, 1985.

"D11696.Pdf." Accessed March 11, 2019. https://www.gao.gov/new.items/d11696.pdf.

Dass, Ram. *Be Here Now*. New York, NY: Harmony, 1978.

"Dr. Rauni Leena Luukanen-Kilde on Mind Control - YouTube." Accessed August 3, 2017. https://www.youtube.com/.

Dyer, Jay. *Esoteric Hollywood II: More Sex, Cults & Symbols in Film*, 2018.

"Elana Freeland." Accessed May 25, 2018. https://www.elanafreeland.com.

Emoto, Masaru. *The Hidden Messages in Water*. Illustrated edition. New York: Atria Books, 2005.

endtimetalks. "TRANSHUMANISM / HUMAN 2.0." *End Time Talks* (blog), January 3, 2021. https://endtimetalks.com/2021/01/03/transumanism-human-2-0/.

Engdahl, F. William. *Manifest Destiny: Democracy as Cognitive Dissonance*. mine.books, 2018.

"Esoteric Hollywood: Sex, Cults and Symbols in Film: Jay Dyer: 9781634240772

Estulin, Daniel. *Tavistock Institute: Social Engineering the Masses*. Walterville, OR: Trine Day, 2015.

Farrell, Joseph P. *Hidden Finance, Rogue Networks, and Secret Sorcery: The Fascist International, 9/11, and Penetrated Operations*. Kempton, IL: Adventures Unlimited Press, 2016.

Fitts, Catherine Austin. "Dillon Read & Co. Inc. And the Aristocracy of Prison Profits," 2006, 124.

Flynn, Lieutenant General Michael T., and Michael Ledeen. *The Field of Fight: How We Can Win the Global War Against Radical Islam and Its Allies*. Reprint edition. St. Martin's Griffin, 2017.

Gedgaudas, Nora T. *Primal Body-Primal Mind: Empower Your Total Health The Way Evolution Intended*. Revised edition. Portland, OR: Primal Body-Primal Mind Publishing, 2009.

"Gilens_and_page_2014_-Testing_theories_of_american_politics.Doc.Pdf." Accessed February 22, 2018. https://scholar.princeton.edu/sites/default/files/mgilens/files/gilens_and_

page_2014_-testing_theories_of_american_politics.doc.pdf.

Giza Death Star. "Giza Death Star," September 29, 2016. https://gizadeathstar.com/.

Dryburgh.com. "Global Capital Class Destroying Independent Income Using SARS-CoV-2," January 14, 2021. https://dryburgh.com/catherine-a-fitts-global-capital-class-destroying-independent-income-using-the-magic-virus/.

Golovin, Yuri I., Natalia L. Klyachko, Alexander G. Majouga, Marina Sokolsky, and Alexander V. Kabanov. "Theranostic Multimodal Potential of Magnetic Nanoparticles Actuated by Non-Heating Low Frequency Magnetic Field in the New-Generation Nanomedicine." *Journal of Nanoparticle Research* 19, no. 2 (February 11, 2017): 63. https://doi.org/10.1007/s11051-017-3746-5.

Griffin, G. Edward. *The Creature from Jekyll Island Update 5th Edition Published in 2010 by G. Edward Griffin - Exact Book Featured on Glenn Beck Program.* 5 edition. Amer Media, 2010.

World Without Cancer; The Story of Vitamin B17. Third Edition edition. Westlake Village, CA: American Media, 1974.

Gross, Bertram. *Friendly Fascism: The New Face of Power in America.* First Printing edition. Boston: South End Press, 1999.

Group, Special Study, and Leonard C. Lewin. *Report from Iron Mountain on the Possibility and Desirability of Peace.* Place of publication not identified: Doubleday, 1969.

Halperin, Mark, and John Heilemann. *Double Down: Game Change 2012.* 1st edition. New York: Penguin Press, 2013.

Huntington, Samuel P. *The Clash of Civilizations and the Remaking of World Order.* New York: Simon & Schuster, 2011.

Ibrahim, Raymond, and Victor Davis Hanson. *Sword and Scimitar: Fourteen Centuries of War between Islam and the West.* Illustrated edition. New York, NY: Da Capo Press, 2018.

Jay's Analysis. "Jay's Analysis." Accessed May 14, 2017. https://jaysanalysis.com/.

Jett, Wayne. *The Fruits of Graft: Great Depressions Then and Now.* 1st edition. Los Angeles: launfal Press, 2011.

Johnson, Matthew Raphael. *"A Circle of Betrayal, Cowardice and Deceit" – On the 100th Anniversary of the Ritual Murder of the Russian Royal Family.* Hromada Books, 2018.

Johnson, Paul. *Intellectuals.* 1st U.S. ed edition. New York: Harpercollins, 1989.

"Jordan Peterson Speech at the 2019 PragerU Summit - YouTube." Accessed May 25, 2019. https://www.youtube.com/watch?v=avInTfCd92Q.

Jr, Robert F. Kennedy. *The Real Anthony Fauci: Bill Gates, Big Pharma, and the Global War on Democracy and Public Health.* Skyhorse, 2021.

Kalimtgis, Konstandinos, U. S. Labor Party Investigating Team, and David Goldman. *Dope, Inc.: Britain's Opium War Against The U.S.* 1st edition. New York: New Benjamin Franklin House Pub. Co, 1978.

Kehoe, Adam. "What We Know About The High-Altitude Balloons Recently Lingering Off America's Coastlines." The Drive. Accessed August 21, 2021. https://www.thedrive.com/the-war-zone/40638/what-we-know-about-the-high-tech-balloons-lingering-off-the-coasts-of-the-u-s-recently.

"Kirby Analytics - Home." Accessed May 20, 2018. http://www.kirbyanalytics.com/.

Lanza, Robert, and Bob Berman. *Biocentrism: How Life and Consciousness Are the Keys to Understanding the True Nature of the Universe.* 1 edition. Dallas, Tex.: BenBella Books, 2010.

BIBLIOGRAPHY

Liang, Qiao, and Wang Xiangsui. *Unrestricted Warfare: China's Master Plan to Destroy America*. Reprint ed. edition. Brattleboro: Echo Point Books & Media, 2015.

Sidney Powell. "LICENSED TO LIE: Exposing Corruption in the Department of Justice (Second Edition Paperback)."

"Lizards Eat Butterflies: An Antidote to the Self-Help Addiction|Paperback." Barnes & Noble. by Dr. David E. Martin

Lobaczewski, Andrew M. *Political Ponerology*. Edited by Laura Knight-Jadczyk. Red Pill Press, 2012.

Lundberg, Ferdinand. *The Rich and Super-Rich*. n/a, 1973.

Marcuse, Herbert, and Douglas Kellner. *One-Dimensional Man: Studies in the Ideology of Advanced Industrial Society, 2nd Edition*. 2nd edition. Boston: Beacon Press, 1991.

Martin, Malachi. *Hostage to the Devil: The Possession and Exorcism of Five Contemporary Americans*. Reissue edition. San Francisco, Calif.: HarperOne, 1992.

Marx, Karl, and Friedrich Engels. *The Communist Manifesto*. New edition edition. New York: International Publishers Co, 2014.

McCoy, Alfred W. *The Politics of Heroin: CIA Complicity in the Global Drug Trade*. Revised edition. Chicago: Lawrence Hill Books, 2003.

McGowan, David, and Nick Bryant. *Weird Scenes Inside the Canyon: Laurel Canyon, Covert Ops & the Dark Heart of the Hippie Dream*. Illustrated edition. London: Headpress, 2014.

McLuhan, Marshall, and Lewis H. Lapham. *Understanding Media: The Extensions of Man*. Reprint edition. Cambridge, Mass: The MIT Press, 1994.

McRae, Ronald M. *Mind Wars: The True Story of Government Research into the Military Potential of Psychic Weapons*. 1st edition. New York: St Martins Pr, 1984.

M.D, Jose M. R. Delgado. *Physical Control of the Mind: Toward a Psychocivilized Society*. CreateSpace Independent Publishing Platform, 1970.

Meyer, Karl. "The Opium War's Secret History." *New York Times*, June 28, 1997, sec. Opinion. http://www.nytimes.com/1997/06/28/opinion/the-opium-war-s-secret-history.html.

"Microcosm and Medium." Accessed May 6, 2021. https://www.lulu.com/en/us/shop/joseph-p-farrell/microcosm-and-medium/paperback/product-1nzew9n6.html?page=1&pageSize=4.

"MICROWAVE MIND CONTROL by Tim Rifat." Accessed November 27, 2018. http://whale.to/b/rifat.html.

Military.com. "Be Ready To Raise Your Right Hand." Military.com. Accessed May 22, 2018. https://www.military.com/join-armed-forces/swearing-in-for-military-service.html.

Mulford, Prentice. *Thoughts Are Things & The God In You*. Radford, VA: Wilder Publications, 2008.

Nageswari, K Sri. "Biological Effects of Microwaves and Mobile Telephony," 2003, 11.

Nesbit, Jeff. "Google's True Origin Partly Lies in CIA and NSA Research Grants for Mass Surveillance." Quartz. Accessed July 2, 2021. https://qz.com/1145669/googles-true-origin-partly-lies-in-cia-and-nsa-research-grants-for-mass-surveillance/.

"No More Fake News Jon Rappoport Investigative Reporter." Accessed October 2, 2017. http://nomorefakenews.com/.

OConnell, Kelly. "Socialism's God—Karl Marx: Was He Stupid, Insane…or Possessed?" Canada

Free Press. Accessed August 9, 2020. https://canadafreepress.com/article/socialisms-god-karl-marx-was-he-stupid-insane...or-possessed.

Peter Gumley on Bojo, the British Deep State and the American Empire. Accessed September 6, 2021. https://rumble.com/vlau2g-peter-gumley-on-bojo-the-british-deep-state-and-the-american-empire.html.

Pike, Albert. *Morals And Dogma.* Orkos Press, 2013.

YouTube. "Powers & Principalities Playlist (Tim Kelly & Joe Atwill)." Accessed June 7, 2019. http://www.youtube.com/playlist?list=PLvg8eyC7StzTDikjUhvccZJly9kCJ3u3B.

Quigley, Carroll. *Anglo-American Establishment.* San Diego, CA: Dauphin Publications Inc., 2013.

Rafalko, Frank J. *MH/CHAOS: The CIA's Campaign Against the Radical New Left and the Black Panthers,* n.d.

Rufo, Christopher F. "Critical Race Theory: What It Is and How to Fight It." *Imprimis* (blog), April 13, 2021. https://imprimis.hillsdale.edu/critical-race-theory-fight/.

"Rules for Radicals: A Practical Primer for Realistic Radicals: Saul D. Alinsky: 9780679721130

Rummel, R. J. *Death by Government: Genocide and Mass Murder Since 1900.* 5th PRINTING edition. New Brunswick: Routledge, 1997.

Russell, Bertrand. *The Impact of Science on Society.* Reprint edition. London ; New York: Routledge, 2016.

Schultz, Daniel J. *How To Get Into The Real Ball Game Of Politics Where You Live To Help President Donald J. Trump Make America Great Again.* Independently published, 2017.

Schwab, Klaus, and Thierry Malleret. *COVID-19: The Great Reset.* Cologny/Geneva: ISBN Agentur Schweiz, 2020.

Scruton, Roger. *An Intelligent Person's Guide to Philosophy.* First American Edition. Allen Lane The Penguin Press, 1996.

Solari Report. "FASAB Statement 56: Understanding New Government Financial Accounting Loopholes." Accessed March 11, 2019. https://constitution.solari.com/fasab-statement-56-understanding-new-government-financial-accounting-loopholes/.

Solzhenitsyn, Aleksandr. *The Gulag Archipelago,* n.d.

Sounds, Strange. "20,000 5G Satellites to Be Launched Sending DANGEROUS BEAMS of Intense Microwave Radiation ACROSS THE WORLD - Strange Sounds." *STRANGE SOUNDS - AMAZING, WEIRD AND ODD PHENOMENA* (blog), January 31, 2019. http://strangesounds.org/2019/01/5g-satellites-space-problem.html.

Sowell, Thomas. *Applied Economics: Thinking Beyond Stage One.* 2nd ed. edition. New York: Basic Books, 2003.

Lockheed Martin. "Space Fence." Accessed September 3, 2019. https://www.lockheedmartin.com/en-us/products/space-fence.html.

Staniloae, Dumitru. *Orthodox Dogmatic Theology: The Experience of God, Vol. 1: Revelation and Knowledge of the Triune God.* 1 edition. Brookline, Mass: Holy Cross Orthodox Press, 1998.

Stone, Sean, Guido Preparata, and Richard Grove. *New World Order: A Strategy of Imperialism.* Reprint edition. Walterville, OR: Trine Day, 2016.

Strauss, William, and Neil Howe. *The Fourth Turning: An American Prophecy - What the Cycles of History Tell Us About America's Next Rendezvous with Destiny.* Reprint edition. New York: Broadway Books, 1997.

BIBLIOGRAPHY

"Study Suggests Medical Errors Now Third Leading Cause of Death in the U.S. - 05/03/2016." Accessed March 24, 2019. https://www.hopkinsmedicine.org/news/media/releases/study_suggests_medical_errors_now_third_leading_cause_of_death_in_the_us.

Sutton, Antony. *America's Secret Establishment: An Introduction to the Order of Skull & Bones*. Walterville: Trine Day, 2004.

Talbot, David. *The Devil's Chessboard: Allen Dulles, the CIA, and the Rise of America's Secret Government*. Harper Perennial (Harper Collins Publishers), 2015.

Taylor, Mark. *The Trump Prophecies: The Astonishing True Story of the Man Who Saw Tomorrow...and What He Says Is Coming Next: UPDATED AND EXPANDED*. 2nd ed. edition. Defender Publishing, 2019.

"Temperature Analysis of 5 Datasets Shows the 'Great Pause' Has Endured for 13 Years, 4 Months | Watts Up With That?" Accessed March 3, 2019. https://wattsupwiththat.com/2014/07/29/temperature-analysis-of-5-datasets-shows-the-great-pause-has-endured-for-13-years-4-months/.

"The Carbon Dioxide Level Is Dangerously Low | Human Events." Accessed March 2, 2022. http://archive.humanevents.com/2014/03/24/the-carbon-dioxide-level-is-dangerously-low/.

"The Corbett Report." Accessed October 9, 2017. https://www.corbettreport.com/.

"The End of All Evil: Jeremy Locke: 9780977745104: Amazon.Com: Books."

Board of Governors of the Federal Reserve System. "The Fed - Is the Federal Reserve Act Going to Expire?" Accessed May 27, 2021. https://www.federalreserve.gov/faqs/is-the-federal-reserve-act-going-to-expire.htm.

"The Hundred-Year Marathon: China's Secret Strategy to Replace America as the Global Superpower: Pillsbury, Michael: 9781250081346

"The Invisible Rainbow: A History of Electricity and Life: Firstenberg, Arthur: 9781645020097

"The Law Illustrated: Bastiat, Frédéric: 9798714320958

Physics-Astronomy.com. "The Milky Way Is Moving Through The Universe At 2.1 Million Kilometers Per Hour." Accessed February 5, 2020. http://www.physics-astronomy.com/2017/07/the-milky-way-is-moving-through.html.

"The Orthodox Study Bible - Hardcover Edition." Accessed September 13, 2018. https://www.christianbook.com/the-orthodox-study-bible-hardcover-edition/9780718003593/pd/003590.

"The Philosophy Of Freedom: Rudolf Steiner: 9781257835126

StrongFirst. "The School of Strength." Accessed August 27, 2021. https://www.strongfirst.com/.

"The Solari Report Blog | The Solari Report Blog." Accessed April 20, 2017. https://solari.com/blog/.

"The Tavistock Institute of Human Relations: Shaping the Moral, Spiritual, Cultural, and Political. A by John Coleman (2006-08-02)

"Christianity and Classical Culture: The... Book by Jaroslav Pelikan."

"From Darwin to Hitler: Evolutionary... Book by Richard Weikart."

"Obedience to Authority: An Experimental... Book by Stanley Milgram."

"The Secret Knowledge: On the Dismantling... Book by David Mamet."

TRANCE Formation of America: True Life Story of a Mind Control Slave. Revised edition. Place of publication not identified: Reality Marketing, Incorporated, 1995.

The Conservative Woman. "Twenty-Year Genetic Trail behind Covid's Creation," July 13, 2021. https://www.conservativewoman.co.uk/twenty-year-genetic-trail-behind-covids-creation/.

Tzu, Sun. *The Art of War.* Edited by James Clavell. New York: Delacorte Press, 1983.

"Under an Ionized Sky: From Chemtrails to Space Fence Lockdown: Elana Freeland: 9781627310536

University, Michigan State. "MSU Scholars Find $21 Trillion in Unauthorized Government Spending; Defense Department to Conduct First-Ever Audit." MSUToday.

Valentine, Douglas. *The CIA as Organized Crime: How Illegal Operations Corrupt America and the World.* Atlanta, GA: Clarity Press, 2017.

Valentine, Douglas. *The Phoenix Program.* Open Road Distribution, 2016.

Vance, J. D. *Hillbilly Elegy: A Memoir of a Family and Culture in Crisis.* Reprint edition. Harper Paperbacks, 2018.

Vance, Laurence M. "Why Not Five Percent?" The New American, July 14, 2014. https://thenewamerican.com/why-not-five-percent/.

Wax, Amy. "Are We Free to Discuss America's Real Problems?" *Imprimis* (blog), January 18, 2018. https://imprimis.hillsdale.edu/are-we-free-to-discuss-americas-real-problems/.

Webb, Gary, and Maxine Waters. *Dark Alliance: The CIA, the Contras, and the Crack Cocaine Explosion.* 2nd edition. New York, NY: Seven Stories Press, 1999.

Wells, H. G., Malcolm Farmer, and Martin Pettit. *Anticipations by H. G. Wells: Anticipations by H. G. Wells.* CreateSpace Independent Publishing Platform, 2018.

"What On Earth Is Happening." Accessed April 22, 2017. http://www.whatonearthishappening.com.

Wolfe, John Truman. *Crisis by Design; The Untold Story of the Global Financial Coup.* Roberts Ross Publishing, 2010.

Wood, Patrick. "Reflexive Law: Sustainable Development Has Conned Us All." *Freedom Advocates* (blog), August 29, 2014. https://www.freedomadvocates.org/reflexive-law/.

Wood, Patrick M. *Technocracy Rising: The Trojan Horse Of Global Transformation.* Mesa, Ariz.: Coherent Publishing, 2014.

Wu, Tim. *The Master Switch: The Rise and Fall of Information Empires.* Reprint Edition. Vintage, 2010.

Yan, Li-Meng, Shu Kang, Jie Guan, and Shanchang Hu. "Unusual Features of the SARS-CoV-2 Genome Suggesting Sophisticated Laboratory Modification Rather Than Natural Evolution and Delineation of Its Probable Synthetic Route," n.d., 26.

Zatz, Noah. "Working at the Boundaries of Markets: Prison Labor and the Economic Dimension of Employment Relationships." SSRN Scholarly Paper. Rochester, NY: Social Science Research Network, December 19, 2007. https://papers.ssrn.com/abstract=1075842.

Index

Index

Index

Index

Index

Index

Index

Index

Index

Index

Index

Index

Index

Index

Index

Index

Index

Index

Index

Index

Index

About the Author

Bruce graduated from University of Wisconsin–Madison in 1980 with a Bachelor of Science Degree in Civil and Environmental Engineering. Prior to engineering school, he worked toward majors in Biology and English at University of Wisconsin – Stevens Point. Bruce started writing at his daughter's suggestion after practicing as a licensed Professional Engineer for nearly four decades and is now retired from project management, heavy civil construction, and civil design engineering. Bruce is happily married (47 years), with two children, one grandson, and lives with Nan, an artist in Coolidge, Arizona.

Bruce, along with his partner, is an alternative energy developer, having been issued U.S. Patent 8,381,523 B2 on February 26, 2013. The patent is for a self-contained, dry geothermal heat harvesting technology capable of supercritical temperatures and pressures offering significantly improved control features and electricity output over conventional geothermal energy methodologies utilizing geothermal reservoir brines. The only environmental emission of this as yet, untested, but patented system is clean water with estimated generation costs as low as $0.008/kWh.

Raised Roman Catholic in Stevens Point, Wisconsin, now tending Orthodox; analysis and suggested **remedies** in *Beyond All Isms* lean heavily toward the author's biased view, that serious societal difficulties stem primarily from humanity's misunderstanding of interrelationships between human nature, *Natural Law*, *Natural Revelation*, and *Supernatural Revelation*. This misunderstanding of how good and evil function in our world, aided by Luciferian influence, clouds individual and group perception, spiritual discernment, and coherent thinking with regard to humanity's role in the material and spiritual realms.

Though work on *Beyond All Isms* began in 2015, its many questions were inaugurated in 1968 while reading Ferdinand Lundberg's, *The Rich and the Super-Rich*. The first draft of *Beyond All Isms* was a three volume, 1,100 page, encyclopedic analysis of how America's 1776 could lead to a 1984 Orwellian dystopia, but has been trimmed to a more functional, reader friendly introduction to its controversial material.

Bruce's author website is: https://brucekolinski.com/
Bruce's energy website is: http://zgroupenergy.com/

www.ingramcontent.com/pod-product-compliance
Lightning Source LLC
Chambersburg PA
CBHW030349130626
46549CB00004B/1424

* 9 7 9 8 9 8 5 0 7 3 6 0 7 *